# Lecture Notes in Computer Science

Edited by G. Goos and J. Hartmanis

## 301

J. Kittler (Ed.)

# Pattern Recognition

4th International Conference
Cambridge, U.K., March 28–30, 1988
Proceedings

# Springer-Verlag

Berlin Heidelberg New York London Paris Tokyo

CR Subject Classification (1987): I.5.0–5, I.4.3–9, I.2.10

ISBN 3-540-19036-8 Springer-Verlag Berlin Heidelberg New York
ISBN 0-387-19036-8 Springer-Verlag New York Berlin Heidelberg

Printing and binding: Druckhaus Beltz, Hemsbach/Bergstr.
2145/3140-543210

# PREFACE

Pattern recognition is traditionally considered to cover all aspects of sensory data perception ranging from data acquisition, through preprocessing and low level analysis, to high level interpretation. Owing to its breadth and important application potential, the field of pattern recognition has been attracting considerable attention of researchers in academia and industry and consequently it has been witnessing a rapid growth and perpetual development. The need for dissemination of the latest results is being served by a host of international conferences on pattern recognition. One such series of meetings is regularly held in the United Kingdom under the auspices of the British Pattern Recognition Association.

This volume contains papers presented at the BPRA 4th International Conference on Pattern Recognition held in Cambridge, 28-30 March 1988. Alongside the conventional topics of Statistical and Syntactic Pattern Recognition, contributions address issues in the hot subject areas of Adaptive Learning Networks, Computer Vision, Knowledge Based Methods and Architectures for Pattern Processing, and among others, report progress in the application domains of Document Processing, Speech and Text Recognition and Shape Analysis for industrial robotics. It is believed that the collection is not merely a report on current activities but that it will also be an important source of inspiration for future developments in the field of pattern recognition.

Guildford, March 1988                                                                              Josef Kittler

# TABLE OF CONTENTS

## Classification Techniques

## Syntactic and Structural

## Image Restoration and Enhancement

## Speech and Text

## Applications

# IS VISION A PATTERN RECOGNITION PROBLEM?

R Wilson

University of Warwick

Coventry CV4 7AL, England

## Abstract

It is argued that traditional pattern recognition methods are inadequate for the tasks confronting computer vision. In an effort to overcome their limitations, a new approach has been developed, in which the concept of pattern is replaced by the group-theoretical notions of representations and invariants. By applying these ideas to the symbolic representation of images, it is possible to derive some very general constraints on the effectiveness of symbolic descriptions from the structure of the image vector space and the transformations which act upon it. The theory is illustrated with some simple examples and then applied to a number of practical problems, including feature description, texture analysis and segmentation. The paper is concluded with a discussion of some generalisations and extensions.

## Computational Approaches to Vision

Everyone who reads this is likely to be familiar with the 'generic' pattern recognition system illustrated in Fig 1. It consists of two parts: a feature extractor which has the image vector v as input and outputs some transformation u=Fv of the input vector; the feature vector u is then input to the classifier, which signals to the user some class label c identifying the input vector. Typically, the transformation F is linear, or consists of a linear transformation followed by some simple non-linearity, such as a squarer. The vector u may have higher or lower dimension than v. The input v may be the whole image, a neighbourhood in the image or even a sequence of images — it makes no difference in principle. Similarly, the class labels c may be numeric or strings, such as 'granny' or 'yellow taxi'. Again, this is a matter of detail. So is the precise form of classifier: it could be statistical, it could take context into account (ie classes of neighbouring vectors), it may be supervised and so on [1]. The important point is that the general pattern recognition system consists of two parts: one continuous and generally singular transformation, whose main job is normally seen as one of data reduction, and one discrete transformation which converts the reduced data to a symbolic form (a label).

Seen at this level of generality, how could there possible by anything wrong with such a model? At this level of generality, comes the response, why bother with two boxes — why not stick both components in one and say "the input is the image data, the outputs are symbols"? It is just about as useful as a description of the problem. Of course, nobody supposes that real vision systems look like that. Everyone recognises that many levels of symbolic description are needed in order to solve problems like recognising grannies or

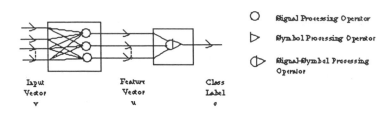

Input
Vector
v

Feature
Vector
u

Class
Label
ω

Fig 1. The traditional pattern recognition system

yellow taxis. Thus an alternative model has evolved for vision (Fig 2) [2], [3]. It clearly has much more expressive power than the original. For example, whereas the simple model of Fig 1 falls into the famous 'granny cell' paradox of requiring a separate label for each of the indeterminate number of distinct views of granny, the more complex symbolic processing of Fig 2 builds up the description step by step, in increasing levels of abstraction, with symbols at low levels, such as zero crossing labels [2], being combined to give '2.5-d', '3-d' and ultimately 'object-centred' descriptions of the components of granny and thence to granny herself. In other words, rather than equate granny symbolically with a huge set of distinct image vectors, granny is represented as the conjunction of a somewhat smaller set of elementary symbols: "if the zero-crossing at $(x_0,y_0)$ is of type $A_0$, that at $(x_1,y_1)$ of type $A_1$, ..., that at $(x_i,y_i)$ of type $A_i$, ..., then it must be granny". Such models are typical of the current generation of vision systems.

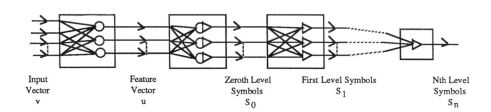

Input
Vector
v

Feature
Vector
u

Zeroth Level
Symbols
$S_0$

First Level Symbols
$S_1$

Nth Level
Symbols
$S_n$

Fig 2. Vision as a symbol processing problem

This focusing of attention onto purely symbolic processing is not without its drawbacks, however. In recent years, a number of voices have been raised against the 'inflexibility', 'sequentiality' and general 'unnaturalness' of symbolic reasoning as embodied in present AI methodology. The advocates of neural networks have been particularly vehement in this regard (eg [4], [5]), Indeed on the more radical wing of the PDP (Parallel Distributed Processing) community, the suggestion has been made that symbols are only of a 'virtual' nature — the 'real problems' are better solved without them [4]. This has led to yet a third architecture for vision, which is illustrated in Fig 3. The significant features of this approach seem to be (i) the complete removal of explicit symbolisations, and (ii) random connectivities. In this view, 'granny' is neither the disjunction of a huge number of global patterns nor the conjunction of a large number of elementary symbols, but an 'equilibrium state' of a network, arrived at after what may be a rather lengthy training process.

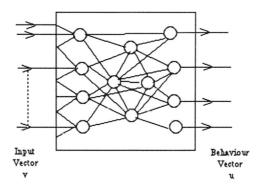

Input
Vector
v

Behaviour
Vector
u

Fig 3. Vision as a neural net problem

It may not be immediately apparent to the reader that, despite their diversity, these three approaches have a common feature, particularly as the shared feature is common by virtue of its absence. The missing component in these theories is a concern with the relationship between the symbolic representation, which is the goal of any perceptual processing (even if the symbols are 'virtual'), and the signal vectors from which that symbolic representation is to be inferred. This theme, which was implicit in Granlund's original work on the representation of image structure [6], has been evolving slowly over the last ten years or so (eg [6]-[13]), to a point where it is now possible to examine in some generality the fundamental problems in the symbolic representation of signals and to explore their consequences for vision systems. The idea behind this work is a simple one: a symbol is supposed to represent some image property or feature faithfully, in the sense that a transformation of the image will induce a corresponding transformation of the symbol, but at the same time remaining invariant to other transformations of the image. For example, suppose a given symbol represents the orientation of a feature in the image (eg 'edge at 45°'). Then if the image is rotated by 45° this should induce a 'rotation' of the symbol (to 'edge at 90°'). On the other hand, the symbol should not change if, for example, the mean luminance of the image changes or if some noise is added to it. Now since there is in principle complete freedom in the choice of symbols, it is meaningful to ask questions like "what are the fundamental constraints on symbolic representation?", "what is the best set of symbols to represent a given image property?", or "how can different types of symbols be combined in a meaningful way?". Clearly the answer to these questions lies in the structure of the signal space and the transformations which act upon it. Some progress has been made in this area (eg [9]-[13]) and it is the purpose of this paper to summarise that progress to date, both at a theoretical and a practical level. Much remains to be done — the theory is far from complete. Some generalisations are therefore discussed.

## The Symbolic Representation of Images

## What Do Symbols Represent?

The central idea in this work is a very simple one: to be useful, a symbol must faithfully represent some derived image property (eg position, class, colour) while at the same time remaining invariant to a host of transformations of the image, all of which produce some change of the image data. Now it frequently happens that such transformations occur in groups and it is the theory of group representations which provides the notions of representation and invariant upon which the following development is based [14]. Most of the results, however, apply even in the absence of a group structure.

To make matters more precise, let an (N x N) image be a vector dimension $N^2$

$$v = (v(0) \; v(1) \; v(2) \; ... \; v(k) \; ... \; v(N^2-1))' \tag{1}$$

where ´ denotes transpose and the image coordinates (k,l) are related to the vector coordinate m by

$$m = kN + 1 \qquad\qquad 0 \le k,l < N \tag{2}$$

(In fact, it makes no difference in the discussion below whether v is the whole image, a part of an image, or even a sequence of images.) A symbolic representation of the image S(v) is a mapping from the space $R^{N^2}$ of images to a set of symbols

$$S(v) : R^{N^2} \xrightarrow{S} \{S(u) : u \in R^{N^2}\} \tag{3}$$

The set of symbols $\{S(u) : u \in R^{N^2}\}$ may be finite or infinite. What is important to note straight away is that the operation of symbolisation splits the vector space into equivalence classes $V_i$

$$R^{N^2} = \underset{i}{U} V_i \tag{4}$$

where $\underset{i}{U}$ is the union operator and

$$V_i = \{v : S(v) = s_i\} \tag{5}$$

is the set of all vectors v with the same symbolic representation (see eg [12], [13]).

Now the first requirement on the operation of S(.) is that is faithfully represents a certain set of $\mathcal{T}_R$ of transformations $T_R \in \mathcal{T}_R$ of the image. That is, the operation of $T_R$ on v should induce a change of label for v, from $s_i = S(v)$ to some new label $s_{i_R}$, but in so doing it must preserve the equivalence classes $V_i$. In other words, if $T_R$ is such a transformation then if, for some i

$$S(V) = s_i \qquad\qquad v \in V_i \tag{6}$$

then

$$S(T_R v) = s_{i_R} \qquad i_R \neq i \qquad \forall v \in V_i \tag{7}$$

and so a transformation is induced on the sets $V_i$

$$T_R V_i = V_{i_R} \qquad \forall i \tag{8}$$

or, in brief,

$$S(T_R v) = T_R S(v) \qquad \forall v \in R^{N^2} \tag{9}$$

Thus to each symbol $S(v)$, there corresponds a symbol $T_R S(v)$ which is induced by the transformation: the transformation *relabels* the equivalence classes, but does *not* change their structure. This must be true for each $T_R \in \mathcal{T}_R$. Only in such a case can the symbols be said to *represent* the property expressed by the transformations.

Representation of wanted properties is only half the story, however. The second part is equally important. There are many transformations $T_I \in \mathcal{T}_I$ to which the symbols should remain invariant, that is,

$$S(T_I v) = S(v) \qquad \forall T_I \in \mathcal{T}_I, \quad \forall v \in R^{N^2} \tag{10}$$

Such transformations obviously map members of a given equivalence class into each other and so

$$T_I V_i = V_i \qquad \forall i \qquad \forall T_I \in \mathcal{T}_I \tag{11}$$

An ideal symbolic representation will have these two characteristics — faithful representation of one set of transformations and invariance to another set. Before considering the extent to which this ideal can be realised, it may be helpful to use a concrete example as an illustration. The simplest is one with which everyone is familiar — the average. The symbolic nature of an average is less obvious perhaps in image processing than in everyday life — "the *average* family has 2.18 children", "the *average* wage is £150.11 p.w." are clearly symbolic statements — they don't refer to any actual family or wage earner. In image analysis, of course, averaging is usually seen as a signal processing operation. It does have a symbolic content, however, in the above sense. Assuming for simplicity that image intensities are integers, the average intensity of an image is just

$$A(v) = N^{-2} \sum_{k=0}^{N^2-1} v(k) \tag{12}$$

and the symbols $A(.)$ are just rational numbers. The set of transformations $T_A$ which the average represents are just those defined by the affine transformations

$$T_\alpha v = v + \alpha d \tag{13}$$

where $d' = (1\ 1\ 1\ ...\ 1)$ is the constant vector and $\alpha$ is an integer. To see this note that

$$A(T_\alpha v) = A(v) + \alpha \tag{14}$$

On the other hand, A(.) is invariant to all permutations Q of elements of v, since

$$A(Qv) = A(v) \tag{15}$$

where

$$(Qv)' = (v(0_q) \, v(1_q) \, \ldots \, v(k_q) \, \ldots) \tag{16}$$

and the permutation Q is defined by the re-ordering $k \rightarrow k_q$ of elements of v. Thus the simple notion of average can also be interpreted as a symbolic representation. Indeed it is perhaps the simplest non-trivial example of a symbol.

Generalising the average, it is clear that any symbolisation based on the point-wise statistics of the image is similarly invariant to permutations. Defining the histogram vector of the image $\eta_v$

$$\eta_v = (\eta_v(0) \, \eta_v(1) \, \ldots \, \eta_v(k) \, \ldots) \tag{17}$$

whose kth component

$$\eta_v(k) = \text{card} \, \{v(i) : v(i) = k\} \tag{18}$$

is just the number of elements of v with intensity k, it is clear that if S(.) is a function only of $\eta(v)$

$$S(v) = s(\eta_v) \tag{19}$$

then for any permutation Q

$$S(Qv) = S(v) \tag{20}$$

In other words, statistical classifications, whether parametric or not (eg [1],[12]) are invariant to permutations. In general, a statistical classification yields a symbolisation which consists of a set of pairs

$$S(v) = \{(\mu_0, \eta_0), (\mu_1, \eta_1), \ldots, (\mu_k, \eta_k)\} \tag{21}$$

where $\mu_k$ is the class mean and $\eta_k$ is the number of pixels in the kth class. Frequently, however, such a symbolisation is not considered sufficient as an image description — it is also desired to represent the position of the classes. In order to make sense of this requirement, it is necessary to define position in terms of a set of transformations. This is easily done by defining the shift or translation operators X and Y by

$$Xv = (v(N\text{-}1) \, v(0) \, v(1) \, \ldots \, v(N\text{-}2) \, v(2N\text{-}1) \, v(N) \, v(N\text{+}1) \, \ldots)' \tag{22}$$

$$Yv = (v(N) \, v(N\text{+}1) \, \ldots \, v(2N\text{-}1) \, v(2N) \, v(2N\text{+}1) \, \ldots)' \tag{23}$$

where for simplicity the vertical (Y) shifts and horizontal (X) shifts are taken to be cyclic. Now as things stand, the representation of eqn (21) is clearly invariant to shifts

$$S(Y^n \, X^m \, v) = S(v) \tag{24}$$

If, however, the class information contained in S(v) is 'projected back' onto the image, by classifying each pixel independently, it is possible to arrive at a new description $S_1(v)$, say, in which the number of points in class k, $\eta_v(k)$, is replaced by the addresses of points in the kth class, giving

$$S_1(v) = \{(\mu_0, \{(x_{00},y_{00}),(x_{01},y_{01}),\ldots(x_{0n_0-1},y_{0n_0-1})\}),$$
$$(\mu_1,\{(x_{10},y_{10}),(x_{11},y_{11}),\ldots(x_{1n_1-1},y_{1n_1-1})\}),\ldots\}$$

(25)

The new symbol $S_1(v)$ obviously represents position, since

$$S_1(Y^nX^mv) = \{(\mu_0,\{(x_{00}+m,y_{00}+n),(x_{01}+m,y_{01}+n),\ldots\}),\ldots$$
$$(\mu_k,\{(x_{k0}+m,y_{k0}+n),(x_{k1}+m,y_{k1}+n),\ldots\}),\ldots\}$$
$$= Y^nX^mS_1(v)$$

(26)

The new representation $S_1(.)$ has a different behaviour with respect to permutations, however. Any permutation $Q_1$ which only exchanges pixels within classes

$$Q_1 : (x_{ki},y_{ki}) \rightarrow (x_{kj},y_{kj}) \qquad \forall\, k \ \text{ for some } i, j\ 0 \le i,j < \eta_k$$

(27)

leaves $S_1(.)$ unchanged

$$S_1(Q_1\, v) = S_1(v)$$

(28)

but all permutations $Q_2$ which exchange pixels between regions

$$Q_2 : (x_{ki},y_{ki}) \rightarrow (x_{lj},y_{lj}) \qquad k \ne l \ \text{ for some } i, j$$

(29)

are represented by $S_1(.)$

$$S_1(Q_2v) = Q_2\, S_1(v)$$

(30)

Thus the invariance of S(.) with respect to permutations is lost when the description $S_1(.)$ is used. This is obviously inevitable if $S_1(.)$ is to represent position. Whereas the description S(.) is purely statistical, $S_1(.)$ by virtue of its representation of position loses its purely statistical character: it is no longer invariant to arbitrary permutations. This is an important lesson — representation and invariance are two sides of the same coin — changing one can affect the other. In particular, the conjunction of class and position information, as in the symbols $S_1(.)$, frequently leads to problems. This will be considered in more detail below.

A final simple example is another one of particular relevance in pattern recognition. A frequently used method in image recognition is pattern matching [1]. In this model, the patterns, which might be a common feature, such as an edge, are represented by a set of pattern vectors $\{u_i\}$. These are convolved with the image vector v to give a set of output images $\{g_i\}$ upon which the symbols are based. Thus

$$g_i = u_i * v \tag{31}$$

or in full

$$g_i(x,y) = \sum_{x'=0}^{N-1} \sum_{y'=0}^{N-1} u_i\ (x',y')v(x-x',y-y') \tag{32}$$

In the simplest case, the output images $g_i$ are subject to some point-wise nonlinearity to give a symbol $S_u(.)$, which is a list of locations for each pattern $u_i$ at which $u_i$ 'matches' the image. This representation actually looks quite like that of $S_1(.)$, eqn (25)

$$S_u(v) = \{(0,\{(x_{00},y_{00}),(x_{01},y_{01}),...(x_{0n_0-1},y_{0n_0-1})\}),$$
$$(1,\{(x_{10},y_{10}),(x_{11},y_{11}),...(x_{1n_1-1},y_{1n_1-1})\}),...\} \tag{33}$$

The shift invariant character of the convolution operation guarantees that $S_u(.)$ represents position, as in eqn (26),

$$S_u(Y^m\ X^n\ v) = Y^m\ X^n\ S_u(v) \tag{34}$$

In this case, however, there is no question that $S_u(.)$ represents permutations — an arbitrary permutation $Qv$ will alter the convolution images $g_i$ in an unpredictable way. The 'class' component of $S_u(.)$ is just the index i of the pattern. In a typical case, the $u_i$ might correspond to line and edge features of different orientations [7],[15]. In a more complex case, several convolution images $g_i$ might be combined to give a more elaborate representation, without affecting the basic structure (eg [7], [8]). The problem in all of these cases is the same — ambiguity. What happens when more than one feature is in the 'window' represented by the pattern $u_i$? The effective window widths $\Delta x$ and $\Delta y$ can be defined, for a pattern $u_i$ centred at $(0,0)$, by

$$(\Delta x)^2 = \sum_{x=0}^{\frac{N}{2}-1} \sum_{y=0}^{N-1} x^2\ u_i^2(x,y) \Big/ \sum_{x=0}^{\frac{N}{2}-1} \sum_{y=0}^{N-1} u_i^2(x,y) \tag{35}$$

$$\Delta y = \sum_{x=0}^{N-1} \sum_{y=0}^{\frac{N}{2}-1} y^2\ u_i^2(x,y) \Big/ \sum_{x=0}^{N-1} \sum_{y=0}^{\frac{N}{2}-1} u_i^2(x,y) \tag{36}$$

It is well known from signal theory that these widths are inversely related to the corresponding frequency bandwidths $\Delta\omega_x$, $\Delta\omega_y$, through the uncertainty principle (eg [9], [16]). Thus for any finite bandwidth pattern there is a window of uncertainty in position. Although it is possible to get 'super-resolution' within this window by thresholding [1], using zero-crossings [2] or, more elegantly, by local centroid [8], these nonlinear operations guarantee interference whenever two features lie within $(\Delta x, \Delta y)$ of each other, even if

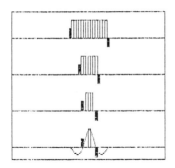

Fig 4. Ambiguity in zero-crossings from DOG operator. Filled symbols show signed zero-crossings in convolution of filter (continuous line) with lines of various widths (open symbols).

the features are of the same type (Fig 4). On the other hand, the only 'features' of 'infinite' bandwidths have uniform Fourier spectra - impulses and random or pseudorandom sequences. Even if there were no noise in the image, they would hardly constitute an interesting set of features for pattern analysis. When the image is noisy, there is in any case a requirement that the pattern matching be noise-insensitive and this inevitably implies a loss of bandwidth [12],[17]. The conclusion is that although it would appear at first sight that the uncertainty in position caused by the finite window width of the patterns can be avoided, this can only be done by assuming that there is only 1 event within a given window. When this assumption is false, then ambiguity results. If the conclusion is correct even when there is no noise in the image, it is true a fortiori when noise is present. Uncertainty is not just *a* problem in symbolisation it is *the* problem, which must now be considered in more depth.

## The Origins of Uncertainty

In order to deal with the problem of uncertainty, it is necessary to uncover how it arises in the process of inferring symbols from image data. On the surface, there would appear to be two types of uncertainty: ambiguity of the type discussed above and noise. Are they really different? What is 'noise'? These are the questions which must now be addressed.

In keeping with the above approach, a somewhat unconventional view will be taken of 'noise'. It will be regarded as a transformation of the image, to which an *ideal* symbolisation should remain invariant, but to which practical symbolisations are not invariant. To make this notion more precise, define an *ideal* symbolisation S*(.) with respect to a pair of sets of transformations $A \in \mathcal{A}$, $B \in \mathcal{B}$ as one which represents A and is invariant to B

$$S^* (Av) = A S^* (v) \qquad \forall A \in \mathcal{A} \qquad \forall v \qquad (37)$$

$$S^* (Bv) = S^* (v) \qquad \forall B \in \mathcal{B} \qquad \forall v$$

The set $\mathcal{B}_n \subset \mathcal{B}$ of noise transformations with respect to a *realisable* symbolisation S(.) is then defined as those transformations $B_n \in \mathcal{B}_n$ for which

$$S(B_n v) \neq S(v) \qquad B_n \in \mathcal{B}_n \subset \mathcal{B} \qquad (38)$$

Typically such transformations $B_n$ are regarded as additive, such as white Gaussian noise. In the present context, a more convenient model is the group of permutations Q of the image, which was described above. As an example, Fig 5 shows a black-and-white image with a single edge and a corresponding permutation of that image. Clearly the permutation could be regarded as a noisy version of the original. In this regard, it is worth noting that while the class symbols S(.) based on statistical classification, eqn (21), were shown to be invariant to permutations, (eqn (20)) those containing a position component, $S_1(.)$ (eqn (25)) were only invariant to within class permutations (eqn (28)-(29)). Note that this is true however the classification of pixels is done — it is an *inherent* property of the symbols, which is *independent* of the way those symbols are computed. This suggests that there are general principles at issue, which can be discussed without examining every conceivable method of symbolising an image.

To take this line of reasoning, it is, however, necessary to impose some very general restriction on 'allowable' symbolisations. Thus a symbolisation S(.) will be called *realisable* if the following conditions on its equivalence classes $V_i$ (eqn (5)) are fulfilled: for each equivalence class $V_i$ there exists a finite set $\{v_{ij} : 0 \leq j < N_i\}$ of vectors such that

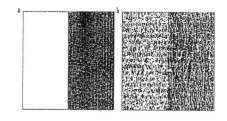

Fig 5.  (a) image with single vertical boundary
         (b) permutation of (a) based on 128*128 blocks

(i)  The equivalence class $V_i$ can be represented as a union of open balls $\beta_\delta$ of radius $\delta$ centred on the vectors $v_{ij}$

$$V_i = \underset{j}{U} \beta_\delta (v_{ij})$$
(39)

where for some norm $\|.\|$

$$\beta_\delta (v) = \{u : \| u - v \| < \delta \}$$

(ii)  The symbol associated with any vector $v \in V_i$ in the ith class is a function only of v and the set $\{v_{ij}\}$ of representative vectors

$$S(v) = S(v, v_{00}, v_{01}, ..., v_{i0}, v_{i1}, ..., v_{kl}, ...)$$
(40)

As an example of realisable symbolisations, those based on the distances $\|v-v_{ij}\|$ or inner products $(v, v_{ij})$ are obvious candidates. Since any symbolisation can be approximated by one based on distance, this definition of realisability seems reasonable. In effect, it simply means that the computation of the symbols is finite.

Returning to the ideal symbolisation, note that it satisfies

$$S^*(ABv) = S^*(BAv) = AS^*(v) \qquad \forall \ A \in \mathcal{A}, B \in \mathcal{B}, v$$
(41)

In other words, under the operation of taking a symbol, the transformations A and B commute. This raises a general question: under what conditions can a *realisable* symbolisation satisfy this demand?

For the sorts of transformations considered so far, which are nonsingular and either linear (T represented by a matrix operator) or translations in $R^{N^2}$ (T represented by adding a fixed vector to each vector), it turns out that there is a general result.

Theorem: An ideal symbolisation $S^*(.)$ with respect to sets of nonsingular transformations $\mathcal{A}$ and $\mathcal{B}$ which are linear or translations can only be realised if the transformations commute, that is if

$$AB = BA \qquad\qquad \forall\ A \in \mathcal{A}, B \in \mathcal{B}$$

Proof: There are 3 cases to consider: both A's and B's are translations, both are linear transforms or one set are linear and the other are translations. These have to be treated separately.

1.　Both $\mathcal{A}$ and $\mathcal{B}$ consist of translations.
　　In this case

$$\begin{aligned} Av &= v + a & \forall\ A \in \mathcal{A} \\ Bv &= v + b & \forall\ B \in \mathcal{B} \end{aligned} \qquad\qquad (42)$$

　　and obviously

$$ABv = (v + b) + a = (v + a) + b = BAv \qquad\qquad (43)$$

　　so that trivially

$$ABv = BAv \qquad\qquad (44)$$

　　and hence, for any $S(.)$

$$S(ABv) = S(BAv) \qquad\qquad (45)$$

2.　Both $\mathcal{A}$ and $\mathcal{B}$ consist of linear transformations.
　　In this case $A \in \mathcal{A}$ and $B \in \mathcal{B}$ can be represented by matrices, which do not commute, in general [18]. That is for arbitrary $T_1, T_2$

$$T_1 T_2 v \neq T_2 T_1 v \qquad\qquad \forall\ v \qquad\qquad (46)$$

　　Now consider an arbitrary $A \in \mathcal{A}$ and $B \in \mathcal{B}$. Then either they commute

$$ABv = BAv \qquad\qquad (47)$$

　　in which case for any $S(.)$

$$S(ABv) = S(BAv) \qquad\qquad (48)$$

　　or at least the equivalence classes must be conserved, so that

$$ABV_i = BAV_i \qquad\qquad \forall\ i \quad \forall\ A, B \qquad\qquad (49)$$

In other words, the operators AB and BA must take vectors $v \in V_i$ into vectors $u \in V_i$. For a realisable symbolisation this implies that, for some k

$$ABv_{ij} = BAv_{ik} \qquad\qquad \forall\ i, j \quad \forall\ A, B \tag{50}$$

where $\{v_{ij}\}$ is the set of vectors representing $V_i$. Since A and B are nonsingular, eqn (50) can be rewritten as

$$A^{-1}B^{-1}ABv_{ij} = v_{ik} \qquad\qquad \forall\ i, j \quad \forall\ A, B \tag{51}$$

or simply

$$Cv_{ij} = v_{ik} \tag{52}$$

Now a similar relation holds for $v_{ik}$, viz

$$Cv_{ik} = C^2 v_{ij} = v_{il} \tag{53}$$

and by induction, since the set $\{v_{ij}\}$ is finite, for some n one must have

$$C^n v_{ij} = v_{ij} \qquad\qquad \forall\ i, j \tag{54}$$

Thus $v_{ij}$ is an eigenvector of $C^n$ with eigenvalue 1 [18]. Now the set $\underset{i}{U}\ \{v_{ij}\}$ of all of the representative vectors must be complete, since by eqn (39), for any $V \in R^{N^2}$, there is some i, j such that

$$\|v - v_{ij}\| < \delta \tag{55}$$

In other words, the set $\underset{i}{U}\ \{v_{ij}\}$ forms a basis for $R^{N^2}$ [18]. But then from eqn (54), it follows that

$$C^n v = v \qquad\qquad \forall\ v \in R^{N^2} \tag{56}$$

and so

$$C^n = I \tag{57}$$

or

$$AB = BA \qquad\qquad \forall\ A \in \mathcal{A}, B \in \mathcal{B} \tag{58}$$

and so for a realisable symbolisation $S^*(.)$ to exist, the transformations must commute.

3.   Finally, consider the case where one set A consists of translations and the other consists of linear transformations. In this case

$$ABv = Bv + a \tag{59}$$

$$BAv = Bv + Ba \tag{60}$$

Then if a is an eigenvector of B, with eigenvalue 1

$$Ba = a \qquad (61)$$

it follows that A and B commute. If this is not the case, then again consider the effects of A and B on the representative vectors $v_{ij}$ of a realisable symbolisation. In this case, by similar reasoning to that above there is some k such that

$$Bv_{ij} + a = Bv_{ik} + Ba \qquad \forall\, i, j \ \forall\, a \in \mathcal{A}, B \in \mathcal{B} \qquad (62)$$

or

$$v_{ij} = v_{ik} + a_1 \qquad (63)$$

and so by induction for some n

$$v_{ij} = v_{ij} + na_1 \qquad \forall\, i, j \qquad (64)$$

and hence

$$a_1 = (I - B^{-1})a = 0 \qquad \forall\, a, B \qquad (65)$$

so that for a realisable symbolisation to exist, eqn (61) must be satisfied and $A \in \mathcal{A}, B \in \mathcal{B}$ must commute.

It has thus been shown that under very restricted assumptions about symbolisations, there are only limited cases where ideal symbolisations exist, namely those where the transformations in the two sets commute. This is a result very much in accord with the spirit of group representation theory [14].

If the transformations do not commute, of course, then the equivalence classes are not preserved and uncertainty is the result. This happens whether the transformations correspond to noise or whether they simply represent incompatible properties [9]. One case where this is always a problem is where the symbols are actually formed by conjunction of two separate symbols (cf the example in the introduction of 'granny' as a conjunction of zero-crossing symbols). Here the problem is hidden by the fact that, for example, one symbol $S_x(.)$, say, might represent position

$$S_x(Y^m X^n v) = Y^m X^n S_x(v) \qquad (66)$$

while the other, $S_c(.)$ represents some 'class' (eg gray level [10], orientation [7] or frequency [8], [11]). Then combined symbols are formed, which attempt to represent both

$$S(v) = S_x(v) \cap S_c(v) \qquad (67)$$

The question then arises: do the new symbols $S(.)$ preserve the representation and invariance properties of the components $S_x(.)$ and $S_c(.)$? The only way to guarantee that the answer is yes is that all the relevant transformations ($A_x, B_x, A_c, B_c$ in the notation used in the theorem) commute, [8], [12]. Only then can it be guaranteed that, for example

$$S(Xv) = S_X(Xv) \cap S_C(Xv) = X(S_X(v) \cap S_C(v)) \tag{68}$$

Another way of seeing the difficulty is by considering the operations which can lead to the definition of a conjunctive symbol such as $S(.)$ of eqn (67). There are 3 ways of computing $S(.)$, as illustrated in Fig 6. Either $S_X(.)$ and $S_C(.)$ can be computed in parallel, or in series, with either $Sx(.)$ or $Sc(.)$ first. Unless the transformations commute, there is no way to guarantee that all 3 methods give the same answer. If they do not, who is to choose which is correct?

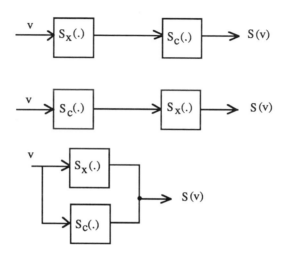

Fig 6.   Three ways to compute a conjunction of two symbols.

## Dealing with Uncertainty

It follows from the above discussion that the uncertainty problems which beset vision are largely impossible to avoid — it frequently happens that it is easy to show by a direct examination of the relevant transformations that ideal symbolic descriptions cannot be realised. This rather negative result has to be set against the common sense experience that human beings are really quite good at seeing. Perhaps then, there are ways to deal with the problem, now it has been recognised. The general principles which have been found important in solving the uncertainty problem are illustrated here by reference to a range of practical applications. The description of those applications is necessarily brief — the interested reader may find fuller coverage in the cited references.

## 1. Intermediate Representations

The first thing to appreciate about symbolic representations is that they do not have to be either completely global, (as in classical statistical methods (cf eqn (25)) or the Fourier transform), or completely localised. Indeed one of the main flaws in the representation $S_1(.)$ was just the way it combined a purely global statistical classification with independent classification of each pixel. At its simplest, for example, it is possible to convolve the image with a smoothing filter, based on a localised window function $w(x,y)$

$$w(x,y) \geq 0 \qquad \forall\ x, y \qquad (69)$$

$$\sum_x \sum_y w(x,y) = 1 \qquad (70)$$

$$\sum_x \sum_y (x^2+y^2)w^2(x,y) = r_w^2 \qquad (71)$$

The first two conditions on w need no comment. The third requires w to preserve a degree of spatial localisation. It is well known [9], [16] that the extent to which this is possible depends on the bandwidth of w, through the uncertainty principle.

In what sense is the result u

$$u = v*w \qquad (72)$$

of such a smoothing an intermediate representation? In the first place, if the bandwidths of w in vertical and horizontal directions are $B_X$ and $B_Y$, then it is possible to subsample u at intervals $m_X \sim \frac{1}{2B_X}$, $m_Y \sim \frac{1}{2B_Y}$.

But the subsampled version, $u_1$, say, now only represents shifts of v by multiples of $m_X$ and $m_Y$

$$S_1(Y^m X^n u_1) = Y^{km_Y} X^{lm_X} S_1(u_1) \qquad (73)$$

where

$$m = km_Y + p \qquad |p| < m_Y/2 \qquad (74)$$

$$n = lm_X + q \qquad |q| < m_X/2$$

whereas the classification of the unsmoothed image represented position faithfully (eqn (26)). On the other hand, if u is not subsampled, the blurring introduced by w will simply cause classification errors in boundary regions, in any case. Similarly, considering the effects of noise as being permutations, as in eqn (29), then if the number of pixels swapped is small (ie low noise variance) then on average only one or no swap will occur within the effective window radius $r_w$ of the filter. The averaging effect of the filter will then reduce the difference between the permuted pixels and their neighbours, so that in an ideal case

$$S_1(Qu_1) = S_1(u_1) \qquad \forall\ Q \in \mathcal{G} \qquad (75)$$

where $G$ is the set of 'high probability' permutations. Thus if the symbolic representation of v based on the smoothed and subsampled vector $u_1$ is denoted $S_2(.)$, then its intermediate position between $S(.)$ and $S_1(.)$ of eqns (21), (25) is shown in table 1 below

| Symbolisation | S( ) | S_2( ) | S_1( ) |
|---|---|---|---|
| Represents | gray level (H) | gray level (H) | gray level (H) |
| | | position (M) | position (H) |
| Invariant to | shifts of position | sparse perms + | interclass perms |
| | all perms | interclass perms | |

Table 1  Summary of 3 symbolic descriptions.  Letters in brackets indicate resolution (L = Low, M = Medium, H = High)

The concept of local smoothing can be extended to deal with quantities other than magnitude.  By defining a window centred at an arbitrary frequency $(\omega_x, \omega_y)$ in the Fourier domain, it is possible to generalise the window $w(x,y)$ to a 'local frequency window' $w(x,y,\omega_x,\omega_y)$

$$w_{\omega_x\omega_y}(x,y) = w(x,y) \exp[j(\omega_x.x+\omega_y.y)] \tag{76}$$

Convolving a set of such 'quadrature filters' [7], [16] with the image results in general in a new vector $\underline{u}$, which unlike v consists of a vector at each spatial location

$$\underline{u} = (\underline{u}(0)\ \underline{u}(1)\ ...\ \underline{u}(N^2-1))' \tag{77}$$

where $\underline{u}(k)$ is an M-d vector

$$\underline{u}(k) = (u_{\omega_{x0}\omega_{y0}}(k)\ u_{\omega_{x1}\omega_{y1}}(k)\ ...\ u_{\omega_{xM-1}\omega_{yM-1}}(k))' \tag{78}$$

and

$$u_{\omega_{xm}\omega_{ym}}(x+Ny) = v * w_{\omega_{xm}\omega_{ym}} \qquad 0 \le m < M \tag{79}$$

is the result of convolving v with the window centred on $(\omega_{xm},\omega_{ym})$.  In most applications of this method, however, it is not $\underline{u}$ itself, but the vector of local energies $\underline{u}_2$ which is used

$$\underline{u}_2(k) = (|u_{\omega_{x0}\omega_{y0}}(k)|^2\ |u_{\omega_{x1}\omega_{y1}}(k)|^2...) \tag{80}$$

The significance of this is illustrated in Fig 7, where it can be seen that just as in the case of the smoothing filter, the magnitudes of the convolutions $\underline{u}_2$ have a 'local shift invariance' of the type defined in eqns (72)-(74).

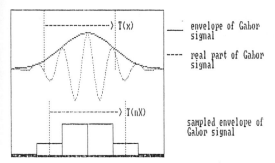

Fig 7. Removal of phase from Gabor signal induces local translation invariance - the arbitrary translation $T(x)$ in the continuous domain is represented by the translation $T(nX)$ by a whole number of sample periods in the sampled domain.

Note, however, that whereas in the case of averaging it is the image itself which displays local translation invariance, through subsampling, when $\underline{u}_2$ is used, it is no longer the image, but a local property, such as orientation [7] or texture [11] which inherits the shift invariance. In effect, the use of the *nonlinear* squaring operation raises the *order* of the invariant property from a first order one (gray scale) to a second order one (texture). Such methods form the basis of many symbolic representations. One which is particularly useful is orientation [7], [8]. The symbolic representation in this case is found by a reduction of the M-d vector $\underline{u}_2(k)$ to a 2-d vector $\underline{t}(k)$

$$\underline{t}(k) = \sum_{m=0}^{M-1} |u_{\omega_{xm}\omega_{ym}}(k)|^2 \, \underline{\omega}_m$$

(81)

where [7]

$$\omega_{xm}^2 + \omega_{ym}^2 = \gamma^2 \qquad\qquad 0 \le m < M$$

$$\arctan(\omega_{x_m}, \omega_{y_m}) = \frac{\pi}{m}$$

(82)

and

$$\underline{\omega}_m = (\omega_{xm}, \omega_{ym})$$

(83)

The symbolic representation of local orientation, $\theta(v)$, is then the image of angles

$$\theta(v) = \text{Arg}(\underline{t}) = (\text{Arg } \underline{t}(0) \ \text{Arg } \underline{t}(1) \ldots \text{Art } \underline{t}(N^2-1))'$$  (84)

Knutsson has shown that, provided the correct filters are used, $\theta(v)$ is a faithful representation of orientation [7]. Thus if $R_\psi$ is the transformation rotating an image by an angle $\psi$, then

$$\theta(R_\psi v) = R_\psi \theta(v)$$  (85)

Similarly, it can be seen from the above arguments that the symbols $\theta(.)$ are invariant to shifts by amounts less than one quarter the inverse bandwidths

$$\theta(Y^m X^n v) = \theta(v) \qquad\qquad \text{if } m < \frac{1}{4B_Y} \quad n < \frac{1}{4B_X}$$

(86)

Fig 8. Vector representation of orientation.

An example of such a representation of an image is shown in Fig 8, which illustrates both the original and the horizontal (left) and vertical components of the vector image $\underline{t}$. Methods based on representations showing 2nd order shift invariants have also been applied successfully to texture analysis [11], stereopsis and motion [19]-[21]. In these cases, it has been possible to establish that the symbolic representation faithfully represents the desired 2nd order property, at the cost of a loss of resolution in position, as in eqns (73), (74). Hence by means of intermediate representations, it is possible to trade off representative power in respect of one set of transformations against that in respect of a second set. In the cases discussed above, this amounts to an increase in the ability to say 'what' is in an image at the expense of the ability to say precisely 'where' it is. However, it is clear in all of these cases that uncertainty remains, both in terms of local shift invariance and in the sense of ambiguity problems — there may be more than one 'event' inside the window (Fig 4).

## 2. Hierarchies of Representation

A fundamental problem with such methods is that they are based on sets of 'features' $w_{\omega_x \omega_y}(x,y)$ which are either incomplete, as in the case of averaging, or at best complete. This implies that the M features in a representation such as $\underline{u}$ (eqn (78)) are linearly independent or orthogonal — they are not 'looking at the same thing'. As there is no way of telling whether their 'answers' fit together or not, the ambiguity problem remains.

An obvious solution to this difficulty is to use an overcomplete representation, so that each 'event' shows up in a number of 'windows'. In the language of representation and invariance, this means using not just one level of intermediate description, but many. The most familiar example of such a description is the quad-tree (Fig 9). Note how the gray level histogram, which is completely ambiguous in the original image, clearly reveals the three regions at the top level of this tree. In effect, the different levels of the tree represent different points in the trade-off between resolution in position (in the sense of eqn (73)) and resolution in gray level statistics. However, it is not enough to use only the top and bottom levels of the tree, for the reason illustrated in Fig 10. It is only by having a range of scales of representation that it becomes possible to disambiguate the symbolic description. This is illustrated most clearly in Fig 10, which shows the successful segmentation of a pair of black circles on a constant background, with a large amount of additive noise. At the top level of the (truncated) tree, which is only 16 x 16 pixels, the two circles merge to form a single 'object'. It is only by tracking the boundary down the tree that the two objects are recognised as separate. This method is fully described in [10], [12].

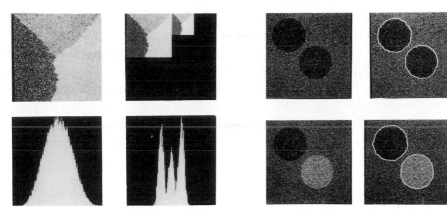

Fig 9. Gray level histograms at top and bottom of gray level quad-tree.

Fig 10. Resovling ambiguities by the use of many scales in quad-tree segmentation of discs.

One interesting way of viewing the levels of a quad-tree emphasises the symbolic nature of the averaging process, as discussed previously (eqns (12), (14)). Thus if $A_i(.)$ is the ith level of the quad-tree, considered as a symbolic representation, then it can be found by successive averaging and subsampling operations

$$A_i(v) = A(A_{i-1}(v)) = A^2(A_{i-2}(v)) = A^i v \qquad (87)$$

where A is the linear operator representing the combination of averaging and subsampling. Thus in a rather trivial sense, the symbolic description at level i of the tree is found by an operation on that at level (i 1) and so on.

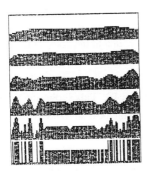

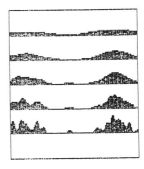

Fig 11. The need for higher order invariants. Averaging at different scales cannot discriminate between centre and surround

Fig 12. Second order invariants can solve problems on which first order methods fail. Averages at different scales of local variance measure.

This suggests a natural extension to higher order invariants, which has indeed turned out to be very valuable in practice. The idea is illustrated in a simple one dimensional case in Figs 11 and 12. Note that in this case the difference between the centre and surround regions is not one of average intensity but of variability, or texture. Thus a simple gray level tree fails to resolve the two regions (Fig 11). On the other hand, a second order tree, based on the squared difference between levels 0 and 1 of the original tree (ie a 'local variance' estimate) now reveals the two regions quite clearly. This is therefore a first order hierarchy of description, but based on a second order property. Now consider Fig 13. In this case, the difference between centre and surround is that the centre region has a slowly varying mean level, while the surround is constant. Both are noisy, however. In this case, first order hierarchies based on either the signal itself or on the local variance between levels 0 and 1 fail to discriminate. Local variation between higher levels in the first order tree does show up the difference — each line in Fig 14 is the average squared difference between that level and the level below in Fig 13. Such a representation corresponds not to uniformity of gray scale, nor even to uniformity of texture, but uniformity of variation of gray scale.

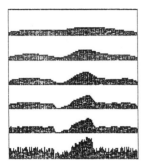

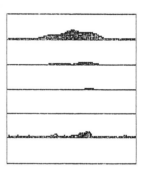

Fig 13. Centre contains a uniform variation which prevents discrimination from surround by magnitude alone.

Fig 14. Local variance estimate at appropriate scale gives clear discrimination of centre and surround.

Such generalisations, which were first discussed by Granlund [6], [23], lead to the development of a 'hierarchy of hierarchies' in which various orders of invariants are expressed in a progressive way, starting with the image and the first order hierarchy based on it (quadtree) then taking second order properties at various levels of the first order hierarchy and building first order hierarchies based on them and so on. Although this ambitious program is not yet complete, it has been applied to the construction of a mutlilevel orientation representation (Fig 15) [26], which is far more robust in noise than the original. A similar multilevel approach has been adapted to stereopsis [19] and to texture segmentation [11], [12] (Fig 16). The most general form explored thus far is illustrated in Figs 17 and 18. This shows the representation of an image in terms of a series of levels, each of which is a complete 'local spectral' representation of the image at a given resolution: it is to the quad-tree what the generalised window (eqn (76)) is to the window function $w(x,y)$ [25]. Operations upon this representation lead to new forms of invariant and simplify the task of disambiguation. From the simple averaging hierarchy of eqn (87), there has emerged a general form of symbolic hierarchy (Fig 19)

$$S(v) = S_n(S_{n-1}(S_{n-2}(...S_0(v)))...)$$

(88)

Using such general methods, it is possible to represent not simply 'consistency of gray level' or 'consistency of texture' but 'consistency of variation of texture' or 'consistency of variation of orientation' and so on.

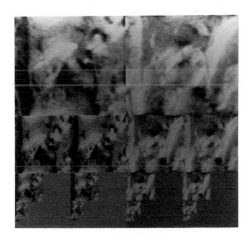

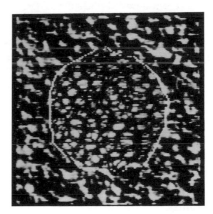

Fig 15. Multilevel orientation representation is robust in noise.

Fig 16. Segmentation of texture using generalised quad-tree.

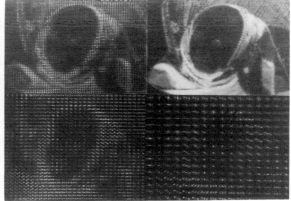

Fig 17. Quad-tree of image containing structure and texture

Fig 18. Multilevel local spectral representation of image shown in Fig 17.

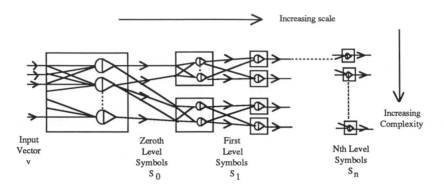

Increasing
Complexity

Input
Vector
v

Zeroth
Level
Symbols
$S_0$

First
Level
Symbols
$S_1$

Nth Level
Symbols
$S_n$

Fig 19.  Vision as a hierarchy of representation and invariance

## 3. Probability

While such methods do help to reduce uncertainty, they cannot remove it completely.  This means that the equivalence classes $V_i$ cannot be formed — a given vector v may 'belong' to more than one class.  The conventional solution to this problem is to introduce probability.  Thus to each vector v, there is a probability $p_i(v)$ that it belongs to the ith class

$$p_i(v) = \text{Prob } \{v \in V_i\} \tag{89}$$

This replaces the problem of finding ideal symbolisations (eqn (37)) with that of finding those which have minimum uncertainty (eg [9], [12]).

This approach raises many questions about which models are appropriate and the range of answers found in the literature indicates that the answers are not easily found.  This topic deserves a paper in its own right, but there is one fundamental issue which is particularly germane to the present discussion.  It concerns the interpretation of probability in vision.  Two plausible, but radically different, semantic models are available.

### 3.1 The Single Symbol Interpretation

This is without doubt the most often used interpretation.  Indeed, it seems to follow from the very definition of probability.  It is that a given image (or image neighbourhood) has a single 'correct' symbolic description, which is hidden from the observer by the ambiguous nature of the processes intervening between the observer and the object of his observation.  In this view, $p_i(v)$ means 'the probability that the ith symbol is the correct interpretation of the image v'.  This is not only plausible, it also leads to a whole range of estimages, from maximum likelihood to expected value, for the symbol in question.  In fact it can lead to interpolation of symbols which do not have an explicit representation: vernier acuity.  For example, both the orientation symbol $\theta(v)$ of eqn (84) and a position estimate based on local centroid were combined [8] to give a symbolic description with sub-pixel position resolution and an angular resolution of the order of $1° - 2°$.  This is far above the resolution implied by the uncertainty principle.  In both cases, these estimates are essentially a form of expected value. Thus if $s_i$ is the symbol associated with vectors $v \in V_i$, then the new symbol $\bar{s}$ is

$$\bar{s} = \sum_i p_i(v) \, s_i \qquad\qquad (90)$$

in the scalar case. In general, $s_i$ and $\bar{s}$ may be vectors (cf eqn (81)) or even tensors [22]. Now of course such interpolation only makes sense when the symbols S(.) are embedded in some form of manifold. It is not clear, for example, what the correct interpolation between a teacup and a river would be. This is a problem for another day, however. The immediate difficulty with such interpolations is that they simply reintroduce ambiguity. Thus the single symbol interpretation, applied at whatever level of description, from single pixel to whole image, leads straight back to the problems with which the introduction of probability was supposed to deal.

## 3.2 The Multiple Symbol Model

The alternative to the single symbol model is obvious: there is no unique symbol describing the image (nor any part of it). This approach flies in the face of the conventional view of probability. In some respects, it is more akin to 'Quantum' reasoning than classical statistical reasoning (see eg [9]). What it implies is that, at each level of symbolic description, the observer must be prepared to support more than one symbol. Methods for implementing such descriptions range from that employed in the GOP architecture [23], which attaches to the interpolated symbol $\bar{s}$ a measure of dispersion, to a full 'wavefunction' description, which stores all of the probabilities $p_i(v)$ (eg [9], [13]). There is some evidence that biological systems employ the latter approach, at least at low levels of description [13]. It is at present an open question whether either of these approaches, or perhaps one lying somewhere between, is best. What is certain is that they are fundamentally different from the conventional 'single symbol' formalism.

## Conclusions

This study began as an attempt to explore the complex relationship between the symbolic descriptions which are the goal of a vision system and the input signals which are the data from which those descriptions must be inferred. It has been shown that there are fundamental constraints on the process of symbolic description, which can be overcome to a certain extent by employing hierarchical methods, but which always leave an element of uncertainty in the representation. The model of vision which has emerged from this work (Fig 19) is like none of the naive approaches described in the introduction and yet it shares elements with each of them. For example, this model of vision is not simple pattern recognition (in the sense of Fig 1) unless 'pattern' is generalised to the notion of 'invariant' discussed above. If that generalisation is allowed, then the two approaches are not so very different. Similarly, although the sharp distinction between 'signal' and 'symbol' processing implied by the model of Fig 2 has been deliberately blurred, the new model shares with that of Fig 2 a recognition of the need for many levels of symbolic representation and invariance, describing not simply more local or global features, but different orders of complexity — 'uniformity', 'uniformity of variation', 'variation of uniformity of variation' and so on.

Finally, like the neural net model of Fig 3, there is a much greater use of 'soft' non-linearities, like squaring, and signal processing methods, but this is not because 'symbols are bad', but rather because the symbolic representations which have been needed so far only require such operations. It hardly needs saying that the program described here is incomplete: 'granny' as a set of 'invariant properties' sounds plausible, but has a degree of circularity. Saying that 'granny' is 'the collection of all those properties which are always there when granny is in the picture' is a bit like saying 'granny is granny'. It is true, but unhelpful. It is fair to conclude that, while the new approach has not reached this level of description, it does focus on the right issue — how to relate the symbols at any level to the signals from which they are derived — and that it has shown some encouraging results at low levels of description. The rest is a matter of faith.

## Acknowledgement

This work was supported by SERC and IBM (UK) Ltd. Many sincere thanks are due to Professor Gösta Granlund of Linköping University, whose pioneering ideas have inspired and informed much of the work presented here, and to Dr Hans Knutsson, also of Linköping University whose contribution has also been enormous. Thanks also to Mike Spann, Andrew Calway and Simon Clippingdale for their hard work in obtaining some of the results.

## References

1. Duda, R. O., Hart, P. E., Pattern Classification and Scene Analysis, New York, Wiley, 1973.

2. Marr, D., Vision, San Francisco, Freeman, 1982.

3. Barrow, H. G., Tenenbaum, J. M., Computational Vision, Proc. IEEE, 69, 5, 572-595, 1981.

4. Rumelhart, D. E., McClelland, J. L., Parallel Distributed Processing Vol. 1, Cambridge, M.I.T., 1986.

5. —, PDP Vol. 2, Cambridge, M.I.T., 1986.

6. Granlund, G. H., In Search of a General Picture Processing Operator, Comp. Graphics and Image Proc., 8, 155-173, 1978.

7. Knutsson, H., Filtering and Reconstruction in Image Processing, Linköping Univ., Ph.D. Thesis, 1982.

8. Wilson, R., Knutsson, H., Granlund, G. H., The Operational Definition of the Position of Line and Edge, Proc. 6th Int'l Conf. on Patt. Rec., 846-849, Munich, 1982.

9. Wilson, R., Granlund, G. H., The Uncertainty Principle in Image Processing, IEEE Trans. on Patt. Anal. and Machine Intell., PAMI-6, 758-767, 1984.

10. Spann, M., Wilson, R., A Quad-tree Approach to Image Segmentation that Combines Statistical and Spatial Information, Patt. Recog., 18, 257-269, 1985.

11. Wilson, R., Spann, M., The Finite Prolate Spheroidal Sequences and their Applications pt I, II, (Accepted for publication) IEEE Trans. on Patt. Anal. and Machine Intell., 1987.

12. Wilson, R., Spann, M., Image Segmentation and Uncertainty, Chichester, Research Studies Pr., 1988.

13. Wilson, R., Knutsson, H., Uncertainty and Inference in the Visual System, (Accepted for publication) IEEE Trans. on Sys. Man and Cybern., 1987.

14. Weyl, H., The Theory of Groups and Quantum Mechanics, New York, Dover, 1950.

15. Frei, W., Chen, C. C., Fast Boundary Detection: A Generalisation and a New Algorithm, IEEE Trans. Comp., C-26, 988-998, 1977.

16. Gabor, D., Theory of Communication, Proc. IEE, 93, 26, 429-441, 1946.

17. Canny, J., A Computational Approach to Edge Detection, IEEE Trans. Patt. Anal. and Machine Intell., PAMI-8, 679-698, 1986.

18. Nering, E. D., Linear Algebra and Matrix Theory (2nd Ed.), New York, Wiley, 1970.

19. Wilson, R., Knutsson, H., Uncertainty and Inference in the Visual System II: Motion and Stereopsis without Matching, To be published.

20. Adelson, E. H., Bergen, J. R., Spatiotemporal Energy Models for the Perception of Motion, J. Opt. Soc. Am. A, 2, 284-299, 1985.

21. Watson, A. B., Ahumada, A. J., Model of Human Visual-Motion Sensing, J. Opt. Soc. Am. A, 2, 322-342, 1985.

22. Knutsson, H., A Tensor Representation of 3-d Structure, IEEE ASSP Soc. Workshop on Multidimensional S.P., Noordwijkerhout, Holland, 1987.

23. Granlund, G. H., Knutsson, H., Contrast of Structural and Homogeneous Representations, in Physical and Biological Processing of Images, ed. O. Braddick, Berlin, Springer-Verlag, 282-303, 1983.

24. Jauch, J. M., Foundations of Quantum Mechanics, Reading, Addison-Wesley, 1968.

25. Calway, A. D., Hierarchical Descriptors for Nonstationary 1 and 2-d Signal Processing, Warwick Univ. Comp. Sci. Rept. no. RR108, 1987.

26. Clippingdale, S., Wilson, R., Quad-tree Image Estimation: a New Image Model and its Application to Minimum Mean Square Error Image Restoration, Proc. 5th Scand. Conf. on Image Anal., 699-706, Stockholm, 1987.

An Integrated Image Segmentation/Image Analysis System

By P.D.S. Irwin and Dr A.J. Wilkinson


Department of Electrical and Electronic Engineering
Queens University, Belfast

Abstract

The paper describes an integrated image segmentation/image analysis system.  A
segmentation algorithm which operates by tuning it's output to a pre-defined
mathematical optimum is firstly outlined.  Implementation of a rule-based image
analysis system which makes use of the data computed during the segmentation process
is then discussed.  A pyramidal data structure is suggested in which the image data
flows from the base upwards with the control data used in analysing the image moving
in the reverse direction.  It is hoped that by means of this approach the image
analysis process will be capable of exerting a degree of control over the segmentation
algorithm leading to a more flexible system.

1.  Introduction


The process of automatically analysing an image is one which is common to a wide
variety of application areas such as automatic inspection, robotic vision, target
tracking etc.  Systems developed to solve image analysis problems can in the main be
described by the functional diagram of Figure 1.1(a), where the problem is divided
into two distinct processes:
(1)  The digitised array of brightness values representing the image is segmented by
assigning individual pixels to a limited number of classes.  This classification
process could involve producing edge/non-edge pixels or perhaps dividing the pixels
into classes dependent on grey-level value, texture measures or even motion vectors.
(2)  The segmented image is then examined by a feature extraction system which
produces the data upon which the required decisions can be based.
Of the wide variety of image segmentation algorithms described in the literature
(refs 1, 2, 3) the majority deal with the segmentation of a single image in isolation.

---

(This work is being carried out as part of a collaborative project with Short Brothers
Plc, Missile Systems Division, Montgomery Road, Belfast).

Broadly speaking these techniques, whether they be feature based (e.g. grey-level thresholding or colour segmentation) or image domain based (e.g. region growing or split and merge schemes), produce a segmented image by applying specific parameters and rules to the original image. The values of the parameters being either pre-defined or evaluated from the original image data. In applications where a sequence of images is being segmented any adaptive parameters or thresholds selected in the segmentation of previous frames can be used again on subsequent images and can be gradually up-dated as necessary rather than being recalculated for each individual frame.

This feedback of information concerning the values of the parameters is however a low-level mathematical process which does not in any way interact with the image analysis part of the system. The segmentation process therefore receives no information about it's performance from the point of view of the 'higher-level' analysis system further along the processing chain. Although the segmentation process may tune it's performance to produce some mathematically 'optimal' output there is no guarantee that the image analysis system is making any sense of the segmented images produced. This lack of feedback may not create a problem in well controlled environments where there are a finite number of possible scene inter-pretations. In the analysis of complex scenes however it would seem a reasonable assertion that if the image analysis process were able to feed back information concerning the performance of the segmentation algorithm, an improved system would result. This would allow the segmentation process to be optimised from the point of view of the analysis process rather than in some mathematical sense. It is not however desirable that the image analysis process completely controls the segmentation process since the analysis system may then begin to 'see' what it wants to see as opposed to what is actually there. However, if some form of limited control is applied it should hopefully allow a more meaningful segmentation to result. The work described therefore aims to produce an image analysis system which will allow the feedback loop of figure 1 .1 (b) to be connected, even if only in some limited form. Discussion of the philosophy behind this approach to image analysis is left to references 4, 5 and 6.

By defining the segmentation algorithm as one which assigns each pixel to one of a limited number of grey-levels, the image analysis part of the system is presented with the possibility of controlling the number and position of these allowable grey-levels. An image segmentation algorithm which uses a purely mathematical system to control the positions of the allowable levels is firstly described in section 2. Section 3 then outlines work currently underway aimed at producing an algorithm which would allow these grey levels to be controlled (at least partially) by a rule based system incorporated into the image analysis part of the overall system.

## 2. A Framework for Image Segmentation

### 2.1 The General Concept

The primary concern of the segmentation process is the reduction of the grey-level data to a size and form which contains as much relevant information as possible, whilst sufficiently reducing the processing burden on the image analysis system. It is intended that this data reduction is achieved in such a way as to allow the other goals stated in the introduction to be incorporated to some degree. The segmentation of an image can be viewed as an edge detection process where the edges of the important objects in the scene are located directly or as a region segmentation process where the edges are defined by the boundaries of the continuous regions produced. Since direct edge detection techniques produce broken boundaries which are notoriously difficult to analyse it is therefore not unexpected that region segmentation techniques are more frequently applied in the majority of applications. Both types of operator are however attempting to locate the same boundaries within the image and it is this edge/region-boundary coincidence which is utilised in the algorithm described. A framework has been developed within which a region operator may be combined with an edge detection operator - Figure 2.1 shows the functional structure of the algorithm. The region segmentation may be defined as a pixel classification problem where each pixel is assigned to one of 'n' grey levels. The edge detection operator must be capable of producing a value for the edge content at each pixel location within the image i.e. essentially performing a digital different-iation of the image array. The region operator performs the actual segmentation (thus producing closed region boundaries) with the independently generated differential array being used to control the process.

The algorithm proposed acts as follows:

A set of allowable grey levels is defined (say 2 initially) and the region operator transforms the grey-level image into a segmented image by assigning each pixel to one of these grey levels. The boundary pixels in the segmented image are then extracted and compared with the corresponding pixels in the separately generated edge array, producing an 'edge score' (E) for the current segmentation. The grey-level assigned to any given pixel in the segmented image is compared with the original grey-level value of that pixel producing a difference score (D). It is obviously desirable to maximise the value of E, therefore maximising the edge/region-boundary coincidence, whilst simultaneously minimising the value of D, the error between the segmented and the original images. These values are therefore combined to form the function:

$$C = E - \lambda D \tag{1}$$

which is then maximised over the number and position of the allowable grey-levels to produce the final segmented image.

## 2.2 Implementation Details

Typical Operators used to implement the functional blocks shown in Figure 2.1 are described below:

(the $m * m$ pixel image is described by the array $I(x, y)$)

1. The edge operator transforms the image $I(x, y) \rightarrow e(x, y)$ the differential array. This can be achieved using any of the standard differential operators (reference 7) - all of the examples shown use a Sobel operator.

2. The region operator transforms the image $I(x, y) \rightarrow I'(x, y)$ the segmented image. Each pixel in $I'(x, y)$ is set to one of the n allowable grey-levels $(l(j))$. In the examples shown below the region operator is a simple minimum error classifier i.e. each pixel is set to its nearest allowable grey-level.

3. The algorithm control block performs the following operations:

   (a) A boundary image $B(x, y)$ is created from $I'(x, y)$ where
   
   $B(x, y) = 0$ for non-boundary pixels in $I'(x, y)$
   $\qquad = 1$ for boundary pixels in $I'(x, y)$
   
   (This is achieved directly by local neighbour comparison over a 4-connected neighbourhood)

   (b) The edge and difference values are evaluated:

$$E = \frac{\sum_{x, y} e(x, y) B(x, y)}{\sum_{x, y} B(x, y)} \qquad (2)$$

$$D = \frac{\sum_{x, y} \left| I(x, y) - I'(x, y) \right|}{m * m} \qquad (3)$$

The number and positions of the allowable grey-levels are then varied in such a way as to maximise the function C where:

$$C = E - \lambda D \qquad \lambda = \text{a weighting constant} \qquad (4)$$

(a value of $\lambda = 5.0$ was used in the results shown below)

It is possible to perform this maximisation using a simple hill-climbing algorithm. Figure 2.2(b) shows the values of C plotted for a two level segmentation of the image in Figure 2.2(a). A smooth curve is produced with three local peaks in the cost function each corresponding to the segmentations shown. This means that provided the initial positioning of the two allowable levels is reasonable the global optimum of C should be

easily attainable using a hill-climbing technique. The initial positioning of
the allowable levels is based on an analysis of the grey-level histogram of the
first image encountered in any given image sequence. The histogram is initially
plotted at a very coarse resolution using only 10 values to cover the entire grey-
scale. If two or more local peaks are obtained on the histogram then these values
are used as the initial allowable grey levels. In cases where only one local peak
is obtained the histogram is replotted at progressively finer resolutions until
the necessary two or more local peaks occur (a more detailed discussion of initial
level selection is contained in ref. 8). When the initial levels selected have been
tuned to their optimum position a decision on whether or not to add further levels
will be taken by the algorithm controller. This decision will be based on the
information extracted from the segmented image (described in section 3) and will
depend upon the degree to which the current segmentation has been 'understood' by
the analysis part of the system. (The technique used to select new allowable grey
levels is also described in ref. 8).

The algorithm has so far been described as a sequential tuning process which
takes place within the time period of a single frame, however this is to be applied
to the segmentation of a sequence of images. Since neighbouring images within this
sequence are extremely similar and since at each iteration of the tuning process a
segmented output is obtained it is possible to perform each iteration on a newly
acquired frame. This means that the tuning of the grey-levels is an on-going process
with the position of the global maximum gradually changing due to the slight
variations in the incoming frames.


3. Analysing the Segmented Image

In applications where the image environment is fairly well controlled, such as in
automatic insepection systems or robotic vision systems segmentation techniques
such as that outlined above may well yield a segmented image which is sufficient for
the analysis system to act upon. Analysis of more complex outdoor scenes may
however require the feed-back loop described by Figure 1.1(b) to be introduced for
better understanding of the scene. The analysis technique outlined below is being
developed with the ultimate aim of allowing this interaction with the segmentation
algorithm to take place. A pyramidal approach has been adopted in trying to label or
'understand' the segmented image. This approach is not new and has often been
advocated in the literature as an efficient means of region representation
(reference 9, 10). Much has also been published describing pyramidal multi-processor
hardware though details of the actual data extracted in specific pattern recognition
problems is often omitted (references 11, 12, 13 and 14).

3.1 Data Flow Within the Pyramid

The data extracted from the segmented image forms a pyramid of progressively
decreasing resolution. The original image, the segmented image and the edge array
(described in section 2) form the base of the pyramid (see Figure 3.1). The level
above the base is divided into a series of non-overlapping windows and data
calculated from the pixels enclosed by each window is passed upward to this level.
Another series of non-overlapping windows producing an even lower resolution makes
up the next level and again data relevant to the area covered by each window is
calculated and passed upward. The window sizes used are shown in Figure 3.1 - these
values have been chosen entirely arbitrarily. It would appear that the optimum
window domensions depend to a great extent on the likely dimensions of the objects
being viewed in the scene though no work has as yet been performed on attempting to
calculate optimum dimensions.

The full resolution image is examined as a series of 8 x 8 non-overlapping
windows. Each allowable grey-level occurring within a given window produces the
following data:

npix    - the number of pixels set to the level in question.
dplus   - the value of D (as described in section 2) using only pixels where
            $I'(x, y) > I(x, y)$
dminus  - the value of D (as described in section 2) using only pixels where
            $I(x, y) < I'(x, y)$
Elevel  - the value of E (as described in section 2) using only pixels which
            border the level in question.

These values are calculated for each level within each of the windows. This process
is not as time consuming as it may appear since each value has already been
partially evaluated during calculation of the cost C. A small amount of extra
processing will be required to calculate the values separately for each level and in
a window form. At the intermediate (8 x 8 window) resolution a connectivity array
is computed for each grey-level occurring in the scene. This array links windows
containing pixels of the  same  grey-level  provided these pixels are within  a
thresnold distance from the boundary dividing the two windows. The threshold set
will depend upon the expected size and spacing of the relevant objects in the scene
as well as the noise content of the image. As an example consider Figure 3.2 which
shows the top of a fir tree outlined against he sky. It is obviously desirable
that the tree is regarded as a single entity by the connectivity array. Therefore
'floating' branches, such as those in window D4 (See Figure 3.2), are regarded as
being connected to the main body of the tree (window D5) provided both windows
contain 'tree' pixels within a threshold distance from the boundary between the two
windows. This approach will obviously lead to errors in other cases - as an example
consider Figure 3.3 (c) or (d) where the sky and bright reflection from the left side

of the block of flats will be regarded as a single entity. The array must therefore be examined by assuming that broken links are permanently broken but that links which are connected are not permanent and indeed pixels of the same level within a window need not be part of the same object.

The lowest resolution array at the top of the pyramid will simply contain values representing the number of pixels of each level appearing in each of the 4 x 4 composite windows. This allows a very broad overview of the character of the scene and can allow surprisingly powerful deductions to be made concerning the scene contents.

## 3.2 Analysis of the Data Within the Pyramid

Consider the segmentation of the image in Figure 3.3 (a) - the 2, 3 and 4 level segmentations are shown in Figure 3.3 (b), (c) and (d). The data extracted from these segmented images is analysed from the top of the pyramid downward.

The low-resolution data at the top of the pyramid produces broad suggestions as to the image contents. These hypotheses can then be confirmed or denied by analysis of the desired sections of the more detailed data deeper in the pyramid. The analysis of the image is therefore to a great extent 'data driven'.

To decide upon the relative weighting given to information from the various sources and the way in which the data is combined, a training set of images will be required. By manually assigning labels to each of the regions within the segmented images and then comparing the data within the pyramid for the various labels, the rules by which a given system operates may be deduced. Development of such an application specific analysis system is currently underway using a commercially available expert system shell (capable of rule induction) to assist in producing an efficient rule set.

## 4. Conclusions

As was stated in the introduction the ultimate aim of this work is to produce an integrated segmentation/analysis system in which the analysis part of the system can feed back performance information to the segmentation process. This goal will hopefully be attainable by allowing the image analysis system to completely control the number of and partially control the positions of the 'allowable grey levels' (as described in section 2). A degree of 'top-down' control over the actual segmentation process would therefore be achieved.

The pyramidal approach to data extraction would appear to present an efficient and flexible means of analysing the relevant data. In practical terms it is hoped that this approach will lead to an application specific system capable of producing a much more flexible response to images which are poorly defined and therefore difficult to segment and analyse. It is also expected that more general purpose systems adopting this approach would be able to make sense of a much wider range of images.

References

1. R M Haralick and L G Shapiro, 'Survey: Image Segmentation Techniques' Computer Vision, Graphics and Image Processing, Vol. 29, No. 1, p 100-132 1985.
2. S Zucker, 'Region Growing: Childhood and Adolescence' Computer Graphics and Image Processing, Vol. 5, (1976) p 382-399.
3. K S Fu and J K Mai, 'A Survey on Image Segmentation' Pattern Recognition, Vol. 13 (1981) p. 3-16.
4. W K Pratt, 'Digital Image Processing', J Wiley and Sons (1978).
5. D H Ballard and C M Brown, 'Computer Vision' Section 10.4, Prentice-Hall, New Jersey 1982.
6. P H Winston (Editor), 'The Psychology of Computer Vision', McGraw-Hill, New York, 1975.
7. A Rosenfeld and A C Kak, 'Digital Picture Processing', Vol. 2, Sec. 10.2, Academic Press, 1982.
8. P Irwin , 'Development of a Parallel algorithm, for real-time target Detection in Minimal Processing Applications'. 54th AGARD Avionics Panel Symposium on Electro-Optical Systems and Image Analysis for Airborne Applications, Athens, October 1987.
9. P Cohen and E Feigenbaum, 'The Handbook of Artificial Intelligence', Vol. 3, Sec. 13E, Pitman Books, 1982.
10. D Ballard and C Brown, 'Computer Vision' (Section 10) Prentice-Hall, New Jersey, 1982.
11. L Uhr, 'Multicomputer Parallel Arrays, Pipelines and Pyramids for Pattern Recognition in 'VLSI and Modern Signal Processing', Ed. S Kung, J Whitehouse, T Kailath, p. 406-421, 1985.
12. C Dyer, 'Pyramid Algorithms and Machines' p. 409-420.
13. S Tanimoto, 'Programming Techniques for Hierarchical Parallel Image Processors, p. 421-429. (Both in Multicomputers and Image Processing' by K Preston and L Uhr, Academic Press, 1982).
14. A Rosenfeld, 'Expert' Vision Systems: Some Issues' Computer Vision Graphics and Image Processing, Vol. 34, No. 1, 1986, p 99-117.

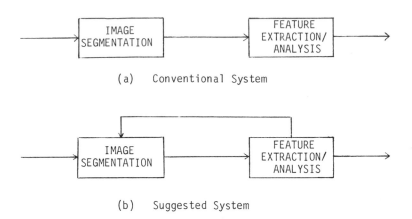

(a)    Conventional System

(b)    Suggested System

Figure 1.1    Functional Diagrams of Image Processing Systems

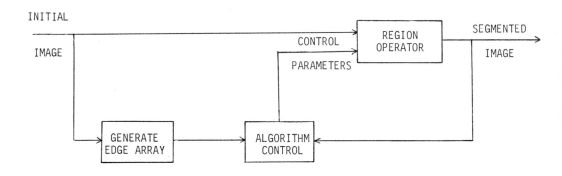

Figure 2.1    Functional Diagram of Proposed Algorithm

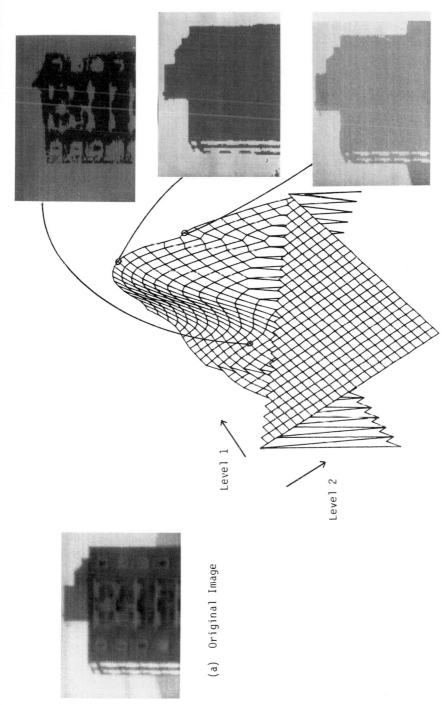

35

(a) Original Image

(b) Image Cost Function for a 2-Level Segmentation - Three Local
Maxima were obtained representing the 3 images shown.

Level 1

Level 2

Figure 2.2 Plot of Typical Image Cost Function

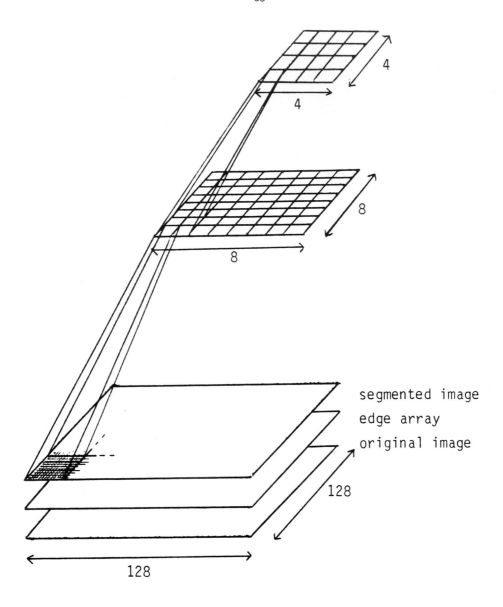

4

4

8

8

segmented image
edge array
original image

128

128

Figure 3.1   Pyramidal Approach to Data Extraction

37

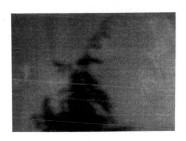

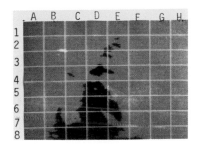

(a)  Original Image

(b)  2-Level Segmentation (with
      windows superimposed)

Figure 3.2  Example of Disjointed Segmentation

(a)  Original Image

(b)  2-Level Segmentation

(c)  3-Level Segmentation

(d)  4-Level Segmentation

Figure 3.3    Example Segmentation

# A fast algorithm for the automatic recognition of heat sources in satellite images

## L.Hayes and A.P.Cracknell

**Department of Applied Physics and Electronic & Manufacturing Engineering,
University of Dundee, Dundee DD1 4HN, Scotland U.K.**

## Abstract

A fast algorithm has been implemented for the automatic recognition of heat sources using data from the Advanced Very High Resolution Radiometer (AVHRR) of the TIROS-N series of meteorological satellites. Channel 3 of the AVHRR measures radiation in the mid-infrared part of the spectrum (3.8 μm wavelength) and is sensitive to high temperature heat sources even when these occupy a very small part of the instantaneous field of view. The use of channel 3 of the AVHRR for the detection of heat sources is well documented but to date these heat sources have been identified by operator interpretation of hard copy or other display media. The algorithm described obviates the need for manual interpretation or display facilities. Attention is given to the avoidance of spurious results arising out of the problem of pixel dropout and other non-systematic noise.

The algorithm has important implications in that it facilitates the detection of wildfires and agricultural burning and the monitoring of gas disposal operations on a routine and cost-effective basis. Known heat sources, such as oil and gas production sites and refineries, are able to be monitored continually, while maverick heat sources can be reported in near-real time. This is particularly useful where fire reporting services are poorly developed.

## 1. Background

As the effect of wildfires can be catastrophic, there is a need for immediate information relating to the presence and location of heat sources to facilitate effective wildfire management. Environmental concern may call for regular monitoring of controlled burning in an agricultural context or in gas disposal operations, the effect of which may not be immediately obvious. Remotely sensed thermal infrared data provide a means by which large areas may be quickly and repetitively monitored, different sensing systems being available appropriate to the scale of the operation. This paper considers the automatic recognition of heat sources in digital thermal imagery using AVHRR data to demonstrate the technique over very large, continental scale, areas.

Theoretical consideration of the spectral interval most suitable for the detection of forest fires (Kondratyev *et al.*, 1972) shows that the optimal spectral regions are those of 3.5 - 4.2 μm and 4.4 - 5.0 μm. The maximum thermal emission of fires is localised within these wavelength bands, which conveniently correspond to atmospheric transmission windows. Channel 3 of the AVHRR records radiation in the former spectral region over a wide field of view (110°), which corresponds to a swath width of approximately 3000 km on the ground.

Kondratyev *et al.* (*ibid.*) investigated the possibilities of using infrared scanning radiometers for the detection of incipient forest fires from aircraft and found that these sensors provided a reliable method of fire detection, having the special advantage of being able to reveal the source of burning which might, in visible wavebands, be obscured by smoke.

Matson and Dozier (1981) have demonstrated the ability of the AVHRR to detect heat sources even when these are much smaller than the instantaneous field of view (IFOV) of the sensor. Matson *et al.* (1984) report the use of AVHRR data in a semi-operational feasibility study for monitoring fires over the western U.S.A. Most fires, which were detected by the investigation of a video display of channel 3 and channel 4 data, were found to be controlled burning but first notice of a wildfire was provided in several instances. Other studies report the use of AVHRR channel 3 data for the identification of steel mills (Matson and Dozier, *op. cit.*), oil production platforms (Muirhead and Cracknell, 1984a), agricultural burning (Muirhead and Cracknell, 1985), and land clearing (Matson *et al.*, 1987). A review of the use of channel 3 data is given by Muirhead and Cracknell (1984b).

## 2. Procedure

A small hot target appearing within the field of view of the AVHRR is recorded as a characteristic spike having large amplitude and a narrow basewidth (see fig. 1). This characteristic spike may be identified digitally by utilizing simple image processing techniques. The amplitude of the spike is a crude measure of the brightness temperature within the IFOV but does not necessarily relate directly to the actual temperature of the heat source. The basewidth is similarly not necessarily suggestive of the size of the heat source. As the IFOV of the AVHRR includes an area more than a kilometre square (see, for example Hayes and Cracknell, 1984 for an illustration of IFOV dimensions) a small but intense heat source may provoke a response commensurate with a larger but cooler heat source. The relationship between the size of the heat source, its temperature and the IFOV may not be established using channel 3 data alone. An algorithm for determining the black body temperature of the heat source is given by Dozier (1981).

The peak brightness temperature of the spike and the brightness temperature difference between the peak and the background or underlying surface together enable heat sources to be identified in

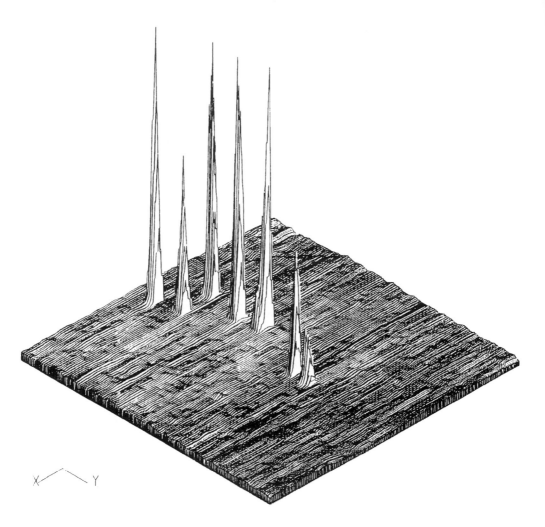

**Figure 1** Temperature surface representation of gas flaring operations in
a small part of the North Sea showing an enhanced view of the

the AVHRR data. These properties represent a primitive connectivity pair allowing automatic knowledge-based identification of heat sources in AVHRR data.

## 2.1 Peak brightness temperature

In the first instance, only high temperature heat sources need be considered as potential heat sources. Accordingly, a threshold, or brightness temperature cutoff, may be chosen in order to restrict the algorithm to the consideration of high temperature heat sources only. For the AVHRR data the lower the digital number the greater the brightness temperature and associated likelihood of the pixel representing a heat source. The relation between the digital number (DN) and the brightness

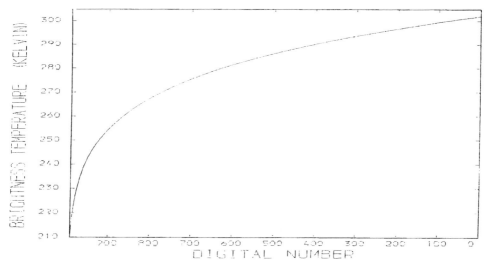

**Figure 2** Relationship between digital number and brightness temperature for NOAA-7 AVHRR Channel 3.

temperature is shown in fig. 2 for NOAA-7 data. This relationship is established by calculating the satellite-received radiance from the calibration data in the data stream and relating this radiance to the brightness temperature using the Planck and normalised detector response functions. It should be noted that a particular DN may not readily be related to absolute temperatures because of the combined effects of atmosphere, path length, emissivity, and size of IFOV. It is also important to note that brightness temperatures in excess of approximately 302 K will saturate the sensor. The number of potential heat sources indicated by the algorithm is likely to relate to the brightness temperature cutoff set. After exhaustive investigation of several AVHRR scenes a cutoff at DN 100 was selected. From figure 2 it may be ascertained that the actual cutoff value selected need not necessarily be precise as in this portion of the curve changes in DN correspond to only small changes in brightness temperature. For this reason it would not seem to be necessary to adjust the cutoff from scene to scene. Figure 3 provides an indication, for a complete range of sensor-target geometries, of the relationship between the number of heat sources reported by the algorithm and the DN cutoff set (the ordinate) and the threshold set for the difference between the peak and the background (abscissa). There being no 'typical' scene, more relevance should be attached to the shape of the curves than to the actual number of heat sources. The small step at DN = 100 would appear to indicate a natural cutoff between those brightness temperatures associated with natural terrestrial radiation and those associated with heat sources, drop out, or sensor saturation.

## 2.2 Difference between peak and background.

In the second instance the brightness temperature difference between the potential heat source and the background is thresholded. This is necessary because of the influence of reflected solar radiation particularly in the case of specular reflection. The reflected solar component may cause apparent temperature gradients to be recorded where these do not in fact exist. This apparent temperature gradient can be accounted for by changes in reflection coefficients with changes in illumination

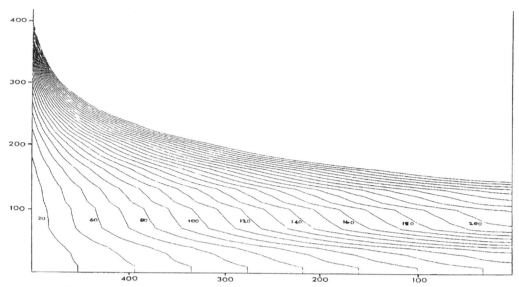

**Figure 3** Algorithm sensitivity measured in terms of the number of heat
sources reported showing a non-linear relationship between
the digital number cutoff set (ordinate) and the threshold set for
the digital number difference between a heat source and its
background. The number of potential heat sources reported increases from the bottom left (low digital number cutoff and high
difference from background threshold) to the top right (high
digital number cutoff and low difference from background threshold).

angle (solar zenith and azimuth) which may in the extreme provide conditions of specular reflection.

This temperature difference threshold provides a measure of the sensitivity of the algorithm since it
determines the minimal value of thermal contrasts that are to be reported by the algorithm. The
probability of detecting a false signal will relate to this sensitivity threshold and figure 3 reflects the
increase in the number of potential heat sources with decrease in the threshold. The function of the
temperature difference threshold is to define the amplitude and basewidth of the spike associated
with potential heat sources. The amplitude of the spike is simply the mean of the background sub-
tracted from the temperature of the peak. The basewidth is considered in terms of the number of
pixels affected by a heat source. An optimal size for the number of pixels to be incorporated into the
calculation of the background value will be determined by this basewidth and by consideration of
the contextual nature of the background; this would to some extent include a trade-off for computational efficiency. In the course of the development of this algorithm several hundred heat sources
have been investigated in AVHRR data and it was observed that less than ten pixels are affected by
any single heat source. As the IFOV of the AVHRR gives rise to pixels a kilometre or more on the
ground, the effect of a heat source will be seen typically only in a single pixel, but not unusually in
adjacent pixels as well. A 5 by 5 pixel window was selected as the point spread function (PSF) for
the algorithm because it is both symmetrical and represents the minimum size appropriate in a
trade-off for computational efficiency.

The combination of the two thresholds - brightness temperature and difference from the background - provides a measure by which the characteristic data spike may not only be identified but also checked to ensure that it is commensurate with a high temperature heat source, providing a context-dependent heat source/non-heat source identification. The knowledge structure for heat source detection in AVHRR data is depicted in fig. 4.

---

**IF:**    The pixel value is less than the threshold set
      *And* the difference from the background is greater
           than the difference value set
      *And* the pixel does not represent noise or dropout
**THEN:**  The pixel represents a potential heat source

**IF:**    The pixel value is equal to zero
      *And* the neighbouring pixels are unaffected
**THEN:**  The pixel represents noise or dropout

**IF:**    The standard deviation of the background is small
**THEN:**  The neighbouring pixels are unaffected

---

**Figure 4**  Knowledge structure for heat source detection in AVHRR channel 3

## 3.  Implementation

Several procedures were considered to achieve automatic recognition of heat sources. The characteristic data spikes may be regarded as a form of non-periodic noise represented by low digital numbers. Noise in an image may readily be identified with the aid of an appropriate filter. A quick method of noise identification takes the form of a simple low pass filter achieved by spatial neighbourhood averaging. The pixels in the vicinity of a candidate pixel are averaged to provide a background value against which the candidate pixel is compared. This moving average may be programmed in a very efficient recursive form. The difference between the central pixel and the surrounding pixels is calculated within the moving PSF window. While both positive and negative differences are likely to occur, it is only the negative differences that are likely to include heat source candidates.

Consider the convolution of a PSF comprised of a 5 by 5 array with the image along a given scan line (fig. 5). The amplitude of the PSF is 1/25 to maintain the average image grey level during processing. A straightforward calculation of the averages at each point would require 24 additions. However, if the average of the pixels in each of the columns of the PSF is saved and updated the 24 additions need to be computed once only at the beginning of the scanline. Each subsequent average is calculated as the previous average minus the old average in the first column plus the new average in column 5. Thus, except for the first output pixel of each line, only five additions and one subtraction are needed to calculate each output pixel. The computational advantage of the recursive algorithm over the direct calculation for a 5 by 5 PSF is therefore a factor of 4. The recursion is also applied in the vertical direction, further increasing its efficiency.

Isolated zero-value pixels and lines in the digital data may be caused by bit loss in data transmission or other electrical problems. 'Drop-out' or noise pixels usually have zero value indicating data loss

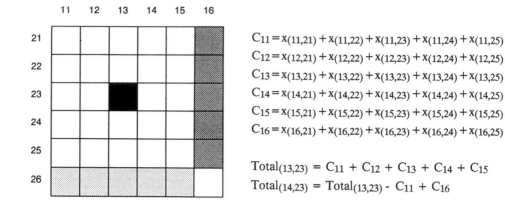

$$C_{11} = x_{(11,21)} + x_{(11,22)} + x_{(11,23)} + x_{(11,24)} + x_{(11,25)}$$
$$C_{12} = x_{(12,21)} + x_{(12,22)} + x_{(12,23)} + x_{(12,24)} + x_{(12,25)}$$
$$C_{13} = x_{(13,21)} + x_{(13,22)} + x_{(13,23)} + x_{(13,24)} + x_{(13,25)}$$
$$C_{14} = x_{(14,21)} + x_{(14,22)} + x_{(14,23)} + x_{(14,24)} + x_{(14,25)}$$
$$C_{15} = x_{(15,21)} + x_{(15,22)} + x_{(15,23)} + x_{(15,24)} + x_{(15,25)}$$
$$C_{16} = x_{(16,21)} + x_{(16,22)} + x_{(16,23)} + x_{(16,24)} + x_{(16,25)}$$

$$Total_{(13,23)} = C_{11} + C_{12} + C_{13} + C_{14} + C_{15}$$
$$Total_{(14,23)} = Total_{(13,23)} - C_{11} + C_{16}$$

**Figure 5** Software implementation of algorithm

while alternatively in the case of channel 3 of the AVHRR a digital number of zero may indicate pixel saturation (see fig. 2). Noise pixels may be differentiated from saturated pixels by considering the deviation of the neighbouring pixels. Pixels surrounding a saturated pixel will themselves be affected by the source of the saturation except in the case of drop out or other noise.

A standard Tukey median filter was investigated as an alternative identification technique - the difference between the central pixel and the median being calculated in order that the isolated heat sources themselves would not affect the median value. Isolated pixels that are different from their nearest neighbours were again readily identified, but the median filter was found to suffer from the shortcoming that where there are several affected pixels in a group not all will be reported in every case.

Identification schemes employing the standard deviation of the background pixels were also investigated in an attempt to provide an automatic and contextually determined setting of the sensitivity of the algorithm. While a difference from the background threshold set in terms of the standard deviation of the background represents an improvement on a predefined difference from the mean, the trade-off of additional computational effort may not be seen to be worthwhile for general applications of the algorithm. An extension of the algorithm to include channel 4 data has not been considered for the same reason. Heat sources detected by the algorithm in Northern England on 17th May 1980 are shown in fig. 6.

## 4.   Limitations of the AVHRR implementation

While heat sources may be identified within minutes of the satellite overpass, several hours (as a function of latitude) may elapse between satellite overpasses. Response times in minutes are generally required. To complicate matters heat sources are obscured by all but thin cloud. While heat sources may be detected through haze and mist, cloud penetration is the exception rather than the norm.

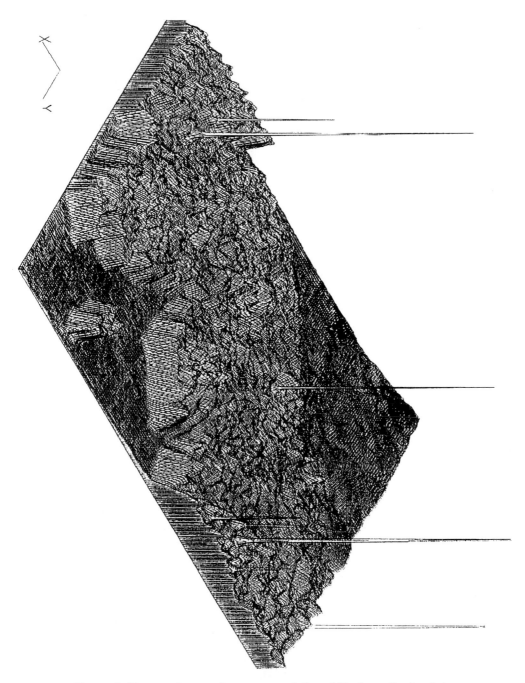

**Figure 6** Temperature surface representation of Northern England showing heat sources detected by the algorithm described from an
excerpt of AVHRR channel 3 data for 17th May 1980. The heat
sources have been accentuated to facilitate their differentiation
from the background

A further consideration is that there may not always be sufficient thermal contrast to enable the detection of every heat source, particularly in areas affected by specular reflection of the Sun from cloud, sea, or land surfaces. However, Sun-target-sensor geometries limit affected parts of a scene to relatively small areas which are non-coincident in successive overpasses. Moreover, since specular reflection does not occur at longer wavelengths thermal contrasts might be investigated in confirmation in congruent channel 4 or 5 data if necessary as an extension to the technique developed by Dozier (*op. cit.*). Hot desert surfaces afford less thermal contrast and may, on hot summer days, necessitate the revision of the general thresholds set although only the afternoon pass is likely to be affected.

The presupposition is that the AVHRR data are available in digital form, but at the same time it would seem that the algorithm would be most applicable in areas outwith the reception area of existing facilities. It should also be mentioned that there is an element of doubt concerning the continuing availability of AVHRR data after 1992 (Rose, 1985). Presently two satellites provide four or more overpasses each day although as a function of latitude, more data sets may in fact be available, up to 12 separate sets of imagery being available for the U.K. daily. The (U.S.) National Oceanic and Atmospheric Administration (NOAA) has guaranteed the maintenance of the TIROS-N series until 1992, whereafter there is a possibility that the two-satellite system may be reduced to a single satellite for financial reasons. This would limit the number of overpasses available for analysis. A further possible limitation will be encountered if data from a proposed additional near infrared channel are substituted for the channel 3 data during daylight operation (Popham, 1984).

The present paper is addressed solely to the recognition of heat sources. While heat sources may be enumerated automatically using the algorithm described, the problems associated with the identification of the heat sources in terms of a terrestrial reference system remain. The automation of this second stage of the process is the subject of ongoing investigation.

## 5. Implications

The algorithm facilitates the near-real time discrimination of wildfires and agricultural burning and the monitoring of gas disposal operations. The simplicity of the algorithm allows it to be implemented on very modest processors, obviating the need for elaborate image processing systems and operator interpretation of output in graphic form as in previous studies.

Known heat sources, such as oil and gas production sites and refineries, are able to be monitored continually, while heat sources outside the usual pattern can be reported within minutes of the satellite overpass. The algorithm has also found application in providing information on gas disposal at exploration sites, where information is otherwise very closely guarded by the site operators.

While the algorithm has been developed for use in conjunction with AVHRR data, the technique would be extendable to alternative mid-infrared data sources. As implemented, the largest benefits of the algorithm are to be found in areas where the fire reporting services are poorly developed, and where agricultural practices do not preclude burning.

# References

Dozier, J.; 1981, A Method for Satellite Identification of Surface Temperature Fields of Subpixel Resolution. Remote Sensing of Environment, 11, 221-229.

Hayes, L., and Cracknell, A.P., 1984, A Comparison of TIROS-N Series Satellite Data and LAND-SAT data over Scotland. Proceedings of the EARSeL/ESA Symposium on Integrative Approaches in Remote Sensing, Guildford, Surrey, (ESA SP-214), pp 63 -74.

Kondratyev, K. Ya., Dyachenko, L.N., Binenko, V.I., and Chernenko, A.P., 1972, Detection of Small Fires and Mapping of Large Forest Fires by Infrared Imagery, Proceeding of the VI International Symposium on Remote Sensing of Environment, Environmental Research Institute of Michigan, Ann Arbor, Michigan, 1297 - 1303.

Matson, M., and Dozier, J., 1981, Identification of Subresolution High Temperature Sources Using a Thermal IR Sensor. Photogrammetric Engineering and Remote Sensing, 47, 1311-1318.

Matson, M., Schneider, S.R., Aldridge, B., and Satchwell, B., 1984, Fire Detection Using the NOAA-Series Satellites. NOAA Technical Report NESDIS 7, January 1984, Washington, D.C.

Matson, M., Stephens, G., and Robinson, J., 1987, Fire detection using data from the NOAA-n satellites, Int. J. Remote Sensing, 8, 961-970.

Muirhead, K., and Cracknell, A.P., 1984a, Identification of Gas Flares in the North Sea using Satellite Data, Int. J. Remote Sensing, 5, 199-212.

Muirhead, K., and Cracknell, A.P., 1984b, Gas Flares and Forest Fires - The Potential of AVHRR band 3, Proceedings of the Tenth Anniversary International Conference, Remote Sensing Society, pp 411-419.

Muirhead, K., and Cracknell, A.P., 1985, Straw Burning over Great Britain Detected by AVIIRR, Int. J. Remote Sensing, 6, 827-833.

Popham, R.W., 1984, NOAA Satellites - Past, Present and Future, Report on the U.K. AVHRR Data Users Meeting, Meteorological Office/Remote Sensing Society, Oxford.

Rose, L., 1985, Space Application and Remote Sensing Office, Office of Advanced Technology, Department of State, Washington D.C., *pers. com.*

# TEXTURE CLASSIFICATION BY LOCAL SURFACE FITTING

Tieniu TAN, Anthony G CONSTANTINIDES

Signal Processing Section, Dept. of Electrical Engineering

Imperial College, London SW7 2BT

**ABSTRACT:** *We present in this paper a new algorithm for texture classification based on local surface fitting of images. At the first step, surface fitting is defined in a predefined local neighborhood and is done at every pixel generating a number of coefficient data fields or texture feature images; Then, texture features are extracted from these feature images and used for texture classification. Initial experimental results show that the algorithm is simple, compact and flexible. It is also suitable for parallel implementation.*

## 1. INTRODUCTION

Texture is observable in all physical surfaces and exists in various kinds of images from satellite multispectral data to microscopic images. It is a fundamental property in many disciplines. However, a formal definition or a model with reasonable complexity has not yet been found. This may be because of the huge number of attributes associated with textures and the lack of the clear understanding of the mechanisms of human visual perception of textures.

For various approaches to texture analysis, HARALICK [1] classifies them into two major groups: Statistical Approaches and Structural Approaches. Recently in [3], TAN suggests three major categories namely Classical Statistical Approach, Structural Approach and Model-Based Approach. Statistical methods consider a texture field as a certain distribution of gray intensity variations and are the most widely used ones; Structural approaches, on the other hand, view a texture field as an arrangement of a set of textural primitives according to some replacement rules, and are usually computationally more complicated; Different from both statistical and structural approaches, model-based approaches are more recent, yet impressive results have been obtained in the content of both texture classification and segmentation by these methods [2, 3]. For details of these approaches, we refer to [1, 2, 3, 4].

In this paper, a new algorithm for texture classification is suggested based on the approximation of digital image data by continuous functions (image surface fitting). It is believed that a digital image field (2-D data array) can be embedded in a continuous function. Since continuous functions are mathematically easy to manipulate, a number of image surface approximation techniques have been suggested and applicable in various fields such as image interpolation, image restoration, image segmentation and image feature extraction (edge detection) [5, 6]. Under most of these circumstances, surface fitting is performed globally, i.e., on the entire image plane. However, surface fitting can be equally applied locally on some sub-image plane or local regions. Although EDEN *et al* [7] have correctly pointed out that a local continuous image representation may also be used to extract edges or local texture properties, no formal procedure concerning the application of local image representation for texture analysis has been established, and no experimental results have been reported of course. Here, with the introduction of local surface fitting, we attempt to remedy this.

The paper is organized as follows. Section 2 provides the framework of local surface fitting. General results of local fitting parameter estimation and the relations between LSF and texture analysis are given; In section 3, we give a case study of the results obtained in the preceding section. We choose polynomials as basis functions; Following section 3, section 4 discusses the problem of texture feature extraction from LSF, and the relation between the features extracted and some important visual texture features are established. Then in section 5, we summarize the experimental results by local polynomial surface fitting; Finally, section 6 concludes the paper.

## 2. LOCAL SURFACE FITTING (LSF)

Let $k \in (1,2,\ldots,K)$, $l \in (1,2,\ldots,L)$, a digital image field will be denoted by $F(k,l)$ with $(k,l) \in KxL$, and $F(k,l) \in (0,1,2,\ldots,Q-1)$. A connected sub-image or region with area A and boundary B will be denoted by $\eta$, where A is the total number of pixels in $\eta$, i.e.,

$$A = \#\{ (k,l), (k,l) \in \eta \}$$

If we assign unity quality to all pixels $(k,l) \in \eta$, the centroid $(i,j)$ of region $\eta$ may be defined as follows

$$i = [\sum_{(k,l) \in \eta} k]/A, \qquad j = [\sum_{(k,l) \in \eta} l]/A$$

(1)

In order to re-index the pixels in $\eta$, we define the following

$$r = k-i;$$
$$c = l-j;$$
$$f(r,c) = F(r+i,c+j) = F(k,l)$$

(2)

where $(i,j) \in KxL$ is the centroid of $\eta$, $(k,l)$ the index pair in the original image field F(k,l) and (r,c) the relative coordinates of (k,l) in η w.r.t (i,j). A region specified by (1) and (2) will be called a **Coordinated Local Neighborhood**, and will be explicitly denoted by $\eta_B(i,j)$ since the region is uniquely determined by the centroid and the boundary. To proceed further, two points should be noticed. It can be easily seen from (1) and (2) that the centroid (i,j) has been actually defined as the origin (0,0) of the coordinated local neighborhood $\eta_B(i,j)$; Second, if B is symmetrical w.r.t. (i,j), we will have

$$\sum_{(r,c)\in\eta_B(i,j)} r = 0, \quad \sum_{(r,c)\in\eta_B(i,j)} c = 0$$

(3)

Now, if let z=f(r,c), then (r,c,z) may be visualized as a point in $R^3$ space. In other words, $\eta_B(i,j)$ defines a discrete surface described by z=f(r,c) and bounded by B. However, being discrete is a severe obstacle for many mathematical manipulations. So, we seek a continuous surface which can approximate z=f(r,c) to any desired extent. Let us represent such a continuous surface as

$$\hat{f}(r,c,\bar{a}_T) = \bar{a}_T^T \cdot \bar{f}(r,c)$$

(4)

where $\bar{a}_T = [a_1 \ a_2 \ \dots \ a_T]^T$ is the parameter or coefficient vector and $\bar{f}(r,c) = [f_1(r,c) \ f_2(r,c) \ \dots \ f_T(r,c)]^T$ is a known function vector (function basis). Then, Least Square fitting of z=f(r,c) by $\hat{f}(r,c)$ gives us the fitting coefficient [8,13]:

$$a_t = \frac{\sum_{(r,c)\in\eta_B(i,j)} f_t(r,c) \cdot [f(r,c) - \sum_{s=1,s\neq t}^{T} a_s f_s(r,c)]}{\sum_{(r,c)\in\eta_B(i,j)} f_t^2(r,c)}$$

(5)

Regarding (5), several remarks are in order. The coefficient $a_t$ calculated by (5) depends on the absolute position of $\eta_B(i,j)$ in the original image field F(k,l), i.e., $a_t$ is a function of (i,j), which we have omitted for the sake of simplicity; Secondly, in order to get the coefficients, we need to solve T linear equations, in other words, coefficient $a_t$ is a linear combination of pixel values f(r,c) in $\eta_B(i,j)$ since all $f_s(r,c), s=1,2,\dots T$ are deterministic; Finally, if for $\eta_B(i,j)$, $f_s(r,c)$ satisfies

$$\sum_{(r,c)\in\eta_B(i,j)} f_s(r,c) \cdot f_t(r,c) = E\delta(t-s)$$

(6)

i.e., they are orthogonal to each other, then we will have simpler solutions for $a_t$ :

$$a_t = \frac{1}{E} \cdot \sum_{(r,c) \in \eta_B(i,j)} f_t(r,c) f(r,c)$$

$$(7)$$

Note, in deriving (7), (5) and (6) have been used. Operations specified by (5) will be termed as Local Surface Fitting abbreviated by LSF. It should be pointed out that more general form of $\hat{f}(r,c,\bar{a}_T)$ can be used giving more general results [13].

Now, if we shift $\eta_B(i,j)$ over the field $\bar{F}(k,l)$ by a unity step, i.e., by one pixel vertically or horizontally, a coefficient field $a_t(i,j)$ is obtained. Therefore, after LSF has been performed at each pixel $(i,j)$, the original image field $F(k,l)$ has been "transformed" or "mapped" into T coefficient fields $a_t(i,j)$, $t=1,2,\ldots,T$. Since different texture fields will certainly exhibit distinct surface characteristics, we may expect these coefficient fields contain useful textural information. Consequently, these T coefficient fields will be formally referred to as Texture Feature Images. A number of useful texture features may be extracted from these feature images as will be discussed in Section 4.

## 3. A CASE STUDY: POLYNOMIAL APPROXIMATION

In this section, we will illustrate the LSF procedure presented in the preceding section using polynomial functions. For simplicity, $\eta_B(i,j)$ is defined to be a 3x3 block centered at pixel $(i,j)$ with area A=9. It is obvious that in the case of square block, the centroid of $\eta_B(i,j)$ and the center of the block are coincided. We define the known function vector $\bar{F}(r,c)$ as polynomial functions. For example, if T=6, we may define $\bar{F}(r,c)=[f_1(r,c) \ f_2(r,c) \ \ldots \ f_6(r,c)]^T$ as

$$f_1(r,c)=1$$
$$f_2(r,c)=r$$
$$f_3(r,c)=c$$
$$f_4(r,c)=r \cdot c$$
$$f_5(r,c)=r^2$$
$$f_6(r,c)=c^2$$

$$(8)$$

Let the parameter vector be denoted by

$$\bar{a}_T =[a_{00} \ a_{10} \ a_{01} \ a_{11} \ a_{20} \ a_{02}]^T$$

then, (4) can be written as

$$\hat{f}(r,c,\bar{a}_T)=\bar{a}_T{}^T \bullet \bar{f}(r,c)$$

$$=a_{00}+a_{10}r+a_{01}c+a_{11}rc+a_{20}r^2+a_{02}c^2$$

(9)

This means the discrete surface $z=f(r,c)$ on $\eta_8(i,j)$ will be fitted by a second order polynomial function. We call LSF specified by (9) **Local Polynomial Fitting (LPF)**. By substituting (8) in (5), solving the resulting 6 linear equations and recalling (2), we finally have (for detail, see [12])

$$a_{00}(i,j)=\tfrac{1}{9}[-F(i-1,j-1)+2F(i,j-1)-F(i+1,j-1)-F(i-1,j+1)$$
$$+2F(i-1,j)+5F(i+j)+2F(i+1,j)-F(i+1,j+1)+2F(i,j+1)]$$
$$a_{10}(i,j)=\tfrac{1}{6}[-F(i-1,j-1)-F(i+1,j-1)-F(i,j-1)$$
$$+F(i,j+1)+F(i-1,j+1)+F(i+1,j+1)]$$
$$a_{01}(i,j)=\tfrac{1}{6}[F(i-1,j-1)+F(i-1,j)+F(i-1,j+1)$$
$$-F(i+1,j+1)-F(i+1,j)-F(i+1,j-1)]$$
$$a_{11}(i,j)=\tfrac{1}{4}[-F(i-1,j-1)+F(i+1,j-1)+F(i-1,j+1)-F(i+1,j+1)]$$
$$a_{20}(i,j)=\tfrac{1}{6}[F(i-1,j-1)-2F(i-1,j)+F(i+1,j-1)+F(i,j-1)$$
$$-2F(i,j)+F(i,j+1)+F(i-1,j+1)-2F(i+1,j)+F(i+1,j+1)]$$
$$a_{02}(i,j)=\tfrac{1}{6}[F(i-1,j-1)+F(i-1,j)+F(i+1,j-1)-2F(i,j-1)$$
$$-2F(i,j)-2F(i,j+1)+F(i-1,j+1)+F(i+1,j)+F(i+1,j+1)]$$

(10)

Where $F(\bullet,\bullet)$ is the pixel sample in the original image field. Note, (10) actually defines 6 image transforms or 6 2-D FIR filtering operations, which are special examples of linear **Local Vector Mapping** defined in TAN [3]. After operations of (10) have been done at every pixel, we obtain 6 texture feature images

$$a_{00}(i,j),\ a_{10}(i,j),\ a_{01}(i,j),\ \ldots,\ a_{02}(i,j)$$

## 4. LSF TEXTURE FEATURES

### 4.1 Definitions of LSF Texture Features

As we discussed in previous sections, LSF generates T coefficient data fields which are termed as Texture Feature Images. Although more sophisticated procedures can be adopted to extract useful texture features from the generated T feature images, we only define some simple features which all are the first order statistics of the feature images and found to be adequate for the purpose of texture classification. More precisely, we define the first four central moments as the features extracted from each feature image. Mathematically, we write

Texture Feature No.1 $TF_1$ :

$$TF_1 = \frac{1}{KxL} \cdot \sum_{(i,j)} a_t(i,j)$$

(11a)

Texture Feature No.2   $TF_2$ :

$$TF_2 = \frac{1}{KxL} \cdot \sum_{(i,j)} [a_t(i,j) - TF_1]^2$$

(11b)

Texture Feature No.3   $TF_3$ :

$$TF_3 = \frac{1}{KxL} \cdot \sum_{(i,j)} [a_t(i,j) - TF_1]^3 / TF_2$$

(11c)

Texture Feature No.4   $TF_4$ :

$$TF_4 = \frac{1}{KxL} \cdot \sum_{(i,j)} [a_t(i,j) - TF_1]^4 / TF_2$$

(11d)

Where $TF_3$ and $TF_4$, i.e., the skewness and Kurtosis have been normalized w.r.t. $TF_2$ the variance. Calculations of $TF_1$, $TF_2$, $TF_3$ and $TF_4$ for every $a_t(i,j)$ produce 4xT texture features, which we will call LSF texture features.

## 4.2  *LSF Texture Features vs. Visual Texture Features*

In any case, a good texture feature set should be consistent with human visual perception, in other words, texture features extracted should have a good indication of visual characteristics of the given texture field. Six common visual texture features are coarseness, contrast, directionality, line-likeness, regularity and roughness [9]. For a particular texture field, only one or few of them is dominant. However, experimental results reveal that in almost all situations, coarseness, directionality and regularity are the three most important features. So, in the first place, any useful texture feature set should reflect these important visual texture properties. In [3], it is shown that the skewness $TF_3$ of $a_t(i,j)$ is a good measure of the randomness, directionality and/or regularity of the original texture field. Random, irregular textures have small $TF_3$ while for directional and regular textures, $TF_3$ takes large value. In addition, we may claim that LSF $TF_1$ features can be made to match any one of the visual texture features mentioned above. One may be easily convinced by the following arguments. Since $TF_1$ (mean value) of $a_t(i,j)$ is a measure of the contribution of $f_t(r,c)$ to the fitting function $\hat{f}(r,c,\bar{a}_t)$, it is also a measure of the characteristics inherent in $f_t(r,c)$ of the original field $F(k,l)$. For example, in the function vector $\bar{f}(r,c)$, let $f_1(r,c)$ be a coarse surface (having rich low frequency components), $f_2(r,c)$ be a directional surface and $f_3(r,c)$ be a regular surface, then $TF_1$ from $a_1(i,j)$ measures the coarseness of $F(k,l)$, $TF_1$ from $a_2(i,j)$ measures the directionality and $TF_1$ from $a_3(i,j)$ measures the regularity etc..

## 5. *TEXTURE CLASSIFICATION: Experimental Results*

In this section, we summarize the experimental results obtained by using the defined texture features from LPF. Since $a_{00}(i,j)$ is found to contains little textural information especially for histogram-equalized textures, features from $a_{00}(i,j)$ have not been considered. We have then 4x5=20 texture features. Experimental results are given in the common form of classification confusion matrix and occasionally in the form of classification accuracy matrix.

### 5.1 *DATA SET*

Ten natural texture samples taken from BRODATZ [10] are used in the experiments. All samples are of size 128x128 and quantized into 8 bits (256 gray levels). Histogram Equalization has been done for all samples to compensate for the lighting differences and other distortions. For the trainning purpose, 75 texture samples for each texture class are derived from the original texture set. These 75 samples consists of 49 32x32 samples, 25 64x64 samples and 1 128x128 sample. LSF (LPF) is performed and $TF_1$, $TF_2$, $TF_3$ and $TF_4$ are calculated for all 75 samples. Then the average of the 75 values for each feature is taken as the corresponding feature value of the underlying class.

### 5.2 *CLASSIFIERS*

A number of classifiers are well developed and used for a long time. For design of a particular classifier, we refer to FUKUNAGA [11]. In this paper, we have only used two very simple classifiers because our interest lies mainly in the investigation of the relative abilities of our LSF texture features to texture classification rather than the performance of various different classifiers. The first one, called the Minimum Aggregate Squared Difference Classifier denoted by MASDC , is defined by

$$\text{Assign } \bar{F} \text{ 'to' class } i, \text{ iff}$$
$$D(i) = \min_{1 \leq k \leq 10} [D(k)]$$
$$D(k) = [\bar{F} - \bar{F}_k]^T \cdot [\bar{F} - \bar{F}_k]$$

(12)

and the second is called the Minimum Aggregate Absolute Difference Classifier denoted by MAADC and defined as

Assign $\overline{F}$ 'to' class i, iff

$$D(i)= \underset{1 \leqslant k \leqslant 10}{Min} [D(k)]$$

$$D(k)=\sum_{j=1}^{N} \left| f(j)-f_k(j) \right|$$

(13)

Where $\overline{F}=[f(1)\ f(2)\ \dots\ f(N)]^T$ is the feature vector of the unknown texture pattern; $\overline{F}_k=[f_k(1)\ f_k(2)\ \dots\ f_k(N)]^T$ is the feature vector of the known texture class k. Note, MASDC is usually called the **Minimum Euclidean Distance Classifier** and MAADC is sometimes called the 'City Block' Distance Classifier. They are indeed different from each other since the following is usually true

$$\left| a-b \right| + \left| c-d \right| \neq (a-b)^2+(c-d)^2$$

(14)

## 5.3  RESULTS

To test the textural discriminating abilities of the features extracted from the LPF feature images, 90 unknown texture samples, 10% of which are from each class, are used in the experiments. Table I shows the classification accuracies by individual LPF texture features. For example, at the fourth row and the third column, we have 72.22% which is the classification accuracy using only feature $TF_2$ from feature image $a_{11}(i,j)$ . Since, we use only one texture feature, that is N-1, MASDC and MAADC give the same results. It is encouragingly to note that some LPF texture features are very powerful on their own in terms of high classification accuracies. LPF $TF_2$s and some $TF_4$s are examples. Table II to V present the classification confusion matrices by using LPF $TF_1$s , $TF_2$s , $TF_3$s and $TF_4$s respectively. In the notation x/y in these tables, x is the number of correct texture class assignments by MASDC and y is the number by MAADC. Similarly, in "Accuracy = x/y ", x is the classification accuracy in percentile by MASDC and y is the accuracy by MAADC. In addition, all blank boxes are 0/0. Based on these results, we would like to make the following remarks:

(1) In all cases, MAADC gives better performances than MASDC in terms of classification accuracy. Using LPF $TF_2$s , we obtained error-free classification by MAADC while the accuracy is 96.67% by MASDC;

(2) LPF $TF_1$s are not much useful for texture discrimination since in both MASDC and MAADC, classification accuracy is very low (lower than 15%);

(3) LPF $TF_2$s are the most powerful texture features compared with $TF_1$s , $TF_3$s and $TF_4$s . Classification performances of LPF $TF_2$s by both classifiers are indeed very impressive; and

(4) LPF $TF_3$s and $TF_4$s give comparable and also very good results.


## 6. CONCLUSIONS

Because of its importance, texture analysis has received increasing attentions from various fields. Texture classification, being a subtask of texture analysis, has been an active area of research. In this paper, we present a new algorithm for texture classification based on the concept of Local Surface Fitting (LSF). The texture features defined are simple in nature and yet found to be very powerful for discriminating different textures. In addition to the high performance of classification, the algorithm has proved to be compact (small number of texture features used) and flexible (possibility of performance improvement by using appropriate $\eta_B(i,j)$ and fitting function $\hat{f}(r,c,\overline{a}_T)$ ) . It is also suitable for parallel implementation since only local information of a given image $F(k,l)$ is involved in Local Surface Fitting.

## REFERENCES


[1]  **R.M.HARALICK**, Statistical and Structural Approaches to Texture, Proc. of IEEE, vol.67, pp.786-804, 1979.

[2]  **L.V.GOOL** et al., Survey: Texture Analysis Anno : 1983, CVGIP, vol.29, pp.336-357, 1985.

[3]  **T.N.TAN**, Texture Analysis Survey and Local Vector Mapping Algorithms, TR-01-TNT, SPABSS/EE/ICST, March 1987.

[4]  **H.WECHSLER**, Texture Analysis: a Survey, SP, vol.2, pp.271-282, 1980.

[5]  **R.M.HARALICK** and **L.WATSON**, A Facet Model for Image Data, CGIP, vol.15, pp.113-129, 1981.

[6]  **M.KOCHER** and **R.LEONARDI**, Adaptive Region Growing Technique Using Polynomial Function for Image Approximation, SP, vol.11, pp.47-60, 1986.

[7]  **M.EDEN** et al., Polynomial Representation of Picture, SP, vol.10, pp.385-393, 1986.

[8]  **P.LANCASTER** and **K.SALKAUSKAS**, Curve and Surface Fitting: an introduction, Academic Press, Orlando, FL, 1986.

[9]  **H.TAMURA** et al., Texture Features Corresponding to Visual Perception, IEEE Trans. SMC, vol. SMC-8, pp.460-472, 1978.

[10]  **P.BRODATZ**, Textures: A Photographic Album for Artists and Designers, Dover, New York, 1966.

[11]  **K.FUKUNAGA**, Introduction to Statistical Pattern Recognition, Academic Press, New York, 1972.

[12]  **T.N.TAN**, Texture Classification By Local Surface Fitting, TR-04-TNT, SPABSS/EE/ICST, September 1987.

**Table I**   Classification Accuracy
by
LPF Texture Features

| Moment / Feature Class | MEAN TF1 | VARIANCE TF2 | SKEWNESS TF3 | KURTOSIS TF4 |
|---|---|---|---|---|
| $a_0(i,j)$ | 8.89% | 61.11% | 55.56% | 60.00% |
| $a_{01}(i,j)$ | 10.00% | 65.56% | 31.11% | 61.11% |
| $a_1(i,j)$ | 15.56% | 72.22% | 42.22% | 58.89% |
| $a_{20}(i,j)$ | 8.89% | 53.33% | 42.22% | 51.11% |
| $a_{02}(i,j)$ | 14.44% | 61.11% | 36.67% | 55.56% |

**Table II**   Classification Confusion Matrix

FEATURE MOMENT(S) USED:  all LPF TF1s    Accuracy = 13.33% / 14.44%

| Texture | Wood Grain | hand-made Paper | d53 | Cotton Canvas | Straw | Beach Sand | Herring-bone | Calf | Grass Lawn | Pressed-oore |
|---|---|---|---|---|---|---|---|---|---|---|
| Wood Grain | 2/1 | | 2/3 | 1/1 | 0/1 | | 3/3 | 1/0 | | |
| hand-made Paper | | | 1/1 | 1/1 | 1/1 | 4/4 | 0/2 | 2/1 | 0/1 | |
| d53 | 3/2 | | 1/2 | | | 0/1 | 4/4 | | 1/0 | |
| Cotton Canvas | 4/3 | 0/1 | 0/1 | | 1/1 | | 2/1 | | | 2/2 |
| Straw | 1/0 | | 1/2 | 1/0 | | 0/2 | 3/3 | 1/1 | | 2/1 |
| Beach Sand | | | | 2/1 | 2/1 | 1/2 | 3/3 | 1/1 | | 0/1 |
| Herring-bone | | | | | | 4/5 | 4/3 | 1/1 | | |
| Calf | | | 1/1 | 0/1 | | | 1/1 | 4/5 | | 3/1 |
| Grass Lawn | | | 0/1 | 1/0 | | 2/3 | 3/3 | 3/2 | | |
| Pressed-oore | 6/4 | | | 2/4 | | | | 1/1 | | |

**Table III**   Classification Confusion Matrix

FEATURE MOMENT(S) USED:  all LPF TF2s    Accuracy = 96.67% / 100%

| Texture | Wood Grain | hand-made Paper | d53 | Cotton Canvas | Straw | Beach Sand | Herring-bone | Calf | Grass Lawn | Pressed-oore |
|---|---|---|---|---|---|---|---|---|---|---|
| Wood Grain | 9/9 | | | 0/0 | | | | | 0/0 | |
| hand-made Paper | | 9/9 | | | | | | | | |
| d53 | | | 9/9 | | | | | | | |
| Cotton Canvas | | 0/0 | | 6/9 | | | 3/0 | | | |
| Straw | | | | | 9/9 | | | 0/0 | | |
| Beach Sand | | | | | | 9/9 | | | | |
| Herring-bone | | | | | | | 9/9 | | | |
| Calf | 0/0 | | | | | | | 9/9 | | |
| Grass Lawn | | | | | 0/0 | | | | 9/9 | |
| Pressed-oore | | | | | | | | | | 9/9 |

**Table IV**   Classification Confusion Matrix

FEATURE MOMENT(S) USED:  all LPF TF3s    Accuracy = 92.22% / 92.22%

| Texture | Wood Grain | hand-made Paper | d53 | Cotton Canvas | Straw | Beach Sand | Herring-bone | Calf | Grass Lawn | Pressed-oore |
|---|---|---|---|---|---|---|---|---|---|---|
| Wood Grain | 9/9 | | | | | | | | | |
| hand-made Paper | | 9/9 | | | 0/0 | | | | | |
| d53 | | | 9/9 | | | | | | | |
| Cotton Canvas | | | | 9/9 | | | | | | |
| Straw | | | | | 9/9 | | | | | |
| Beach Sand | | 0/1 | | | | 5/5 | | 3/2 | 1/1 | |
| Herring-bone | | | | | | | 9/9 | | | |
| Calf | | | | | | | | 9/9 | | |
| Grass Lawn | | 1/1 | | | | 0/1 | | 8/7 | | |
| Pressed-oore | | 1/0 | | | | | | 1/1 | | 7/8 |

**Table V**   Classification Confusion Matrix

FEATURE MOMENT(S) USED:  all LPF TF4s    Accuracy = 87.78% / 95.56%

| Texture | Wood Grain | hand-made Paper | d53 | Cotton Canvas | Straw | Beach Sand | Herring-bone | Calf | Grass Lawn | Pressed-oore |
|---|---|---|---|---|---|---|---|---|---|---|
| Wood Grain | 2/9 | | 7/0 | | | | | | | |
| hand-made Paper | | 9/9 | | | 0/0 | | | | | |
| d53 | | | 9/9 | | | | | | | |
| Cotton Canvas | | | | 9/9 | | | | | | |
| Straw | | | | | 9/9 | | | | | |
| Beach Sand | | | | | | 7/7 | | | 2/2 | |
| Herring-bone | 0/0 | | | | | 1/1 | 7/7 | | | 1/1 |
| Calf | | | | | | | | 9/9 | | |
| Grass Lawn | | | | | | | | | 9/9 | |
| Pressed-oore | | | | | | | | | | 9/9 |

Table I-V:   LSF Texture Classification Accuracy and Confusion Matrices

# RANGE IMAGE SEGMENTATION AND CLASSIFICATION VIA SPLIT-AND-MERGE BASED ON SURFACE CURVATURE

Hyun S. Yang

Dept. of Electrical and Computer Engineering
University of Iowa
Iowa City, IA 52242, U. S. A.

## ABSTRACT

Surface curvatures have been widely used for the purpose of segmenting and classifying range images. However, since surface curvatures include the second order derivatives, they become unreliable in the presence of noise, yielding false segmentation and/or classification of the range images. In this paper we investigate the sensitivity of the surface curvatures to the noise, and provide some observations on the characteristics of surface curvatures in the presence of noise. Following these observations, we then propose a scheme for reliable range image segmentation and classification. This scheme first differentiate planar region from curved region using planarity test. Surface curvatures are then computed only from the points belonging to the curved region, and mean curvature sign image (MCSI) and Gaussian curvature sign image (GCSI) are generated. Segmentation is done using split-and-merge operations on a quadtree representation of the MCSI. The sign of the Gaussian curvature is incorporated with the segmented MCSI to give a classification of the region. In the preliminary classification stage, the distribution of the Gaussian curvature signs are considered for each segmented region of the segmented MCSI. In the secondary classification stage, unclassified regions from the preliminary classification are classified using split-and-merge operations based on predominant Gaussian curvature signs.

## I. INTRODUCTION

Recently, three-dimensional vision techniques based on range information have been receiving a lot of attention by many researchers working in computer vision, robotics, and artificial intelligence [11,12,13,14,15]. Particularly, in such areas as industrial and navigational robotics where a robot must be capable of handling 3-D environment, range information have been playing a vital role.

Range information, in comparison with the photometric data, has several advantages as follows: (1) *it encompasses intrinsic characteristics of the object shape;* (2) *it is free from artifacts such as contrast reduction and shadow effect that are common in the photometric data;* (3) *it can be used to generate useful 3-D object features such as local surface normal and local surface curvature.* Due to the advantages described above, range information becomes very crucial when the objects are inherently 3-D in nature and/or when the objects in a scene are not sufficiently well separated.

Of many different schemes for representing 3-D object or scene, surface-based representation schemes have received more attention lately, because range image is inherently topological description of the 3-D surface shapes. Many schemes, in relation to 3-D object recognition and scene analysis, that exploit surface features like local surface orientation and local surface curvature have been proposed [1,3,5,6,8,9,10,17].

In surface-based representation, surface curvatures (Gaussian and mean curvatures) have been known extremely useful -- they are viewing direction independent entities. Local surface shapes can be classified into eight different types by using the surface curvature signs [3]. Further, surface curvature histograms can categorize surfaces into more specific types such as spherical, elliptical, cylindrical, conical, and toroidal [17]. Due to the aforementioned advantages of surface curvatures, they have been widely applied for the purpose of range image segmentation and classification, 3-D object recognition, and 3-D scene analysis. In most applications, signs of both Gaussian and mean curvatures are simultaneously used for local surface classification.

However, since surface curvatures include the second order derivatives, they are very sensitive to the noise. More often than not, when one deals with real range images that suffer from both quantization error and noise, this drawback of surface curvatures makes even the classification of the planar surface from the curved one fairly complex, the reason being that setting the proper threshold between zero and non-zero curvatures is not easy. Although smoothing range images before computing surface curvatures can alleviate this sensitivity, it still remains as an annoying problem. In this paper, we propose a scheme by which one can reliably segment and classify range images using surface curvatures in the presence of noise. the proposed method is developed based upon our observations on surface curvature characteristics in the presence of noise.

This paper is organized as follows: in Section II we briefly review surface curvatures as differential geometry point of view and how one can estimate surface curvatures from the range image; in Section III we discuss the problem of using surface curvatures in the presence of noise and provide some observations; in Section IV we show how one can quickly and reliably measure the planarity at each point in the range image; in Section V we propose a strategy for reliable range image segmentation and classification using surface curvatures, together with experimental results.

## II. SURFACE CURVATURE ESTIMATION

Surface curvatures stand for the mean curvature and the Gaussian curvature. The mean curvature and the Gaussian curvature are the local second-order surface characteristics that possess several desirable invariance properties and can be used to classify surface shapes. These two curvatures are invariant to changes in surface parameterization and to translations and rotations of object surfaces. A most noteworthy feature of these two curvatures is that their signs can be exploited to differentiate a surface region into one of eight basic types, these being *flat, peak, pit, minimal, ridge, saddle-ridge , valley, and saddle-valley* [3].

In the following, we will first briefly discuss the expressions for the first and the second fundamental forms that uniquely characterize and quantify a general smooth surface and then, using the coefficients in these forms, we will show how the Gaussian and mean curvatures are related to the first and the second partial derivatives of a range map.

An explicit parametric representation of a surface in $E^3$ is described as:

$$\mathbf{x}(u,v) = (x(u,v), y(u,v), z(u,v)) \tag{1}$$

The first fundamental form is given by

$$I(du,dv) = d\mathbf{x} \cdot d\mathbf{x}$$
$$= (\mathbf{x}_u du + \mathbf{x}_v dv) \cdot (\mathbf{x}_u du + \mathbf{x}_v dv)$$
$$= E du^2 + 2F dudv + G dv^2 \tag{2}$$

where

$$E = \mathbf{x}_u \cdot \mathbf{x}_u$$

$$F = \mathbf{x}_u \cdot \mathbf{x}_v$$
$$G = \mathbf{x}_v \cdot \mathbf{x}_v \qquad (3)$$

E, F and G are called *the first fundamental coefficients.*

While the first fundamental form does not contain partial derivatives of $\mathbf{x}$ higher than the first, the second fundamental form encompasses the second order partial derivatives of the surface and is given by

$$\mathrm{II}(du,dv) = -d\mathbf{x} \cdot d\mathbf{N}$$
$$= -(\mathbf{x}_u du + \mathbf{x}_v dv) \cdot (\mathbf{N}_u du + \mathbf{N}_v dv)$$
$$= L du^2 + 2M dudv + N dv^2 \qquad (4)$$

where

$$L = \mathbf{x}_{uu} \cdot \mathbf{N}$$
$$M = \mathbf{x}_{uv} \cdot \mathbf{N}$$
$$N = \mathbf{x}_{vv} \cdot \mathbf{N} \qquad (5)$$

with

$$\mathbf{N} = \frac{\mathbf{x}_u \times \mathbf{x}_v}{|\mathbf{x}_u \times \mathbf{x}_v|} \qquad (6)$$

being the surface normal at $\mathbf{x}(u,v)$. L, M and N are called *the second fundamental coefficients.*

It is clear that the coefficients E, F, G, L, M, and N completely determine the two fundamental forms. We will now represent the Gaussian and the mean curvatures in terms of these fundamental coefficients. The Gaussian curvature, denoted by K, is given by

$$K = \frac{LN - M^2}{EG - F^2} \qquad (7)$$

and the mean curvature, denoted by H, is given by

$$H = \frac{EN + GL - 2FM}{2(EG - F^2)} \qquad (8)$$

It is clear that the numerical computation of K and H requires that we first calculate the first, second and mixed derivatives of $\mathbf{x}(u,v)$.

Assuming $\mathbf{x}(u,v)$ to be of form $(u,v,z(u,v))$, a form that corresponds to what is known as a graph surface (which is also known as a Monge patch), computation of the derivatives of $z(u,v)$ can be done by first fitting a quadratic function to the range data and then computing analytically the derivatives of this fitted surface [2,3].

These computations can be combined into the form of a separable window convolution operation, making a fast implementation feasible. For our experiments, to compute the first, second and mixed derivatives, we have used windows derived from the quadratic facet model; detail as to how those windows are generated is referred to [3].

## III. SURFACE CURVATURE WITH NOISY RANGE IMAGE

This section discusses the problems in using the surface curvatures for the purpose of range image segmentation and classification in the presence of noise. For testing the sensitivity of the surface curvatures to the noise, we have used synthetic image. Following Hoffman and Jain [8], we assume the standard deviation of the noise in the real range image is about 4 when the range image is quantized as 256 levels; we added this type of Gaussian noise to the synthetic data to generate a more realistic noisy range image.

First, we generated a 128x128 plane corrupted by Gaussian noise with zero mean and standard deviation 4. We estimated mean and standard deviation of the Gaussian and the mean curvatures computed from this noisy range image by using different sizes of windows (3x3 and 5x5) derived from the quadratic facet model. We also estimated both curvatures after we smoothed noisy range image using the nearest neighbor smoothing technique suggested by Hoffman and Jain [8]. Table 1 shows that Gaussian curvature is more sensitive to the noise than mean curvature; ideally, both curvatures must be zero, however, mean and standard deviation of the Gaussian curvature are greater than those of the mean curvature in most cases. Certainly, smoothing and/or adopting larger size windows alleviate the sensitivity of the surface curvatures to the noise.

To compare the sensitivity of surface curvatures in the presence of noise on the planar and curved surfaces, we also generated a synthetic range image that consists of a sphere (radius 30) and the background plane, whose ranges are quantized as 256 levels. We also generated noisy image by adding the Gaussian noise. Figs. 1a and b show the Gaussian and the mean curvatures computed along the 75th row after we smoothed the noisy image using nearest neighbor smoothing; note that the center of the sphere is at (60,64).

Analyzing these curvature plots, one might conclude that it might be very difficult to set the proper threshold between zero curvature and non-zero curvature. (Note that one can classify local surface shapes into eight different categories only if the distinction between non-zero and zero curvatures is feasible.) Fig. 2 illustrates a curvature sign image generated from the smoothed range image of a sphere by setting the best threshold for zero curvature. Apparently, classification was not reliable at all. Particularly, background plane has been segmented into too many false segments. If one directly try range image segmentation on this image exploiting surface curvatures, too many inconsistent segments would be generated.

Although experiments we conducted for testing the sensitivity of the surface curvatures to the noise might not be sufficient to exhibit all the problems included, we could make some observations through these experiments.

- Smoothing noisy range image is required before surface curvatures are computed; simple averaging is not satisfactory since it tends to smooth rather heavily, rendering gently curved regions into planar regions.

- Values of the Gaussian and the mean curvatures computed from the noisy range images are very unreliable; even after smoothing they still remain unreliable.

- The mean curvature is less sensitive to the noise and gives more reliable values in the presence of noise than the Gaussian curvature; this is probably because the mean curvature is the average of two principal curvatures, and averaging tends to reduce noise sensitivity.

- Signs of the Gaussian and the mean curvatures are more sensitive to noise in planar and gently curved regions than in highly curved regions. This is to be expected since a small perturbation due to noise can make a planar patch concave or convex, but curved regions, especially the highly curved regions, are less susceptible to this artifact.

- Immunity of surface curvatures to noise increases with the size of the windows used for determining partial derivatives, however, large windows require more arithmetic, yielding more computation time, and furthermore, cause edge effects.

Observations described above lead us to develop different strategy for range image segmentation and classification from the conventional method that exploits both curvature signs simultaneously; this strategy will be described in detail in Section V.

## IV. PLANARITY MEASUREMENT

As described in the previous section, surface curvatures become very unreliable in the presence of noise; particularly on the planar regions. To overcome this difficulty, at the beginning of the segmentation, we better distinguish planar regions from curved ones using more reliable method than surface curvatures. This is done by measuring the planarity at each point of the range image. Planarity measurement can be done by determining the best fitting plane to the NxN region and summing up the errors between the range data and the fitted plane. The best fitting plane equation can be obtained by minimizing the fitting errors. As described in [7], the resulting parameters of the best fitting plane equation become:

$$a = \frac{3}{M(M+1)(2M+1)^2} \sum_{i=-M}^{M} x \sum_{j=-M}^{M} z(x,y)$$

$$b = \frac{3}{M(M+1)(2M+1)^2} \sum_{j=-M}^{M} y \sum_{i=-M}^{M} \Sigma z(x,y)$$

$$c = \frac{1}{(2M+1)^2} \sum_{i=-M}^{M} \sum_{j=-M}^{M} z(x,y)$$

where the equation of the best fitting plane is

$$z = ax + by + c$$

and $z(x,y)$ is the range value at $(x,y)$. Also $M = (N-1)/2$. Assuming range image as Monge surface results in $x=i$ and $y=j$; therefore, $z(x,y) = z(i,j)$.

The fitting error is then measured by

$$J = \sum_{i=-M}^{M} \sum_{j=-M}^{M} ( z(i,j) - ai - bj - c)^2$$

In our experiment, for planarity measurement, we have used the same size region as the one we used for estimating surface curvatures. In fact, planarity measurement only requires little extra computation since $a = x_u$ and $b = x_v$, and c is nothing but the average of the range values in local region. In Fig. 3a is shown the fitting errors measured along the 75th row of the smoothed synthetic range image of a sphere used in Section III. We have used 7x7 window to compute a, b, and c. Apparently, this measurement can reliably distinguish planar region from curved region (Fig. 3b).

## V. STRATEGY FOR RELIABLE RANGE IMAGE SEGMENTATION AND CLASSIFICATION

The overall scheme for segmenting and classifying noisy range image is shown in Fig. 4, and is discussed below.

The raw range image is subjected to nearest-neighbor smoothing, proposed by Hoffman and Jain [8], for reducing the effect of noise. Although this smoothing technique is not as effective as averaging for the purpose of removing noise, it preserves small curvatures better. The smoothed image is then tested for local planarity as discussed in Section IV. The planarity test is motivated by the fact that surface curvatures computed in noise-corrupted planar regions are very unreliable. In addition, it saves some computation time, for surface curvatures need not be determined in regions that are found to be planar.

The next step is to determine the mean and Gaussian curvatures in the non-planar regions of the image. The curvatures are computed using the equations of Section II. The magnitudes of the curvatures of the smoothed image are still quite unreliable, and only their signs are used in the segmentation process. All curvature values whose magnitudes are below a threshold are set to zero and signs are extracted from the rest. This step yields two images: the mean curvature sign image (MCSI) and the Gaussian curvature sign image (GCSI). The sign images are processed further to remove noise-like signs, using a variation of mode filtering; if five or more points in the 8-neighborhood of a point have the same sign, the point under consideration is also given that sign.

We now segment the image based on the MCSI (Gaussian curvature signs are not reliable enough to be used at this stage). Segmentation is done using quadtree- based split-and-merge operations on the MCSI. Regions are split if they do not contain a large predominance of a particular mean curvature sign. Adjacent regions with the same mean curvature are merged.

In the final stage, the algorithm attempts to classify each region of the segmented image into one of eight different surface types. In order to do so, the predominant mean and Gaussian curvature signs should be determined for each region. The mean curvature sign of each region is determined in the segmentation step above. If there is a strong majority of Gaussian curvature signs in each region, it can be classified.

If the Gaussian curvature sign of a region is indeterminate, it needs to be further segmented. The unclassified regions are subjected to a secondary segmentation and classification step; these regions are split. To avoid fragmentation in areas where the Gaussian curvature signs are not reliable, the regions are split no further when they reach a size of 4x4. Any sub-region with a predominant Gaussian curvature sign is labeled according to that sign. Indeterminate regions are merged to adjacent labeled regions. At this stage all regions in the segmented image have been labeled by a Gaussian curvature sign or have been split into sub-regions that are so labeled.

The mean and the Gaussian curvature sign pairs are combined for each region (or sub-region) in order to classify it into one of eight surface types.

We have applied this classification strategy to a synthetic range image comprising a spherical and a cylindrical region. The synthetic image was corrupted by Gaussian noise of mean zero and standard deviation four. The noisy image was cleaned by nearest-neighbor smoothing, and the smoothed image was segmented and classified. A confidence level of 90% was used to decide the mean curvature of the sign of a region; if the majority sign in a region was less than this percentage, the region was split further. The Gaussian curvature sign of regions in the segmented image were determined using a confidence level of 80%. Subsequent classification gives five major surface types. The spherical and cylindrical regions and the planar background are classified correctly as peak, ridge, and planar surfaces respectively. The edge regions are classified into saddle valley and saddle ridge surfaces. Some isolated points that look like impulse noise can be merged into their neighboring regions by setting a threshold on the smallest acceptable size for a region.

In Fig. 5 is illustrated a segmented and classified range image obtained following the proposed strategy.

## VI. CONCLUSION

In this paper we discussed the difficulties in using surface curvatures for the purpose of range image segmentation and classification in the presence of noise. We then proposed a strategy that can segment and classify noisy range images more reliably than the conventional methods. In the future we would like to test our strategy for real complex range images.

# VII. REFERENCES

[1]  H. Asada and M. Brady, "The Curvature Primal Sketch," IEEE Workshop on Computer Vision: Representation and Control, 1984, pp. 8-17

[2]  P. R. Beaudet, "Rotationally Invariant Image Operators," *Proc. Intl. Joint Conf. Pattern Recognition,* Nov. 1978, pp. 579-583.

[3]  P. J. Besl and R. C. Jain, "Invariant Surface Characteristic for 3D Object Recognition in Range Images," *Computer Vision, Graphics, and Image Processing,* Vol 33, 1986, pp. 33-80.

[4]  K. L. Boyer, H. S. Yang and A. C. Kak, "3-D Vision for Pile Analysis," Purdue University Technical Report, TR-EE-84-17, 1984.

[5]  T. J. Fan, G. Medioni and R. Nevatia, "Description of Surfaces from Range Data using Curvature Properties," *Conf. on Computer Vision and Pattern Recognition,* 1986, pp. 86-91.

[6]  O. D. Faugeras and M. Hebert, "The Representation, Recognition, and Positioning of 3-D Shapes from Range Data," in *Techniques for 3-D Machine Perception,* A. Rosenfeld ed., North-Holland, 1985.

[7]  R. M. Haralick and L. Watson, "A Facet Model for Image Data," *Computer Graphics and Image Processing,* Vol. 15, 1981, pp. 113-129.

[8]  R. Hoffman and A. Jain, "Segmentation and Classification of Range Images," *IEEE PAMI,* Vol. PAMI-9, Sept. 1987, pp. 608-620.

[9]  B. K. P. Horn and K. Ikeuchi, "The Mechanical Manipulation of Randomly Oriented Parts," *Scientific America,* 1984, pp. 100-111.

[10]  B. K. P. Horn, "Extended Gaussian Images," *Proceedings, IEEE,* Dec. 1984, pp. 1671-1686.

[11]  A. C. Kak and J. S. Albus, "Sensors for Intelligent Robotics," *Handbook of Industrial Robotics,* S. Nof ed., John Wiley, New York, 1984.

[12]  A. C. Kak, K. L. Boyer, C. H. Chen, R. J. Safranek and H. S. Yang, "A Knowledge-Based Robotic Assembly Cell," *IEEE EXPERT* spring 1986, pp. 63-83.

[13]  D. Nitzan, A. E. Brain and R. O. Duda, "The Measurement and Use of Registered Reflectance and Range Data in Scene Analysis," *Proc. IEEE,* Vol. 65, pp. 206-220, 1977.

[14]  A. Pugh ed. *Robot Vision,* IFS Ltd. and Springer-Verlag, 1983.

[15]  A. Rosenfeld ed., *Techniques for 3-D Machine Perception,* North-Hollander, 1986.

[16]  H. S. Yang, K. L. Boyer and A. C. Kak, "Range Data Extraction and Interpretation by Structured Light," *1st Conference on Artificial Intelligence Applications,* Dec, 1984, pp. 199-205.

[17]  H. S. Yang and A. C. Kak, "Determination of the Identity, Position and Orientation of the Topmost Object in a Pile," *Computer Vision, Graphics and Image Processing,* Nov. 1986, pp.

| image<br>window,<br>curvature | | before<br>smoothing | after<br>smoothing |
|---|---|---|---|
| 3x3 | GC | (-0.5, 7.8) | (-0.12, 1.57) |
| | MC | (0.015, 1.67) | (0.0011, 0.82) |
| 5x5 | GC | (-0.084, 0.55) | (-0.033, 0.25) |
| | MC | (0.0011, 0.49) | (-0.0007, 0.35) |

Table 1: Means and standard deviations of the Gaussian curvature and mean curvatures computed by different sizes of windows with and without smoothing; the first item in the bracket is the mean while the second item is the standard deviation.

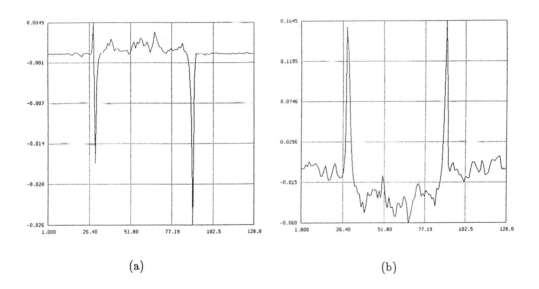

(a)                                                    (b)

Fig. 1: Gaussian (a) and mean (b) curvatures computed along the 75th row of the smoothed synthetic range image (128x128) of a sphere. Note that the center of the sphere is at (60,64).

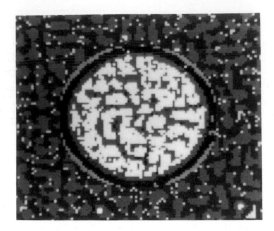

Fig. 2: Illustrated here is the curvature sign image generated from the smoothed range image of a sphere. Image has been classified into 8 different regions depending on the signs of surface curvatures. Note that, particularly, planar region (background) has been classified very unreliably.

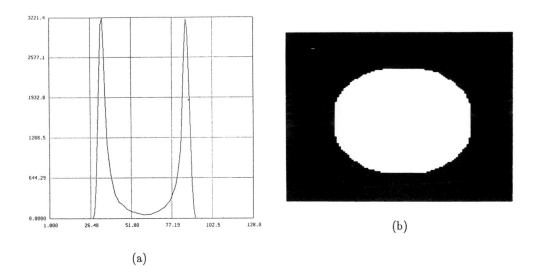

(a)

(b)

Fig. 3: (a) Shown here is the planarity measured along the 75th row of the smoothed range image. (b) Binary image showing planar region (black) and curved region (white) determined by using the planarity test.

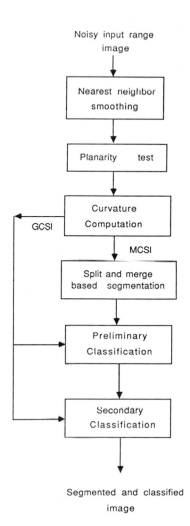

Noisy input range image

Nearest neighbor smoothing

Planarity test

Curvature Computation

GCSI

MCSI

Split and merge based segmentation

Preliminary Classification

Secondary Classification

Segmented and classified image

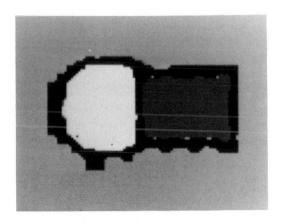

Fig. 5: Shown here is a segmented and classified image of a shape, comprising spherical and cylindrical surfaces, obtained following our strategy. Different gray levels have been used to label segmented and classified regions.

Fig. 4: Depicted here is the block diagram describing the proposed strategy for reliable range image segmentation and classification using surface curvatures and planarity measurement.

# AN ENHANCED LINEAR MODEL EDGE DETECTOR

M.H.A.Assal, E.Horne, M.C.Fairhurst
Electronic Engineering Laboratories
University of Kent,
Canterbury, Kent. CT2 7NT

## 1. INTRODUCTION

An edge in an image can be defined as the boundary between two regions with distinctive gray levels. Many modules in a typical vision system depend on the performance of an edge detector, and consequently there has been substantial effort directed towards improving the performance of existing edge detectors or developing new techniques. One technique based on the linear model has been proposed by Kay and Lemay [1]. The size of this linear model operator is a 3x3 array of pixels which defines the extent of the local domain over which the evidence about the existence of an edge is gathered. It is well known that the noise characteristics of an operator depend on its size. The larger the operator, the more effective it is in reducing random noise, but it is also more likely to overlap several edges or corners simultaneously and thus degrade its resolution capability. In applications requiring higher detectability and localisation of high curvature edges 3x3 neighbourhood edge detectors are the most popular. The important feature of the linear model edge detector is its invariability to multiplicative changes in the gray scale values of the image so that threshold based histogram segmentation is not required. Consequently this edge detector presents a satisfactory solution to the problem of the threshold selection.

This paper will describe and evaluate a modified form of a linear model edge detector. Section 2 gives a description of the linear model edge detector, while in Section 3 some of the problems associated with this detector are discussed and proposed solutions to these problems are introduced. Section 4 contains a performance analysis of the original linear model and the proposed modified version. Section 5 reviews the results obtained and their implications.

## 2. THE LINEAR MODEL EDGE DETECTOR

The description of the problem of edge detection in terms of the linear model discussed by Kay and Lemay [1] depends on the analysis of the variances of the three following models:

a) Vertical model, b) Horizontal model, c) Reduced model (i.e. constant image subregion).

Figure 1 shows the pixel means for each model, where an analysis of the variances of these three models provides a convenient method of comparing the fit of a set of pixel intensities in a 3x3 array to one of these models.

The observed pixel values for each of the above three models from the viewpoint of the general linear model [2] may now be expressed as:

a) For the vertical model:

$$
Y = \begin{bmatrix} y_1 \\ y_2 \\ \cdot \\ \cdot \\ \cdot \\ y_9 \end{bmatrix} = \begin{bmatrix} 1 & 0 \\ \tfrac{1}{2} & \tfrac{1}{2} \\ 0 & 1 \\ 1 & 0 \\ \tfrac{1}{2} & \tfrac{1}{2} \\ 0 & 1 \\ 1 & 0 \\ \tfrac{1}{2} & \tfrac{1}{2} \\ 0 & 1 \end{bmatrix} \begin{bmatrix} \mu_0 \\ \mu_1 \end{bmatrix} + \begin{bmatrix} \epsilon_1 \\ \epsilon_2 \\ \cdot \\ \cdot \\ \cdot \\ \epsilon_9 \end{bmatrix}
$$

$$\qquad \qquad X \qquad \Theta \qquad \Sigma$$

b) For the horizontal model:

$$
Y = \begin{bmatrix} y_1 \\ y_2 \\ \cdot \\ \cdot \\ \cdot \\ y_9 \end{bmatrix} = \begin{bmatrix} 1 & 0 \\ 1 & 0 \\ 1 & 0 \\ \tfrac{1}{2} & \tfrac{1}{2} \\ \tfrac{1}{2} & \tfrac{1}{2} \\ \tfrac{1}{2} & \tfrac{1}{2} \\ 0 & 1 \\ 0 & 1 \\ 0 & 1 \end{bmatrix} \begin{bmatrix} \mu_0 \\ \mu_1 \end{bmatrix} + \begin{bmatrix} \epsilon_1 \\ \epsilon_2 \\ \cdot \\ \cdot \\ \cdot \\ \epsilon_9 \end{bmatrix}
$$

$$\qquad \qquad X \qquad \Theta \qquad \Sigma$$

c) For the reduced model:

$$
Y = \begin{bmatrix} y_1 \\ y_2 \\ \cdot \\ \cdot \\ \cdot \\ y_9 \end{bmatrix} = \begin{bmatrix} 1 \\ 1 \\ \cdot \\ \cdot \\ \cdot \\ 1 \end{bmatrix} \begin{bmatrix} \mu \end{bmatrix} + \begin{bmatrix} \epsilon_1 \\ \epsilon_2 \\ \cdot \\ \cdot \\ \cdot \\ \epsilon_9 \end{bmatrix}
$$

$$\qquad \qquad X \qquad \Theta \qquad \Sigma$$

where

$Y$ = 9×1 vector of observable random variables representing the actual pixel intensities in a 3x3 image subregion.

$X$ = 9×k matrix of known fixed numbers depending on the assumed model.

$\Theta$ = k×1 vector of unknown parameters (model parameters).

$\Sigma$ = 9×1 unobservable vector of Gaussian random variables. ( $\epsilon_1, \epsilon_2, \cdots, \epsilon_9$ are the statistical errors which account for the failure of a model to provide an exact fit. Each of these random variables $\epsilon_i$ is NID(0,$\sigma^2$).

$K$ = the number of parameters of the model.

$K$ = 1 for the reduced model ($\mu$).

$K$ = 2 for either the vertical or horizontal model ($\mu_0$ & $\mu_1$).

The model is usually of interest in relation to testing some hypothesis concerning $\Theta$. Formally the testing of NH (null hypothesis) against AH (alternative hypothesis) may be considered [3]. In the case of the linear model edge detector Kay and Lemay proposed the following:

$$\text{NH} \longrightarrow H_0 : [1 \quad -1] \begin{bmatrix} \mu_0 \\ \mu_1 \end{bmatrix} = 0 \qquad \text{i.e. no edge present } (\mu_0 = \mu_1 = \mu)$$

$$\text{AH} \longrightarrow H_1 : [1 \quad -1] \begin{bmatrix} \mu_0 \\ \mu_1 \end{bmatrix} \neq 0 \qquad \text{i.e. edge present } (\mu_0 \neq \mu_1)$$

The important result obtained from the work cited is the description of the edge detection problems in terms of the linear model and the outcome is the composite hypothesis test for both the vertical and horizontal edge models:

$$l_v = \left( \frac{\hat{\hat{\sigma}}^2 - \hat{\sigma}_v^2}{\hat{\sigma}_v^2} \right) \left( \frac{n - K}{r} \right) \tag{1}$$

$$l_h = \left( \frac{\hat{\hat{\sigma}}^2 - \hat{\sigma}_h^2}{\hat{\sigma}_h^2} \right) \left( \frac{n - K}{r} \right) \tag{2}$$

where

$l_v$ is the test statistic for the vertical edge.

$l_h$ is the test statistic for the horizontal edge.

$\hat{\hat{\sigma}}^2$ is the variance estimate of the reduced model.

$\hat{\sigma}_v^2$ is the variance estimate of the vertical model.

$\hat{\sigma}_h^2$ is the variance estimate of the horizontal edge model.

(n-K) is the degree of freedom of the denominator and is constant for the assumed models, (in this case n-K = 7).

r is the degree of freedom of the numerator and is also constant for the assumed models, (r = 1).

The quantity $\left( \dfrac{\hat{\hat{\sigma}}^2 - \hat{\sigma}^2}{\hat{\sigma}^2} \right)$ simply represents the rescaled version of the reduction in residual sum of squares due to enlarging the model (i.e. from the reduced to either the vertical or horizontal edge model) and it has been shown in [2] and [3] that this ratio follows the F-distribution. Each of these two test statistics will provide a measure of the degree of fit for each of the two assumed edge direction models in comparison with the reduced model.

After computing the two test statistics $(l_v, l_h)$, they are compared with a threshold value $(\lambda)$ which is chosen to maintain a given probability of false alarm (i.e. erroneous detection of an edge) to declare the presence or absence of an edge according to the following:

$$\max \{l_v, l_h\} > \lambda \text{ decide edge present}$$
$$< \lambda \text{ decide no edge present.}$$

Further details can be found in Kay and Lemay [1].

# 3. PROBLEMS ASSOCIATED WITH THE LINEAR MODEL AND SOME PROPOSED SOLUTIONS

There are two main disadvantages associated with this detector:

1.     Test statistic values calculated for both the vertical and the horizontal edge models are severely sensitive to the edge orientation, as shown in Figure 2. As a result the detector has difficulty in discerning diagonal edges, and this contributes to an impaired detection performance.

Figure 3 shows the average intensities of different pixels of a 5x5 central edge model which is used for measuring the sensitivity of the linear model test statistic values to the edge orientation. This 5x5 central edge model follows the same principle as the 3x3 and the 2x2 central edge models used by Abdou and Pratt[4] but it is suitable for testing the sensitivity to the edge orientation of an edge detector utilising a 3x3 or a 5x5 image subregion.

2.     There is no way to disqualify low contrast detected edge points which can be formed either by intensity quantisation or shadows.

The origin of the first difficulty concerning the ability of the linear model to detect diagonal edges is its assumption of the existence of only vertical and horizontal edge models, as indicated in Section 2. It is possible, however, to augment the model by postulating the existence of a diagonal edge model, as shown in Figure 4.

It is not intended to form a completely new model for the diagonal edges, but it is apparent that the appearance of diagonal edges can be enhanced by rotating the pixels within a 3x3 image subregion under test one step clockwise or counter- clockwise as Figure 4 shows, with the result that diagonal edges will appear as vertical or horizontal edges. Consequently, it is possible to calculate another two statistic values $(l_{d1}, l_{d2})$ for diagonal edges using the same equations as apply to the vertical and horizontal test statistic values $(l_v, l_h)$ introduced in Section 2. Therefore, a decision concerning the presence or absence of an edge will be made according to the rule:

$$\max \{l_v, l_h, l_{d1}, l_{d2}\} > \lambda \text{ decide edge present}$$
$$< \lambda \text{ decide no edge present.}$$

Figure 5 shows the relationship between $l_v$ and $l_{d1}$ and the edge orientation angle, illustrating the complementary nature of these two test statistics which is the essential factor in the enhancement of the detector performance. It is clear from Figure 5 that the threshold $(\lambda)$ may be raised to a value higher than the one used by the original model for judging the presence of an edge while keeping the detector capable of detecting edges in all directions. In turn, this will result in reducing the value of the probability of false alarm $(P_{FA})$ associated with each test. Figure 6 shows the result of applying both the original linear model edge detector and the proposed modified version, which additionally accounts for diagonal edges, on a test image containing the central edge model shown in Figure 3 which has been rotated from 0 degrees to 180 degrees. From this experiment it is clear that the number of edge points detected by the proposed version of the model is always higher than that detected by the original detector at the same test statistic threshold value. Figure 7 shows the plot of the number of edge points detected by both versions as a function of the threshold value.

The second problem noted earlier concerned the disqualification of unwanted low contrast edge points due to intensity quantisation and shadows which may be detected when a discrete image array is processed by the linear model edge detector. It is possible to enhance or accentuate these discontinuities of the image function f(x,y) by using one of the enhancement/ thresholding edge detectors such as the well-known Sobel operator [5] and then, if the enhanced discontinuity is less than some threshold (t) an edge is deemed absent at that point, in spite of its detection by the linear model detector. The enhancement/thresholding edge detectors spatially process a discrete image array to produce a set of gradient functions, and calculating the gradient of the image function is the most commonly adopted method in image processing to enhance image discontinuities [6]. The gradient of an image function f(x,y) at coordinates (x,y) is defined as the vector:

$$G\left[f\left(x,y\right)\right] = \begin{bmatrix} \dfrac{\delta f}{\delta x} \\ \dfrac{\delta f}{\delta y} \end{bmatrix}$$

The two important properties of the gradient are:

1.    The vector G[f(x,y)] points in the direction of the maximum rate of increase of the function f(x,y).

2.    The magnitude of G[f(x,y)] is given by:

$$mag\left[G\right] = \left[\left(\dfrac{\delta f}{\delta x}\right)^2 + \left(\dfrac{\delta f}{\delta y}\right)^2\right]^{\frac{1}{2}}$$

which equals the maximum rate of increase of f(x,y) per unit distance in the direction of G.

In fact, it is sufficient only to use the approximated gradient formula given by:

$$mag\left[G\right] \approx \left[\left|\left(\dfrac{\delta f}{\delta x}\right)\right|\right] + \left[\left|\left(\dfrac{\delta f}{\delta y}\right)\right|\right]$$

for the purpose of disqualifying the unwanted low contrast edge points.

The calculation of the direction of the gradient α(x,y), given by:

$$\alpha\left(x,y\right) = \tan^{-1}\left[\dfrac{\left|\left(\dfrac{\delta f}{\delta y}\right)\right|}{\left|\left(\dfrac{\delta f}{\delta x}\right)\right|}\right]$$

will generate an added important feature to the proposed modified linear model required for the process of linking the detected edge points. Furthermore, this may be useful for other machine vision modules.

Finally, the ultimate decision about the presence or absence of an edge will not only depend on the degree of fitting to the model at the assumed directions but also on the amplitude of the edge enhanced array. Therefore, the edge is judged present at a point (x,y) if and only if

$$\max \left\{ l_v, l_h, l_{d1}, l_{d2} \right\} > \lambda \ AND \ mag \left[ G \right] > t$$

otherwise an edge is deemed absent at that point.

## 4. FIGURE OF MERIT COMPARISON

It is instructive to use the figure of merit introduced by Pratt [7] to evaluate the performance of the two versions of the linear model and additionally, to compare their performances with the Sobel edge detector. The scalar function of this figure of merit (F) is given by:

$$F = \frac{1}{\max \left( I_1, I_A \right)} \sum_{i=1}^{I_A} \frac{1}{1 + \alpha d^2}$$

where $I_1$ and $I_A$ represent the number of ideal and actual edge map points respectively, $\alpha$ is a scaling constant, and $d$ is the separation distance of an actual edge point normal to a line of ideal edge points. This function is normalised so that F=1 for a perfectly detected edge. The advantages of this figure of merit as discussed by Abdou [8] are:

1.   It is sensitive to different types of edge error ( fragmented, offset or smeared ).

2.   It allows each edge detector to be tuned to its best capabilities, which guarantees a fair comparison. The analysis as introduced by Abdou and Pratt[4] is based on two test images, one of which contains a vertical edge and the other a diagonal edge. The vertical edge test image, shown in Figure 8, consists of a 64x64 pixel array over a 0 to 63 amplitude range with a vertically oriented edge of variable contrast and slope placed at its centre. Independent Gaussian noise of standard deviation $\sigma$ is added to the edge image, and the signal-to-noise ratio is defined as

$$SNR = \left( \frac{h}{\sigma} \right)^2$$

where $h$ is the edge height.

A test image for a diagonal edge is shown in Figure 8 and consists of a 128x128 pixel array generated with the same signal and noise models used in the vertical edge test image. To simplify the comparison of the results obtained by each test image the number of edge points is chosen to be the same in the two cases. Thus, edge pixels in the diagonal edge test image are only counted in a centrally located square and the diagonal distance $d$ is normalised by the factor $\sqrt{2}$ to account for the discretisation differences. Figure 9 shows the experimental results obtained by applying the original linear model, the proposed modified version of the linear model and the Sobel edge detectors to this set of test images. The height $h$ is equal to 25, and Gaussian noise is added to the edge test image with signal-to-noise ratio 1,2,5,10,20,50 and 100 respectively.

This experiment shows that the performance of the proposed linear model detector is superior to the original version, especially at high signal-to-noise ratios. From Figure 9 it is clear that the original linear model detector does not account for diagonal edges, as expected, while the proposed modified version does take account of these. The improvement of the figure of merit values at high signal-to-noise ratios, where low contrast edges are likely to occur, due to adding a Sobel detector to the proposed model in order to disqualify low contrast edges are also shown in Figure 9.

## 5. CONCLUSION

The linear model edge detector has been discussed as one of the edge detectors with a performance that is relatively unaffected by lighting changes.For this reason its use in on-line applications where illuminations levels may vary ( for example, in an automatic warehousing environment) is very attractive. Furthermore, the linear model detector offers the high resolution typically provided by the 3x3 window edge detectors and consequently, in applications where the use of larger size detectors (e.g. the 5x5 Nevatia-Babu operator [9]) is more likely to overlap several edges, the linear model detector is preferable.

In this paper the performances of both the original linear model and a proposed modified version have been measured and it has been demonstrated that the modified version accounts for diagonal edges and that its performance is superior at high signal-to-noise ratios.

Future work will concentrate on further evaluating the proposed detector, particularly with regard to real images where performance in relation to physical characteristics, geometric properties, and so on can be assessed. It is also proposed to study strategies for the implementation of this type of operator, where it is envisaged that utilising parallel processing techniques will offer many potential benefits.

## REFERENCES

1. S.M.Kay & G.J.Lemay, " Edge detection using the linear model ", IEEE Trans. Acoustics, Speech and Signal Processing, ASSP-34, 1221-1227, 1986

2. F.A.Graybill, " Theory and application of the linear model ", MA: Duxbury, 1976

3. S.Weisberg, " Applied linear regression ", Wiley, New York, 1980

4. I.E.Abdou & W.K.Pratt, " Quantitative design and evaluation of enhancement/thresholding edge detectors ", Proc.IEEE, 67, 753-763, 1979

5. R.O.Duda & P.E.Hart, " Pattern classification and scene analysis ", Wiley, New York, 1973

6. R.C.Gonzalez & P.Wintz, " Digital Image Processing ", Addison-Wesley, 1987

7. W.K.Pratt, " Digital Image Processing ", Wiley, 1978

8. I.E.Abdou " Quantitative methods of edge detection ", Univ. Southern California, Los Angeles, USC Report 830, July 1978

9. R.Nevatia & K.R.Babu, " Linear feature extraction and description ", Comput. Graphics Image Processing, 13, 257-269, 1980

| | | |
|---|---|---|
| $y_1$ | $y_2$ | $y_3$ |
| $y_4$ | $y_5$ | $y_6$ |
| $y_7$ | $y_8$ | $y_9$ |

(a) Locations of pixels in a 3 x 3 array.

| | | |
|---|---|---|
| $\mu_0$ | $\dfrac{\mu_0 + \mu_1}{2}$ | $\mu_1$ |
| $\mu_0$ | $\dfrac{\mu_0 + \mu_1}{2}$ | $\mu_1$ |
| $\mu_0$ | $\dfrac{\mu_0 + \mu_1}{2}$ | $\mu_1$ |

(b) Pixel means for vertical edge model

| | | |
|---|---|---|
| $\mu_0$ | $\mu_0$ | $\mu_0$ |
| $\dfrac{\mu_0 + \mu_1}{2}$ | $\dfrac{\mu_0 + \mu_1}{2}$ | $\dfrac{\mu_0 + \mu_1}{2}$ |
| $\mu_1$ | $\mu_1$ | $\mu_1$ |

(c) Pixel means for horizontal edge model

| | | |
|---|---|---|
| $\mu$ | $\mu$ | $\mu$ |
| $\mu$ | $\mu$ | $\mu$ |
| $\mu$ | $\mu$ | $\mu$ |

(d) Pixel means for the reduced model (constant image subregion)

Fig. 1

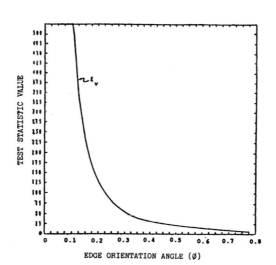

Fig. 2

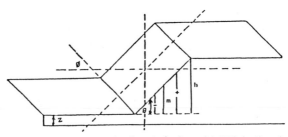

Fig. 3 (a) Two dimensional central edge model ('h' is the edge height, 'm' equals h/2, '+' values between 'm' and 'h', '-' values between '0' and 'm', $z = 0$)

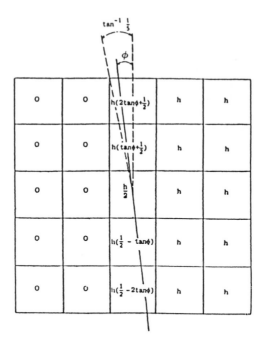

Fig. 3(b)

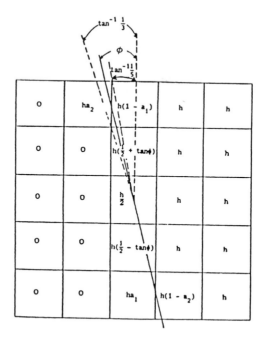

$$a_1 = \frac{(1 - 3 \tan\phi)^2}{8 \tan\phi}$$

$$a_2 = \frac{(5 \tan\phi - 1)^2}{8 \tan\phi}$$

Fig. 3(c)

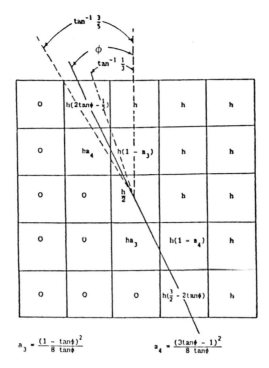

$$a_3 = \frac{(1 - \tan\phi)^2}{8 \tan\phi} \qquad\qquad a_4 = \frac{(3\tan\phi - 1)^2}{8 \tan\phi}$$

Fig. 3(d)

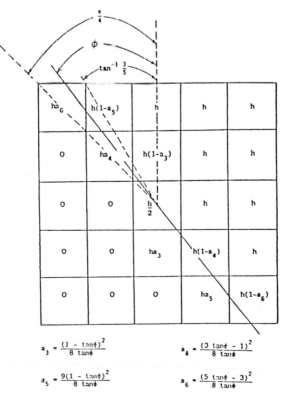

$$a_3 = \frac{(1 - \tan\phi)^2}{8 \tan\phi} \qquad\qquad a_4 = \frac{(3 \tan\phi - 1)^2}{8 \tan\phi}$$

$$a_5 = \frac{9(1 - \tan\phi)^2}{8 \tan\phi} \qquad\qquad a_6 = \frac{(5 \tan\phi - 3)^2}{8 \tan\phi}$$

Fig. 3(e)

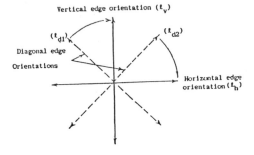

(a) Pixel means for diagonal edges.

(b) Edge orientations ($\ell_v$, $\ell_h$, $\ell_{d1}$, $\ell_{d2}$).

Fig. 4

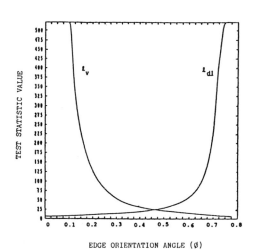

Fig. 5

The Threshold Value : 27

a)Original Linear Model

```
zzmhh   zz+hh   zz+hh   z-hhh   z-hhh   z-hhh   z+hhh   -+hhh   -+hhh
zzmhh   zz+hh   zz+hh   zz+hh   zz+hh   z-+hh   z-+hh   z-hhh   z-hhh
zzlhh   zzlhh   zzlhh   zzlhh   zzlhh   zzlhh   zzOhh   zzOhh   zzOhh
zzmhh   zz-hh   zz-hh   zz-hh   zz-hh   zz-+h   zz-+h   zzz+h   zzz+h
zzmhh   zz-hh   zz-hh   zzz+h   zzz+h   zzz+h   zzz-h   zzz-+   zzz-+

mhhhh   +hhhh   +hhhh   hhhhh   hhhhh   hhhhh   hhhhh   hhhhh   hhhhh
zmhhh   -+hhh   -+hhh   -+hhh   ++hhh   +hhhh   +hhhh   hhhhh   hhhhh
zzOhh   zzOhh   zzOhh   z-0+h   z-1+h   z-1+h   z-1+h   --1++   --1++
zzzmh   zzz-+   zzz-+   zzz-+   zzz--   zzzz-   zzzz-   zzzzz   zzzzz
zzzzm   zzzz-   zzzz-   zzzzz   zzzzz   zzzzz   zzzzz   zzzzz   zzzzz

hhhhh   hhhhh   hhhhh   hhhhh   hhhhh   hhhhh   hhhhh   hhhh+   hhhh+
hhhhh   hhhhh   hhhhh   hhhh+   hhhh+   hhh++   hhh+-   hhh+-   hhh+-
mmlmm   ++1--   ++1--   h+1-z   h+1-z   h+1-z   h+0-z   hhOzz   hhOzz
zzzzz   zzzzz   zzzzz   -zzzz   -zzzz   --zzz   +-zzz   +-zzz   +-zzz
zzzzz   zzzzz   zzzzz   zzzzz   zzzzz   zzzzz   zzzzz   -zzzz   -zzzz

hhhhm   hhh+-   hhh+-   hhh+z   hhh-z   hhh-z   hhh-z   hh+zz   hh+zz
hhhmz   hhh-z   hhh-z   hh+-z   hh+-z   hh+zz   hh+zz   hh+zz   hh+zz
hhOzz   hhOzz   hhOzz   hhOzz   hhlzz   hhlzz   hhlzz   hhlzz   hhlzz
hmzzz   h+zzz   h+zzz   h+-zz   h+-zz   hh-zz   hh-zz   hh-zz   hh-zz
mzzzz   +-zzz   +-zzz   h-zzz   h+zzz   h+zzz   h+zzz   hh-zz   hh-zz
```

b)Modified Linear Model

```
zzmhh   zz+hh   zz+hh   z-hhh   z-hhh   z-hhh   z+hhh   -+hhh   -+hhh
zzmhh   zz+hh   zz+hh   zz+hh   zz+hh   z-+hh   z-+hh   z-hhh   z-hhh
zzlhh   zzlhh   zzlhh   zzlhh   zzlhh   zzlhh   zzlhh   zzlhh   zzlhh
zzmhh   zz-hh   zz-hh   zz-hh   zz-hh   zz-+h   zz-+h   zzz+h   zzz+h
zzmhh   zz-hh   zz-hh   zzz+h   zzz+h   zzz+h   zzz-h   zzz-+   zzz-+

mhhhh   +hhhh   +hhhh   hhhhh   hhhhh   hhhhh   hhhhh   hhhhh   hhhhh
zmhhh   -+hhh   -+hhh   -+hhh   ++hhh   +hhhh   +hhhh   hhhhh   hhhhh
zzlhh   zzlhh   zzlhh   z-1+h   z-1+h   z-1+h   z-1+h   --1++   --1++
zzzmh   zzz-+   zzz-+   zzz-+   zzz--   zzzz-   zzzz-   zzzzz   zzzzz
zzzzm   zzzz-   zzzz-   zzzzz   zzzzz   zzzzz   zzzzz   zzzzz   zzzzz

hhhhh   hhhhh   hhhhh   hhhhh   hhhhh   hhhhh   hhhhh   hhhh+   hhhh+
hhhhh   hhhhh   hhhhh   hhhh+   hhhh+   hhh+-   hhh+-   hhh+-   hhh+-
mmlmm   ++1--   ++1--   h+1-z   h+1-z   h+1-z   h+1-z   hhlzz   hhlzz
zzzzz   zzzzz   zzzzz   -zzzz   -zzzz   --zzz   +-zzz   +-zzz   +-zzz
zzzzz   zzzzz   zzzzz   zzzzz   zzzzz   zzzzz   zzzzz   -zzzz   -zzzz

hhhhm   hhh+-   hhh+-   hhh+z   hhh-z   hhh-z   hhh-z   hh+zz   hh+zz
hhhmz   hhh-z   hhh-z   hh+-z   hh+-z   hh+zz   hh+zz   hh+zz   hh+zz
hhlzz   hhlzz   hhlzz   hhlzz   hhlzz   hhlzz   hhlzz   hhlzz   hhlzz
hmzzz   h+zzz   h+zzz   h+-zz   h+-zz   hh-zz   hh-zz   hh-zz   hh-zz
mzzzz   +-zzz   +-zzz   h-zzz   h+zzz   h+zzz   h+zzz   hh-zz   hh-zz
```

'O' means an undetected edge point,
'1' means a detected edge point.

Fig. 6

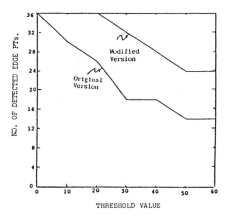

Fig. 7

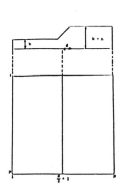

(a) Vertical Edge Test Image (N = 64)

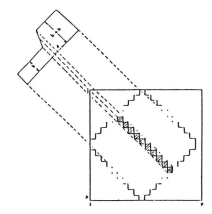

(b) Diagonal Edge Test Image (N = 128)

Fig. 8

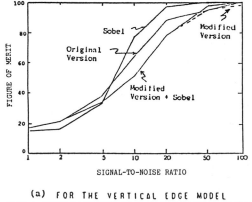

(a) FOR THE VERTICAL EDGE MODEL

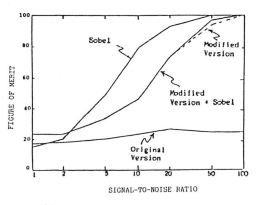

(b) FOR THE DIAGONAL EDGE MODEL

Fig. 9

# Decision Feedback in Adaptive Networks

B. Kani  and  Manissa J. Dobree Wilson

Department of Electrical and Electronic Engineering

Brunel University

Uxbridge, Middlesex UB8 3PH

## Abstract

The application of decision feedback to artificial vision operators known as adaptive windows is considered. The open-loop adaptive window is reviewed and a simple behaviour model evaluated. This simple model is then used to predict the behaviour of an adaptive window with feedback. Requirements for Optimal closed-loop performance are presented.

## Introduction

Adaptive windows are artificial vision operators extensively used in the field of image processing (Aleksander & Wilson [85]), texture discrimination (Kani & Wilson [87]), stereopsis (Wilson [85]) and general multicategory pattern classification problems. A frequent problem in applying adaptive windows is that of poor confidence levels of discrimination compared with those of natural vision. This problem occurs frequently in complex texture discrimination where patterns of different classes have a high degree of similarity. Consider the  simple example of discriminating between the characters 5 and 3. Fig.1 highlights the area of high discriminatory information.

discriminatory features

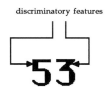

Fig.1 Discriminatory information

It would be quite useful to increase the amount of discriminatory information and hence enhance discrimination performance. One way to do this would be to associate a fixed label with each training pattern of a particular class as shown in Fig.2.

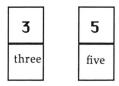

Fig.2 Label association

During classification the system is presented with a pattern belonging to one of the classes. The system then tries to associate the correct label with the pattern to be classified.  The label associated during

Decision feedback in adaptive networks

training should therefore be the expected response of the system. Adaptive windows in their usual configuration can only produce numerical responses possibly in the form of a histogram as shown in Fig.3.

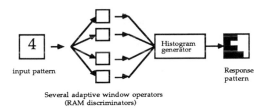

**Fig.3 Histogram response**

The longest bar in the histogram is used to classify the input pattern as belonging to a particular class. It is therefore reasonable to associate training patterns with the ideal response of the adaptive window as shown in Fig.4

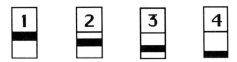

**Fig.4 Pattern association**

During classification a pattern is presented to the system and a histogram is generated at the output. This histogram can now be fed back in order to enhance the original decision. This is shown in Fig.5

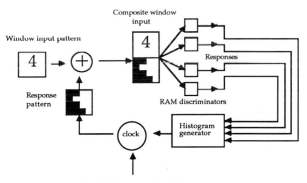

**Fig.5 Histogram feedback**

## Introduction to Adaptive Windows

The basic structure of the adaptive window is shown in Fig.6. The window has a resolution of x by y pixels each connected to one of the address inputs of a set of RAMs according to some mapping function (usually random). The number of input lines to each RAM is called the **tuple size**. The window can take samples from the input image at any position.

Decision feedback in adaptive networks

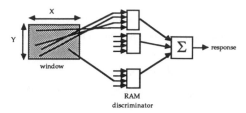

**Fig.6 The Adaptive Window operator**

There are two phases involved in using adaptive windows. The first is the training phase during which the window is shown many samples from the image. The second is the classification phase where the RAM responses to test patterns are analysed. In multicategory classification problems several adaptive window operators are used, each representing one class of patterns.

## Training phase of the adaptive window

During this phase, the window samples the image at many random positions. These samples form the training set. At each position the pixel values form addresses to each RAM, where the addressed location is set to one. This signifies an important property of adaptive windows, ie, the fact that only one bit is stored for a subpattern of size = tuple size. The training phase is completed when sufficient samples are taken from the input image. These samples may be taken from one image or several images belonging to the same class.

One has to be careful not to saturate the adaptive window during the training phase by overtraining. Full saturation takes place when all the RAM locations are set to one, ie, in which case there would be no information stored in the RAMs. In order to avoid saturation one is forced to increase tuple size or take fewer training samples. The speed with which the system is saturated depends on the diversity of the patterns in the training set. One way to avoid saturation is to use a technique that takes into account the frequency of occurrence of subpatterns during the training phase.

## Enhanced adaptive window

The standard adaptive window completely ignores the number of times a subpattern may occur during training, ie, no information is kept in the RAMs regarding the frequency of occurrence of subpatterns. If, as in the adaptive window, however, one does record the frequency of occurrence of subpatterns, saturation can be avoided at even very low tuple sizes as shown in Kani & Wilson [87]. The penalty paid is that the RAM locations must now be wider than one bit in order to store this information. The width of each RAM should satisfy :

$$2^{(RAM\ width\ in\ bits)} >= \text{size of the training set}$$

## Classification phase of the adaptive window

During the classification phase, the window samples the image to be classified in many random positions. These samples constitute the test set of the adaptive window. During this phase the pixel values address RAM locations and the output bits of the RAMs form the response vector. The number of ones in the response vector is the response of the adaptive window. The average response of the adaptive window is then obtained by averaging the responses over the entire test set.

**Decision feedback in adaptive networks**

<u>Response of the open-loop system</u>

During classification a single RAM will output a one if all of its address lines are connected to the common area between the test pattern and any training patterns. Therefore, the response of a single RAM is the probability of its N address lines being connected to the overlap area as shown in Fig.7.

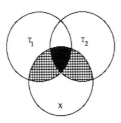

**Fig.7 Overlap areas**

For clarity Fig.7 shows the case of only two training patterns $T_1$ and $T_2$ with a test pattern X. It is obvious that the area common to X and $T_1$ or X and $T_2$ should contribute towards the response. The response of a single RAM to test pattern X has previously been shown to be given by equation (1), (Aleksander & Wilson [85]).

$$P(X) = P(N,x_1,R) + P(N,x_2,R) - P(N, x_{12},R) \text{------------------------------------------------------------ (1)}$$

where :

$P(X)$ is the probability of generating an output of 1 from a specific RAM in response to a test pattern X.

$P(N,Q,R)$ is the probability of connecting N randomly selected points in a specific area of Q points in a total area of R points, which is equal to :

$$\frac{Q!(R-N)!}{R!(Q-N)!}$$

which is approximately equal to :

$$(Q / R)^N$$

and

$x_1$ = common area between X and $T_1$.

$x_2$ = common area between X and $T_2$.

$x_{12}$ = common area between X , $T_1$ and $T_2$.

The negative term is due to the intersection of $x_1$ and $x_2$ (black area in Fig.7) which is needed in order to avoid double counting in calculating the probability. We may now generalize equation (1) for the case of three and then for the general case of T training patterns :

$$P(X) = P(N,x_1,R) + P(N,x_2,R) + P(N,x_3,R) - P(N,x_{12},R) - P(N,x_{13},R) - P(N,x_{23},R) + P(N,x_{123},R)$$

## Decision feedback in adaptive networks

Note the alternating sign of the groups of terms.

We may now generalize this to the case of T training patterns :

$P(X) =$

$+ P(N,x_1,R) + \ldots + P(N,x_T,R)$

$- P(N,x_{12},R) - \ldots - P(N,x_{1T},R) - P(N,x_{23},R) - \ldots -P(N,x_{2T},R) -\ldots - P(N,x_{T-1\ T},R)$

$+ P(N,x_{123},R) + \ldots + P(N,x_{12T},R) + P(N,x_{134},R) + \ldots + P(N,x_{13T},R) + \ldots+ P(N,x_{T-2\ T-1\ T},R)$

.

.

$+ (-1)^T P(N,x_{123\ldots T},R)$

The above formula may be compacted as follows :

$$P(X) = \sum_{j=1}^{T}(-1)^{j+1} . P(j)$$

where

$$P(j) = \sum \left( \prod_{k=1}^{j} A_{a_k} \right)^N \qquad \text{such that } \{a_1,a_2\ldots\ldots a_j \mid \ 1<= a_i <=T\} \text{ -------------- (2)}$$

The above formula is a rather complex series of terms. In Aleksander [83] it is stated that the likely response of a RAM to a test pattern P(x) is approximately equal to :

$$(x_n/ R)^N \text{ ------------------------------------------------------------- (3)}$$

where $x_n$ is the overlap of test pattern X with the training pattern which is closest to X. This approximation introduces an error whose magnitude is not considered in Aleksander [83]. A series of experiments was therefore carried out in order to estimate the size of this error. In these experiments character images of size 24 by 16 pixels were used from a database of handwritten characters provided by the Post Office. In each test the number of training patterns was varied from 1 to 10. The response of the net to a test pattern was then arrived at in three different ways :

1 . Response from the simulated net.

2 . Response from equation (2).

3 . Response from equation (3), ie, Aleksander [83].

The three different responses are shown in Fig.8.

**Decision feedback in adaptive networks**

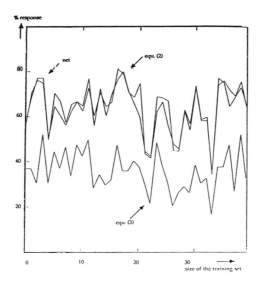

**Fig.8 Theoretical vs experimental results**

It can be seen that the response from equation (2) is very close to the response from the simulated net, demonstrating the validity of the analysis in deriving equation (2). The error produced by the approximate formula, ie, equation (3), however, is quite significant and the curves in Fig.8 reveal a strong dependency on tuple size. Given a fixed tuple size, however, this error is seen to level off with increased training and becomes constant for a given tuple size and a given data set. It would therefore seem reasonable to use the approximate formula and to add an error constant.

## The Closed-loop Adaptive Window

In the closed loop system the response of each adaptive window is fed back to the label area. The mapping between the output of each operator and the label area is unimportant. There should also be no loss of information along the feedback loop, ie, there should be one to one mapping between the output bits and the pixels in the label area.

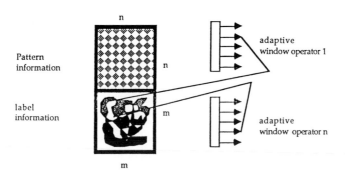

**Fig.9 Random feedback mapping**

Decision feedback in adaptive networks

## The training phase

During the training phase samples of a particular class are placed in the pattern information area and the associated label information, ie, the expected response from the corresponding window is placed on the broken feedback channel. This is repeated for all classes.

## Constraint for maximum information feedback

If no loss of information is to occur during the feedback operation, the label information area should be able to accommodate all the bits coming out of all the RAMs. We must therefore have :

$$K\,(n^2 + m^2)\,/\,N \;=\; m^2$$

which gives :

$$N = [\,(n\,/\,m)^2 + 1\,]\,.\,K$$

where :

K = no of classes

N = tuple size

n = pattern resolution

m = label resolution

Fig.10 shows a plot of this equation with the ratio (n/ m) as a parameter. There is a limit to which one can increase the tuple size in adaptive windows (usually 16) without requiring a massive amount of memory, and according to Fig.10 this puts a limit on the maximum number of categories for classification. The graph of Fig.10 illustrates the following points :

(1) For n/m -> 0, ie, the label area is very much larger than the pattern information area, optimum feedback is achieved at N = K.

(2) For N < K there would always be loss of information resulting in degraded performance, ie, non-optimal feedback.

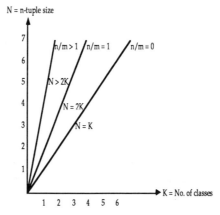

**Fig.10 Optimal feedback**

## Response calculation in the closed-loop system

It was stated in the previous section that the feedback mapping into the label area is immaterial, we therefore adopt a mapping that would depict the responses of the adaptive windows in the form of a histogram in the label area as shown in Fig.11. The size of the label area is chosen to be the same as the

## Decision feedback in adaptive networks

image area and a four category classifier is considered. $X_t$, $Y_t$, $Z_t$ and $M_t$ represent the normalized responses, ie, the proportion of RAMs outputting a one in a particular operator.

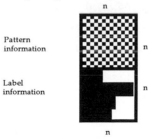

**Fig.11 Histogram map**

The response of the window at time $t+1$ may be expressed in terms of responses at time t in the following manner :

$$X_{t+1} = (\text{ overlap })^N + \text{ error} \text{ --------------------------------------------------------------------- (4)}$$

$$= \{ [n^2FX + n^2/4(X_t) + n^2/4(1 - Y_t) + n^2/4(1 - Z_t) + n^2/4(1 - M_t)] / [2n^2] \}^N + e_x$$

$$= \{ 1/2 \, FX + 1/4 \, (3 + X_t - Y_t - Z_t - M_t) \}^N + e_x$$

Where FX is the overlap of the test pattern in the image area with the closest pattern in the training set. Since we are using this approximation an error has to be introduced into the equation (4). We will therefore have a set of equations representing the behaviour of the closed loop system with respect to time as follows :

$$X_{t+1} = [1/2 \, FX + 1/8 \, (3 + X_t - Y_t - Z_t - M_t)]^N + e_x$$

$$Y_{t+1} = [1/2 \, FY + 1/8 \, (3 + Y_t - X_t - Z_t - M_t)]^N + e_y$$

$$Z_{t+1} = [1/2 \, FZ + 1/8 \, (3 + Z_t - Y_t - X_t - M_t)]^N + e_z$$

$$M_{t+1} = [1/2 \, FM + 1/8 \, (3 + M_t - Y_t - Z_t - X_t)]^N + e_m$$

As stated in the previous section, the above errors could be estimated for a given data set and tuple size.

### Confidnce calculation in the closed-loop system

Assuming $X_T$ and $Y_T$ are the highest and next highest responses after these responses have stabalized, confidence is defined as follows :

$$C_{closed} = \lim (X_t - Y_t) / X_t = (X_T - Y_T) / X_T \text{ ------------------------------------------------------- (5)}$$

In order to calculate confidence therefore, we evaluate the above set of equations. This was done by starting with $X_0 = Y_0 = Z_0 = M_0 = 0$ and then calculating subsequent values of new responses until they stabilized.

### Confidence calculation in the open-loop system

Assuming X and Y are the highest and next highest responses :

$$X = [(n^2FX + n^2) / (2n^2)]^N + ex$$

$$Y = [(n^2FY + n^2) / (2n^2)]^N + ey$$

The open-loop confidence is therefore given by :

$$C_{open} = (X - Y) / X = 1 - [(1/2FY + 1/2)^N + ex]/[(1/2FX + 1/2)^N + ey] \text{ ------------------------------------ (6)}$$

**Decision feedback in adaptive networks**

**Confidence improvement over the open-loop system**

Confidence improvement is given by :

$$[(C_{closed} - C_{open}) / C_{closed}] = 1 - (C_{open} / C_{closed})$$

where $C_{open}$ and $C_{closed}$ are given by equations (5) and (6) respectively.

Fig.12 shows the variation of confidence improvement for different tuple-size and overlap values. It shows that maximum improvement takes place at **N = 2K**

where :

   N = tuple size

   K = no. of classes

This is in total agreement with the results from the graphs in Fig.10 for (n/m = 1), since we have used the same resolutions for image and label areas in deriving equations (5) and (6), giving optimal feedback for N=2K.

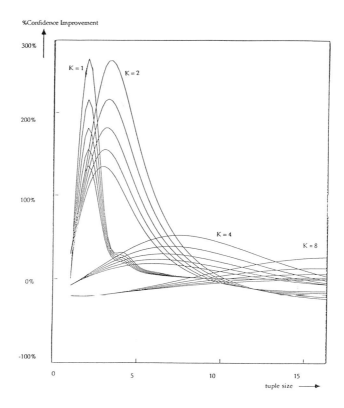

Fig.12 Confidence improvement

## <u>Summary and Conclusions</u>

In this paper the effect of decision feedback on adaptive networks has been considered. Optimal feedback has been hypothesized in terms of maximum information feedback and verified by analysing the closed loop system. In order to describe the behaviour of networks of adaptive windows under decision feedback it is necessary to formulate the operation of the open loop adaptive window. The equations describing the open loop system were found to be too cumbersome to be used in the analysis of the closed loop system. An approximate formula was therefore used and the approximation error was estimated. Using these equations we have been able to verify results obtained using the idea of maximum information feedback.

## REFERENCES

Aleksander, I. and M.J.D. Wilson [1985], "Adaptive Windows for Image Processing." IEE Proc. E., Comput. & Digital Tech., vol 132 No.5. p 233-245.

Aleksander, I. [1983] "Emergent Intelligent Properties of Progressively Structured Pattern Recognition Nets." Proc. BPRA 2nd Int. Conf. on Patt. Rec. Oxford.

Wilson, M.J.D. [1985] "Adaptive Windows : Edges, Stereopsis and Stripes." BPRA , Third Int. Conf., St Andrews, 1985.

Kani, B and Wilson, M.J.D [1987] "Adaptive Windows for Texture Discrimination." Proc. of the third Alvey vision conf., Cambridge. p 251-257.

# DYNAMICS OF HOPFIELD ASSOCIATIVE MEMORIES

M. R. B. Forshaw
Department of Physics and Astronomy
University College London
Gower Street, London WC1E 6BT

## 1. Introduction

This paper is concerned with a particular class of quasi-neural network (QNN), namely the Hopfield auto-associative memory, and its behaviour with time when it is presented with a partial or complete pattern which has to be identified.

The Hopfield paradigm, first described in 1982 [1], has been the subject of extensive investigation [e.g. 2-5]. It is a model of a network of binary threshold logic units (TLUs) with weighted connections between the units. It is assumed that the units have all-to-all connectivity and that the system evolves from a starting state by means of serial, element-by-element, updating. It is of particular interest for several reasons. First, it is similar in structure to infinite-range spin glasses. These have been extensively studied by solid-state theorists, who have used techniques which are based on Sherrington-Kirkpatrick [SK] replica-symmetric thermodynamics [e.g. 6]. Many authors have used these techniques to obtain predictions for the equilibrium states of the Hopfield network. These predictions have largely been borne out by computer simulations of networks with up to 4000 units [3,4].

A second reason for studying the Hopfield network and its close relatives is that they offer insights into the workings of 'real', organic, neural networks [e.g. 7]. Although the details of the TLUs are drastically different from the structure of real neurons, it appears that the cooperative behaviour of the Hopfield network is qualitatively similar in some ways to the behaviour which is believed to occur in real neural nets.

A third reason for detailed consideration of the Hopfield network is that it forms a useful theoretical starting point for the development of systems which may eventually turn out to have practical significance in terms of realisable hardware. This is the reason behind the work described in this paper. Several groups have designed or built prototype associative memory systems which explicitly or implicitly acknowledge the Hopfield paradigm [e.g. 8].

The Hopfield network is mainly considered to be a type of associative memory. Patterns (usually random) are stored in the network by modifying the interconnection weights according to the Hebb rule [1]. The network is then started with an 'initial value' condition, with the states of the TLUs being set to correspond to all, or part, of one of the stored patterns. The system then evolves iteratively, by serial updating of the units, to a final steady state. If the final steady state of the network corresponds to one of the original patterns (with perhaps a small number of errors) then the pattern is considered to have been recognised. It has been found that, for a network with N units (nodes), up to approximately

N/7 patterns can be stored and retrieved with good reliability. When more than this number of patterns is stored, then the retrieval rate of the system drops very rapidly — the final state of the system has only a small correlation or overlap with the 'correct' pattern. By storing less than the maximum number of patterns the network can be made to recognise incomplete or noisy patterns [9-12].

Most theoretical analyses have been concerned with predicting the equilibrium properties of the Hopfield network, that is to say the most stable states of the system. It is known that the network usually takes only a few complete update cycles (that is, from N to a few times N serial node updates) to reach equilibrium when the system is not fully loaded [4]. It is also known that the system dynamics undergoes 'critical slowing' when the number of stored patterns is close to the maximum. Such behaviour is characteristic of a phase transition from one mode of behaviour to another [3-6]. However, apart from [9-12], not very much work has been published about the dynamical behaviour of the system, whether it is used at maximum or at less-than-maximum capacity. In [11] the parallel dynamics of a Hopfield network were analysed for two iterations: the theory became too complex to permit further analysis. The effect of imperfect pattern inputs has recently been considered in some detail in [12], which dealt mainly with the limiting cases of either one or an infinite number of iteration cycles, and for N tending to infinity. It is the purpose of the present paper, to provide some additional experimental and theoretical information about the dynamics of Hopfield networks for arbitrary network sizes and for arbitrary times during the evolution of the system. It is assumed in this paper that the element states are +1 or −1, rather than the values (+1,0) which were used in Hopfield's original paper. This modification, which has been suggested by several authors [e.g. 1,2,9], permits the capacity to be doubled while enabling the element thresholds to be set to zero.

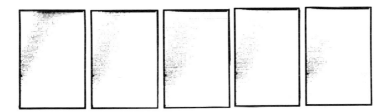

Figure 1. How a Hopfield network evolves with time.

## 2. Simulation Results

Figure 1 is an example of the behaviour of a small Hopfield network with N = 100 nodes and P = 10 stored random patterns. This figure represents the cumulative results of 2,000 different runs with the same values of N and P. The plots show the probability of the network having a particular state after 1,2,3,4 and 8 iterations. The system is started with an initial state, then allowed to evolve, using serial updating of each element (node) in turn. After N such updates, one complete cycle of iteration has taken place. The starting states were chosen by taking each of the 10 stored patterns in turn, then randomly inverting a proportion of the elements to produce a corrupted version of the prototype pattern. The horizontal axis represents the initial overlap between the prototype pattern and the corrupted version of that pattern. The overlap $C_0$ varies from 0 (50% of the elements inverted) at the left to 1 (a complete match) at the right. The ordinate $C_n$ measures the overlap after n = 1,2,3,4 and 8 cycles of iteration. It ranges from 1 at the top to –0.5 at the bottom (the results are antisymmetric about the point (0,0)). The purpose of this form of presentation is to permit investigation of how well the QNN recognises incomplete or corrupted versions of the stored patterns. Other results using this format can be found in [9,10].

Ideally the system would start (at iteration 0) from a point along the diagonal line joining (0,0) to (1,1) and rapidly evolve to a horizontal line along the top of the graph. It can be seen that starting patterns with large values of $C_0$ evolve to a perfect match within a few iteration cycles, while more corrupted patterns initially appear to be attracted to the prototype pattern, then evolve away from this attractor and finish up clustering around $C_n = 0$, as the iteration number n increases. The results for other values of the ratio $\alpha$ = P/N are qualitatively similar, except that the region of 'perfect recall' is larger with smaller values of $\alpha$. For values of $\alpha$ beyond about 0.14 almost no patterns are recalled perfectly, even when the initial state of the system overlaps perfectly with one of the stored patterns. The network also exhibits critical slowing around $\alpha_{crit}$ = 0.14, with many more cycles of iteration being needed to achieve stability. Beyond $\alpha_{crit}$, the final states of the system cluster around a small but non-zero overlap value, even for starting states which are identical to one of the prototype patterns. See [3,4] for experimental results for this particular set of starting conditions and for large values of N.

The behaviour of the system when parallel (synchronous) updating is used is similar but not identical. Figure 2 contains some examples of how a network with N = 200 and P = 20 evolves with serial and with parallel updating (further simulations are still in progress). In [10] it was reported that the two types of updating showed no significant differences. With larger numbers of simulations it can be seen that there are noticeable differences between results obtained with the two types of updating, though the final results are broadly similar.

It is well-known [1] that the Hopfield network can be considered to evolve in a state 'landscape' containing energy minima which correspond more or less exactly to the prototype stored patterns. From an arbitrary starting point the system will 'move downhill' until it finds the nearest stable energy minimum. Figure 3 is a diagrammatic representation of the topography of the energy surface for a QNN with a set of stored patterns: the true surface is of course multi-dimensional. A particular pattern, pattern 1 for example, corresponds to a relative minimum of the energy surface. We may expect to find, at some distance away from the valley for pattern 1, other valleys for patterns 2,3,...,P. There will also be 'false' minima, which correspond to spurious patterns as far as the associative memory capability of the QNN is concerned.

The following diagrams are quantitative representations of various subsets of cuts through the topography of the energy surface. 'Horizontal distance' is measured in terms of the Hamming distance h of some state of the QNN from a particular prototype stored pattern, and the 'height' of the state is measured by its energy:

$$\mathbf{E}^\beta = -0.5 \sum_{i=0}^{i=N} \sum_{j=0}^{j=N} W_{ij} s_i^\beta s_j^\beta$$

where $\beta$ denotes a particular pattern or system state, $s_i$ denotes the value (±1) of each element of the pattern, and $W_{ij}$ is the symmetrical weight on the arc connecting elements i and j. It is convenient to consider the diagrams as 'radial' plots of the projections of sets of contours, which vary with azimuth and radius about a central feature (the energy of the pattern of interest).

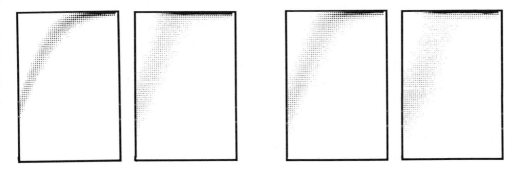

Figure 2. This figure illustrates some of the differences which are observed in the dynamics of a Hopfield network when parallel and sequential updating are used. The axes are the same as in Figure 1. The lefthand pair of plots are for parallel (synchronous) updating and the righthand pair for serial updating. The left plot of each pair shows the accumulated results of 1000 runs after one iteration. The right plot of each pair is for four iterations. The network size was 200 and the number of stored patterns was 20.

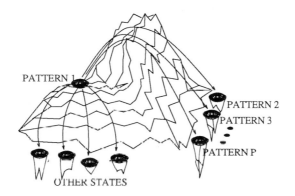

Figure 3. A qualitative representation of the multidimensional energy surface of a Hopfield net. The stored prototype patterns would ideally lie at the bottom of 'basins of attraction', but spurious attractors also occur, particularly as the number of stored patterns increases.

Figure 4 shows how the absolute energy E of a QNN varies with Hamming distance h from the stored pattern prototypes as the system state is progressively converted from each pattern to that of its negative counterpart. The six plots shown are for a network with N = 100 elements and having P = 1,2,5,10,15 and 20 stored random patterns respectively. Two hundred energy values were computed for each Hamming distance, with different elements having their states randomly inverted for each value. The energy ranges from $0.1(0.5N^2)$ at the top to $-1.1(0.5N^2)$ at the bottom. The abscissa extends from a Hamming distance of zero to the maximum distance (N) from the prototype. The plots are fundamentally symmetrical about (h = N/2): there is an artefactual error for the two rightmost columns in each plot.

This figure shows how an energy barrier separates a prototype pattern and its negative counterpart, each having the same relatively low energy. Because each prototype is chosen at random there is a

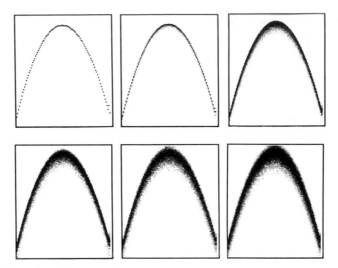

Figure 4. Selected profiles through the energy landscape of a Hopfield associative memory. The ordinate is proportional to the energy of the system; the abscissa is the Hamming distance from each of the prototype patterns. The plots are for N = 100 and P = 1,2,5,10,15 and 20 patterns. Only those profiles are shown which lie on paths which connect a prototype pattern and its negative.

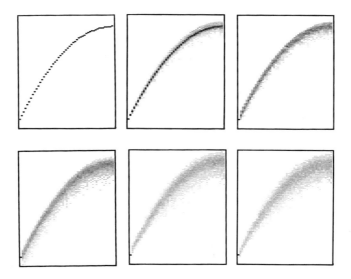

Figure 5. As Fig 4, but here the Hamming distances extend only from 0 to N/2, while the energies are measured relative to each prototype pattern. (Thus the lefthand points, for h = 0, all coincide.)

scatter, of the order of PN, in the energy of each prototype. Essentially the same data is presented in Figure 5, but now the energies are plotted relative to those of the appropriate prototypes, so that the leftmost points, with zero Hamming distance, coincide. The abscissa in these plots only extends from h = 0 to h = N/2. It can be seen that, as the number of stored patterns increases, the probability of the prototype

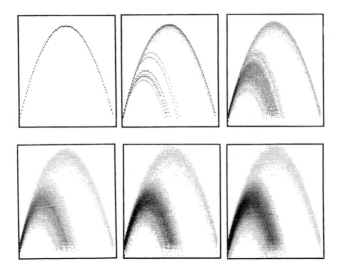

Figure 6. Selected profiles through the energy landscape of a Hopfield network. The ordinate is proportional to the system energy; the abscissa is the Hamming distance from each of the prototype patterns. The plots are for $N = 100$ nodes and $P = 1,2,5,10,15$ and 20 stored patterns. Only those profiles are shown which lie on paths which connect a prototype to its negative or to any one of the other prototypes or their negatives.

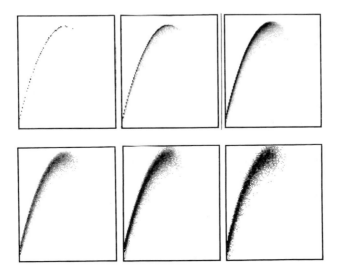

Figure 7. As Fig 6, but for paths which connect each prototype pattern to an arbitrarily-chosen random pattern with equal probabilities of +1, −1 states.

patterns being the states of lowest energy decreases: there are states, a few units of Hamming distance away from the prototypes, with lower energy.

In generating these plots a particular set of directions has been chosen from the N-dimensional state space. In Figures 4 and 5 only those paths have been chosen which connect a prototype pattern and its negative. Such paths are only a small subset of the N! routes by which one may depart from a given pro- totype. Figure 6 shows the cumulative E–h plots, for N = 100 and P = 1,2,...,20 as before, when paths are taken from each prototype to each of the other prototypes and their negatives. Because any two pro- totypes are separated by a Hamming distance of approximately N/2, most of the parabolic barriers end near h = N/2, except for the, decreasingly important, paths between each prototype and its own negative.

There are many states of the system which do not lie on the routes which connect a prototype pat- tern and its negative, or on the routes from that pattern to the other prototypes (or their negatives). Fig- ure 7 is an E–h plot for system states which depart from the prototypes along random directions, i.e. towards states which are not prototypes. It can be seen that there is only a small probability of a system state, which does not match or partly match one of the prototypes, being a low energy state of the system. This does not preclude the possibility of other minima, for example those due to mixture states which have been predicted or observed by several authors [e.g. 3,10]. Indeed, it is believed that mixture states will make a significant contribution to the energy landscape as $\alpha$ increases towards $\alpha_{crit}$.

## 3. Discussion of Results

It should be noted that Figures 4-7 are obtained with constant numbers of samples at each value of h, whereas the actual number of possible states varies enormously along each of the possible paths. For example, in Figure 7 the density of points would vary approximately as $_h^N C$, while in Figure 6 the density of points would vary with h approximately as $_h^{h_0} C$, where $h_0$ is a Gaussian-distributed random variable with mean N/2 and variance proportional to P. Despite this apparent misrepresentation of the state den- sities, the plots in fact provide a useful guide in deriving a theory for the dynamics of the network.

It is possible to make some qualitative predictions about the dynamical behaviour, even without any analytical description of the shape of the E–h maps. When only a small number of patterns are present then the system, if started halfway up the slope in Figure 4, for example, will travel, not more than one Hamming unit at a time, down towards the nearest attractor. It will therefore reach the region of the energy minimum in about $h_0$ single-element updates, if it is not trapped by some spurious local minimum. Figure 5 shows that, in the region of the prototype, there is a finite probability of there being states with lower energy than that of the prototypes. Figure 6 provides confirmation of the observation [e.g. 5] that the energy barriers between prototype states decrease as the number of stored patterns increases. For small values of $\alpha$ Figure 7 will apply: most partial patterns will lie on the 'upper branch' of the E–h plot and can only evolve towards smaller h values. Thus states which lie within a distance $h \approx N/2$ of a given prototype will be captured by that prototype. As $\alpha$ increases then the possibility increases that states at larger values of h may initially move left towards the chosen prototype, then 'drift' to the right, towards some other prototype pattern. Allied with this is the increased probability that start- ing states which are very close to a prototype may drift away from the prototype. As $\alpha$ increases towards 0.14 so the probability of 'punchthrough' from one prototype to another increases. (Figure 6 does not include the effect of possible mixture states.) Finally, we may note that the energy topographies of Figures 6 and 7 should really be combined, with probability densities which are functions of h, P and N. Preparation of plots with the appropriate weighting factors is still in progress.

## 4. Elements of a Theory of the Dynamics

References [1,2,9,10] provide simple and fairly accurate descriptions of the dynamical behaviour of the network for one cycle of iteration, but could only be extended to two or more cycles with considerable difficulty. Reference [11] provides a prediction of the behaviour for up to two cycles of parallel updating, but the mathematics is extremely complicated. Reference [12] considers the basin of attractions of the prototype states in some detail, but is mainly concerned with states which are attracted within one cycle and with arbitrarily large values of N. Apart from reference [13], the only other theoretical predictions are those based on the SK model and apply strictly only to the equilibrium properties of infinitely large networks. Thus any theory which could predict the dynamical behaviour at arbitrary update times, and for arbitrary network sizes, is likely to be quite useful.

The author suggests that the behaviour of Hopfield networks can usefully be predicted on a probabilistic basis, by considering them to undergo biased random walks through an energy landscape, with a finite and predictable probability of being trapped in some local energy minimum. The theory is still in preparation, but some elements can be described. The system energy E is considered as an inhomogeneous Markov process, evolving towards lower energy with a transition probability which is a function of N, P and h. At any given Hamming distance h from the probabilistically averaged prototype, the system will have a certain probability of moving one unit towards the prototype, of moving one unit away from the prototype, or of being trapped. Starting from a particular value of h at time zero, the system energy undergoes a random walk. As the number of individual element updates increases, i.e. as discrete time increases from zero, the probability of the system energy being able to change will progressively decrease, while the chances of it being trapped will progressively increase.

Figure 8 is a qualitative representation of how the experimental results of Figure 1 might be explained in terms of the energy landscape. Figure 6 is used as a basis (though it must be appreciated that this is not a plot of the complete landscape). The system is started at time zero with a corrupted pattern of known Hamming distance from a protoype. As time increases (1,2,...,8,...,∞) the probability of finding the pattern at a particular energy and Hamming distance from the prototype should evolve as shown diagrammatically on the right of Figure 8. These qualitative predictions are not inconsistent with the corresponding vertical cuts through the plots shown in Figure 1.

## 5. Conclusion

It is unlikely that the Hopfield model will be of much practical use as a stand-alone associative memory for pattern recognition purposes. Its importance lies in its conceptual significance: since 1982 nearly all of the publications in this field have acknowledged the relevance of this model. Several papers have recently described modifications to the Hebb programming rule, to permit the storage of correlated patterns. Such systems are much more likely to be of use for pattern recognition, either as algorithmic models to be run on existing computers or perhaps as small-scale VLSI implementations. There are several factors which are important when assessing the importance of an associative memory. These include its pattern-storage capacity, its algorithmic or hardware complexity, its ability to recognise imperfect input patterns, and its response time. The present paper is intended to make a contribution towards describing the behaviour of the last two factors.

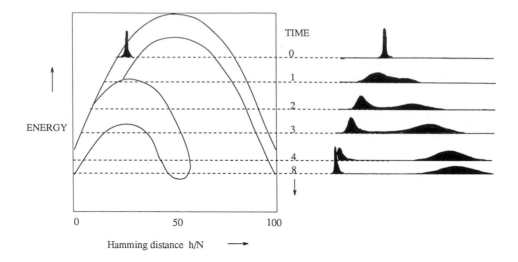

**Figure 8.** A qualitative representation of how a Hopfield net might evolve, starting from a particular point in the energy landscape. The lefthand plot is based upon Figure 6, the righthand plot is based upon vertical cuts through Figure 1, for $C_0 \approx 0.25$. The system evolves towards states of lower energy (with a small but finite probability of being trapped in some metastable local energy minimum). Eventually, as time tends to infinity, no changes occur in the probability of the system having a given value of Hamming distance from a particular prototype.

## Acknowledgments

The author is grateful to T. J. Fountain for helpful discussions and to M. Recce for the provision of reference 13. The work was carried out as part of Alvey Contract No. MMI/033.

## References

1. J. J. Hopfield, Neural networks and physical systems with emergent collective computational abilities, *Proc. Natl. Acad. Sci. USA 79*, 2554-2558 (1982).
2. G. Weisbuch and F. Fogelman-Soulié, Scaling laws for the attractors of Hopfield networks, *J. Physique Lett. 46*, L623-L630 (1985).
3. D. J. Amit, H. Gutfreund and H. Sompolinsky, Statistical mechanics of neural networks near saturation, *Ann. Phys. 175*, 30-67 (1987).
4. A. D. Bruce, E. J. Gardner and D. J. Wallace, Dynamics and statistical mechanics of the Hopfield model, *J. Phys. A: Math. Gen. 20*, 2909-2934 (1987).
5. D. Grensing, R. Kühn and J. L. van Hemmen, Storing patterns in a spin-glass model of neural networks near saturation, *J. Phys. A: Math. Gen. 20*, 2935-2947 (1987).
6. S. Kirkpatrick and D. Sherrington, Infinite-ranged models of spin glasses, *Phys. Rev. B17*, 4384-4403 (1978).
7. J. Buhmann and K. Schulten, Associative recognition and storage in a model network of physiological neurons, *Biol. Cybern. 54*, 1-17 (1986).

8. H. P. Graf, L. D. Jackel, R. E. Howard, B. Straughn, J. S. Denker, W. Hubbard, D. M. Tennant and D. Schwartz, VLSI implementation of a neural network memory with several hundreds of neurons, *Neural Networks for Computing*, ed. J. S. Denker, pp. 182-187. Amer. Inst. Phys. Conf. Proc. 151, New York (1986).

9. M. R. B. Forshaw, Pattern storage and associative memory in quasi-neural networks, *Pattern. Recogn. Letts. 4*, 427-431 (1986).

10. M. R. B. Forshaw, Pattern Storage and Associative Memory in Quasi-Neural Networks, *WOPPLOT 86 — Parallel Processing: Logic, Organization and Technology*, ed. J. D. Becker and I. Eisele, pp. 185-197. Springer-Verlag, Berlin (1987).

11. E. Gardner, B. Derrida and P. Mottishaw, Zero temperature parallel dynamics for infinite range spin glasses and neural networks, *J. Physique 48*, 741-755 (1987).

12. R. J. McEliece, E. C. Posner, E. R. Rodemich and S. S. Venkatesh, The capacity of the Hopfield associative memory, *IEEE Trans. IT-33*, 461-482 (1987).

13. J. D. Keeler, Basins of attraction of neural network models, *Neural Networks for Computing*, ed. J. S. Denker, pp. 259-264. Amer. Inst. Phys. Conf. Proc. 151, New York (1986).

# CONVERGENCE IN A LEARNING NETWORK
# WITH PATTERN FEEDBACK

**L. Masih & T.J.Stonham**
**Department of Electrical  Engineering,**
**Brunel University.**
**Uxbridge, Middx. UB8 3PH**

## ABSTRACT

An architecture based on networks of logic functions is proposed with the output of the network forming a model or archetype image of the class of pattern stimulating the net. Frequency of occurrence information which relates the output of each function to the number of times the stimulus sampled in the test pattern has occurred during the training phase is used. This is shown to have significant advantages over simple binary systems and networks with progressively decreasing connectivity during training-the so called 'ageing 'effect. The frequency of occurrence networks are no longer sensitive to the sequence or order of the training categories and have a greatly improved noise stability. The network is assessed with real world data made up of some hundreds of examples of machine printed numerals.

## 1. Introduction

Cellular networks of processing elements often referred to as neural networks,offer an alternative information processing structure to the serial Von-Neuman computer structure. They are particularly relevant to areas where an algorithmic description of a process cannot be predefined. This may arise due to the excessive complexity of the data or our lack of knowledge of its structure.  A network in which a behaviour emerges from a training strategy offers a potential for intelligent processing which can,in some ways,be compared with human intelligence. The essential similarity is that a consistent description or labelling has to be applied to a set of fuzzy input stimuli which have recurring features recognisable by human inspection but which prove to be intractable to deterministic analysis. Pattern recognition is a typical example of this type of problem. The letter **A** can be written or printed in almost infinite number of different ways. No two hand printed examples will ever be identical. To a human,character recognition is a trivial sub-conscious process,yet it defies algorithmic description in all but the most highly constrained situations where one has to resort to high quality single font prints. Other pattern recognition tasks have proved to be even less amenable to deterministic strategies.Some examples are speech and speaker recognition,face identification,and even smell detection which are all possible by humans implying that some operation on the real world data leads to its correct labelling or recognition. Human recognition processes are unlikely to be unravelling in the foreseeable future. We have a severe lack of understanding of the structure and essential features of both the data and the human processor. In order to make some progress in artificial systems,there has recently been a revived interest in neural models and the development of processing networks based loosely on our currently perceived structure of the brain. Such networks adapt during a training or learning phase in which clustering or converging properties are set up.In the limit one aims to converge from potentially infinite set of real world data to a single descriptor. In character recognition,for example,all possible versions of the letter **A** should be labelled with a single descriptor which,in computer form,would be the ASCII code '260'.

Single layer networks of logic functions( Figure 1) provide a solution for many specific pattern recognition problems. However,the neural analogy is best described as being loose. The representation of a neuron with a simple logic element is a considerable simplification of the currently perceived function of the cell. The binary process is,of course,appealing from a technological point of view as it is amenable to VLSI fabrication and networks of hundreds of thousands of functions can quite easily be set up within single programmable logic circuits.

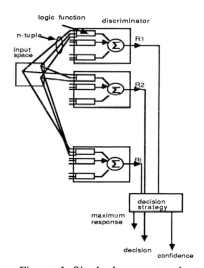

Figure 1 Single layer network

This paper will explore a feedback architecture based on Boolean networks which generate internal models or representation of the input data. The models are combined with an external stimulus and reinput and cycled through the network. Given a potentially infinite set of fuzzy real world data,the aim is to converge to a single or limited set of states. A technique for weighting the function outputs is introduced which gives a measure of the certainty with which pixels in the output image,the model,are set to black(1) or white(0).A strategy for reinstating the pixels of the external stimulating image depending on the pixel probabilities of the internal model,is introduced. The system is evaluated using a data base of examples of unconstrained multi-font printed alphanumerics,using approximately four hundred examples per character class.

## 2.Pattern Feedback Architecture

The pattern feedback architecture for a single layer network(Figure 2) comprises a number of combinational logic functions(implemented in bit organised memory elements,so that each bit respresents a minterm). Each logic function has a set of n inputs(**n-tuple**) to which it will respond with either a '0' or '1'. The output depends upon whether the input is a minterm of the function. Training is achieved by applying typical examples of patterns and driving the teach terminals from a fixed model pattern. Note that the contents of the logic functions are set randomly(with 0/1) initially to ensure that the net is unbiased towards any particular pattern category. For example , if the contents were set to zero then the net would converge towards the all zero pattern,since the taught patterns may only alter a small number of locations within the individual functions.

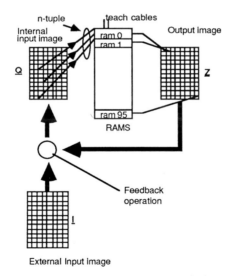

Figure 2 Binary output pattern feedback architecture

In previous work(ref 2) a frequency of occurence count has been used in the training stages as an alternative to another process known as "**Ageing**"(ref 1). This ageing process was used to reduce the dominance of the last taught pattern ,a problem inherent in binary nets. This involves an exponential reduction in the number of taught functions within the net as the teaching progresses. But this idea of functions being removed does not seem acceptable as a suitable solution and is unlikely to be analogous to the natural system.

A frequency of occurrence strategy was used to alter the bit patterns within the functions,depending on the frequency of the n-tuples seen during training. This strategy overcomes the problem of the last seen pattern dominating the net. There are however other deficiencies encountered when the architecture generates a binary output $Z$. Firstly the convergence properties depend on the bit densities of the external input $I$ ,the output $Z$ and the logical operation in the feedback path.

If $P(Z_i)$ and $P(I_i)$ are the probabilities that the $i^{th}$ pixel in $Z$ and $I$ respectively are set to 1,then an AND operation

$Z_i$ AND $I_i \rightarrow 0$     if $P(Z_i),P(I_i) < 1$

whereas an OR operation

$Z_i$ OR $I_i \rightarrow 1$     if $P(Z_i),P(I_i) > 0$

The practical effect is that an AND operation biasses the convergence to white output whereas OR tends towards black output of the image.

Secondly there is a noise magnification problem in the binary system. This is caused by the 1 to n mapping of the network,so that each pixel in the internal input is connected to n n-tuple functions. Hence a one bit change due to noise on the input will cause n functions to change on the output image. This seriously effects the clustering performance of the binary output network. This effect can be illustrated by the following example:

. Given an ORed feedback operation

. the net is trained on the following pattern as input $I$
and desired output $Z$.

. Testing the trained net with the following pattern

will result in the net following the trajectory -

The system does not converge to the model pattern. Since we have a 1 to n (in this case n=8) mapping between input and output,the 1 pixel of noise will cause a maximum change of eight pixels in the output image. Since the feedback operation is a logical OR, this initial one bit change will never disappear and can only accumulate. Hence the net will never converge to the model pattern.

The architecture in Figure 3 is a modified form of that shown in Figure 2. The logic functions output a frequency of occurrence count of each n-tuple sample occurring during training. If an n-tuple sample is to be set to zero as defined in the model pattern then the minterm counter in the logic function is decremented. If logical 1 is required on the output the counter is incremented. After all training patterns have been shown,the functions contain +ve and -ve values. When an input pattern is presented,all the functions respond with negative values for white pixel and positive values for black pixel in the output $Z$. The output image is now a vector of response magnitudes with high +ve values implying a black output pixel,high -ve values for a white pixel and near zero values representing an uncertainty or don't care condition.

The external input image in this case is no longer in binary form,but has pixel values in the range $-K < I_i > +K$ indicating the probability of 0 or 1 pixel values. This convention is used so that the external image is compatible with the output image and to control dominance of the external input on the convergence of the net. The external image is added to the output image

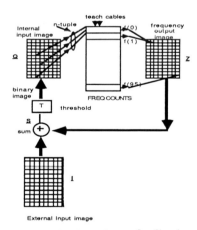

Figure 3 Frequency output pattern feedback architecture

and the new internal image ( binary) is produced by thresholding (T) in the following way : assume ,

|threshold |= T (% of maximum frequency encountered in the functions)

External input image $I = < I_0$ .......... $I_{95} >$    where $I_i \in (-K,+K)$

Output image $Z = < Z_0 \ldots\ldots Z_{95} >$ where $Z_i$ is the frequency of occurrence data

The Sum vector is $S = Z + I = < S_0 \ldots\ldots S_{95} >$

and the Internal input image $Q$ is

$$Q = < Q_0 \ldots\ldots\ldots Q_{95} > \quad\text{where}\quad Q_i \in (0,1)$$

such that:

$$Q_i = \begin{cases} 1 & \text{iff } s_i > +T \\ 0 & s_i < -T \\ \text{otherwise (ie. } -T < S_i < +T) \\ 1 & i_i > 0 \\ 0 & i_i < 0 \end{cases}$$

This frequency output architecture overcomes the problem illustrated earlier with the binary output in that the spurious noise outputs will be filtered out by the threshold. The output which are in error are regarded as those with low responses and in this case a selection is made to reinstate the external input pixels corresponding to the error pixels. This produces a new internal input which comprises of reinstated external and output (thresholded) pixels. Hence the feedback operation consists of a selection of the output and the external image pixels to reduce the emphasis on the bit density of the external images.

## 3. Clustering performance

The performance of each of the two different architectures, shown in Figure 2 and 3 can be assessed by the amount of clustering achieved. One way of measuring this,is to calculate the average Hamming distance between the model and the input or final state(internal image when the net stabilises) pattern,as shown below :

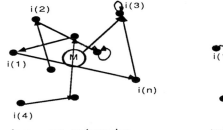

random    net trajectories

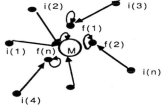

trained net trajectories

let, $H(M,I(i))$ - be the Hamming distance between model M and external input
pattern $I(i)$.

$H(M,Q(i))$ - be the Hamming distance between model M and final stable
pattern on the internal input image retina.

given a total of 'p' test samples -
average of initial fuzzy data:

$$\overline{x}(i) = \frac{\sum\limits_{j=1}^{p} H(M,I(j))}{p}$$

average after convergence:

$$\overline{x}(f) = \frac{\sum\limits_{j=1}^{p} H(M,Q(j))}{p}$$

For this set of experiments, both frequency and binary based architectures were trained on 400 examples of the numerals '0','2' and '3's with an n-tuple size of 8. The models selected to drive the teach cables were as shown below :

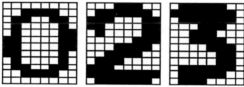

Each of the nets were then tested on examples of 100 patterns (not in training set) belonging to each class and $\overline{x}(i)$ along with $\overline{x}(f)$ evaluated for the data. The results (as shown in Figure 4) show that the frequency model produces more tighter clusters than with the binary output architecture,although the Interclass distance in both cases remains the same. This is to say that the Hamming distance seperation between the classes remains relatively unchanged.

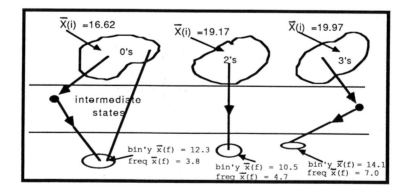

Figure 4 State space clustering

The problems arising with the binary architecture is two-fold. The first is the identification of the feedback operation,although the operation has shown dependency upon the bit density of the external image(ref 2). The second being the problem of noise magnification,which is overcome by the frequency based network.

## 4. Noise magnification

The noise magnification problem can be resolved by using the frequency output architecture and hence the overall performance of the net is significantly better than the binary output architecture. The way in which the problem is resolved is given in the example below:

If the train and test patterns are

.   assume the training pattern is presented 10 times so enabling the frequencies to build up

.   the threshold selected is 50%

.   testing with one bit noise added,will cause the following trajectory of images before the net stabilises on the model pattern.

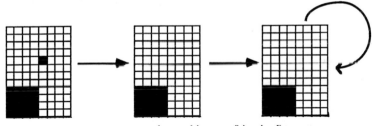

new internal images (binarised)

The reason that the net has converged to the model pattern is that a decision is made whether the firing function is a correct output or simply noise. In the case of noisy output, the pixels corresponding to those positions are replaced with the external image.

Hence, the frequency model has the capability to remove noise initially encountered in the external image and improves clustering, better than the binary output architecture.

## 5. Characteristics of the frequency based system

The behaviour of the frequency output net is dependent on the number of distinct classes it has been taught on and the value of the threshold which controls the dominance of the input. Two graphs showing these effects are given in Figure 5 and 6.

The graph of Figure 5 shows the rate of convergence decreases as the number of classes are increased. For this experiment the net is trained initially on 400 examples of numeral $0$,n-tuple size 8 and tested with 100(not in training set) examples belonging to the same class. The convergence($1/\bar{x}$(f)) is calculated for the final images. The net is then trained on additional data consisting of 400 examples of $2$'s. Again the net is tested with the previous 100 examples of $0$'s and again the convergence calculated. This is repeated until a number of classes have been taught.

The convergence rate of the net is large resulting in tighter clusters for a low number of classes,but decreases as the number of classes is increased. The reason for this being that since there is only one set of functions an increase in number of classes is likely to increase the probability of conflict were the same input minterms require differing outputs for different classes. Similar results are obtained when testing with 100 examples of the numeral $2$ and then $3$.

The second graph (Figure 6) shows the rate of convergence with change in selected threshold. The net was trained on 400 examples of numeral $0$'s,n-tuple size 8. The net is then tested on 100 examples of $0$'s and the convergence($1/\bar{x}$(f)) calculated at each increment in threshold percentage. The procedure was then repeated with examples of the numerals $2$'s and $3$'s.

The net shows that maximum convergence(tighter clusters) is encountered for a given threshold after which increasing threshold will result in increasing dominance of the external image on the

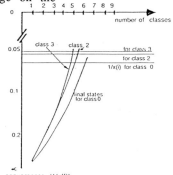

Figure 5 Rate of convergence with increasing classes

internal image and a reduction in the amount of clustering. The threshold is seen to vary between 0 and 100%. If the threshold is at 0%,then this implies that all the output frequencies are above the threshold and the net is not influenced by the external input pattern after the first iteration. However,if the threshold is at 100% then the external input image pixels are re-instated on the input to the net in all cases except where an invariant pixel occurs throughout the training set. This is highly improbable with real data. The net in this case is behaving like an open loop. Hence the patterns do not converge and the final state convergence($1/\bar{x}$(f)) is the same the initial convergence.

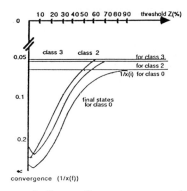

Figure 6 Rate of convergence with variable threshold

## 6. Conclusion

The frequency of occurrence network has substantially increased noise immunity compared with the binary architecture. The feedback operation in a binary system is shown to be dependent upon the bit density of the data to be processed. This limitation requires that the teacher has pre-knowledge of the data to be processed. In this case an inappropriate feedback function may result in divergence even for simple examples.

The frequency architecture,however,overcomes these problems by having the output image as a vector of frequency counts. These frequency counts give an indication of how strong or confident a response is from a function. By the thresholding operation,only the confident responses are carried forward as part of the next input to the net. The selection of the threshold gives the teacher the ability to optimise the rate of convergence.

As a result of overcoming the limitations encountered with the Binary output network,the frequency output network shows a significant increase in performance. Typical improvements in the clustering ability were seen to be of the order of a factor of 3 in the evaluation experiments.

As a preprocessor for pattern recognition hardware ,clustering of this extent will significantly reduce the diversity of real world data and no doubt lead to improved pattern recognition performance.

## References

1. Fairhurst, M.C.,'Natural pattern clustering in digital learning nets'.Electronic letters, 1971, Vol. 7, P724.

2. Stonham, T.J., Wilkie, B.A. and Masih, L, 'Higher order Adaptive Networks- Some aspects of multi-class and feedback systems'.Proceeding of the Third Alvey Vision Conference,Cambridge, 1987, P245.

# GREY SCALE N TUPLE PROCESSING

James Austin

Dept. Computer Science

University of York, York, UK

## ABSTRACT

This paper describes a generalisation of the binary N tuple technique originally described by Bledsoe and Browning (1). The binary N tuple technique has commonly been used for the classification (2) and pre-processing (3) of binary images. The extension to the method described here allows grey level images of objects to be classified using the N tuple method without first having to convert the image to an intermediate binary representation. The paper illustrates the methods use in image preprocessing.

## Introduction

The binary N tuple pattern recognition process was originally described by Bledsoe and Browning (1), and has been applied to a number of image processing tasks such as character recognition (4), face recognition (2), and scene analysis (5). The N tuple process may be seen as a simple perceptron (8) with a non-linear pre-processing transform. Thus, it is an adaptive classifier, which must be trained on a subset of the patterns to be recognised. It has two major advantages over the perceptron, first, it learns each training pattern quickly and, secondly, it is able to classify patterns that fall into the category of 'exclusive or' problems (9).

However, the N tuple method has always been limited to processing binary images; grey scale images may only be processed by the method if they are first converted to a binary representation (see 3). The method described here requires no intermediary binary representation of the grey scale data.

Although the binary N tuple process has been shown to be adequate in a number of applications there are a number of cases where it is insufficient, requiring the full grey scale information to be used in the classification process. For instance, in the classification of edge features where it is necessary to determine the angle and 'sharpness' or slope of an edge. This information is only present in the grey scale domain.

## Binary N tuple process

The binary N tuple process as described by Bledsoe and Browning (1) and Aleksander (2) may be seen as a two stage process. The pre-processing stage performs a non-linear transform on the input image. The resultant image is then processed using a simple perceptron with binary weights. The addition of the pre- processor allows the perceptron (a linear classifier) to classify non-linearly separable data (i.e the 'exclusive or' or parity problem).

The binary N tuple process takes as its input a binary image. From this image a set of tuples are formed. Each tuple is made up of N elements from the image. The origin of each pixel in the image used to make up each tuple is defined once. Normally the origin of each pixel is selected in a random manner, each pixel only contributing to one tuple. The optimal size of N depends on the characteristics of the data and the generalisation properties required (1).

Each tuple may be denoted $D_{k,N}$. For each image there are $N_{max}$ number of tuples where $N_{max} = i/N$, i being the number of elements in the image.

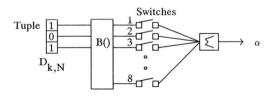

Fig 1: One N tuple processing unit, U.

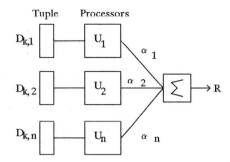

Fig 2: An N tuple classifier.

Fig. 1 shows one tuple and the processing associated with it (N = 3). The first stage B() assigns one state, S, to the tuple in accordance with table 1*. The tuple size, N, equals 3 in this case, giving a total of $2^3$ possible states for each tuple.

The next stage in fig. 1 shows a set of switches. Each switch is used to record the occurrence of a particular state, S, assigned by B(). There are $2^N$ switches to record all the possible states of the tuple. The output from the switches are OR'ed by the summing unit to produce an output $\alpha$. For each of the $N_{max}$ tuples there is one of the processing units, U, shown in fig 1. Fig. 2 shows how the outputs of all the units are summed to produce an output R, the response for the classifier.

There are two phases of operation of the system, teaching and testing. Teaching causes the system to learn an input pattern so that during subsequent presentation and testing it may be recognised.

When a pattern is presented for teaching, the image is broken into N tuples and each tuple assigned a

---

* The function B() may be defined formally. If the N tuple, $D_{k,N}$, is represented as a binary (base 2) number, the state of the tuple is given as its decimal (base 10) equivalent.

| State Table | | | |
|---|---|---|---|
| State | Tuple element values | | |
| | i | j | j |
| 1 | 0 | 0 | 0 |
| 2 | 0 | 0 | 1 |
| 3 | 0 | 1 | 0 |
| 4 | 0 | 1 | 1 |
| 5 | 1 | 0 | 0 |
| 6 | 1 | 0 | 1 |
| 7 | 1 | 1 | 0 |
| 8 | 1 | 1 | 1 |

Table 1 : The state table for the binary N tuple
function B(), for an N tuple size of 3.

state, S, as described above. Each state is recorded on the switches shown in fig. 1 by closing the switch connected to the line associated with the tuple state. As further patterns are taught into the system more switches are closed.

Once a number of patterns have been taught, classification on an unknown pattern may take place. This process, called testing, uses the summing devices shown in fig. 1 and 2. First the image is broken into tuples and the function B() applied as during teaching. A state, S, will now be assigned to each tuple. This is reflected in fig. 1 as an output line of the B() processor going to 1. If the active output wire coincides with a closed switch, a logical 1 is passed to the output of the processing unit, $\alpha_n$. This is repeated for all tuples and the total number of $\alpha$ at logical 1 summed. This value appears as a response, R, as shown in fig 2. This value represents how well the input matches the previous images presented. Normally a number of classifiers are used, one for each pattern class to be classified. The classifier which gives the largest R value indicates the class of the input pattern.

The process of teaching and testing may be defined formally.

$P_{r,i}$ : The r'th input pattern P of size i. $P_{r,i} = 1$ or 0 in the binary N tuple process.

$D_{k,N}$ : Pattern P is broken into k vectors or tuples each of N in size, where $k_{max} = i/N$ and $k_{min} = 0$.

B() : Some function that assigns one state S to each N tuple group,

where $S_{min} = 0$ and $S_{max} = 2^N$ in the binary N tuple process.

$W_{k,t}$ : A vector of weights, where $t_{min} = 0$ and $t_{max} = S_{max}$. $W_{k,t}$ is 0 or 1.

Teaching : the image P is supplied and transformed into the tuples D. Then

$$W_{k,t} = 1 \text{ where } t = B(D_{k,N}) \text{ for all k, } k_{min} \text{ to } k_{max}.$$

This is repeated for all k patterns P in the training set.

Testing : again the image P is transformed into the tuples D. Then

$$R = \sum_{k=0}^{k=k_{max}} W_{k,t} \qquad \text{where } t = B(D_{k,N}). \tag{A}$$

where R is the response from the classifier.

One classifier as described above may be used to discriminate between two patterns. More are used to classify a large number of patterns. For more details of the N tuple process and its generalisation and classification properties see (1,4,9).

The heart of the binary N tuple process is the function B() which translates a given N tuple group into a state S. The function is exactly described by the state table in table 1. The function only takes binary tuples, to be able to process grey scale patterns using the N tuple process it is necessary to replace the function B() used in the binary process for a function that will take grey scale values.

**Grey scale N tuple processing**

The grey scale N tuple process described here was originally described by Austin (5) where it was used as a pre-processing operation to an associative memory in a scene analysis system. It is described here as a general form of grey scale N tuple processing.

In grey scale images each pixel may take on any integer value between 0 and $I_{max}$, where $I_{max}>1$. If a set of tuples is formed from such an image as described above, the tuple element values will be non binary and thus the binary N tuple process cannot be used.

It is a simple matter to threshold the N tuple at some pre-defined or actively defined value, and use the binary N tuple function B() to assign one of $2^N$ states to the N tuple. For example, the grey scale N tuple 4,4,2,1 could be thresholded at 2 to generate the binary N tuple 1,1,1,0. generating the state 14 after application of B(). However, if the threshold is set to 3, the binary N tuple would become 1,1,0,0 giving the state 12 after application of B(). The sensitivity of this method to the level chosen for the threshold rules it out as a practical method. For instance, the method would not cope with variations in overall light levels between teaching on one example pattern and testing on another. Even if the image that was tested was exactly the same apart from the overall light level, the classification process would fail. To overcome this it is possible to teach all example patterns over all light levels. However, this would be a slow and inaccurate method.

To overcome this problem the following grey level state assignment function G() has been developed which takes a grey level N tuple $G'_{k,N}$ and assigns it to one state S'. Consider a general 4 tuple which has the elements A,B,C,D that has been derived from a grey level image. If A,B,C and D can take on the values $I_{min}$ to $I_{max}$, then the N tuple may be sorted into a list of descending element values; this ordering will represent one state, S', of the N tuple. For instance, consider the N tuple 4,3,1,2. The labels are assigned A,B,C,D to each element respectively, then the tuple sorted by value to produce the list A,B,D,C. The order of this list represents the state of the N tuple. The state is equivalent to the state of the binary N tuple produced by the function B().

Each tuple in the image is sorted in this way, Each particular ordering of a tuple represents one state, S'. The total possible number of states an N tuple may be assigned is a function of the tuple size, N, and is given by :

$$S'_{max} = \sum_{k=1}^{N} k! \, S_2(N,k) \tag{B}$$

where $S_2(N,k)$ is the Stirling number of the second kind and is given by :

$$S_2(N,k) = \begin{cases} 1 \text{ if } k=1 \text{ or } k=N \\ S_2(N-1,k-1) + k.S_2(N-1,k) \text{ thereafter} \end{cases}$$

To perform grey scale N tuple processing the function G() replaces the function B() in the formal definition of teaching and testing. Exactly the same procedures may then be used, only now a grey scale image is supplied.

**Reduction of the Number of States**

Although the grey scale N tuple function G() described above may be used in grey scale image classification it suffers from a number of problems. The first of these relates to the number of states each grey scale N tuple can generate by the application of G(). (i.e $S'_{max}$), and the subsequent amount of storage needed in a classification system using the method. As an example, a typical 256 by 256 pixel image would be broken into 16384 tuples where the tuple size is 4. Each tuple generates a possible 75 states, thus one classifier would require 75 * 16384 switches, approximately $1.2 \times 10^6$. A typical implementation (2) of the N tuple method uses 1 bit of conventional computer memory to store the state of one switch, thus one classifier would require 150 k bytes of storage. Furthermore, it can be seen from equation B that the memory used raises factorially with the size of the tuple. This storage requirement may be reduced using a number of data packing techniques (6). However, there is a simple extension to the method that allows a reduction of the number of states each tuple may be assigned, using the concept of 'ranks'. A rank here is used to define a threshold region between which some values may lie. i.e. if a rank had an upper value of 4 and a lower value of 2 the rank interval would be 2 to 4. There may be many (non-overlapping) ranks between two values X and Y, the number of which is given as $\rho$. At the extreme this extension reduces the function G() to be exactly equivalent to the function performed by the binary N tuple function B().

The state assignment procedure for reducing the number of states a tuple may be assigned is best explained with the aid of an example. Consider the following grey level 4 tuple : A = 8, B = 7, C = 2, D = 1.

The following procedure is followed to find the state the tuple belongs to;

i) Find the maximum responding tuple element, Max. and the minimum responding tuple element, Min. i.e Max = A = 8, Min = D = 1.

ii) Find the 'rank interval', I,

$$I = \frac{Max - Min}{\rho}$$

Where $\rho$ is the number of ranks required

$$i.e. \quad \frac{8-1}{2} = 3.5$$

iii) From these values a ranking table can be constructed, which contains $\rho$ ranking intervals or threshold regions of size I. The tuple elements are then placed within these regions depending on the elements values. i.e

| Ranking Table | | |
|---|---|---|
| Rank | Ranking interval | tuple elements |
| 1 | 1 to 4.5 | C,D |
| 2 | 4.5 to 8 | A, B |

The ordering of the tuple elements over the ranked regions represents one particular state of the tuple; in this example there are two ranks, A and B in the second rank, C and D in the first rank. An example of all the possible state assignments of a 3 tuple using the procedure above (with $\rho = 3$ and $N = 3$) is shown in table 2. The precise state number given to each line in the table is chosen arbitarily from the range 1 to $S''_{max}$, and remains fixed.

| state | Rank | | |
|---|---|---|---|
| | 1 | 2 | 3 |
| 1 | A | B | C |
| 2 | A | C | B |
| 3 | B | A | C |
| 4 | B | C | A |
| 5 | C | B | A |
| 6 | C | A | B |
| 7 | AB | C | |
| 8 | C | AB | |
| 9 | A | BC | |
| 10 | BC | A | |
| 11 | B | AC | |
| 12 | AC | B | |
| 13 | A | | BC |
| 14 | BC | | A |
| 15 | B | | AC |
| 16 | AC | | B |
| 17 | C | | AB |
| 18 | AB | | C |
| 19 | ABC | | |

Table 2
Example ranking for the grey scale N tuple process, N = 3, = 3.
Each element of the tuple is labelled A,B and and C respectively.
Two tuple elements that appear in the same table positions have the same value.

The total number of states that may be assigned to one tuple using the new procedure is :

$$S''_{max} = \rho^N - (\rho - 1)^N$$

which results in values of $S''_{max}$ less than $S'_{max}$ for low values of $\rho$.

It was pointed out above that the functions G() and B() may be equivelent, this occours when the nuber of ranks equals 2, then $S'_{max}=S''_{max}+1$. The one state diffence occoures when all the tuple elements are equal, these tuples are given the same state by G() but different states by B(). (Concider the states assigned to the two tuples 1,1,1,1 and 0,0,0,0 when passed to the the function G() with R = 2, and then to the function B().)

The value of $\rho$ is set subjectively, as is the size of N the tuple size. The effect of different sizes of $\rho$ is shown in the examples of edge detection.

It will be noted from the above example that an N tuple element can fall on a boundary between two ranks or threshold regions. When this occurs it is not possible to assign a state to the tuple in question. On these occasions the tuple can be assigned more than one state, the state when the tuple element is forced into the upper rank and the state when it is forced into the lower rank. This method makes pattern classification robust, because it is equally likely that successive patterns shown to the system will force the indeterminate tuple element either way.

**The Incorporation of N Tuple Confidences**

Consider two grey scale N tuple samples taken from an image of an object lying on a background that has an almost uniform intensity profile. One tuple samples pixels from an edge that defines the shape of the object, the other samples from the background. Two tuple samples from the image might be as follows (N = 4) :

Edge tuple (i) : A = 10, B = 15, C = 100, D = 120

Background tuple (ii) : A = 1, B = 3, C = 4, D = 1

If a grey scale N tuple process is used with $\rho$ = 2 the states assigned to the two tuples relate to the orderings :

C,D/A,B - tuple (i)

B,C/A,D - tuple (ii)    (upper rank/lower rank)

It is obvious that the tuple which samples from the edge is more important in the classification of the object than the tuple sample taken from the background. This information is reflected in the individual tuple element values; tuple (i) has a range of tuple element values from 10 to 120, where as tuple (ii) range from 1 to 4. However, this information is not passed to the response, R, of the N tuple process (see fig 2) as R is merely a count of the number of tuples from the present image which were present during teaching. Each tuple has an equal effect on the outcome of the classification. It is useful to add confidances to the tuple to be used during classification (testing), which reflect the 'strength' of the N tuple. The confidances may be derived for each tuple and equals C = Max element value – Min element value. The confidance may be incorporated in the response R during testing by altering equation (A) in the following way :

$$R = \sum_{j=0}^{j=K_{max}} W_{j,t} \times C_k \quad \text{where } t = G(D_{k,N})$$

In this way the N tuple process is biased towards N tuples which are more 'defined' and so more likely to be important features in the scene.

**Image Processing Example**

The grey scale N tuple technique may be used in a number of applications. The following example shows its use as an adaptable edge operator.

**Edge Detection**

A simple image of 5 grey level bars is shown in fig 3, captured using a Vidicon camera and associated frame store, thus it is not a 'clean' image. It is 128 x 128 pixel square with a grey scale resolution of 256. Plot 1 shows how the grey level information varies along the line x = 64 in the image. To allow the recognition system to recognise the edge boundaries in the image a grey scale N tuple processing system was used which consisted of a small 8x8 pixel window which was scanned over the image. The recognition process used 4 pixels per N tuple, with a rank size as shown later.

The recogniser was trained on an example of an edge in the scene. To do this the input window of the recogniser was trained with its centre at the following 3 coordinates in the image, 64,40; 64,42; 64,38. (fig 3

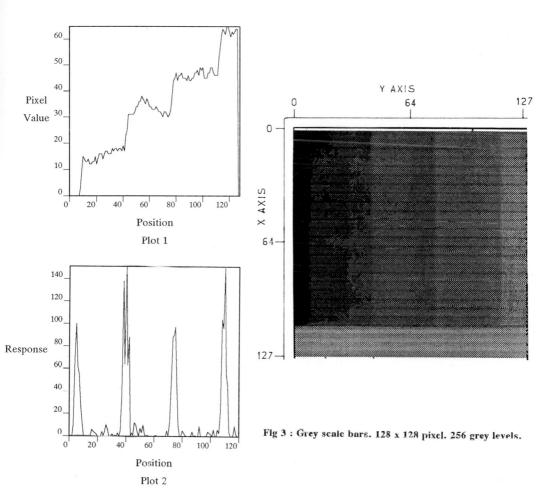

Fig 3 : Grey scale bars. 128 x 128 pixel. 256 grey levels.

has the coordinate axis marked for reference.)

After training, the recogniser's window was scanned across the line x=64 in the same image, in one pixel steps. At each step the recogniser was tested and its response noted. The results of scans using a number of different recogniser set-ups are shown in table 3.

Table 3

| Exp. | Ranks | Confidence used ? | E | | | | M | $\beta$ |
|---|---|---|---|---|---|---|---|---|
| | | | 1 | 2 | 3 | 4 | | |
| 1 | 2 | No | 14 | 16 | 14 | 14 | 10 | 40% |
| 2 | 2 | Yes | 165 | 170 | 170 | 180 | 40 | 75% |
| 3 | 4 | No | 10 | 16 | 10 | 11 | 3 | 70% |
| 4 | 4 | Yes | 100 | 150 | 100 | 150 | 10 | 90% |

| | |
|---|---|
| Exp. | experiment number |
| Ranks | number of ranks used in recogniser |
| Confidence used | whether or not tuple confidances were used. |
| E | peak value where an edge is detected |
| M | maximum peak where an edge is not present. |
| $\beta$ | confidence |

Experiments 1 and 3 show an overall lower response than expts. 2 and 4 due to the use of confidence in the testing procedure.

Table 3 indicates how well each style of recogniser is at separating edges from flat areas, by giving a confidance figure. This is, $\beta = \dfrac{X - M}{X}\%$

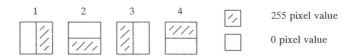

Fig. 5 : Patterns taught (1-4) into recogniser

**Fig 4 : Image of books, 128 x 128 pixel.**

**256 grey levels.**

**Fig 6 : Result of applying grey scale recogniser**

**taught on the images in fig 5 to the image in fig 4.**

where X is the minimum recogniser response where an edge is detected (minimum of E in table 3). In other words, for all the places where an edge should be detected over the total scan of the recogniser, the minimum recogniser response is noted. M is the maximum response from the recogniser over all regions where an edge should not be detected.

The results show an number of important points. First, the larger the number of ranks used, then the higher is the 'selectivity' of the recogniser. Compare expts. 1 and 3; the use of the larger rank in expt 3 has resulted in a far better selection of the edge from the background, as reflected in the confidances for the two expts, 40% and 70% respectively.

The discussion of the recogniser pointed out that the recogniser will detect weak edges and strong edges with equal response. While this can be an advantage in some situations, the use of confidances will make the method sensitive to the strength of edges. The effect of the use of confidances is shown by comparing expt. 1 with 2 and 3 with 4. Both expts. show a better selectivity between the edge and the background when the confidance of the tuple is passed to the response, reflected in the confidance figures, 40% compared to 75%, and 70% compared to 90%. A plot of the results of scanning the recogniser over the image with the set up as in expt. 4 is shown in plot 2.

To show the edge detector operating on a scene, fig 4 was convolved with a grey scale recogniser of window size 8 x 8 pixels, N tuple size of 4 and 2 ranks per tuple. Confidances were not used in the recognition process. The recogniser was taught on the patterns shown in fig 5. The output of the recogniser is shown in fig 6. The recogniser has also been used to recognise textures after training the system on typical examples of the textures to be recognised (10).

## Conclusions

The results of the examples show how the grey scale N tuple technique may be successfully used in pre-processing applications. Furthermore, the operator may be trained on examples of the data to be recognised, thus freeing the user from the need to describe the patterns to be processed formally, as an algorithm or a mathematical definition.

## Acknowledgements

Thanks are due to Bill Freeman for the calcluation of $S'_{max}$.

## References

1, Bledsoe, W. W., I, Browning, "Pattern Recognition and Reading by Machine." Proc. Eastern Joint Computer Conf., Boston, Mass., pp. 225-232, 1959.

2, Aleksander, I., W. V. Thomas., P. A. Bowden, "WISARD, a Radical Step Forward in Image Recognition", Sensor Review, Vol. 4, No. 3, pp 120-124.

3, Wilson, M. D., "Adaptive Windows: Edges, Stereopsis and Stripes", Pattern Recognition Letters, No. 4, 1986, pp351-358.

4, Ullamnn, J. R.,, "Experiments with the N Tuple Method of Pattern Recognition", Trans. IEEE Computers C-18 (12), pp 1135-1137, 1969.

5, Austin, J., "The Design and Application of Associative Memories for Scene Analysis", PhD, Department of Electrical Engineering, Brunel University, August 1986.

6, Austin, J., "ADAM: A Distributed Associative Memory for Scene Analysis", Proc. First annual conference on Neural networks, San Diego, CA, USA, 1987.

7, Aleksander, I., Stonham, T. J., "Guide to Pattern Recognition Using Random-access Memories", Computers and Digital Techniques, Feb 1979, Vol. 2, No. 1. pp29-40.

8, Minsky, M.,Papert S,, "Perceptrons", MIT Press, 1969.

9, Stonham, T. J., "Practical Pattern Recognition", in "Advanced Digital Information Systems", chapter 6, Eds. Aleksander I. et. al., Prentice-Hall int., 1985.

10, Austin, J. "Image Pre-processing With a Generalised Grey Scale N Tuple Operator", Dept. Computer Science internal report, University of York, 1987.

# CHANGE DETECTION IN DIGITAL IMAGERY USING THE ADAPTIVE LEARNING NETWORKS

Nael K. Asker/Nabeel T. Hendow
Space and Astronomy
Research Center
Baghdad, Iraq

Mahmuod H. Al-Muifraje
Military Technical
College,
Baghdad, Iraq

## ABSTRACT

This paper reports research conducted on the problem of change detection in digital imagery. The detection of changes is very important in any applications which require comparison of many images of the same scene. The problem requires an approach which is flexible and can adapt to varying data trends. The system is based on the adaptive learning networks which are an implementation of the N-tuple method of pattern recognition.

Several experiments were carried out to optimize the net parameters and test the performance of the net for this application. A new mapping structure for the N-tuple was devised to cope with insignificant scattered changes that might occuring a scene. Also the size of the minimum detectable object in a scene was also determined.

## INTRODUCTION:

The problem of change detection presents itself in the analysis of data from imaging sensors that view the same area repeatedly. It involves comparing two or more images of the same scene to identify the change that has taken place.

An automatic change detection system would relieve the interpreter of a great burden by identifying the change areas and possibly describe the change.

Besides its importance for military survaillance, other applications include urban planning, weather prediction, land resource management, industrial parts recognition and medical image interpretation.

Most of the early work on change detection concentrated on aerial imaging sensors [1,2]. These require highly accurate image registration and extensive corrections for geometric distortions generated by the system and the terrain. Both of these operations are arithmetically intensive.

For determining whether significant changes have occured, several techniques have been proposed. Simple subtraction of the two images was used, and the difference image was classified [3]. In [4] the Kolmogrov-Smirnov (K-S) test was used to compare two Landsat images of the same area. The K-S test evaluates whether two samples have been drawn from the same population, and hence can detect the presence of change.

In [5] Kawamure discusses a change detection system for use in urban development. He divides the area into small cells, and identifies the change in each cell depending on three parameters; correlation coefficient, entropy and high intensity probability. All the above methods require intensive calculations.

Several methods have been proposed for studying tomographic and nuclear medicine images [6,7]. However, they are optimized for the problem at hand and not general procedures.

It should be noted that all the above methods depend on comparing two images, one as reference and the other for testing. In time varying environments no one image can give a good description of a scene. This is because a number of insignificant changes can occur randomly in the scene which cannot be accounted for. The application of specific rules and algorithms becomes more complex and time consuming. Thus the need for more general adaptive approach became apparent. The response of this approach is evolved from a representative set of the data to be encountered.

In this paper a new technique is proposed. The system can "learn" from multiple coverages of the scene, and then can identify whether a new coverage is significantly different from other coverages. The system is based on the adaptive learning networks (ALNs) which are an implementation of the N-tuple method of pattern recognition [8,9]. No formal definition and correction for the inaccuracies of the imaging system and terrain are required. This is replaced by a training procedure with reference to known examples to the scene to be encountered. Also the ALN digital hardware implementation in the form of memory elements can be redily and cheaply achieved and its inherent parallel structure makes it extremely fast in operation.

This paper investigates the implementation of a change detection system using the ALNs. This novel approach to change detection has shown good discrimination capility even in the presence of distortions and added noise. The size of minimum change which can be detected in various noise levels is determined.

## 2. ADAPTIVE LEARNING NETWORKS (ALNs):

2.1 Principle of Operation

The basic theory of ALNs will be revised here. More details can be found in [10].

Assume an image array of (R) pixels is divided into (K) groups of (N) pixels each. Every such group is said to form an N-tuple. The state of the N-tuple is defined by the values of the constituent pixels. Hence for B bits per pixel, $2^{NB}$ states are possible for an N-tuple.

It is assumed throughout that each pixel is selected for one N-tuple only, hence

$$K=R / N$$

The selection of pixels to form an N-tuple may be random or ordered in certain method to extract certain features from the image. It should be noted that this mapping of pixels is done once at the beginning of a task and remains fixed throughout.

The first step is reaining the system using a few examples of the pattern. For each training pattern, the state of every N-tuple is stored. Thus, for T training patterns, T states are obtained for every N-tuple. In fact the number of different states may be less than T, since two different training patterns may have some of their tuples in identical states.

When the system is presented with an unidentified image, the states of the N-tuples of the image are compared to those of the training patterns. The number of common states is an indication of similarity of the testing pattern with the training pattern. It is called the response of the system and varies between O and R.

The confidence may be defined as:

confidence = response/ maximum response

The confidence level thus calculated can be used for the detection of change in images by setting a suitable threshold on its value. An unidentified image will be classified as a changed or unchanged version of the scene depending whether the confidence obtained is above or below the threshold.

The flexibility of the system arises from the fact that for every N-tuple, the system has approximately T possible states and hence an unidentified object will be correctly classified if its N-tuples are made from any combination of the possible states from different training patterns. This important property of the net is known as the generalization capability, and it allows the net to classify patterns other than those in the training set. However, the generalization capability is highly dependent on the size and quality of the training data [10,11]. Increasing the number of training patterns results in an improvement in classification accuracy until an optimum number of training patterns has been presented to the system whereafter classification begins to fall off. Many other parameters affect the performance of the net, such as N-tuple size, the connection mapping and the decision logic. These effects are discussed elswhwew in literature [12,13].

2.2 A Note on Implementation

A major attraction of the ALN is the possibility of a simple low-cost hardware implementation using memory elements. Such as implementation for binary images is shown schematically in fig.(1). Each N-tuple requires $2^N$ memory bits which are addressed by the pixels forming the N-tuple. Hence each location forms a possible state for the tuple.

Training is carried out tuple by tuple where a logic 1 is stored in each location whose state occurs during training.

For testing, the memory elements are put in the read state, and the memory is addressed same as above. A logic 1 is obtained at the output of each tuple whose state has occured during training. The outputs are added to form the response of the net.

Images with grey level can be implemented in the same manner, but a coding scheme will be required for the grey level, and the memory required will be approximately doubled for every doubling of grey levels [14].

A software implementation on a general purpose computer is also possible where approximately same amount of memory will be required, but the response will be much slower.

3. PERFORMANCE OF THE NET FOR CHANGE DETECTION

3.1 Experimental Set-up

It was decided to take an experimental approach, since it was considered that a theoretical model would not be able to cope with the effects of varying training patterns or imaging conditions. The first step for experimenting with the net is to provide training data of a particular scene. This requires several images of the scene which constitute a representative set of the scene including the effects of conditions or system inaccuracies.

To generate such data the system whose block diagram is shown in fig.(2) was used. The input to the video camera consisted of a black and white photograph of a scene in Iraq shown in fig.(3). The

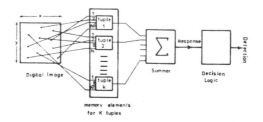

Fig. 1    Block Diagram of an Adaptive Learning Network

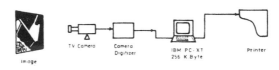

Fig. 2    Data Acquisition and Analysis System Block
          Diagram.

Fig. 3    Black and white photograph of a Scene in Iraq.

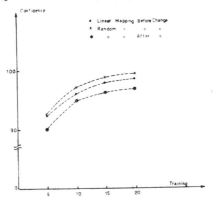

Fig. 4    The Effect of Number of Training Patterns on the
          Confidence Level for Linear and Random Mapping.

Table 1    Confidence Level for the Four Quarters at
           Different Signal to Noise Level

| Noise Level | Confidence % Before Change | Confidence % After Change |
|---|---|---|
| No Noise | 100<br>100<br>100<br>100 | 90.521<br>100<br>100<br>100 |
| S/N = 200 | 96.588<br>96.351<br>96.398<br>96.303 | 87.488<br>96.351<br>96.398<br>96.303 |
| S/N = 100 | 93.365<br>92.891<br>92.701<br>93.128 | 84.36<br>92.891<br>92.701<br>93.128 |
| S/N = 50 | 86.54<br>85.782<br>86.493<br>86.445 | 78.531<br>85.782<br>86.493<br>86.445 |
| S/N = 30 | 78.246<br>77.915<br>78.626<br>77.915 | 71.043<br>77.915<br>78.626<br>77.915 |
| S/N = 10 | 48.862<br>47.915<br>47.394<br>44.408 | 44.929<br>47.915<br>47.394<br>44.408 |

digitizer obtains the image in 256 grey levels which are subsequently thresholded to two binary levels and limited to size (90 x 75) pixels.

Thirty images were obtained, ten of them were selected randomly as test data. Another set of test data was prepared by inserting a twenty pixel object to represent change in the above images. The remaining twenty images were used as training data. A net simulation program on an IBM PC-XT was used.

3.2 Parameter Selection and Initial Performance

Several experiments were carried out to select the net parameters for best performance; the criterion being the ability of the net to decide for or against the presence of change. The decision is based on a threshold value on the confidence level as mentioned in section 2.1. The net was trained with a varying number of the training patterns, and different N-tuple size. It was then tested with the ten unchanged testing patterns and the percentage of changed tuples (confidence) was calculated, and averaged over the ten images. The experiments were repeated with the change test patterns. The difference in confidence between the two sets of images was taken as the measure of the net discrimination capability . The results are shown in figures 4,5 and can be summarized as follows.

A- From fig.4 it is clear that the confidence improves as the number of training patterns is increased. The diagram shows the results for the case where the number of pixels per tuple (NT) is eight. Similar experiments were carried out for NT = 4,6 and 10. The results give a similar trend. This is because more training will give added information to the system about the tested scene and the imaging system, which will subsequently improve the confidence of the system.

B- From figure 4, random mapping of the tuples seems to produce better results than linear horizontal mapping. This is expected since the features in a scene are randomly distributed.

C- Fig. 5 compares the confidence levels obtained using different N-tuple sizes. In addition to affecting the performance, the choice of N-tuple size affects the memory requirement since for every pixel increase in tuple size the required memory almost doubles. From the figure it is noted that the absolute confidence decreases as tuple size is increased from 4 to 10. NT=8 shows the sharpest change in confidence between changed and unchanged test images, and hence will be expected to give best change detection performance.

D- When a moderately sized change occurs in a scene, the decrease in confidence is too low to be taken as a threshold value. This results from the fact that change of a few pixels is insignificant (as a percentage) compared to the image dimensions (in our case 90 x 75 pixels). Considering that the net may be operating in noisy environments it became necessary that steps are taken to optimize the performance of the net and hence increase the confidence level so that a realistic threshold may be set. This problem will be tackled in the next section.

## 3.3 Optimized Mapping for Change Detection

The experiments in the earlier section reveal that by proper training, the effect of differing conditions and inaccuracies in the imaging can be accounted for. However, the relative change in confidence is highly affected by the size of the change. This is further complicated by the possibility of existence of a number of insignificant changes in a scene. For example, in a residential area a few scattered houses may have been repainted or added or removed. These appear as scattered changes in the scene and will modify the confidence level obtained, although their effect should be neglected; i.e. they act as additive noise on the system besides that of the imaging system.

Initial experiments suggested that the net performance will be degraded in the presence of randomly distributed additive noise. To overcome this, a new mapping for the N-tuple was suggested. This takes advantage of the random spatial distribution of noise. While any significant change will tend to be clustered in a certain area, insignificant changes are expected to be randomly distributed.

The modifies mapping is as follows:-

Divide the image into four sections either horizontally or vertically. Then form a separate network for each quarter as shown in fig.(6). It should be noted that this new mapping does not requires extra memory space. Perform training as in previous section

During testing a confidence level will be obtained for each section separately. This confidence value will be indicative of the change or noise present in that section. Considering that noise tends to be randomly distributed across the image it will tend to affect the confidence of all the sections uniformly, while if some change has occured in one of the sections it will affect the confidence of that section only. Hence the difference in confidence between the sections is indicative of the change that occured in the section. A threshold can be set which is based on the difference in confidence between the sections. This will make it possible for the net detect change even in noisy environments.

Several experiments were carried out to test this structure. The same training data set was used but with the modified mapping. To simulate the effect of insignificant changes, randomly distributed noise of varying magnitude was added to the test images. Experiments were carried out with and without the presence of a twenty pixel object in the first quadrant. The results are shown in table-1.

It is noted that the confidence level in each section is decreased as the noise level increases. However, this decrease is uniform between the four sections when no object is present, while the section which has a change inserted is markedly different from the rest. This fully agrees with previous assumptions and hence a threshold can now be set based on the difference in confidence between the sections. Fig.(7) shows the effect of varying the noise level on the minimum difference in confidence between a section which has a change inserted, and any other section in the image. The figure shows that apart from very high noise levels a reasonable threshold can be set for change detection.

3.4 Size of Detectable Changes

Having deviced an algorithm for change detection it is essential that the size of minimum detectable change for a given threshold is obtained. The threshold value will correspond to a certain reliability in detection. However, there is no optimum method for selecting a threshold value since it will be very dependent on the nature of change and the image. Furthermore, an exhaustive search of all the assignments proves to be difficult. Nevertheless some indication can be obtained in the light of experimentation, and it was decided to use a threshold value of 5% for the difference in confidence between sections as the threshold for the presence of change.

The experiments in the earlier section reveal that the confidence obtained is still dependent on the noise level, hence the size of the minimum detectable object will be dependent on the noise level in the image. Fig. (8) depicts the minimum size plotted against the noise level in the image. For the results to be independent of image size, the size of change in pixels has been normalized by the image size. As expected the size increases as the noise level increases, but remains within reasonable bounds except for high noise levels (S/N <= 30) were it starts to increase sharply.


DISCUSSION:

A successful implementation of a change detection system would give the system all the attractive features of the net. Firstly the system

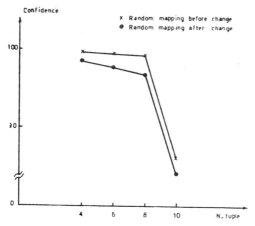

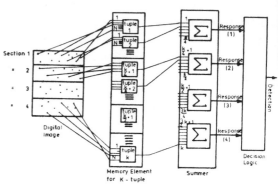

Fig. 6    Optimized Mapping for Change Detection

Fig. 5    Effect of N-tuple Size on Confidence Level for
Random Mapping.

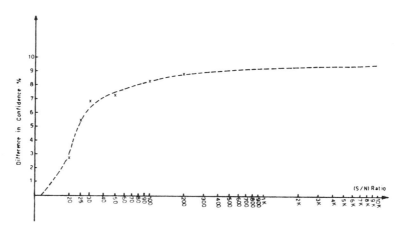

Fig. 7    Difference in Confidenec for Different Signal to
Noise (S / N) Ratio.

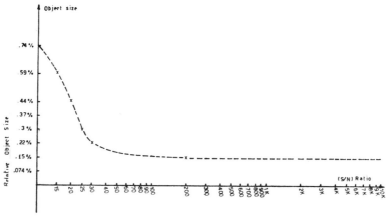

Fig. 8    Detectable Object Size for Different Signal to
Noise (S/N) Ratio.

will be highly flexible and adaptable. No formal corrections will be required for environmental changes or system inaccuracies, and its performance can be easily altered to cope with varying data. Another main advantage is then possible implementation as a dedicated hardware machine at relatively low cost using memory elements only. Such an implementation is discussed in detail in [15]. This makes it suitable for real-time applications.

As confirmed by our experiments, the performance of the net is highly dependent on the training data. The training set should be adequate in size and gives a good description of the scene. It should be noted that the memory requirement is independent of the size of training data, since there is no direct storage of images.

Generally, the performance of the net for change detection seems to be adequate. The net was capable of discriminating change from system inaccuracies due to the recuring nature of the inaccuracies, and hence the training was able to improve the performance. However, if the variations in the inaccuracies within the image are limitless and random in nature and thus difficult to describe by training, then one has to depend on the spatial features of image and noise. This was achieved in the second set of experiments by devising a new mapping structure.

The system was assessed using binary images. However, extension of the system to cope with grey level images can be easily implemented.

## 5. CONCLUSIONS:

This research has investigated the problem of automatic change detection using the adaptive learning networks. An attempt was made in order to make the presentation of general nature and hence suited to a wide variety of problems. Due to the non-deterministic nature of the problem an experimental approach was adopted.

The training and the testing data were obtained using digitized video image of a photograph. All the net parameters were optimized for best performance.

Generally, the net was found to be capable of detecting changes in the presence of system inaccuracies if good training is available.

Also the system performance in the presence of scattered insignificant changes in the image was investigated and a new mapping structure was presented. The size of minimum detectable change was determined after setting a threshold on the confidence values obtained.

## REFERENCES :

1- Shepard, J.R., "A concept of change detection", photogrammetric Eng., vol.30, pp 648-651, July 1964.

2- Lillestrand, R.L., "Techniques for change detection", IEEE Trans. Comput., vol.c-21 pp 654-659, July 1972.

3- Anuta, E. and Bauer, N., "An analysis of temporal data for crop sciences classification and urban change detection", Laboratory for Applications of Remote Sensing, Purdue University, West lafaytte, Indiana, 1973.

4- Eghbal, H.J., "K-S test for detecting changes from Landsat Imagery Data", IEEE Trans. on Systems, Man and Cybernetice, vol.SMC-9, pp 17-23, Jan. 1979.

5- Kawamura, J.G., "Automatic recognition of changes in urban development from aerial photographs", IEEE Trans. Systems, Man, and Cybernetics, vol.SMC-1, pp 230-239, July 1971.

6- Frei, W., Singh, M. and Shibata, T. "Digital Image Change Detection", Optical Engineering vol.19, No.3, pp. 331-337, May-June 1980.

7- Abutaleb, A., Frey, D. and Spicer, K., "Adaptive noise cancelling for change-detection in image sequences", proc. of eleventh Annual Northeast Bioengineering conference, pp 248-251, 1985.

8- Bledsoe, W. and Browning, I. "Pattern recognition and reading by machine", Eastern joint computer conference pp 225-231, 1959.

9- Aleksander, I. and Albrow, R. "Pattern recognition with adaptive logic circuits" IEE/NPL conf. on pattern recognition.

10- Aleksander, I. and Stonham, T.J. "A Guide to Pattern recognition using random access memories" IEE proceeding on computers and digital techniques, vol.2 no.1, 1979.

11- Aleksander, I. "Microcircuit Learning computers", Mills and Boon Ltd., 1971.

12- Ullmann, J.R. "Experiments with N-tuple method of pattern recognition", IEEE Trans. Computers, vol.c-18, pp.1135-1137, Dec. 1969.

13- Nappey, J.A., "Aspects of N-tuple character recognition for a blind reading aid", Ph.D. Thesis, Brunel University, UK, 1977.

14- Aleksander, I. and Dobree Wilson, M.J., "Adaptive window for image processing" IEE proceedings, vol.132, pt. E. No.5, Sep. 1985.

15- Aleksander, I., "Advanced Digital Information System", Prentice / Hall International, London, 1985.

# IMAGE SEGMENTATION USING CAUSAL

# MARKOV RANDOM FIELD MODELS

Pierre A. Devijver
Philips Research Laboratory
Brussels, BELGIUM

## 1   Introduction

This paper summarizes some of our recent work on the image restoration and segmentation problems under the assumption that real imagery can be adequately represented by *hidden Markov mesh random fields* (MMRF) models. We develop coherent approaches to both problems of *i)* image segmentation and restoration and *ii)* model acquisition.

Here, we return to an image model we have investigated in two previous papers. In [1] we outlined labeling algorithms for 2nd order MMRF's and this work was extended to 3rd order MMRF's in [2]. Both these papers outlined labeling solutions that could be implemented in *real-time*. However, the huge amount of computation required by the algorithm proposed in [2] detracted very substantially form its attractiveness. Also, both these papers left the learning problem unanswered. Accordingly, our first goal here will be to outline a labeling algorithm for a 3rd order MMRF image model which achieves minimal complexity and can be implemented in *real-time*; more precisely, the algorithm can be made to operate with a fixed time-lag relative to image data acquisition (in standard raster scan). We shall also exhibit a simple deterministic relaxation technique which permits reaching — in an iterative manner — a local maximum for the joint probability of image measurements and labels configuration. On the other hand, we shall propose a coherent learning technique which permits to estimate the parameters of the MMRF which provides the best fit to actual image data. Theoretical developments will be illustrated by restoration and segmentation results on artificial and real images.

## 2  Image Model and Problem Statement

We briefly specify our image model: Let $V_{M,N} \doteq \{(m,n)|1 \leq m \leq M, 1 \leq n \leq N\}$ denote the finite, $M \times N$ integer lattice. Equivalently, let $(m,n)$ designate the pixel at the intersection of row $m$ and column $n$ in a $M \times N$ image. Associated with pixel $(m,n)$ are a label $\lambda_{m,n}$ and a feature vector $X_{M,N}$. We use $\Lambda_{M,N}$ and $X_{M,N}$ to denote $M \times N$ arrays of labels $\lambda_{m,n}$ and feature vectors $X_{m,n}$ respectively. Labels specify *properties* and some possible interpretations are "background versus object", "edge versus non-edge", or "the index of the region the pixel belongs to". Observations can be gray-levels, multi-spectral reflectance measurements, texture descriptors, etc. As a rule, labels are not observable, nor are they explicitly available from the input data (observations).

We regard $\Lambda_{M,N}$ as a sample realization of a homogeneous, third order MMRF:

**Definition 1** *A third order MMRF is defined by the property*

$$P(\lambda_{m,n}/\{\lambda_{k,\ell} \mid k < m \text{ or } \ell < n\}) = P\left(\lambda_{m,n} \middle/ \begin{array}{cc} \lambda_{m-1,n-1} & \lambda_{m-1,n} \\ \lambda_{m,n-1} \end{array}\right)$$

*where, as in all that follows, boundary conditions are assumed to be obvious enough and are not specified.*

By analogy with the 1–D Markov chain, it is seen that the part of the array which is regarded as the *past* for pixel $(m,n)$, consists in all sites above or to the left of $(m,n)$. The MMRF is "third order" because of the dependence of $\lambda_{m,n}$ upon the labels of *three* neighboring sites. We also assume that the model is spatially homogeneous. Thus, let $S$ be the finite state-space of the MMRF, i.e., the set of labels available, $\vartheta \doteq |S|$, and $q, r, \cdots, w, y, z \in S$. Then, homogeneousness enables us to write $P_{q/r,s,t}$ as a short for $P(\lambda_{m,n} = q/\lambda_{m-1,n} = r; \lambda_{m-1,n-1} = s; \lambda_{m,n-1} = t)$ uniformly in $(m,n)$.

MMRF's have a number of properties:

**Property 1** *For any $(m,n) \in V_{M,N}$,*

$$P(\Lambda_{m,n}) = \prod_{k=1}^{m} \prod_{\ell=1}^{n} P\left(\lambda_{k,\ell} \middle/ \begin{array}{cc} \lambda_{k-1,\ell-1} & \lambda_{k-1,\ell} \\ \lambda_{k,\ell-1} \end{array}\right).$$

**Property 2** *For any* $(m, n) \in V_{M,N}$

$$P(\lambda_{m,n} / \{\lambda_{k,\ell} \mid k \neq m, \ell \neq n\}) = P\left(\lambda_{m,n} \middle/ \begin{array}{ccc} \lambda_{m-1,n-1} & \lambda_{m-1,n} & \lambda_{m-1,n+1} \\ \lambda_{m,n-1} & & \lambda_{m,n+1} \\ \lambda_{m+1,n-1} & \lambda_{m+1,n} & \lambda_{m+1,n+1} \end{array}\right).$$

**Property 3** *The rows (columns) in each set of $k$ consecutive columns (rows) of a homogeneous MMRF form a stationary $k$-dimensional vector Markov chain.*

**Property 4** *For $1 \leq i \leq M + N$, let $\Lambda_i^{(d)} \doteq \{\lambda_{m,n} \mid (m, n) \in V_{M,N}, m + n = i\}$, i.e., the ith sub-diagonal of $\Lambda_{M,N}$. Then,*

i) *under appropriate boundary conditions, the diagonals of a 3rd order MMRF form a 2nd order Markov chain, viz., $P(\Lambda_i^{(d)} / \{\Lambda_j^{(d)} \mid j = 1, \cdots, i - 1\}) = P(\Lambda_i^{(d)} / \Lambda_{i-1}^{(d)}, \Lambda_{i-2}^{(d)})$;*

ii) *conditionally upon $\Lambda_{i-1}^{(d)}$ and $\Lambda_{i-2}^{(d)}$, elements of $\Lambda_i^{(d)}$ are mutually independent but*

iii) *they may become dependent if the elements of any $\Lambda_j^{(d)}$ with $j > i$ are instantiated.*

We shall make the assumption that the original, noise-free image was corrupted by conditionally independent noise: Let $S$ serve as an index set for the distributions $p_\lambda(X)$, i.e., we take the distribution of the observation $X_{m,n}$ to be $p_q(X_{m,n})$ when $\lambda_{m,n} = q$. Moreover, we assume that conditionally upon $\lambda_{m,n}$, $X_{m,n}$ is independent from $\lambda_{k,\ell}$ and $X_{k,\ell}$ for any $(k, l) \neq (m, n)$. Readily, this assumption implies $P(\boldsymbol{X}_{m,n} / \boldsymbol{\Lambda}_{m,n}) = \prod_{k=1}^{m} \prod_{\ell=1}^{n} p_{\lambda_{k,\ell}}(X_{k,\ell})$ and from the theorem of the total probability, one can see that the likelihood $p(\boldsymbol{X}_{M,N})$ of any sample realization is given by

$$p(\boldsymbol{X}_{M,N}) = \sum_{\boldsymbol{\Lambda}_{M,N}} \prod_{m=1}^{M} \prod_{n=1}^{N} P\left(\lambda_{m,n} \middle/ \begin{array}{cc} \lambda_{m-1,n-1} & \lambda_{m-1,n} \\ \lambda_{m,n-1} & \end{array}\right) p_{\lambda_{m,n}}(X_{m,n}), \qquad (1)$$

where the summation runs over all possible label assignments $\boldsymbol{\Lambda}_{M,N}$ in $\boldsymbol{V}_{M,N}$. The sum in (1) has $\vartheta^{M \times N}$ terms, each of which is the product of $2MN$ factors. Thus direct evaluation of this probability by a brute force approach would prove intractable for all but the most trivial problems.

Two problems will presently be addressed. The first one is that of estimating the parameters of the model that best fits actual image data $\boldsymbol{X}_{M,N}$. The second one is that of devising efficient schemes for computing maximum a posteriori probability (MAP) label estimates. As the solution of the former requires that of the latter, these problems will be treated in reverse order.

As far as labeling is concerned, we shall first exhibit a *real-time* algorithm. Clearly, the real-time requirement precludes MAP estimation of pixel-labels based on the full image data $X_{M,N}$. (This would impose postponing any labeling until the entire image has been observed.) A viable alternative would be to base the computation on the information available from the upper left quarter-plane $V_{m,n}$ and to estimate $\lambda_{m,n}$ from the probability distribution $P(\lambda_{m,n}/X_{m,n})$. This would be acceptable from the viewpoint of the labeling problem but quite too drastic a simplification as far as the learning problem is concerned. As a compromise, we will propose a scheme which exploits the information available from the extended upper left quarter-plane $V_{m+1,n+1}$ by making MAP estimation based on the distribution $P(\lambda_{m,n}/X_{m+1,n+1})$. Subsequently, we will formulate a simple iterative technique which permits successive updating by deterministic relaxation in such a way as to drive the overall labeling to a local maximum of the posterior probability. Both labeling techniques will be illustrated by experimental results which lead us to question the desirability of the second approach.

# 3  Labeling Algorithms

## 3.1  A real-time algorithm

Let us temporarily assume that all model parameters are known to us. Prior to attempting the computation of $P(\lambda_{m,n}/X_{m+1,n+1})$ we shall address the problem of computing the posterior probability for the occurrence of $\lambda_{m,n} = q$, given the realization $X_{m,n}$ of image measurements in the upper left quarter-plane $V_{m,n}$. We introduce a simplified notation, viz., $\mathcal{F}_{m,n}(q) \doteq P(\lambda_{m,n} = q/X_{m,n})$. As in the case of the likelihood of $X_{M,N}$ in Eq. (1) it is clear that the complexity of computing $\mathcal{F}_{m,n}(q)$ is exponential in $m \times n$. Therefore, we shall introduce a simplifying assumption which will enable us to *linearize* the computational complexity. In what follows, this complexity is reduced to a theoretical minimum of $\mathcal{O}(\vartheta^4)$ operations per pixel.

For $m > 1$ and $n > 1$, let $V_{\overline{m,n}}$ denotes the truncated upper left quarter-plane $\{(k, \ell) \in V_{m,n} | k \le m \text{ and } \ell \le n, (k, l) \ne (m, n)\}$, that is, $V_{m,n}$ with pixel $(m, n)$ removed, and similarly for $X_{\overline{m,n}}$. Define $\mathcal{G}_{m,n}(r, s, t) \doteq P(\lambda_{m-1,n-1} = s, \lambda_{m-1,n} = r, \lambda_{m,n-1} = t/X_{\overline{m,n}})$. Readily, $\mathcal{F}_{m,n}(q)$ and $\mathcal{G}_{m,n}(r, s, t)$ are related as

$$\mathcal{F}_{m,n}(q) \propto \sum_{r,s,t} \mathcal{G}_{m,n}(r, s, t) P_{q/r,s,t}\, p_q(X_{m,n}) \quad \Longleftrightarrow$$

| | $n$ |
|---|---|
| | $\vdots$ |
| | $s$ \| $r$ |
| $m$  $\cdots$  $\cdots$ | $t$ \| $q$ |

Let us also define $\mathcal{M}_{m,n}(q,r,t) \doteq P(\lambda_{m-1,n} = r, \lambda_{m,n-1} = t, \lambda_{m,n} = q/\boldsymbol{X}_{m,n})$, for $m > 1$ and $n > 1$, $\mathcal{Y}_{m,n}(q,t) \doteq P(\lambda_{m,n-1} = t; \lambda_{m,n} = q/\boldsymbol{X}_{m,n})$, for $m \geq 1$ and $n > 1$, and $\mathcal{Z}_{m,n}(q,r) \doteq P(\lambda_{m-1,n} = r, \lambda_{m,n} = q/\boldsymbol{X}_{m,n})$ for $m > 1$ and $n \geq 1$.

Eventually, let also $\boldsymbol{X}^{(c)}_{m-1,n} \doteq \{X_{(k,\ell)}|1 \leq k \leq m - 1, \ \ell = n\}$ and $\boldsymbol{X}^{(r)}_{m,n-1} \doteq \{X_{(k,\ell)}|k = m, \ 1 \leq \ell \leq n - 1\}$, viz., the $m - 1$ and $n - 1$ first pixels in column $n$ and row $m$ respectively.

We may now formulate our simplifying assumption leading to the linearization for the complexity of computing $\mathcal{F}_{m,n}(q)$: Given $(s, \boldsymbol{X}_{m-1,n-1})$, we shall assume that $(r, \boldsymbol{X}^{(c)}_{m-1,n})$ and $(t, \boldsymbol{X}^{(r)}_{m,n-1})$ are mutually independent. There follows

$$\mathcal{G}_{m,n}(r,s,t) \propto \frac{\mathcal{Y}_{m-1,n}(r,s)\mathcal{Z}_{m,n-1}(t,s)}{\mathcal{F}_{m-1,n-1}(s)}$$

and this together with

$$\mathcal{M}_{m,n}(q,r,t) \propto \Sigma_s \, \mathcal{G}_{m,n}(r,s,t) P_{q/r,s,t} \, p_q(X_{m,n}) \quad \mathcal{Y}_{m,n}(q,t) = \Sigma_r \, \mathcal{M}_{m,n}(q,r,t)$$
$$\mathcal{F}_{m,n}(q) = \Sigma_t \, \mathcal{Y}_{m,n}(q,t) = \Sigma_r \, \mathcal{Z}_{m,n}(q,r) \quad \mathcal{Z}_{m,n}(q,r) = \Sigma_t \, \mathcal{M}_{m,n}(q,r,t)$$

is a well-formed *real-time* recurrence on $m$ and $n$ for computing $\mathcal{G}_{m,n}(\cdot,\cdot,\cdot)$, hence $\mathcal{F}_{m,n}(q)$ for any $m > 1$ and $n > 1$. (Clearly, boundaries require a special treatment.)

As far as the computational complexity is concerned, a simple examination reveals that it is $\mathcal{O}(\vartheta^4)$. One could have anticipated that by adopting a 3rd order MMRF model we would be bound to examine all possible combinations of $\lambda_{m,n}$ and its North, North-West and West neighbors. There are $\vartheta^4$ such combinations. Thus $\mathcal{O}(\vartheta^4)$ is a lower bound to the model intrinsic complexity. In this sense, our simplifying assumption has enabled us to achieve minimal complexity. In terms of memory requirements, $[\vartheta(\vartheta + 1)(2N + 1)]$ storage is needed to save past values of $\mathcal{F}_{k,\ell}$ and $\mathcal{Y}_{k,\ell}$ for $k = m - 1, \ell = n - 1, \cdots, N$, and $k = m, \ell = 1, \cdots, n - 1$.

## 3.2 A look-ahead technique

We have pointed out above that the implementation of a sensible learning scheme will require the computation of the *look-ahead* probability

$$\mathcal{L}_{m,n}(s) \doteq P(\lambda_{m,n} = s/\boldsymbol{X}_{m+1,n+1}) \quad \Longleftrightarrow$$

|  |  | $n$ $+$ $1$ |
|---|---|---|
|  |  | $\vdots$ |
|  | $s$ | $r$ |
| $m+1$ $\cdots$ | $\cdots$ $t$ | $q$ |

Using the same simplified notation as above we have

$$
\begin{aligned}
\mathcal{L}_{m,n}(s) &= P(\lambda_{m,n} = s / X_{m+1,n+1}) = \sum_{q,r,t} P(q,r,s,t / X_{m+1,n+1}) \\
&\propto \sum_{r,t} P(r,s,t / X_{\overline{m+1,n+1}}) \sum_q P_{q/r,s,t}\, P_q(X_{m+1,n+1}) \\
&= \sum_{r,t} \mathcal{G}_{\overline{m+1,n+1}}(r,s,t) \sum_q P_{q/r,s,t}\, P_q(X_{m+1,n+1}),
\end{aligned}
$$

with adjustments at the boundaries. Thus, $\mathcal{L}_{m,n}(s)$ can be obtained as soon as the computation of $\mathcal{G}_{\overline{m+1,n+1}}(\cdot,\cdot,\cdot)$ has been accomplished with the real-time part of the algorithm. This involves a fixed time-lag of $N+1$ sampling intervals. The additional work effort is again of the order of $\mathcal{O}(\vartheta^4)$. No extra-storage is needed. At this stage, MAP estimates $\hat{\lambda}$ of pixel labels $\lambda$ are obtained by the rule $\hat{\lambda}_{m,n} = q$ if $q = \mathrm{argmax}_{q'} \mathcal{L}_{m,n}(q')$. This is nothing but the Bayes rule corresponding to the zero–one loss function. This algorithm has been implemented and experimental results will be outlined later on.

## 3.3  Optimization by deterministic relaxation

So far, we confined ourselves to labeling techniques which proceed pixelwise. While these techniques generally give good results, they may produce labelings which are not even consistent with the assumed model. We shall now adopt quite a different approach, one which attempts to optimize the labeling over an entire image by iterative optimization.

Iterative optimization proceed by making local changes to some current labeling in such a way as to increase the probability of the entire image. To simplify things, let $I_q$ stand for an arbitrary labeling of $V_{M,N}$ which has the configuration

$$
\begin{matrix}
s & r & z \\
t & q & y \\
u & v & w
\end{matrix}
$$

centered about some arbitrary location $(m,n)$, and let $P(I_q)$ designate the joint probability of that labeling and the image data, i.e.,

$$
P(I_q) = \prod_{k=1}^{M} \prod_{\ell=1}^{N} P\left( \lambda_{k,\ell} / \frac{\lambda_{k-1,\ell-1} \ \ \lambda_{k-1,\ell}}{\lambda_{k,\ell-1}} \right) p_{\lambda_{k,\ell}}(X_{k,\ell}),
$$

where some of the labels are as shown above. Note that the right hand side is one of the terms in the sum in (1). Next, suppose that we modify the current labeling by changing $q$ into $q'$ at pixel $(m,n)$. Let $I_{q'}$ designate this new labeling and $P(I_{q'})$ be its probability. It is easy to see that

$$
\frac{P(I_q)}{P(I_{q'})} = \frac{P_{q/r,s,t} P_{y/z,r,q} P_{v/q,t,u} P_{w/y,q,v} P_q(X_{m,n})}{P_{q'/r,s,t} P_{y/z,r,q'} P_{v/q',t,u} P_{w/y,q',v} P_{q'}(X_{m,n})},
$$

and if this ratio is less than one, this update has produced a labeling whose probability is higher. This rule can be applied to each pixel in turn to provide a complete updated labeling. This process — which for obvious reasons is bounded to converge to some local maximum of $P(I)$ — can be repeated for a fixed number of cycles or until convergence to produce the final "estimate" of the labeling of $V_{M,N}$.

Several advantages may be claimed for this kind of procedure [1]: First, it is simple, both conceptually and computationally. Second, it depends only on the local rather than the global characteristics of the image. Third, the image data $X_{m,n}$ are retained and used at every stage of the procedure as distinct from relaxation methods which apply repeated spatial smoothing to the initial $I$ without further reference to the image data. Fourth, it has been our experience that, with a good initial estimate, convergence is fairly rapid, usually demanding no more than, say, three to five iterations. (In our experiments, the initial labeling is taken to be the one produced by the look-ahead algorithm described above.)

In principle, the order in which pixels are visited for updating is irrelevant. However, it is tempting to proceed in such a way that successive updates are statistically independent. This goal can be achieved to a certain extent with Besag's coding sets. Consider the arrangement:

$$
\begin{array}{ccccccccc}
\cdot & \times & \cdot & \times & \cdot & \times & \cdot & \times & \cdot & \times \\
\cdot & \cdot & \cdot & \cdot & \cdot & \cdot & \cdot & \cdot & \cdot \\
\cdot & \times & \cdot & \times & \cdot & \times & \cdot & \times & \cdot & \times \\
\cdot & \cdot & \cdot & \cdot & \cdot & \cdot & \cdot & \cdot & \cdot
\end{array}
$$

It is then immediately clear that, for a third order MMRF image model, variables associated with the $\times$ pixels, given the values at all other pixels, are mutually independent, and all pixels can be visited by four shifts of the coding framework.

## 4   Learning Algorithms

Our next problem is that of estimating the model parameters. The method that is described hereafter is an extension of a learning technique that we have developed under the assumption that the image is modeled by a hidden Pickard random field [3]. The formulation of an EM re-estimation algorithm for model parameters will serve as a starting point for a simpler algorithm based on a *decision directed* (DD) approach. [This DD algorithm could also be interpreted as following from a (hypothetical) ergodic theorem for MMRF's.]

To simplify things, we temporarily assume that the random process associated with the states is represented by $\vartheta$ *discrete* distributions $p_q(\xi_i) = P(X_{m,n} =$

$\xi_i/\lambda_{m,n} = q$), $q \in \mathcal{S}$, $1 \leq i \leq I$, $1 \leq m, n \leq M, N$. Let $\boldsymbol{\Pi}$ stand for the likelihood $p(\boldsymbol{X}_{M,N})$ as given in Eq. (1). We shall formulate our learning problem as that of finding the parameter values which maximize $\boldsymbol{\Pi}$ under the appropriate constraints, e.g., $\Sigma_q P_q = 1$, $\Sigma_q P_{q/t} = 1 \; \forall t$, $\Sigma_q P_{q/r,s,t} = 1 \; \forall r, s, t$, etc. By using the method of Lagrange multipliers it can be seen that the solution takes the form

$$P_q = \frac{P_q \partial \boldsymbol{\Pi}/\partial P_q}{\Sigma_{q'} P_{q'} \partial \boldsymbol{\Pi}/\partial P_{q'}} \qquad P_{q/t} = \frac{P_{q/t} \partial \boldsymbol{\Pi}/\partial P_{q/t}}{\Sigma_{q'} P_{q'/t} \partial \boldsymbol{\Pi}/\partial P_{q'/t}}$$

$$P_{q/r,s,t} = \frac{P_{q/r,s,t} \partial \boldsymbol{\Pi}/\partial P_{q/r,s,t}}{\Sigma_{q'} P_{q'/r,s,t} \partial \boldsymbol{\Pi}/\partial P_{q'/r,s,t}} \qquad p_q(\xi_i) = \frac{p_q(\xi_i) \partial \boldsymbol{\Pi}/\partial p_q(\xi_i)}{\Sigma_{q'} p_{q'}(\xi_i) \partial \boldsymbol{\Pi}/\partial p_{q'}(\xi_i)}$$

(Here as hereafter, we omit the re-estimation formula to be used along the first column. It can be obtained by symmetry from the formula for the first row.) By evaluating the partial derivatives and making the substitutions we obtain the solution in the form of implicit equations, viz.,

$$P_q = \frac{P(\lambda_{1,1} = q/\boldsymbol{X}_{M,N})}{\Sigma_{q'} P(\lambda_{1,1} = q'/\boldsymbol{X}_{M,N})}$$

$$P_{q/t} = \frac{\Sigma_{n=2}^{N} P(\lambda_{1,n-1} = t, \lambda_{1,n} = q/\boldsymbol{X}_{M,N})}{\Sigma_{n=2}^{N} \Sigma_{q'} P(\lambda_{1,n-1} = t, \lambda_{1,n} = q'/\boldsymbol{X}_{M,N})}$$

$$P_{q/r,s,t} = \frac{\Sigma_{m=2}^{M} \Sigma_{n=2}^{N} P\left( \begin{matrix} \lambda_{m-1,n-1} = s & \lambda_{m-1,m} = r \\ \lambda_{m,n-1} = t & \lambda_{m,n} = q \end{matrix} /\boldsymbol{X}_{M,N} \right)}{\Sigma_{m=2}^{M} \Sigma_{n=2}^{N} \Sigma_{q'} P\left( \begin{matrix} \lambda_{m-1,n-1} = s & \lambda_{m-1,m} = r \\ \lambda_{m,n-1} = t & \lambda_{m,n} = q' \end{matrix} /\boldsymbol{X}_{M,N} \right)}$$

$$p_q(\xi_i) = \frac{\Sigma_{m,n|X_{m,n}=\xi_i} P(\lambda_{m,n} = q/\boldsymbol{X}_{M,N})}{\Sigma_{m,n} P(\lambda_{m,n} = q/\boldsymbol{X}_{M,N})}$$

It should be clear that these formulae, if ever implemented, should be used in an iterative way: current parameter values should be used to compute the right hand sides thereby yielding new, updated parameter values.

These formulae call for a number of comments. First of all, they all involve the posterior probabilities for labels given the observations over the entire image, and we do not know of any scheme that could allow us to compute these. Second, these formulae would preclude any attempt at real-time processing as they require the whole image to be observed prior to initiating the estimation. Third, it has been our experience that the probability of pixel $(m, n)$ being in state $q$ given all the observations $\boldsymbol{X}_{M,N}$ is fairly well approximated by the probability of the same event, given only the *look-ahead* observations $\boldsymbol{X}_{m+1,n+1}$. By making the appropriate changes in the above equations, we obtain

$$P_q = \frac{P(\lambda_{1,1} = q/\boldsymbol{X}_{2,2})}{\Sigma_{q'} P(\lambda_{1,1} = q'/\boldsymbol{X}_{2,2})}$$

$$P_{q/t} = \frac{\sum_{n=2}^{N-1} P(\lambda_{1,n-1} = t, \lambda_{1,n} = q / X_{2,n+1})}{\sum_{n=2}^{N-1} \sum_{q'} P(\lambda_{1,n-1} =, \lambda_{1,n} = q / X_{2,n+1})}$$

$$P_{q/r,s,t} = \frac{\sum_{m=2}^{M-1} \sum_{n=2}^{N-1} P \left( \begin{array}{cc} \lambda_{m-1,n-1} = s & \lambda_{m-1,m} = r \\ \lambda_{m,n-1} = t & \lambda_{m,n} = q \end{array} / X_{m+1,n+1} \right)}{\sum_{m=2}^{M-1} \sum_{n=2}^{N-1} \sum_{q'} P \left( \begin{array}{cc} \lambda_{m-1,n-1} = s & \lambda_{m-1,m} = r \\ \lambda_{m,n-1} = t & \lambda_{m,n} = q' \end{array} / X_{m+1,n+1} \right)}$$

$$p_q(\xi_i) = \frac{\sum_{m,n | X_{m,n} = \xi_i} P(\lambda_{m,n} = q / X_{m+1,n+1})}{\sum_{m,n} P(\lambda_{m,n} = q / X_{m+1,n+1})}$$

At this stage, the computation of all the probabilities involved could be achieved with the algorithm of the preceding section. Unfortunately, these formulae still involve an excessive amount of computation for anything more than binary images: e.g., it can be seen that computing $P \left( \begin{array}{cc} \lambda_{m-1,n-1} = s & \lambda_{m-1,n} = r \\ \lambda_{m,n-1} = t & \lambda_{m,n} = q \end{array} / X_{m+1,n+1} \right)$ requires integrating out 5 state variables and raises the total complexity to an impressive $\mathcal{O}(\vartheta^9)$ operations per pixel. Therefore, for the want of a more efficient solution, we shall content ourselves here with the kind of approximation by which the Isodata clustering procedure can be derived from the EM algorithm for iid data. The resulting algorithm will be typical of the class of procedures that are known under the name of *decision directed* (DD) algorithms.

The DD re-estimation technique is based on the assumption that labeling with the current values of the parameters is done *with probability one*. In other words, assigning some labels to a given pixel excludes the possibility of that pixel bearing any other label. This technique transforms the above re-estimation formulae into *counting* formulae. If we let $\mathbf{I}[(\cdot)]$ be the *indicator* function for the event $(\cdot)$ and let the labeling be performed with the algorithm described above using the current parameter values, the DD re-estimation formulae can be written as:

$$P_q = \begin{cases} 1, & \text{if } \hat{\lambda}_{1,1} = q \\ 0, & \text{otherwise} \end{cases}$$

$$P_{q/t} = \frac{\sum_{n=2}^{N} \mathbf{I}[\hat{\lambda}_{1,n-1} = t, \hat{\lambda}_{1,n} = q]}{\sum_{n=2}^{N} \mathbf{I}[\hat{\lambda}_{1,n-1} = t]}$$

$$P_{q/r,s,t} = \frac{\sum_{m=2}^{M} \sum_{n=2}^{N} \mathbf{I} \left[ \begin{array}{cc} \hat{\lambda}_{m-1,n-1} = s & \hat{\lambda}_{m-1,n} = r \\ \hat{\lambda}_{m,n-1} = t & \hat{\lambda}_{m,n} = q \end{array} \right]}{\sum_{m=2}^{M} \sum_{n=2}^{N} \mathbf{I} \left[ \begin{array}{cc} \hat{\lambda}_{m-1,n-1} = s & \hat{\lambda}_{m-1,n} = r \\ \hat{\lambda}_{m,n-1} = t & \end{array} \right]}$$

$$p_q(\xi_i) = \frac{\sum_{m,n | X_{m,n} = \xi_i} \mathbf{I}[\hat{\lambda}_{m,n} = q]}{\sum_{m,n} \mathbf{I}[\hat{\lambda}_{m,n} = q]}$$

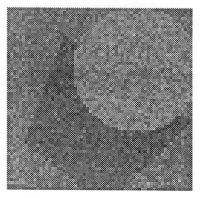 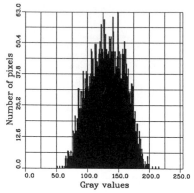

Figure 1. An artificial image and the corresponding histogram.

Our experiments were performed under the additional assumption that gray-levels within a region were normally distributed. Re-estimation formulae for the mean values $\mu_q$ and variances $\sigma_q$ were the standard ones, namely,

$$\mu_q = s_q^{(1)}, \quad \sigma_q^2 = s_q^{(2)} - \mu_q^2 \quad \text{where} \quad s_q^{(\alpha)} = \frac{\sum_{m=1}^{M} \sum_{n=1}^{N} \mathbf{I}[\hat{\lambda}_{m,n} = q] X_{m,n}^{\alpha}}{\sum_{m=1}^{M} \sum_{n=1}^{N} \mathbf{I}[\hat{\lambda}_{m,n} = q]}$$

for $\alpha = 1, 2$. It should be evident that one iteration of the DD learning technique can be implemented at the negligible cost of some counting and averaging operations which can be synchronized with the labeling operations.

## 5  Some Experimental Results

The labeling and learning algorithms were implemented in PASCAL and extensive experimentation was carried out. In all experiments, the only prior information that was made available at the start was the number of desired states and the assumption that observations were drawn from Gaussian distributions (with unknown means and variances).

The choice of initial values for the parameters is quite critical. In our current implementation this choice is specified as follows:

i) $P(\lambda_{1,1} = q) = 1/\vartheta \ \forall q$, $P(\lambda_{1,n} = q/\lambda_{1,n-1} = q') = 0.5$ for $q' = q$ and $1/2(\vartheta - 1)$ otherwise; $P_{q/r,s,t} = 0.5$ for $q = r = s = t$, $1/2(\vartheta - 1)$ for $r = s = t \neq q$, and $1/\vartheta$ in all other cases.

ii) $\mu_q$ is set equal to the $(q/(\vartheta + 1))$th quantile of the cumulated gray-level histogram of the input image.

iii) $\sigma_q = (\mu_\vartheta - \mu_1)/2(\vartheta - 1) \ \forall q \in \mathcal{S}$. (Mean values are assumed to be, on the average, two standard deviations away from each other.)

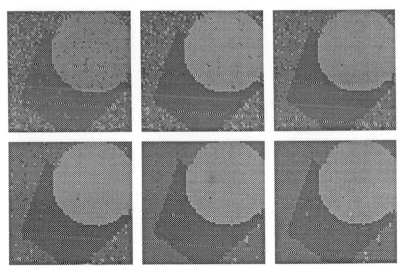

Figure 2. Segmentation results for artificial image.

Our first illustration concerns an artificial $64 \times 64$ three-level image which is shown in Figure 1 together with the corresponding gray-level histogram whose uni-modality shows that there is little hope of much good coming from any kind of attempt at thresholding the input image. Restoration results are shown in Figure 2. Proceeding from left to right, the upper row in Figure 2 displays the labeling obtained by using the model parameters estimated at the end of the 1st, 2d and 3rd learning iterations. The results in the lower row were obtained after the 4th, 6th and 8th learning iterations. These results are of interest on two grounds: First, they show a quasi perfect restoration in spite of the high level of overlap between the components of the histogram. Second, they exemplify well the behavior of the algorithm in terms of directivity of the convergence. The upper row in Figure 2 shows that, at the beginning, the learning algorithm starts by erring almost blindly in the high dimensional parameter space. However, once a good direction is found, convergence is extremely rapid as can be seen from the lower half of Figure 2.

Our second illustration shows the segmentation results for a real $128 \times 128$ eight-bit image of an airplane. The histogram (not shown) is a complicated mixture of peaks and flat regions. Parts of the object we are interested in — the plane — are very poorly contrasted against a changing background. A six-state segmentation was asked for and the results are shown in Figure 3. The original image is in the upper left corner. Proceeding from left to right and top to bottom are shown the labeling results with the parameters obtained at the end of every other learning iteration.

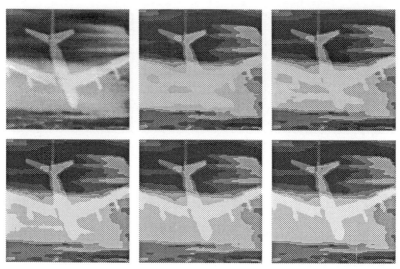

Figure 3. Segmentation results for the "airplane" image.

Again two comments are in order. First, this sequence of results corroborates our previous findings about the lack of directivity in the early stage of the learning algorithm. Second, in this particular instance, it is very tempting to relate this problem to the huge number of parameters to be estimated, for instance, 1296 probabilities of the $P_{q/r,s,t}$ type. It should be pointed out that segmentation results do not seem to be very sensitive to the accuracy of the parameter estimates: it has been our empirical experience that segmentations obtained after little perturbations of optimal values cannot be distinguished from the original ones. From a practical standpoint, this remark has enabled us to fix the number of learning iterations a priori while obtaining consistently good segmentation results.

Our last illustration displays the segmentations obtained by the deterministic relaxation algorithm of Section 3.3 for both the artificial and the airplane images. For this experiment, the model parameters were those obtained at the end of the learning illustrated above, and the initial configurations were those produced by the algorithm of Section 3.2 and illustrated by the pictures in the lower right corners of Figures 2 and 3. The results shown in Figure 4 are those obtained after convergence of the algorithm, that is when a complete sweep over the image does not produce any re-labeling, a situation that is usually obtained after no more that 3 iterations.

For what concerns the artificial image, deterministic relaxation removes some labeling errors in the middle of uniform regions. However it has very detrimental influence in its way of handly regions boundaries. In a word, this optimization process does not improve the quality of the restoration.

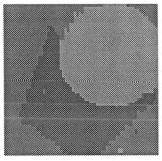 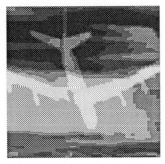

Figure 4. Segmentation results obtained by deterministic relaxation
for the artificial and airplane images

For what concerns the airplane image, the net result of the application of discrete relaxation is a clear tendency at producing rectangular regions. This is particularly visible in the lower and lower right part of the image. Our interpretation of this behavior is that the optimization process is a kind of attempt at "overfitting" a Markovian structure to an image which, at the start, is all but Markovian.

In a sense, the good quality of the segmentation obtained with the look-ahead algorithm should be attributed to the fact that the model allows us to exploit some statistical dependence between neighboring pixels while the slight degradation resulting from our attempts at "optimizing" the labeling reflects the fact that the model should not be given excessive weight compared to the input data.

# References

[1] J. Besag, "On the statistical analysis of dirty pictures," paper read at the SERC Research Workshop on Statistics and Pattern Recognition, Edinburgh, July 1985.

[2] P.A. Devijver, "Probabilistic labeling in a hidden second order Markov mesh," in *Pattern Recognition in Practice II*, E. Gelsema, and L.N. Kanal Eds., Amsterdam: North Holland, 1985, pp. 113–123.

[3] P.A. Devijver, "Segmentation of binary images using third order Markov mesh image models," in *Proc. 8th Internat. Conf. on Pattern Recognition*, Paris, Oct. 1986, pp. 259–261.

[4] P.A. Devijver, and M.M. Dekesel, "Learning the parameters of a hidden Markov random field image model : A simple example," in *Pattern Recognition Theory and Applications*, P. Devijver and J. Kittler Eds., Heidelberg: Springer, 1987, pp. 141–163.

# PREDITAS — SOFTWARE PACKAGE FOR SOLVING PATTERN RECOGNITION AND DIAGNOSTIC PROBLEMS

P. Pudil, S. Bláha, J. Novovičová
Institute of Information Theory and Automation
Czechoslovak Academy of Sciences
182 08 Prague 8

## SUMMARY

A general purpose software package "PREDITAS" is presented, aimed at solving a wide range of pattern recognition and diagnostic problems with respect to constraints and requirements imposed by practice. The theoretical background of the feature selection technique and stepwise decision rule employed in the PREDITAS system is outlined, together with the reasons for the necessity to combine theoretically based procedures with heuristic ones at some stages of the global solution.

## INTRODUCTION

Growing demands for solving a great variety of practical problems of a decision-making character, which cannot be solved for some reason analytically, stimulated the development of a general purpose software package for their solution, which would aim to be as far as possible universal and problem free. A statistical pattern recognition approach to the solution of this class of problem has been adopted, in accordance with general practice.

Since our principal application field has been medicine, where the well established term "diagnostic problem" is commonly used, we have incorporated this term into the name of the software package "PREDITAS" (Pattern REcognition and DIagnostic TAsk Solver). Though a general medical diagnostic problem can be formulated in terms of statistical pattern recognition, we use the term "diagnostic" explicitly in order to stress the formal analogy.

There exists a broad spectrum of statistical pattern recognition methods that differ widely in their assumptions about data set structure, in their computational complexity, etc. Our goal has not been to develop a software package that would be based on completely new original methods, but rather to design a practicable system, incorporating certain new ideas into the already known theoretical results.

Due to the impossibility of an exact mathematical formulation of each phase of the overall solution, our approach is a combination of both theoretically based and heuristic procedures. It is the result of a long experience in solving various pattern recognition problems in close cooperation with specialists in various application fields, whose valuable opinions and comments have been incorporated in the present version of the PREDITAS system.

# 1. REQUIREMENTS AND CONSTRAINTS IMPOSED BY PRACTICE

Frequent discussions with potential users of the software package have resulted in a number of constraints, imposed by the needs and requirements of practice. A system with ambitions to be useful for everyday practice should fulfil these requirements, and should be designed with respect to the corresponding constraints. Without claiming completeness, let us state briefly at least the principal conditions to be met:

1/ The resultant solution supplied to the user should be as simple as possible, computable quickly even on a very small personal computer, easily interpretable and finally, perhaps most importantly, it should leave some space for the user himself, allowing him to take the final decision and thus to participate in the solution.

2/ A reject option, equivalent to not taking a decision in the case where the probability of misclassifying a certain pattern would be higher then an apriori set limit, should be included in the system. It should also be possible to set these limits independently for both classes in terms of probabilities of misclassification, or in terms of admissible average risk if the latter is preferred.

3/ The sample size is usually too small for a given dimension of original data (this problem has been studied e.g. by Kanal, Chandrasekar (1971) and Foley (1972)). It results in the necessity of feature extraction or selection, as well as in difficulties with usage of multidimensional probability estimation methods.

4/ The dimension of original measurement can be rather high, in quite a few applications it was of the order of one hundred. A feature extraction or selection algorithm should be able to cope with this dimension.

5/ Components of original multidimensional measurement vectors cannot be supposed to be statistically independent. This fact must be respected by the feature selection algorithm.

6/ Experts from application fields prefer decision-making on the basis of meaningful interpretable features to decision-making by means of some mathematical abstractions. This issue is especially sensitive in most medical applications. Priority has therefore been given to feature selection instead of feature extraction, even if the latter can generally yield a slightly more discriminative set of features. Moreover, only feature selection enables one to exclude completely some of the original measured variables and thus to cut the cost of data acquisition.

7/ The system should not only provide a list of features ordered according to their significance for classification (respecting of course complicated multidimensional statistical relations among them), but should help as well in choosing the optimum number of features for classification (the dimensionality of classifier). Since the answer to this partial but important problem cannot be always unique and theoretically justified, the user should be provided at least with some heuristic procedure allowing him to assess a few possible solutions offered by the system and to choose the most suitable one according to his own scale of preferences.

8/ The algorithmic and computational complexity of the system of programs should not prevent the finding of a solution within a reasonable time limit even for high dimensions.

9/ Finally, the two principal stages of the solution – feature selection and derivation of the classification rule should be interconnected as much as possible and not solved independently, which is usually the case. This condition has not been raised by practice, but it follows from the experience of leading experts in the pattern recognition field (Kanal (1974)).

In connection with these conditions there is one point to be mentioned. In a multiclass problem, optimum feature subsets for discrimination of two particular classes are generally not the same for different pairs of classes. For this reason only a dichotomic problem is considered in the PREDITAS system, which does not represent any serious limitation since any multiclass problem can be transformed into a sequence of dichotomic problems.

The philosophy and the corresponding architecture of the PREDITAS system have resulted from the endeavour to fulfil the above named conditions. These conditions have greatly influenced not only the algorithmic realization but also the underlying theory employed in PREDITAS, which will be briefly described in the following paragraphs.

## 2. FEATURE SELECTION

The well known aim of the feature selection process is to reduce the dimensionality of the feature space without greatly influencing the performance of the classifier. Furthermore, removing redundant and irrelevant features can increase the reliability of the classifier, as well as its feasibility. The features are selected by an optimizing process requiring a criterion function and a search procedure (Kanal (1974), Devijver, Kittler (1982)).

Most of the published methods for feature selection use criterion functions which are based on the assumption that the complete information about the probabilistic structure of the classes is available. The feature selection procedure used in PREDITAS respects the fact that in most practical situations this assumption is not fulfilled. Our feature selection procedure is based on the criterion function called the "measure of discriminative power"

$$\lambda = \text{tr } \hat{S}_W^{-1} \hat{S}_B \tag{1}$$

where $\hat{S}_W$ and $\hat{S}_B$ denote the sample average within-class scatter matrix and the sample between-class scatter matrix, respectively (Pudil, Bláha (1981)). This criterion is equal to the maximum value of the Fisher's discriminant ratio

$$F(w) = w^T \hat{S}_B w \ / w^T \hat{S}_W w \tag{2}$$

with respect to the vector $w$ (Anderson, Bahadur (1962)).

In our technique the criterion for a feature subset evaluation is directly tied to the classifier performance.

As far as the feature selection technique itself is concerned, it is well known that only exhaustive searching of all the possible combinations can guarantee the maximum value of the criterion. This is of course hardly feasible, especially in the cases of large dimensions and thus various search techniques are employed.

The PREDITAS system has the option of choosing any of four sequential searching procedures, either backward (sequentially rejecting features) or forward (sequentially adding features). Two of them are basic ones – step optimal, while the remaining two (so called "floating" methods) represent a heuristic improvement aimed at a closer approximation of the optimum subset for any dimension (Pecinovský, Pudil, Bláha (1982)). All the methods are based on the maximization of the criterion (1) and enable to order single features according to their discriminating power. Moreover, they yield results facilitating the user's decision on the optimum number of features, as will be mentioned in the following paragraph.

## 3. CLASSIFICATION

Suppose we have a finite training set $X_n$ of classified samples, $X_n = \{x_l\}_{l=1}^{n}$, $x_l \in \mathbb{R}^d$. Assume the probabilities of two classes $P_i$, $i=1,2$, are known or have been estimated, and the conditional density $p_i(x)$ of the class $\omega_i$, $i=1,2$, is unknown.

The classification procedure in the PREDITAS system is realized using a sequence of m decision rules $\{{}^kR\}_{k=1}^{m}$, where each ${}^kR$, $k=1,2,\ldots,m$ is derived from its own training set $X_{nk}$ .

A brief description of the steps in our technique for the design of the k-th decision rule, $k=1,2,\ldots,m$, is as follows:

Step 1: Compute the vector ${}^k w \in \mathbb{R}^d$ which gives the greatest value of the Fisher's discriminant ratio (2).

Step 2: Project all elements of the training set $X_{nk}$ on the line with direction ${}^k w$ using equation

$$ {}^k w^T x_l = y_l, \quad l=1,2,\ldots,n^k $$

and denote the transformed training set by $Y_{nk}$ .

Step 3: Obtain an estimate $\hat{p}_i(y,{}^k w)$ of the transformed conditional density function $p_i(y,{}^k w)$, $i=1,2$.

Step 4: Determine the points ${}^k w_1$ and ${}^k w_2$, ${}^k w_1 < {}^k w_2$, ${}^k w_i \in \mathbb{R}^1$, $i=1,2$, on ${}^k w$ in the following way:

for all $y \leqq {}^k w_1 \wedge y \in Y_{nk}$

$$\hat{P}_r\hat{p}_r(y,{}^kw)/\hat{P}_{3-r}\hat{p}_{3-r}(y,{}^kw) \overset{\geq}{=} c_r \qquad (3)$$

holds for the corresponding r (either r=1 or r=2);
for all $y \overset{\geq}{=} {}^kw_2 \wedge y \in Y_n$

$$\hat{P}_s\hat{p}_s(y,{}^kw)/\hat{P}_{3-s}\hat{p}_{3-s}(y,{}^kw) \overset{\geq}{=} c_s \qquad (4)$$

holds for the corresponding s (either s=1 or s=2). The constants $c_r$, $c_s$ are determined by the permitted two types of probability of misclassification or by the loss associated with misclassification.

Step 5: Classify the samples from $X_{nk}$ using the following decision rule ${}^kR$:

Assign $\mathbf{x}$ to the class ${}^k\alpha_1$, if $\mathbf{x} \in R({}^k\alpha_1) = \{\mathbf{x} \in \mathbb{R}^d : {}^k\mathbf{w}^T\mathbf{x} \leq {}^kw_1\}$
Assign $\mathbf{x}$ to the class ${}^k\alpha_2$, if $\mathbf{x} \in R({}^k\alpha_2) = \{\mathbf{x} \in \mathbb{R}^d : {}^k\mathbf{w}^T\mathbf{x} \geq {}^kw_2\}$
where ${}^k\alpha_1 = \omega_1$ if r=1 and ${}^k\alpha_1 = \omega_2$ if r=2 in (3); ${}^k\alpha_2$ is defined analogously.
Reject to classify $\mathbf{x}$ if $\mathbf{x} \in R({}^k\alpha_0) = \{\mathbf{x} \in \mathbb{R}^d : {}^kw_1 < {}^k\mathbf{w}^T\mathbf{x} < {}^kw_2\}$

The regions $R({}^k\alpha_1)$, $R({}^k\alpha_2)$, $R({}^k\alpha_0)$ are thus determined by two hyperplanes perpendicular to ${}^k\mathbf{w}$ and intersecting the vector ${}^k\mathbf{w}$ at the points ${}^kw_1$ and ${}^kw_2$.

Step 6: Discard from $X_{nk}$ all the samples that have been classified using the decision rule ${}^kR$. Let $X_{nk+1}$ denote the remaining subset.

Step 7: Repeat the procedure for the training subset $X_{nk+1}$.

The above described process of generating the sequence of the decision rules starts from the training set $X_n = X_{n1}$ and continues until all the elements of the original training set $X_n$ are classified or any of the terminating conditions are fulfilled.

The problem of classifying a new pattern $\mathbf{x}$ is solved by using the above defined sequence of the respective decision rules as follows:

Assign $\mathbf{x}$ to the class ${}^j\alpha_i$ if $\mathbf{x} \in R({}^k\alpha_0) \wedge \mathbf{x} \in R({}^j\alpha_i)$
for all k, $1 \overset{\leq}{=} k < j \overset{\leq}{=} m$, i=1,2
Reject to classify $\mathbf{x}$ if $\mathbf{x} \in R({}^k\alpha_0)$ for all $1 \overset{\leq}{=} k \overset{\leq}{=} m$.

Details about this classification procedure can be found in Bláha, Novovičová, Pudil.

# 4. ARCHITECTURE AND USAGE OF PREDITAS SYSTEM

The PREDITAS system consists of four problem independent programs used in succession, where the results of one program are utilized in the following one:

1/ DATANAL – performs a basic statistical analysis of the input data set and constitutes the training set in its standard form.

2/ MEDIP – performs the analysis of feature significance for discrimination, taking into account mutual dependence, and determines the optimum subset of features. Altogether four different methods are available as described above. They can be used either independently or in combination according to the character of the data.

3/ SEDIF – determines a stepwise decision rule for any given subset of features. It computes in each step the optimum discriminative direction and the discriminative function, evaluates the error probability and prints out the final overall solution in the form of a summary table.

4/ CLASSIF – is designed for the application of the derived decision rule and, unlike the previous programs requiring a bigger computer, it is rather simple and can be implemented even on a programmable pocket calculator. In cases where a small personal computer is available, a dialogue mode can be utilized and the graphical mode of the solution can be easily tailored to suit any special needs of the user. The essential point is that every particular decision (classification of a new pattern) is associated with a computed degree of decision reliability.

The first three programs actually represent the learning or training phase, while the last one corresponds to the working or application phase.

As far as the user of the software is concerned, he is actually supposed to utilize only the CLASSIF program. However, as we have already mentioned, there are certain parts of the overall solution where a limited manoeuvring space is left to the user. According to our experience users prefer to be able to influence within certain limits the solution themselves, rather than to be given automatically just one solution without any justification. This is quite an important psychological issue, which is e.g. well treated in expert systems.

Beside these psychological reasons there are of course also theoretical and practical reasons for leaving a user with an option to choose the most suitable solution himself. The different criteria and conditions to be fulfilled are often contradictory and are given intuitively different preferences by individual users. In order to design a system that would yield the optimum solution quite automatically, it would be necessary to employ a multicriterial approach, which has not been found feasible since the users are not generally able to assess their scales of preferences of individual criteria explicitly.

Apart from the possibility of influencing the feature selection process by particular restrictions and conditions, this philosophy has been used in the phase of determining the optimum number of features selected for the classifier. Since criteria of discriminant analysis do not have a direct relationship to the probability of misclassification, the feature selection technique used enables one to determine certain bounds within which the optimum dimension should be chosen. These bounds are set according to the values of the separability criteria as the function of the number of features (in practice the shape of the graphical function of separability can be conveniently utilized). A few variants of feature subsets are usually verified from the point of view of the corresponding quality of classification and the user can be given corresponding results with an accompanying commentary. While a certain variant can yield a lower value of the average risk, another may be connected with a slightly higher average risk but on the other hand its degree of reliability may be higher too. The user is thus given clearly defined values to substitute into his own preference scale and may choose the solution accordingly.

A similar situation can arise in cases where the user is unable to assess explicitly the average loss connected with rejecting a decision, which is quite frequently the case. This results in the need to choose from among a few variants of the solution differing by estimates of probabilities of misclassification and by estimates of reject rate (where these two values have obviously opposite trends). Again, this choice depends strongly on the particular application.

To conclude, we state that two distinct phases of the overall solution can be considered. The possibility of making corrections in the training phase on the basis of application phase results is obviously essential. Thus, the process of arriving at a final solution is an iterative process with some feedback loops built in. A block diagram of just such a "global" solution is presented in Bláha, Pudil, (1984). Active participation of the user in these feedback decisions is made possible with the help of the User Manual, which has been written to be comprehensible to a broad spectrum of users (Bláha, Pudil (1987)).

## 5. APPLICATIONS

The PREDITAS system has been successfully tested in a number of problems, mainly from the field of medicine. Various problems of differential diagnostics in perinatology, internal medicine, gynaecology and neurology have been solved, as well as various classification problems in geology, remote sensing, power engineering and economics.

## REFERENCES

(1) Anderson T., Bahadur R.: Classification into two multivariate normal distributions with different covariance matrices. The Annals of Math. Statistics, Vol.33, 420–431, 1962.
(2) Bláha S., Pudil P.: The PREDITAS system and its use for computer-aided medical decision making. In: Medical Decision Making: Diagnostic Strategies and Expert Systems, edited by J.H.Van Bemmel, F. Grémy, J. Zvárová. North-Holland, Amsterdam 1985 (Proceedings of the IFIP-IMIA International Conference).
(3) Bláha S., Pudil P.: PREDITAS – User Manual (in Czech), Research Report No.1331, Prague 1987.
(4) Bláha S., Novovičová J., Pudil P.: PREDITAS – Theory and practice of diagnostic task solving (to appear )
(5) Devijver P.A. and Kittler J.: Pattern Recognition – A Statistical Approach. Prentice-Hall, Englewood Cliffs, New Jersey 1982.
(6) Foley D.: Considerations of sample and feature size. IEEE Trans. Inf. Theory, Vol. IT-18, 618–626, (1972).
(7) Kanal L., Chandrasekar B.: On dimensionality and sample size in statistical pattern classification. Pattern Recognition, Vol. 3, 225–234, 1971.
(8) Kanal L.: Patterns in pattern recognition 1968-1974. IEEE Trans. on Pat. Recog. IT-20, 697- 722, 1974.
(9) Pecinovský R., Pudil P., Bláha S.: The algorithms for sequential feature selection based on the measure of discriminative power. Proceedings of DIANA Symposium, Liblice 1982.
(10) Pudil P., Bláha S.: Evaluation of effectiveness of features selected by discriminant analysis methods. Pattern Recognition, Vol. 14, Nos 1-6, 700-703, 1981. (Special Issue: Proceedings of 1980 Pattern Recognition Conference, Oxford).

# PROCESSING POOR QUALITY LINE DRAWINGS BY LOCAL ESTIMATION OF NOISE

M. E. Dunn and S. H. Joseph

Department of Mechanical Engineering, University of Sheffield,
Mappin Street, Sheffield S1 3JD

## Summary

The problem of extracting the best data from poor quality line originals at the lowest possible resolution is considered. The form of the
grey level histogram from such originals is examined, especially the
shape of the peak corresponding to the white background. The viabil-
ity of deriving a threshold for display from simple measurements of
the location and width of this peak is demonstrated. A more accurate
method for these measurements is described, and the improvement in
thresholding upon its application to originals with variations in background noise level across the image is shown. The accuracy of the
methods is quantified.

## Introduction

A line drawing or a page of text is an intentionally bi-level object,
so an obvious first stage in interpreting its image is to restore the
binary nature of the original by thresholding. The work in this paper
was inspired by the requirement to handle poor quality originals in the
interpretation of engineering drawings. These originals may have been
reproduced by dyeline or electrostatic copying, and may be large and
detailed. There is thus a premium on being able to extract the maximum
of useful information at minimum resolution in the presence of high
noise levels. Under these conditions thresholding is not straightforward. The significance of the grey level of a given pixel may need to
·be assessed in the context of a later interpretation stage; early
binarisation would preclude such a possibility.

Our response to this situation has been to extract basic statistical data that would be used for thresholding, but only to use it to
normalise the image, not to binarise it. The subsequent interpretation stages thus have access to the full grey level image, together
with the statistical data. It is of course possible to use the data
to binarise the image, as we have done for the illustrations in this
paper, to provide a ready human assessment of the quality of the data.

## The approach

In setting a threshold for binarisation it is hoped to establish a white level (of the background), a black level (of the line or character) and then bisect these with a threshold level. For some images this can be done by compiling a grey level histogram [1] and identifying peak values corresponding to black and white, together with a valley between at which the threshold is set. However, for line drawings the black peak is too weak and diffuse to produce a marked valley between it and the white peak (see fig. 1). Various methods of histogram enhancement to bring out this valley have been proposed [2]. As drawing quality becomes poorer and noise levels higher the search for the black peak becomes harder [3]. This is recognised in a practical thresholding system [4] where the threshold reverts to a value independent of black level when the black areas are weak. Our approach has been to measure the position and width of the white peak, and to refer grey levels to those values. The decision between black and white can then be made in terms of a 'likelihood of being white'.

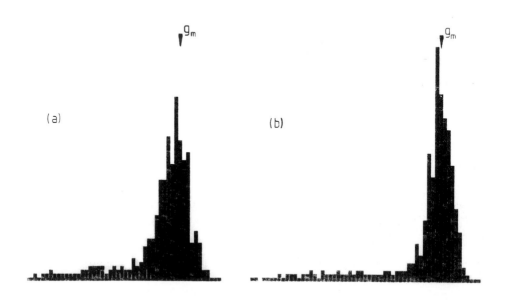

Figure 1:    Grey level histograms of areas (a) and (b) in Fig. (2)

The image

The image is obtained by digitisation of a CCTV image at 768 x 576 x 7 bit resolution using a 'Pluto' frame grabber. The image is transferred into a Whitechapel MG1 (32016 processor at 8 MHz) and held in RAM. The processing routines are written in 'C' and the image is accessed as a single array. An example of a typical difficult image is shown in fig. (2). There are variations in light level, camera response, background noise, background grey level and line density across the image.

Lighting and camera response variations are extraneous to the image and should be taken out by localising the image analysis. This is readily done, since they are also long range effects compared to the line widths present. The variations in background noise and grey level are both short and long range. It is not possible to take out the short range variations by simple localisation without also taking out the lines that it is the goal of the whole process to capture. The lines in this image are at most ten pixels wide.

Figure 2:    The area of original drawing under consideration

The range of localisation allowed is also limited at the bottom by the effects of small sample size: to locate the mean of a histogram to within half a grey level with 95% confidence requires about 150 points in a sample of Normally distributed data. The top limit of the range of localisation depends on original image quality, which has been chosen in the present case to be poor (a low cost camera, normal room lighting). Examination of the image using pseudocolour and manually set thresholds indicated that a sub area 64 x 64 pixels (i.e. dividing the original into 9 x 12 sub areas) possessed a suitably uniform background level. There is thus some scope for successful localisation using histogramming in this image. Grey level histograms of two such sub areas are shown in fig. (1).

## Local Histogramming - a first method

Although the histograms have a marked peak, the data quality does not permit its location by identifying the maximum population of the original histogram. To overcome this, a smoothed histogram was formed by averaging the original over three grey levels, and the modal grey level, $g_m$, for this histogram was found. $g_m$ is marked in fig. 1. It can be assessed as an estimate for white peak location by displaying a picture thresholded at $g_m$. The result should contain nearly equal numbers of black and white pixels in the nominally white areas. A difference of only one grey level between display threshold and white peak location gives a clear imbalance between black and white in those areas. This visual assessment gave apparent white peak locations that coincided with $g_m$ to within ±1 grey level. We use $g_m$ as a preliminary measure of white peak location.

To measure the background noise level, the halfwidth of the white peak in the smoothed histogram was estimated by measuring its halfwidth at half its height (see fig. (3). This halfwidth is approximately 1.2 $\sigma$ for normally distributed data of standard deviation $\sigma$. Values of halfwidth varied from 2 to 5 across the image but did not seem to relate to the obvious variations in background noise. They could be made more consistent by increasing the smoothing of the histogram, but at the expense of systematically broadening the peak. In view of this, the average value

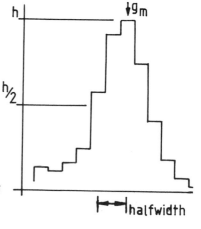

Fig. 3.

of halfwidth over all 108 sub areas, was used for image assessment. In
an image such as this the clearest way to display the data is to offset
it so that average white level is zero, and invert it so that black is
positive.  This done, the grey level at any pixel is a measure of its
significance for subsequent line capture.  Furthermore, this significance can be quantified by reference to the width of the white peak.
The results of thresholding the image of fig. (2) at 3 x average half-
widths are shown in fig. (4).

Figure 4:    Obtained by thresholding fig. 2 at 3.6 x global noise
             standard deviation

The advantage of the method of white peak width assessment are shown
by the uniformity and low level of noise.  At this threshold a noise
level of 1 pixel in 5000 would be expected from a normally distributed
white peak.  The user can be confident that any attempt to set a substantially whiter threshold, say in the areas where text is faint, will
invoke substantial noise.  Indeed, if the user wishes to do this, they
can estimate the expected higher noise level by assuming the white peak
to be normally distributed with standard deviation about halfwidth /1.2.
This aspect of the image assessment will be taken further in the next
section.

The limits of this first approach are also seen in fig. (4), in that
the noise level in the original of fig. (2) does vary systematically,
there being a higher noise level to the left of the image due to the

copying procedure. So although this approach deals with the existence of noise, and adapts to its overall level, it it not accurate enough for local noise measurement.

## Local Histogramming: improving accuracy

The estimates of white peak position and width formed above are rapid, robust and approximate. They rely on the histogram having a strong peak whose top and sides (to half way down) stand out clearly from the surroundings. This is well satisfied by the images we are concerned with. However, the accuracy of our initial methods can readily be improved.

The mean and variance of these histograms can be easily evaluated in the usual way, but that would not measure the properties of the white background because of the black pixels that lie in the tail of the distribution on the left of the white peaks in fig. 1. However, it should be possible to truncate the histogram to a window around the white peak, calculate the statistics of the truncated histogram, then allow for the truncation on the basis of some model of the white peak. Such a window is illustrated in fig. 1: if its width is 2x. We may refer to the mean and variance of the truncated histogram as $m(x)$ and $v(x)$ respectively.

If the white peak were Normally distributed $\left[ \phi(t) = \frac{1}{\sqrt{2\pi}\sigma} e^{-t^2/2\sigma^2} \right]$, $v(x)$ would have a relationship to x that depends on $\sigma$: for $x \ll \sigma$, $\phi(t)$ is approximately constant so $v(x) \cong v_c = 1/3 \; x^2$. As x increases towards $\sigma$, $\phi(t)$ reduces and $v(x)$ falls away from $v_c$. So if we examine $f(x) = \frac{v(x)}{v_c(x)}$ as x increases, the value of x at which f falls to a given value should be proportional to $\sigma$. This is confirmed by examining $v(x)$ for a Normal distribution.

$$v_n(x) = \sigma^2 \left[ 1 - \frac{xe^{-x^2/2\sigma^2}}{\int_o^x e^{-t^2/2\sigma} \; dt} \right]$$

So, putting $x/\sigma = h$; $f_n(x) = \frac{v_n(x)}{1/3 \; x^2} = \frac{3}{h^2} \left[ 1 - \frac{he^{-h^2/2}}{\int_o^h e^{-t^2/2} \; dt} \right]$ .

A graph of $f_n(x)$ is shown in fig. 5(a). Suppose now that a Normally distributed peak stands out from a histogram so that it can be located by the methods of the previous section. We can centre our window at $g_m$ and explore the variation of $v(x)$ with x. The graph of $f(x) = v(x)/v_c(x)$ against x will have the form of fig. 5(a) with a width proportional to the unknown $\sigma$. The above procedure is readily implemented,

with suitable adaption to discrete data. m(x) and v(x) are found for
windows of width 1, 3, 5 ... centred initially at $g_m$. For a window of
unit width, the mean will always be at the centre of the window. As
width increases, the mean may differ from the centre by more than 0.5.
In this case the window is recentred by one grey level so that the mean
is kept within 0.5 of the centre. Values of f(x) from this procedure
are shown in fig. 5(b) for the histogram of fig. 1.

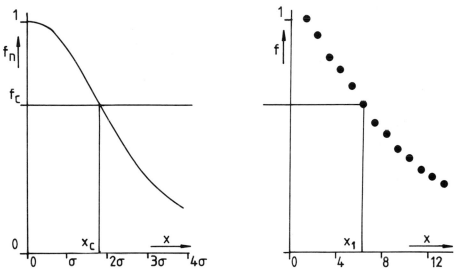

Figure 5: (a) $f_n(x)$    (b) f(x) for the histogram of fig. 1(a)

It now remains to fit the curve of 5(a) to the data of 5(b) and deduce
σ for a Normal model of the white peak. In view of the quality of the
data in fig. 5(b), a simple approach to the fitting was taken: that of
matching the abscissae at a suitable ordinate. Examining fig. 5(a) we
see that the maximum slope of $f_n(x)$ occurs at $x = x_c \cong 1.8\sigma$ where
$f_n(x_c) = f_c \cong 0.642$. Thus if we seek $x_1$ such that $f(x_1) = f_c$ in fig. 5(b)
we may deduce the standard deviation as $\sigma_c = x_1/1.8$. This was done
firstly by interpolation between values of f(x) either side of $f_c$. The
abscissa $x_1$ is clearly suitable from the form of $f_n(x)$ alone, but there
are other considerations: a large abscissa will include more of the
histogram in the calculation of f(x), reducing random error, but may
also infringe on the black pixels in the tail of the histogram, introducing systematic overestimate of σ. In effect, $x_1$ is a safe value
designed to reduce random error: it includes 92% of a Normal white peak,
and it coincides with the maximum slope of the theoretical curve. The
possibility of systematic overestimation due to the black pixels was
considered less undesirable, and more susceptible to correction by
further refinements to the procedure. A check on operation of the

procedure was carried out by fitting a regression line to the values.
of f, centred on $x_1$. The magnitude of the residuals of the regression
was found to decrease to a minimum as the number of points in it rose
above three, then to increase as the form of f became non linear. A
new estimate for standard deviation, $\sigma_r$, was found from the intersection
of this minimal residual line with $f = f_c$.

The results showed clearly that the increased noise in the left part
of the image due to copying was detected and that local standard deviations were usable. The results of thresholding the image at 3.6 x local
standard deviation are shown in fig. (6). The operation of the local
noise measurement is demonstrated by examining sub areas of fig. (6).
High noise (area a, $\sigma_c$ = 3.5) and low noise (area b, $\sigma_c$ = 2.7) are shown
enlarged in fig. (7) at (ii)a and (ii)b for this method; for comparison in the
same figure at (i)a and (i)b are shown the results of the previous (non-
local) method. Thus the localisation of noise estimation has enabled
improved localisation of thresholding.

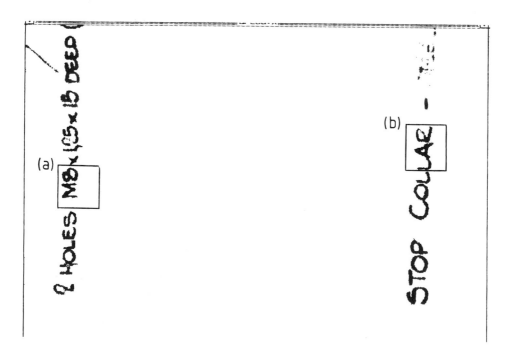

Figure 6: Obtained by thresholding fig. 2 at 3.6x local noise
standard deviation

(i)                                          (ii)

Figure 7:   Enlarged views of (i) fig. (4) and (ii) fig. (6) at areas
            (a) and (b) of fig. (6)

## Evaluation of results

Although the results are visually satisfactory, the problem of assessing
their accuracy remains.  To tackle this, images of nominally white
paper were captured.  Values of mean ($m$) and standard deviation ($\sigma$)
were obtained from the classic formulae (1) and (2) for comparison
with those from our own methods ($g_m$, $m_w$ and $\sigma_c$, $\sigma_r$).  The influence of
sample size was examined, from 100 to 4096 data points.  Results were
compiled from multiple subsamples within many sub areas of the image.
In discussing these we will use the word 'scatter' to denote the standard deviation of a set of such results: this is to avoid confusion
when discussing the scatter of a standard deviation.

   The estimate of white peak position by the mode of the smoothed histogram ($g_m$) was found to be unbiased, and to have a scatter of about
0.5 grey levels at all sample sizes.  The estimate via the windowed
histogram ($m_w$) was also unbiased, but had smaller scatter: about 10%
greater than $m$, the classic value.  So, for example, the scatter in $m_b$
was approximately 0.25 at a sample size of 100, and decreased inversely
as the square root of sample size.

   The measurements of standard deviation by interpolation and by regression ($\sigma_c$ and $\sigma_r$) were found to be equally good.  The residuals in

$\sigma$ in the regression were better than 5% for five points. They both produced values not significantly different from, but slightly scattered with respect to, the classical $\sigma$. For example, for a sample of 100 points the scatter of $\sigma_c/\sigma$ was 12%, reducing to 6% for a 1000 point sample. For this latter sample size, the classic scatter of $\sigma$ was 0.14 grey levels about a mean of 2.2 grey levels.

Further tests on consistency were carried out on images containing linework. These produced an increase in scatter of the mean (typically by 30% for $m_w$), but no significant increase in scatter for $\sigma_c$.

## References

1. T. Pavlidis, Structural pattern recognition, Springer Verlag, 1977.
2. J. S. Weszka and A. Rosenfield, Histogram modification for threshold selection, IEEE Trans. Systems Man Cybernetics, 9, 38-52 (1979).
3. J. Kittler, J. Illingworth and J. Foglein, Threshold selection based on a simple image statistic, Comput. Vision Graphics. Image Process 30, 125-147 (1985).
4. M. R. Bartz, The IBM 1975 Optical Page Reader, Part II: Video thresholding system, IBM J. Res. Develop., 12, 354-363 (1968).

# A Color Classification Algorithm for Color Images

Shoji Tominaga

Department of Psychology, Stanford University

Stanford, California 94305, USA

## Abstract

We describe a color classification algorithm that partitions color image data into a set of uniform color regions. The algorithm uses a recursive method to detect clusters of color data. The algorithm can be divided into two main steps. First, we map the device dependent image data into an approximately uniform perceptual color space. Second, we apply a recursive histogram analysis to the data represented in this perceptually uniform space. The histogram analysis is designed to identify the spatial subregions within the image that correspond to a uniform color. Once a region has been identified, the corresponding data are removed and the histogram analysis is repeated on the remaining data set. The performance of the algorithm is discussed with respect to a test image.

## 1. Introduction

We describe an algorithm that accepts high resolution color images as input, and yields a new representation of the data in the form of a set of spatial regions, each described by a single color value. The algorithm is designed so that the number of colors used to represent the spatially uniform color regions in the output image is quite small (say 4 bits per spatial region) compared to the number of colors used to specify the data in the input image (say 24 bits per pixel). The ability to classify spatial regions of the input image into a small number of uniform regions can be useful for several problems including data reduction, image segmentation, and feature extraction [1],[2],[3],[4].

The algorithm can be divided into two main parts. First, the input image data are mapped from device coordinates into an approximately uniform perceptual color space defined in terms of hue, lightness, and saturation. Examples of perceptually uniform spaces are the Munsell color system or the CIE-L*a*b* color system in color science. The mapping we describe is quite close to the Munsell system, but somewhat more convenient for numerical processing. Second, we classify connected spatial subregions of the image based on their color specifications in the uniform color space. Using a method based on histogram analysis, we seek spatial regions in the image that can be classified as a uniform region based on both (1) their similarity in color and (2) their identification as a cluster in the uniform color space. The histogram analysis for extracting uniform regions is recursive. Following the identification of a class, we remove the data identified with the class from the data set and apply the histogramming method to the remaining data. The final output consists of a set of uniform color regions.

## 2. Color Specifications

There are several systems for a perceptually uniform color space defined by hue, lightness, and saturation. The Munsell color system is based on such psychological ordering of object colors. The three attributes called Munsell Hue (H), Value (V), and Chroma (C) make a space of cylindrical coordinates. Fig. 1 shows the chromaticity plane by (H, C). There exists no analytical formula for conversion between the tristimulus values and Munsell attributes, but only a table [5]. Hence a direct-mapping method was derived to assign observed RGB signals to Munsell attributes for each pixel in an image quickly [6].

We first define an observation space of the color signals by a five (or four)-dimensional vector

$$\mathbf{s} = [\, 1, (\rho_{B/W}{}^{1/3}), \rho_R^{1/3}, \rho_G^{1/3}, \rho_B^{1/3} \,]^T, \tag{1}$$

where the first element is a constant bias, and $\rho_i$ $(i = (B/W), R, G, B)$ are the effective reflectances obtained from an imaging device. $T$ denotes matrix transposition. Let $p$ be a three-dimensional

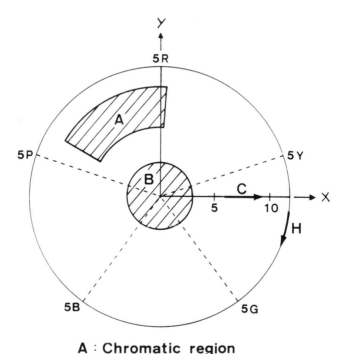

A : **Chromatic region**
B : **Achromatic region**

Fig.1 Chromaticity plane of the Munsell color system.

column vector representing Munsell space as

$$\mathbf{p} = [\, x, y, z\, ]^T = [\, C \, \sin(\tfrac{2\pi}{100}H), \ C \, \cos(\tfrac{2\pi}{100}H), V \,]^T. \qquad (2)$$

Then a mapping from the observation space into Munsell space is described by

$$\mathbf{p} = \mathbf{F}\,\mathbf{s}. \qquad (3)$$

The matrix $\mathbf{F}$ is a 3x5 (or 3x4) transformation matrix defining the mapping, which is determined based on measurements of color samples.

Although the Munsell system provides perceptually uniform spacing with respect to each dimension of HVC, it is not such a metric space as the Euclidean space. In this study, we define a formula which represents a color difference between two colors $\mathbf{P}_1$ and $\mathbf{P}_2$ as follows:

$$d_M = (\,(x_1 - x_2)^2 + (y_1 - y_2)^2 + 4\,(z_1 - z_2)^2\,)^{1/2}. \qquad (4)$$

Another similar formula is found in Ref.[7]. We use the above formula for a performance index of color classification.

## 3. Classification Method

### (1) Attributes and histogram features

An image can be expanded in terms of HVC (or HLS) by the mapping of observed RGB signals into a perceptual space pixel-by-pixel. The statistical distribution of color pixels in the color space is represented by using a set of one-dimensional histograms on attributes. The three histograms of HVC are mutually independent. These possess individual features as the cylindrical coordinate system. Fig.2 shows a typical shape of histograms for Munsell attributes. Note that Hue histogram is cyclic in a modulus of the domain [0,100]. Value histogram takes zero at both ends of the domain [0,10], because the ideal black (0) and white (10) are unrealized. Chroma histogram descends steeply as C nears zero. The upper bound of the domain is not fixed.

A cluster of pixels in the color space should make a peak in each histogram by projecting the three-dimensional space onto each of the attribute axes independently. Appearance of peaks depends on the direction of projection in a space. In other words, a cluster which is apparent in the original space may be projected in such a manner that it is not evident on any one axis. This problem seems to be inevitable in mathematics. While, from an image analysis viewpoint, effectiveness of the three perceptual attributes has been shown in feature extraction of natural color images.

As shown in Fig. 1, this coordinates partition a color space into a set of cylindrical or funnel-shaped color blocks for detecting color clusters. A color block for chromatic color is bounded by six coordinate surfaces which are determined by two pairs of H, V, and C. The block for achromatic color is determined by V and C values only. A straightforward way to avoid missing small clusters by this sampling is to use additional axes with a different projection from HVC. These axes should be rectangular coordinates (x, y). Five attributes {H, V, C, x, y} are a complete set of color features in the perceptual space to make histograms of an image. Usually all histograms are normalized to have the same domain [0, 100]. For x and y, the origins $(x,y = 0)$ are transformed into the center value of 50. If computation is expensive, first three attributes of the set may be chosen for analysis.

**(2) Algorithm**

The color classification takes place by the sequential detection of uniform color regions in the image. A uniform region is extracted by a histogram analysis using the attribute data. Once the data have been identified they are removed from the data set and the histogram analysis is repeated on the

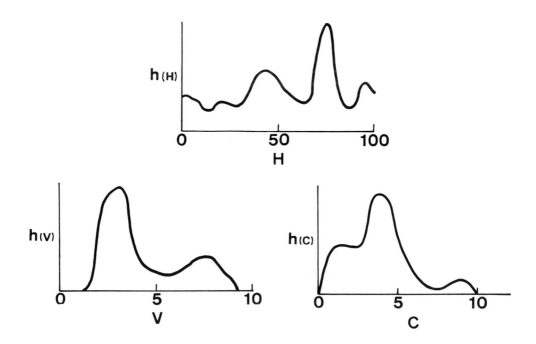

Fig.2 Typical histogram shapes of Munsell attributes.

remaining image data. Fig. 3 shows the flow chart of the color classification process. The operation at each stage is explained below. The peak analysis of histograms is described in detail in a separate section.

1. First we initialize a color label array $img(i,j)$ and a mask array $imgw(i,j)$. The mask array determines whether an image point is still considered to be part of the data set, or whether it has already been classified. Following each iteration the data points in $img(i,j)$ without labels are set in $imgw(i,j)$ to permit further color classification.

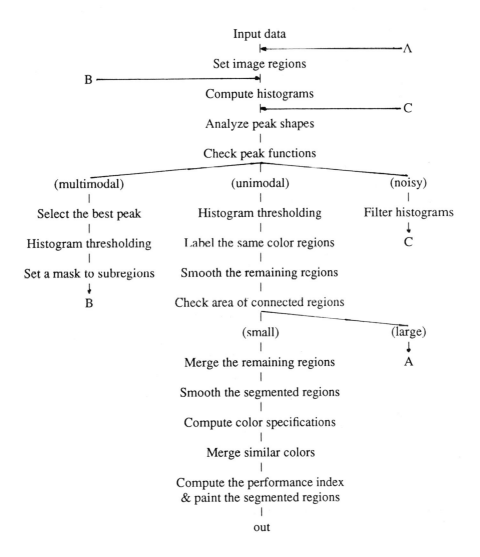

Fig.3 Flow chart of the color classification process.

2. The histogram for each attribute in the uniform color space is computed for those data whose mask is set.

3. The histograms are analyzed to find significant peaks. To determine the peaks we first perform a smoothing operation on the histogram to decrease random fluctuation. Then the histogram peaks are identified. The peak function is computed for each of the candidate peaks. The exact methods of specifying the histogram peaks are described below in more detail.

4. The peak function is checked, and the mode of histograms is classified into three cases.

5. In one case, if any histogram is multimodal, the most significant peak in a set of histograms is selected. A pair of thresholds of the attribute is computed from the positions of two valleys at the sides of the main peak. The peak area is cut out, and the image is split using the thresholds. A mask for describing the extracted subregions is created on $imgw(i,j)$. We then continue with the histogram computation.

6. In a second case, if all histograms are noisy and have no well-defined peaks, then the peak analysis is repeated again after further filtering the histograms.

7. In the third case, all histograms are unimodal or some of them have no peak. In this case we classify the data as belong to one color cluster. The image is split using the thresholds of attribute corresponding to the most significant peak. The segmented regions with uniform color are labeled on $img(i,j)$. One step color classification ends.

8. After classifying the image data, there will be a number of small isolated regions which can be ignored as noise. We smooth out these regions without a color label by using a region merging operation based on color difference.

9. An area for each of connected regions which remains without a label is checked. If all the areas are less than a threshold value $areathd$, the finishing process, described in step 10, is executed. Otherwise, the classification is continued for the remaining regions.

10. To complete the  process all regions without a label are merged into the neighboring regions with color labels on $img(i,j)$. Then smoothing is applied to all the segmented regions with color labels. This smoothing is a type of merging. That is, if the area of a region is less than $arethd$, and also the minimum color difference to one of the neighbors is less than $thd$, then the color label is replaced with the neighbor's one on $img(i,j)$.

11. Color specification for each color label is computed as the average color specification over regions with the same label. If the color specifications are within $thd$, it is considered as over-classification. Normally it is necessary to merge the similar colors into one label. This process accompanies with correction of $img(i,j)$ and some tables.

12 We evaluate the results of color classification and image segmentation. The average color difference is computed between the original image and the estimated one, which is represented by the

extracted color only. Finally the segmented regions with uniform colors are painted, where HVC is converted to RGB color. Thus the estimated image is displayed on a monitor.

### (3) Peak analysis of a histogram

The quality of color classification depends greatly on the performance of peak detection in a histogram  For this classification procedure we must determine a group of values near the peak, not simply the peak position only. The peak area is normally defined as the domain between two valleys at the sides of a peak, so that thresholds are the attribute values corresponding to the bottom positions of valleys.

A histogram is first filtered, and then a search is made for all the peaks and the valleys. A cyclic processing is performed for the hue histogram only. In this paper, to detect the peak areas, we do not adopt a functional fitting approach (e.g., see p.394 in [2]), but employ a more direct way based on the shape of histograms. This is because  it is difficult to fit a more than bimodal histogram to a functional form like a mixture of Gaussians. Fig. 4 shows an example of the peak area in a histogram. A main peak area is regarded as V1 to V7 where P4 is the main peak. The other peaks and valleys should be neglected. Here we have made two operations: One handles the case of a shallow valley between two high peaks like P2-V3-P4, and the other treats the case of a small peak on the sloping side of a high peak like P4-V5-P6. In both operations, the relationship of peak and valley heights are checked in combination with heights of the neighboring peaks and valleys. As a result, only one large peak and two deep valleys are left, and a main peak is determined.

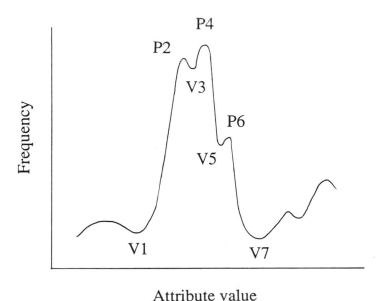

Fig.4 Example of the peak area in a histogram.

Next, to choose the most significant peak from candidates, a criterion function is computed for each peak area. The definition is given as

$$f = \frac{S_p}{T_a} \frac{100}{FWHM},$$ (5)

where $S_p$ indicates an area between two valleys, and $FWHM$ is the full-width at half-maximum of a peak. Moreover $T_a$ denotes the overall area of a histogram (the total number of pixels). This function includes a term representing the size $(S_p/T_a)$ and sharpness $(100/FWHM)$ of the peak area.

## 4. Experimental Results

The flower image shown in Fig. 5 has been used for analysis. The image is mapped into the Munsell color system, and color classification is performed by the histogram analysis using five Munsell attributes. The histograms of Hue, Value, Chroma, x, and y are first computed for a 128x128 original image. The main peak in the y histogram is chosen as the most significant peak, and used for initial thresholding. The peak function takes a value of 13.4. A big color cluster which corresponds to the background, is extracted after four iterations of the histogram analysis procedure.

The remaining regions are smoothed with the thresholding $thd = 3.0$, and $areathd = 10$. The color extraction has been repeated, and after twenty iterations the process was terminated. The remaining regions without a color label are merged. Furthermore the segmented regions are smoothed with the

Fig.5 Part of the morning glory picture.

same thresholds. The average color specifications are computed for twenty color regions. Then two colors are merged into one. Table 1 shows the final results of color classification. There are 19 colors used in the final image. The performance index is 1.303. Fig. 6 demonstrates the results of image segmentation, where the original image is split into 134 connected regions.

Table 1 Color classification results.

| Color No. | Munsell specifications | Coordinates | | | Area |
|---|---|---|---|---|---|
| 1 | 3.1PB 1.7/ 3.2 | -2.91 | -1.34 | 1.66 | 5951 |
| 2 | 3.5GY 4.4/ 2.3 | 2.26 | -0.50 | 4.42 | 3552 |
| 3 | 3.9RP 4.0/ 8.4 | -5.35 | 6.42 | 3.98 | 2165 |
| 4 | 5.6B 5.5/ 1.9 | -1.16 | -1.48 | 5.54 | 945 |
| 5 | 2.8P 7.5/ 1.8 | -1.73 | 0.31 | 7.48 | 924 |
| 6 | 9.3G 2.4/ 1.7 | 0.61 | -1.63 | 2.42 | 761 |
| 7 | 9.6B 6.9/ 1.7 | -1.39 | -1.06 | 6.90 | 629 |
| 8 | 8.1G 5.2/ 1.5 | 0.64 | -1.36 | 5.19 | 258 |
| 9 | 0.8YR 4.7/ 2.1 | 0.75 | 1.94 | 4.72 | 178 |
| 10 | 0.1B 3.5/ 1.8 | -0.57 | -1.71 | 3.54 | 152 |
| 11 | 0.3GY 3.8/ 5.1 | 5.07 | -0.10 | 3.84 | 148 |
| 12 | 3.0R 2.6/ 6.9 | -0.85 | 6.81 | 2.58 | 140 |
| 13 | 5.9YR 2.6/ 2.3 | 1.46 | 1.80 | 2.60 | 124 |
| 14 | N 6.0/ 1.3 | 0.60 | -1.14 | 6.00 | 124 |
| 15 | N 2.1/ 0.9 | 0.53 | 0.78 | 2.09 | 109 |
| 16 | 9.5P 6.1/ 4.4 | -3.67 | 2.48 | 6.12 | 145 |
| 17 | N 3.6/ 1.3 | 0.00 | 1.32 | 3.59 | 32 |
| 18 | 4.6YR 3.2/ 3.4 | 1.95 | 2.83 | 3.21 | 25 |
| 19 | 7.7Y 5.3/ 5.2 | 5.12 | 0.74 | 5.33 | 22 |

Fig.6 Image segmentation results.

The same procedure was run using the first three attributes, {H,V,C}. The set of only three attributes results in a larger number of classified colors and almost the same performance index. The segmentation results are a little more complicated in comparison with Fig. 6. The use of {V, x, y} results in a less number of colors and large residual errors. It is a rough segmentation.

## 5. Conclusion

The present paper has described a color classification algorithm for partitioning an image into a set of uniform color regions. The method uses a recursive histogram technique to detection clusters of perceptual attributes in a spatially uniform color space. The color space attributes are hue, lightness, and saturation that are derived by a mapping from the device dependent input data.

The features of the present algorithm are briefly summarized as follows:
(1) A perceptually uniform color space is used.
(2) Color classification and region segmentation are combined.
(3) All histograms are treated in the same way except for the cyclic process of hue.
(4) Region merging is performed on color difference.
(5) The color specifications are reliable for color analysis.

The present algorithm is written in C, and runs on Sun Microsystem computers under UNIX. The Color Analysis Package [8] was used to develop the algorithm.

## Acknowledgments

I thank A. Schwartz and B. Wandell for their help with this project. This work was supported, in part, by a grant from the National Aeronautics and Space Administration, NCC-307, to Stanford University.

## References

[1] R. Nevatia, Machine Perception, Prentice-Hall, Englewood Cliffs, NJ, 1982.
[2] M.D. Levine, Vision in Man and Machine, McGraw-Hill, New York, 1985.
[3] R. Ohlander, K. Price, and D.R. Reddy, Picture segmentation using a recursive region splitting method, Computer Graphics and Image Processing , vol.8, pp.313-333, 1978.
[4] Y. Ohta, T. Kanade, and T. Sakai, Color information for region segmentation , Computer Graphics and Image Processing, vol.13, pp.224-241, 1980.
[5] G. Wyszecki and W.S. Stiles, Color Sciences, John Wiley&Sons, New York, 1982.
[6] S. Tominaga, Expansion of color images using three perceptual attributes, Pattern Recognition Letters, vol.6, pp.77-85, 1987.
[7] D.B. Judd, and G. Wyszecki, Color in Business, Science, and Industry, John Wiley&Sons, New York, 1975.
[8] D.H. Brainard, and B.A. Wandell, The color analysis package (submitted).

# Fuzzy Set Methods in Pattern Recognition

James M. Keller and Hongjie Qiu
Electrical and Computer Engineering
University of Missouri-Columbia
Columbia, MO  65211

## Abstract

Dealing with uncertainty is a common problem in pattern recognition.  Rarely do object descriptions from different classes fall into totally disjoint regions of feature space.  This uncertainty in class definition can be handled in several ways. In this paper we present several approaches to the incorporation of fuzzy set information into pattern recognition.  We then introduce a new technique based on the fuzzy integral which combines objective evidence with the importance of that feature set for recognition purposes.  In effect, the fuzzy integral performs a local feature selection, in that it attempts to use the strongest measurements first in the object classification.  Algorithm performance is illustrated on real and synthetic data sets.

## 1.    Introduction

The classification of objects from extracted features  occupies a fundamental position in many areas of research interest and practical application.  There are numerous approaches to the pattern recognition problem, [1]-[4] which can be organized by the different types of criterion functions which are used.  Traditional approaches include decision theoretic methods, based on standard, or crisp, set theory, probabilistic techniques utilizing random models for uncertainty, and syntactic methods which rely on formal language theory.  In the ideal case--well separated classes of tightly clustered objects--almost any recognition technique will work.  However, this case is rarely found in real data.  Hence, whatever approach is taken, knowledge about the structure and distributions of the data is extremely useful, if not crucial, to the successful classification of the objects of interest.

Fuzzy set theory was introduced by Zadeh in 1965 [5] as an alternative means of describing those situations where the defining characteristics of the sets themselves are vague or imprecise, and has been successfully used in many applications [3,4,7,10].  In this paper, we first present some of these methods for pattern recognition.  We then present a new fuzzy pattern recognition algorithm which is based on the fuzzy integral with respect to a Sugeno measure.

## 2.   Fuzzy Sets in Pattern Recognition

Given a universe U of objects, a conventional "crisp" subset A of U is commonly defined by specifying the characteristic function of A, $u_A:U \rightarrow \{0,1\}$. Fuzzy sets are obtained by generalizing the concept of a characteristic function to a membership function $u:U \rightarrow [0,1]$. Most crisp set operations and set properties have analogs in fuzzy set theory.

Given a set of sample vectors $\{x_1, \ldots, x_n\}$, a fuzzy c partition of these vectors specifies the degree of membership of each vector in each of c classes. It is denoted by the c x n matrix U where $u_{ik} = u_i(x_k)$ for i = 1, ..., c, and k = 1, ..., n is the degree of membership of $x_k$ in class i. The following properties must be true for U to be a fuzzy c partition:

$$\sum_{i=1}^{c} u_{ik} = 1; \qquad 0 < \sum_{k=1}^{n} u_{ik} < n; \qquad u_{ik} \in [0, 1].$$

The most frequently used and documented fuzzy classification technique is the fuzzy c-means clustering algorithm [4]. It is an unsupervised approach which, like its crisp counterpart, looks for clusters in feature space by successively placing together all vectors which are "close to" the cluster center established for each class. In the crisp c-means, the vectors are assigned to respective clusters, while in the fuzzy c-means, their memberships in each class are updated during the iteration. The cluster centers then become a weighted average of the sample data [4]. Iterations continue until the process stabilizes.

In many pattern recognition problems, the classification of an input pattern is based on data where the respective sample sizes of each class are small and possibly not representative of the actual probability distributions, even if they are known. Under many circumstances, the K-nearest neighbor (K-NN) algorithm [6] is used to perform the classification. This decision rule provides a simple nonparametric procedure for the assignment of a class label to the input pattern based on the class labels represented by the K-closest neighbors of the vector.

One of the problems encountered in using the K-NN classifier is that normally each of the sample vectors is considered equally important in the assignment of the class label to the input vector. The fuzzy K-nearest neighbor algorithm [7] assigns class membership to a sample vector rather than assigning the vector to a particular class. The advantage is that no arbitrary total assignments are made by the algorithm. In addition, the vector's membership values provide a level of assurance to accompany the resultant classification. The basis of the algorithm is to assign membership as a function of the vector's distance from its K-nearest neighbors and those neighbors' memberships in the possible classes [7].

The labeled samples can be assigned class memberships in several ways. First, they can be given complete membership in their known class and nonmembership in all other classes. Other alternatives are to assign the samples' membership based on distance from their class mean or based on the distance from labeled samples of their own class and those of the other class or classes [8].

There are other instances in classification problems where linear decision boundaries are desired. The classical perceptron technique [9] is an iterative training algorithm which, given two classes of patterns attempts to determine a linear decision boundary separating the two classes. If the two sets of vectors are linearly separable, the perceptron algorithm is guaranteed to find a separating hyperplane in a finite number of steps [1]. However, if the two sets of vectors are not linearly separable, not only will the perceptron algorithm not find a separating hyperplane, but there is no method for knowing when to terminate the algorithm to obtain an optimal or even a good decision boundary.

The vectors that cause the classes to overlap are primarily responsible for the erratic behavior of the perceptron algorithm. In many cases, these same vectors are also relatively uncharacteristic of the respective classes, yet they are given full weight in the perceptron algorithm. By basing the amount of correction to the weight vector on the fuzzy memberships, vectors whose class is less certain will have less influence in determining the weight vector. In the crisp perceptron, the correction step is $W \leftarrow W + cx_j$. In order to incorporate the membership function values into the correction step, in [10] we modify this step so that it becomes

$$W \leftarrow W + |u_{1j} + u_{2j}|^m cx_j \qquad \text{where m is a positive constant.}$$

Like the crisp perceptron, the fuzzy perceptron will find a separating hyperplane in a finite number of iterations in the linearly separable case [10].

## 3. Fuzzy Measure and Fuzzy Integral

In this section we introduce a new classification technique which combines explicit evidence presented by features, or combinations of features with the relative degree of importance of these features.

A fuzzy measure g generalizes a probability measure by replacing the additivity condition with a weaker condition, that is, if $A \subset B$ then $g(A) \leq g(B)$, [11]. A particularly useful set of fuzzy measures is due to Sugeno [11].

Let $g_\lambda$ be a fuzzy measure satisfying the addition property:

If $A \cap B = \Phi$, then $g_\lambda (A \cup B) = g_\lambda (A) + g_\lambda (B) + \lambda g_\lambda (A) g_\lambda (B)$,

for some $\lambda > -1$. Then $g_\lambda$ is called a Sugeno measure.

Suppose X is a finite set, $X = \{x_1, \ldots, x_n\}$, and let $g^i = g_\lambda(\{x_i\})$. Then the set $\{g^1, \ldots, g^n\}$ is called the fuzzy density function for $g_\lambda$. Using the above definitions one can easily show that $g_\lambda$ can be constructed from a fuzzy density function by

$$g_\lambda(A) = [\prod_{x_i \in A} (1 + \lambda g^i) - 1]/\lambda,$$

for any subset A of X.  Using the fact that $X = \bigcup_{i=1}^{n} \{x_i\}$, $\lambda$ can be determined from the equation

$$1 = [\prod_{i=1}^{n} (1 + \lambda g^i) - 1]/\lambda . \tag{1}$$

Let h: X -> [0,1].  The fuzzy integral of h over X with respect to $g_\lambda$ is defined in [11] by:

$$\int_X h(x) 0 g_\lambda = \sup_{\alpha \epsilon [0,1]} [\alpha \wedge g_\lambda (F_\alpha)], \text{ where } F_\alpha = \{x \epsilon X \mid h(x) \geq a\}.$$

If X is a finite set, $X = \{x_1, \ldots, x_n\}$, arranged so that

$h(x_1) \geq h(x_2) \geq \ldots \geq h(x_n)$, then

$$\int_X h(x) 0 g_\lambda = \bigvee_{i=1}^{n} [h(x_i) \wedge g_\lambda ( X_i )] \tag{2}$$

where $X_i = \{x_1, \ldots, x_i\}$.  Also, given $\lambda$ as calculated above, the values $g_\lambda ( X_i )$ can be determined recursively as

$$g_\lambda ( X_1 ) = g_\lambda (\{x_1\}) = g^1 ; \tag{3a}$$

$$g_\lambda ( X_i ) = g^i + g_\lambda ( X_{i-1} ) + \lambda g^i g_\lambda ( X_{i-1} ) \text{ for } 1 < i \leq n. \tag{3b}$$

In general, fuzzy integrals are nonlinear functionals (although monotone) whereas ordinary (e.g., Lebesque) integrals are linear functionals.  It is this nonlinear subjective evaluation potential of the fuzzy integral which we utilize in pattern recognition applications.

4.    The Fuzzy Integral Algorithm

Let X be an object described by n features, $X = \{x_1, \ldots, x_n\}$.  For each pattern class $w_j$, let $u_j$: X -> [0,1].  Thus, $u_j$ is an objective partial evaluation of X from class $w_j$, that is, for each feature $x_i$, $\mu_j(x_i)$ measures the membership of X in $w_j$ from the standpoint of a single feature value $x_i$.  This partial evaluation is combined with the subjective measure $g_{\lambda j}$ which represents the important degree of the subset $X_i = \{x_1, \ldots, x_i\}$ of X.  For example, $g_{\lambda j}( X_1 ) = g_{\lambda j}(x_1)$ expresses the extent to which a viewpoint of feature $x_1$ is important in evaluating objects from class $w_j$, and for i > 1, $g_{\lambda j}( X_i ) = g_{\lambda j}(\{x_1, \ldots, x_i\})$ expresses the degree to which the set of viewpoints $\{x_1, \ldots, x_i\}$ contribute to the recognition of objects from class $w_j$. The fuzzy integral value,

$$e_j = \mathop{V}_{i=1}^{n} [u_j(x_i) \wedge g_{\lambda j}(X_i)], \tag{4}$$

gives a nonlinear evaluation of the degree to which object X belongs to class $w_j$.

There are many ways to generate the membership functions which provide the direct evidence of classification, including the methods described in section 2. For this report, we chose to calculate these functions from the feature histograms.

For each feature, a training set of samples was used to generate feature histograms for both classes. If the histograms show fairly small overlap, then an S-function [12] is generated using the minimum and maximum feature values for each class to calculate the memberships. When the histograms of the feature values of the training set exhibit more overlap, a $\pi$ function is used to compute the initial memberships. In [7-8], Keller et al., used a method based on the k-nearest neighbor approach to generate the membership values for training vectors. Also, in [13], we used automated histogram analysis of the three color components of an image to generate both the memberships and densities.

The Sugeno measure $g_{\lambda j}$ for each class is generated from a fuzzy density function $\{g_j^1, \ldots g_j^n\}$ by equation 3 with $\lambda$ calculated from equation 1. The class fuzzy densities for each feature are obtained subjectively from feature histogram analysis. In short, the greater the degree of separability exhibited by the histogram, the larger the importance degree, and hence the density value, which was given to the feature.

5.  Results

Three labeled data sets were utilized to test the algorithms. The data set IRIS is that of Anderson first used by R. A. Fisher to illustrate the concept of linear discriminant analysis [14]. There are fifty vectors per class in this data set. The IRIS23 data set is a subset of the IRIS data. It includes classes two and three, the nonseparable classes, of the IRIS data.

The TWOCLASS data set is an artificially generated normally distributed set of vectors. This data set was included because classification results from a Bayes classifier were available to use in the comparison. This data set contains 121 samples per class.

The results of the fuzzy classifications are reported in terms of the simplest crisp partition, where a sample vector is assigned to the class of maximum membership.

The results obtained from the fuzzy c-means, the fuzzy K-NN and the fuzzy perceptron are summarized below. Detailed description of more extensive experiments and comparison to crisp techniques can be found in [7,8,10]. Table I displays the outcome of running the crisp K-means algorithm on the IRIS and TWOCLASS data. The confusion matrices for the fuzzy K-means are almost identical. The advantage gained in the fuzzy version is that the partition is fuzzy, and hence, there is additional information available in a final decision procedure.

Figures 1 and 2 show features 3 and 4 from the overlapping classes of the IRIS and TWOCLASS data sets respectively. Also, a fuzzy perceptron boundary is displayed for each class. Table II illustrates the termination problems of the crisp perceptron on nonseparable data. Since it will never terminate, we stopped at the several intervals and determined the misclassification rates. Table II shows these outcomes for the IRIS 23 samples, but similar results have been obtained on other data [10]. We see that the fuzzy perceptron procedures a good boundary where the only misclassified vectors occur in the overlap region.

Table III displays some of the results obtained from the crisp and fuzzy K-NN rules. Two types of initialization were used for the fuzzy algorithm. The first, called crisp initialization, was to assign each training vector a membership of 1 in its true class, and 0 in the other. The second method used a 3-nearest neighbor variation to assign the initial class memberships [7]. The testing was accomplished using a "leave-one-out" methodology. From the table we see that the fuzzy k-nearest neighbor using a fuzzy initialization scheme produced the best results with the added benefit of final class memberships.

To test the new fuzzy integral algorithm we added another data set, labeled FLIR containing two measurements extracted from objects in forward looking infrared (FLIR) images. The set consisted of 64 targets and 48 clutter windows.

The results from running the fuzzy integral algorithms are summarized below. In determining the initial class memberships for the features in the IRIS set, an S-function was used for features 1, 3, and 4 for both classes. The memberships for feature 2 were generated with a $\pi$-function. For the TWOCLASS data, $\pi$-functions were used for features 1 and 2 while memberships for features 3 and 4 were calculated with S-functions. Finally, S-functions were used for both features in the FLIR set.

In testing the algorithm, three situations were considered for generating the fuzzy density function values $g_j^i$. The first case, representing a baseline, assigned equal weight to each feature for each class such that the weights sum to one. This condition implies $\lambda_j = 0$ for each j. The second and third situations allowed the density values to reflect subjective opinions of feature strength based on histogram separability with the distinction that in the third case, the feature weights need not sum to one. The representative values chosen are shown in Table IV. The results of running the fuzzy integral algorithm under these three situations are displayed in Table V. The vectors were assigned to the class of

largest fuzzy integral value.  However, if fuzzy decisions are desired, the fuzzy
integral values themselves provide a good means of measuring class membership.  It
can be seen from this data that providing nonuniform subjective density values is
advantageous for better classification results.  The classification rates for the
three data sets compare favorably with those for the crisp and fuzzy K-nearest
neighbor algorithms, the fuzzy perceptron, and for the TWOCLASS set, with the Bayes
classifier for which the data was originally designed.

## 6.  Conclusions

Several approaches to pattern classification have been presented where the
underlying basis for the uncertainty is fuzzy set theory.  The resulting crisp
partitions generated from the fuzzy outcomes compare very favorably with crisp or
probabilistic techniques.  An added advantage of these methods is that the final
memberships provide a natural degree of typicalness of the input pattern to the
respective classes.

The new method based on the fuzzy integral offered an alternate approach.
Instead of treating each feature identically, it can stress those features or sets
of features which supply the most evidence toward the determination of class
membership.  This is a convenient framework to produce different nonlinear
classification rules for different classes within the same problem and with the same
overall feature set.

TABLE I
Confusion Matrices for the K-Means Algorithm

| | IRIS[1] | | | | TWOCLASS[2] | |
|---|---|---|---|---|---|---|
| | 1 | 2 | 3 | | 1 | 2 |
| 1 | 50 | 0 | 0 | 1 | 114 | 7 |
| 2 | 0 | 48 | 2 | 2 | 15 | 106 |
| 3 | 0 | 14 | 36 | | | |

[1]Terminated in three iterations.  [2]Terminated in ten iterations.

TABLE II.  Comparison of crisp and fuzzy perceptron or IRIS23 Data

| Type of Perceptron | Number of Iterations | Number of Misclassifications Out of 100 |
|---|---|---|
| Fuzzy, features 3-4 | 237 | 6 |
| Crisp, features 3-4 | 200 | 43 |
| | 300 | 36 |
| | 400 | 41 |
| | 500 | 37 |
| | 600 | 22 |
| | 1000 | 24 |
| | 1500 | 18 |
| | 3000 | 18 |

TABLE III
Results of K-Nearest Neighbor Classifiers
Number of Misclassified Vectors

| K | Crisp | | Fuzzy-(1) | | Fuzzy-(2) | |
|---|---|---|---|---|---|---|
| | I | T | I | T | I | T |
| 3 | 6 | 21 | 6 | 22 | 6 | 19 |
| 5 | 5 | 20 | 5 | 21 | 4 | 19 |
| 7 | 5 | 19 | 5 | 21 | 4 | 19 |
| 9 | 6 | 21 | 4 | 21 | 4 | 18 |

I - IRIS23 data (four features)
T - TWOCLASS data (four features)
(1) - crisp initialization
(2) - fuzzy 3-nearest neighbor initialization

TABLE IV.  Subjective Densities for Fuzzy Integral

| Data Set | Class | Case 2 Densities | | | | Case 3 Densities | | | |
|---|---|---|---|---|---|---|---|---|---|
| | | $g^1$ | $g^2$ | $g^3$ | $g^4$ | $g^1$ | $g^2$ | $g^3$ | $g^4$ |
| IRIS23 | $W_1$ | .1 | 0 | .5 | .4 | .1 | .1 | .6 | .4 |
| | $W_2$ | .1 | 0 | .5 | .4 | .1 | .1 | .6 | .4 |
| TWOCLASS | $W_1$ | 0 | 0 | .45 | .55 | .1 | .1 | .6 | .4 |
| | $W_2$ | .1 | 0 | .55 | .35 | .1 | .1 | .6 | .4 |
| FLIR | $W_1$ | .4 | .6 | -- | -- | .5 | .7 | -- | -- |
| | $W_2$ | .7 | .3 | -- | -- | .8 | .5 | -- | -- |

Table V.  Fuzzy Integral Classification Results

| Data Set | Case 1 | | Case 2 | | Case 3 | |
|---|---|---|---|---|---|---|
| | Number Mis-classifed | Classi-fication Rate | Number Mis-classified | Classi-fication Rate | Number Mis-classified | Classi-fication Rate |
| IRIS | 4/7 | 89% | 3/1 | 96% | 3/1 | 96% |
| FLIR | 6/6 | 89% | 6/3 | 92% | 6/3 | 92% |
| TWOCLASS | 5/26 | 87% | 9/11 | 92% | 12/15 | 89% |

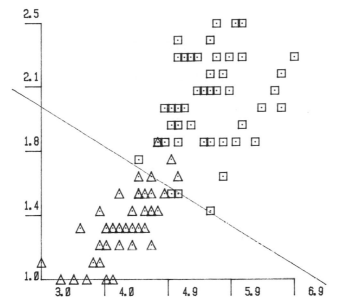

Figure 1.   IRIS23 date with fuzzy perceptron boundary.

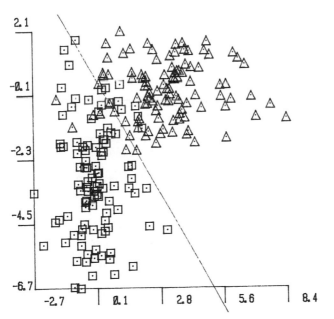

Figure 2.   TWOCLASS data with fuzzy perceptron boundary.

References

1.  J.T. Tou and R.C. Gonzalez, Pattern Recognition Principles, Reading, MA: Addison-Wesley, 1974.

2.  K.S. Fu, Syntactic Methods in Pattern Recognition, New York: Academic Press, 1974.

3.  A. Kandel, Fuzzy Techniques in Pattern Recognition, New York: John Wiley and Sons, 1982.

4.  J.C. Bezdek, Pattern Recognition with Fuzzy Objective Function Algorithms, New York: Plenum Press, 1981.

5.  L.A. Zadeh, "Fuzzy Sets," Inf. Control, Vol. 8, pp. 338-353, 1965.

6.  T.M. Cover and P.E. Hart, "Nearest neighbor pattern classification," IEEE Trans. Inform. Theory, vol. IT-13, pp. 21-27, Jan. 1967.

7.  J. Keller, M. Gray, and J. Givens, Jr., "A fuzzy k-nearest neighbor algorithm," IEEE Trans. Systems, Man, Cybern., Vol. SMC-15, No. 4, July 1985, pp. 580-585.

8.  J. Keller and J. Givens, "Membership function issues in fuzzy pattern recognition," Proc. International Conference on Systems, Man and Cybernetics, Tuscon, 1985, pp. 210-214.

9.  F. Rosenblatt, "The perceptron: A perceiving and recognizing automation," Cornell Univ., Ithaca, NY, Project PARA, Cornell Aeronaut. Lab. Rep., 85-460-1, 1957.

10. J. Keller, and D. Hunt, "Incorporating fuzzy membership functions into the perceptron algorithm," IEEE Trans. Pattern Anal. Machine Intell., Vol. PAMI-7, No. 6, 1985, pp. 693-699.

11. M. Sugeno, "Theory of fuzzy integral and its applications," Ph.D. Thesis, Tokyo Institute of Technology, 1974.

12. L.A. Zadeh, "Calculus of fuzzy restructions," in Fuzzy Sets and Their Applications to Cognitive and Decision Processes, L.A. Zadeh, K.S. Fu, K. Tanaka, and M. Shimura, Eds., London: Academic Press, 1975, pp. 1-26.

13. H. Qiu and J. Keller, "Multiple Spectral image segmentation using fuzzy techniques", Proc. North American Fuzzy Information Processing Society Workshop, W. Lafayette, IN, 1987, pp. 374-387.

14. R.A. Fisher, "The use of multiple measurements in taxonomic problems," Ann. Eugenics, Vol. 7, pp. 179-188, 1936.

# A Fuzzy Hybrid Model for Pattern Classification

*Prasenjit Biswas*

Dept. of Computer Sc. and Engg.
Southern Methodist Univ., Dallas, TX75275, USA

*Arun K. Majumdar*

Dept. of Computer Science,
Univ. of Guelph, Guelph, Ontario, Canada

## ABSTRACT

In this paper we propose a hybrid model for pattern classification. The model is hybrid in the sense that the first phase of the classifier uses a supervised learning algorithm for establishing the fuzzy separability of pattern classes based on the Fuzzy set theoretic approach producing hierarchical binary decision trees; and the second phase uses a syntactic approach. The effectiveness of the model is demonstrated by using it for recognition of handprinted Devanagri[1] characters. The principle of classifier design described in this paper establishes a methodology for identifying the boundary of transition from the geometric to the structural approach in such hybrid classification schemes.

## 1. Introduction

The methodologies that have been developed for Pattern recognition could be broadly classified as Syntactic methods, Statistical methods and Fuzzy set based techniques [4,6,8,9,10]. Typically a problem in pattern recognition is solved using one of these techniques. When one of these techniques is used to solve a pattern recognition problem for a reasonably large number of classes, the classifier design tends to get extremely complex. There had been proposals for hierarchical complexity decomposition for such problems, so that different methods could be used in appropriate phases of the decomposed problem [5]. In such an exercise in decomposition, it could become difficult to identify the transition boundaries between these different phases.

In this paper, we propose a technique for complexity decomposition and apply the proposed design principle to the development a hybrid classifier for recognition of handprinted Devanagri characters. There are reports on hybrid classifier design in the literature [4,8], where primarily statistical information has been used to form stochastic grammars and maximum likelihood or Baye's decision rules have been used in syntactic methods. The classifier proposed here is hybrid in a different sense.

In the first phase of the proposed classifier, we use a fuzzy set based method to establish fuzzy separability [1] of the pattern classes. When it is established that certain classes are not fuzzy separable, syntactic recognition is used for classification.

Fuzzy set based methods have been particularly suitable when it is not reasonable to assume class density functions and statistical independence of features, and available training set is small [6,9,10].

## 2. The Membership Function

A fuzzy subset A of a universe of discourse $\Omega$, is characterized by a membership function [10] $\mu_A : \Omega \rightarrow [0,1]$ which associates with each element of X of $\Omega$ a number $\mu_A(X)$ in the interval $[0,1]$. The subset A might be considered to be having an ill-defined boundary so that an element X belongs to the set with a degree of membership. We will be concerned with L fuzzy pattern classes $C_i$ [i=1,...L] in the feature space. Each of these L classes is defined by a set of prototype vectors (corresponding to the training patterns).

---

[1] Devanagri is the script for Hindi, one of the official languages of India.

In the design of the first phase of the classifier we are primarily concerned with the estimation of a suitable membership function that appropriately partitions the feature space. To decide the classification of an unknown pattern X into one of the fuzzy classes $C_i$, we will use the following criterion. We decide X to be a member of class $C_j$ if --

$$\mu_{C_j}(X) = \underset{i}{\text{Max}} \ [\mu_{C_i}(X)] \tag{1}$$

In this paper we will consider a membership function for an input pattern X, for the pattern class $C_i$ as --

$$\mu_{C_i}(X) = [1 + D(X, C_i)]^{-1.0} \tag{2}$$

where $D(X, C_i)$ is a similarity measure of X to $C_i$.

The measure $D(X, C_i)$ is assumed to be of the type --

$$D(X, C_i) = \left( \frac{1}{M} \sum_{j=1}^{M} \left\{ P_{ij} \tilde{d}_{ij}(X) \right\}^2 \right)^{0.5}, \tag{3}$$

where $\tilde{d}_{ij}(X) \in R^+$ is the measure of similarity of X to $C_i$ in the $j$th dimension. The terms $p_{ij}$'s in the similarity measure are the unknown parameters in the membership function. In the discussions to follow, we will refer to these parameters as directional correcting parameters (DCP's) as they are introduced in the similarity measure to represent the directional sensitivity of class $C_i$ in the $j$th dimension. In the following section we will present a Supervised Learning Algorithm (SLA) for estimating the DCP's from a set of training patterns.

The choice of a similarity measure is subjective in nature and typically depends on the type of problem under consideration [6,9,10]. The total similarity measure (3) is a linear combination of the similarities in each axis of measurement. It should be noted that this, however, is not a serious restriction as various types of measure reported in the literature could be expressed in this form [9,10].

## 3. The Supervised Learning Algorithm (SLA)

A Supervised Learning Algorithm is used to estimate the DCP's, using sets of training patterns (labeled $T_i$) from each class $C_i$. Initially the DCP's are assumed to be M-dimensional *unit* vectors. Each DCP vector $p_i$ is sequentially modified by a sequence of training patterns (say, $S_i$). The SLA estimates the vector $p_i^*$ for each class $C_i$ such that the scalar product $|p_i^T \cdot \tilde{d}_i(X)|$ satisfies the following condition --

$$\left. \begin{array}{ll} |p_i^T \cdot \tilde{d}_i(X)| \leq a_i & \text{if} \quad X \in_f C_i \\ |p_i^T \cdot \tilde{d}_i(X)| \geq b_i & \text{if} \quad X \notin_f C_i \end{array} \right\} \tag{4}$$

where $a_i < b_i$ and $a_i$, $b_i$ are positive real numbers. The symbol $\in_f$ is distinguished from the classical set theoretic notation $\in$. The notation $X \in_f C_i$ means that X is a training pattern known to be a member of the fuzzy class $C_i$.

**Definition 1**: Two fuzzy classes $C_i$ and $C_j$ are fuzzy separable (denoted by $C_i \backslash\backslash C_j$) if there exists a $p_i^*$ such that condition (4) is satisfied with $p_i = p_i^*$ for some $a_i$ and $b_i$. The DCP vector $p_i^*$ is called the solution DCP vector.

Let $p_i(r)$ be the DCP vector when the rth labeled sample $X_r$ is presented to the trainer and $p_i(r+1)$ represent the final value of the DCP vector at the end of the rth step of the learning algorithm executed with the training sample $X_r$. Within the rth learning step, the DCP vector is iteratively modified till condition (4) is satisfied. The procedure adopted for the iterative modification within the rth learning step is given below --

PROCEDURE SLA

$$l_r:=0;$$
if $X_r \in {}_fC_i$ and $[p_i^T(r)\cdot\tilde{d}_i(X_r)] > a_i$ then

L1:    while $[p_i^T(r+1)\cdot\tilde{d}_i(X_r)] \leqslant a_i$ do
   $l_r:=l_r+1;$
   for $j=1, M$ do
     $p_{ij}(r+1):=|p_{ij}(r)-l_r\nu\tilde{d}_{ij}(X_r)|;$
   od;
  od;
 else
   if $X_r \in {}_fC_i$ and $|p_i^T(r)\cdot\tilde{d}_i(X_r)| < b_i$ then

L2:    while $[p_i^T(r+1)\cdot\tilde{d}_i(X_r)] \geqslant b$ do
   $l_r:=l_r+1;$
   for $j=1, M$ do
     $p_{ij}(r+1):=|p_{ij}(r)+l_r\nu\tilde{d}_{ij}(X_r)|;$
   od;
  od;
 else $p_i(r+1):=p_i(r);$
 fi;
fi;

In the above procedure $\nu$ is a real valued scalar factor. We have shown earlier [1] that upper limit of $\nu$ needs some restriction for $l_r$ to be finite in the loops shown above.

The value of $\nu$ needs to be less than $\operatorname*{Min}_i \left| \dfrac{a_i}{\hat{d}_i} \right|$, where

$$\hat{d}_i = \operatorname*{Max}_{X_r \in C_i} \sum_{j=1}^{M} [\tilde{d}_{ij}(X_r)]^2.$$

From definition 1 it follows that if
$C_1 \backslash\backslash [C_{j_r} | j_r \in \{1, 2, ... L\}$ and $j_r \neq i]$ , there exists $a_i$, $b_i$, $p_i^*$ such that condition (4) is satisfied. The conditions for convergence of the SLA is stated in the following lemma.

**Lemma 1** [1]: The sequence of $p_i$ (r) generated by the SLA converges to the solution DCP vector $p_i^*$ if --

(a)  $C_i \backslash\backslash C_j$  and
(b)  $R_{ii}$ and $R_{ij}$ are closed, bounded, and convex sets [where $R_{ij}=\{\tilde{d}_i(X) | X \in {}_fC_j \}$; $R_{ij} \subset R^M$ ]
[The interested reader may see the proof in [1] ].

In view of the simple decision criterion (1), we introduce additional constraints on $a_i$ and $b_i$ and it could be easily shown that condition (4) could be rewritten as --

$$\left. \begin{array}{ll} \mu_{C_i}(X) \geq Z_i & \text{for } X \in {}_fC_i \\[2mm] \mu_{C_i}(X) < Z_i & \text{for } X \notin {}_fC_{j_r}, \ j_r \in \{1,2,..,L\} \text{ and } j_r \neq i \end{array} \right\} \qquad (5)$$

where

$$Z_i = \frac{M}{M+a_i\sqrt{M}} = \frac{M}{M+b_i+\theta} \quad [\theta > 0 \text{ is an infinitesimally small quantity }].$$

The condition (5) ensures that the training patterns will be correctly classified when decision criterion (1) is used. The parameter $Z_i$ will be referred to as the *threshold membership value*. So a stricter definition of fuzzy separability is as follows:

**Definition 2**: Two fuzzy subclasses $C_i$ and $C_j$ are fuzzy separable, if there exists a $p^*_i$ such that condition (5) is satisfied for some value of $Z_i$.

## 4. Hierarchical Partitioning of the Feature Space

The notion of hierarchical partitioning of feature space is similar to classification methods based on piecewise linear discriminant functions. In the last two sections we have established the condition of separability of pattern classes under consideration and indicated the method for estimating the membership function. But in most realistic situations (for $L \leq 3$), it is not possible to achieve such distinct partitioning of the feature space. In such cases it becomes necessary to hierarchically partition the feature space. The principle could be best illustrated by a simple example involving three fuzzy pattern classes $C_1$, $C_2$ and $C_3$. Let us assume the following conditions --

(i) $C_1 \setminus\!\setminus C_2$; $C_2 \setminus\!\setminus C_3$ and $C_1 \setminus\!\setminus C_3$

(ii) $C_1 \setminus\!\setminus (C_2 \cup C_3)$; $C_2 \setminus\!\setminus (C_1 \cup C_3)$ and $C_3 \setminus\!\setminus (C_1 \cup C_2)$.

In such a situation it is possible to estimate $\mu_1$ and $Z_1$ that establishes the separability of $C_1$ and $C_2$. For an input pattern $(X \in_f C_2)$ we could decide whether it belongs to $\{C_1 \cup C_3\}$ or $\{C_2 \cup C_3\}$, using $\mu_1$ and $Z_1$. In this case it will be classified to the group $\{C_2 \cup C_3\}$. Similarly it is possible to estimate $\mu_2$, $Z_2$ (as $C_1 \setminus\!\setminus C_3$) and $\mu_3$, $Z_3$ (as $C_2 \setminus\!\setminus C_3$. Thus the pattern X can be now classified using $\mu_3$, $Z_3$. The example demonstrates that in most realistic situations, where hierarchical partitioning is required, it is necessary to construct binary decision trees, where a membership function $\mu_i$ and a decision threshold $Z_i$ will be associated with each node of the tree.

Due to brevity of presentation, we will not present the algorithm used to form the multilevel binary decision tree for an L class problem. But is is quite obvious that if the SLA is used to establish the conditions of separability and estimation of $\mu_i$ and $Z_i$, it becomes computationally non trivial for any real life problem where L is reasonably large.

### 4.1. Fuzzy Clustering

To reduce the complexity of the problem the proposed classifier forms L fuzzy clusters based on unit DCP vectors and then the SLA is used to form the decision trees for each of these clusters. A large training set (with equal number of representatives from each of the L classes) is used to form the fuzzy clusters. The DCP vector is considered to be a unit vector and the training patterns are classified according to the decision function (1).

The result of classification is used to form a confusion matrix CF. The diagonal elements $CF_{i,i}$ represent the percentage of training samples labeled $T_i$ that were correctly classified as members of class $C_i$. Similarly an entry $CF_{i,l}$ $(i \neq l)$ represents the percentage of labeled samples $T_i$ that were incorrectly classified as members of class $C_l$. A column labeled $C_l$ of the matrix is used to form the fuzzy cluster $C'_l$. The training patterns belonging to this cluster are the patterns of class $C_l$ that were correctly recognized and the patterns of all the other classes that were misclassified to be members of class $C_l$. Thus $C'_l = \bigcup_{i=1}^{L} C_i^l$, where $C_i^l$ represents the training patterns of $C_i$ classified as members of lth class. The decision trees $DT_i$'s are formed for each of these fuzzy clusters $C'_l$.

The complexity of the construction of the decision tree is greatly reduced as we will be forming L decision trees. Moreover, the condition of fuzzy separability needs to be established for fewer classes in a cluster $C'_l$, as typically the number of confusing classes in the cluster will be much less than L.

## 5. The Syntactic Phase

In the last three sections we described the the principle underlying the design of the first phase of the classifier. The design process clearly indicates the steps involved in the hierarchical complexity decomposition.

In the first phase of classification, an unknown pattern is assigned a decision tree $DT_l$ if $\mu_{C_l}(X) = \underset{i}{Max} [\mu_{C_i}(X)]$, using unit DCP vectors in the membership function. Now the decision tree is used for final classification. When it so happens that a leaf of the decision tree has more than one class associated with it, an unknown pattern reaching that leaf cannot be further classified. We introduce a syntactic recognizer phase of the classifier to solve the above mentioned problem. In general it is not necessary to consider the complete pattern for syntactic analysis. A zone in the feature frame is selected that reflects structural dissimilarities of the pattern classes under confusion.

We consider the leaves of the decision trees are numbered from left to right and $LF(i,n)$ is the $n$th leaf of the decision tree $DT_i$. Now we associate a set of grammars $G(i,n)$ with the leaf $LF(i,n)$. If the leaf $LF(i,n)$ is associated with m subclasses, then we derive $(m-1)$ distinct grammars for the leaf under consideration. The grammar corresponding to the subclass $C_i^j$ associated with the $n$th leaf is denoted as $GC_i^j(n)$.

If, in the first phase of the classifier, an input pattern reaches a leaf $LF(i,n)$ associated with m subclasses, a prespecified zone of the pattern is encoded as a string of syntactic pattern primitives and the string is parsed with respect to the set of grammars $G(i,n)$. If the string gets correctly parsed using the grammar $GC_i^j$, then the input pattern is classified to be a member of the class $C_i$.

## 6. A Fuzzy Hybrid Model for Recognition of Handprinted Devanagri

In this section we present the design of a hybrid classifier based on the principles discussed in the earlier sections. The pattern classes under consideration are 35 of the most commonly occurring characters of the Devanagri alphabet. As shown in figure 1, each of the 35 characters have been assigned labels $T_1$, $T_2$ ... $T_{35}$. The fuzzy pattern class associated with the labeled sample $T_i$ will be denoted as $C_i$ $(i = 1 ... 35)$.

### 6.1. Phase I

As the aim of the approach is to decompose the problem of recognition into simple subproblems, an extremely simple feature extraction procedure is adopted. The measurement grid with equally spaced reference axes are shown in figure 2(a). Each of the 24 reference axes is further subdivided into five equal parts by concentric circles of increasing radii. The number of intersections of a pattern on an axis is considered as the feature of that pattern in that particular axis of measurement. The points of intersections of the circles with the axes of measurement are considered as the reference points. Due to resolution restrictions, more than one intersections of the pattern and a reference axis between two consecutive reference points on that axis is considered to be a single intersection. Hence, the maximum number of intersections that contribute to the feature measurement on that axis is limited to five. Figure 2(b) and 2(c) shows a character type $T_8$ and the corresponding feature vector respectively.

Figure 1: 35 characters of the Devanagri Alphabet.

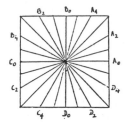

Figure 2a.

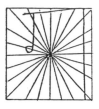

Figure 2b.

$$\overset{A_o}{\underset{}{}} \qquad \overset{B_o}{\underset{}{}} \qquad \overset{C_o}{\underset{}{}} \qquad \overset{D_o}{\underset{}{}} \qquad {}^T$$
$$\left[ 1,1,1,1,1,1,1,1,2,1,1,2,1,0,0,0,0,0,0,0,0,1,1,1 \right]^T$$

Figure 2c.

Altogether 600 handwritten data sheets were collected from writers in the age group of 15-50 years. Out of these 70% was found to be satisfactory. From the satisfactory data sheets 200 samples of each of the 35 classes were randomly selected for design of the classifier and the remaining samples were used for testing the classifier. The training sample set and the test sample set were exclusive of each other. The details of constraints for data collection and feature extraction are not included in this paper [2].

### 6.1.1. The Membership Function

The forms of the membership function and the total similarity measure used in the classifier design are as shown in equations (2) and (3). In the present context, the similarity measure $d_{ij}(X)$ along each axis is defined as --

$$\tilde{d}_{ij}(X) = \underset{\forall k \in N}{\text{Min}} \; |d^i_j(x_j, k)|,$$

where k is the number of intersections and $N = \{0,1,...5\}$. (Note: The set N depends on resolution of the scanner) As suggested in [7], we incorporate some available statistical information in the similarity measure. The following choice of the function $d^i_j : N \times N \rightarrow R^+$ was found to be suitable --

$$d^i_j(0,0) = [1/f^i_j(0)] - 1$$
$$d^i_j(0,k) = [k/f^i_j(k)] \qquad \text{for } k \neq 0 \text{ and } k \in N \qquad\qquad (6)$$
$$d^i_j(n,k) = |n*w_k - k| \qquad \text{for } n, k \in N$$

In (6), the function $f^i_j : N \rightarrow [0, 1]$ determines the relative frequency of intersections on the $j$th axis for the $i$th class. The relative frequencies are obtained from 200 samples of each class. The factor $w_k$ is defined as --

$$w_k = f^i_j(k) \quad \text{if } |n*f^i_j(k) - k| \leq |n-k|$$
$$\text{otherwise} \quad w_k = [1/f^i_j(k)] \qquad\qquad (7)$$

The above choice reflects the fact that the similarity measure primarily depends on the relative frequency of intersections. It is so chosen that

$$d^i_j(x_j, k) \geq |x_j - k| \quad \text{and} \quad \{d^i_j(x_j - k) - |x_j - k|\} \text{ increases}$$

as the relative frequency of k intersections on the $j$th axis for the $i$th class decreases.

## 6.1.2. Fuzzy Clustering

In this stage of the design the membership function is used with unit DCP vectors and the training patterns are classified according to the decision criterion (1). The result of classification is collected as a 35X35 confusion matrix. As the matrix is large we show some example compressed columns of the matrix in figure 3. Only those elements that are greater than 2 are included in the compressed column vector. As explained in section 4.1, 35 fuzzy clusters are formed using the columns of the confusion matrix. It should be noted that in the above process of classification, the training patterns that form a particular subclass in the fuzzy cluster are precisely known.

As shown in figure 3, the fuzzy cluster $C'_{12}$ consists of the subclasses $C_{12}{}^{12}$, $C_{19}{}^{12}$, $C_{20}{}^{12}$ and $C_{32}{}^{12}$. Similarly the cluster $C'_6$ consists of seven different subclasses.

$$
\underline{T6} \qquad\qquad \underline{T12} \qquad\qquad \underline{T35}
$$

$$
\begin{bmatrix}
(T1) & 13 \\
(T6) & 83 \\
(T7) & 15 \\
(T26) & 25 \\
(T27) & 7 \\
(T30) & 7 \\
(T32) & 5
\end{bmatrix}
\qquad
\begin{bmatrix}
(T12) & 72 \\
(T19) & 20 \\
(T20) & 7 \\
(T32) & 5
\end{bmatrix}
\qquad
\begin{bmatrix}
(T7) & 8 \\
(T24) & 15 \\
(T26) & 10 \\
(T27) & 10 \\
(T30) & 5 \\
(T32) & 25 \\
(T33) & 12 \\
(T35) & 83
\end{bmatrix}
$$

Figure 3.

## 6.2. Generation of Decision Trees

The principle of hierarchical partitioning of the feature space was discussed in section 4. The SLA is used to estimate the $\mu_i$'s and $Z_i$'s for separating the subclasses in the fuzzy clusters $C'_1$'s. Actually various $Z_i$'s are selected over the range $[0 , 1]$ for estimating the DCP vectors with repeated cycling (10 cycles in this experiment) of the training set. Finally the threshold membership value is estimated using a least square error criterion [2].

The decision tree $DT_{12}$ corresponding to the cluster $C'_{12}$ is shown in figure 4. It may be observed that at node 1.1, it is only possible to establish the fuzzy separability of the subclass $C_{12}{}^{12}$ with subclasses $C_{20}{}^{12}$ and $C_{32}{}^{12}$ [i.e., $C_{12}{}^{12} \backslash\backslash \{ C_{20}{}^{12} , C_{32}{}^{12}\}$. Hence, as discussed in section 4, the subclass $C_{19}{}^{12}$ is included in both the nodes 1.1 and 1.2.

Once the complete set of decision trees was obtained, the design of the first phase of the classifier was complete. Altogether 27 decision trees had to be generated, out of which 13 trees were of two or three levels. Maximum number of subclasses found in any fuzzy cluster was 9 for $C'_{14}$, follwed by 8 subclasses for $C'_{35}$ and 7 subclasses for $C'_6$.

It was found that five of these decision trees [ $DT_i$ for $i = 6,9,13,14,35$ ] had more than one subclass associated with some of the leaf nodes. For instance, $DT_{35}$ had leaf node associated with the subclasses $C_{32}{}^{35}$ and $C_{35}{}^{35}$. As mentioned earlier, existence of a leaf node with more than one subclass associated with it implies that the classes are not fuzzy separable. The phase 2 of the classifier was designed to classify those patterns that reach leaves of the decision trees with more than one subclass associated with them. In the second phase syntactic classification is done using structural differences of those patterns in a specific zone of the feature frame.

## 6.3. Phase II of the Classifier

In this phase we consider only a particular zone of the patterns (under confusion) that reflect structural differences. For simplicity, we restrict ourselves to the zone between reference axes $C_0$ to

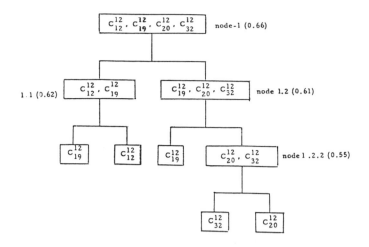

**Figure 4: Decision tree DT$_{12}$**

$D_0$ ($90^c$) as shown in figure 5(a). A different set of features (pattern primitives) is used in this phase. The set of linguistic pattern primitives ( $t_1$, $t_2$,...., $t_8$ ) is shown in figure ... the primitives were defined between adjacent *reference points* (cf. phase I). We have adopted a variation of Freeman's chain coding [4] scheme to encode the portion of the pattern in the specified zone to strings of primitives. The search for the starting point of the trace was always performed from the outer boundary of the reference frame starting from the axis $C_0$ and following the order $C_0$ , $C_1$ ,...,$D_0$. The coding of the string started with the trace and terminated for either of the following conditions :

(a) a discontinuity in the path is found,

(b) trace reaches the boundary of the zone,
(c) traces reaches a junction point which has already been traversed.
An example encoding is shown in figure 5(b).

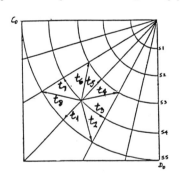

Figure 5a.

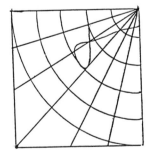

Figure 5b.

## 6.4. Syntactic Analysis in Phase II

As discussed in section 5, learning in this phase corresponds to inference of grammars $G(i , n)$ using the training patterns that reach the leaf $LF(i , n)$ of the decision tree $DT_i$. A novel grammatical inference procedure based on some results on the equivalence of rational and recognizable formal power series was used in this phase [3]. The description of the inference procedure is beyond the scope of this paper.

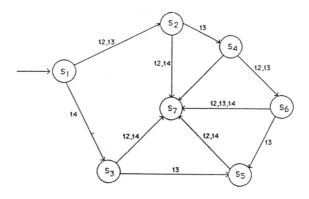

**Figure 6:  The DFSA for G(35,2).**

As an example, we will consider the decision tree $DT_{35}$. The only leaf that is associated with more than one subclass is the leaf LF(35,2). The subclasses associated with the leaf are $C_{32}{}^{35}$ and $C_{35}{}^{35}$ . In this case the set G(35,2) consists of only one generative regular grammar that corresponds to the subclass $C_{32}{}^{35}$ (for the specified zone). The strings that are used to infer G(35,2) are as follows:

{ $t_1t_2t_3$ , $t_4t_3t_2$ , $t_2t_3t_3$ , $t_3t_3t_2$ , $t_2t_3t_2$ }.

The deterministic finite state automaton (DFSA) inferred from these strings is shown in figure 6.

Similarly sets of DFSA's were inferred that were associated with the decision trees $DT_i$ [ i = 6, 13, 14, 17]. Altogether nine different DFSA's had to be inferred that corresponded to the grammars --- $GC_1^6$ , $GC_{26}^6$ , $GC_{32}^6$ , $GC_7^{13}$ , $GC_7^{14}$ , $GC_{21}^{14}$ , $GC_{18}^{17}$ and $GC_{32}^{35}$ .

The classification process in this phase is best explained using an example. Let us consider an input pattern which gets assigned to $DT_{35}$ (in the first phase of classification) reaches the leaf LF(35,2) of the decision tree. In the second phase, a coded string of the input pattern (in the zone $C_0$---$D_0$) is obtained and is presented to the automaton corresponding to the grammar $GC_{32}^{35}$. If the string is accepted, the input pattern is classified to be a member of the class $C_{32}$, otherwise it is classified as a member of the class $C_{35}$. A similar logic holds for leaves with more than two classes. In fact, in the present experiment, maximum number of subclasses associated with any of the leaves was only three.

## 7. Results

Once the classifier was designed, two hundred more samples of each class were presented for recognition. The percentage of correct recognition for each of the 35 classes is shown on Table I.

The performance of the classifier was found to be reasonably good for all the character types except $T_{21}$ and $T_{30}$. The low values for the recognition rate for these two classes is due to the fact that the syntactic analysis was not effective for the subclasses $C_{21}^9$ and $C_{30}^9$ associated with LF(9,4). The syntactic analysis would have been effective if the zone between the axes $B_0$ and $C_0$ (90°) were considered.

## References

[1]  P. Biswas and A. K. Majumdar, "A Supervised Learning Algorithm for Hierarchical Classification of Fuzzy Patterns," Information Sciences, Vol. 30, No. 2, 1984.

[2]  P. Biswas, "A Fuzzy Hybrid Model for Pattern Classification with Application to Recognition of Handprinted Devanagari," Ph.D. Dissertation, Jawaharlal Nehru Univ., New Delhi, 1981.

[3] P. Biswas and A. K. Majumdar, "Synthesis of Minimal DFSA for a Finite Sample: A Formal Power Series Approach," (submitted) available as Technical Report 87-CSE-23, Dept. of Computer Science, SMU, Dallas, TX.

[4] K. S. Fu, "Syntactic Pattern Recognition and Applications," Prentice Hall, 1982.

[5] L. N. Kanal and B. Chandrasekharan, "On Linguistic, Statistical and Mixed Models for Pattern Recognition," in Frontiers of Pattern Recognition, Academic Press, 1972.

[6] Abraham Kandel, "Fuzzy Techniques in Pattern Recognition," John Wiley, 1982.

[7] A. Kandel and W. J. Byatt, "Fuzzy Sets, Fuzzy Algebra and Fuzzy Statistics," Proc. IEEE, Vol. 66, No. 12, Dec. 1978.

[8] J. Mantas, "Methodologies in Pattern Recognition and Image Analysis -- A Brief Survey," Pattern Recognition, Vol. 20, No. 1, 1987.

[9] S. K. Pal and D. K. Dutta Majumdar, "Fuzzy Mathematical Approach to Pattern Recognition," John Wiley (Eastern), 1986.

[10] L. A. Zadeh et al. (Eds.), "Fuzzy Sets and Their Application to Cognitive and Decision Process," Academic Press, 1975.

| Pattern Class | Correct Recognition (%) | Pattern Class | Correct Recognition (%) |
|---|---|---|---|
| $c_1$ | 91 | $c_{19}$ | 90 |
| $c_2$ | 94 | $c_{20}$ | 87 |
| $c_3$ | 94 | $c_{21}$ | 74 |
| $c_4$ | 92 | $c_{22}$ | 93 |
| $c_5$ | 89 | $c_{23}$ | 89 |
| $c_6$ | 94 | $c_{24}$ | 93 |
| $c_7$ | 91 | $c_{25}$ | 92 |
| $c_8$ | 89 | $c_{26}$ | 86 |
| $c_9$ | 91 | $c_{27}$ | 88 |
| $c_{10}$ | 92 | $c_{28}$ | 89 |
| $c_{11}$ | 89 | $c_{29}$ | 86 |
| $c_{12}$ | 90 | $c_{30}$ | 76 |
| $c_{13}$ | 90 | $c_{31}$ | 87 |
| $c_{14}$ | 88 | $c_{32}$ | 85 |
| $c_{15}$ | 90 | $c_{33}$ | 88 |
| $c_{16}$ | 86 | $c_{34}$ | 86 |
| $c_{17}$ | 94 | $c_{35}$ | 92 |
| $c_{18}$ | 89 | | |

Table I:  Recognition Results.

# ON THE ROLE OF PATTERN IN RECOGNIZER DESIGN

Timothy D. Ross
Air Force Wright Aeronautical Laboratories
(AFWAL/AART-2)
Wright Patterson AFB, Ohio 45433

Prof. Alan V. Lair
Air Force Institute of Technology (AFIT/ENC)
Wright Patterson AFB, Ohio 45433

## Abstract

Recognizer design is well established as an engineering
discipline.  Pattern is widely appreciated as a common sense idea.
However there is a lack of consensus on the technical meaning of
pattern in recognizer design.  As a step towards a more generally
acceptable concept of pattern, we wish to address the role of patterns
in this engineering problem.  To begin, we develop the literal
meanings of pattern.  We especially distinguish the uses to which
pattern is put and the objects to which pattern is applied.  One use
of pattern is as a class of objects.  The other use is as a
description of the order in an object.  Objects of interest in the
recognition design problem include measurements, class-labels,
measurement into class-label mappings and sets of such mappings.  The
different uses of pattern and the different objects to which pattern
applies can be combined to form the various literal meanings of pattern
recognition.  One of the literal meanings (measurement classification)
basically matches its use in reference to traditional recognition
machines.  However the various literal meanings are quite autonomous
and a different interpretation (description of the measurement to
class-label mapping) is much more practically consequential.

## INTRODUCTION

Recognizer design is about constructing machines that map large
(possibly infinite) sets that we call "measurements" into small (always
finite) sets we call "class-labels", when the dominant factor is the
pattern-ness of this mapping.  [1] clarified this measurement into
class-label mapping concept and we use it here in exactly the same
sense.  But what is "pattern-ness"?  Watanabe [2] provides a recent
discussion of many of the views of pattern.  Some more frequent
interpretations are based on similarity, structure, reductionism, or

simplicity.

However there is no widely accepted technical view of pattern.
The word pattern has become almost vestigial in some modern recognizer
design contexts, e.g.[3], it is simply the object to be recognized.
Most engineering Pattern Recognition texts do not define pattern in
isolation.  For example, in a survey of 31 engineering Pattern
Recognition books, all having "pattern" in their title, only 5 had the
isolated word "pattern" in their indices.  Those that do treat
"pattern" as an isolated concept, tend to do so as part of a
philosophically oriented introduction rather than as a basis for
technical developments.

However we believe the concept of pattern has a special role to
play in recognition.  That is, "pattern recognition" is different from
just "recognition".  This paper explores this special role.  While we
stop short of proposing a technical definition of pattern, we hope to
contribute to a more precise use of this very important concept in the
engineering Pattern Recognition context.

For this paper we want to use pattern in the general sense of
regularity, order, or structure.  In the near future we will propose a
more formal definition of pattern along these lines [4] and argue that
the traditional views are special cases of this.  However, for now, we
take this view without special justification, consider it a common
sense view of pattern if you will.  Watanabe [2] used pattern in this
sense when mentioning iron filings in the presence of a magnet.
Garner [5] used pattern in this sense in his ink blot versus geometric
figure example.

COMMON SENSE PATTERNS

There is a common sense idea of pattern, especially to those
outside the Pattern Recognition community (the study of Pattern
Recognition seems to lead one to a more specific but less essential
view).  Garner exploited this common sense idea of pattern in
experiments involving visual and auditory stimuli.  Without prior
training in what a pattern is, Garner's subjects were able to rate the
pattern-ness of the various stimuli with high consistency [5,p.188].

There is a significant gray area between patterns and non-patterns
with respect to this common sense view.  This is helped somewhat by
comparing the pattern-ness of two objects rather than classifying them
absolutely as patterned or non-patterned.  However we will also carefully construct the examples to avoid this gray area.  That is, highly
patterned examples will be compared to highly unpatterned examples.

Our common sense notion of pattern includes an expectation of
certain practical consequences.  For people, patterns are easier to
recognize, learn, remember, etc.  We expect similar practical
consequences for machine processing of patterns.

As indicated in [6], having to list all the elements is the
essence of an unpatterned set.    We are reminded of this fundamental
role of pattern when we consider a problem which is not patterned.
For example, suppose we are given recent U.S. census results, then asked
to build a classification algorithm to map social security numbers (the
measurements) into whether or not the individual resides east or west
of the Mississippi River (the class-label).    The lack of pattern-ness
limits us to a brute force table look-up.    Contrast this with
classifying the same set of numbers into even and odd.    Here a very
simple algorithm will perform the exact classification.    Clearly the
presence or absence of patterns fundamentally determines our approach
to a problem.    Friedman[7], in discussing Switching Theory, refers to
patterned functions as "modular".

KINDS OF OBJECTS
    "A pattern is, by definition, a complex of n things, where n is a
number greater than or occasionally equal to 2."[8,p6].    [2,p137] also
notes that patterns are important "in a system consisting of partial
subsystems."    Therefore we limit our consideration of pattern to
objects with parts.    That is, some internal structure is necessary
before an object can be a pattern.
    What kinds of objects do we want to consider as possibly
patterned?    Our engineering problem is about mapping measurement into
class-labels.    This suggests three object types: measurements, class-
labels, and measurement into class-label mappings.    In order to show
mappings as elements in a pattern, we consider collections of
measurement into class-label mappings as a fourth object type.    This
fourth object is practically important for a multi-purpose system, that
is, a single machine which will (in different configurations) represent
any one of a set of mappings.    In this case, the relationship of our
mapping to other mappings in the set (i.e. inter-mapping) may be as
important as the internal (i.e. intra-mapping) pattern-ness of our
mapping.
    For each of the four object types we will identify the whole and
the parts, give examples and explore the relationship between the
objects as concerns their pattern-ness.

Patterned                Unpatterned
Figure 1   Measurements

The first object is the measurement.    Virtually all kinds of
measurements are used in Pattern Recognition (especially images and

audio signals).   The "whole" measurement is the entire input to the
algorithm which computes a class-label.    The parts of a measurement
depend on the type of measurement (e.g. a digitized image may have
pixel parts).    We can demonstrate that individual measurements may be
patterned with examples.    The left measurement in Figure 1 is more
patterned (based on the common sense view) than the right measurement.
This is similar to the first kind of seeing-one-in-many [2,p16].

    The second object we consider is a class (intra-class or inter-
measurement patterns).    "Class" is nearly as loaded with imprecise
meaning as "pattern" [2], however for our purposes we may completely
characterize a class by the set of measurements we wish to associate
with that class-label.    The "whole" in this case is the set of measurements and the "parts" are the various individual measurements belonging to that class.    Again we illustrate patterned and unpatterned
classes with examples.    We would probably say the left class of Figure
2 is more patterned (i.e. the class of even numbers less than 20) than
the right class.    Notice the individual measurements in either of
these classes do not have parts (allow us to consider the two digit
numbers as single symbols), therefore are unpatterned.

        {2,4,6,8,10,12,14,16,18}    {1,2,4,8,9,10,13,15,18}


            Patterned                    Unpatterned
                Figure 2   Classes


    The third object is the entire measurement into class-label
mapping (intra-mapping or inter-class patterns).    The "whole" is the
set of ordered pairs that is the mapping.    The parts are the
individual ordered pairs.    The examples (Figure 3) which illustrate
patterned and unpatterned mappings have integer measurements; thus
again, the individual measurements are not patterned.    Similarly the
individual classes have only a single measurement, thus are also
unpatterned.    This is similar to the second kind of seeing-one-in-many
[2,p16].

| m | f(m) |   | m | f(m) |
|---|------|---|---|------|
| 1 | 1    |   | 1 | 7    |
| 2 | 4    |   | 2 | 9    |
| 3 | 9    |   | 3 | 14   |
| 4 | 16   |   | 4 | 27   |
| 5 | 25   |   | 5 | 32   |

        Patterned                    Unpatterned
                Figure 3   Mappings

The final object we consider is a set of measurement to class-label mappings (inter-mapping patterns). The "whole" for this object is the set of mappings and the "parts" are the individual mappings. Figure 4 exemplifies a patterned set of mappings (i.e. $f_{i+1}(x) = f_i(x)+1$, all addition modulo 4) and an unpatterned set. As before the constituent elements (mappings in this case) are individually unpatterned.

| m | f0 | f1 | f2 | f3 |
|---|----|----|----|----|
| 0 | 0  | 1  | 2  | 3  |
| 1 | 2  | 3  | 0  | 1  |
| 2 | 3  | 0  | 1  | 2  |
| 3 | 1  | 2  | 3  | 0  |

| m | f0 | f1 | f2 | f3 |
|---|----|----|----|----|
| 0 | 3  | 0  | 2  | 1  |
| 1 | 2  | 3  | 1  | 0  |
| 2 | 0  | 1  | 3  | 3  |
| 3 | 1  | 2  | 0  | 2  |

Patterned                              Unpatterned

Figure 4   Set of Mappings

OBJECT RELATIONS

Notice each of these objects may be patterned without implying the constituent elements are patterned. In the intra-class example, the individual measurements were not patterned. In the intra-mapping example, the individual measurements and classes were not patterned. In the inter-mapping example, the individual mappings were not patterned. Clearly, constituent element pattern-ness is not necessary for the parent object to be patterned.

| measurements | class f | g |
|---|---|---|
| | A | 5 |
| | A | 3 |
| ⋮ | ⋮ | ⋮ |
| | A | 8 |
| | B | 2 |
| ⋮ | ⋮ | ⋮ |
| | Z | 6 |

Figure 5   Mappings on Patterned Measurements

It is possible (even common) for patterned constituents to be a factor in the pattern-ness of the parent object. For example, the measurements of Figure 5 are patterned and this is connected with the pattern-ness of the mapping f.

However also notice that patterned constituents are not a sufficient condition for a patterned parent object. For example, the measurements of Figure 5 are patterned, but the mapping (g) based on these, is not patterned.

Since a class is effectively a subset of a measurement to class-label mapping, there is a certain necessary relation between the pattern-ness of these two. However, in general, the pattern-ness of constituent parts is neither necessary nor sufficient for the pattern-ness of the parent object. This statement with measurements as parts and the measurement to class-label mapping as the parent object is especially relevant to the role of pattern in traditional recognizer design. That is, patterned measurements are neither necessary nor sufficient for a patterned measurement to class-label mapping.

## USE OF PATTERN

Pattern is most commonly used in engineering texts in the sense of a template or a mold, e.g.[3,9,10]. This is a special case of the more general concept we are discussing, see [2,11].

We will identify two distinct uses of "pattern", both of which are semantically based on the common sense idea of pattern.

The first use of pattern is as a patterned object. This is exemplified by a statement like "{0,1,1,2,3,5,8,13,21} is a pattern". The object itself is declared to be a pattern. In this case, a pattern is an element of the class of highly patterned objects. "Is a pattern" can be read "is a patterned object". This sense of pattern is defined in terms of patterned; we rely on the common sense idea to give meaning to patterned. For this use of pattern, pattern recognition is the same as classification. That is, to recognize a pattern is to recognize an object (which happens to be a pattern) or to classify the object.

The second use of pattern is as a statement of the order in an object, which we call pattern description. Pattern is used in this sense in the question "what is the pattern in {0,1,1,2,3,5,8,13,21}?". An acceptable answer to this question might be "$x(i+1)=x(i)+x(i-1)$". Here we are interested in a statement of the underlying structure or order of the object in question. The pattern is a description of this structure. Again we rely on the common sense view of pattern to give meaning to structure and order. For this use of pattern, pattern recognition is the discovery of the underlying order or structure in an object. That is, pattern recognition is the process of finding the patterned quality of an object.

Unlike a patterned object, pattern description is distinct from the object. For example, {0,1,1,2,3,5,8,13,21} is not a pattern in the pattern description sense, rather "$x(i+1)=x(i)+x(i-1)$" is the pattern of {0,1,1,2,3,5,8,11,21}. Also notice the above sequence and

{0,2,2,4,6,10,16,26,42} are distinct as patterned objects (i.e. distinct objects), but have the same pattern description. Patterned object and pattern description are two distinct uses of the common sense notion of pattern.

## LITERAL PATTERN RECOGNITION

Having laid out these two aspects of pattern, we can now characterize what it literally means to recognize a pattern. There are eight possible meanings of pattern (four objects by two uses). Therefore, we can talk about the measurements being patterned, or we can talk about the description of how the measurements are patterned, or we can talk about a class being patterned, etc. The meaning of pattern recognition depends on the sense of pattern we are using and the kind of object involved.

We want to focus on two particular points in this space of pattern use. One point, we think reflects closely the traditional perspective of recognition machines. Without diminishing the practical importance of traditional recognizers, we feel a second, quite distinct, point reflects the fundamental pattern recognition problem.

The first point has measurements as the object types and uses pattern in the sense of a patterned object, i.e. the measurement classification (measurement object, patterned object use) point. This is the sense of pattern recognition most often used in engineering Pattern Recognition texts, e.g.[3,12,13]. In fact, pattern and measurement are used almost synonymously in these texts. This seems to be the sense in which most pattern recognition machines are referred to. Taking character recognition as an example, the measurements are patterned objects (as in Figure 1) and the machine recognizes the measurements. In this sense of pattern recognition, machine pattern recognition is the product of the engineering problem. Machine pattern recognition is a reality in this sense.

The other special point in our literal pattern recognition space is the mapping description (measurement to class-label mapping object, pattern description use) point. Here we interpret pattern recognition to mean the process of finding a description of the pattern in the measurement to class-label mapping. Consider the "realization problem" of recognizer design [1]. Finding a pattern description is analogous to finding a low cost realization. Therefore this sense of literal pattern recognition is important in the design of a recognition machine, and not in its operation. That is, pattern recognition is an integral part of making these machines, but the machine itself does not do pattern recognition. Human designers are primarily responsible for pattern recognition in this sense. Of course we do have analytical and machine procedures for constructing parts of recognizers. However, the Pattern Recognition engineer's most important tools are the innate human abilities. For example, there are analytical tools for pruning a set of features, but initial definition of the features depends largely upon unassisted human decisions. Similarly, there are off-the-shelf parsers. However, the definition of the primitives (and of course the decision to use a syntactic description in the first place) depends on non-analytical human abilities. Therefore, machine pattern recognition is not a reality in the mapping description sense.

## CONCLUSION

Pattern is a special state of affairs which has important practical consequences. Pattern has a number of interpretations, all based on this special character. Two of these interpretations are especially relevant to the engineering discipline of recognizer design.

The interpretation most prevalent in the engineering field is what we called measurement classification (measurement object, patterned object use). While this is one of the correct literal interpretations, is it consistent with our common sense idea of pattern? That is, does pattern-ness in this sense ensure the existence of a classification algorithm better than a brute force table look-up? To demonstrate that it does not, consider one of the standard engineering problems, character recognition. We know there are patterns here of the practically important kind. Assume the patterns of importance are intra-measurement patterns. Now consider a different mapping using the exact same measurement set. If the assumption is true, then this second mapping has the practically important patterns, even if it is a random association of measurements and class-labels (as in g of Figure 5). That is, the measurements are unchanged, thus the intra-measurement pattern-ness is unchanged. However the patterns we were to exploit for pattern recognition do not exist in the second mapping. We would be forced to use a table look-up to recognize these "patterns". Therefore intra-measurement patterns are not the patterns of importance.

This contrasts the other literal interpretation, mapping description (measurement to class-label mapping object, pattern description use), which is exactly the pattern-ness whose recognition is of practical importance. That is, recognition of a pattern (in the pattern description sense) in the measurement to class-label mapping is exactly what we need to solve (and for there to exist a solution to) our engineering problem.

The two interpretations of pattern recognition reflect rather different technical maturities. There exist machines doing pattern recognition in the measurement classification sense. However for pattern recognition in the mapping description sense, we not only do not have machines, but people must do it relying on innate rather than analytical tools.

Finally consider whether or not measurement classification (and most of traditional recognizer design) is extensible to the more practically consequential mapping description problem. We found that measurement pattern-ness is neither necessary nor sufficient for mapping patterns. Also patterned object recognition outputs a label or a single symbol, whereas pattern description outputs a statement in a language. Clearly these are two fundamentally different processes. All this suggests that traditional recognizers are not directly applicable to recognizing patterns in their most practically consequential and essential sense.

## Acknowledgments

We wish to acknowledge Ralph Bryan of AFWAL/AART, Prof. Matthew Kabrisky of AFIT's Electrical Engineering Dept. and Prof. John Jones of AFIT's Mathematics Dept. for the contributions they made through informal discussions and careful review of this paper. We also wish to express appreciation for the continued support of AFWAL/AART managers Arthur Duke and John Jacobs.

## References

[1] T. Ross and A. Lair, "Definition and Realization in Pattern Recognition System Design", Proceedings of the 1987 IEEE International Conference on Systems, Man and Cybernetics, pp.744-748, October 1987.

[2] S. Watanabe, Pattern Recognition: Human and Mechanical, Wiley, New York, 1985.

[3] P. Devijver and J. Kittler, Pattern Recognition: A Statistical Approach, Prentice-Hall, Englewood Cliffs, New Jersey, 1982.

[4] T. Ross, Elementary Properties of Realization Patterns, Air Force Institute of Technology, Wright-Patterson Air Force Base, Ohio, Dissertation(in preparation).

[5] W. Garner, "Good Patterns Have Few Alternatives", Current Trends in Psychology, I. Janis (ed), William Kaufmann Inc., Los Altos, Calif., 1977, pp.185-192.

[6] B. Batchelor (ed), Pattern Recognition: Ideas in Practice, Plenum Press, London, 1978, p.1.

[7] A. Friedman, <u>Fundamentals</u> <u>of</u> <u>Logic</u> <u>Design</u> <u>and</u> <u>Switching</u> <u>Theory</u>, Computer Science Press, Rockville, Maryland, 1986, p.87.

[8] L. Uhr, "Pattern Recognition" in <u>Pattern</u> <u>Recognition</u>, L. Uhr(ed), Wiley, New York, 1966.

[9] J. Bezdek, <u>Pattern</u> <u>Recognition</u> <u>with</u> <u>Fuzzy</u> <u>Objective</u> <u>Function</u> <u>Algorithms</u>, Plenum Press, New York, 1981.

[10] T. Pavlidis, <u>Structural</u> <u>Pattern</u> <u>Recognition</u>, Springer Verlag, New York, 1977.

[11] L. Kanal and B. Chandrasearan, "On linguistic, statistical and mixed models for pattern recognition", <u>Frontiers</u> <u>of</u> <u>Pattern</u> <u>Recognition</u>, S. Watanabe (ed), Academic Press, New York, 1972.

[12] K. Fu, <u>Syntactic</u> <u>Pattern</u> <u>Recognition</u> <u>and</u> <u>Applications</u>, Prentice-Hall, Englewood Cliffs, New Jersey, 1982.

[13] T. Young and K. Fu (eds), <u>Handbook</u> <u>of</u> <u>Pattern</u> <u>Recognition</u> <u>and</u> <u>Image</u> <u>Processing</u>, Academic Press, New York, 1986.

# A STATISTICAL STUDY IN WORD RECOGNITION

F J Smith and C J Clotworthy
Department of Computer Science
The Queen's University of Belfast
Belfast BT7 1NN, Northern Ireland

## 1. INTRODUCTION

Whole word recognisers usually work by comparing the template for an unknown word with a range of templates for words in a stored dictionary [1, 2, 3]. A distance score is produced for each template and a decision is taken on which is the likely word, depending upon the scores. Most recognisers use a minimum distance or closest match criterion to specify the successful word, although some systems extend this and use an ordered list of the best candidates [4].

If the number of words in the dictionary is limited and if they are acoustically diverse, this approach can be quite successful with high recognition scores reported in the literature [2]. This approach for word recognition can also be used for other pattern recognition applications [5].

However, there is one difficulty with scores or distances. Let us assume that a spoken word is compared with three words $w_1$, $w_2$ and $w_3$ in a dictionary, with scores 130, 145 and 190 respectively. Then $w_1$, with the lowest score, is the most probable. What the scores do not tell us, on their own, is a measure of this probability, ie the numerical probability that $w_1$ is correct or indeed the probability that $w_2$ or $w_3$ might be correct. Probability would be much more meaningful than distances to humans and it would also have the major advantage that it can be used in the theoretical development, based on Bayes' rule, which we come to in the next section.

We therefore think it is important to study the problem of obtaining probabilities from a word recogniser rather than simply scores or distances.

## 2. BAYES' RULE

Let $\underline{x}$ be a sample vector representing a word input to a recogniser, and let $\{w_i\}$ represent the set of words in the dictionary. From Bayes' Rule the probability that a particular word $w_i$ is correct, given the signal vector $\underline{x}$, is

$$P(w_i:\underline{x}) = P(w_i).P(\underline{x}:w_i)/P(\underline{x}) \tag{1}$$

where $P(w_i)$ is the probability of $w_i$ being spoken, $P(\underline{x}:w_i)$ is the probability of the recogniser acquiring vector $\underline{x}$ if word $w_i$ was spoken and $P(\underline{x})$ is the probability that $\underline{x}$ was measured. This last value $P(\underline{x})$ is very small, but otherwise it is unknown. However, this is not important as we only wish to compare different values of $P(w_i:\underline{x})$; thus by normalisation we can write

$$P(w_i:\underline{x}) = \frac{P(w_i) \cdot P(\underline{x}:w_i)}{\sum_j P(w_j) \cdot P(\underline{x}:w_j)} \tag{2}$$

The first term, $P(w_i)$ is the probability that $w_i$ is spoken in the environment in which the enunciation is made. If it is taken at random from the dictionary as in a random test of the recogniser, then all words in the dictionary are equally likely and

$$P(w_i) = 1/N \tag{3}$$

for all i where N is the number of words in the dictionary. However, if the word occurs in the middle of a sentence and is preceded by certain words and followed by certain others, then the syntax and semantics of the language used on either side of the spoken word, will determine this environment. In this case the probability $P(w_i)$ will vary a great deal with word $w_i$; for example many words will have a probability of zero because they are not possible grammatically (for example the word 'of' should not follow the word 'the'). Systems have been implemented successfully using statistics on bi-grams or tri-grams, ie sets of two or three words to estimate the probability $P(w_i)$. These have been quite successful [6].

This last approach is clearly the one to adopt for continuous text (and we are studying this in Belfast) but for the limited experiment reported in this paper, we will assume that each word is spoken separately and randomly from our vocabulary of words so that $P(w_i) = 1/N$; thus

$$P(w_i:\underline{x}) = KP(\underline{x}:w_i)/N \tag{4}$$

where K is a normalising constant.   This enables us to study the term P($\underline{x}$:$w_i$) which has not been given much previous attention in the literature, apart from some related work by Cox [7] and a very early conference paper by the authors [8] (this paper corrects and substantially adds to that paper).

## 3.   PROBABILITY DISTRIBUTION

The probability distribution of obtaining any vector $\underline{x}$ for a word $w_i$, can be expressed in terms of a multivariate normal distribution

$$P(\underline{x}|w_i) = (2\pi)^{m/2} \mid C \mid^{-\frac{1}{2}} \exp \left[-\tfrac{1}{2}(\underline{x}-\mu)^T C^{-1}(\underline{x}-\mu)\right] \qquad (5)$$

where m is the dimension of vector $\underline{x}$, $\underline{\mu}$ is its mean value and C is the covariant matrix for the measurements.   This can be reduced to its principle components by writing it in the form

$$P(\underline{x}|w_i) = (2\pi)^{-m/2} \left(\prod_{i=1}^{m} \lambda_i^{-\frac{1}{2}}\right) \exp \left[-\tfrac{1}{2} \Sigma \; y_i^2/\lambda_i\right] \qquad (6)$$

where $\lambda_i$ are the latent roots and $y_i = \underline{v}_i.(\underline{x} - \underline{\mu})$   where $\underline{v}_i$ are the latent vectors.

When we realise that the vector $\underline{x}$ has hundreds and possibly thousands of components and that therefore the covariant matrix C is extremely large, it is clear that it is difficult to use the first of these equations in practice (although attempts have been made to do so [9]). Even the second equation, equation (6), is not amenable to practical computation because of the amount of time required in finding the latent roots and latent vectors.

We have therefore investigated a major simplification of the distribution in terms of the principal components.   We have assumed that the distribution has spherical symmetry in a smaller number of dimensions, that is that the number n of $\lambda_i$ values have all the same value, $\sigma^2$ and that the remainder are all zero.   We make this assumption and then   test the hypotheses to see if it has some validity.

The probability now has the much simpler form of a normal distribution and P($\underline{x}$:$w_i$) is replaced by a simpler function, the probability that a distance is obtained for a particular word, P(d:$w_i$).   This can be written as follows

$$P(d:w_i) = A_n \ d^{n-1} \ \exp \ (-d^2/2 \ \sigma^2) \tag{7}$$

where $\sigma^2$ is the variance and $A_n = \Gamma(n/2)^{-1} \ 2^{1-n/2}/_\sigma \ n$. The extra term $d^{n-1}$ is a dimensional term and must be added as we need to integrate over the hypersphere $\underline{x} - \underline{\mu} = d$ to normalise the equation.

## THE EXPERIMENT

We carried out an experiment to check that a measured distribution function corresponded to the approximate multidimensional Gaussian distribution of Equation (7). It was decided to study the 12 words in table 1 in detail; they were chosen to have as much phonetic diversity as possible and to be mono-syllabic. Each word was spoken by a single speaker 300 times and the sound recorded on a cassette tape. A head worn noise cancelling microphone was used in a quiet environment and to avoid distortion if a word was spoken too many times at one session, the 300 samples of each word were recorded over several sessions and several days.

An isolated word acquisition system was used which consisted of a pre-amplifier with high frequency pre-emphasis, feeding a 16-channel filter bank (based on an LSI device described by Hin et al [10]), sampled by an 8-bit analogue to digital converter every 10 ms. A PDP 11/23 mini-computer was used to store and analyse the word vectors and a simple energy-based word boundary detection algorithm was used to locate word endings. The words were amplitude normalised and sampled in 25 spectral frames for ease of comparison.

Using this computer system a mean word vector was calculated for each of the 12 words and used as a word template. Since there were 16 frequencies and 25 time intervals, the vector consisted of 400 numbers, which were approximated by integers. Distances for each word vector from its mean value were then computed using dynamic time warping (Velichko and Zagoruiko [11]). A distribution table was then formed into a histogram, an example of which is shown in figure 1 for one of the 12 words. The histograms for all the other words looked similar. The histogram was then fitted with a n-dimensional Gaussian distribution formula, as in Equation (7) and values of n and determined. In Table 1 we also give a list of the peak positions and of the values of n and $\sigma$.

## GAMMA DISTRIBUTION

An examination of figure 1 shows that the n-dimensional Gaussian formula fits the histogram fairly well, but there are two discrepancies at the two ends of the distribution at large distances the frequencies represented by the histogram are too high and at short distances, the frequencies are too low. We found these discrepancies in all of the words measured. No combination of n and $\sigma$ could be chosen to correct these distortions. The reason for the distortion was discovered partly by chance.

To investigate a formula which might be faster to compute, we attempted to fit the distribution using the simpler multi-dimensional Gamma distribution function of the form

$$P(d:w_i) \quad = \quad B_n \; d^{n-1} \; \exp \; (-d/\sigma) \tag{8}$$

where $B_n = 1/(n-1)! \; \sigma^n$. We found that we were able to fit the experimental distribution more accurately with this Gamma distribution than with the apparently better theoretical Gaussian formula. This is illustrated in Figure 2.

The reason can be explained by reference to Figure 1 where we have also shown the more common one-dimensional Gaussian distribution function;

$$P = A_1 \; \exp \; (-d^2/2\sigma^2) \tag{9}$$

where the value of $\sigma$ is chosen to be the same as for the multi-dimensional curve on the same graph.

It can be seen that this new distribution has already fallen close to zero at values of $\sigma$ where most of the contribution comes to the n-dimensional distribution. That most of the contribution comes from large d is a dimensional effect because of the large volume of n-dimensional hyper-space at large values of d. However, this means that the Gaussian formula is only being used in its far wing which is not used in most experiments, and thus our common assumption and experience of the validity of a Gaussian distribution may not apply.

The correct distribution for a finite number of measurements is the Student distribution [13]; the Gaussian distribution is widely used only because it is a good approximation to the Student distribution, and easier to calculate.  The Student distribution has the form

$$\text{Stu}(t) = C_f (1 + t^2/f)^{-(f+1)/2} \qquad (10)$$

where C  is a constant, f is the number of measurements and
$t = (x-\mu)/\sigma$ .  In this $\mu$ is the mean value of x.  It is easily shown
that this takes the Gaussian form in the limit as f approaches
infinity [13].  However, for a limited number of measurements, say 50
or 300 measurements, we found that the Student distribution
approximates more accurately to a Gamma  distribution in the far
wings. The Gaussian distribution deviated by orders of magnitude in
the region where most measurements lay in our case, between t = 2 and
t = 7 and fall off too rapidly at large distances.

We therefore reached the unexpected result that the Gamma
distribution, besides being easier to calculate, was a better
approximation for our purpose than the Gaussian and we used this in
our later calculations.  However, we also carried through some
calculations of probability with the Gaussian function, but since it
did not fit the experimental data quite as closely and particularly
because it fell off too quickly at large distances,  we were not
surprised to find some of the probabilities to be inaccurate [12].

**PRINCIPLE COMPONENT ANALYSIS**

To investigate if the values of n obtained from our experiments were a
real approximation to the dimensional space of the vectors x we
carried out a principle component analysis on the co-variant matrices
for the 10 words. An example of the principle eigenvalues obtained for
one word – the word "keep" – is given in table 2.  These show that the
16th eigenvalue falls off to approximately 1% of the maximum value.
If we make the assumption that the dimensions, p,  of the principle
components is determined approximately by the number of eigenvalues
giving about 90% of the total sum of all the eigenvalues, then we find
that the dimensions n obtained by fitting the distributions are very
roughly in agreement with the principle component dimensions. To make
n = p, the percentage of the total number of eigenvalues needed varies
between 86% and 95% for the 12 words.

This indicates that we have found another method of determining the
dimensions of the vectors; it also tells us that one of these words
can be represented by a vector of approximately 16 numbers, rather
than 400, but it does not tell us  any easy way of choosing the 16
numbers apart from the calculation of eigenvectors.  Unfortunately

work with co-varient matrices with 400 x 400 elements to find eigenvectors is unrealistic for real time operation.

This result made us more confident that our decision, as a first approximation, to assume spherical symmetry when using a multi-dimensional distribution was justified.

## OBTAINING PROBABILITIES FROM SCORES

The next and final step was to use the values of $\sigma$ and n obtained from our measurements to calculate a probability from the scores or distances, d.

We first enlarged our dictionary to 223 words and after finding that the distribution did not vary greatly, when using 50 measurements rather than 300, we used only 50 for each of the words. The distributions were curve fitted and values of n and $\sigma$ determined for all 223 words.

When the 50 enunciations of each word were being taped, four extra words were spoken in each case. These were subsequently used as 892 "unknown words" and the recogniser produced distances d, for these unknown words from the mean template obtained for the 223 words in the dictionary. The probabilities were determined from the formula

$$P_i(w:d) = K \, \sigma_i^{-n_i} \exp(-d/\sigma_i) \qquad (11)$$

where $\sigma^2_i$ and $n_i$ are the variance and dimension of word $w_i$ in the dictionary where w is the unknown word and where K is chosen to normalise the measurements (to make the sum of the probabilities equal 1).

However, we quickly found that this gave nonsensical results with probabilities varying by many orders of magnitude more than we would have expected. This was caused by using a varying $n_i$ value. An examination of Table 1 shows that n varies between 10 and 34 and since $d \approx 500$, $\sigma^{-n}$ varied by over 50 orders of magnitude! It was immediately clear that we could not compare words in different dimensional spaces - such comparisons did not make sense. We found that the average value of n for all words was approximately 15 and that the curve fits to all distributions and indeed probabilities obtained at the end of our computation did not vary greatly with n. So we chose this average value $n_i = 15$ for all words, recomputed the best $\sigma_i$ value to fit each distribution and recalculated the probabilities using Equation (11). The results are illustrated in Tables 3, 4, 5, 6, 7 and 8. These show that the scores appear to have been replaced by meaningful probabilities in the great majority of cases. In a small number of examples the probability measure reverses the order given by the distances, mostly correctly, a few incorrectly. But it is more important in all these cases that the uncertainty is indicated and measured. Only in 24 cases out of 892 (about 3%), does the probability measure fail, ie giving a low probability to a correct word (eg 0.001 in Table 8). These are unusual pronunciations which occur in the far wing of the distribution. It appears that in this region the Gamma distribution still underestimates the probability. One with a smaller kurtosis is needed.

**ACKNOWLEDGEMENTS**

We thank British Telecom for support of a CAST studentship for one of us (CJC). Thanks are also due to the Department of Education, Northern Ireland for the studentship.

We are indebted to John Fleming of BT for correspondence which helped with the development of the theory.

**REFERENCES**

1. Shearme J N and Leach P F, 1968. Some experiments with a simple word recognition system. IEEE Trans Audio Electroacoust, AU-16, 256-261.

2. White G M and Neely R B, 1976. Speech recognition experiments with linear prediction, bandpass filtering and dynamic programming. IEEE Trans Acoust Speech, Signal Processing, ASSP-24, 183-188.

3. Kuhn M H and Tomachewski H H, 1983. Improvements in isolated word recognition. IEEE Trans Acoust, Speech, Signal Processing, ASSP-31, 157-167.

4. Aldefeld B, Levinson S E and Szymanski T G, 1980. A minimum-distance search technique and its application to automatic directory assistance. Bell Syst Tech J, vol 59, 1343-1356.

5. Bow Sing-Tze, 1984. Pattern recognition, Marcel Dakker, NY, p9.

6. Jelinek F, 1976. Continuous speech recognition by statistical

methods.   Proc IEEE vol 64, 532-556.

7.   Cox S J, 1986.   Estimating the error-rates of isolated-word template-matching speech recognisers.   BT Report R18/005/86.

8.   Clotworthy C J and Smith F J, 1986.   Spoken word variation and probability estimation.   Proc IEEE Inter Conf on Speech Input/output, London,   27-30.

9.   Damper R I, McDonald F L, 1984.   Statistical clustering procedures applied to low-cost speech recognition.   J Biomed Eng, vol 6, 265-271.

10.   Hin L T, Tseng H, Cox D B, Viglione S S, Conrad D P and Runge R G, 0001983.   A monolithic audio spectrum analyser.   IEEE Trans Acoust Speech, Signal Processing, ASSP-31, 288-293.

11.   Velichko V M and Zagaruiko N G, 1970.   Automatic recognition of 200 words.   Int J Man-machine Stud, vol 2, 233-234.

12.   Clotworthy C J, 1987.   Thesis to be submitted.

13.   Balmer M G, 1967.   Principles of Statistics, 2nd Ed, Oliver and Boyd, Edinburgh, p.133.

## TABLE 1

Value of dimension n and variance $\sigma^2$ obtained by curve fitting the distributions, as in Figure 1, with an ndimensional distribution for 10 words

| Word | GAUSSIAN N | $\sigma$ | GAMMA N | $\sigma$ |
|------|------------|----------|---------|----------|
| ASK  | 11 | 601 | 21 | 94  |
| BUS  | 18 | 552 | 35 | 67  |
| COW  | 14 | 437 | 27 | 60  |
| DOG  | 9  | 575 | 17 | 101 |
| FISH | 8  | 964 | 16 | 168 |
| KEEP | 9  | 663 | 17 | 115 |
| MAKE | 8  | 605 | 14 | 120 |
| PULL | 9  | 530 | 17 | 92  |
| SUN  | 6  | 906 | 11 | 198 |
| THAT | 6  | 693 | 11 | 153 |
| TOY  | 11 | 462 | 21 | 72  |
| WALK | 13 | 403 | 24 | 58  |

## TABLE 2

The first 16 eigenvalues $\lambda_i$ of the 400 x 400 covariant matrix for the word "keep".

| i | $\lambda_i$ ($\times 10^3$) | i | $\lambda_i$ ($\times 10^3$) |
|---|------|----|-----|
| 1 | 3860 | 9  | 121 |
| 2 | 1450 | 10 | 104 |
| 3 | 716  | 11 | 90  |
| 4 | 441  | 12 | 78  |
| 5 | 393  | 13 | 64  |
| 6 | 312  | 14 | 57  |
| 7 | 262  | 15 | 49  |
| 8 | 174  | 16 | 41  |

## TABLE 3

Examples of distances and probabilities where the probability added significantly to the information available, typical of about 97% of the 892 tests

Spoken word : "WE"

| WORD | DISTANCE | PROBABILITY |
|------|----------|-------------|
| WE   | 1565     | 0.536       |
| BE   | 1624     | 0.342       |
| ME   | 1842     | 0.018       |
| TEA  | 1889     | 0.002       |
| HE   | 1959     | 0.001       |

Spoken word : "DRAWS"

| WORD  | DISTANCE | PROBABILITY |
|-------|----------|-------------|
| DRAWS | 1476     | 0.999       |
| DRAW  | 1956     | 0.0003      |
| DOG   | 2179     | 0.0001      |
| DOGS  | 2217     | 0.0001      |

## TABLE 4

Examples of 24 cases out of 892 where the probability measure correctly reversed the candidate order from the recogniser

Spoken word : "AT"

| WORD | DISTANCE | PROBABILITY |
|------|----------|-------------|
| PAT  | 1926     | 0.245       |
| AT   | 1931     | 0.517       |
| CAT  | 2094     | 0.145       |
| HELP | 2105     | 0.048       |

TABLE 5

Examples of 42 cases out of 892 where the probability and distance measures both order the words incorrectly but the probability measure indicates considerable uncertainty

Spoken word : "I"

| WORD | DISTANCE | PROBABILITY |
|------|----------|-------------|
| OUR | 1575 | 0.142 |
| I | 1643 | 0.211 |
| HOW | 1647 | 0.258 |
| BY | 1659 | 0.192 |
| FARM | 1708 | 0.182 |
| NOW | 2010 | 0.0001 |

TABLE 6

Examples of 15 cases out of 892 where the distance and probability measure both fail to identify the correct word, but the correct word has a high probability

Spoken word : "TAKES"

| WORD | DISTANCE | PROBABILITY |
|------|----------|-------------|
| CAKES | 1867 | 0.758 |
| TAKES | 1980 | 0.241 |
| PIGS | 2456 | 0.001 |

TABLE 7

Examples of 20 cases out of 892 where the probability measure incorrectly orders the words, but still indicates a measure of uncertainty

Spoken word : "HOW"

| WORD | DISTANCE | PROBABILITY |
|------|----------|-------------|
| HOW | 1731 | 0.380 |
| FARM | 1745 | 0.525 |
| OUR | 1854 | 0.001 |

TABLE 8

Examples of 24 cases of of 892 where both distance and probability measure fail

Spoken word "HOW"

| WORD | DISTANCE | PROBABILITY |
|------|----------|-------------|
| OUR | 1296 | 0.781 |
| FARM | 1456 | 0.191 |
| ARE | 1661 | 0.019 |
| HOW | 1689 | 0.001 |

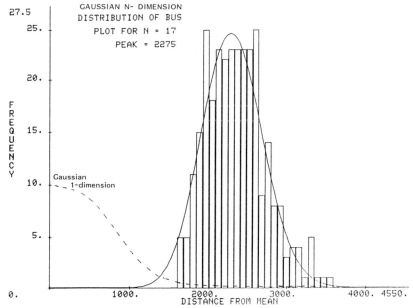

FIGURE 1 : Measured distribution for the word BUS and N-dimensional Gaussian Fit.
Also shown is the equivalent 1-dimension Gaussian Distribution for the
same σ (not to scale) showing the N-dimensional Fit is in the far wing.

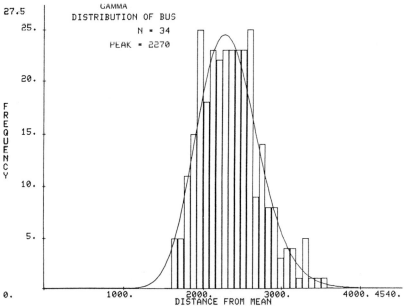

FIGURE 2 : N-dimensional Gamma Fit to the measured distribution for "BUS".
It is slightly better than the Gaussian distribution, particularly
for large distances.

# Feature Extraction From Line Drawing Images

[1]Kelvin J. Goodson[†]   and   [2]Paul H. Lewis

[1]Department of Electronic Engineering,
Dorset Institute of Higher Education, Bournemouth BH1 3NG,
United Kingdom
and
[2]Department of Electronics and Computer Science,
University of Southampton, Southampton SO9 5NH,
United Kingdom

## Abstract

This paper describes progress towards an automatic system for extracting line features from line drawing images. A semi-automatic system for tracking lines and for building features from the resulting line fragments has been developed. Operator intervention is required to guide the feature building when ambiguities arise. A knowledge based system, which works alongside the semi-automatic system, can execute some of the decision making tasks in place of the operator and as the knowledge base is increased the need for operator intervention will diminish.

## 1 Introduction

Line drawings can be found in many forms including maps, charts, cartoons, technical drawings, circuit diagrams and sketches. Although several approaches to automatic feature extraction have been described elsewhere, they have frequently been concerned with drawings where the feature geometry is well known; for example in character recognition [1], electrical schematics [2] and linear feature extraction [3,4].

Attempts to extract features of arbitrary geometry from complex drawings such as maps have mainly involved high cost facilities and often resulted in substantial operator intervention [5]. The aim here is to develop a general and relatively low cost system for extracting features from line drawing images with a diminishing need for user intervention. In the first instance the application area has been the extraction of contours and coastlines from images of hydrographic charts.

Three stages are involved in the approach. In the first, a line tracker is implemented to extract line fragments from the image. Although some line trackers perform well in specific circumstances, most have difficulty in handling lines of arbitrary geometry and produce a collection of line fragments rather than a complete and reliable continuous chain code. In the second stage a semi-automatic feature extraction system (SAFE) is developed to build features from the list of line fragments produced by the tracker. When ambiguities of interpretation

---

[†]Now at The University of Southampton.

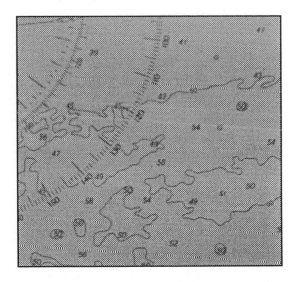

Figure 1: Raw Chart Image

arise or when feature codes have to be assigned, human intervention is solicited via a user friendly interface. The SAFE system can be used to extract features reliably but still involves substantial human assistance.

The third stage involves the development of an intelligent knowledge based system (IKBS) which works in collaboration with the SAFE system. When the SAFE system requires assistance the IKBS is consulted first. If it can resolve the problem then human interaction is not required. If the IKBS fails to satisfy a goal from SAFE then human intervention is again solicited. As the rule base is developed the need for human intervention should decrease.

## 2  Implementation of a Line Tracker

The possible non-automated routes for obtaining feature representations are to hand digitise the information using a digitising table or to use commercially available semi-automatic digitisation techniques; for example those based on Laser Scanning devices. However, these approaches are either heavily labour intensive or involve very expensive equipment. Amin and Kasturi [6] have recently described a system for map data processing which falls between these extremes but they use simple test maps and adopt a conventional approach to algorithm development. Our specific aim is to explore the use of image processing and knowledge based techniques for feature extraction at relatively low cost and with a minimum amount of user interaction.

Figure 1 shows a 256 × 256 image with 64 grey levels obtained using a monochrome video camera. The essential requirement is to devise an algorithm which will detect a line from the image and represent it by some explicit code with correct spatial positioning of the line as an important criterion. The tracker should ideally follow a continuous contour from its start to end point without fragmentation. Since no character recognition is used at present, the human operator should simply need to enter the depth reading for each contour feature to complete the procedure.

Several line extraction algorithms have been described in the literature in recent years. In general they make some constraining assumptions about the images considered or the features

Figure 2: Line fragments from the Tracker

to be extracted. For example, some assume binary images [7,8] while others assume only linear line features [3,4] are to be extracted. The approach adopted as the starting point for the extraction process in the current work was based on a tracker which begins by blurring the image with a gaussian filter to give lines a convex topographic profile [9]. This profile has the property that pixels on the profile exceed the average of their eight connected neighbours by non-negligible amounts. It should thus be possible to identify line pixels and then *walk along the ridge* of the convex line profile to extract the line detail. An adaptive threshold is applied to isolate points on the ridge top and distinguish them from homogeneous regions and background. Finally a ridge walking line tracker is initiated to produce a chain coded representation of the extracted lines.

Some of the line fragments extracted from part of figure 1 during the tracking process are shown in figure 2. Breaks between fragments are made visible by imposing a 10 pixel gap. For a variety of reasons, the tracked segments consist of fragments of lines rather than a continuous line feature. One reason is that the raster scan operation in the tracking algorithm first encounters a pixel in a line at a local maximum in that line; the line will first be tracked in the direction with maximal grey level and then a new segment will be started to follow the line in the opposite direction. Fragmentation can also be caused by the thresholding operation within the tracking routine. It may be that a line which should obviously be continuous is not recognised as such because it does not quite meet the thresholding criteria. A further reason is that the line in the image is interrupted by graphics; perhaps a depth indication to mark a contour or an intersection with a map grid line or compass rose.

For the features in the image to be correctly represented, the fragmented chain codes of the feature must be correctly linked to form a single feature representation. This stage often involves decisions based on high level knowledge about the attributes of features found in the image.

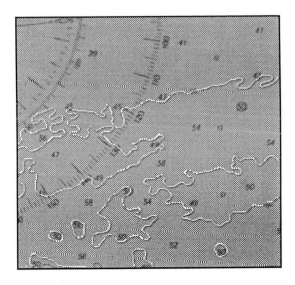

Figure 3: The SAFE system in Operation

# 3 Development of a Semi-Automatic Feature Extraction (SAFE) System

The approach used in the semi-automatic feature extraction system (SAFE) is to face the user with the original raw video image: in this case, a portion of a chart. To initialise the system the user associates a previously generated file of line segment chain codes with the displayed image. The system starts in an automatic mode and selects a segment with which to begin building a feature. As a line segment is added to the current feature it is displayed graphically over the video image of the map in a higher grey level so that the user can see the features being built automatically.

The SAFE system then searches for extensions to the feature. Candidate line segments are linked if their end points are within a given tolerance and no competing fragments are in the vicinity. No user interaction is required until an ambiguity is encountered or until no line segment is found to continue the feature. When this happens the SAFE system displays what it considers to be the most likely candidate for continuation of the feature and invites confirmation from the user. If the response is negative the image is regenerated over the graphic display and the next candidate displayed in the same manner, up to a maximum of five candidates. In the case when all candidates are rejected or no line segments can be found to continue the feature, the system drops into manual mode in which the user may direct the system explicitly through a menu of options. Facilities available include the direct selection of a line segment to be linked into a feature, explicit modification or extension of a feature and a low level feature manipulator for correcting errors in the feature building process. Finally the menu includes an option to close and save a feature and add a feature code.

Figure 3 shows the screen during the running of the SAFE system. Features either under construction or completed are shown highlighted.

# 4 Knowledge based extension to the SAFE system

The semi automatic system involves a considerable amount of operator intervention since, whenever an ambiguity is encountered the judgement of the operator is required. Typically the operator may indicate that a particular gap is not relevant and the contour should continue across it, or that two line segments should be connected because the visual continuity of the lines suggests that they should be.

In order to make such decisions the operator uses either well founded rules based on the chart topology or else he applies rules of thumb which he knows from experience will be correct.

In order to reduce the level of operator intervention an intelligent knowledge based system(IKBS) has been developed, which the SAFE system can consult in the event of a problem or ambiguity. Only if the IKBS fails to give the necessary direction is the human operator consulted. Several authors have considered the application of knowledge based techniques to image analysis. For example, Nazif and Levine [10] describe a rule-based system for low-level image segmentation. Some of the novel aspects of the approach described here are the use of line fragments as the primitive for rule-based feature building and the interaction between the SAFE system and the IKBS, ensuring that a fully usable system is available even during the rule-base development phase which can often be lengthy.

The IKBS is a rule-based system which uses backward chaining to satisfy goals. Uncertainties in facts and rules are handled using certainty factors in a manner similar to that adopted in the well known expert system, MYCIN [11].

Conventionally, expert systems are consultative systems in which the user effectively has a conversation with the expert system at the keyboard. In our approach the feature extraction system consults the IKBS automatically by passing it goals to be satisfied, and receives in return a certainty factor for the goal submitted. An example of a typical rule is

```
IF function endseparation(linefeatureA, lineB) LT 2
THEN isconnected(linefeatureA, lineB) is true CF 0.9
```

This rule says that if the end point of a line is within 2 units of of the end point of a feature then the line and the feature should be connected with a certainty factor of 0.9. A goal to establish whether a particular line and a particular feature should be connected might take the form

```
isconnected(linefeature5, line18)
```

An ambiguity caused by the SAFE system not knowing which of two lines to follow might cause SAFE to submit two goals to the IKBS. It would select the one which returns the highest certainty factor, providing it is significantly different from the next highest value and also exceeds a preset threshold.

In this way, some of the decision making tasks of the operator are being replaced by the IKBS and as the rule-base is extended the need for operator interaction is reduced.

# 5 Conclusions

A system (SAFE) has been developed to extract features from line drawing images in a semi-automatic way. The system can be used to build features reliably but is labour intensive. A knowledge based system has been developed to interact with the SAFE system providing some of the decision making which would otherwise be performed by the operator. As the rule base is extended the need for operator interaction will gradually diminish. The system could have applications to general feature extraction and object recognition tasks in image analysis.

# References

[1] R. W. Smith, "Computer processing of line images: A survey," *Pattern Recognition*, vol. 20, pp. 7–15, 1987.

[2] H. Bley, "Segmentation and preprocessing of electrical schematics using picture graphs," *Comp. Vision, Graphics and Image Proc.*, vol. 28, pp. 271–288, 1984.

[3] R. Nevatia and K. Babu, "Linear feature extraction and description," *Computer Graphics and Image Processing*, vol. 13, pp. 257–269, 1980.

[4] B. J. Burns, A. R. Hanson, and E. M. Riseman, "Extracting straight lines," *IEEE Transactions on Pattern Analysis and Machine Intelligence*, vol. 8, pp. 425–455, July 1986.

[5] M. C. Fulford, "The FASTRAK automatic digitising system," *Pattern Recognition*, vol. 14 No1-6, pp. 65–74, 1981.

[6] T. J. Amin and R. Kasturi, "Map data processing: recognition of lines and symbols," *Optical Engineering*, vol. 26, no. 4, pp. 354–358, 1987.

[7] L. Caponetti, M. T. Chiaradia, A. Distante, and M. Veneziani, "A track-following algorithm for contour lines in digital binary maps," in *Digital Image Analysis*, (S. Levialdi, ed.), pp. 149–154, Pitman, 1984.

[8] S. Suzuki, M. Kosugi, and T. Hoshino, "Automatic line drawing recognition of large-scale maps," *Optical Engineering*, vol. 26, no. 7, pp. 642–649, 1987.

[9] L. Watson, K. Arvind, R. Ehrich, and R. Haralick, "Extraction of lines and regions from grey tone line drawing images," *Pattern Recognition*, vol. 17, pp. 493–507, 1984.

[10] A. M. Nazif and M. D. Levine, "Low level image segmentation : an expert system," *IEEE Transactions on Pattern Analysis and Machine Intelligence*, vol. 6, pp. 555–577, September 1984.

[11] E. H. Shortliffe, *Computer-Based Medical Consultations:MYCIN*. New York: American Elsevier, 1976.

# SYNTAX ANALYSIS IN AUTOMATED DIGITIZING OF MAPS

Thomas Bjerch and Torfinn Taxt

Norwegian Computing Center

Oslo, Norway

## Abstract.

To enter analog maps into well-structured cartographic databases several consequtive steps of data processing have to be performed. The processing starts with scanning, binarization and vectorization. Thereafter, segmentation and recognition of the unintelligent vectors must be done before the building of the database can be started. The recognition step usually involves many separate recognition tasks such as recognition of isolated iconic symbols, of iconic symbol orientation, straight lines and height contour lines. Often, a large part of these tasks still have to be solved by manual labelling of the vector structures interactively.

In this paper we report on a special syntactic approach to automate some recognition tasks that frequently arise in the digitizing of maps. We have used this method, called syntax directed translation schemata, to automate the recognition of numbers with one decimal, correct some single symbol classification errors and to find legal descriptions of parcel codes on cadastral maps.

We conclude that syntax directed translation schemata are good tools to reduce substantially the interactive work load in the recognition step of map digitizing.

## 1  Introduction.

Automated digitizing of analog maps consists of many sequential steps. The main steps are scanning, binarization, vectorization, segmentation, recognition of all symbolic information and finally building of a cartographic database. One of the big bottlenecks in this sequence is the recognition step. It usually involves many separate recognition tasks such as recognition of isolated iconic symbols, of iconic symbol orientation, straight lines and height contour lines. Several of these tasks still have to be solved by manual labelling of the structures interactively.

In this paper we report on the successful application of a syntax directed translation schema ($SDTS$) to the automatic recognition of numbers with punctation and one decimal. We have also used $SDTSs$ in the automatic correction of single symbol classification errors and to find legal symbol map codes.

# 2 Methods.

*The statistical classification system.* The statistical classification system for the recognition of single iconic symbols is described in detail in [4]. A recent extension of the system, allowing automatic training, is published by [3].

In brief, the system recognizes handwritten symbols correctly in about 99 % of all cases, provided an appropriate feature extraction method has been chosen. The symbol recognition system is designed in a classical way. Initially, it has to be trained for the classification task in question, either manually or automatically, to find the relevant probability density function of each symbol class. Bayes' optimal classification rule with the possibility for doubt and outliers are used in the classifier.

*The syntax analyser.* The kernel of the syntax analyzer is a parser for syntax directed translation schemata (*SDTS*), see [1]. A *SDTS* can be viewed upon as a grammar where each production in the grammar has a description part.

*Formally a SDTS can be defined as a 5-tuple : $T = (N, \Sigma, \Delta, R, S)$, where*

$N$ - *is a finite set of non-terminal symbols.*
$\Sigma$ - *is a finite input alphabet.*
$\Delta$ - *is a finite output alphabet.*
$R$ - *is a finite set of rules of the form $A \rightarrow \alpha, \beta$, where*

- $A \in N$
- $\alpha \in (N \cup \Sigma)^*$
- $\beta \in (N \cup \Delta)^*$
- *the non-terminals in $\beta$ are also present in $\alpha$.*

  *$A, \alpha$ and $\beta$ are denoted as production symbol, production part and description part*

$S$ - *is a special non-terminal in $N$, namely the starting symbol.*

It should be noted that the requirement *"the non-terminals in $\beta$ are also present in $\alpha$."* is a more loose requirement than normally required for *SDTSs*. The normal requirement is *"the non-terminals in $\beta$ are permutations of the non-terminals in $\alpha$".*
A translation form of T is defined as :

1. *$(S, S)$ is a translation form, and the two $S$'s are said to be associated.*

2. *If $(\alpha A \beta, \alpha' A \beta')$ is a translation form with the two $A$'s associated, and if $A \rightarrow \gamma, \gamma'$ is a rule in R, then $(\alpha \gamma \beta, \alpha' \gamma' \beta')$ is a translation form. The non-terminals of $\gamma$ and $\gamma'$ are associated in the transformation form as they are associated in the rule. The non-terminals in $\alpha, \beta, \alpha'$ and $\beta'$ are associated as they were in the old transformation form.*

The translation defined by $T$ is the set of pairs :

$$\{ (x, y) \mid (S, S) \overset{*}{\Longrightarrow} (x, y),\ x \in \Sigma^* \text{ and } y \in \Delta^* \}$$

The *SDTSs* can be viewed as a method for transforming derivation trees in an input grammar to derivation trees in an output grammar. Given an input sentence $x$, a translation for

| Production symbol | Production part | Description part |
|---|---|---|
| $\langle S \rangle$ | $\rightarrow$ $\langle car \rangle$ | Car:$\langle car \rangle$ |
| $\langle S \rangle$ | $\rightarrow$ $\langle boat \rangle$ | Boat |
| $\langle car \rangle$ | $\rightarrow$ $BMW\langle col \rangle$ | $BMW(\langle col \rangle)$ |
| $\langle car \rangle$ | $\rightarrow$ FIAT$\langle col \rangle$ | FIAT($\langle col \rangle$) |
| $\langle col \rangle$ | $\rightarrow$ r | red |
| $\langle col \rangle$ | $\rightarrow$ b | blue |
| $\langle boat \rangle$ | $\rightarrow$ Windy | WINDY |

Figure 1: *Example of a SDTS.* $\langle \ \rangle$ *enclose non–terminal symbols.* $\langle S \rangle$ *is the start non–terminal symbol that all sentences must be derived from.*

$x$ can be obtained by constructing a derivation tree for $x$, then transforming the derivation tree into a tree in the output grammar, and then taking the frontier of the output tree as a translation for $x$.

A *SDTS* in the implemented syntax analyzer is given by the user with the set of rules $R$ in the format seen in figure 1. $N$, $\Sigma$ and $\Delta$ are given implicitly. $N$ is the set of all non–terminals used in $R$. $\Sigma$ ($\Delta$) is the set of all terminals used in the production parts (description parts). The start symbol is always defined as $S$.

Figure 2 shows an example of analyzing (and describing) the two strings "BMWr" and "Windy" with the *SDTS* shown in figure 1. Note that the description of the non–terminal $\langle boat \rangle$ is not included in the result description because $\langle boat \rangle$ is not present in the description part of the rule $\langle S \rangle \rightarrow \langle boat \rangle$ , Boat.

If there for a non–terminal in a description part, exists more than one occurrence of the same non–terminal in the production part, it is necessary to specify which non–terminal in the production part a non–terminal in the description part is referring to (the association must be defined), see figure 3.

*Grouping.* The result of the statistical symbol recognition is single symbols with an associated class. To be able to use any grammar in a meaningful way, the grammar must be presented with a string of symbols that is logically connected. The formation of such strings we call grouping. The grouping algorithms will not be discussed here.

# 3    Results.

The syntax analyzer has been successfully used for solving several different tasks in the automated digitizing of maps. Below three examples on such applications are given.

*Insertion of decimal points.* On some maps there are symbol strings consisting of either text or height numbers. Usually, each of the height numbers is given with a certain accuracy, and therefore has a fixed number of decimals. However, during the preceeding steps in the digitizing process, the punctation is normally filtered out as noice.

We used a syntax directed translation schema (fig. 4) to check if any symbol string

Sentence : "BMWr"

$$((\langle S \rangle, \langle S \rangle)) \Rightarrow (\quad \langle \text{car} \rangle \qquad , \quad \text{Car:}\langle \text{car} \rangle \qquad )$$
$$\Rightarrow (\quad \text{BMW}\langle \text{col} \rangle \quad , \quad \text{Car:BMW}(\langle \text{col} \rangle) \quad )$$
$$\Rightarrow (\quad \text{BMWr} \qquad , \quad \text{Car:BMW}(\text{red}) \quad )$$

Description : "Car:BMW(red)"

Sentence : "Windy"

$$((\langle S \rangle, \langle S \rangle)) \Rightarrow (\quad \langle \text{boat} \rangle \quad , \quad \text{Boat} \quad )$$
$$\Rightarrow (\quad \text{Windy} \quad , \quad \text{Boat} \quad )$$

Description : "Boat"

Figure 2: *Analyzing / description examples. The symbol " $\Rightarrow$ " means that the transformation form at the right side is produced from the previous transformation form with one application of a rule.*

$$\langle \text{exp} \rangle \quad \rightarrow \quad \langle \text{exp} \rangle / \langle \text{exp} \rangle \quad , \quad \langle \text{exp:1} \rangle \text{ divided by } \langle \text{exp:2} \rangle$$

Figure 3: *Example of use of occurrence number.*

$$
\begin{array}{lll}
\langle S \rangle & \rightarrow & \langle \mathrm{num}* \rangle \langle \mathrm{num} \rangle \quad \langle \mathrm{num}* \rangle . \langle \mathrm{num} \rangle \\
\langle S \rangle & \rightarrow & \langle \mathrm{num} \rangle \qquad\qquad .\langle \mathrm{num} \rangle \\
\langle \mathrm{num}* \rangle & \rightarrow & \langle \mathrm{num} \rangle \langle \mathrm{num}* \rangle \quad \langle \mathrm{num} \rangle \langle \mathrm{num}* \rangle \\
\langle \mathrm{num}* \rangle & \rightarrow & \langle \mathrm{num} \rangle \qquad\quad\ \langle \mathrm{num} \rangle \\
\langle \mathrm{num} \rangle & \rightarrow & 0 \qquad\qquad\quad\ 0 \\
\langle \mathrm{num} \rangle & \rightarrow & 1 \qquad\qquad\quad\ 1 \\
\langle \mathrm{num} \rangle & \rightarrow & 2 \qquad\qquad\quad\ 2 \\
\langle \mathrm{num} \rangle & \rightarrow & 3 \qquad\qquad\quad\ 3 \\
\langle \mathrm{num} \rangle & \rightarrow & 4 \qquad\qquad\quad\ 4 \\
\langle \mathrm{num} \rangle & \rightarrow & 5 \qquad\qquad\quad\ 5 \\
\langle \mathrm{num} \rangle & \rightarrow & 6 \qquad\qquad\quad\ 6 \\
\langle \mathrm{num} \rangle & \rightarrow & 7 \qquad\qquad\quad\ 7 \\
\langle \mathrm{num} \rangle & \rightarrow & 8 \qquad\qquad\quad\ 8 \\
\langle \mathrm{num} \rangle & \rightarrow & 9 \qquad\qquad\quad\ 9 \\
\end{array}
$$

Figure 4: *A syntax directed translation schema for decimal point insertion.*

on the map was such a number. As a result, we could replace the symbol string with a number (the description), having the decimal point inserted at the right place.

On the actual maps only numbers with one decimal after the decimal point were present. In all cases where the symbol string consisted of all the correct digits of the number, but with no decimal point, all decimal points were correctly inserted. Furthermore, no strings that originally were text were recognized as numbers.

However, about 10 % of all numbers were not found by the syntax analysis. This was not caused by the syntax analyser, but by the preceeding steps in the digitization. There were three main reasons for this. First some digits were not classified as symbols or misclassified because they were too severely distorted. Second, misclassifications in the symbol recognition caused replacement of letters for digits, and also digits with other digits. Third, sometimes the grouping algorithm failed to form the correct group of classified symbols. For example, a single group was considered as two groups by the grouping algorithm, and therefore got two decimal points.

*Correction of classification errors.* On some maps there is a fixed syntax of legal symbol strings. A *SDTS* can then be used to check if any string is legal and simultaneously correct some strings for commonly occuring classification errors (e.g. "B" subsituted with "8", and "1" substituted with "I").

In the digitization of one large map series with such a fixed syntax of legal strings, a particular *SDTS* was applied to correct some classification replacement errors between "1" and "I", "B" and "8", "2" and "z", and finally "z" and "Z" (see fig. 5).

This syntax analyser corrected a large fraction of all classification errors. However, for the same reasons as described in the first example, not all classification errors could be corrected automatically.

*Description of parcel codes.* On a series of cadastral maps the parcels were labeled with parcel codes consisting of a string of symbols. The codes had a fixed structure with

| $\langle S \rangle$ | $\rightarrow$ | $\langle$num$*\rangle$ | $\langle$num$*\rangle$ |
|---|---|---|---|
| $\langle S \rangle$ | $\rightarrow$ | G8 | GB |
| $\langle S \rangle$ | $\rightarrow$ | B8 | BB |
| $\langle S \rangle$ | $\rightarrow$ | 8B | BB |
| $\langle S \rangle$ | $\rightarrow$ | Qz | QZ |
| $\langle S \rangle$ | $\rightarrow$ | Q2 | QZ |
| $\langle$num$*\rangle$ | $\rightarrow$ | $\langle$num$\rangle\langle$num$*\rangle$ | $\langle$num$\rangle\langle$num$*\rangle$ |
| $\langle$num$*\rangle$ | $\rightarrow$ | $\langle$num$\rangle$ | $\langle$num$\rangle$ |
| $\langle$num$\rangle$ | $\rightarrow$ | 0 | 0 |
| $\langle$num$\rangle$ | $\rightarrow$ | 1 | 1 |
| $\langle$num$\rangle$ | $\rightarrow$ | $I$ | 1 |
| $\langle$num$\rangle$ | $\rightarrow$ | 2 | 2 |
| $\langle$num$\rangle$ | $\rightarrow$ | 3 | 3 |
| $\langle$num$\rangle$ | $\rightarrow$ | 4 | 4 |
| $\langle$num$\rangle$ | $\rightarrow$ | 5 | 5 |
| $\langle$num$\rangle$ | $\rightarrow$ | 6 | 6 |
| $\langle$num$\rangle$ | $\rightarrow$ | 7 | 7 |
| $\langle$num$\rangle$ | $\rightarrow$ | 8 | 8 |
| $\langle$num$\rangle$ | $\rightarrow$ | 9 | 9 |

Figure 5: *Error correcting SDTS.*

subcodes, and could therefore in principle be checked automatically by a *SDTS*.

However, the codes were often duplicated several times within the parcel (see fig. 6). Furthermore, the parcels also frequently contained other types of symbol codes such as street names. It was not possible to sort these different types of symbol codes within a parcel, before giving the single code to the STDS for recognition of parcel codes. The grouping software also regularly produced permutations of subcodes within a given candidate parcel code.

The task was therefore to find the correct code from several strings of symbols where the code symbols could be permuted within a given string. The string could also contain entirely irrelevant information for the interpration of the parcel code.

The problem was solved by splitting it into three consecutive parts. First, each individual string inside a parcel was parsed by a *SDTS* which looked for legal subcodes. The result of the parsing was either that the symbol string consisted of only legal subcode descriptions, a mixture of legal subcode descriptions and parts of the string having no description at all, or that the entire string was illegal with no description at all.

Following the checking and description of all symbol strings within the parcel border, the string descriptions were sorted. Based on the sorting, equal subcode descriptions and illegal strings could be removed. This resulted in a number of different and unordered subcode descriptions which might together constitute a legal parcel code. A second *SDTS* was therfore used finally to check the subcodes and see if they together could produce a legal description of a parcel code. (The *SDTSs*, used for this example, were found to be too big to be included here.)

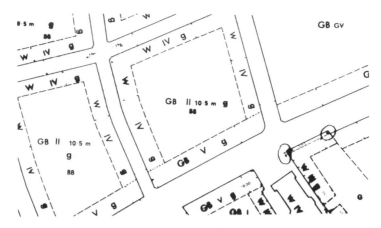

Figure 6: *Codes describing areas. Published with kindly permission from* MDADV-Wien.

During the initial application of this strategy, no interactive inspection and correction of the single symbol classification was done before the use of the above scheme. However, with this approach, symbol substitution errors within a parcel often resulted in misinterpretations of the parcel codes. This was probably because many parcels contained up to 20 symbol strings, giving a large chance for an error in the descriptions produced, when a few subsitution errors were present.

Note, however, that not all substitution errors will lead to an error in the description of the *SDTS*. For example, this is the case when a particular parcel code is duplicated within the parcel boundary, and one of them has a symbol substitution error and is described as illegal.

Based on the initial experience, the interactive correction of symbol classification errors was performed before the searching for the parcel codes in later applications. When the input symbol strings were error free, no errors were encountered in the descriptions of the parcels.

## 4 Discussion.

In this paper we have demonstrated the practical usefulness of syntax directed translation schemata (*SDTSs*) in the automatized digitization of maps. Both some of their limitations and possibilities have been exposed.

Their performance is very dependent on the quality of the preceding steps in the digitization process. In particular, errors in the symbol recognition caused by fusion of two starting symbols into one symbol candidate or the splitting of one starting symbol into two, are hard to correct using *SDTSs*. Such errors often causes the *SDTS* to fail.

On the other hand, frequently occuring substitution errors in the statistical classification, such as occuring between "B" and "8", may be corrected very efficently using a *SDTS*. However, this is only so when such errors occur in a context which may be formalized by a grammar.

*SDTSs* also allow reinsertion of small, but essential signs lost during the early digitization steps. But again, this is only possible as long as such signs are lost in a unique context.

Our present experience with *SDTSs* strongly indicates that they may be generalized to take into account geometrical restrictions efficiently as well as the present syntactical context restrictions applied in this paper. We conclude that syntax directed translation schemata is already a useful tool in automated map digitizing and will be even more so in the near future. *SDTSs* can be used efficiently to reduce the interactive work load substantially in the recognition step of map digitization.

# References

[1] A. V. Aho, & J. D. Ullman, *The Theory of Parsing, Translation and Compiling.* Volume 1. Prentice-Hall, 1972.

[2] K. S. Fu, *Syntactic Methods in Pattern Recognition,* Academic Press, 1974.

[3] L. N. Hjort, & T. Taxt, *Automatic training in statistical pattern recognition,* IV International Conference on Image Analysis and Pattern Recognition, (Proc. Sicily, Italy, 1987, *In press*).

[4] E. Holbæk-Hanssen, K. Bråten, & T. Taxt, *A general software system for supervised statistical classification,* the 8th International Conference on Pattern Recognition (Proc. Paris, 1986).

[5] A. Nijholt, *Context–Free Grammars.* Springer–Verlag, 1980.

# Ackowledgements.

We are indebtet to *SysScan* and *the Royal Norwegian Council for Scientific and Industrial Research* for partly financing this research.

A FAST BINARY TEMPLATE MATCHING ALGORITHM FOR DOCUMENT IMAGE DATA COMPRESSION

Murray J.J. HOLT

Department of Electronic and Electrical Engineering
Loughborough University of Technology
Loughborough, Leics. LE11 3TU, England

Abstract

In the coding of digital facsimile documents, a number of non-information-preserving codes have been proposed which make use of the repetition of binary patterns corresponding to printed or typewritten text characters. The success of such a scheme depends on the accuracy and speed of the template-matching algorithm which decides whether one pattern may be substituted for another without loss of context or legibility. This paper proposes a template-matching algorithm whose accuracy compares favourably with that of other reported algorithms, and whose execution time is significantly faster in computer simulations. The proposed algorithm is particularly well suited to realisation in parallel hardware.

INTRODUCTION

Equipment for the digitisation of office documents has existed for decades, and is now a common feature of the office environment. Typically, documents are scanned at a resolution of 200 points per inch (ppi), each point being assigned one of two quantisation levels (black or white). An A4-size page digitised in this way generates approximately 4 million bits, or half a megabyte, of data. Without compression, the mass digitisation of documents is therefore unattractive, and image data compression is essential for realising the potential capacity of document archiving and transmission systems.

The CCITT Recommendation T-6 for facsimile transmission via noiseless channels includes a loss-less coding standard, MRC-II, and a mixed mode proposal where ASCII codes are used for the text and MRC-II for the graphics [1]. The latter scheme generates 3-4 times the compression of the former, but requires optical character recognition (OCR). Omni-font OCR is relatively expensive and often requires a high-resolution or low-noise digital image. Other OCR techniques need to be trained specifically for each typeface used. A general-purpose mixed-mode compression scheme for Group-4 facsimile is not readily achievable for a number of reasons: resolution down to 200 ppi must be tolerated, documents of varying quality need to be handled, and a-priori knowledge of the typefaces is not normally available. In addition, many documents contain symbols for which there is no ASCII representation, such as algebraic symbols and foreign alphabets.

An alternative approach which avoids these problems is symbol pattern-matching [2], which for a scanned text document achieves compression typically three times as high as that obtainable with MRC-II [3-5]. The digital image is first segmented into symbols, and each symbol is compared with previously segmented symbols in an adaptive library of prototype symbol patterns. Initially, the library is empty, and the first symbol in the image is inserted directly into the library. For each subsequent symbol, if a matching library symbol is found, only the identification of the library symbol and the position of the current symbol are encoded, thereby improving the compression. If no matching library symbol is found, the current symbol is encoded in its entirety and added to the library. Once all symbols in the image have been encoded, the remaining black objects in the image, collectively termed the 'non-symbols' or 'residue', are encoded by another procedure.

A crucial operation in such a scheme is template matching, in which the pattern of an incoming symbol is compared point-by-point with the short-listed library patterns. Owing to sampling and quantisation noise, separate occurrences of the same symbol in a document rarely produce identical patterns in the digital image. If the matching algorithm is to associate the different manifestations of a particular symbol, it must therefore tolerate some variation between patterns.

The manner in which this tolerance is specified is crucial to the success of the matching algorithm. Too little tolerance can result in rejections of matches between patterns which in fact correspond to identical symbols. This in turn results in duplicate copies of symbols being included in the library, thereby reducing the compression. On the other hand, if the tolerance is too great, matching errors can occur, with the catastrophic consequence of symbols being incorrectly substituted in the reconstructed image.

In existing compression schemes, the template matching algorithms are based on the error map, obtained by logical Exclusive-Or operations between corresponding bits in the appropriately registered binary patterns. The error map is therefore a binary pattern in which the '1's, also known as error pels, correspond to pels which differ in the two symbol patterns, and the '0's correspond to pels which are the same in both patterns. The existing algorithms fall into two main types, depending on whether global or local criteria are employed in obtaining the matching decision from the error map.

One established algorithm based on global criteria is the Combined Symbol Matching (CSM) algorithm [3]. This computes a weighted count of the error pels, in which higher weights are given to clustered error pels. A match is rejected if this count exceeds a threshold, which varies as a function of symbol size, obtained from a training process. It has been found that when patterns sampled from small characters and from noisy images are included in the training set, any threshold function which eliminates matching errors also leads to a rejection rate of typically 36%. The recently proposed Weighted And-Not (WAN) algorithm [5,6], which uses similar criteria, reduces the rejection rate in such circumstances to 24%, but this still results in an unnecessarily high proportion of duplicated symbols in the library.

In other algorithms, such as the Pattern Matching and Substitution (PMS) algorithm [4], the matching decision is based on local criteria. A match is rejected if a feature characteristic of a mismatch occurs anywhere in the error map, regardless of the symbol size. This results in fewer rejections than the CSM and WAN algorithms, but the matching error rate can be unacceptably high, especially in the case of small characters where the characteristic features can be obscured by noise.

This paper presents an alternative template matching algorithm, which improves on the matching error rate of the PMS algorithm without seriously increasing the rejection rate. The proposed algorithm also reduces the processing overhead associated with template matching, which is the most time-consuming activity in the encoding process. The algorithm is based mainly on local criteria, but also uses global size information to determine which set of criteria to apply.

PROPOSED ALGORITHM

We first briefly describe the PMS algorithm [4] to which the proposed algorithm is related. To obtain the error map, the two patterns may be superimposed in a number of positions - up to nine different registrations of any pair of patterns are tested. The matching criteria are applied at each registration until either the match is accepted or all valid registrations have been tested. At each registration, a match is rejected if either of the following features is detected:

(1)   (Rule PMS1) An error pel whose eight nearest neighbouring positions include four or more error pels

(2)   (Rule PMS2) An error pel which both (i) has two neighbouring error pels which are not adjacent to each other, and (ii) is centred in a 3x3 neighbourhood in which all 9 pels have the same colour in one of the two symbol patterns.

In practice, Rule PMS1 is sufficient to eliminate a large majority of distinct symbol pairs, but Rule PMS2 is included for pairs of symbols whose differences occur only in narrow strokes or gaps. The proposed method is derived by replacing one or both of these rules with alternative rules, which have proved more accurate and efficient over a variety of test image data.

The first modification involves replacing Rule PMS1 with an alternative rule whose implementation is considerably simpler. Instead of counting errors in the eight neighbours of each error pel, the alternative rule examines pels in 2x2 neighbourhoods of the Exclusive-OR map. If any such neighbourhood contains four error pels, the match is rejected. This is the FEP (Four Error Pels) rule, illustrated in Figure 1. The FEP rule is faster to implement than the PMS1 rule, since, for each error pel, the number of neighbouring error pels to be inspected is reduced from eight to just three. The FEP rule essentially allows a margin of no more than one pel's width between corresponding edges in the two patterns. Any area of the error map where corresponding symbol edges are two or more pels apart is bound to generate at least one 2x2 block of error pels (except in the case of narrow, one-pel-thick, strokes and gaps in a symbol pattern, where significant differences are detected by Rule PMS2).

The second modification concerns Condition (ii) of Rule PMS2, which tests a 3x3 neighbourhood in both symbol patterns for nine pels of the same colour. The modified rule inspects just five pels in each symbol – the cental pel, and the four pels immediately above, below, left and right of it. Condition (i) – that the error pel has at least two non-adjacent neighbouring error pels – is unchanged in the modified rule, which we call the FPN (Five-Pel Neighbourhood) rule. The FPN rule is therefore a tightening of Rule PMS2, in an attempt to trap some of the matching errors made by the PMS algorithm for small characters. It is also more computation-ally efficient, since it reduces the number of pels to be inspected in the symbol patterns when testing Condition (ii).

Figure 2 shows a distinct symbol pair for which a match is rejected by the FPN rule. The error map contains no error pels which satisfy Rule PMS1, nor does it contain any 2x2 neighbourhoods satisfying the FEP rule. However, the ringed pel in the error map satisfies both conditions of the FPN rule. Condition (ii) is satisfied by the marked pels in the pattern of the letter 's'. Note that in this example, Condition (ii) of Rule PMS2 is not satisfied. Consequently, the PMS algorithm incor-rectly matches these symbols, while the proposed FPN rule correctly rejects the match.

Our initial experiments have shown that the FPN rule results in fewer matching errors than the PMS algorithm, but causes a greater number of rejections, especially among larger symbols, resulting in an overall increase in the library size compared with the PMS algorithm. We also noted that the matching errors which result from the PMS algorithm, but which are avoided by the FPN rule, occur almost entirely in smaller characters of no more than 1.5 mm in width.

These observations led to the proposal of a Combined Size-Independent Strategy (CSIS), in which a mismatch is detected by a combination of the FEP rule with either of the FPN or PMS2 rules. The FPN rule is applied only in cases where the width or height of either symbol is twelve pels or less. For larger symbols, the more relaxed PMS2 rule is applied instead. Figure 3 gives a flow-chart for template matching by the CSIS algoirithm. Note that the FPN or PMS2 rule is only applied in cases where the computationally simpler FEP rule does not result in a rejection.

## COMPRESSION SCHEME

The proposed template matching algorithm is incorporated into a simulated compression scheme, which otherwise follows the method of Johnsen et al. [4], except in two aspects of the coding specification. Apart from template matching, described above, the important functions of the simulated scheme are segmentation, screening, library management, coding and decoding, which are explained below.

For the purpose of segmentation, a symbol is defined as a connected set of black pels entirely surrounded by white pels and not exceeding a certain prescribed window size. Symbols thus defined can be conveniently segmented by boundary tracing. Once processed, a symbol is 'deleted' from the digital image by changing black pels to white within the external contour of the symbol. The window size is fixed at 32x32 pels (for a resolution of 200 pels per inch). This is sufficient for all 'body copy' text symbols, and also for many larger symbols used in occasional headings.

Because the template matching of symbol patterns is the most time-consuming activity in the compression process, symbol pattern-matching is implemented as a two-level strategy. The first level, known as screening, selects from the library an ordered short-list of candidate symbols for which a match with the current symbol is feasible. The second level obtains the final matching decision by a template match of the current symbol against each candidate symbol in turn. The screening is designed so that the probability of a matching library symbol being excluded from the short-listed candidates is negligible. The introduction of screening therefore rarely affects the accuracy or compression of the scheme, but it improves the comput-ational efficiency by reducing the number of template matches required to process each symbol. The screening algorithm in the simulated scheme compares four easily measured features of a symbol pattern: the width and height (in pels), and the numbers of horizontal and vertical internal white runs. The short-list is then made up of candidate library symbols whose features are sufficiently close to those of the current symbol. The candidate symbols are then ordered by increasing feature distance, and in the event of a tie, by decreasing frequency of use.

The encoding and decoding apparatus are required to store simultaneously the exact pattern of every library symbol. A consistent library management strategy must therefore be implemented in both the encoder and decoder in the event of the library becoming full. In the simulated scheme, the capacity of the library is 512 symbols of up to 32x32 pels each. After the processing of any scan line containing symbols, the library is sorted by decreasing frequency of use. In the event of the library becoming full, the least frequently used symbol is discarded from the library each time an incoming symbol is to be inserted. Provided the same strategy is implemented in both the encoder and the decoder, the image is still reconstructable from the modified library.

The coding scheme used in the simulation is summarised in Table I. For a full explanation of these codes, the reader is referred to the PMS scheme of Johnsen et al.

[4], since the code specification is identical to that method, with two exceptions:

(i)   In the library pattern description, the extended bit-pattern is coded row-by-row, using the CCITT two-dimensional code (MRC).  The PMS code allows column-by-column coding of the bit-pattern if this gives more compact code for the symbol. It was decided that the small saving in code achieved by this option does not justify the computational overheads involved in implementing it.

(ii)  The non-symbols, or residue, are coded separately by the MRC-II code, which is applied to the entire image buffer once all symbols have been coded and deleted. In the PMS scheme, non-symbols are partitioned into symbol-sized segments which are then matched and coded in the same way as symbols.  In typical office documents, the residue will consist of company logos, sketches, signatures and other cursive script. Repeated bit-patterns occur very rarely in such imagery, and the PMS treatment of the residue is likely to result in a large increase in the library size with no improvement in compression.

## Table I

### Codewords used in simulated compression scheme

| Category | Item | | Code | Bits |
|---|---|---|---|---|
| Symbol | Symbols flag | | 0/1 | 1 |
| Position | No more symbols | | 111 | 3 |
| | Vertical | 0 | 0 | 1 |
| | displacement | -1 | 10 | 2 |
| | | +1 | 11 | 2 |
| | Horizontal position of each symbol | | 00000000000– 11010111111 | 11 |
| Symbol | New symbol | | 00100 | 5 |
| identification | Same symbol | | 000 | 3 |
| | Relative | (1-16) | 1xxxx | 5 |
| | index in | (17-32) | 010xxxx | 7 |
| | sorted | (33-64) | 0011xxxxx | 9 |
| | library | (65-128) | 00101xxxxxx | 11 |
| | | (129-512) | 011xxxxxxxx | 12 |
| Library pattern | Height | (1-32) | 00000-11111 | 5 |
| description | Symbol pattern | | MRC | Variable |
| Residue | Residual image | | MRC | Variable |

The <u>decoder</u> is equipped with an image buffer, equal in size to a digitised document, which is initialised with zeros (white pels) everywhere. Symbol patterns are reconstructed from the code are held in a separate buffer as a library which is managed in an identical manner to the encoder. Symbol patterns from the library are substituted in the image buffer as required. The MRC-coded residue is then decoded line-by-line, in a separate scrolling two-line buffer, and each reconstructed line of the residue is superimposed in the image buffer.

RESULTS AND COMPARISONS

The compression scheme described above has been simulated on an ICL Perq computer. The simulation program was written in Pascal, and makes extensive use of the Raster-Op utility [7] whose micro-coded implementation improves the speed of the template matching algorithms. The CSIS method has been compared with the existing CSM, WAN and PMS algorithms, by applying the simulated scheme to three test documents containing different sizes and styles of text, as shown in Figure 4. The numbers of symbol patterns segmented in the three documents are (A) 1,489, (B) 2,865, and (C) 2,054. The CSM and WAN algorithms were both trained by the method described in ref. [5], using a training set which includes character patterns sampled from all three test documents.

Table II

Comparison of Template Matching Algorithms

| Test document | Coding scheme | Matching algorithm | Compression factor | Library symbols | Matching errors | Encode time (m:s) |
|---|---|---|---|---|---|---|
| A | MRC-2 | – | 20.7 | – | – | 1:22 |
| " | | CSM | 55.1 | 225 | 0 | 9:57 |
| " | Symbol | WAN | 57.9 | 211 | 0 | 12:00 |
| " | matching | PMS | 71.7 | 115 | 0 | 6:15 |
| " | | CSIS | 72.2 | 111 | 0 | 4:16 |
| B | MRC-2 | – | 6.9 | – | – | 1:45 |
| " | | CSM | 13.4 | 395 | 0 | 18:15 |
| " | Symbol | WAN | 15.1 | 313 | 0 | 16:30 |
| " | matching | PMS | 16.8 | 200 | 12 | 9:15 |
| " | | CSIS | 16.8 | 203 | 0 | 6:31 |
| C | MRC-2 | – | 13.0 | – | – | 2:14 |
| " | | CSM | 36.4 | 351 | 2 | 14:55 |
| " | Symbol | WAN | 38.0 | 287 | 2 | 14:37 |
| " | matching | PMS | 42.6 | 199 | 12 | 10:27 |
| " | | CSIS | 43.4 | 190 | 6 | 7:22 |

The results are given in Table II, which also quotes the compression obtained by the standard MRC-II coding algorithm applied to each document. In each case, the compression factor is obtained by dividing the size in pels of the original digitised document, by the length in bits of the compressed code. The number of symbol patterns in the library, after all symbols have been coded, is also quoted. The column headed 'Matching errors' gives the number of incorrectly substituted characters in the image as reconstructed from the compressed code. The encode time is the excution time for the simulation program, which excludes any disk input/output operations.

The CSIS algorithm is clearly faster, and produces higher compression, than any of the other algorithms tested. It also eliminates matching errors, except in the case of Document C, which contains regions of small thin characters which prove difficult to match accurately. For that document, the matching errors are still reduced compared with the PMS algorithm, and the error rate (0.21%) may well be acceptable for certain applications. The CSM and WAN algorithms, which as a result of training have reduced the error rate even further, are significantly less efficient than CSIS in terms of both speed and compression.


DISCUSSION

The proposed algorithm has been shown to be effective over a range of character sizes and styles. The small characters in document C, for which the algorithm produces matching errors, should arguably have been scanned at a higher resolution in the first place. The algorithm has yet to be tested for the higher resolutions in the Group-4 specification (250, 300, 400 and 480 ppi). It is likely to require modification for the highest two resolutions, where a margin of more than one pel's width may be reqired for the naturally occurring differences between patterns of similar symbols.

In the simulation program, the micro-coded Raster-Op utility is used in all four template matching algorithms. A reduction in time is observed with the CSIS algorithm since it involves fewer Raster-Op calls and less high-level arithmetic than the other algorithms. Since Raster-Op is functionally related to Single-Instruction/Multiple-Data (SIMD) parallel architectures, such as the DAP [8], the CSIS algorithm is clearly amenable to realisation in such architectures.

The symbol pattern matching approach to compression does not always improve over the standard methods, especially for documents in which there is a predominance of handwriting or graphics. Such images can however be coded more efficiently by other techniques, such as thinning the black lines and coding their skeletons. A technique of this type has been combined with symbol pattern-matching in a hybrid coding scheme for binary document images [9]. In simulations, the compression achieved by the hybrid scheme exceeds that of MRC-II by a factor of typically 3.5 for text documents, 1.5 for non-text, and 2.5 for documents containing both text and non-text regions.

## ACKNOWLEDGEMENT

The work described in this paper was funded by International Computers Ltd., Systems Strategy Centre, Bracknell, England.

## REFERENCES

[1] BODSON, D., DEUTERMANN, A.R., URBAN, S.J. and CLARKE, C.E., 'Measurement of data compression in advanced Group-4 facsimile systems', Proc. IEEE, 1985, Vol.73, No.4, pp.731-739.

[2] ASCHER, R.N. and NAGY, G.: 'A means for achieving a high degree of compaction on sign-digitized text', IEEE Trans. Comput., 1974, Vol.C-23, pp.1174-1179.

[3] PRATT W.K., CAPITANT, P.J., CHEN, W., HAMILTON, E.R. and WALLIS, R.H.: 'Combined symbol matching facsimile data compression system', Proc. IEEE, 1980, Vol.68, pp.786-796.

[4] JOHNSEN, O., SEGEN, J. and CASH, G.L.: 'Coding of two-level pictures by pattern-matching and substitution', Bell System Tech. J., 1983, Vol.62, pp.2513-2547.

[5] HOLT, M.J.J. and XYDEAS, C.S.: 'Recent developments in image data compression for digital facsimile', ICL Technical Journal, May 1986, Vol.5, No.1, pp.123-146.

[6] HOLT, M.J.J.: 'Symbol pattern matching', UK Patent Application No.8525509, filed 16 Oct. 1985.

[7] NEWMAN, W.M. and SPROULL, R.F.: Principles of Interactive Computer Graphics, 2nd Edn., McGraw-Hill, Tokyo, 1981, Chapter 18.

[8] REDDAWAY, S.F.: 'DAP and its application to image processing', Image Processing Symposium, RSRE Malvern, 1983, Paper 6.3.

[9] HOLT, M.J.J. and XYDEAS, C.S.: 'An efficient hybrid code for document image data compression', in preparation.

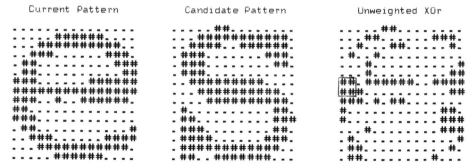

FIGURE 1    Illustration of the FEP rule – one example of a four-error-pel neighbourhood is marked in the XOr map

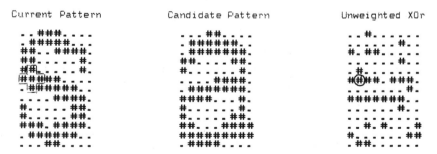

FIGURE 2    Illustration of the FPN rule – the ringed pel in the XOr map satisfies Condition (i), and its five-pel neighbourhood, marked in the current symbol pattern, satisfies Condition (ii)

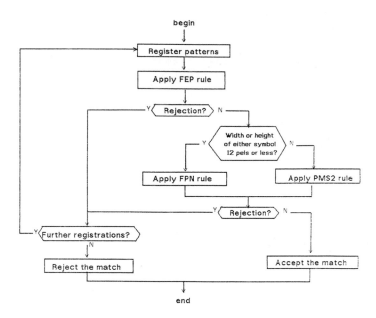

<u>FIGURE 3</u>    Flow-chart for the CSIS template matching algorithm

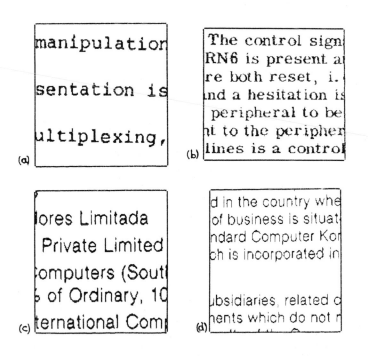

<u>FIGURE 4</u>    Enlarged sections of the test documents:   (a) Document A;  (b) Document B;
        (c),(d) Document C (containing two sizes of text).
Each enlarged section corresponds to a one-inch square in the original document.

# RECOGNITION SYSTEM FOR THREE-VIEW MECHANICAL DRAWINGS

Kiyoshi Iwata, Masanari Yamamoto and Michiko Iwasaki
FUJITSU LABORATORIES LTD.
1015 Kamikodanaka, Nakahara-ku, Kawasaki 211, JAPAN

## 1. INTRODUCTION

Drawings for CAD systems can be either logic-dependent or figure-dependent. For instance, electric circuit diagrams or sequence diagrams for chemical plant engineering are classified as logic-type drawings, and pattern diagrams for printed circuit board or maps are figure-type drawings. Three-view mechanical drawings contain both logic and figure information superposed in a complicated way. Therefore, to analyze mechanical drawings, not only the figure elements must be identified, but the drawing must be interpreted using features and knowledge of the three-view drawings. By contrast, other types of drawings can be recognized by the more localized features [1--3]. Thus, drawing interpretation is indispensable for mechanical drawings which are written using three-view drawings because we don't necessarily indicate dimensions on each view, and further abbreviate dimensions or figures that are redundant.

Several mechanical drawing recognition systems have been reported [4--6], but many did not offer good interpretations and could only be used on simpler drawings. We have just developed a prototype system for inputting and analyzing three-view mechanical drawings that we believe is superior to other systems [7--8]. The subsequent chapters outline the processing in the mechanical drawing recognition system and the experimental results for the plate work drawings.

## 2. OVERVIEW OF MECHANICAL DRAWING RECOGNITION SYSTEM
### 2.1 Applicable Drawings

In general, mechanical drawings are drawn in accordance with various standards. However, to implement a practical drawing recognition system, we established new rules which should not inconvenience designers too much.

Six types of line segment can be used: object line, hidden line, dimension line, extension line, leader, and center line. Lines may be solid, broken, or dot-dash lines of any thickness. A center line may be a solid or dot-dash line. Solid lines may be used for straight lines, circles, and arcs, but broken and dot-dash lines may only be used for straight lines. Alpha-numeric characters are used to designate figures and dimensions. Symbols are used to designate the machining methods: precision, finish, and welding methods.

## 2.2 System Configuration

In a mechanical drawing, the shape of the object is represented by line segments, symbols, and characters. Therefore, before the entire drawing can be recognized, each figure element must be correctly segmented and identified. However, it is also necessary to understand the relationship between different figure elements and the meaning of character strings in order to get adequate information about the ralationships between elements. Therefore, the system must perform two functions: (1) segment and identify each figure element, and (2) interpret the entire geometry according to the relationships between the three views and the characteristics of the three view drawing.

Figure 1 shows the system developed to serve this purpose. The section for segmenting and identifying figure elements converts binary images into vectors. It then subjects the resulting vector data to graphic processing on a bottom-up basis to determine the attribute of each line segment and recognize characters and symbols. The section for drawing interpretation relates the figures to each other on a top-down basis while referencing the knowledge base containing the rules to be applied to figure elements and notation on mechanical drawings, thus determining the shape of the object.

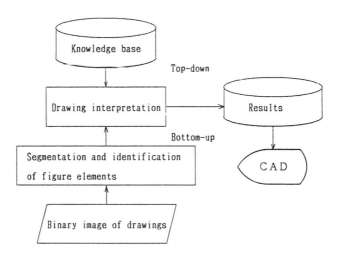

Figure 1   Configuration of the mechanical drawing recognition system

## 3. SEGMENTATION AND IDENTIFICATION OF FIGURE ELEMENTS

In this phase, line segments, characters, and symbols are segmented from the image of the drawings. The characters and symbols are encoded. For each line segment, the coordinates of its endpoints are determined to obtain a vector representing it, and also its attributes are identified.

Figure 2 shows the processing flow. The drawing is scanned to get the image data at 10 dots/mm. The image data is now thinned, and then converted to vector data by polygonal approximation. The obtained vectors are checked for their interconnections. If the rectangular area enclosed by a set of interconnected vectors is relatively small, it is defined as an isolated figure. Otherwise, it is an unisolated figure.

Isolated figures are classified according to their elements, which include characters, broken lines, and dot-dash lines. Next, candidates of broken and dot-dash lines in the isolated figures are checked for their continuity to unisolated figures. This is to identify hidden lines represented by broken lines and center lines represented by solid or dot-dash lines. For character candidates, a character string is extracted through character recognition.

Line segments in unisolated figures are assumed to be dimension lines or leaders if they relate to a character string of isolated figures. Arrows at the end of the line segments and extension lines perpendicular to the line segments are then recognized. Finally, for

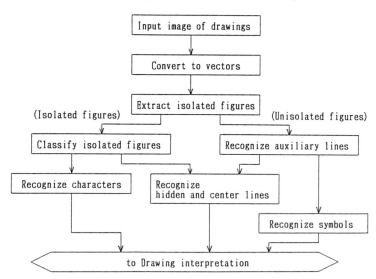

Figure 2    Processing flow for figure elements

unisolated figures with inidentified attributes, symbols are segmented according to local features. The figures with no end points are regarded as object lines. Otherwise, line segments are regarded as undefined because their attributes cannot be identified. The data about line segments, characters, and symbols obtained by recognition processing is passed to the subsequent drawing interpretation process.

## 4. DRAWING INTERPRETATION
### 4.1 System Configuration

The drawing interpretation procedure receives the results of the preceding figure element segmentation and recognition phase, links the figure elements according to the rules applicable to three view drawings, identifies the shape of the drawn object, and passes the geometric data to the CAD and solid model generation systems.

Figure 3 shows the structure of the drawing interpretation system. In this phase, the drawings are interpreted using a knowledge base, which is represented by production type knowledge database. The processor starts by compiling and then executing the necessary procedures. It then stores the results in a shared data area. The processing modules are executed repeatedly until definite geometrical data is obtained. Processing ends when the shared data area is filled with completed information.

The knowledge base includes processing procedures, processing modules, and definition information. The processing procedures are the actual processing requirements which are represented by a production type knowledge database. Processing modules are a group of

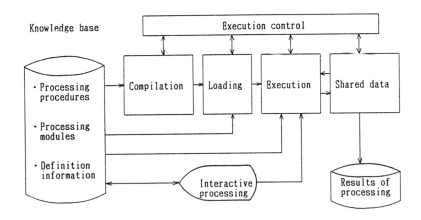

Figure 3   System configuration for drawing interpretation

subroutine packages for drawing interpretation. Definition information includes processing parameters and definition of character strings to be referenced during processing module execution.

The shared data area is accessed by all processing modules for drawing interpretation. The shared data is composed of basic data (character strings, symbols, and grouped data of object lines and auxiliary lines ), high-level data ( results of interpretation ), low-level data (vector data at the lowest level of figure element), and link data tables, specifying the relationship between different types of data.

## 4.2 Drawing Interpretation Algorithm

This section describes the drawing interpretation algorithm, which is composed of geometric interpretation modules that use the meaning of character strings, object dimension determination modules that consider the relationship between the three views, and addition modules that add the omitted line segments. At each step, the processing module for drawing interpretation has several thresholds, ranging from strict to loose interpretations. More likely shapes are adopted earlier, thus, the interpretation quickly converges.

(1) Geometric interpretation using the meaning of character strings

The abbreviations given in table 1 indicate the shapes and sizes of objects. This abbreviated character strings are interpreted to identify the indicated shape and size. The format of the character string is determined by referencing the character string formats in the knowledge base. The fixed character string is compared with the corresponding shape, and then the size and shape of the designated

Table 1　Abbreviations used on this system

| Item | Abbreviation | Example |
|------|-------------|---------|
| Non-proportional | # | #1000 |
| Long hole | LH | 2−LH10×30 |
| Drill hole | DH | DH−$\phi$10×8 |
| Long bore | LB | LB10×25 |
| Square hole | SH | 2−SH−10×15 |
| Dowel | DW | DW−$\phi$10×8 |
| Countersunk hole | CSH | CSH10 |
| Counterbore | CB | $\phi$5×$\phi$8×10−CB |
| Sphere | SP | SP−$\phi$25 |

figure is determined finally. If the actual shape is inconsistent with the shape determined by the character string, the system corrects drawing information with emphasis placed on shapes, or asks the user for assistance.

(2) Object dimension determination by using the three views

In general, dimension indications on three view mechanical drawings are simple (even omitted in some cases). However, the system cannot understand the shape of a figure unless the dimensions of all line segments are specified. To obtain the shape of a figure, dimensions which are not explicitly specified are determined according to the characteristics of three view drawings.

Dimension determination

This sub-module has two methods for determining dimensions: (1) On each view, the dimension of line segments specified by character and auxiliary line are determined, and (2) If dimensions on one view cannot be used to directly determine a line length, the dimensions are determined according to the relationship between the three views.

First, the endpoints of the line segments on each view are projected onto the I and J axes of the two dimensional plane, then normalized. Dimension calculation tables (FI, FJ, $\cdots$ , RJ) are generated for the I and J axes according to the normalized endpoint coordinates, as shown in figure 4. This table gives the distance between endpoints. A distance which is unkown can be determined by simple addition and subtraction of known distances.

If unkown distances remain, dimension calculation tables are generated for the X, Y, and Z axes of the three dimensional coordinates, by relating the endpoint I and J coordinates determined

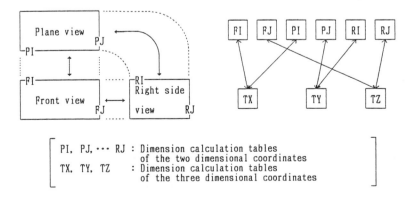

$$\begin{bmatrix} \text{PI, PJ,} \cdots \text{RJ : Dimension calculation tables} \\ \qquad\qquad\quad \text{of the two dimensional coordinates} \\ \text{TX, TY, TZ} \qquad \text{: Dimension calculation tables} \\ \qquad\qquad\quad \text{of the three dimensional coordinates} \end{bmatrix}$$

Figure 4    Relationship between the three views

on one view to those on the other views considering the relationship between the three views, as shown in figure 4. Using these tables TX, TY, and TZ, the unkown distances are determined as in the case of dimension calculation on one view.

## Dimension determination using symmetry

Symmetry is considered when determining the dimension of a line segment which crosses a center line, or when determining the dimension of a figure, such as a hole, located away from any center line. If the symmetry conditions are satisfied, the type and size of the known figure are reflected on those of the unknown figure, and then the dimensions between endpoints and the type and size of figure are determined.

## (3) Addition of the omitted line segments

On mechanical drawings, line segments are omitted if they make it difficult to understand the drawings. This makes the three views inconsistent. These inconsistencies are not distinguishable from those to mis-recognition or a drawing error. To solve this problem, our system has two modes available. In one mode, the system asks the user for assistance. The other mode is used only when plate work drawings are applied. It adds line segments where necessary to remove inconsistencies.

As shown in figure 5, line segments are added where a plate thickness is indicated on the plate work drawing (A in figure 5), or where a hole is indicated ( B in figure 5 ). First, the system determines whether the omitted line is an object line or a hidden line

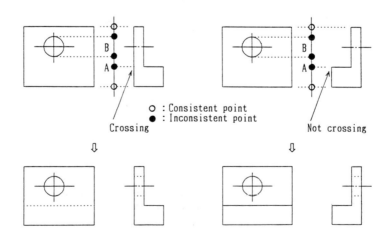

Figure 5    Addition of the omitted line segments

by scanning between inconsistencies in the direction perpendicular to the corresponding axis on the drawing. If there is an intersection with another line segment in the scanning interval, a hidden line is added, and if not, an object line is added.

## 5. EXPERIMENTAL RESULTS

Figure 6 shows the experimental results on a three view drawing of the plate works. In this figure, (a) is an image of original drawing, (b) shows the results of auxiliary line extraction during drawing interpretation, and (c) shows the results of object interpretation. On figure 7, (a) shows the results of interpretation of character strings, and (b) shows the results of determining unknown dimensions and adding the omitted line segments. Satisfactory results of recognition were obtained from three view drawings, especially of plate works, when the drawings conformed to some reasonable and practical rules.

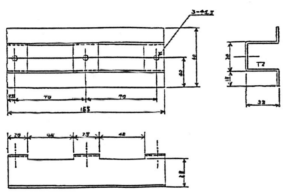

(a) Original image data of plate work drawing

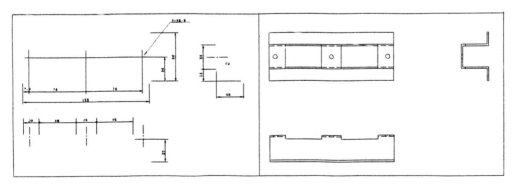

(b) Result of interpretation
(auxiliary lines)

(c) Result of interpretation
(object and hidden lines)

Figure 6    Experimental results for plate work drawing

Figure 8 shows the results of a three dimensional model generated using the object interpretation results of this system.

## 6. CONCLUSIONS

We have just developed an automatic interpretation system that interprets three-view drawings which conform to some reasonable and practical rules. Experimental results on the plate work drawings were satisfactorily obtained, and the extracted object was verified to be correct by generating a three-dimensional model.

## ACKNOWLEDGEMENTS

This works were carried out as a project of the Information Technology Promtion Agency, Japan. We would like to thank the members of the consulting group for their technical advice, and also give our thanks to Mr. Minejima, FUJITSU LABORATORIES LTD.

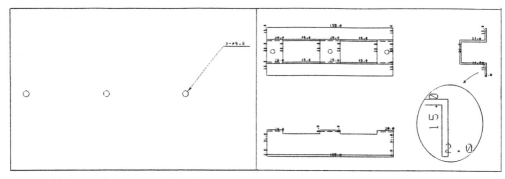

(a) Geometric interpretation by using a character string

(b) Determination of unkown dimensions and addition of the line segments

Figure 7    Processing examples of drawing interpretation

Figure 8    Three dimensional model generation for the result of figure 6 (c)

## REFERENCES

[1] T.Masui, et al., "Recognition System for Design Chart drawn on Section Paper", Proc. 5th ICPR, pp.121-130, 1980.

[2] S.Shimizu, et al., "Logic Circuit Diagram Processing System", Proc, 6th ICPR, pp.717-719, 1982.

[3] H.Harada, et al., "Recognition of Freehand Drawings in Chemical Plant Engineering", Proc. CAPAIDM, pp.146-153, 1985.

[4] T.P.Clement, "The Extraction of Line-Structured Data from Engineering Drawing", Pattern Recognition, Vol.14, 1981.

[5] M.Ito, et al., "Understanding Machine Drawings using a Planning Network and a Geometric Modeller", IECE. PRL84-51, 1980 (in Japanese).

[6] H.Alfeis, J., "Automated Conversion of Drawing into CAD Models in Mechanical Engineering Design", Proc. Data Processing in Design '87, Vol.5, pp.91-104, 1986.

[7] M.Iwasaki, et al., "Development of an Automatic Input System for Mechanical Part Drawings - Segmentation and Recognition of Figure Elements-", IEICE. PRU87-23, 1987 (in Japanese).

[8] M.Yamamoto, et al., "Development of an Automatic Input System for Mechanical Part Drawings - Drawing Understanding-", IEICE. PRU87-24, 1987 (in Japanese).

# A HEURISTIC ALGORITHM FOR STROKE EXTRACTION

Xiaofeng Yin     Dongzhuang Su
Beijing Information Technology Institute
Weizikeng Dewai Beijing P.R. of China

## Abstract

An algorithm for extraction of strokes of handwritten and printed Chinese characters is described. The main idea is based on the heuristic information of Chinese character structure. Experiment shows that strokes can be extracted efficiently according to the heuristic strategy. The general distribution of terminal points is analysed by means of Polya's theorem. The improved algorithm in speed by combining the stroke extraction with thinning is also discussed.

## 1. Introduction.

Feature Extraction plays a key role in Pattern Recognition. For recognition of both printed and handwritten Chinese characters, it is also a very important and complicated task to extract stable and efficient features (1). As we know, all Chinese characters can be represented by a set of line segments called strokes. Therefore we intuitively take them as recognition features and many researchers have made use of this idea. (2)(3).

In this paper we present a heuristic algorithm for stroke extraction. The main idea is to use the ratio of standard stroke length to real standard length as the major heuristic to extract strokes with bottom-up methods. The general distribution of terminal points is analysed by means of Polya's theorem. We also discuss how to quicken the algorithm by combining extraction with thinning. The algorithm can be applied for Chinese character recognition and structural shape analysis in pattern recognition.

## 2. Heuristic Information for Stroke Extraction.

After a Chinese character is scanned into a binary image of M*M pixels, the stroke extraction actually can be considered as a search procedure for irregular line segments.

Many factors affect the precise solution of stroke extraction (4). The unlimited variability of writing style is the hardest one to deal with and exhaustive search methods are not feasible. Therefore we try to take heuristic methods and make good use of structural knowledge of Chinese characters as heuristic information for stroke extraction.

We believe that a heuristic is a piece of knowledge capable of suggesting plausible actions to follow and implausible actions to avoid. (5) Here we employ the following attributes as heuristic for stroke extraction.

1. Terminal Points

Here terminal points represent both start and end points of a stroke, which contain the start and end position of a stroke and define its length and direction.

2. Degree of Terminal Points

Terminal points can act as one or more start or end points. They are also able to hold concurrent posts for both start and end point. The degree of a terminal point is referred to as the number of times of terminal points acted as start and end point.

3. Equality of start and end point of strokes

Although a strict order does exist when one writes a character, but we ignore it in the recognition. We treat start and end points equally and take any one from two terminal points of a stroke as start or end point.

4. Density and Length

The matrix density of a Chinese character is the sum of the black pixels in the matrix. Stroke density stands for the sum of the black pixels which compose the stroke. The standard stroke length denotes the geometric distance between start and end points. The

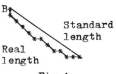

Fig.1

real stroke length designates the distance along stroke black pixels. The standard and real stroke length are illustrated in Fig.1.

3. Extraction Strategies.

If we know the stroke start and end points, the stroke search would be very easy; and we would simply need to determine the "path" connectivity between them. Therefore we can see that the crux for stroke search is how to detect the start and end points. The approach can be generalized in the following questions:

a. How to find a start point efficiently by using the heuristic information?

b. How to find an end point correctly corresponding to the searched start point?

The answers to the question above are also essential steps in our algorithm. For question a., given all terminal points in the matrix of a Chinese character, we abide by the following heuristic strategies to search the stroke points:

S1: Take the terminal points with the smallest degree as start point among elements of terminal point set.

S2: For these points with the same degree, take the one that lies in the sensitive area where the start point may appear with the greatest possibility as a start point.

For question b., we assume: ep: end points; dis(x,y): geometric distance function; den(x,y): real distance; T: set of terminal points; then we have the heuristic strategies to search the end points:

E1: Distance: select the nearest one to the start point as end point, that is:

$$ep=MIN(dis(sp,p)\bigwedge(p \text{ in } T)).$$

The stragey is easy to compute but does not map the connectivity of strokes and can not accommodate the variability of writing style. For long stroke it takes too much unnecessary calculation and judgement.

E2: Connectivity: select the point connected with the start point as end point, that is:

$$ep=(connect(sp,p))\bigwedge(p \text{ in } T).$$

This strategy can not accommodate the variability of writing style either. Though the connectivity is taken into account the solution is still offen non-unique.

Combining E1 and E2, we proposed E3:

E3: Ratio of standard stroke length to real stroke length, let:

$$LD(x,y)=dis(x,y)/den(x,y),$$
$$ep=MIN(\,|1-LD(sp,p))\,|\,)\bigwedge(p \text{ in } T).$$

Here standard length reflects the distance and real length the connectivity and their ratio embodies the degree of posibility of the terminal points to be a corresponding end point which accommodates the variation of writing style with small amount of computing.

After finding the start point, we set up a candidate set of matching end points by untilizing the possible directions of end points so as to reduce the computing.

From the above discussion of heuristic information we have seen that the algorithm is a bottom-up procedure from terminal points to strokes, which can be outlined as follow:

1). Find out all the terminal points;

2). Select a start point according to the degree and position of terminal points;

3). Select the end point according to the ratio of standard length to real length;

4). Analysis and extract strokes.

We have assumed that all the terminal points have been found, but how to find them for step 1 mentioned above? This is what we will discuss next.

4. Analysis of Terminal Points.

First we probe the general distribution of black pixels of the 8-neighborhood around a black pixel.

By creating a one to one relation between the 8 pixels around a black pixel and the vertices of a regular octagon, the problem can be converted into a coloring problem for vertices of regular octagon with black and white colors so that the general distribution of black and while pixels can be obtained through finding the coloring number irrespective of permutation.

Polya's theorem offers a general solution for coloring problems. (6) To utilize the Polya theorem, we specify the following permutations:

Type 1. revolving around the central point of regular octagon, shown in Fig. 2.

$a_1 = (1)(2)(3)(4)(5)(6)(7)(8)$        $(0^\circ)$

$a_2 = (1\ 2\ 3\ 4\ 5\ 6\ 7\ 8)$        $(45^\circ)$

$a_3 = (1\ 3\ 5\ 7)(2\ 4\ 6\ 8)$        $(90^\circ)$

$a_4 = (1\ 4\ 7\ 2\ 5\ 8\ 3\ 6)$        $(135^\circ)$

$a_5 = (1\ 5)(2\ 6)(3\ 7)(4\ 8)$        $(180^\circ)$

$a_6 = (1\ 6\ 3\ 8\ 5\ 2\ 7\ 4)$        $(225^\circ)$

$a_7 = (1\ 7\ 5\ 3)(2\ 8\ 6\ 4)$        $(270^\circ)$

$a_8 = (1\ 8\ 7\ 6\ 5\ 4\ 3\ 2)$        $(360^\circ)$

Type 2. Revolving around the connecting line of opposite verticies, shown in Fig.3.

$a_9 = (1)(5)(4\ 6)(3\ 7)(2\ 8)$

$a_{10} = (2)(6)(1\ 3)(5\ 7)(4\ 8)$

$a_{11} = (3)(7)(1\ 5)(2\ 4)(6\ 8)$

$a_{12} = (4)(8)(1\ 7)(2\ 6)(3\ 5)$

Type 3. Revolving around the connecting line between middle points of opposite edges, shown in Fig.4.

$a_{13} = (1\ 8)(4\ 5)(3\ 6)(2\ 7)$

$a_{14} = (1\ 2)(5\ 6)\ (4\ 7)(3\ 8)$

$a_{15} = (1\ 4)(2\ 3)(5\ 8)(6\ 7)$

$a_{16} = (1\ 6)(2\ 5)(3\ 4)(7\ 8)$

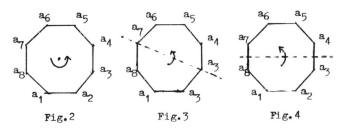

Fig.2          Fig.3          Fig.4

Based on the definitions above, we have:

Theorem: let $S_8 = (1,2,3,4,5,6,7,8,)$

$G = (a_1, a_2, a_3, \ldots a_{15}, a_{16})$, '*' is a binary operation, $a_i * a_j$ represents permutation formed by first applying $a_i$, then $a_j$ to $S_8$, then G is a permutation group on $S_8$.

Proof: Constructing the operation table of G (shown in Table 1), the followings can be drawn from the table:

1. the $a_1$ is the primitive element of G;
2. for all $a_i, a_j, a_k$ in G,   $a_i * (a_j * a_k) = (a_i * a_j) * a_k$;
3. for all $a_i$ in G, only one $a_j$ in G exists, meeting: $a_i * a_j = a_1$;
4. for all $a_i, a_j$ in G, $a_i * a_j$ in G.

We concluded that G is a group.

Now we take the generating function's expression of Polya's theorem to examine coloring number's general distribution: $L = 16$;

Table 1.

| * | $a_1$ | $a_2$ | $a_3$ | $a_4$ | $a_5$ | $a_6$ | $a_7$ | $a_8$ | $a_9$ | $a_{10}$ | $a_{11}$ | $a_{12}$ | $a_{13}$ | $a_{14}$ | $a_{15}$ | $a_{16}$ |
|---|---|---|---|---|---|---|---|---|---|---|---|---|---|---|---|---|
| $a_1$ | $a_1$ | $a_2$ | $a_3$ | $a_4$ | $a_5$ | $a_6$ | $a_7$ | $a_8$ | $a_9$ | $a_{10}$ | $a_{11}$ | $a_{12}$ | $a_{13}$ | $a_{14}$ | $a_{15}$ | $a_{16}$ |
| $a_2$ | $a_2$ | $a_3$ | $a_4$ | $a_5$ | $a_6$ | $a_7$ | $a_8$ | $a_1$ | $a_{13}$ | $a_{14}$ | $a_{15}$ | $a_{16}$ | $a_{12}$ | $a_9$ | $a_{10}$ | $a_{11}$ |
| $a_3$ | $a_3$ | $a_4$ | $a_5$ | $a_6$ | $a_7$ | $a_8$ | $a_1$ | $a_2$ | $a_{12}$ | $a_9$ | $a_{10}$ | $a_{11}$ | $a_{16}$ | $a_{13}$ | $a_{14}$ | $a_{15}$ |
| $a_4$ | $a_4$ | $a_5$ | $a_6$ | $a_7$ | $a_8$ | $a_1$ | $a_2$ | $a_3$ | $a_{16}$ | $a_{13}$ | $a_{14}$ | $a_{15}$ | $a_{11}$ | $a_{12}$ | $a_9$ | $a_{10}$ |
| $a_5$ | $a_5$ | $a_6$ | $a_7$ | $a_8$ | $a_1$ | $a_2$ | $a_3$ | $a_4$ | $a_{11}$ | $a_{12}$ | $a_9$ | $a_{10}$ | $a_{15}$ | $a_{16}$ | $a_{13}$ | $a_{14}$ |
| $a_6$ | $a_6$ | $a_7$ | $a_8$ | $a_1$ | $a_2$ | $a_3$ | $a_4$ | $a_5$ | $a_{15}$ | $a_{16}$ | $a_{13}$ | $a_{14}$ | $a_{10}$ | $a_{11}$ | $a_{12}$ | $a_9$ |
| $a_7$ | $a_7$ | $a_8$ | $a_1$ | $a_2$ | $a_3$ | $a_4$ | $a_5$ | $a_6$ | $a_{10}$ | $a_{11}$ | $a_{12}$ | $a_9$ | $a_{14}$ | $a_{15}$ | $a_{16}$ | $a_{13}$ |
| $a_8$ | $a_8$ | $a_1$ | $a_2$ | $a_3$ | $a_4$ | $a_5$ | $a_6$ | $a_7$ | $a_{14}$ | $a_{15}$ | $a_{16}$ | $a_{13}$ | $a_9$ | $a_{10}$ | $a_{11}$ | $a_{12}$ |
| $a_9$ | $a_9$ | $a_{14}$ | $a_{10}$ | $a_{15}$ | $a_{11}$ | $a_{16}$ | $a_{12}$ | $a_{13}$ | $a_1$ | $a_3$ | $a_5$ | $a_7$ | $a_8$ | $a_2$ | $a_4$ | $a_6$ |
| $a_{10}$ | $a_{10}$ | $a_{15}$ | $a_{11}$ | $a_{16}$ | $a_{12}$ | $a_{13}$ | $a_9$ | $a_{14}$ | $a_7$ | $a_1$ | $a_3$ | $a_5$ | $a_6$ | $a_8$ | $a_2$ | $a_4$ |
| $a_{11}$ | $a_{11}$ | $a_{16}$ | $a_{12}$ | $a_{13}$ | $a_9$ | $a_{14}$ | $a_{10}$ | $a_{15}$ | $a_5$ | $a_7$ | $a_1$ | $a_3$ | $a_4$ | $a_6$ | $a_8$ | $a_2$ |
| $a_{12}$ | $a_{12}$ | $a_{13}$ | $a_9$ | $a_{14}$ | $a_{10}$ | $a_{15}$ | $a_{11}$ | $a_{16}$ | $a_3$ | $a_5$ | $a_7$ | $a_1$ | $a_2$ | $a_4$ | $a_6$ | $a_8$ |
| $a_{13}$ | $a_{13}$ | $a_9$ | $a_{14}$ | $a_{10}$ | $a_{15}$ | $a_{11}$ | $a_{16}$ | $a_{12}$ | $a_2$ | $a_4$ | $a_6$ | $a_8$ | $a_1$ | $a_3$ | $a_5$ | $a_7$ |
| $a_{14}$ | $a_{14}$ | $a_{10}$ | $a_{15}$ | $a_{11}$ | $a_{16}$ | $a_{12}$ | $a_{13}$ | $a_9$ | $a_8$ | $a_2$ | $a_4$ | $a_6$ | $a_7$ | $a_1$ | $a_3$ | $a_5$ |
| $a_{15}$ | $a_{15}$ | $a_{11}$ | $a_{16}$ | $a_{12}$ | $a_{13}$ | $a_9$ | $a_{14}$ | $a_{10}$ | $a_6$ | $a_8$ | $a_2$ | $a_4$ | $a_5$ | $a_7$ | $a_1$ | $a_3$ |
| $a_{16}$ | $a_{16}$ | $a_{12}$ | $a_{13}$ | $a_9$ | $a_{14}$ | $a_{10}$ | $a_{12}$ | $a_{11}$ | $a_4$ | $a_6$ | $a_8$ | $a_2$ | $a_3$ | $a_5$ | $a_7$ | $a_1$ |

$$P = \frac{1}{16}\left((B+W)^8 + 4(B^8+W^8) + 2(B^4+W^8) + 2(B^4+W^4)^2 + 5(B^2+W^2)^4 + 4(B+W)^2(B^2+W^2)^3\right)$$

where B and W denote black and white color separately and any distribution can be obtained from P. The method used here can also be applied to investigate the m-neighborhood.

Regarding the demands of terminal points, we only study the following situations:

a. containing only one black pixel:

the factor of $B^1W^7$: $1/16(C(8.1)+4\times2)=1$;

b. containing two black pixels:

the factor of $B^2W^6$: $1/16(C(8.2)+5\times C(4.1)+4\times4)=4$;

c. containing three black pixels:

the factor of $B^3W^5$: $1/16(C(8.3)+4\times2\times3)=5$.

We only search the above terminal points in our algorithm at this stage.

5. Algorithm

Before depicting the algorithm, some definitons should be presented.

Definition 1. Let: $d(x)$ be the set of possible end points for start point $x$; search $(x,y)$, the procedure to determine the connectivity, then the candidate set $Cond(x)$ is $Cond(x)= \{y \mid (search(x,y)=true)\wedge(y$ in $d(x))\}$.

Definition 2. For any $x,y$ in T, if $search(x,y)$ true, then $BES_{ij}(x,y)$ is the black pixel matrix of "path" $x-y$, where:

$BES_{ij}(x,y)=1$, if pixel on "path" x-y;

$BES_{ij}(x,y)=0$, others.

Definition 3. Let (i,j) be a black pixel in the matrix of a Chinese character, if $BES_{ij}(p,q)\neq 0$ and $BES_{ij}(x,y)\neq 0$, and $BES_{ij}(p,q)\neq BES(x,y)$, then (i,j) called a common pixel in the matrix, a matrix consiting of common pixels is called a common matrix.

The following is the outline of the algorithm:

C:     thinned input Chinese character matrix;

CD:    density function;

FIND: Terminal Point finding procedure;

HS:    heuristic function for start points;

HE:    heuristic function for end point;

R:     common matrix;

ANA:  storke analysis procedure;

```
        Algorithm       HSE;
        BEGIN
          T:=FIND(C);
          WHILE CD(C)≠0     DO
          BEGIN
            sp:=HS(T);
            ep:=HE(Cond(sp);
            ANA(sp,ep);
            C:=CxBES(sp,ep)+R;
          END;
        END.
```

# 6. Experiment

The experiment was conducted on a VAX/11-750 computer using 105 handwritten Chinese characters stored in a 32x32 matrix.  The terminal point and stroke extraction were carried out after thinning.

Four primary types of strokes, horizontal, vertical, right-falling and left-falling strokes were extracted, and more complex strokes can also be picked up through synthesizing these primary strokes.  For 105 handwritten Chinese characters the total number of strokes is 1106 and 97 strokes were not extracted correctly.  The correct rate is 91.2%.

The algorithm was unable to extract some strokes correctly because:

a. thinning results were not real skeleton in some areas so that terminal points were confused or lost;

b. strokes were too close to separate.

There are two means to solve the above problems:

a. devising a thinning algorithm with entire skeleton output;

b. enhancing resolution of input devices.

Experiment shows the algorithm is able to extract the complicated strokes efficiently and has great potentials to develop further.

## 7. Considerations for algorithm quickening

The major problem to consider here is how to combine the thinning with stroke extraction and to do them parallelly.

In the general case, strokes are extracted after thinning or without thinning (7), the former costs a great deal of computing time and the latter will lose many important features and be not suitable for hardware implementation as it is sequential.

A quick thinning algorithm is proposed in (8) where most of the stroke information can be obtained during the thinning so we can try to combine thinning with stroke extraction.

### 7.1 Fast thinning.

We simply identify some related concepts and operations briefly to form the algorithm for fast stroke extraction. More details for fast thinning can be found in (8) and (9).

Definition 4. Interval: one or many black pixels along the horizontal direction constitute a stroke interval which can be described by the coordinates of start and end points or width and its middle point.

Definition 5. Overlapping: let $s_i$ and $e_i$ be the start and end points of the intervals, then intervals $(s_i, e_i)$ and $(s_j, e_j)$ will be overlapping if both following inequalities hold:

$$s_i < e_j \text{ and } s_j < e_i$$

Definition 6. degree of overlapping: the number of intervals which overlap with the same interval (below or above).

Definition 7. line adjacency graph: The nodes of the line adjacency graph correspond to intervals and branches connect nodes if the corresponding intervals are adjacent lines. Fig. 5 shows an example of LAG.

Definition 8. vertical path: A vertical path of LAG is where the width of all nodes is below a given threshold $w_o$ and the number of nodes exceeds a given value $N_o$.

Definition 9. Horizontal path: A horizontal path of LAG is one where the width of all

Fig.5 LAG

nodes exceeds a threshold $N_o x V_s$, the number of nodes is below $w_o/v_s$, and nodes on either side of the path have width greater than or equal to $w_o$.

Definition 10. Diagonal path: A diagonal path of the LAG with slope $\emptyset$ is one where all the centers are approximately collinear, the slope of the line passing through them is $\emptyset$, the width of all the nodes is below $w_o x \sin(\emptyset)$, and their number exceeds $N_o x \cos(\emptyset)$.

We list the thinning algorithm as follows to investigate what can be performed for stroke extraction when thinning:

Algorithm   Fast Thinning

1). Form the LAG

2). Find paths consisting of nodes according to the degree of overlapping.

3). Extend paths with definition 8,9 and 10.

4). For horizontal paths, find their middle points and extend to their original width.

7.2   Fast stroke extraction

The following is the operations we considered can be conducted during thinning:

1). 1-degree terminal points analysis: these points can be extracted directly from the degree of overlapping of intervals and be labeled in step.1.

2). extraction of isolating strokes: these strokes can be extracted directly in step. 2, step. 3 with few discrimination added and some horizontal path extending time will be saved in step.4.

3). Attribute labeling: in step 3, many of the nodes have been examined and the path's types the nodes attach to have also been obtained, therefore we can label the attributes of the skeleton's pirels to faciliate the stroke extraction.

Based on the discussion above, the quickened algorithm of stroke extraction can be described as follows for the original binary matrix of a Chinese character:

1). Form LAG and label 1-degree terminal points;

2). Find paths and label isolated strokes and the types of skeleton pixels;

3). Delete isolating strokes and resume the horizontal paths;

4). HSE.

As some of strokes have been extracted during the fast thinning and much useful information acquired for use in the next stroke extraction this improved algorithm will certainly be faster than the previous single HSE.   Further experiments need to be made to prove it.

The whole algorithm is also highly parallel.   Most of the operations in each step are independent and can be implemented by hardware efficiently.

8. Conclusion

The algorithm HSE described previously has produced promising results which is powerful  for both printed and handwritten Chinese characters and can tolerate variation of writing style.   The idea of combining HSE with fast thinning shows a great potentials for success with inherent parallel nature.

However some aspects remain to be improved:

1). False terminal points should be detected at the early stage of the algorithm to reduce the error rate of stroke extraction.

2). More quantitive information should be used for stroke extraction.   We have gained some statistical results reflecting the pattern of stroke variation (10).

## 9. Acknowledgement

The authors would like to express their thanks to Professor Xiling Zhou and Professor Qiangnan Sun for their careful reading and encouragement. We also thank Mr. Xiaohong Mao for his help and advice.

## 10. References

(1) X.F. Yin, C.D. Yan, D.Z. Su. "Feature extraction and distribution of a primary Chinese character set". Journal of Chinese information Processing. Vol.1, No.1, 1986.

(2) X.Z.Chang. etc. "The automatic recognition of handprinted Chinese character-a method of extracting an ordered sequences of strokes" Pattern Recognition Letters 1. 1983.

(3) Leow Wee-Kheng. "Syntactic approach to Chinese character recognition". Proc. of ICCC'86. Singapore.

(4) C.Y. Suen etc. "Advances in recognition of handwritten characters". Proc. of ICPR. 1978.

(5) D.B. Lenat. "The nature of heuristics". Artificial Intelligence. No.4 Vol. 20. 1983.

(6) D.I.A. Cohen. "Basic Techniques of Combinatorial Theory". John Wiley & Sons. 1978.

(7) Fang-hsuan Cheng etc. "Three stroke extraction methods for recognition of handwritten Chinese characters". Proc. of ICCC'86. Singapore.

(8) Xiaofeng Yin etc. "A quick thinning algorithm for Chinese characters". Proc. of 2nd National conference on Computer Graphics and Pattern Recognition. 1986.

(9) Theo Pavlidis. "Algorithms for Graphics and Image Processing". Computer Science Press. 1982.

(10) Xiaofeng Yin, Dongzhuang Su. "Stroke Analysis of Handwritten Chinese character by Regression Method" Proc. of ICCIP'87, Vol.2, Beijing.

# AN ANALYSIS OF METHODS FOR IMPROVING

# LONG-RANGE CONNECTIVITY IN MESHES

T. J. Fountain
Department of Physics and Astronomy
University College London
Gower Street, London WC1E 6DT

## 1. Introduction

The two-dimensional mesh-connected processor array is well-suited for performing low-level image processing algorithms which involve near-neighbour operations, but poorly matched to those which are functions of data at long distances. In attempting to overcome this problem, designers of such systems have utilised a number of different schemes for adding better long-range communications to the basic mesh. Schemes which have been implemented include sets of orthogonal buses; dual-channel processors and a superimposed hypercube. Other methods which are being developed include directly switchable connections between PE input and output channels and simulated quadtree connectivity.

The properties of these arrangements can be very different and it is the purpose of this paper to review the various proposals and to develop a comparative analysis of their performances. Because the aim is to determine the validity of each approach, rather than the quality of particular implementations, an attempt will be made to remove technological factors from the comparison. The paper commences with a statement of the basic problem which is to be overcome, followed by a survey of the methods which have been proposed or implemented for so doing. The final sections comprise an analysis of the properties of the various methods.

## 2. Data-Passing in Pure Meshes

Three alternative methods which have been used for connecting the processors in a mesh are shown in Figure 1. Because it is the most widely used, and because it is the simplest to analyse, the discussion here will be based on that shown in (b) — the four-connected orthogonal system. In fact, unless other differences are incorporated, the data-passing properties of the alternatives are very similar. A further assumption which is made is that each processor can simultaneously output and receive one, and only one, bit of data. This accurately reflects the true facts in the great majority of systems and permits a common baseline to be used in the present analysis.

Each data transfer is assumed to comprise a read from memory, a transfer operation and a write to memory. If each of these operations takes the same time (a single clock cycle of the system), then the total time taken is three clock cycles. During this time the maximum number of bits which can be transferred is equal to the number of PEs in the array (say $N^2$) and the distance over which each bit is

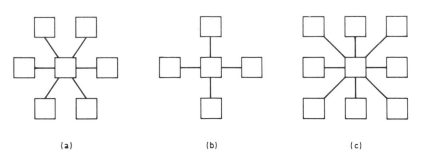

(a)        (b)        (c)

Figure 1   Alternative Near-Neighbour Connection Schemes.

transferred is one inter-processor distance.  This operation corresponds to shifting a (single-bit) image by one pixel along one of the two orthogonal axes.  A corresponding long-range function might be to shift a line of data, originating at one edge of the array, to the opposite edge.  This would involve moving N bits of data over a distance of (N−1) units and the time required would be 3(N−1) clock cycles.

An alternative type of operation, which frequently occurs in both short- and long-range versions, is the accumulation of a local neighbourhood of data at each PE.  For the smallest (3 x 3) neighbourhood in our archetypal array, the time required is 12 clock cycles for the NSEW neighbours, plus 24 clock cycles for the diagonal neighbours.  The total time is therefore 36 clock cycles.  It should be noted that two factors can reduce this time.  First, if the eight connections shown in Figure 1(c) are present, the time is reduced to 24 cycles.  Alternatively, if some flexibility of addressing is permitted, advantage can be taken of the fact that diagonal neighbours have already made part of their journey in the guise of orthogonal neighbours of other PEs.  If this fact is utilised, the time required can again be reduced to 24 cycles.

For the largest possible 'neighbourhood' operation, where the data from every pixel must be accumulated in a single PE, the time required can be calculated as follows.  In the first part of the operation, the image is shifted step by step (say) leftwards over the array.  At each step, data is stored until eventually all the data from the image has been accumulated in the leftmost column of the array.  In the second part of the operation, columns of data are shifted (say) downwards over the array (in fact, complete arrays are moved, but only the leftmost column is significant).  After N columns have each been shifted by N−1 processors, all data from the original array has been accumulated in one (the bottom lefthand) PE.  The time for the first part is simply 3(N−1) cycles, whereas the time for the second part is 3N(N−1) cycles, giving a total of $(3N^2-3)$ cycles.

A final operation worth considering is that of broadcasting a (binary) value from one PE to all others.  Assuming, for the sake of simplicity, that the value to be broadcast lies in one corner of the array, it can be transmitted to all others in its own row or column in 3(N−1) cycles.  The row or column data can then be passed to all others in a further 3(N−1) cycles, giving a total time of 6(N−1) cycles.

In order to give some feel for the magnitude of these figures, we need to assume a value for N. Systems have been marketed by a variety of companies [1–4] in which N lies between 32 and 256.  A representative figure is therefore taken to be N = 128.  Inserting this into the results calculated above we obtain the times given in Table 1. Both the advantages and the shortcomings in the performance of the mesh, when used to interconnect an array of processors, are apparent from these figures. However, the very large figure for accumulation of the 128 x 128 neighbourhood may be somewhat misleading. It should be noted that, even if zero time were taken for data transmission, merely loading the array of data into the chosen PE would take $N^2-1$ cycles, one third of the total figure. Nevertheless, it is apparent that data shifting can be a time-consuming process in a mesh-connected array, and it may therefore be worthwhile considering methods of improvement.

Table 1   Times for Representative Operations on a Mesh.

| Operation | Time (cycles) |
|---|---|
| Shift an image 1 pixel | 3 |
| Shift a line 127 pixels | 381 |
| Accumulate 3 x 3 | 24 |
| Accumulate 128 x 128 | 49 149 |
| Broadcast | 762 |

## 3. A Variety of Solutions

The problem of improving long-range connectivity has been considered by the designers of mesh processors since the earliest efforts and, in fact, most of the systems which have been produced incorporate some arrangements to deal with the problem. One of the earliest proposals, the Illiac III system [5], had a direct path from input to output, bypassing the PE storage devices. CLIP4 [6] incorporated a second processor in each PE as a data transmission channel which allowed data to flow through the array without constant storage and retrieval. Both the DAP systems [7] and GRID [8] incorporate orthogonal data buses which can pass data directly across the width of the array. More recently, the Connection Machine [9] superimposes a (partial) n-cube network over the array, although in this case the original motivation considered the n-cube connections as the main data-passing medium, with the mesh as a secondary aid to debugging. Finally, two recent proposals, YUPPIE from IBM [10] and PAPIA2 [11], use a means of direct switching between the mesh connections to avoid through-processor delays. In the case of YUPPIE this is principally intended for mapping arbitrary graphs onto the structure, while the PAPIA2 system is intended to simulate pyramid connectivity. However, each could certainly be used to improve long-range connections in a variety of ways. There are, then, at least four different methods available to improve mesh connectivity. Perhaps the easiest to consider is the X-Y bus arrangement.

## 3.1 X-Y buses

The typical arrangement of orthogonal buses in a mesh array is shown in Figure 2. In this form, common to the DAP and GRID systems, each bus line may be driven by only one PE but may drive up to (N-1) PEs. The example of shifting a line of data from one edge of the array to the other can therefore be accomplished in three clock cycles. However, use of the facility to accumulate an

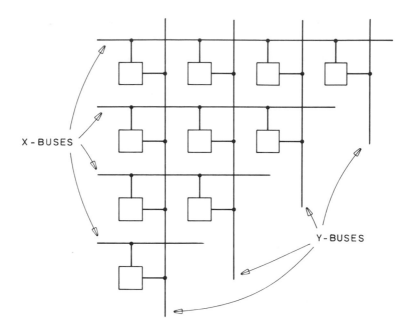

Figure 2   Connections by Orthogonal Buses.

N x N neighbourhood requires exactly the same number of cycles ($3N^2{-}3$) as would use of the mesh. Broadcasting a value from one to all processors takes just six cycles.

### 3.2 Global propagation

The only systems which have incorporated this technique are those in the CLIP series built at University College London and marketed by Stonefield plc.   The idea utilises the dual processor nature of the CLIP PE, shown in Figure 3.   A signal which is initiated at a given PE (or at the edge of the array) can pass through other elements of the array without being stored and retrieved from memory, but can then be stored in the memory of one or more target PEs.   The way in which this is achieved is fully explained in [6], while the effect on the performance of the notional array considered here would be as follows.   Transmission of a line from one side of the array to the other needs one cycle for memory read, (N–1) cycles for data transmission and one cycle for memory write — total time required (N+1) cycles. The time needed for accumulation of data in an N x N neighbourhood is actually increased substantially by the use of global propagation.   This is principally because data must still flow through each PE, rather than being able to bypass it.   For the sake of completeness, the minimum time for the operation using this facility would be approximately one half of $N^3$.   However, the time taken to broadcast a value from one PE to all is reduced to 2(N+1) cycles.

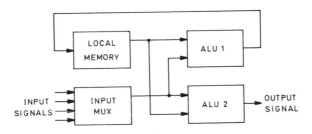

Figure 3   A CLIP4-Style Dual ALU Processor.

Two facts should be noted here.   In the only implementations of this system to date (the CLIP series), the ratio between memory access time and data transmission time is very different from that assumed here (1:1), the actual ratio being 20:1.   This greatly increases the value of the facility in the CLIP systems.   Similarly, the CLIP PEs in fact embody selectable gates as inputs rather than multiplexers, and the ability of these gates to channel data from more than one input simultaneously again improves the value of the global propagation facility.   In the CLIP implementation, then, the line shifting time becomes (N/20+2) cycles and the broadcast time is (N/10+4) cycles.   These results serve to illustrate the fact that, although an analysis of the sort carried out here may be self-consistent, the impact of implementational details on the results may be significant.

### 3.3 N-cube connections

The notion of n-cube connectivity between a set of PEs is a perfectly good one in its own right [12], but the Connection Machine has demonstrated that it can also be combined with mesh connectivity to yield improved overall properties.   Partly because of the scale of the system and partly because of the different viewpoint of the designers, however, the Connection Machine itself has sixteen times as many mesh-connected PEs as it has hypercube nodes.   For the sake of consistency I shall consider a system which has equal numbers of each, as shown in Figure 4.

One of the basic properties of the n-cube structure is that the maximum number of links along a row or column of an N x N PE array is $\log_2 N$ and, in the implementation chosen here, this is the number of links between PEs at the ends of the rows.   The time required to shift a line from one edge to the next is therefore $3\log_2 N$ cycles.  The times required to broadcast data and to assemble data over an N x N neighbourhood are more difficult to compute and depend, to some extent, on assumptions about the processors. To retain as much consistency as possible, let us suppose that a PE can place the same data onto all its output lines simultaneously, but can still only receive a single bit at a time.  Under these circumstances, the time taken to broadcast data to all other PEs is $3\log_2 N^2$ cycles.

One way to accumulate a full N x N neighbourhood would be to utilise this broadcast function $N^2$ times, giving a total time of $3N^2\log_2 N^2$ clock cycles.   For any substantial N, this is far longer than the time taken using the mesh connections.   It is, of course, true that a hypercube includes a mesh, but a system in which some of the hypercube connections formed the mesh would be less rich than one in which both mesh and hypercube were present in parallel.

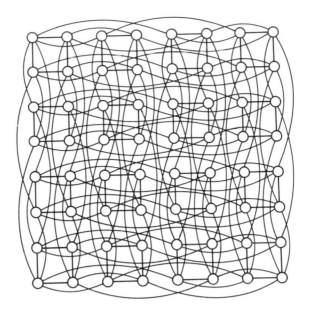

Figure 4   Hypercube Connections in an 8 x 8 Array.

## 3.4 Switched connections

The technique proposed here is illustrated in Figure 5.  In the most general case, any input to a PE can be routed directly to any output.  The facility can either be locally controlled, in which case a variety of different sub-configurations can be mapped onto the array simultaneously, or globally controlled in order to change the array configuration from one specific arrangement to another.  In the present context it is the latter method which is of significance.

Since this technique allows any PE to be bypassed at will, the time required to shift a line of data from one edge of the array to the other is almost exactly 3 clock cycles, irrespective of array size.  It is, however, true that there will be some residual delay occasioned by the switching at each PE.  Since the switching circuits can be minimally simple, this delay can be approximated as 1/100 cycles per PE.  For our example of N = 128, the total shifting time is therefore increased to 4.28 cycles, which, if array operation is synchronous, implies an effective time of 5 cycles.

Whether the time for broadcast of data is reduced below that of the mesh depends on a detail of implementation.  If data which is bypassing a PE is also presented as a potential input to the PE and therefore to its store, then the time is reduced to twice that required to shift a line, i.e. 10 cycles.  Since this arrangement is rather easy to implement, it will be assumed here.  The time required to accumulate an N x N neighbourhood using the switching facility would be approximately $5N^2-5$ cycles, the approximation again concerning the differing delays incurred by switching signals through varying numbers of PEs.

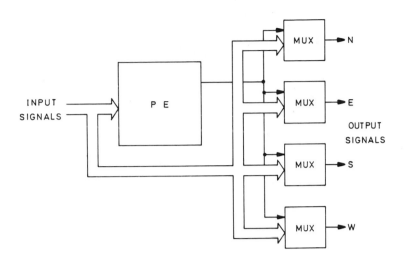

Figure 5   A Method for Direct Switching between Neighbour Connections.

## 4. Comparative Analysis

In the above sections, the properties of the alternative mesh enhancements considered here were illustrated by their performance on a few standard operations. A comparison between these times is necessary but not sufficient for a complete analysis of the systems. For this, it may be best to begin with the costs incurred by enhancement.

### 4.1 Physical costs

The additional costs incurred by enhancing the mesh connectivity fall into two classes. The first, and probably the more significant, are those caused by the changes required to the PEs themselves. To provide a baseline for assessing these, Figure 6 illustrates the makeup of a 'typical' bit-serial PE. The number of transistors required to implement each section of the circuit is shown in brackets. The presence of local data memory as part of the circuit requires some discussion. All mesh-connected arrays have some local memory associated with each processor, but the amount varies widely from system to system. I have made the assumption here that the memory can be considered in two parts — cache memory which is associated closely with the processor and main memory which is treated separately. From this viewpoint, most actual processors have a similar amount of cache memory, between 32 and 128 bits. I have therefore assumed a value of 64 bits for our 'typical' PE.

The total number of transistors for the standard PE is therefore about 215. The additional circuits required to implement an X-Y bus arrangement can take two forms. In the first case the buses carry only data, and an expansion of the input multiplexing arrangements is all that is required on the data paths. However, each PE must also be provided with an addressing mechanism, which is costly in terms of extra circuits. The alternative is to use the buses for both data transmission and addressing — PEs can then be selected either individually or by groups on the same rows or columns. This can be achieved with a

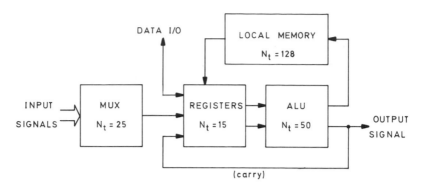

Figure 6   A Typical Bit-Serial Processing Element.

($N_t$ = number of transistors)

much simpler address decoder and is therefore to be preferred. In this latter case, the extra number of transistors required overall is about 25. The additional circuits required to implement a global propagation arrangement consist mainly of an extra ALU which operates in parallel with the principal ALU. The number of transistors needed for this enhancement is about 75. For the arrangement suggested above using n-cube connections, the only additional cost is incurred by a (fairly substantial) expansion of the PE input multiplexing arrangements. The extra number of transistors is approximately 75. One possible arrangement for implementing bypass switches in a mesh is shown in Figure 5. For the general arrangement shown, the additional number of transistors needed is about 150.

The second area of additional costs is associated with the extra wires needed for each particular enhancement. In fact, only two of the arrangements discussed here need extra wires: the X-Y bus and the n-cube. For the bus arrangement, the extra costs are minimal, comprising two extra connection points per PE and 2N wires distributed evenly over the array. In the case of the n-cube, an additional $2\log_2 N$ connection points per PE are needed, together with $N^2\log_2 N$ wires. An additional cost is incurred by the non-homogeneous nature of the extra connections. The author has been unable to discover a realistic method of quantifying these extra wiring costs. Table 2 merely notes which arrangements involve extra costs of this sort.

## 4.2 Fundamental properties

In order to obtain some idea of the likely worth of any particular enhancement to connectivity, one alternative to calculating the performance for particular operations is to estimate the fundamental parameters of the arrangement. The first of these is the data bandwidth which, in the present circumstances, is a simple function of the extra number of wires involved in each implementation (since one bit of data can be transmitted by each wire in unit time). The calculation is extremely simple and results in the figures given in Table 2. A second parameter is the spanning distance, defined here as the (average) distance, in terms of pixels, over which the enhanced connection net can transmit the amount of data implied by the bandwidth figure, in a single operation (i.e. in three clock cycles).

Table 2   Comparative Properties of Alternative Enhancements.

| Property | Mesh | X-Y bus | Global | n-cube | Switch |
|---|---|---|---|---|---|
| Shift a line 127 pixels | 381 | 3 | 129 | 21 | 5 |
| Accumulate 128 x 128 | $5 \times 10^4$ | $5 \times 10^4$ | $1 \times 10^6$ | $7 \times 10^5$ | $8 \times 10^4$ |
| Broadcast data | 762 | 6 | 258 | 42 | 10 |
| Added PE costs | (215) | 25 | 75 | 75 | 150 |
| Added wiring costs | | yes | no | yes | no |
| Data bandwidth | $2 \times 10^4$ | 128 | 0 | $2 \times 10^3$ | 0 |
| Spanning distance | 1 | 128 | 128 | 32 | 128 |

## 4.3 Summary

The various properties which have been calculated in this paper are summarised in Table 2. In considering the implications of this table, it must be borne in mind that a number of (somewhat arbitrary) assumptions have been made in arriving at these figures. Although the assumptions have been consistent, this does not guarantee their suitability for each case. For any particular type of enhancement, it might be possible to identify one area where a concentration of facilities would be of disproportionate benefit. However, given this proviso, it is apparent that substantial improvements in global performance can be achieved for relatively small costs in a number of ways.

The X-Y bus arrangement offers the best figures for line shifting and broadcast of data, minimal increased processor cost and a balanced combination of bandwidth and spanning distance. Its main drawback is the requirement for additional wiring, although this is probably not great. The system of switching inputs to outputs gives similar performance figures, although at increased cost, but probably offers substantial additional advantages if local control permits differently switched subsets. Global propagation can only compete with the alternatives if the implementation conditions are appropriate, as described in section 3.2. The superimposed n-cube offers moderate performance on the chosen tasks for a moderate increase in processor complexity. It is also the only arrangement which incorporates an additional bandwidth comparable with that of the original mesh. This, together with a less homogeneous distribution of wiring, probably gives it an advantage in less uniformly structured operations, although such an advantage would depend on additional complexity of control.

## 5. Conclusions

Mesh connectivity in an array of processors is ideal for many low-level image processing operations where the output at each point is a function of locally concentrated data. For operations where data must be moved substantial distances about the array, however, the usual mesh connectivity can be rather inefficient. A number of alternative arrangements have been proposed which can overcome these problems. In some cases (e.g. the addition of X-Y buses) improvements in long-range connectivity are the main intention of the enhancement; in other cases (e.g. the n-cube connectivity of the Connection

Machine), there are other reasons for the added complexity and the improvements in low-level data shifting come as a bonus.

This paper has demonstrated that, given equality of technical factors, each of the proposed arrangements has a unique balance of advantages and disadvantages. Before summarising these, three points should be noted. First, for no arrangement does the added complexity improve the time taken to accumulate large neighbourhoods of data at each PE. Second, the comparative performance of some arrangements can be significantly improved by slight changes in the 'ground rules'. Finally, although all the proposals offer greatly improved spanning distances, none offers a substantial increase in total bandwidth. This last implies that all the arrangements are better at moving small data sets than large.

With these points in mind, Table 3 ranks the various arrangements for a number of properties. In conclusion it is worth noting that, for each of the enhancements described here, very large improvements in performance on selected operations are available for rather small increases in (hardware) costs. This certainly indicates that such improvements to the original 'pure' mesh concept are worthwhile, but it should not be forgotten that there are hidden costs in terms of added algorithmic complexity, which may not be negligible.

Table 3   Ranking of Enhancements.

| Arrangement | Shifting/Broadcast | Costs | Bandwidth | Distance |
|---|---|---|---|---|
| X-Y bus | 1 | 1 | 2 | 1 |
| Global | 4 | 2 | 3 | 1 |
| n-cube | 3 | 3 | 1 | 4 |
| Switch | 2 | 4 | 3 | 1 |

## References

1. Active Memory Technology, Reading, Berks, DAP - Technical Literature, (1987).
2. Stonefield Systems PLC, Horsham, Sussex, CLIP - Technical Literature, (1987).
3. Goodyear Aerospace Corporation, Akron, Ohio, MPP - Technical Literature, (1987).
4. Thinking Machines Corporation, Cambridge, Mass., Connection Machine - Technical Literature, (1987).
5. B. H. McCormick, The Illinois pattern recognition computer - ILLIAC III, *IEEE Trans. EC-12*, 791-813 (1963).
6. M. J. B. Duff and T. J. Fountain (Eds.), *Cellular Logic Image Processing*. Academic Press, London (1986).
7. S. F. Reddaway, DAP - a distributed array processor, *Proc. 1st Annual Symp. on Computer Architecture, Florida*, 61-65 (1973).
8. T. J. Fountain, *Processor Arrays: Architectures and Applications*. Academic Press, London (1987).
9. W. D. Hillis, *The Connection Machine*. MIT Press, Cambridge, Mass. (1985).
10. H. Li and M. Maresca, Polymorphic-Torus Architecture for Computer Vision, IBM Research Report RC 12492 (#56120), T J Watson Research Center, Yorktown Heights, NY 10598 (1987).
11. V. Cantoni, Private communication, (1987).
12. N. Mokhoff, Concurrent computers make scientific computing affordable, *Computer Design*, 59-60 (April 1985).

# Implementation and use of software scanning on a small CLIP4 processor array.

J. Buurman, R.P.W. Duin

Pattern Recognition Group, Faculty of Applied Physics

Delft University of Technology

The Netherlands

## Abstract.

For a small CLIP4 processor array, algorithms are described that perform scanning over large images. Two algorithms are shown: a shift out algorithm developed by Stonefield Systems PLC., and a shift through algorithm, which is presented here for the first time. A simple hardware alternative to shifting, half scan addressing, is shown to offer a significant speed advantage.

It is shown that software scanning suffers from a severe drawback: it has a high overhead for simple neighbourhood operations. However, techniques are available to reduce the overhead to values, comparable with those of the hardware scanning CLIP4S system. These require the user to know the neighbourhood size needed for his operations, and the maximal neighbourhood allowed (a system constant). For point- and complex neighbourhood operations, software scanning can be faster than hardware scanning. An advantage of software scanning is its flexibility (in image size and sorts of operations), which also offers the possibility to do data dependent processing and recursion.

It is concluded that software scanning can be an alternative to hardware scanning, especially when flexibility is of value.

## 1. Introduction.

For some time, mesh connected processor arrays have been used in image processing. However, arrays with a sufficient size for common images have remained a rarity. As a result of this, ways have been developed to map an image onto a smaller array. Two solutions can be distinguished:

- The crinkle or pyramidal mapping (see Pass[1] and fig.1.1.), where the whole image is mapped onto the array at once, so that regions of adjacent pixels reside in one processing element.
- The window mapping (see fig. 1.2.), where the image is split up into regions the size of the array. Each region (called a scan) is processed successively by the array. The array is thereby scanning across the image.

The crinkle mapping can make no use of a possible feature of some processor arrays in which each processing element (p.e.) may access several neighbours simultaneously, because in this mapping the neighbour p.e.s in general do not contain the adjacent pixels. Because of this, crinkling is less suitable for arrays that offer this feature. In the window mapping, neighbouring pixels are mapped onto neighbouring p.e.s by which an optimal use can be made of the hardware connection pattern.

In this paper we will restrict ourselves to the window mapping and scanning. The main problem with scanning is the passing of values between adjacent pixels in different scans for neighbourhood operations. There are several ways to implement scanning. The two main classes are:

- Scanning by hardware. This is mostly done by one-dimensional arrays scanning each instruction across the image.
- Scanning by software. For speed reasons, it is better not to do this for each instruction separately. A larger algorithm, which we will call an operation, is executed completely for each scan before the next scan is processed. These operations can be the same as would be executed on a non-scanning array. The array is in general a two-dimensional mesh. Scanning by software can be supported by special hardware, but optimal hardware (such as the MPP's staging memory, see Potter[2]) is very complex. The scanning software itself may be executed by the host or by the array.

Scanning by the host, which is also serving other tasks, is rather slow. In this paper, software scanning by the array is examined. Two algorithms for pure software scanning and one method of simple hardware support are presented in chapter 2. The algorithms and a simulation of the hardware have been implemented on a CLIP4 system (see Duff[3]). CLIP4's most characteristic feature is that each processing element may access eight neighbouring processing elements in parallel. This is reflected in the algorithm length of simple operations. The scanning algorithms are compared with respect to scanning overhead, along with a hardware scanning system, the CLIP4S (see Fountain et.al.[4]). In chapter 3 the use of software scanning is discussed. This allows conclusions to be drawn in chapter 4.

## 2. Scanning algorithms.

Let us assume that we want to process an image of $N*N$ pixels with a small, two dimensional processor array of $n*n$ p.e.s.. The pixels have $p$ bits values. Because the image is larger than the processor array, it is divided into $s$ scans. On this image we want to perform an algorithm of length $m$ steps, each step equal to one typical processing cycle of length $t_S$. Such a basic algorithm will be called an operation.

Scanning an operation is only problematic when the operation is a neighbourhood operation, so that p.e.s processing a pixel also need values of pixels adjacent in the image. This is indicated by the overlap $w$: for a $(2w +1)*(2w+1)$ neighbourhood operation, at most $w$ pixels in every direction can be in a different scan (see fig. 2.1).

A scanning algorithm should divide the image into $c$ manageable areas called *chunks*. For each chunk, a solution for the neighbour problem is given where the edge pixels, necessary to process the chunk correctly, are made available. For a description of scanning algorithms that is independent of the image size, we will use the number of steps taken to perform the operation on a complete image, divided by the number of scans. This number of steps per scan, $M$, can in general be written as:

$$M = \alpha + \beta * m, \qquad (2.1)$$

where $\alpha$ and $\beta$ are constants determined by the scanning algorithm. $\alpha$ is a measure of the amount of work involved

in partitioning the image into chunks. $\beta$ indicates how efficient the chunk partitioning is. A value of 1 indicates that the operation is only performed once per scan, large values implicate a less efficient algorithm. Each of these chunks must be prepared for processing and after processing be sent to the output. A measure of the performance of the scanning algorithm is the scanning overhead factor $A$, given by

$$A = M / m. \qquad (2.2)$$

An overhead factor of 1 means that there is no overhead: processing the image takes as long as processing all the scans. This is theoretically possible for point operations. For neighbourhood operations, the case is more complicated as on the edges of chunks, values must be present to allow edges to be processed correctly. This requires a shifting of the pixels in the chunks. Some algorithms are described below.

### 2.1. Shift out.

A shift out algorithm uses a shift operation where data shifted out of the array is lost. A good algorithm, which has been developed by Stonefield Systems PLC. for their CLIP4 systems is the following:

The image is divided into chunks of size $(n-w)*(n-w)$, which is the maximum amount of data the array can process correctly. This means that the chunk partitioning is maximally efficient. The number of chunks $c$ is

$$c = \left/ \frac{N - 2w}{n - 2w} \right/^{2}, \qquad (2.3)$$

where $/x/$ denotes the first integer higher than or equal to $x$.

Each chunk resides in one, two or four scans. The different parts are fetched, shifted to the appropriate place and or-ed together, see fig. 2.2. After processing, the result is divided into parts and stored in different output scans. The number of shift operations is proportional to the number of bitplanes and the image size. The number of program steps of a shift operation is taken to be $k_{so}$, the total number of steps per scan $M_{so}$ is given by

$$M_{so} = \frac{c}{s} * (B + a * n * p * k_{so} + m ), \qquad (2.4)$$

where $B$ is a constant overhead for bookkeeping which is generally small and $a$ is a constant of maximally 8 for a

4-connected array and an infinite image and smaller in all other cases. Properties of this algorithm are:
- Number of steps only dependent on the overlap through the number of chunks.
- Large number of shifts necessary.
- Maximally efficient chunk partitioning.

## 2.2. Shift Through.

If a different shift operation is used a different algorithm becomes possible. A shift through operation is a shift where data shifted out of the array is carried to another scan. This operation is more complicated than a shift out and is very dependent on the array architecture, because values have to be moved from one side of the array to the other side. A good algorithm is the following:

The image is partitioned into chunks of size $2n*2n$, so that chunk boundaries are in the middle of scans. This means that some efficiency in chunk partitioning is traded against a shorter algorithm. The processing takes place on $3*3$ scans subimages: the scan edges are copied using $2w$ shift throughs from the middle scan outward so that each pixel can be processed correctly somewhere in the subimage, see fig. 2.3. The scan shifted out from remains unchanged. All nine scans are operated upon, and the result is shifted in again. This requires $48w$ shift throughs. The algorithm length per scan $M_{st}$ is equal to

$$M_{st} = \frac{1}{4} * \left( B + 48 * w * p * k_{st} + 9 * m \right), \quad (2.5)$$

where $k_{st}$ is the length of a shift through operation (in program steps). Properties of this algorithm are:
- Number of steps proportional to the overlap size ($w$).
- Relatively low number of shifts.
- Chunk partitioning efficiency not optimal.

## 2.3. Half scan addressing.

As the numbers of shifts in all shift algorithms are quite large, ways were sought to avoid these. An architecture that would allow every part of the image to be transferred to the array without shifts would be very complex. A small change in the array architecture would allow an instantaneous shift over half the array size, $n/2$, see fig. 2.4. Chunks have size $n/2*n/2$, which is not very efficient. This can be implemented in the following way:

The array is connected to an external memory which contains the image. If this memory is only $n/2 * n/2$ bits wide, four quarters of a chunk with their edge pixels can be fetched from different scans by addressing the correct

quarters subsequently, see fig. 2.5. This is only a minor extension of the array controller's complexity. The algorithm has to divide the image into chunks, read each chunk, process it and write the result. For an infinitely large image, the number of chunks $c$ approximates $4s$. The algorithm length $M_{hsa}$ would be

$$M_{hsa} = B + 4 * m, \quad (2.6)$$

where the bookkeeping term $B$ is significant due to the absence of shifting. Properties of half scan addressing are:
- Number of steps not dependent on the overlap.
- No shifting required.
- Not very efficient in chunk partitioning.

## 2.4. Implementation.

Shift out and shift through algorithms and a simulation of half scan addressing have been implemented on the Delft University CLIP4 processor array. This array has the following properties:
- Dedicated controller realizing a typical processing cycle $t_S$ (including array control) of approximately 10 μs.
- The length of typical binary operations ranges from 1 - 100 $t_S$, for other kinds of arrays which do not access eight neighbours at a time we may expect 10 - 1000 $t_S$ for a similarly defined $t_S$. Typical 8-bit grey value operations range from 50-5000 $t_S$. Since these operations do not make such intensive use of parallel connections to neighbours, we may expect similar values for other arrays. Some operation lengths are shown in table 1.
- 8-connected array, leading to a value of 4 for $a$.
- Shift outs take one instruction, so $k_{so} = 1$. There is no hardware to support shift through, resulting in an value of about 7 for $k_{st}$.

The Delft array is somewhat a-typical because it is not square. It is a 64*32 array processing images of up to 256*256 pixels. Since the shift through implementation was never developed into a universal program, the bookkeeping term $B$ cannot not be given. For the half scan addressing implementation, it is

$$B = 30 + 10 * p, \quad (2.7)$$

For 256*256 images, 2.4-6 become

$$M_{so} = 50 + 240 * p + 1.4 * m, \quad (2.8)$$

$$M_{st} = 73 * p + 2.2 * m, \quad (2.9)$$

$$M_{hsa} = 27 + 10 * p + 3.3 * m. \quad (2.10)$$

It should be noted that differences in the bookkeeping term are caused by differences in the implementations. Of course, one solution requires more bookkeeping than the other. However, this term is only of importance for half scan addressing. Other differences are due to the fact that the images are not of infinite size. From eqs. 2.8-10, the scanning overhead can be derived using eq. 2.2.

## 2.5. CLIP4S.

Another CLIP4 system that also uses scanning is the CLIP4S system described by Fountain et.al.[4] The CLIP4S is a 512*4 array processing 512*512 images. Each array instruction is scanned across the image by hardware using edge stores. Although this principle is entirely different the scanning overhead can still be estimated:

For a 128 scans image, a binary neighbourhood operation takes 14 ms. This instruction would take 10 μs on a non-scanning CLIP4. However, Fountain[5] estimates that a speed-up of about 2.5 is achieved because the host system (acting as the controller) can operate while the array is scanning. The resulting scanning overhead is

$$A_{4S} = \frac{14*10^3}{128 * 10 * 2.5} = 4.4. \quad (2.11)$$

CLIP4S has a similar overhead for point operations. This property is not shared by software scanning, because the edge problem does not occur in this case.

## 2.6. Comparison.

For a number of operations, the execution times for all systems and without scanning are given in table 1. For all scanning methods, a 256*256 image has been assumed. CLIP4S times were taken from Fountain et.al.[4], scaled down for the proper image size. Times given in italics were estimated using eq. 2.11. It can be seen that for simple operations, the shifting and bookkeeping determine the execution time, whereas for complicated operations, the chunk partitioning is decisive. For these operations, the overhead caused by the scanning per instruction of CLIP4S is also important. For point operations, software scanning only has some bookkeeping overhead. This means that for all but the most simple operations, it is faster than hardware scanning.

Operation lengths have been measured by the author for standard software. For point operations, only the shift out times have been given. Since point operations do not have problems with edges, the only thing the software has to do is transport scans. The speed of this does not depend on the scanning method but on the actual implementation. Times for the shift out implementation are considered to be representative for software scanning.

For all systems the scanning overhead as a function of the neighbourhood operation length is shown in figs. 2.6 and 2.7 for binary and 8 bit images, respectively. It can be observed that:

- only for complex neighbourhood operations, the efficient use of chunks is of importance. From the figures mentioned earlier we see that this does not apply to most operations. For simple neighbourhood operations, software scanning has a high overhead.
- for these operations, hardware scanning with edge stores is most efficient. The order of the software scanning methods depends on the operation. Conclusions about the different software methods are postponed until chapter 3, when their use has been discussed.

| operation description | no scanning | shift out | shift through | half scan addr | CLIP4S (hardware) |
|---|---|---|---|---|---|
| binary move | 10 μs | 8.5 | - | - | 2.8 |
| 8-bit add | 150 μs | 17.5 | - | - | 27.5 |
| 8-bit multiply | 2.6 | 95 | - | - | *370* |
| 8-conn. erosion | 15 μs | 90 | 24 | 13 | 3.5 |
| 8-bit sobel filter | 1.5 | 650 | 292 | 190 | 210 |
| 8-bit 3*3 median | 36 | 1980 | 2700 | 3800 | *5000* |

Table 1. Execution time for all scanning methods and without scanning, for several operations for a 256*256 image and 2048 p.e.s. Times in ms, unless otherwise stated.

# 3. Use of software scanning.

The software scanning methods described above have the following properties:
- Scanning at the operation level.
- Large overhead for simple operations.
- Overhead independent (half scan addressing) or nearly independent (shift out) of the overlap size.

Based on these properties the following techniques can be given to use software scanning effectively:

## 3.1. Grouping of operations.

Since simple operations are scanned at a high overhead, and increasing the overlap does not raise it (by much), it is useful to perform several operations in one scanning. There is of course a limit to this gain because the numbers of pixels producing valid output of the array decreases with increasing overlap. For software scanning, the optimal overlap for a group of simple operations is about $\sqrt{n}$, a system constant. Half scan addressing limits the overlap to $n/4$. Since the length of a shift through algorithm is proportional to the overlap, this property cannot be used. Therefore shift through algorithms are less preferable.

## 3.2. Data dependent processing.

When complex operations are scanned, software scanning allows different operations on different chunks. For instance, an operation may not be executed when the chunk is empty, or an iterated operation may be stopped when a stable result has been obtained. Depending on the contents of a scan, one of several operations may be executed, giving an effect similar to that of processor arrays with an enable bit. It can be shown[6] that when small objects are processed, the behaviour of the array becomes that of a non-scanning array, plus a fixed extra time overhead.

## 3.3. Recursion.

Another possibility with software scanning is recursion: the results after operating upon one chunk may be written back to the input image and used by the next chunk. This method of scanning allows the realization of global transformations, such as the CLIP4 global propagation, or distance transforms.

## 3.4. Flexibility.

An important advantage of two-dimensional software scanning is its flexibility: unlike linear arrays, the image size is free; unlike hardware scanning, data dependent scanning is possible; recursion is possible. When a processor array is used as a universal system, not for a special application only, these are important qualities.

## 3.5. An example: the skeleton.

The skeleton algorithm described by Arcelli et.al.[7] is very suited to the CLIP4 processor architecture. One iteration consists of the matching of eight different masks on the image, each time removing those pixels that fit. On the Delft CLIP4 array (64*32 p.e.s) it has been implemented using the shift out scanning algorithm described above.

First, scanning was tried once for every mask fitting, the most primitive operation of the algorithm which uses an overlap of 1. Second, because the overhead was relatively independent of the overlap, operations were grouped until the sum of their overlaps was equal to the system's optimal overlap (8). This resulted in scanning once per skeleton iteration. Finally, iterations were grouped. This is possible because the masks are related. All eight masks never remove a layer of more than two pixels (see Hilditch[8]), resulting in a 5*5 neighbourhood operation (overlap 2). When the data is unevenly distributed across the image, the time per iteration may even be lower, because in scans where nothing changes, the operation is terminated early (data dependent processing). The final operation is:

```
count = 4
do
        fit all masks and remove fitting pixels
        count = count - 1
until ((nothing has changed) or (count = 0))
if (something changed during the last iteration)
        flag global unfinished
```

There is also a global check to see if anything has changed, the scanning continues until nothing has changed in the entire image. The number of iterations per operation (4) is the result of

$$no.\ of\ iterations = \frac{optimal\ overlap}{overlap\ of\ iterations}, \qquad (3.1)$$

where the optimal overlap is a system constant which is in this case 8.

The obtained results are listed in table 2. Unless otherwise stated a 256*256 image is used. Using grouping of operations the scanning overhead has been reduced to 5.5. Using data dependent processing, the execution time per iteration may be reduced even further. If the data is distributed very unevenly, a longer algorithm using a smaller overlap (such as the border parallel algorithm suggested by Hilditch) may be justified.

| description | time per iteration | scanning overhead |
|---|---|---|
| without scanning (64 * 32 image) | 286 µs | - |
| scanning per mask (overlap 1) | 820 ms | 90 |
| scanning per iteration (overlap 8) | 140 ms | 16 |
| scanning per 4 iterations (overlap 8) | 50 ms | 5.5 |

Table 2. Execution time per iteration and scanning overhead for the Arcelli algorithm.

## 3.6. Consequences for the comparison.

From the techniques described above, conclusions can be drawn about the different algorithms. Since grouping of operations is useful when an optimal overlap exists, an algorithm length almost independent of the overlap is a preferable quality. This means that for arrays where the shift through is a complicated operation, a shift out algorithm should be preferred. When a shift through is simple, the absolute length of this algorithm is decisive. As an alternative to shifting, half scan addressing offers a significant decrease in scanning overhead for most cases.

## 4 Conclusions.

In chapter two, several methods of scanning have been examined. For all point operations except the most simple ones, software scanning is faster than hardware scanning. For simple neighbourhood operations, hardware scanning with edge stores showed to be the fastest method. Software scanning has a high overhead for these operations, a problem that is reduced by half scan addressing. Complicated neighbourhood operations have low software scanning overheads, this follows from the fact that they consist mostly of point operations. For these operations however, efficient chunk partitioning is important. Software scanning provides this and can thereby be faster than hardware scanning.

As was shown in chapter three, techniques are available to reduce the overhead to values, comparable with that of hardware scanning. These require the user to know the overlap required for his operations, and the maximal overlap. Since the latter is a constant for each system and the former is implied in most operations, this does not seem an unreasonable demand.

Also in chapter three, advantages of software scanning are shown. They are: flexibility (in image size and kinds of operations) and as a result of this, the possibility to do data dependent processing and recursion. Data dependent scanning may be used to an advantage when the data is distributed unevenly over the image. Recursion is a type of operation that is only to a limited extent available on hardware scanning systems.

The results of this comparison are to a certain extent influenced by CLIP4's architecture. The most important factors are:
- The fact that each processing element can access eight neighbours in parallel results in relatively short algorithms for cellular logical operations. For short algorithms, scanning overhead is largest. For complex grey value operations this feature is of little importance.
- The shift through operation may be realized using global propagation, a typical CLIP4 operation. Other arrays could use a wrap-around to make the operation faster, or no support at all, which would make it much slower.

It seems that a similar comparison can be made for other processor arrays.

The authors would like to stress that flexibility is of importance in a field such as scanning, where experience is limited. During their work on scanning, they found several times that the software had to be extended to allow for another class of operations. Limits on the number of input images, the number of output images, the sequence of scanning and the use of recursion had to be avoided. Should a similar need have arisen on a hardware scanning system, where changes are cumbersome and expensive, this could never have been done.

It may be concluded that software scanning can be a real alternative to hardware scanning, especially when flexibility is of value. For most point operations and for complicated neighbourhood operations software scanning can be made faster than hardware scanning.

# References:

1. Pass S.; The GRID computer system. In: Kittler J., Duff M.J.B. (eds.),; Image processing system architecture, Research Studies Press, Letchworth, 1985.
2. Potter J.L.; MPP architecture and programming. In: Preston K. jr., Levialdi S., Duff M.J.B. (eds.); Multicomputers and image processing, Academic Press, London, 1982.
3. Duff M.J.B.; The CLIP4. In: Fu K.S., Ichikawa T., Special computer architectures for pattern processing, CRC Press, 1982.
4. Fountain T.W., Postranecky M., Shaw G.K.;The CLIP4S system, Pattern recognition letters 5, 1987.
5 Fountain T.W.; private communication, 1987.
6. Buurman J. ,1987; Scanning algorithms for the CLIP4 processor array. Thesis, Pattern recognition group, Department of applied physics, Delft University of Technology, 1987.
7. Arcelli C., Cordella L., Levialdi S.; Parallel thinning of binary images, Electr. Lett. 11, 1975.
8. Hilditch C.J.; Comparison of thinning algorithms on a processor array. Image and vision computing 3, 1983.

# Acknowledgement.

This research was made possible by the Netherlands Organization for the Advancement of Pure Research (Z.W.O). The authors would like to thank P.P.Jonker for his contribution to the shift through method.

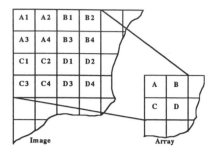

**Fig. 1.1.** The crinkle mapping. Pixels with the same letter correspond to the processing element with that letter.

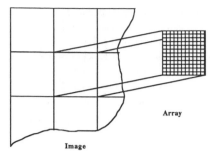

**Fig. 1.2.** The window mapping or scanning. Each area is mapped onto the array successively.

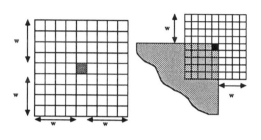

**Fig. 2.1.** (a) A pixel with a $(2w+1)*(2w+1)$ neighbourhood. (b) This pixel has at most $w$ neighbours in each direction in other scans.

**Fig. 2.2.** A shift out algorithm. A chunk is in at most four different scans (left). After shifting (indicated by the arrows) the chunk (right) can be composed by or-ing the four parts together.

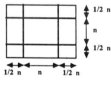

(a) A chunk.

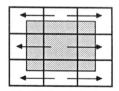

(b1) Shift through (horizontally).

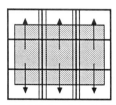

(b2) Shift through (vertically).

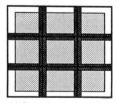

(c) Processing (edge pixels are incorrect).

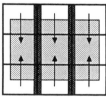

(d1) Shift-in (vertically).

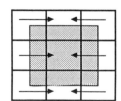

(d2) Shift-in (horizontally).

**Fig. 2.3.** A shift through algorithm. Dark lines denote scan boundaries, the chunk is shaded.

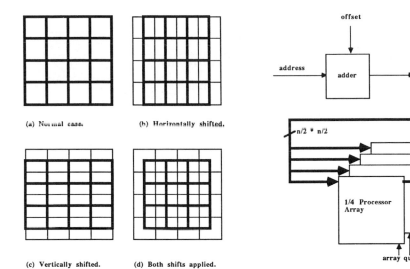

(a) Normal case.  (b) Horizontally shifted.

(c) Vertically shifted.  (d) Both shifts applied.

Fig. 2.4. Possible shifts of the array for half scan addressing.

Fig. 2.5. Possible implementation of half scan addressing.

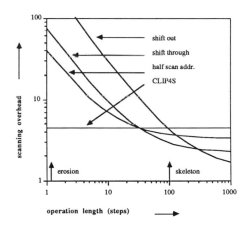

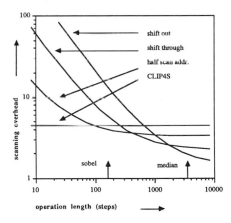

operation length (steps)

operation length (steps)

Fig. 2.6. Scanning overhead as a function of the operation length for binary images (overlap 1). Typical operations range from 1 (erosion) to 100 (4 Arcelli iterations) steps, curves may change as a result of larger overlap as realized by operation grouping.

Fig. 2.7. Scanning overhead as a function of the operation length for 8-bit images (overlap 1). Typical operations range from 50-5000 steps. Indicated are the sobel and median filter from table 1.

# Performing Global Transforms
# On an SIMD Machine

De-lei Lee

Department of Computer Science
York University
North York, Ontario
Canada M3J 1P3

Wayne A. Davis

Department of Computing Science
University of Alberta
Edmonton, Alberta
Canada T6G 2H1

**Abstract**:

This paper addresses the problem of performing global transforms of images on an SIMD machine proposed for image processing [4]. In particular, parallel computation of two-dimensional fast Fourier transform (2-D FFT) is considered. Two of the machine's permissible memory accesses are exploited, which allow the $N$ processing elements of the machine to access two halves of two rows or columns of an $N \times N$ image in the memory system in one memory access. It is shown that in two memory accesses, each processing element is able to obtain two pixels of one of the two rows or columns which are $2^{n-1}$ pixels apart. This access capability in conjunction with the machine's permutation network lead to an efficient algorithm for parallel computation of 2-D FFT through row-column decomposition.

**Keywords**: SIMD machine, permutation network, global transforms, 2-D FFT.

## 1. INTRODUCTION

Global transforms are operations in which each output depends on any portion of the input image. Examples of global transforms are 2-D Fourier transform, Hadamard transforms, and matrix manipulations [7]. The Fourier transform arises in many fields of science and engineering, and a fast method for computing the Fourier transform has long been of great interest. One of the major applications of the

This work was supported in part by the Natural Sciences and Engineering Research Council of Canada under Grants NSERC-A9196 and NSERC-A7634, and by the Institute of Space and Terrestrial Science.

2-D FFT is in computing the convolution of two images X and Y, where X is an input image of dimension $N \times N$ and Y is the convolution kernel of dimension $M \times M$, by making use of the convolution theorem [7]. In this application, it is computationally efficient to first apply a 2-D FFT to image X and image Y, then compute a new image by multiplying pairs of the corresponding elements in these two transformed images, and finally to apply the inverse 2-D FFT to the new image to get the desired convolution. When the kernel size $M$ becomes as large as $N$, the direct convolution method requires $O(N^4)$ arithmetic operations. However, the use of the 2-D FFT will reduce the cost to $O(N^2 \log N)$ in uniprocessor environment. Parallel computation of 2-D FFT on SIMD machines has been studied by a number of researchers [1, 3, 5, 8]. In particular, the well-known STARAN parallel processor [1] can execute the 2-D FFT of an $N \times N$ image in $O(N \log N)$ steps. However, STARAN does not provide a suitable computing structure for neighborhood operations, especially for those with large window size, in image processing applications. It is widely believed that future parallel computers for image processing at the pixel level should possess more flexible architecture on which a variety of image processing algorithms can be efficiently implemented [2, 6].

The purpose of this paper is to show that parallel computation of 2-D FFT can be done in $O(N \log N)$ steps on a proposed SIMD machine [4], using two of the machine's permissible memory accesses. The machine possesses a flexible architecture to support various image processing algorithms. For example, neighborhood operations can be performed at maximum efficiency by making use of other permissible memory accesses of the machine, regardless of the window size [4].

The next section contains some background: the formulation of an $N$ point 1-D FFT, and a brief description of the proposed SIMD machine. Section 3 describes two of the machine's permissible memory accesses which lead directly to an algorithm for computing 1-D FFT of two rows or two columns of an image simultaneously. Parallel computation of 2-D FFT of the image is then presented.

## 2. BACKGROUND

Throughout this paper, let $N = 2^n$, where $n$ is an even number. The elements of $\{0, 1, ..., N-1\}$ will be considered as integers, or $n$-dimensional vectors whose components are either 0 or 1. An $n$-dimensional vector $x_0 \cdots x_{n-1}$ is identified with the integer $x = \sum_{i=0}^{n-1} x_i 2^{n-i-1}$, with $x_0$ being the most significant bit. The vector $x_0 \cdots x_{n-1}$ is also called the binary representation of $x$. Let P represent an image of dimensions $N \times N$, and $P(i, j)$ denote the pixel at the $i$th row and $j$th column of P.

## 2.1 Fast Fourier transform

The 2-D Discrete Fourier Transform (DFT) of P is defined as follows:

$$G(u,v) = \sum_{i=0}^{N-1} \sum_{j=0}^{N-1} P(i,j)\omega^{ui}\omega^{vj},$$

where $\omega$ is a primitive $N$ th root of unity. It can be rewritten as

$$G(u,v) = \sum_{i=0}^{N-1} (\sum_{j=0}^{N-1} P(i,j)\omega^{vj})\omega^{ui}.$$

This indicates that the 2-D DFT of P can be computed by decomposing it into row and column 1-D DFT's, i.e., computing the 1-D DFT of each row of P and storing the result in an intermediate array, then computing the 1-D DFT of each column of the intermediate array. The 1-D DFT of $N$ points is to compute $X(0), X(1), ..., X(N-1)$ when given $x(0), x(1), ..., x(N-1)$ defined by

$$X(i) = \sum_{k=0}^{N-1} x(k)\omega^{ik}.$$

Let the indices $i$ and $k$ be in the binary representation. The decimation-in-time version of the 1-D FFT algorithm [5, 8] is to compute the $n$ vectors defined bellow:

$$T_1(i_{n-1}k_1 \cdots k_{n-1}) = \sum_{k_0} x(k_0 \cdots k_{n-1})\omega^{i_{n-1}k_0 2^{n-1}},$$

and, for $2 \leq s \leq n$,

$$T_s(i_{n-1} \cdots i_{n-s}k_s \cdots k_{n-1}) = \sum_{k_{s-1}} T_{s-1}(i_{n-1} \cdots i_{n-s+1}k_{s-1} \cdots k_{n-1})\omega^Z,$$

where $Z = (\sum_{m=n-s}^{n-1} i_m 2^{n-m-1})k_{s-1}2^{n-s}$. It can be shown that $T_n(i_{n-1} \cdots i_0) = X(i_0 \cdots i_{n-1})$. Thus, to obtain the value of $X(i)$ when given vector $T_n$, it is necessary to reverse the binary digits in the binary representation of $i$ to get a new index $i'$. Then, $X(i) = T_n(i')$. To generate the two elements of $T_s$ whose indices differ only in the $(s-1)$th bit position requires the following computation,

$$T_s(i_{n-1} \cdots i_{n-s+1}0k_s \cdots k_{n-1}) = T_{s-1}(i_{n-1} \cdots i_{n-s+1}0k_s \cdots k_{n-1}) + T_{s-1}(i_{n-1} \cdots i_{n-s+1}1k_s \cdots k_{n-1})\omega^Z \quad (1)$$

and

$$T_s(i_{n-1} \cdots i_{n-s+1}1k_s \cdots k_{n-1}) = T_{s-1}(i_{n-1} \cdots i_{n-s+1}0k_s \cdots k_{n-1}) - T_{s-1}(i_{n-1} \cdots i_{n-s+1}1k_s \cdots k_{n-1})\omega^Z \quad (2)$$

where $Z = (\sum_{m=n-s+1}^{n-1} i_m 2^{n-m-1})2^{n-s}$. The computation presented in (1) and (2) is known as a butterfly operation that computes the two elements of $T_s$ from the two elements of $T_{s-1}$ with only one complex multiplication and two complex additions.

The key for parallel computation of 1-D FFT on SIMD machines is to provide a means by which each processing element can obtain the required pair of points in parallel with others in computing $T_s$

from $T_{s-1}$. The additional difficulty associated with parallel computation of 2-D FFT of P on SIMD machines with $N$ processing elements lies in how to store P in their memory systems so that the row-column decomposition method can be adopted. Ideally, two rows (columns) can be fetched from the memory with two memory accesses, and each processing element is provided with two pixels of the same row (column) which are $2^{n-1}$ pixels apart. This will allow the $N$ processing elements to compute the two $T_1$ vectors from the two rows (columns) in parallel first, and then to compute the two $T_s$ vectors from the two $T_{s-1}$ vectors subsequently, for $2 \leq s \leq n$. As will be seen, the proposed SIMD machine is capable of doing so.

## 2.2 The proposed SIMD machine

The SIMD machine consists of $N$ processing elements, $N$ memory modules of $N$ memory locations each, an interconnection network, and a control unit (CU), as illustrated in Fig. 1, where $PE_k$ and $M_k$ denote processing element $k$ and memory module $k$, respectively.

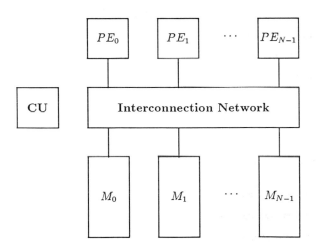

Fig. 1. The SIMD machine.

The single instruction stream is fetched and decoded by the control unit. Control unit instructions are also executed there, and processing element instructions are broadcast to the PE's. Through masking, each processing element has the option to either execute the instruction on its own data or ignore it. The interconnection network consists of $\frac{1}{2}\log N$ stages and allows transfer of data among PE's as well as alignment of data between PE's and the memory modules. It is capable of realizing two classes of mappings, of which one allows processing element $k$ to transfer data to processing element $(k \oplus x)$ for all $k$ in parallel, where $x \in \{0,1, ..., N-1\}$. Permuting data among the processing elements in such a way is essential, especially when $x = 2^{n-s}$, for parallel computation of 1-D FFT as it can be used to pair data for butterfly operations in computing $T_s$ from $T_{s-1}$, for $2 \le s \le n$. There is no intention to describe the machine itself in any detail, a formal description of this machine and its properties can be found elsewhere [4]. Storing the image P in the $N$ memory modules according to the storage scheme proposed in [4], the machine allows its $N$ processing elements to access $N$ pixels of P through the interconnection network in a single memory cycle. The following notations are useful in describing the machine's permissible memory accesses. For any $i \in \{0,1, ..., N-1\}$, let $\xi(i_0 \cdots i_{\frac{n}{2}-1} i_{\frac{n}{2}} \cdots i_{n-1}) = i_{\frac{n}{2}} \cdots i_{n-1} i_0 \cdots i_{\frac{n}{2}-1}$, where both integer $i$ and the value of the function are in binary representation. Next, let $\bar{A}$, $AB$, and $A \oplus B$ denote the bitwise complement of $A$, the bitwise and of $A$ and $B$, and the bitwise exclusive-or of $A$ and $B$, respectively, where $A$ and $B$ are integers in $\{0,1, ..., N-1\}$, namely, they are $n$-dimensional vectors. The following two theorems give the machine's permissible memory accesses. Proofs of the two theorems can be found in [4].

**Theorem 1**: For any two integers $A, l \in \{0,1, ..., N-1\}$, the machine allows processing element $k$ to access $P(\xi(Al \oplus \bar{A} \xi(k)), \bar{A}l \oplus A \xi(k))$ in one memory access for all $k$ in parallel.

**Theorem 2**: For any two integers $A, l \in \{0,1, ..., N-1\}$, the machine allows processing element $k$ to access $P(\xi(Al \oplus \bar{A}k), \bar{A}l \oplus Ak)$ in one memory access for all $k$ in parallel.

## 3. PARALLEL COMPUTATION OF FFT

As the machine has $N$ processing elements, it is desirable to carry out 1-D FFT of two rows (columns) of P simultaneously. In this regard, the processing elements can be configured as two independent groups with one group performing the 1-D FFT of a row (column) of P in parallel with the other group performing the 1-D FFT of another row (column) of P. As suggested in the formulation of 1-D FFT, to compute vector $T_1$ of any row or column of P in parallel requires that each processing element be provided with two pixels of that row or column which are $2^{n-1}$ pixels apart. The following is to show that with exact two memory accesses, two rows or columns of P can be fetched by the processing elements in such a way. In what follows, superscripts are used as repetition factors when describing binary numbers, e.g., $0^2 1^2 = 0011$.

**Corollary 1**: The machine allows its $N$ processing elements to access $N$ pixels of two columns of P in one memory access, with $N/2$ pixels from each column. Furthermore, through two memory accesses, each processing element is able to fetch two pixels of the same column that are $2^{n-1}$ pixels apart.

*Proof*: According to Theorem 1, processing element $k$ can access $P(u,v)$, where $u = \xi(Al \ominus \bar{A}\xi(k))$

and $v = \bar{A}l \ominus A\xi(k)$. Let $A$ satisfy the condition $A = [0^{\frac{n}{2}}10^{\frac{n}{2}-1}]$. Then, replacing $A$ by $[0^{\frac{n}{2}}10^{\frac{n}{2}-1}]$ in $u$ and $v$ yields the following,

$$u = \xi([0^{\frac{n}{2}}l_{\frac{n}{2}}0^{\frac{n}{2}-1}] \oplus \bar{A}[k_{\frac{n}{2}} \cdots k_{n-1}k_0 \cdots k_{\frac{n}{2}-1}])$$

$$= \xi([k_{\frac{n}{2}} \cdots k_{n-1}l_{\frac{n}{2}}k_1 \cdots k_{\frac{n}{2}-1}])$$

$$= l_{\frac{n}{2}}k_1 \cdots k_{n-1}$$

and

$$v = [l_0 \cdots l_{\frac{n}{2}-1}0l_{\frac{n}{2}+1} \cdots l_{n-1}] \oplus A[k_{\frac{n}{2}} \cdots k_{n-1}k_0 \cdots k_{\frac{n}{2}-1}]$$

$$= l_0 \cdots l_{\frac{n}{2}-1}k_0l_{\frac{n}{2}+1} \cdots l_{n-1}.$$

This indicates that for any fixed $l$, processing elements with $k_0$ being zero access $N/2$ pixels of column $l_0 \cdots l_{\frac{n}{2}-1}0l_{\frac{n}{2}+1} \cdots l_{n-1}$, while processing elements with $k_0$ being one access $N/2$ pixels of column $l_0 \cdots l_{\frac{n}{2}-1}1l_{\frac{n}{2}+1} \cdots l_{n-1}$ in one memory access. Now, consider two values of $l$ which are differ only at the $(\frac{n}{2})$th bit position. In one memory access with $l_{\frac{n}{2}}$ being zero, processing element $k$ is able to fetch pixel $0k_1 \cdots k_{n-1}$ of column $l_0 \cdots l_{\frac{n}{2}-1}k_0l_{\frac{n}{2}+1} \cdots l_{n-1}$. In another memory access with $l_{\frac{n}{2}}$ being one, processing element $k$ is able to fetch pixel $1k_1 \cdots k_{n-1}$ of the same column. Since the indices of the two pixels differ only at the first bit position, they are $2^{n-1}$ pixels apart in the column. **Q.E.D.**

**Corollary 2**: The machine allows its $N$ processing elements to access $N$ pixels of two rows of P in one memory access, with $N/2$ pixels from each row. Furthermore, through two memory accesses, each processing element is able to fetch two pixels of the same row which are $2^{n-1}$ pixels apart.

*Proof*: According to Theorem 2, processing element $k$ can access $P(u,v)$, where $u = \xi(Al \ominus \bar{A}k)$ and $v = \bar{A}l \ominus Ak$. Let $A = [01^{n-1}]$, and replace $A$ by $[01^{n-1}]$ in $u$ and $v$. This results in $u = \xi(k_0l_1 \cdots l_{n-1})$ and $v = l_0k_1 \cdots k_{n-1}$. This means that for any fixed $l$, processing elements with $k_0$ being zero access $N/2$ pixels of row $\xi(0l_1 \cdots l_{n-1})$ while processing elements with $k_0$ being one access $N/2$ pixels of row $\xi(1l_1 \cdots l_{n-1})$ in one memory access. Now, consider two values of $l$ which are differ only at the first bit position. In one memory access with $l_0$ being zero, processing element $k$ is able to fetch pixel

$0k_1 \cdots k_{n-1}$ of row $\xi(k_0 l_1 \cdots l_{n-1})$. In another memory access with $l_0$ being one, processing element $k$ is able to fetch pixel $1k_1 \cdots k_{n-1}$ of the same row. Since the indices of the two pixels differ only at the first bit position, they are $2^{n-1}$ pixels apart in the row. **Q.E.D.**

The use of these two corollaries is now illustrated. Let each processing element have four local registers: $I_0$, $I_1$, $O_0$, and $O_1$ to store intermediate results during the computation of $T_s$, for $1 \leq s \leq n$. Next, let $e = l_0 \cdots l_{\frac{n}{2}-1} 0 l_{\frac{n}{2}+1} \cdots l_{n-1}$ and $z = l_0 \cdots l_{\frac{n}{2}-1} 1 l_{\frac{n}{2}+1} \cdots l_{n-1}$. Furthermore, let $T_s^e$ and $T_s^z$, be defined for column $e$ and column $z$ of P, respectively, as $T_s$ defined for vector $x$ in the 1-D FFT formulation, for $1 \leq s \leq n$. According to Corollary 1, in one memory access, processing element $0k_1 \cdots k_{n-1}$ can read pixel $0k_1 \cdots k_{n-1}$ of column $e$ of P into its $I_0$ and processing element $1k_1 \cdots k_{n-1}$ can read pixel $0k_1 \cdots k_{n-1}$ of column $z$ of P into its $I_0$. With another memory access, however, processing element $0k_1 \cdots k_{n-1}$ can read pixel $1k_1 \cdots k_{n-1}$ of column $e$ into its $I_1$ and processing element $1k_1 \cdots k_{n-1}$ can read pixel $1k_1 \cdots k_{n-1}$ of column $z$ into its $I_1$. Now, all processing elements will execute the following two instructions: $O_0 := I_0 + I_1$, $O_1 := I_0 - I_1$. It is easy to see that after the execution of the two instructions, $O_0$ and $O_1$ of processing element $0k_1 \cdots k_{n-1}$ will contain $T_1^e(0k_1 \cdots k_{n-1})$ and $T_1^e(1k_1 \cdots k_{n-1})$, respectively. Similarly, $O_0$ and $O_1$ of processing element $1k_1 \cdots k_{n-1}$ will contain $T_1^z(0k_1 \cdots k_{n-1})$ and $T_1^z(1k_1 \cdots k_{n-1})$, respectively. To compute the remaining $T_s^e$ and $T_s^z$ for $2 \leq s \leq n$, the control unit of the SIMD machine will execute Algorithm A below, where processing element instructions (lines 1-9) are broadcast to the processing elements for execution.

**Algorithm A**

> **begin**
>> **for** $s := 1$ **to** $n - 1$ **do**
>>> **begin**
>>>
>>> 1.      $I_0 := O_0 \quad [\phi^s 0 \phi^{n-s-1}]$;
>>> 2.      $I_1 := O_1 \quad [\phi^s 1 \phi^{n-s-1}]$;
>>> 3.      $O_1 := O_0 \quad [\phi^s 1 \phi^{n-s-1}]$;
>>> 4.      $O_1 \leftarrow O_1 :(0^s 10^{n-s-1})$;
>>> 5.      $I_1 := O_1 \quad [\phi^s 0 \phi^{n-s-1}]$;
>>> 6.      $I_0 := O_1 \quad [\phi^s 1 \phi^{n-s-1}]$;
>>> 7.      $I_1 := I_1 \times \Omega[s]$;
>>> 8.      $O_0 := I_0 + I_1$;
>>> 9.      $O_1 := I_0 - I_1$;
>>>
>>> **end;**
>
> **end.**

In the algorithm above, processing element instructions in company with a mask will be executed by those processing elements whose indices match the mask, e.g., the instruction at line 1 with mask $[\phi^s 0 \phi^{n-s-1}]$ will be executed only by processing elements $k_0 \cdots k_{s-1} 0 k_{s+1} \cdots k_{n-1}$ at the $s$th iteration of the loop, where $\phi$ stands for *don't care*. Other processing elements will ignore this instruction. Instructions without the mask will be executed by all processing elements. In other words, a mask of the form $[\phi^n]$ does not appear explicitly in the algorithm to minimize confusion. The instruction at line 4 is a data transfer instruction, which exchanges the content of $O_1$ of processing element $k_0 \cdots k_s \cdots k_{n-1}$ with that of processing element $k_0 \cdots (k_s \oplus 1) \cdots k_{n-1}$ through the interconnection network [4]. Each processing element makes use of $n-1$ locations of its local memory represented as array $\Omega$ in the algorithm to store precomputed weights required by the $n-1$ butterfly operations. More specifically, $\Omega[s]$ of processing element $k_0 \cdots k_{n-1}$ has the value of $\omega^Z$, where $Z = (\sum_{m=n-s}^{n-1} i_m 2^{n-m-1}) 2^{n-s-1} = (\sum_{m=1}^{s} k_m 2^{m-1}) 2^{n-s-1}$.

**Theorem 3**: Given $T_1^e$ and $T_1^z$, Algorithm A computes the $T_n^e$ and $T_n^z$ simultaneously in $O(\log N)$ time.

The proof of Theorem 3 is given in the Appendix. It should be clear that after $T_n^e$ and $T_n^z$ have been computed, they can be written in place of columns $e$ and $z$ of P, respectively, in two memory accesses according to Corollary 1. As an immediate consequence of corollaries 1, 2, and Theorem 3, the following result follows.

**Theorem 4**: In place computation of $T_n$'s of two columns (rows) of P can be performed simultaneously in $O(\log N)$ time.

Now, in the light of Theorem 4, repeating the process $N/2$ times to P columnwise will replace each column of P by its $T_n$ vector, generating an intermediate array. Then, repeating the process $N/2$ times to the intermediate array rowwise will replace each row by the $T_n$ vector of that row, resulting a new array. The newly obtained array is, however, not the 2-D DFT of P as yet, since some of its columns and rows are not in the right order according to the 1-D FFT formulation previously described. Action must be then taken to bring those columns as well as rows into the correct order. Reordering the new array can be done in $O(N)$ time as follows. First, two other permissible memory accesses of the machine will be used which allow the $N$ processing elements to access a column or row of the new array in one memory access [4]. The processing elements simply exchange column $j = j_0 \cdots j_{n-2} j_{n-1}$ with column $j' = j_{n-2} \cdots j_0 j_{n-1}$ only if $j \neq j'$. The same process is then repeated for the resulting image rowwise. Only at this point, P has been replaced by its 2-D FFT. Consequently, the following theorem follows.

**Theorem 5:** Performing 2-D FFT of P in place can be done in $O(N \log N)$ time.

## 4. CONCLUSION

Two of the machine's permissible memory accesses have been described in this paper, which in conjunction with the machine's interconnection network lead to an efficient parallel algorithm for computing 1-D FFT of two columns (rows) of P in place simultaneously. Based on the parallel 1-D FFT algorithm, a parallel algorithm for computing the 2-D FFT of P has been presented. It should be pointed out that performing the 2-D inverse FFT on the SIMD machine requires only simple modification of the parallel algorithms given.

## Appendix

*Proof of Theorem 3*

The correctness proof is by induction on $s$ that at the end of the $s$th iteration of the loop: (1) $T_{s+1}^e(i_{n-1} \cdots i_{n-s-1} k_{s+1} \cdots k_{n-1})$ is in $O_j$ of pe $0i_{n-1} \cdots i_{n-s} k_{s+1} \cdots k_{n-1}$; and (2) $T_{s+1}^z(i_{n-1} \cdots i_{n-s-1} k_{s+1} \cdots k_{n-1})$ is in $O_j$ of pe $1i_{n-1} \cdots i_{n-s} k_{s+1} \cdots k_{n-1}$, where $j = i_{n-s-1}$. Thus, when $s = n-1$, $T_n^e(i_{n-1} \cdots i_0)$ will be in $O_j$ of pe $0i_{n-1} \cdots i_1$; and $T_n^z(i_{n-1} \cdots i_0)$ will be in $O_j$ of pe $1i_{n-1} \cdots i_1$, where $j = i_0$. The following is to show that induction hypothesis (1) is true. The proof for induction hypothesis (2) is analogous.

**Basis:** Consider the first iteration of the loop ($s = 1$). Recall that $T_1^e(i_{n-1} k_1 \cdots k_{n-1})$ is in pe $0k_1 \cdots k_{n-1}$ with $T_1^e(0k_1 \cdots k_{n-1})$ in $O_0$ and $T_1^e(1k_1 \cdots k_{n-1})$ in $O_1$ before the loop is entered. Entering the loop, pe $00k_2 \cdots k_{n-1}$ moves $T_1^e(00k_2 \cdots k_{n-1})$ to $I_0$ in line 1, and pe $01k_2 \cdots k_{n-1}$ moves $T_1^e(11k_2 \cdots k_{n-1})$ to $I_1$ in line 2, and then moves $T_1^e(01k_2 \cdots k_{n-1})$ to $O_1$ in line 3. Line 4 exchanges the content of $O_1$ of pe $00k_2 \cdots k_{n-1}$ with that of pe $01k_2 \cdots k_{n-1}$. As a result, pe $00k_2 \cdots k_{n-1}$ loads its $I_1$ with $T_1^e(01k_2 \cdots k_{n-1})$ in line 5, and pe $01k_2 \cdots k_{n-1}$ loads its $I_0$ with $T_1^e(10k_2 \cdots k_{n-1})$ in line 6. Thus, after the execution of lines 8 and 9, $T_2^e(i_{n-1} 0k_2 \cdots k_{n-1})$ and $T_2^e(i_{n-1} 1k_2 \cdots k_{n-1})$ will be in $O_0$ and $O_1$ of pe $0i_{n-1} k_2 \cdots k_{n-1}$, respectively.

**Induction step:** From the induction hypothesis, when $s = m - 1$, $T_m^e(i_{n-1} \cdots i_{n-m+1} 0k_m \cdots k_{n-1})$ and $T_m^e(i_{n-1} \cdots i_{n-m+1} 1k_m \cdots k_{n-1})$ are in $O_0$ and $O_1$ of pe $0i_{n-1} \cdots i_{n-m+1} k_m \cdots k_{n-1}$. Consider the iteration of the loop when $s = m$. In line 1, pe $0i_{n-1} \cdots i_{n-m+1} 0k_{m+1} \cdots k_{n-1}$ moves $T_m^e(i_{n-1} \cdots i_{n-m+1} 00k_{m+1} \cdots k_{n-1})$ to $I_0$. And pe $0i_{n-1} \cdots i_{n-m+1} 1k_{m+1} \cdots k_{n-1}$ moves $T_m^e(i_{n-1} \cdots i_{n-m+1} 11k_{m+1} \cdots k_{n-1})$ to $I_1$ in line 2, and then moves $T_m^e(i_{n-1} \cdots i_{n-m+1} 01k_{m+1} \cdots k_{n-1})$ to $O_1$ in line 3. Line 4 exchanges the content of $O_1$ of pe $0i_{n-1} \cdots i_{n-m+1} 0k_{m+1} \cdots k_{n-1}$ with that of pe $0i_{n-1} \cdots i_{n-m+1} 1k_{m+1} \cdots k_{n-1}$. Consequently, in line 5, pe $0i_{n-1} \cdots i_{n-m+1} 0k_{m+1} \cdots k_{n-1}$ loads $I_1$ with $T_m^e(i_{n-1} \cdots i_{n-m+1} 01k_{m+1} \cdots k_{n-1})$ and, in line 6, pe

$0i_{n-1} \cdots i_{n-m+1} 1k_{m+1} \cdots k_{n-1}$ loads $\mathbf{I}_0$ with $T_{m-1}^e (i_{n-1} \cdots i_{n-m+1} 10k_{m+1} \cdots k_{n-1})$. Thus, upon completion of lines 8 and 9, $T_{m+1}^e (i_{n-1} \cdots i_{n-m} 0k_{m+1} \cdots k_{n-1})$ and $T_{m+1}^e (i_{n-1} \cdots i_{n-m} 1k_{m+1} \cdots k_{n-1})$ will be in $\mathbf{O}_0$ and $\mathbf{O}_1$ of pe $0i_{n-1} \cdots i_{n-m} k_{m+1} \cdots k_{n-1}$, respectively. This completes the correctness proof. The analysis of the time complexity is straightforward. **Q.E.D.**

## References

1. K.E. Batcher, "The flip network in STARAN," *Proc. Int'l Conf. Parallel Processing*, pp. 65-71, Aug. 1976.

2. P.E. Danielsson and S. Levialdi, "Computer architectures for pictorial information systems," *Computer*, vol. 14, pp. 53-67, Nov. 1981.

3. L.H. Jamieson, P.T. Tueller, and H.J. Siegel, "FFT algorithms for SIMD parallel processing systems," *Journal of Parallel and Distributed Computing*, vol. 3, pp. 48-71, 1986.

4. D.-L. Lee, *A multiple-processor architecture for image processing,* Ph.D. Thesis, Department of Computing Science, University of Alberta, 1987.

5. M.C. Pease, "An adaptation of the fast Fourier transform for parallel processing," *J.ACM*, vol. 15, pp. 252-264, Apr. 1968.

6. A.P. Reeves, "Parallel computer architectures for image processing," *Computer vision, Graphics, and Image Processing*, vol. 25, pp. 68-88, Feb. 1984.

7. A. Rosenfeld and A.C. Kak, *Digital picture processing,* Academic Press, 1982.

8. H.S. Stone, "Parallel processing with perfect shuffle," *IEEE Trans. Comput.*, vol. C-20, pp. 153-161, Feb. 1971.

# A PARALLEL ARCHITECTURE FOR MODEL-BASED OBJECT RECOGNITION

M.J. Livesey, J. Owczarczyk

Dept. of Computational Science, University of St.Andrews

North Haugh, St.Andrews, Scotland KY16 9SS.

## 1. Introduction

For computation intensive applications, such as computer vision, the high-performance solutions always derive from some form of specialised computer architecture. However, specialisation should not limit system flexibility, another characteristic which is especially important in the early experimental stages of a project when methods and techniques are in a state of flux. There would, however, be no contradiction if the proposed architecture were *scalable*, i.e. the same generic architectural framework could serve as a model for a whole family of systems regardless of system performance. The term *performance* is used here in a wide sense; for example, in a recognition system it refers not only to *implementation efficiency* (speed of recognition in objects per unit time) but also to *method limitations* (what object types can be distinguished by the method) and *noise sensitivity* (how fast the recognition degrades in the presence of noise). Therefore, to be a useful practical concept scalability must be incorporated at all levels: the application level, the algorithmic level, the hardware level, and the programming level.

At the application level scalability simply requires system structure and data flow to be carefully chosen. That is, it should be general to cover all known and anticipated individual cases (within the application) but also specific enough to model an *application-driven* architecture. At the algorithmic level scalability manifest itself as a coherent set of techniques and corresponding algorithms to satisfy various performance requirements, relative to one particular computational model. At the programming level, the language must enable the decomposition of large programs into processes running concurrently on one or more processors, and the specification of the communication between them. Lastly, at the hardware level scalability corresponds to modularity and extensibility of the physical architecture consistent with the requirements of VLSI technology and current trends in parallel and distributed computing.

In this paper we discuss a suitable architecture for model-based object recognition as used in machine (robot) vision, and which encompasses a wide variety of methods and techniques. The scalability criterion is addressed throughout the paper. The main advantage of a scalable architecture is that it permits the system to be tailored to any of a wide range of sub-applications, varying in performance requirements, while still retaining its basic structure. Scalability will undoubtedly speed up the process of transforming research results into a viable industrial product.

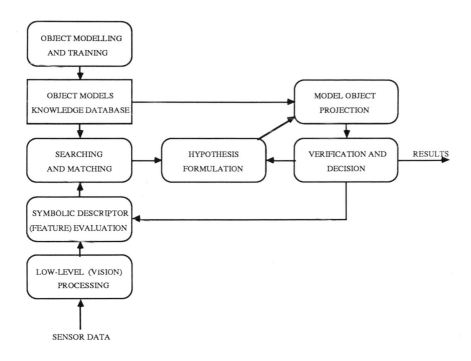

Fig.1. Conceptual structure of model-based recognition

Model-based recognition can be thought as searching for a consistent matching between certain symbolic descriptors derived from sensory data and those derived from object models. What distinguishes various approaches is the type of sensory data (intensity images, range images), the character and number of symbolic descriptors (global, local, relational), the type of constraints used to limit the search space, and the way the recognition process is organized (depth reconstruction, perceptual organization). The conceptual framework of model-based object recognition shown in Fig.1. is general enough to encompass all these approaches. Two recent survey papers [Besl85, Chin86] give an excellent background and describe a variety of present day model-based recognition systems. Current research at the University of St.Andrews [Cole87] is concentrating on three-dimensional object recognition and scene understanding from single intensity images (monocular monochrome vision).

## 2. Computational aspects of model-based recognition

To address the problem of the underlying architecture, it is convenient to distinguish phases of model-based recognition (cf. [Besl85, Brad82, Chin86]). Both phases requi computing power, but of different types.

The first phase, which we call *low-level vision*, is a preprocessing phase and includes enhancement, filtering, image data segmentation. Low-level vision performs repetitive operations on large data sets (images) using numerical algorithms. It demands a fairly uniform distribution of high data-rate memory access, requiring a wide-band memory.

The second *high-level processing*, or *scene understanding*, phase includes searching, matching and verification. The high-level processing tasks operates on lists, graphs and trees rather than two-dimensional arrays. It requires sophisticated decision making, often including combinatorial algorithms, data flow is highly irregular in terms of destination and volume.

The apparent disparity in the computational requirements for the two phases calls for some form of two-level, or *dual paradigm*, physical architecture [Page87]. It should be pointed out, however, that architectures for low-level vision -- which in fact is a part of *digital image processing,* a relatively mature field -- have long been the subject of research and are well developed. Moreover, thanks to regularity and simplicity of its operations, low-level vision lends itself to, and profits to a greater extent from, VLSI technology. Consequently, the performance of present vision systems is not limited by that of low-level vision machines. Indeed, there are a number of scalable parallel architectures which can maintain video rate processing of low-level vision operations. The candidate VLSI architectures for robot vision are reviewed in [Live87]; see also [Brad83, Reev84]. The optimal architecture for the second phase is less obvious, but the computational requirements strongly suggest a multiple-instruction-multiple-data (MIMD) machine.

A two-level architecture raises the *integration problem* of efficiently combining both architectures, which is often addressed in the literature. The approach to a general architecture for vision oriented research advocated in Uhr [Uhr85] combines various single-instruction-multiple-data (SIMD) and MIMD computers into wider networks by using Moore graphs. Such an approach can be viewed as an extension of the *special-function-unit* concept of multiprocessor architectures, also suggested for general image processing systems (see [Reev84] for a review of such systems), where processors are specialised for different functions. Such heterogeneous systems, although giving good performance, do not meet important system criteria such as fault-tolerance and scalability. The integration problem can also be solved by using an architecture which can be reconfigured from a MIMD to a (multiple) SIMD machine [Rice85, Yala85]. Tanimoto [Tani85] suggests a special memory organization and a hardware buffer for efficient data transmission from a mesh-connected SIMD machine into a MIMD system. In [Reev85] it is proposed that the Multicluster system for computer vision will execute low-level vision operations on a MIMD machine without a separate SIMD component. However, we predict that the problem of combining these two architectures will soon disappear, as progress in VLSI technology may lead to new *intelligent* sensors with embedded low-level vision processing; some prototypes already exist [Nudd80].

In this paper we propose a unified architectural framework -- a parallel architecture which exhibits the high throughput required for real-time applications.

## 3. Model-based recognition in a distributed environment

VISTA (VIsion research at ST.Andrews) is an application-driven architecture developed at the University of St.Andrews as a research vehicle for robot vision. It is a tree-structured network of identical computing nodes each of which is physically a (micro)computer system. These nodes share no memory, and communicate only by passing messages over passive links. It is a tree-structured system with the root able to act as a central control; Fig.2 illustrates the scheme for various sizes.

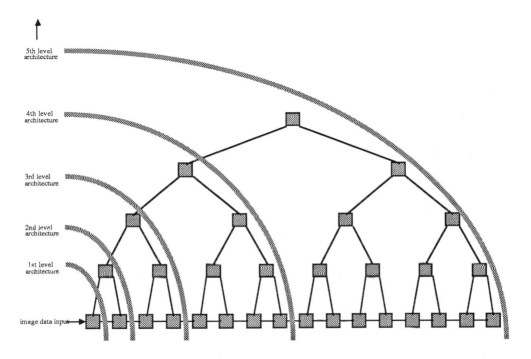

5th level architecture

4th level architecture

3rd level architecture

2nd level architecture

1st level architecture

image data input

Fig.2. VISTA - a general framework

Tree-structured multicomputers possess several practical advantages over other more complex multicomputer networks [Live87b]. The regularity and simplicity of the interconnections facilitates implementation and reduces cost. The structure is modular and readily extensible; high level architectures can be constructed systematically from the lower-level versions. To demonstrate the suitability of such an architecture for model-based recognition, we discuss in greater detail the implementation of a computationally complex recognition method.

For model-based recognition in a distributed environment, as for any distributed problem, it is necessary to discuss four topics, viz: problem decomposition into sub-problems; sub-problem distribution; sub-problem solution; and answer synthesis.

The natural means of problem decomposition is to split with respect to some data domain associated with the application. In model-based recognition we have, among others: object space (subproblem: recognition of a class of objects); descriptor space (subproblem: matching all objects against one descriptor); or constraint space (subproblem: matching under a single constraint). The granularity and simplicity of such decomposition varies with recognition methods, as we shall illustrate below. The relationship between subproblems can be expressed in a *problem graph*. Distribution can then be viewed as mapping the problem graph onto a system graph describing the network interconnections. (Alternatively, a two-stage mapping procedure with an intermediate *virtual graph* can be used.) In general, an efficient mapping strategy will require some knowledge of inter-task communication requirements, since its ultimate goal is to minimize communication overheads -- the unwanted side effect of distributed computation. For each individual recognition method the amount of communication between the problem graph nodes is different. It can be estimated by simulation, and compared with process execution times to give the communication/processing decomposition.

In distributed model-based recognition we interpret all activities as processes; this conforms to the actor model of [Agha85]. There are several types of process, with a number of instances of each type. For example, feature-detection processes operating directly on the image (one per feature), passing information to object-recognition processes (one for each type of object), which in turn send their results to the verification and decision processes. In our system, answer synthesis fits well with the tree structure, and is therefore somewhat simplified.

Lowe [Lowe87] proposes a system that can recognise three-dimensional objects in single grey-scale images from unknown viewpoints. Unlike most other approaches, recognition is accomplished without bottom-up reconstruction of depth information from the visual input. Instead, a perceptual organisation is used to form groupings, a probabilistic ranking then reduces the search space during model-based matching, and finally a process of spatial correspondence brings the projections of three-dimensional models into direct correspondence with the image by solving for the viewpoint and model parameters. The most time-consuming step here is the evaluation of perceptual groupings of line segments. This problem is similar to *optical clustering*, and it has been shown [Dehn86] that given a set of N disjoint line segments, the clusters with respect to a given separation parameter can be sequentially computed in time $O(N\log N)$. The efficiency of a segment clustering implementation on a distributed tree-structured machine depends primarily on good segment distribution. We now describe this distribution process.

The leaves of the tree form a linear array of $2^{n-1}$ processors, where n is the number of levels. Each leaf processor (except the two outermost) is connected to its two neighbours by bidirectional communication links, and is equipped with sufficient local RAM for the leaves collectively to store a single monochrome image with one byte per pixel. If the image is $2^m$ x $2^m$ pixels, each edge node requires $2^{2m+n-1}$ bytes. The image is input at the leftmost leaf in raster-scan mode (row-wise, left-to-right, top-to-bottom), then loaded into the individual node memories prior to computation. This results in the image being partitioned into $2^{n-1}$ vertical strips of $2^{2m-n+1}$ pixels each, with one strip per leaf.

The low-level vision operations (convolution, the Sobel operator and Laplacian for edge detection) are performed by the leaf nodes. For a local operation with a (2k+1)x(2k+1) kernel, a kernel belonging to one strip may overlap an adjacent strip by up to k(2k+1) pixels, requiring this information to be communicated between the corresponding leaves.

The resulting zero-crossing image is transferred to the next level, whose nodes hold lists of edges shared between adjacent strips. This procedure continues towards the root; at each stage edges are retained only if they do not cross the border of the associated image subset, otherwise they are passed to the next level. In this way the linked edges are distributed through the tree for subsequent straight line segment evaluation. This distribution mechanism has several advantages: it leads to a well-balanced workload because segmentation cost is proportional to total edge length; it facilitates concurrent detection of perceptual groupings based on segment endpoint proximity; and it provides hierarchical information about segment distribution which is useful for subsequent scheduling of the tasks that perform matching.

The VISTA experimental system is implemented on transputers [Whit85]. The computation at each node is performed by a set of concurrent processes written in Occam 2 [May87], the transputer system programming language. These processes divide into two categories; the *application* processes, discussed above, and the *support* processes -- see Fig.3. One job of the latter is to buffer communication between application processes at different nodes, to allow them to operate asynchronously. Of course, buffering only absorbs temporary mismatches in data rates; one of the main experimental tasks is to tune the system to a common average data rate (its *throughput*). Another is to try to minimise the standard deviation of the rates to allow a reasonable bound on buffer-size.

Much is often made of the distinction between systems with a *global store*, or *database*, and those *pure distributed* systems without. However, as soon as the database in the former is itself distributed, which becomes necessary to exploit the possibility of concurrent access to independent parts of the database, the distinction rapidly blurs. We have simply a distributed system of actors, each of which may possibly be measured on some spectrum of how "active" or "passive" it is. The VISTA tree therefore has a process/data duality; we can think of it as both a structure of processors and a distributed database. There are two particular consequences of the latter view. The first concerns the individual node software structure. Within a single node, the local data (or at least some of it) acts as a "blackboard" for the processes performing the local computation, of which there may be more than one. The Occam paradigm of point-to-point communication via channels requires that this data be embodied in a separate process. This is the *Store* process of Fig.3, which also serves as a central node-control process.

The second consequence concerns the node degree, which is three for the (internal) nodes of a binary tree. But one of the main aims of our experiment is to achieve a fault-tolerant system, and to this end we employ a fourth link connected to a network "backplane" to provide redundant communication paths [Live87c]. The effect of this is to create a tree of processors connected by a network to a distributed database, where the tree and the database happen to coincide.

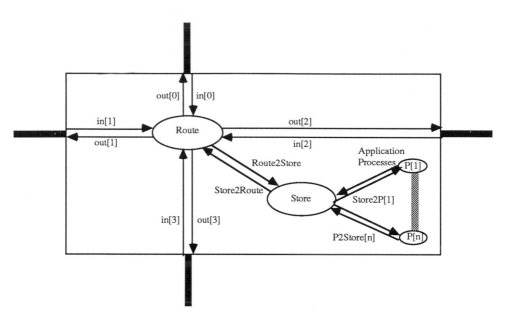

```
PROC Store =
    VAR x, y the.store                          PROC Route( this.node ) =
    WHILE TRUE                                      VAR x
        ALT                                         WHILE TRUE
            Route2Store ? x                             SEQ
                buffer(x)                                   ALT
            ALT i = [1 FOR n]                               ALT i = [0 FOR 4]
                P2Store[i] ? x                                  in[i] ? x
                    SEQ                                         Store2Route ? x
                        y := handle(x)                  IF
                        IF                                  destination(x) = this.node
                            read(x)                             Route2Store ! x
                                Store2P[i] ! y              TRUE
                            message(x)                          out[route(destination(x))] ! x
                                Store2Route ! y
                            TRUE
                                SKIP
```

Fig.3.   Node software structure

## 5. Conclusion

We have presented a general methodological framework of a distributed model-based recognition system. We have stressed the importance of scalability of the system architecture, and suggested how it may be achieved. We have also demonstrated how the hardware, programming and algorithmic levels can be integrated into a coherent application-driven architecture.

## Acknowledgments

The research herein was supported by St.Andrews University Research Committee, Grant No. 0653059.

## References

Ball81    Ballard, D. "Strip trees; a hierarchical representation for curves", *Communication of the ACM,* **24** (1981), 310-321

Besl85    Besl, P., and Jain, R. "Three-dimensional object recognition", *ACM Computing Surveys,* **17** (1985), 77-145

Brad82    Brady, M. "Computational approaches to image understanding", *ACM Computing Surveys,* **14** (1982), 3-71

Brad83    Brady, M. "Parallelism in vision", *Artificial Intelligence,* **21** (1983), 271-283

Chin86    Chin, R., and Dyer, C. "Model-based recognition in robot vision", *ACM Computing Surveys,* **18** (1986), 67-108

Cole87    Cole, A., Dyckhoff, R., Livesey, M.J., and Owczarczyk, J. "An approach to distributed model-based object recognition", Technical Report CS/87/4 (1987), Dept. Comp. Sci., University of St. Andrews

Dehn87    Dehne, F. "Optical clustering", *The Visual Computer,* **2** (1986), 39-43

Live87a    Livesey, M.J., and Owczarczyk, J. "Tree-structured multiprocessors and multicomputers: a survey", *Computers and Artificial Intelligence,* (submitted for publication)

Live87b    Livesey, M.J., and Owczarczyk, J. "Concurrent VLSI architectures for robot vision", Technical Report CS/87/5 (1987), Dept. Comp. Sci., University of St.Andrews

Live87c    Livesey, M.J., and Owczarczyk, J. "Fault-tolerant schemes for parallel architectures", *Electronics Letters* **23** (1987) 1206-1207

Lowe87    Lowe, D. "Three-dimensional object recognition from single two-dimensional images", *Artificial Intelligence,* **31** (1987), 355-395

May87    May, D. "Occam 2 language definition", *INMOS Technical Note,* INMOS Ltd, Bristol, 1987

Nudd80    Nudd, G. "Image understanding architectures", *Proceedings of the National Computer Conference,* 1980, pp. 377-390

Page87    Page, I. "The Disputer: a dual paradigm parallel processor for graphics and vision", in *BCS Conference Documentation; Parallel Processing for Displays,* R. Earnshaw (ed), London, 1987

Reev84    Reeves, A. "Parallel computer architectures for image processing", *Computer Vision, Graphics and Image processing,* **25** (1984), 68-88

Reev85    Reeves, A. "Multicluster: an MIMD system for computer vision", in *Integrated Technology for Parallel Image Processing,* S. Levialdi ed., Academic Press, London, 1985, pp. 39-56

Rice85    Rice, T., and Jamieson, I. "Parallel processing for computer vision", in *Integrated Technology for Parallel Image Processing,* S. Levialdi ed., Academic Press, London, 1985, pp. 57-67

Rose86    Rosenfeld, A. "Computer vision", in *Handbook of Pattern Recognition and Image Processing,* T. Young, and K. Fu (eds.), Academic Press, Orlando, 1986 pp.335-348

Tani85    Tanimoto, S. "An approach to the iconic/symbolic interface", in *Integrated Technology for Parallel Image Processing,* S. Levialdi ed., Academic Press, London, 1985, pp. 31-38

Uhr86    Uhr, L. "Parallel architectures for image processing, computer vision, and pattern perception", in *Handbook of Pattern Recognition and Image Processing,* T. Young, and K. Fu (eds.), Academic Press, Orlando, 1986 pp. 437-469

Whit85    Whitby-Strevens, C. "The transputer", *Proceedings of the 12 Annual Inter. Symp. on Computer Architecture,* Boston, Mass., June 1985, pp. 278-280

Yala85    Yalamanchili, S, and Aggarwal J. "Analysis of a model for parallel image processing", *Pattern Recognition,* **18** (1985), 1-16

# Lapwing - A Trainable Image Recognition System for the Linear Array Processor

*Ian Poole*

Department of Computer Science
University College London, Gower Street, LONDON WC1E 6BT

*Hilary Adams*

Department of Computer Science
University of York, Heslington, YORK Y01 5DD

## ABSTRACT

A trainable recognition system intended for the detection of features in satellite imagery and for potential application to, for example, production line inspection has been constructed. A genetic search algorithm is used to find linear discriminant functions which will partition the pattern space and isolate the required features. The partitions are built up hierachically and represented as a classification tree. The training phase generates programs for the Linear Array Processor permitting subsequent images to be processed rapidly. It is shown that the system can generate a relaxation process to exploit contextual information.

## 1. Introduction

The Lapwing system is designed to recognise image features which are defined by example on a training image. Such a system has potential application to, for example, character recognition and production line inspection. In remote sensing it is common practice to employ nearest neighbour techniques to classify land cover types based on each pixel's spectral characteristics, see eg ref[1]. While such classifiers have a proven worth, they also have severe limitations; they are unable for example to identify linear features (such as roads and rivers), as the key to their recognition lies in the spatial and not the spectral domain.

A major motivation for Lapwing was the desire to perform image feature recognition using the National Physical Laboratory (NPL) Linear Array Processor - hereafter referred to as simply the "LAP"[2].

The LAP has a Single Instruction - Multiple Data (SIMD) architecture and is designed specifically for image processing applications. It consists of a linear array of typically 256 processing elements (PEs). Each can communicate with its two nearest neighbours. Image rows are processed serially, the pixels of a row being operated on simultaneously. Each PE can access a small amount of local memory enabling several lines of the image to be held so that window operations can be performed.

A special purpose programming language - PPL or Picture Processing Language[3] - has been developed at NPL for the LAP. The purpose of the Lapwing system is to generate the PPL code which will enable the LAP to perform the desired recognition task.

The details of the system will be described in the subsequent sections, however the following outline may be found useful.

This work is supported by a SERC CASE studentship in conjunction with the National Physical Laboratory, Teddington.

Hilary Adams is now at Cambridge Electronic Design Ltd., Science Park, Cambridge CB4 4FE.

Paper submitted for the 4th International Conference on Pattern Recognition, March, 1988.

Lapwing is trained on an example image and pre-classified overlay. For each pixel in the training set a pattern vector is extracted made up of the pixel's local neighbourhood - say 7x7. A search is made for 'good' linear partitions of this pattern space. Splitting continues in a hierarchical fashion until an acceptable level of impurity, w.r.t pattern class, is obtained within each terminal partition. The partitions are represented as a classification tree. The combinatorial explosion unleashed by considering such a high dimensional pattern space is mitigated by the use of an adaptive search strategy, namely a Genetic Algorithm (GA).

The system generates a program suitable for execution on the LAP from the classification tree. With this program the LAP is able to classify subsequent images rapidly; typically 0.5 seconds for a 256x256 pixel image.

## 2. Formulation

The formulation used in this paper largely follows ref[4]. Classification is on a per-pixel basis, taking into account the pixel's local neighbourhood.
Thus each pixel can be characterised by a pattern vector x as shown below.

$$
\begin{matrix}
x_{19} & x_{20} & x_{21} & x_{22} & x_{15} \\
x_{18} & x_6 & x_7 & x_8 & x_{24} \\
x_{17} & x_5 & x_0 & x_1 & x_9 \\
x_{16} & x_4 & x_3 & x_2 & x_{10} \\
x_{15} & x_{11} & x_{13} & x_{12} & x_{11}
\end{matrix}
\quad \rightarrow \mathbf{x} =
\begin{bmatrix}
x_0 \\ x_1 \\ x_2 \\ x_3 \\ \vdots \\ x_D
\end{bmatrix}
$$

These pattern vectors are drawn from a potential pattern space $\Omega$, $x \in \Omega$.

Each pixel can belong to one of c possible classes, $\omega_j$, $j=1 .. c$ However, since any multi-class recognition problem can be broken down into separate two class problems, what follows will be restricted to the two class case, c=2.

The training set consists of an example image in conjunction with an 'overlay' to give the desired classification of each pixel. Formally then, the training data is a set of N pairs

$$L=\{(\mathbf{x}, \omega_j)_n \quad n=1..N , \ j=1..2\}$$

The ideal Bayes classifier for the problem would require $P(\omega_j|\mathbf{x}) \ \forall x \in \Omega$, $j=1..2$. This is impractical to say the least. An approximation is to partition the space $\Omega$ into a number of disjoint subsets $\Omega_k$, $k=1 .. K$, covering $\Omega$ and to then estimate $P(\omega_1|\mathbf{x} \in \Omega_k) \ \forall k=1 .. K$. The greater the number of partitions then the closer is the approximation, however this will always be limited by the availability of training data, since each partition must contain a statistically significant number of training data points.

## 3. Classification Trees

The following treatment is adapted from the book by Breiman et al[5]. A review of the decision tree approach to learning can be found in ref[6].

Classification trees are a useful structure for building up pattern partitions in a hierarchical way. Each node, $t$, represents a partition of $\Omega$, $\Omega_t$ and includes an estimate of $P(\omega_1|\ x \in \Omega_t)$. A predicate function, $q_t(\mathbf{x})$ represents the decision function which will split $\Omega_t$ into $\Omega_{t,l}$ and $\Omega_{t,r}$ as follows (assuming $x \in \Omega_t$) :

$$If \ q_t(\mathbf{x}) = true \ \ Then \ \ x \in \Omega_{t,l} \ \ Else \ \ x \in \Omega_{t,r}$$

The two diagrams below show an example classification tree and the form of the partitions it may represent.

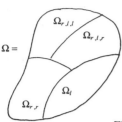
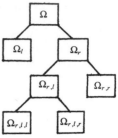

**Figure 1.** A classification tree and equivalent space

## 3.1 Constructing a Classification Tree

A tree is constructed with reference to a training set of classified cases $L$. Intuitively the aim is for each partition $\Omega_k$ to contain cases predominately from class 1 or class 2, ie for $P(\omega_1|\ x \in L_t) \approx 1$ or $0$ where $L_t = \Omega_t \cap L$, that is, $L_t$ is the subset of the training data which falls into $\Omega_t$

The tree is constructed from the top down. Associated with each node is the set $L_t$. The problem is to find a predicate function $q_t(x)$ to divide $L_t$ into $L_{t,l}$ and $L_{t,r}$ so as to reduce the *average split impurity* w.r.t class membership. The average split impurity, $I(t)$ is defined as :

$$I(t) = P(L_{t,l}) \cdot i(t,l) + P(L_{t,r}) \cdot i(t,r)$$

where $P(L_{t,l})$ is the proportion of case falling into $L_{t,l}$ out of the total in $L_t$.

This leaves the *node impurity* function, $i(t)$ to be defined. The form adopted in the present Lapwing system is known as the *Gini* criterion[5] and is defined as follows (for the two class case).

$$i(t) = P(\omega_1|\ x \in L_t) \cdot P(\omega_2|\ x \in L_t)$$

It is important to appreciate that $L_t$ will not generally cover $\Omega_t$, and thus there will be many possible partitions of $\Omega_t$, ie different predicates, which will produce *identical* $L_{t,l}$ and $L_{t,r}$, and thus *identical* $I(t)$. But are they all equally good splits ? This will be addressed in section 4.1.

The tree growing procedure is recursive. Having split a node $t$ into $(t,l)$ and $(t,r)$ the procedure is repeated with each of $(t,l)$ and $(t,r)$ to produce $(t,l,l)$ etc. Ideally the process should continue until each $L_t$ becomes completely pure, even if this means they contain only one member ! Statistically meaningless splits are identified in a subsequent pruning phase. The pruning algorithm used is known as *minimum cost-complexity* pruning, and uses an independent training sample, (see Breiman et al, chapter 3). The tree growing process is expensive however and so is terminated when a node contains less than $N_{min}$ cases of either class. $N_{min}$ is typically set to 30.

## 4. The Splitting Rules

Lapwing is able to search for a linear partition in any orientation. We first express $q(x)$ in the form

$$q(x) = [\ g(x) < C\ ]$$

where $g$ is a scalar function of $x$ and $C$ is a threshold value. To permit the specification of general hyperplanes in $\Omega$ we can define $g(x)$ as

$$g(x) = \frac{v.x}{|v|}$$

From vector algebra $g(x)$ is the perpendicular distance of $x$ from the hyperplane which passes through the origin and has normal vector $v$. Recalling that $x$ represents a square neighbourhood of pixels, it is clear that $v$ can be regarded as a square convolution operator, familiar in image processing. It is known that many image processing operations can be performed with convolution operators and this gives intuitive support for the chosen form of $g$ . As importantly, it is precisely this type of operation at which the LAP excels.

## 4.1 More on the criterion for a good split

It was remarked in section 3 that there are likely to be many different partition surfaces which produce identical split impurities. The relevance of this can be readily appreciated if one considers fig 2 (a).

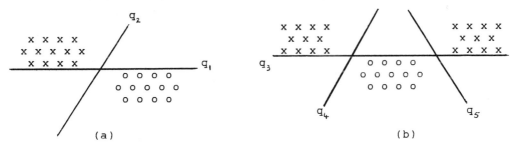

**Figure 2.** Which are the better splits ?

A criterion function based on Gini alone would make no distinction between splits $q_1$ and $q_2$, yet clearly $q_2$ is to be preferred. Although both give perfect classification of the the training set, $q_1$ could be described as "fragile" since only a small shift of the population, caused by a bias in the training set perhaps, could produce large classification errors. $q_2$ on the other hand would tolerate a relatively large shift of the pattern space.

In Figure 2 (b) the Gini criterion would select $q_3$ since this gives perfect class separation; intuition and caution however favours $q_4$ followed by $q_5$. Note that criterion based on maximising the distance between class means would also select $q_3$.

The above discusion seems to suggest that when partitions are to be built up hierachically, as they are in a classification tree, they should be selected so as to pass through *unpopulated* regions of the pattern space, even if this gives poorer class separation at that stage. The following section summarises a criterion function which is used in the Lapwing system to assess the 'fragility' of a partition.

## 4.2 An additional criterion for robustness against simple bias

The simplest and most common form of bias encountered in images is a variation of light intensity across the subject, or a variability of the gain of the image capturing system between images.

We will assume the effect is additive rather than multiplicative, and that it is constant for the pixels of one neighbourhood. The model of bias proposed then, is simply that the pattern vectors $x'$ may become transposed to the patterns x by

$$x' \rightarrow x + bu, \qquad u = \frac{1}{\sqrt{D}} \begin{bmatrix} 1 \\ 1 \\ \cdot \\ \cdot \\ 1 \end{bmatrix}$$

The scalar $b$ is the magnitude of the bias. $b$ will vary from image to image (or even within an image), but we will assume it is normally distributed, with mean zero, standard deviation $\sigma$, ie, $p(b) = \phi_{0,\sigma}(b)$ From this assumption it can be shown[7] that the probability of a pattern vector x crossing the decision boundary due to additive bias is

$$Em = \int_{g(x)=-\infty}^{g(x)=\infty} \overline{\Phi}_{0,\sigma g(u)}(C - g(x)) \cdot p(g(x)) \, dg(x) \qquad where \qquad \overline{\Phi}_{0,\sigma g(u)} = \begin{cases} \Phi_{0,\sigma}(b) , & b < 0 \\ 1 - \Phi_{0,\sigma}(b) , & b \geq 0 \end{cases}$$

$\overline{\Phi}_{0,\sigma}(b)$ can be approximated to zero when $|b| > 2\sigma g(u)$, and the integral limited accordingly.

*Em* is a measure of the proportion of the population which are likely to cross the decision surface as a result of simple additive bias. It penalizes splits which pass close to densely populated regions of the pattern space, the more so if the surface is close to being perpendicular with **u** - ie if it is just an "average and threshold" type of split. It will favour splits which are derived from a **v** such that **v.u** is close to zero. This confirms conventional wisdom that the components of a good convolution operator should sum to zero.

To estimate *Em* it must be applied to $L_t$ rather than $\Omega_t$. *Em* is a function of $L_t$, $g$, $C$ and $\sigma$. The first three are parameters of a potential split at a node $t$, so it will be appropriate to denote this criterion function as $Em_\sigma(t)$. The value of $\sigma$ must be estimated and will depend on the application domain.

Finally note that we have carefully avoided referring to $Em_\sigma(t)$ as the likelihood of *mis-classification* ; it is the likelyhood of *mis-split* at that node alone. However it seems plausible to assume, after the discussion of section 4.1, that minimizing this likely-hood of mis-split is a strategically 'good' thing to do.

### 4.3 The total Cost Function used by Lapwing

The complete cost function used by the Lapwing learning program as the heuristic by which it searches for the best split at each node, is as follows.

$$cost(t) = k_1 I(t) + Em_\sigma(t) + k_z Z(v)$$

$I(t)$ is the Gini criterion, $Em(t)_\sigma$ is the likelihood of miss-split due to additive bias , and $Z(v)$ is a measure of the complexity of the convolution **v** defined as the number of non zero elements it contains. The inclusion of this latter term produces a slight pressure towards simpler convolutions. This is relevant as the LAP does not have a large program store, and the PPL compiler is clever enough not to generate code for zero components of a convolution. At present $k_1$ and $k_z$ are set to 5 and 0.001 respectively.

### 4.4 A 3-D Convolution ?

Thus far we have assumed that the classification is based on only one input image. This would preclude the system's use with multi-spectral (or multi-temporal) data sets which are common in remote sensing. However, if the pattern vector **x** and associated convolution **v** are extended to represent a 3 dimensional structure, then the third dimension can span over, say, three selected spectral bands of the multi-spectral data.

## 5. Searching - Genetic Algorithms

The cost function given in 4.3 forms the criterion by which the predicate $q_t$ can be selected at each node. It seems unlikely that the minimisation of this function would succumb to analysis, and thus a search procedure has been adopted with the given cost function acting as the heuristic to guide the search. The search strategy used is taken from a class generally referred to in the literature as a *Genetic Algorithm*. The key papers on the subject are due to Holland[8, 9]. He approaches the optimisation problem as one of efficiently allocating trials of candidate solutions (assuming that the only significant resource usage is that of evaluating the cost function). He shows that the processes of genetics as seen in sexual reproduction do in fact achieve this efficient allocation of "trials".

Genetic algorithms are being applied to an increasing number of optimisation problems which are characterised by a high dimension parameter space and a multi-modal, non-convex cost function. Smith T.R[10]. has used GAs for the calibration of an information driven model of US interstate migration patterns. In structural engineering Goldberg[11] has optimised the members of a ten member plane truss. Several learning systems have been developed including LS-1[12] which has been applied to bet decision making in draw poker, CS-1[13] which has been used in a maze walking problem, Eurisko[14] from which has developed a novel 3D VLSI AND/OR gate and a medical diagnosis system and RS-1[15] which has been used for robot navigation. A review of applications can be found in ref[16] to which the reader is also refered for a full account of the algorithm to be summarised here.

## 5.1 A general purpose genetic algorithm

Genetic algorithms model the process of evolution. A candidate solution to the optimisation problem is regarded as an *organism* and represented as a *chromosome* built out of a linear sequence of *genes*. A collection (typically ~ 100) of these chromosomes form a *population*. *Development* refers to the mapping of the chromosome representation onto the organism. The fitness of an organism is assessed by a cost function. Chromosomes of different organisms are permitted to *mate* to produce progeny via the genetic operation of *cross-over*. All new chromosomes are subject to possible *mutation* and *inversion*. The algorithm is summarised by the following pseudo-code.

Randomly initialise the population of chromosomes.
REPEAT
    FOR each chromosome in the population DO
        Develop into an organism (candidate solution).
        Evaluate cost function for this organism.
    END.
    Remove a given percentage of the poorest performers from the population.
    Select pairs from survivors in proportion to their fitness to mate and
        produce new chromosomes by crossover.
    Randomly mutate a few of the chromosomes in the population.
    Randomly perform inversions on a few of the chromosomes in the population
UNTIL best organism achieves desired cost OR
    a fixed number of generations have been simulated.

The crossover operation involves a break occurring at exactly corresponding points in the two chromosomes and their rejoining crosswise. The resulting progeny thus inherit aspects of 'the solution' from both parents, with the potential for two successful but partial solutions to be brought together in one organism.

Inversion involves two breaks occurring in a single chromosome and the chromosome reconstituting with the central portion reversed. As each gene is tagged with its gene number, inversion has *no* effect on the organism actually produced by development; however, it permits genes that may operate in a cooperative fashion to be brought closer together and so are less likely to be separated in future crossovers. In genetics this is known as *linkage*.

Mutation is the least important of the genetic operators. The value of a randomly chosen gene is randomly changed. It serves to ensure that all points in the search space are reachable.

## 5.2 Lapwing Specifics

The algorithm described in the previous section is completely general except for the cost function and the 'develop' routine. The former has already been described - it is exactly that given in section 4.3. 'Develop' must generate a candidate solution (an organism) from a given chromosome. In our case the organism is the predicate $q(t)$. Recall that the key component of $q(t)$ is the convolution vector v. (The optimum $C$ for each v is found by an ad-hoc histogramming method). Various ways of mapping a chromosome onto v can be envisaged; presently the simplest method is used - ie mapping individual gene values onto individual components of v. A more subtle method than this one-to-one mapping may give better results; certainly the form chosen is not irrelevant.

The algorithm includes several parameters which must be tuned - namely the population size, the proportion 'killed' at each generation, the mutation rate and the inversion rate. Some work has been done to find optimum settings of these parameters for the "travelling salesman" problem[16] but as yet no general results can be reported. These values have been only roughly tuned in the system at present.

## 6. Generation of Code for the LAP

The LAP is exclusively programmed in PPL - 'Picture Processing Language'. PPL directly supports image convolutions and conditional expressions. It is convenient therefore to represent a classification tree as a nested conditional expression. One of the Lapwing suite of programs takes a classification tree as input and generates the equivalent PPL program. Sample output from a small tree is shown below. The numbers which form the terminal expressions are the probability estimates of class 1 in terminal node k - ie $P(\omega_1| x \in \Omega_k)$, expressed in 255ths. The output from the LAP is therefore a 'probability image', white representing certain class 1, black meaning certain class 2 and the shades of grey in between being varying shades of uncertainty.

```
{ PPL generated from lll g1c1.tre    }
{ 26/8/1987}
{TOPPL  V4.0 (a) 29 th Jul 1987}
apply
  if convolve [  0,  0, -2, -6,  4,  3,  1,
                 0, -4,  1,  1,  0, -4,  4,
                 3, -2,  3, -4, -6,  0, -2,
                -6,  7, -2,  4, -7, -2,  0,
                -6, -2,  2, -1, -3,  1,  1,
                -6,  5, -2,  1,  0,  1,  5,
                -4,  5, -5,  5, -4,  0,  0 ] < -16 then
    if convolve [  0,  1,  5, -1,  0,  0,  7,
                   4,  7,  7, -2,  1,  0,  6,
                   0,  7, -1, -6,  0,  5, -1,
                  -3, -5,  7, -5, -7, -7, -4,
                  -3, -4,  3,  5, -7, -5,  5,
                   5,  2,  1,  6,  5,  0,  4,
                   4,  3, -2, -1, -5,  2,  0 ] < -28 then
      254
    else
      18
  else
    0
end
```

**Figure 3.** Sample PPL program generated from a classification tree

## 7. Context

In almost any image recognition application, pixel labels in close spatial proximity are not statistically independent. Knowledge of the labels of immediate neighbours will usually effect the Bayes probability estimate. It is clear that a consideration of the context within which a label exists can potentially improve the performance of any recognition system - often to a considerable degree.

Methods to exploit contextual dependencies are by necessity iterative in nature, and are generally referred to as 'relaxation labeling'. The literature on the topic is too extensive to review here. Reviews can be found in refs[17] and[18]

### 7.1 The cascade method.

Once a classification tree $\tau^0$ has been grown using learning sets $L^0$ and pruned with $L'^0$, that tree is used to classify the images of $L^0$ and $L'^0$. The probability images in conjunction with the original overlays can be considered to constitute new training sets, $L^1$ and $L'^1$. A second tree $\tau^1$ can thus be grown from $L^1$, pruned on $L'^1$ and then used to classify the the images of $L^1$ and $L'^1$. The process can clearly be continued indefinitely. The result is a sequence of trees, $\tau^0, \tau^1, \tau^2 .. \tau^n$ which can be successively applied to new unclassified images. Each will be converted to PPL and executed on the LAP.

The above has implied that the the training set $L^i$ is constructed only from the results of $\tau_{i-1}$, $(i \neq 0)$. In fact, given the system's ability to deal with more than one input image through the '3-D convolution' concept, the image(s) which make up $L^0$ can be included in all of $L^1 .. L^n$. This may have a stabilizing influence on the process.

In the multi-class situation, $L^i, (i \neq 0)$ will consist of the probability images for each of the C classes, thus enabling the learning program to exploit complex relationships *between* classes.

In-spite of its extreme simplicity, this method appears to work well (see results in next section). Problems of instability are largely avoided since separate trees are grown for each stage of the relaxation process. It has been observed that the sizes of successive trees decrease. Eventually, when all available contextual information has been exploited, one would expect that further learning stages would produce identical trees whose effect would be invariant, though this remains to be verified.

More work is needed to investigate the stability and convergence properties of this process. What does it mean to search for "clusters in probability space" ? Can it be proved that an invariant tree will eventually be produced ? Should the spatial width of the convolution (v) be increased at each stage ?

## 8. Results

The results shown here are for the detection of vertical or horizontal lines amongst much confusing clutter and with the lighting intensity varying across the image. All images are 256x256 pixels.

Three stages of classification are shown. Stages two and three are the results of contextual refinement based on the previous stage results. The training for this task took about 1 hour on an IBM PC-AT. Each classification stage took approximately 0.5 seconds on the LAP.

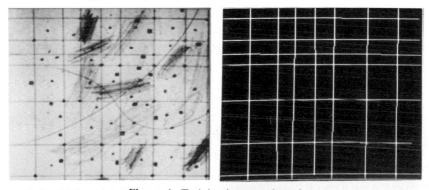

**Figure 4.** Training image and overlay.

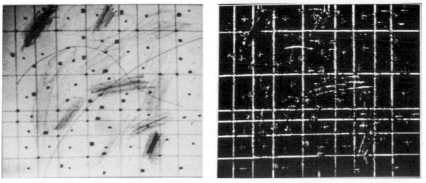

**Figure 5.** Test image and stage one results.

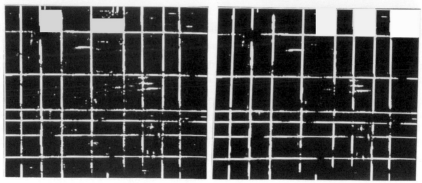

**Figure 6.** Stage two and three results.

## 9. Conclusions

A novel approach to supervised pattern recognition has been described. A Genetic search algorithm is used to find linear discriminant functions which are built up hierachically and represented as a classification tree. The use of a search strategy has permitted the selection criterion for the splits to be experimented with. Multiple training phases have been shown to be effective for the automatic elucidation of contextual relationships, although a theoretical explanation of the procedure is not given.

## Acknowledgments

We would like to acknowledge the help and encouragement of Dr Graeme Wilkinson and Dr Paul Otto (UCL), Mr David Burnett-Hall (York) and Dr Piers Plummer (NPL).

## References.

1.  Curran P J, *Principles of Remote Sensing*, Longman (1985).

2.  Plummer A P, *The Linear Array Processor*, The National Physical Laboratory (1986). DITC h 24.

3.  Plummer P and Dale F, *The Picture Processing Language Compiler*, The National Physical Laboratory. (1984).

4.  Devinjer P A and Kittler J, *Pattern Recognition: A statistical Approach*, Prentice/Hall Int. (1982).

5.  Breiman L, Friedman J, Olshen R, and Stone C, *Classification and regression trees.*, Wadsworth Int. Group (1984).

6.  Quinlan J R, "Induction of Decision Trees", *Machine Learning* **1** (1)pp. 81-106 (1986).

7.  Poole I, *Lapwing - A Prototype Image Recognition System for the Linear Array Processor*, Dept. Computer Science, UCL (1987). Internal Note 2157.

8.  Holland J H, "Genetic Algorithms and the Optimal Allocation of Trials", *SIAM J. of Computing* **2** (2) (1973).

9.  Aleksander, I and Holland, J H, "Adaptation in natural and artificial systems.", *Pattern Recognition Letters* **1**pp. 724, University of Michigan Press. (1975).

10. Smith T R and DeJong K A, "Genetic algorithms applied to information driven models of US migration.", *12th Annual Pittsburgh Conference on Modelling and Simulation.* **3**pp. 955-959 (1981).

11. Goldberg D E, "A tale of two problems : broad and efficient optimisation using genetic algorithms.", *Proceedings of the 1986 Summer Computer Simulation Conference, Reno.*, pp. 44-

48 (1986).

12. Smith S F, "Flexible learning of problem solving heuristics through adaptive search.", *Proceedings 8th International Joint Conference on Artifial Intelligence.*, pp. 422-425 (1983).

13. Holland J H, "Escaping brittleness.", *Proceedings 2nd International Workshop on Machine Learning.*, pp. 92-95, University of Illinois (1983).

14. Lenat D B, "The role of heuristcs in learning by discovery.", *In Machine Learning, an artificial intelligence approach. Michalski R S, Carbonell J G & Mitchell T M.*, , Tioga Press. (1983).

15. Grefenstette J J and Pettey C B, "Approaches to machine learning using genetic algorithms.", *IEEE International Conference on Systems, Man and Cybernetics* 1pp. 55-60 (1986).

16. Adams H P, *The Genetic Algorithm - A Search Strategy: Review, Implementation and Use.*, Dept Computer Science, University of York (1987). MSc thesis..

17. Davis L S and Rosenfield, "Co-operating Processes for Low-Level Vision: A Survey.", *Artificial Intelligence* 17pp. 245-263 (1981).

18. Kittler J and Illingworth J, "Relaxation labelling algorithms - A review", *Image and Vision Computing* 3 (4)pp. 206-216 (1985).

# Linguistic Definition of Generic Models in Computer Vision

P. Fretwell and P.J. Goillau

Royal Signals and Radar Establishment,

St Andrews Road,

Malvern, Worcs, UK,

WR14 3PS

### Abstract

A method has been developed that can take a human description of an object's spatial appearance and produce a PROLOG representation. The object's appearance is currently in terms of an edge map and the English descriptions are stylised accounts of the salient features and combinations of features found in this representation. At present the translation is performed by hand. However, suggestions are made on how this process can be automated. A prototype translator has been implemented. The PROLOG model is expressed as a hierarchy about the object's appearance, terminating in plausible low-level image primitives. A way is proposed of matching the hierarchy against an image for object recognition in isolation from its background. This reduces the search space of features and feature combinations that the matcher has to consider, so avoiding some of the combinatorial problems when using PROLOG. Extensions using fuzzy logic to deal with uncertain image date and the vagueness of natural language are discussed.

## 1   Introduction

There has been great activity in the field of image processing and AI attempting to solve the image interpretation problem. Most results achieved so far have concentrated on simple domains. This simplification has been achieved in a variety of ways but mainly by restricting the class of object to be recognised. Additional techniques need to be developed to deal with the problem of recognition in its generic sense.

The long term objective of this work is to develop tools and techniques for recognition in unconstrained scenes. The main thesis of this work is that unconstrained image interpretation requires novel information structures and processing techniques (Fretwell et al, 1987). It is the purpose of the work to address some of these issues. In particular, it is proposed to develop and demonstrate in principle a suitable knowledge formalism that can be used to represent spatial and non-spatial information for scene interpretation, and secondly to show how this knowledge can be organised and used for recognition. The non-spatial information could include data on the function and context of what is being recognised. Until recently the use of function to represent objects for computer recognition had received little attention in the literature. (See Lowry, 1982, Winston et al, 1983, Adorni et al, 1984, Ingrand et al, 1984, Di Manzo et al, 1985, and more recently Fretwell et al, 1986).

In this paper the following approach is taken. A human-computer interface is used to translate stylised linguistic descriptions of the spatial appearance of objects, generating a form of the description expressed in a logic programming language. The language used in this paper is PROLOG under the POPLOG environment (see Barrett et al, 1985). However, the language FRIL (Fuzzy Relational Inference Language - Baldwin, 1986) is at present being assessed for future use. A taxonomy of subsumption relationships is implicit in the language description. The logic system uses the taxonomy to draw inference about objects from image features extracted from the image by lower level algorithms. In this way the taxonomy is used as a model to match against an image, so providing object recognition.

Using human expertise has been chosen in preference to a machine learning mechanism because current state-of-the-art learning methods cannot cope with the complexity of data presented by a real image.

## 2   Construction of Model

It is first necessary to elicit from human observers their normal English language descriptions of the spatial appearance of the objects concerned. The terms and concepts used in the object descriptions are refined until a bottom level of description is reached. This level represents the interface between the high level object description level and the lower image pixel level. At present it is thought that this intermediate level should comprise two-dimensional features and their interrelationships. Once the object description has been elicited from the human it is transformed by hand from English to PROLOG.

Hand crafting of English car descriptions to PROLOG is appropriate in the short-term, but there are advantages to automatic translation. Naive user descriptions can conveniently be harvested directly into the system, without semantic filtering by the system designer. Knowledge may be added dynamically 'in the field' by extending the hierarchy. In addition to asserting facts and rules the user may ask questions of the system, so giving bidirectional communication.

Typical sentences from example English car description:


"Every car (always) has some wheels".

"A wheel is_(sort_of)_shaped_like an ellipse".


Predicate calculus representation of meaning:


```
all(_1,car(_1) -> exists(_2,wheels(_2) & has(_1,_2)))
exists(_1,wheel(_1) & exists(_2,ellipse(_2) & is_shaped_like(_1,_2)))
```


Partial PROLOG database:

```
car(X)    :-  has(X,wheels).
wheel(X) :-  is_shaped_like(X,ellipse).
```

Figure 1: Translation of English to Predicate Calculus to PROLOG

## 2.1  Domain Specific Example

A prototype automatic translator has been implemented in POPLOG PROLOG to deal with a limited sub-set of English car descriptions, based on Pereira and Warren's (1980) Definite Clause Grammar. The syntax of valid sentences is modelled using a Context Free Grammar (CFG) formalism e.g. sentence to noun phrase, verb phrase (see Winograd, 1983). A successful parse involves decomposing a sentence into its bottom-level linguistic primitives (e.g. determiner, noun, verb) matching these terminal symbols to dictionary entries and linking predicate calculus quantifiers, and then reconstructing a predicate calculus representation of the sentence's meaning. Figure 1 gives an example of the translation for some sentences making up elements of a particular car description.

Predicate calculus is a convenient logic formalism that can be used as an intermediate bridge between English and some further representation which is appropriate to the knowledge representation and reasoning mechanism e.g. PROLOG. A series of standard logical manipulations can be used to rewrite a predicate calculus formula into its precise clausal form (Clocksin and Mellish, 1984). The manipulations comprise removing implications, moving negations inwards, Skolemising, moving universal quantifiers outwards, distributing ANDS over ORS, and finally grouping into clauses. The clausal form of predicate calculus is close to a set of PROLOG clauses.

The translator is limited to sentences covered by the syntax and to words held in the dictionary,

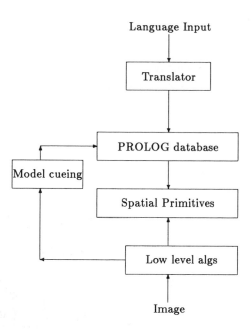

Figure 2: The Matching Paradigm

though both could be extended dynamically with an appropriate user interface. Currently synonyms and non-grammatical input cause the description to be rejected.

## 3 Object Recognition using the Model

The idea behind the matching strategy is to emulate (however roughly) one possible way in which a human could decide if an object fulfilled the stored descriptive definition. Thus the strategy is essentially top-down or model-driven. The problem of finding suitable object descriptions to match against may be alleviated by using a bottom-up or data-driven partial selection process which isolates likely candidates for matching. This cuing problem is considered elsewhere (Fretwell et al, 1988).

The representation used in the preliminary implementation consists of a PROLOG form of the object's spatial description. The relationship between image, language input and model is shown in Figure 2.

```
car(X):-
            roof(X, ROOF_REGION),
            wheels(X ,WHEELS_REGION),
            wheel_arches(X, WHEEL_ARCHES_REGION),
            windows(X, WINDOWS_REGION),
            car_doors(X, CAR_DOORS_REGION),
            under(CAR_DOORS_REGION, ROOF_REGION),
            under(WHEEL_ARCHES_REGION, ROOF_REGION),
            under(WHEELS_REGION, ROOF_REGION),
            under(WHEEL_ARCHES_REGION, WHEELS_REGION),
            contains(WINDOWS_REGION, CAR_DOORS_REGION).
```

Figure 3: Partial PROLOG Representation of Side View of Car

## 3.1   Extended Domain Specific Example

In order to see how the recognition paradigm worked with real images the problem of recognising motor cars in natural and man-made environments was chosen, consistent with membership of Alvey consortium MMI/IP 007. A description of the general side view of a car was proposed. The description is as follows:

"A car usually has a roof. A car always has wheels. Wheels are black. They are sort-of shaped like ellipses. Each wheel is placed at a position near the bottom corners of the car. Sometimes only the bottom half of the wheels are visible. A car sometimes has wheel arches. These are concave regions in the body of the car. The wheel arches are roughly semicircular shapes near the bottom of the vehicle. The wheel arches sometimes mask the wheels. A car usually has doors. A door incorporates a window. The door extends from the top part of the car to near the bottom of the car body. A car always has windows. These are closed shapes that have four sides. The windows are near the top of the car body."

Part of the PROLOG representation of the side view of a car is shown in Figure 3. A plausible set of low level spatial primitives that could be used to locate the car within a series of real images has been proposed. A subset is shown in Figure 4. For the case of the car the spatial primitive procedures have been written with synthetic values. Figure 5 demonstrates part of the automatic recognition process with the spatial definition of a car acting on a synthetic database. The chain of reasoning has been traced using the "spy" facility of POPLOG PROLOG.

```
roof(X, ROOF_REGION)

wheels(X, ROOF_REGION)

etc

Some 2D spatial relationships between regions

under(REGION,REGION)

contains(REGION,REGION)
```

Figure 4: Some Plausible Spatial Primitives for Car

# 4   Discussion and Future Work

At present the method proposed matches the model against object features. If the background were to become cluttered, or more parts were added to the scene, then the matching mechanism would be affected in the following way. The number of combinations of features necessary to identify the object would become exponentially large as the background and other parts in the image contributed more and more features that did not belong to the object. In general, non-closed world situations provide uncertain and inconsistent data. Thus PROLOG with its hard reasoning is not well fitted to the task of relating the model to the image. Therefore, at present a superset of PROLOG called FRIL (Baldwin, 1986) is being assessed. It is hoped that FRIL with its support logic can accommodate the uncertainty and inconsistency found in real images.

Another major limitation of the proposed method is the potential problem caused by the combinatorial explosion of the search time when using PROLOG (or FRIL) to match the object model to the image. It is clear that some heuristic knowledge must be incorporated into the deduction mechanisms to alleviate the search problems, by using whatever prior knowledge is available to generate a best-first search. As has been noted earlier, there are advantages to using non-spatial (e.g. context and function) as well as spatial information in the reasoning process. However, a difficulty of the functional approach appears to be the limited range of objects that can be described adequately by their function. A further difficulty is the problem of implementing suitable functional primitives to interface with the image.

In hand-crafting human object descriptions to PROLOG the system designer applies his own semantic processing which is at present difficult to quantify to extract key concepts and their relationships. With automatic translation of English descriptions there is a problem when mapping the imprecision and vagueness inherent in natural language descriptions (e.g. "sometimes", "mostly") onto the bimodal logic, negation by failure operation of PROLOG. Future work will attempt to map the degree of vagueness onto probabilities in the CFG, using the FRIL package and its support

```
** (1) Call : car(_1)?
** (2) Call : roof(_1, _2)
** (2) Exit : roof(_1, [])
** (3) Call : wheels(_1, _3)
** (3) Exit : wheels(_1, [])
** (4) Call : wheel_arches(_1, _4)
** (4) Exit : wheel_arches(_1, [])
** (5) Call : windows(_1, _5)
** (5) Exit : windows(_1, [])

    .      .

    .      .

    .      .

** (1) Exit : car(_1)
```

Figure 5: PROLOG Matching

logic mechanism to reason about probabilities. In addition the meaning component may be spread over several sentences comprising a paragraph description. Although the Definite Clause Grammar formalism used in the prototype implementation is powerful and general, there are alternative meaning-based approaches (for example Lexical Functional Grammar, Systemic Grammar, Scripts, Case Frame systems) which are being evaluated for comparison.

## 5  Conclusions

A method has been developed that can take human analysis of an object's spatial appearance in the form of a stylised description of salient features and combinations of those features, and generate an equivalent PROLOG representation. A paradigm has been proposed by which the PROLOG model may be matched against an object in isolation from its background. The domain specific problem of recognising cars has been discussed by way of example. The car model consists of the salient edges and combinations of those edges. This description is turned into a PROLOG representation of the object by hand crafting. Suggestions have been made on how the language description to PROLOG translation could be automated, and a prototype system implemented. A superset of PROLOG called FRIL has been proposed to deal with uncertain image data and the vagueness of natural language.

# References

- Adorni, G., Di Manzo, M., Giunchiglia, F., Meson, L., October, 1984, "A conceptual approach to artificial vision", Proc. of the 4th Int. Conf. on Robot Vision and Sensory Controls - RoVisSec 4, London.

- Baldwin, J.F., 1986, "Support logic programming", in Jones, A.I. et al (eds), "Fuzzy sets - Theory and Applications", Proceedings of NATO Advanced Study Institute, Reidel Publishing Co..

- Barrett, R., Ramsey, A., Sloman, A., 1985, "POP-11: A practical language for artificial intelligence", Ellis Horwood, Chichester.

- Clocksin, W.F. and Mellish, C.S., 1984, "Programming in PROLOG" (2nd edn), Springer-Verlag, Berlin.

- Di Manzo, M., Adorni, G., Giunchiglia, F., Ricci, F., 1985, "Building function descriptions : Computer vision", Proc. of the 5th Int. Conf. on Robot Vision and Sensory Controls - RoVisSec, Amsterdam, Netherlands, 29-31 Oct. 1985, pp403-412.

- Fretwell, P., Hearn, D.B., Sleigh, A.C., 1986 "Methods for knowledge representation and inference for image understanding", Oral Presentation at IEE Colloquium on Knowledge-based image processing, Savoy Place, London, 27 January 1986.

- Fretwell, P., Goillau, P.J., Hearn, D.B. and Sleigh, A.C., 1987, "Representation and reasoning using linguistic descriptions of objects", Oral Presentation at BPRA Colloquium on Representing knowledge in vision, Imperial College, London, 7 April 1987.

- Fretwell, P., Bayliss, D.A., Radford, C.J., and Serles, R.W., 1988, "Generic cueing in image understanding", this volume.

- Ingrand, F. and Latcombe, J.C., "Functional reasoning for automatic fixture design", November, 1984, CAM-I 13th. Annual meeting and technical conference, Clearwater Beach, Florida.

- Lowry, M.R., 1982, "Reasoning between structure and function", Proceedings of the DARPA image understanding workshops, pages 260-264. Science Applications Inc., McLean, VA., September.

- Pereira, F.C.N. and Warren, D.H.D., 1980, "Definite Clause Grammars for language analysis - a survey of the formalism and a comparison with Augmented Transition Networks", Artificial Intelligence, 13, pp231-278.

- Winograd, T., 1983, "Language as a Cognitive Process. Volume I: Syntax", Addison-Wesley, Reading, Massachusetts.

- Winston, P.H., Binford, T.O., Katze, B., and Lowry, M., 1983, "Learning physical descriptions from functional definitions, examples and precedents", M.I.T. AI Memo, January 1983.

# A Multiple Hypothesis Rule-Based Automatic Target Recognizer

John Wootton
Carl Carpenter
Gregory Hobson
Emerson Electric Electronics and
    Space Division
8100 West Florissant
St. Louis, MO  63136

James Keller[1]
    Electrical and Computer
       Engineering Department
University of Missouri-Columbia
Columbia, MO  65211

## Abstract

The majority of automatic target recognizers undertaking field evaluation today owe their internal structure to a classical statistical approach.  Although the dimensionality of the variable parameters that each system is subject to is large, little use is made of context and ancillary information such as time of day, sensor, weather conditions and intelligence data.  Such ancillary data can be profitably used to alleviate the algorithmic burden of accommodating the extreme ranges of conditions.

Presented here is a novel approach to include ancillary knowledge into the control structure of an automatic target recognizer (ATR).

## 1.  Introduction.

The application of a rule-based or knowledge-based approach to automatic target recognition represents an on going joint research effort between UMC (University of Missouri-Columbia) and their industrial counterparts at Emerson Electric, Electronics and Space Division.  Automatic target recognition involves the determination of objects in natural scenes in different weather conditions and in the presence of both active and passive countermeasures and battlefield contaminants.  This high degree of variability requires a flexible system control capable of adapting as the conditions change.  The desired flexibility can be achieved with a rule-based system in which the knowledge of the effects of scene content and ancillary information on algorithm choices and parameter values can be modelled and manipulated.  This on-going effort is an outgrowth of earlier activity in automatic target recognition research.  New theoretical and practical tools were developed for the analysis of military scenes, with emphasis placed on methods to deal with uncertainties associated with such imagery [1-5].  The ongoing effort

---

[1]J. Keller was partially supported by a contract A75786-67 from Emerson Electric Electronics and Space Division and an Air Force Office of Scientific Research grant AFOSR-87-0226.

involves incorporating the knowledge and experience gained in working with such imagery and with modelling uncertainties into a rule-based structure for the detection and recognition of objects in military scenes.

The main focus of research in incorporating AI into automatic target recognition has been the use of context to cue the possible likelihood of a target in a given area of the scene [6]-[11]. This paper presents a much different approach to the inclusion of AI technology.

## 2. Approach.

The approach we developed jointly between Emerson Electric Co. and UMC was borne out of several years of independent research in image processing, image analysis, image understanding and artificial intelligence techniques. Because of the large variability in automatic target recognition, no single set of algorithms, no matter how adaptive they could be made, would give consistent, reliable results when subject to the full variety of target conditions and scenario conditions. Yet, it was realized that by having knowledge of the conditions (that could be measured by simple metrics) that an expert analyst could select an appropriate algorithm which could yield an optimal performance.

The known tool for implementing this expert corporate knowledge was a rule based system. We preferred that such a system indicate when it was being subjected to a situation for which there was no supporting research. We asked that the system be structured so that it identified circumstances which were outside its experience. Finally we resolved not necessarily to have a set structure for finding targets and target types but to let the data trigger the rules for finding "potential objects". Once a potential object has been found the system carries multiple hypothesis as regard to the type of the object using a local Dempster-Shafer approach to eventually determine the target type.

## 3. Image Processing Basis.

Classical statistical image processing generally follows the stages of enhancement, prescreening, segmentation and feature extraction followed by detection, recognition and/or identification. Within each stage, the image analysts developed a whole series of algorithms which themselves had adaptive coefficients, or thresholds [12, 13]. Indeed some of these algorithms themselves included simple rule based algorithms.

The systems usually utilize deterministic and/or statistical rules for classification. Little use is made of context and ancillary information such as time of day, season, weather conditions and "intelligence" data. The conventional approach utilizes a training data set as a basis to select processing algorithms, select parameter values, select feature sets and to build decision rules. If an actual situation fell outside of the training set, such a system would make a decision with a relatively high, and likely unacceptable, error probability.

In addition to developing the individual algorithms the analysts also developed measures of performances for evaluating the performance of an algorithm under various circumstances. These "tractability" fundamental parameters are i) size, ii) contrast, iii) clutter, iv) motion, v) shape and vi) color. The real worth of this work was that the image understanding analysts were able to quantify image tractability as a function of image metrics [14, 15]. A set of algorithms could, in general, be selected and their coefficients controlled to give very reasonable performance (-reasonable when compared to human performance-) provided that the set of test images to which the system was subjected were confined to small excursions of the image conditions.

Combining the knowledge of the image processing researchers with that of the scene understanding personnel became the goal of the artificial intelligence team assigned to the task. At the earliest stage the knowledge engineers quantified the knowledge under the general headings of sensor, scene, and objective. The impact of the sensor is self evident. The significance of the scene can be illustrated by comparing the difficulty of finding a man made object in a rural scene as distinct from an urban scene.

The target condition itself plays a dominant role. Apart from its size, its signature against its background is one of the most dominant video features. Clearly a well camouflaged target will present little or no contrast to the ATR which makes the basic task of initial target detection difficult [15]. Conversely a sharply contrasted target is very easy to locate. The weather conditions greatly contribute to this received image contrast. Rain, fog, and BIC (battlefield induced contaminants) all contribute to image degradation.

The final impact upon an ATR structure is the mission objective. In the first level of classification under the objective category we consider detection, recognition and identification. If all that is required is detection then essentially the ATR is faced with a two class problem of target or non-target. Once the target category has been designated as a military set (tanks, APCs, trucks, helicopters, etc.) then every object not recognized as one of that target set is a non-target. If recognition is the requirement, then the ATR has to accommodate a multiclass structure and look for a set of features which can discriminate between those classes selected. Identification of a particular object subclass leads to yet a more tasking problem. In addition to the baseline objective of detection, recognition and identification, the target type and its priority impact the algorithms chosen. For Ground order of battle, targets of opportunity, such as tanks, etc., tend to proliferate in the battlefield. An ATR carried on a high valued asset such as a fighter aircraft, whose objective is to find such targets of opportunity should be optimized to have a very low false alarm rate at the expense of probability of detection. On the other extreme are high value targets such as a mobile nuclear missile site for which one should be prepared to accept a higher probability of detection at the expense of a higher false alarm. Again, ancillary data on the target can greatly ease the target detection and recognition problem. For instance the majority of high value targets such as bridges, POL dumps, etc. have known physical locations. The linking of the knowledge concerning the location of the sensor platform (-aircraft-) and look angle of the sensor can indicate to the ATR that the object should be there geographically. The ATR in this case has much of the responsibility of finding the target removed by the inclusion of inertial navigation data and the knowledge that the target is at that location.

This knowledge was incorporated into an ATR control structure through the use of a rule-based network, or tree, to determine i) the choice of processing algorithms, ii) the order of application of these algorithms, iii) the parameters utilized in these techniques and iv) provide an overall confidence level associated with the final decision. Such a rule-based structure offers the following advantages in ATR applications:

1) efficient use of knowledge directly concerned with relationships of conditions to conclusions or deductions, such as the influence of ancillary factors on selecting features or the image sensor;

2) isolation of (IF...THEN rules) for feature selection from those for selecting a segmentation algorithm;

3) ability to handle uncertainties in terms of probabilities, belief functions or possibility distributions;

4) ability to perform specific goal directed hypothesis testing, for example, different approaches are necessary to decide if an object is a tank, or more generally a target.

4. Description of the Process.

Our early image analysis research had followed a sequential approach. We had found that we could perform considerable enhancement either globally or locally, which would give "pleasing" results to a human observer [16]. However, such preprocessing did little in terms of improving an ATRs overall performance unless it was concerned with removing an artifact generated by the sensor.

We similarly studied many of the common prescreeners and tested them using different sensors against targets in different scenarios [17]. What was learned was that depending on the sensor and the scenario, not only is there an appropriate choice of prescreener but there is also an optimal choice of that prescreener's coefficient [17-18].

Therefore it became evident that we could define a knowledge base structure such that if the sensor was known, and the scene conditions measured, the most appropriate choice of preprocessor and prescreener could be selected.

The next stage became somewhat more complex. We had researched segmentors [14], features extraction [17] and the methods for combining features [17, 18] to determine the detection, recognition or identification of objects in military scenes. In our efforts to optimize the segmentation process we realized that the measure of performance of the segmentor was related to the consistency of the feature it produced for the feature extraction stage [14]. The value of the feature itself depended upon the manner in which that feature separated the chosen class from the other classes. Through considerable testing of a number segmentors (around 20) in conjunction with over 150 features there evolved a consistent set of appropriate feature extractor-segmentor pairs that gave reliable results [14, 17].

The appropriate set of features themselves were predicated upon the class of targets required (i.e. the objective). For each classification problem encountered, target vs. non-target, tank vs. APC, helicopter vs. false alarm, etc., we studied the effects of different collections of features and pattern recognizers on a large data base of military objects. The classifiers included Bayes decision rule, crisp and fuzzy K nearest neighbor and perceptron schemes, and a Dempster-Shafer evidence combination process [4, 5, 18-21]. We then developed rules which paired the decision making procedure with the appropriate feature sets for each subproblem. This in turn demanded an appropriate choice of feature-extractor methodology.

The work in determining the optimal classifiers was based upon extracting the features from the training data into known ranges of values. We faced the dilemma that when features were extracted from test data that did not correspond to the range of data extracted from the training set, then any decision derived from that data is unsubstantiated. To accommodate this we allowed the ATR to address other features which might fall into a range that had been observed from the training data. Should the ATR not find a feature that corresponds to the test data range, it returns an answer of "outside our experience."

As an added robustness feature, we carried multiple hypotheses as to the identity of the potential target. For instance, in determining whether a detection from the prescreener is a target (defined as a tank or an APC) or a false alarm, we examined the possibility that it was a target or a non-target, that it was an APC or a non-APC, that it was a tank or a non-tank. Whatever the objective of system at a particular time, the first piece of evidence acquired is a detector decision (target vs. non-target) using a Bayes Rule with 8 features chosen from our feature set. The rule was trained on approximately 900 targets and around 100 false alarms. The decision made at this stage (together with the Bayes confidence) is used to tailor the resulting evidence acquisition.

From this point on, different pattern recognition problems are solved, and the results combined in a voting scheme individualized to the overall objective of the system. For example, if the objective was to distinguish tanks, APC's and false alarms, then the following subproblems were initiated to provide the evidence for the final vote: tank vs. non-tank, APC vs. non-APCs, targets vs. false alarms, APCs vs. false alarms, and tanks vs. false alarms. In each of these processes, we used four features chosen from our feature set as being good separators of the training data. The evidence combination in each decision process was based on Dempster-Shafer belief theory [21]. For each feature, a simple support function was generated separately for each hypothesis. It is in this support function that information "outside our experience" can be ignored. In fact, the basic probability assignment for the hypothesis under consideration was calculated by a $\pi$-function centered on the interval of the feature axis occupied by the training data. Hence, if this feature value for a test object does not fall into the range of our training data, a vacuous support function is generated. These support functions are combined using Dempster's Rule into a belief function related to this feature. These belief functions are then combined for all features to produce overall beliefs for the hypotheses under consideration. A decision is made to favor the hypothesis with greatest belief. We choose this structure so that spurious values of a few features caused by noise, partial occlusion, etc. will not overly bias the decision, as may happen in a Bayes technique.

There are several rules in the system which combine the decisions generated by those subproblems into a final classification. These rules depend upon the overall objective, and the choice and results of the various subtests. Intuitively, if there is a clear winner with high enough belief, then that hypothesis is chosen. However, there are tie-breaking rules which reflect mission objectives, for example if the object could be either a tank or an APC with about equal support, then call it a tank. There are even rules which override a majority if the evidence from a high priority rule is strong enough. An instance of this type of rule occurs where the object is thought to be a target from Bayes rule, and a tank in the tank vs. non-tank rule (with high enough belief) but is labeled a false alarm by two or three rules which allow false alarm as a hypothesis. In this case, the majority is overridden by the confidence in the target and tank decisions.

5. Implementation and Results.

The rule based system control strategy contained both forward chaining and backward chaining paradigms. The forward chaining approach tends to follow the traditional sequence of steps in image analysis, while the backward chaining mode allows specific tailoring of the system structure for hypothesis generation and testing.

Two basic implementations were made. The first was produced on a Xerox 1108 development machine using common LISP as the underlying language. The second system was implemented in an expert system shell for rapid prototyping with image inputs from the Computer Vision Laboratory equipment at UMC. Our basic prototype system uses 212 rules.

The object recognition portion of the rule base was tested on a sequence of 100 frames containing two tanks and an APC during which the APC moves behind one of the tanks and into and out of a ravine. This sequence of images is considerably different from the data used to "train" the rule base. Using the output of the first part of the rule base, the images were prescreened, and segmented, and the chosen features were extracted. The rule base was executed using different objectives and representative results are displayed in Table I. The format of the table gives the actual object under consideration, the system objective, the result of the target detection stage and the recognition evidence, followed by the final classification. We have suppressed the local Shafer belief values for individual processes and have only reported the partial determination. It can be seen from the table that different system objectives give rise to different recognition processes and interpretation rules. Several instances of system behavior can be be highlighted. There are circumstances when this rule base will not make a partial decision. This occurred when the results of the individual recognition procedures conflicted with the system objective. This can be seen in tests (4), (5), (8) and (10) in Table 1. In each case, an Undecided (Nil) response was generated, and the search for evidence proceeded. With the object labeled APC 1 (8), in the APC vs. tank scenario, the tests tank vs. non-tank and APC vs. false alarm indicate that the result is false alarm, contrary to the objective. The system recorded a Nil decision from the evidence, and proceeded. When it encountered the same confusion in the next set of tests, it produced a final classification of Undecided. (This APC was partially occluded by the ravine). However in the APC vs. false alarm case, a decision was made quickly (This APC's features resembled those of ground clutter due to its occlusion). Now APC 4 corresponds to the APC after it had become completely visible and was correctly classified in all scenarios.

Test (6) from Table I involved a tank in a three class recognition problem. In this case, since false alarm was a viable answer, the inconsistency described above was not present. Hence, there were two votes for false alarm in this case, countered by the one vote for tank. However, the fact that the object was called a target by the detection algorithm (Bayes Decision Rule), and a tank in the tank vs. APC process, together with "high" belief in tank and "low" belief in false alarm, the system correctly identified the object. This is an example of a non-majority decision rule consistent with a mission plan.

6.  Conclusions.

A rule-based approach to automatic target recognition has been presented. The system contained rules which cover the entire image analysis sequence from preprocessing to object identification. The uncertainty in the definition of various objects was modeled with Shafer belief functions and evidence combined using Dempster's rule. Mission objectives dictated the choice of subproblems which were solved prior to the voting rules which finally classified the object. A prototype system was developed and tested on several images taken from a large military image database. The results demonstrated the applicability and flexibility of this approach. We are currently updating both the rule base and the methodologies for determining the partial evidence and final classification.

Acknowledgements:

The authors would like to thank Advait Mogre, Hossein Tahani, Asghar Nafarieh and Jim Givens at UMC for their assistance in the discussions and implementation of this system.

References

1)  R. Crownover and J. Keller, "Fast dimension reduction that preserves undetermined data clusters," Proceedings, SPIE Conference on Advanced Signal Processing Algorithms and Architectures, San Diego, California, August 1986.

2)  J. Keller, R. Crownover, J. Wootton and G. Hobson, "Target recognition using the Karhunen-Loeve transform, " Proceedings, IEEE International Conference on Systems, Man and Cybernetics, Tucson, Arizona, November 1985, pp. 310-314.

3)  J. Keller, R. Crownover and R. Chen, "Characteristics of natural scenes related to fractal dimension," IEEE Transactions, Pattern Analysis and Machine Intell, Vol. PAMI-9, No. 5, Sept. 1987, pp. 621-627.

4)  J. Keller and D. Hunt, "Incorporating fuzzy membership functions into the perceptron algorithm," IEEE Transactions, Pattern Anal and Machine Intell, Vol. PAMI-7, No. 6, November 1985, pp. 693-699.

5)  J. Keller, G. Hobson, J. Wootton, A. Nafarieh and K. Luetkemeyer, "Fuzzy confidence measures in midlevel vision," IEEE Transactions, Systems, Man and Cybernetics, Vol. SMC-17, No. 4, 1987.

6)  P.A. Nagin, A.R. Hanson, and E.M. Riseman. "Region extraction and description through planning," COINS Tech Rep 77-8, Computer and Information Sciences Dept., University of Massachusetts, Amherst.

7)  R.A. Brooks, R. Greiner, and T. Binford. "Progress report on a model-based vision system," Proceedings of the Image Understanding Workshop, 1978, pp. 145-151 (L.S. Baumann, ed.).

8)  D.P. McKeown. "MAPS: The organization of a spatial database system using imagery, terrain and map data," Proceedings: DARPA Image Understanding Workshop, June 1983, pp. 105-127.

9)  D.M. McKeown, and J. McDermott. "Toward expert systems for photo interpretation," IEEE Trends and Applications '83, May 1983, pp. 33-39.

10) A. Rosenfeld and A. Kak. Digital Picture Processing, 2nd edition, Orlando: Academic Press, 1982.

11) R. Duda, and P. Hart, Pattern Classification and Scene Analysis, New York: Wiley & Sons, 1978.

12) K. Luetkemeyer, G. Hobson, and C. Carpenter. "Evaluation of segmentation techniques applied to prescreened areas of multi-sensor imagery," MAECON, Dayton, 1986.

13) G. Waldman, J. Wootton, G. Hobson, and K. Luetkemeyer. "A normalized clutter measure for images," Computer Vision, Graphics & Image Processing (to be published).

14) G. Hobson, and J. Wootton. "Electro optical/infrared automatic feature recognition," IRAD Tech Report, F784, Emerson Electric.

15) G. Hobson, and J. Wootton. "Electro optical/infrared automatic feature recognition," IRAD Tech Report, F785, Emerson Electric.

16) G. Hobson, and J. Wootton. "Electro optical/infrared automatic feature recognition," IRAD Tech Report, F786, Emerson Electric.

17) J. Keller, M. Gray, J. Givens. "A fuzzy k-nearest neighbor algorithm," IEEE Trans System, Man, Cybern, Vol. SMC-15, No. 4, July/August 1985, pp. 580-585.

18) J. Wootton, G. Hobson, K. Luetkemeyer and J. Keller. "The use of fuzzy set theory to build confidence measures in multisensor imagery," IEEE Applied Imagery Pattern Recognition Workshop.

19) G. Shafer. A Mathematical Theory of Evidence, Princeton: Princeton University Press, 1976.

Table I.  Sample Output*

| Actual Object | System Objective | Evidence | | Final Classification |
|---|---|---|---|---|
| | | Detection | Recognition [(process)/result] | |
| Tank 11 (1) | T vs FA | Target | (T vs A)/T (T vs NT)/T | Tank |
| (2) | T vs A | Target | (T vs A)/T (T vs NT)/T (A vs NA)/NA (T vs FA)/T | Tank |
| (3) | T vs A vs FA | Target | (T vs A)/T (T vs NT)/T (A vs NA)/NA (T vs FA)/T | Tank |
| Tank 13 (4) | T vs A | Target | (T vs A)/T (T vs NT)/T (A vs NA)/NA }Nil (T vs FA)/FA | Tank |

(Table I continued)

| | | | | |
|---|---|---|---|---|
| **Tank 22** | | | | |
| (5) | T vs A | Target | (T vs A)/T | |
| | | | (T vs NT)/NT ⎫ | |
| | | | ⎬ Nil | |
| | | | (A vs FA)/FA ⎭ | |
| | | | (A vs NA)/NA ⎫ | |
| | | | ⎬ Nil | |
| | | | (T vs FA)/FA ⎭ | Tank |
| (6) | T vs A vs FA | Target | (T vs A)/T | |
| | | | (T vs NT)/NT ⎫ | |
| | | | ⎬ FA | |
| | | | (A vs FA)/FA ⎭ | |
| | | | (A vs NA)/NA ⎫ | |
| | | | ⎬ FA | |
| | | | (T vs FA)/FA ⎭ | Tank |
| **APC 1** | | | | |
| (7) | A vs FA | False Alarm | (A vs NA)/NA | False Alarm |
| (8) | A vs T | False Alarm | (T vs NT)/NT ⎫ | |
| | | | ⎬ Nil | |
| | | | (A vs FA)/FA ⎭ | |
| | | | (A vs NA)/NA ⎫ | |
| | | | ⎬ Nil | |
| | | | (T vs FA)/FA ⎭ | Undecided |
| **APC 4** | | | | |
| (9) | A vs FA | Target | (T vs A)/A | |
| | | | (A vs NA)/A | APC |
| (10) | T vs A | Target | (T vs A)/A | |
| | | | (T vs NT)/NT ⎫ | |
| | | | ⎬ Nil | |
| | | | (A vs FA)/FA ⎭ | |
| | | | (A vs NA)/A | APC |
| **Clutter** | | | | |
| (11) | T vs A vs FA | False Alarm | (T vs NT)/NT | |
| | | | (A vs FA)/FA | |
| | | | (A vs NA)/NA | False Alarm |
| | | | (T vs FA)/FA | |
| | | | (A vs FA)/FA | |

*Abbreviations:  T - Tank
  NT - Nontank
  A - APC
  NA - nonAPC
  FA - False Alarm

# GENERIC CUEING IN IMAGE UNDERSTANDING

P. Fretwell, D.A. Bayliss, C.J. Radford, R.W. Series,

RSRE,

St Andrews Road,

Malvern,

Worcs,

WR14 3PS

### Abstract

We report an attempt to derive simple low level features which may readily be extracted from an image. The features may be used to provide a classification of objects, so acting as a cue to aid further recognition.

It is shown that such an approach may find applications in the early stages of image analysis for the classification of objects in an open world situation. The method is illustrated by application of classification rules based on an estimate of line wigglyness (fractal dimension) and analysis of the directional edgel statistics.

## 1 Introduction

In image understanding a cue may be defined as a link between one level of object description to a higher level via measurement at the lower level. The ability to reason over uncertain and possibly contradictory inferences derived from this cue analysis will be the subject of a future publication.

In this paper we report the use of a combination of generic features to form specific object cues for the classification of an open world scene. It is shown that taken individually the individual cues provide limited discrimination but certain combinations of them can provide an effective object cue. An edgel representation of the scene which has been edge extracted from a grey level image by the application of a directional edge operator is used as the basis for the study. The edgel representation used has a five bit edge strength component and a three bit (eight directions) directional component.

A simple, computationally inexpensive cueing method that links directional edge information to some as yet unspecified higher level model is proposed. The domain is real images set in natural and semi-natural outdoor environments. This choice of domain poses many difficulties not found in closed world problems such as are encountered in certain industrial part recognition problems in highly structured and controlled environments. One of the many difficulties in the open world scenario is that the background cannot be controlled and this can cause problems when trying to match an object model against the image. Another difficulty the open world can share with the closed world is that of object variability. This may be found at three levels. Most simply, a given object, from a given viewpoint, may take a variety of appearances depending on the illumination. Next, the image will vary with viewpoint. Finally, in most open world situations, there is no unique three dimensional specification of the object and we require to classify objects in terms of their generic structure.

Our approach is not to use an exact representation of the three dimensional shape of the object. Rather, the idea is to use generic image properties of an object class to approximately identify the location and identity of the object in the image. We suggest that such an approach may find applications in the early stages of image analysis for the classification of objects in an open world situation. This will of course be followed by verification of the exact identity and position of the object under scrutiny. A verification method could use a spatial model based approach, see for instance Brooks 1981, Lowe 1985, 1987 and Brisdon 1987 and the related paper Sullivan 1987.

## 2    Related Techniques

The cue rules in the method presented in this paper are based on an estimate of wigglyness of edge features and analysis of directional edgel distribution. Details of this approach appear in the next section. Related work includes that of Knoll and Jain 1986 and more recently Wallace 1987.

Knoll and Jain use binary images of three dimensional flat objects. Using what amount to two dimensional objects overcomes the problems of viewing variability. Their work is close in philosophy to the method proposed in this paper in that they identify common features that objects in a particular class possess. Therefore, identification does not rely on unique features. This means it can cope with some obscuration. The common features in the method are lengths of certain parts of the objects boundaries. This makes the method dependent on some measure of scale. Our method is virtually scale independent and does not rely on the measurement of image edge segments. The breaking up of continuous object lines by edge operators into smaller segments is a major problem when analysing edge maps for image understanding. This non robustness derives from the possible shortfall in the edge operators performance and more importantly from the fact that a pixel value is a product of so may factors. It depends on the objects reflectance, the light source, the orientation of the object with respect to the light source and so on. The method of Knoll and Jain is particularly affected by the output of the edge operator. Our method has a certain robustness to breaking up of the edges.

Wallace 1987 concentrates on the recognition of flat industrial parts based on the identification of binary shape cues. These cues are pairs of line segments in a particular relationship such as roughly joined at right angles. They claim that the method should be robust to partial obscuration because not all the object's boundary is used. However, the model used is quite specific to a particular object and is prone to the problems of object variability. The variability caused by different viewing angles will cause the number of cues for the object to become very large indeed. The technique is used to recognise flat industrial parts. The background is uncluttered and the parts appear alone or in twos in the image. It is not clear what the outcome would be if the background was to become cluttered or more parts were added to the scene. It is probable that the number of combinations of cues necessary to identify the object would become expontentially large as the background and other parts in the image contributed more and more false cues.

In contrast our method uses generic properties of the object image. These image properties are not necessarily unique to the object but they do give an indication of the presence of the object. Various combinations of these image properties can serve to strengthen the belief that a particular object is at a particular position. This means that background properties will influence the cueing but will not necessarily mean that as the background complexity increases the method will take an exponentially increasing amount of time.

A related approach uses a region segmentation together with contextual reasoning to label the regions of the segmentation. (Golden, Fullwood and Hyde 1987, Morton 1987). The output of these methods is a set of bounded regions in the two dimensional image in which an object of interest is thought to be located, along with an initial view point hypothesis.

# 3   Generic Image Cues

A series of cues are desired that can roughly indicate the presence of objects in a large object class. In other words the cue is designed to use only those attributes that all members of the class share. Thus it trades in accuracy for generality. The purpose of this work is to propose several such cues and investigate how they may be combined to produce a more accurate cueing mechanism.

Figure 1: Typical Test Set Car Image          Figure 2: Edgel Map of Typical House Image

## 3.1   Cueing with Edge Wigglyness

Figure 1 is a typical image taken from a test set of 60 images used in this work. Figure 2 is an edgel map of a typical image containing a building taken from the same test set. It was recognised, not surprisingly perhaps, that the buildings and cars had more linear features (mainly, straight lines) while the bushes and trees have more high frequency in their edge structure.

To investigate the applicability of this classification we used an edge extraction operator due to the work of Radford (to be published). This operates first by extracting an edge map from the grey level image using an adaptive directional Sobel operator. This provides a series of edge segments, each of which has information about local direction coded into the output. A second stage has the effect of tracking along the lines and measuring the total change in line direction as a function of line length. This provides a measure of the "wigglyness" of the line which is approximately independent of scale. Wigglyness has an inverse relationship to fractal dimension. Note that the code takes no precautions to detect a wiggly line joined onto a straight line and so is potentially capable of significant enhancement.

Figure 3 shows those edgels that have been classified as "wiggly" while the image in Figure 4 shows only those edges classified as "non-wiggly" by the filter. Note that most of the edge features of the building and car are classified as smooth while much of the detail of the vegetation is classified as wiggly although not exclusively so as noted above. These are primarily due to the joining of edges of differing types. There are various methods which might be used to overcome this problem, for example a statistical analysis of the fractal dimension along a line might be used to look for changes in line character in a manner analogous to the DSRM algorithms used in some region growing algorithms (Godden, Fullwood and Hyde 1987).

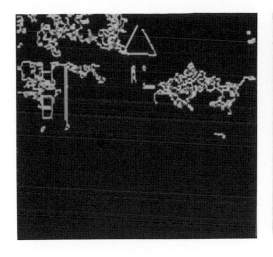

Figure 3: Wiggly Edgels

Figure 4: Non-Wiggly Edgels

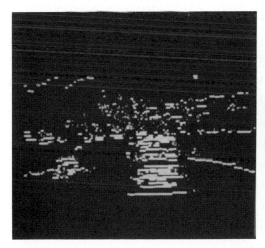

Figure 5: Horizontal Edgels

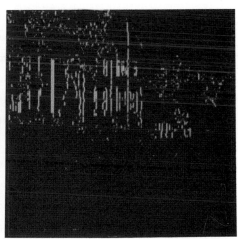

Figure 6: Vertical Edgels

Figure 7: Car Cue

Figure 8: Building Cues

## 3.2 Cueing using Edgel Direction

Analysis of test images after application of the edge operator and wiggle filter revealed that the motor cars and the buildings in the images were responsible for many of the long straight horizontal lines. To study the potential value of the directional edge information, maps were produced of the vertical and horizontal edge components in a variety of images. As the edge operator produces output giving directional information as a three bit output, the maps show edgels within plus or minus 22.5 deg of horizontal or vertical directions

Figure 5 shows the edgels in the typical car image that have horizontal orientation (to within plus or minus 22.5 degrees) while Figure 6 shows the edgels in the typical house image that have vertical orientation. It was noted that the bushes and trees made a significant contribution to the horizontal edgels. The building regions are responsible for long vertical lines while the car and shrubbery regions are responsible for many of the short vertical lines. These findings form the basis of a simple cue for potential cars or buildings within the test data.

The ratio of the number of horizontal edgels to the number of vertical edgels was calculated for the regions that contained cars and buildings. It was found that the ratio for the two different regions was different and also had a value that was fairly constant (within a range of values) over the majority of the test set. This was in spite of the cars having different scale and orientations (within a horizontal plane) within the image. Thus the ratio could be said to have reasonable scale invariance. It was found that if the edgels corresponding to the vegetation were removed the ratio for the car and building regions were more consistent.

From this observation an algorithm was devised that used the vegetation removal procedure and the ratio test for regions of an image to discriminate between car like and non-car like and house like and non-house like.

The algorithm first removes the majority of the edgels corresponding to the vegetation as possible. The parameter governing the edgel operator as well as the vegetation removal is achieved by fixed thresholds. The resulting edgel image is then divided into 64 regular regions. The ratio of horizontal edgels to vertical edgels within each region is calculated. If the region has a ratio that lies outside [1.0,60.0] then the region is said not to contain a car and similarly if the ratio lies outside [0.2,10.0] then the region is said not to contain a building. Finally the largest contiguous set of regions with the appropriate ratio is selected as the cue region.

The algorithm is demonstrated in Figure 7 and Figure 8. The dark regions in Figure 7 correspond to those regions that have not got a ratio that lies inside the car ratio. Figure 8 shows the algorithm for the case of the building. It can be seen that the majority of the indicated region in Figure 7 contain most of the car. Similarly for the case of the building.

## 4 Discussion and Future Work

Cueing based on the ratio of horizontal to vertical edgels within an image is clearly sensitive to variations in the edgel operator output. This in turn is sensitive to changes in grey level caused by lighting, shadows, reflectance and so forth. This potential problem maybe overcome by performing the cueing using several edgel maps of different sensitivities and combining these to obtain a ratio. This approach could allow the cueing method to be independent of hand crafted parameters in the edgel operator.

The cueing is based on analysis of 64 rectangular grid regions in the edgel domain. Unless the object fills a whole number of regions there will be some regions that contain only a small part of the object. This may cause the cueing to disregard those parts of the image. The cueing could be more accurate if there were fewer regions that only contained a small part of the object. This could possibly be achieved by using regions that have been obtained via a region segmentation of the image based on the grey levels. These would in general be non regular regions. This is an area of continuing research.

## 5 Conclusion

Two simple cue rules have been proposed. The first one based on the rate of change of edgel direction. The second is based on a ratio of edgel directions. The first cue can be used to distinguish bushy vegetation from objects that have smooth long lines associated with them (like buildings and cars). The second cue has been shown to roughly discriminate between objects that have long horizontal and vertical lines and others. The cue measures the ratio of the number of horizontal edgels to the number of vertical edgels. The vegetation in the images produces both vertical and horizontal edgels. This is why the cue does not operate well in the presence of vegetation edgels. However, a combination of the vegetation cue followed by linear feature cue improves the performance of the linear feature cue. This has been demonstrated by developing a cue selective between cars and buildings within the test images. This demonstrates one important feature of cues in that the full power is achieved by the application of cues in combination rather than in isolation.

## References

- Brisdon, K,. 1987, "Alvey MMI-007 Vehicle Exemplar: Evaluation and Verification of Model Instances", Proceedings of the third Alvey Vision Conference, 1987, Univ. of Cambridge, 1987, 15-17 Sept. pp 33- 37.

- Goddon, R.J., Fullwood, J.A., Hyde, J., 1987, "Alvey MMI-007 Vehicle Exemplar: Image Segmentation and Attribute Generation" Proceedings of the third Alvey Vision Conference, 1987, Univ. of Cambridge, 1987, 15-17 Sept. pp 5 - 13.

- Knoll, T.F., and Jain, R.C., 1986, "Recognising Partially Visible Objects Using Feature Indexed Hypothesis", R.A., 2,1, March 1986.

- Lowe, D.G., 1985, "Perceptual Organisation and Visual Recognition", Kluwer, Boston,MA.

- Lowe, D.G., 1987, "Three dimensional object recognition from single two dimensional images", Artificial Intelligence, 31, pp 233-395.

- Morton, S.K., 1987, "Alvey MMI-007 Vehicle Exemplar: Object Hypothesis by Evidential Reasoning", Proceedings of the third Alvey Vision Conference, 1987, Univ. of Cambridge, 1987, 15-17 Sept. pp 15 - 25.

- Sullivan, G.D., "Alvey MMI-007 Vehicle Exemplar: Performance and Limitations", Proceedings of the third Alvey Vision Conference, 1987, Univ. of Cambridge, 1987, 15-17 Sept. pp 39 - 45.

# KNOWLEDGE-BASED APPROACH
# FOR ADAPTIVE RECOGNITION OF DRAWINGS

Shin-ichirou OKAZAKI   and  Yoshitake TSUJI

C&C Information Technology Research Laboratories, NEC Corporation

1-1, Miyazaki 4-Chome, Miyamae-ku, Kawasaki, Kanagawa 213, Japan

Abstract: This paper describes the Knowledge-based Adaptive Recognition System for Drawings (KARD), using a computer and an optical scanner, and its application to chemical structural formula. KARD is designed as a test-bed system for a drawings recognition method with constructional knowledge about drawings concerned. In order to adaptively resolve target variety and distortion variety, KARD adopts an objective pattern unit description of rules and data-flow-like activation control mechanism for the rules. KARD application to chemical structural formula recognition, with knowledge about its syntactic restrictions, proves that KARD can not only recognize them but also detect contradictions due to recognition failures in the processes.

## 1. INTRODUCTION

Drawing recognition systems have been developed as a data input technique for use with CAD systems [1-2]. One of the problems involved in developing a drawing recognition system is to cope with the variety inherent in various drawings. The concept variety here includes two meanings. One meaning is target variety, wherein there are many kinds of drawings. Figures indicating symbols or lines are quite different when considered different kinds of drawings. The other meaning is distortion variety, wherein elemental symbols of a specific kind contain a wide variety of shapes, due to being drawn by different draftsmen, or due to pictorial distortions generated by the same draftsman.

To resolve these varieties, it is necessary to improve methods to extract elemental patterns accurately in drawings. It is much more significant to let the system know what the system tries to extract by means of knowledge about drawings concerned. Knowledge-based recognition technique has been mainly researched in the machine vision field, such as natural scene analysis[3-7]. In regard to drawings recognition, because drawings are artificial images used to communicate draftsman's ideas according to specific rules, and because all interpretations for a drawing image must be identical (this is a different aspect from natural scene analysis), the knowledge-based recognition approach is expected to lead to its correct interpretation. That is, defining specifications as described knowledge enables coping with target variety and distortion variety.

KARD is a test-bed system to develop essential functions in the knowledge-based recognition system for drawings, especially representing a topological network. In order to resolve the varieties mentioned above and to retain the recognition efficiency for large drawings, KARD has been designed so that it may have the following features.

(1) General-purpose internal mechanism, such as data structure and processing functions, where they are not designed for a special target drawing.

(2) Objective pattern unit description by "construction rule", which improves modularity to describe and readiness to read.

(3) Data-flow-like activation mechanism, which utilizes modularity of construction rules and improves efficiency to determine which rule is applicable.

This paper describes the system configuration and its behavior in Section 2. Section 3 shows its application to chemical structure formula recognition.

## 2. KARD CONFIGURATION

### 2.1 SYSTEM OVERVIEW

KARD functional blocks are shown in Fig.1. The Primitive Extraction module extracts and symbolizes tiny line elements as figurative primitives from an input image. This can be achieved by using local pattern matching technique. These primitives are put into the Segment Memory module as initial segments. In the Segment Memory, individual results extracted by processes, which usually form a pattern, are represented as a symbolic object, called a "segment", as shown in Fig.2. A segment consists of (1) several other segments that construct it, each called a "sub-segment", (2) any relations with other segments, (3) segment identifiers to classify the corresponding pattern, (4) pattern features, such as positions, direction in the image space, and moments of the pattern. The total segments construct a network by sub-segment links and relation links. Sub-segment links can represent a conceptual hierarchy, such that three lines connected with each other

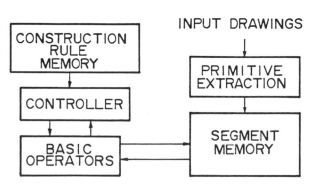

Fig. 1    KARD System Configuration.

construct a triangle. Relation links can represent geometrical and auxiliary relations, such that two lines are in parallel. As pattern feature is based on the pattern moment, features of a newly generated pattern can be easily calculated from its sub-segments' features.

The Basic Operators module contains the basic functional operators necessary for the extraction of patterns, defined by the construction rule explained later. Each individual operator is mostly corresponded with a predicate to describe construction rules with.

These modules are not designed for a special kind of drawings. Therefore, overall construction rules in the Construction Rule Memory module define the target drawing to be recognized. Using structural or restrictive properties of target drawing, it can also absorb the distortion variety for shapes appearing in a specific drawing.

## 2.2 KNOWLEDGE REPRESENTATION FOR DRAWINGS RECOGNITION

Many schemes to represent the specifications can be proposed, such as a model-based scheme with frame-like description, or a production-rule-based scheme. KARD's specification description for a target drawing is rather similar to the production-rule, called "construction rule". The construction rules are placed as an intermediate representation between these schemes and actual extraction processing sequences. This enables avoiding much time being consumed during interpretative processing with such schemes. Every construction rule should be modularly described with respect to a class of desired objective patterns such as triangles, or to a class of mutual relations such as geometrical relation in parallel. This concept is aimed at making explicit what patterns or relations the rule refers to and tries to find. An identifier (ID) specifies the class of segments, each corresponding to a pattern, or relations extracted by a construction rule.

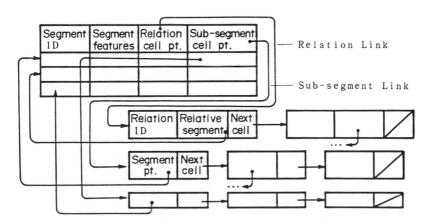

Fig. 2    Internal Network Data Structure for Segments.

Each construction rule contains the following descriptions.

(1) Reference-ID(s) declaration: segment ID(s) and/or relation ID(s), to which predicates referred in the construction rule.

(2) Generation-ID declaration: segment ID or relation ID, generated or modified as a result by the construction rule.

(3) Sequence of predicates the objective pattern satisfies.

(4) Data operations within the Segment Memory for the found objective patterns as sets of segments.

(5) Control predicates, which form a complex predicate from basic predicates.

These objective pattern unit descriptions improve the modularity to describe, compared with conventional procedures, and have interfaces matched to descriptive schemes proposed in the AI field. It also provides ability to execute fast searching for applicable rules by using control mechanism explained in Section 2.3.

Example predicates prepared in KARD are shown in Table I. They can be classified into 5 groups, based on their function. These are

TABLE I    Examples of Predicates Provided in KARD.

| Class | Predicate Name | Meanings |
|-------|----------------|----------|
| 1 | HAS_ID | Segment has indicated identifier. |
|   | HAS_FEATURE | Segment has feature in indicated range. |
|   | HAS_RELATION | Segment has relations with segments. |
|   | HAS_PARENT | Segment has upper segments (it's a subpattern). |
|   | SUBSEGMENT | Sub-segments constructing specified segment. |
|   | COMBINATION | Generates sets of segments of specified number. |
| 2 | CONNECT | Segments connecting with each other. |
|   | CONNECT_TO | Segments connecting to specified segments. |
|   | SAME | Segments which have the same features. |
|   | REPEAT | Segments which appear periodically. |
| 3 | EQUAL | One value is equal to a second value. |
|   | COUNT | Count the number of elements in a segment list. |
|   | ADD | Add two values. |
|   | EXISTS | Whether it exists or not. |
|   | NOT | Reverse truth value. |
| 4 | FOR_ALL | True if all of the segments satisfy predicates. |
|   | FOR_EACH | Apply successive predicates sequence. |
|   | SUCH_THAT | True for segment satisfying predicates sequence. |
| 5 | WINDOW | Spatial range definition for combinative selection |
|   | AREA | Area restriction to specified place for selection. |

(1) selection with IDs, relations, segment structure, or segment features, (2) classification based on the connectivity of or similarity between segment features, (3) numerical operation and comparison, (4) control for making complex predicates, and (5) spatial restriction regarding the size of areas where searches are carried out. For instance, the classification predicate CONNECT means that each segment in the considered set must be properly connected with any other segments in the same set. Furthermore, in the execution, it also indicates the extraction operation for segments satisfying it. Truth value for the predicate CONNECT is identical to determining whether any set of connecting segments can be extracted or not.

The following description is a sequence of predicates finding two lines in parallel. TR1 is a threshold value indicating direction similarity and TR2 is a threshold value indicating distance between two end points. A predicate WINDOW is used to restrict the area where combinations of two lines are made within DX by DY. The first SUCH_THAT phrase means that the number of sets, obtained by clustering with respect to the direction feature, is 1; the directions of two segments are the same. The second SUCH_THAT phrase means that there exist two pairs of end points that are near to each other.

```
HAS_ID $LINE
WINDOW DX DY
COMBINATION 2
SUCH_THAT (
        SAME DIRECTION TR1
        COUNT 1
)
SUCH_THAT (
        SUBSEGMENT $ENDPOINT
        CONNECT TR2
        COUNT 2
)
```

A segment or a set of segments satisfying a sequence of predicates would be stored appropriately into the Segment Memory by data operators, constructing new segment representing higher conceptual hierarchy or being related to other existing segments. Data operations are classified into 4 groups. These are (1) creation of segments, (2) setting up relations, (3) modification of segments or relations, (4) deletion. The SET operation, for example, creates a new segment in the Segment Memory, which consists of its sub-segments. This means generation of a pattern formed with its sub-patterns. The ID for operated segments is explicitly declared on the generation-ID declaration of the rule.

## 2.3 PROCESSING FLOW CONTROL

When any segment is newly generated or modified, the rule, in which the ID for the segment is declared as a reference-ID, will be expected to be meaningful and to be worth trying to apply. Therefore, the KARD controller shown in Fig.1, observes the IDs for newly generated/modified segments or relations. KARD controls rule activation based on the data-flow-like control strategy, as shown in Fig.3. Each construction rule is invoked by symbolic event tokens corresponding to the ID indicated on the rule, as follows.

There are two kinds of symbolic tokens, normal-token and null-token. A normal-token indicates the generation or modification of segments belonging to a class specified by the segment ID, while a null-token indicates failure. The first time a construction rule is invoked, a normal token for each reference-ID of the rule is required. If there is any null-token, the controller will not apply the rule. It only generates a null-token for the generation-ID and send it to other rules referring to it. If any segment or relation satisfying the rule is extracted, a normal-token for the generation-ID is generated and sent to referring rules. If no segment or relation is extracted, a null-token is generated. After the first invocation of a rule, normal-tokens for at least one reference-ID cause extra invocation of the rule. Then, any null-token for the reference-ID is merely absorbed.

The behavior explained above is applied when there is only one construction rule generating an ID. If there are more construction rules generating identical IDs, null-tokens play an important role of invocation. Each rule referring to it waits for the same number of symbolic tokens for the reference-ID as the number of rules generating the identical ID, where either normal-tokens or null-tokens will do. In case that at least one of these symbolic tokens is a normal-token, KARD regards it as a successful extraction of target segments. Therefore, multiple rules can be defined for an objective pattern, and any of them may appropriately extract the target segments.

The control strategy mentioned above basically accomplishes a bottom-up extraction process. It is intentionally given no automatic exclusive mechanism, maintaining that an image in a certain local area takes a unique interpretation at any processing time; it permits multiple interpretations. Although verifying or selective rules must be

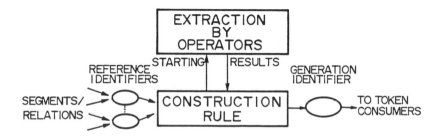

Fig. 3    Construction Rules Activation Control Mechanism.

described so that unique interpretation remains at the end of processing, it is applicable to take an active strategy wherein the system at first generates some possible interpretations as hypotheses and selects a correct one later by using restrictive knowledge regarding the target drawing or extraction reliability.

## 3. APPLICATION TO CHEMICAL STRUCTURE FORMULAE

### 3.1 CONSTRUCTION RULES FOR CSF

A chemical structure formula (CSF) is one of several drawings used in the chemical engineering field. The CSF is usually drawn with characters, special symbols and straight lines. The CSF forms a network made with nodes of strings of characters, nodes represented by line connections, and arcs for lines between nodes. It has some descriptional syntax based on the chemical fundamentals shown below. It is expected that recognition failure can be effectively detected by means of making checks with these syntax.

(1) Strings of characters, each representing a radical, are restricted with respect to their kind.

(2) The sort of nodes automatically defines the number of lines connecting to it.

(3) There are no lines which do not connect to a string, at any end.

(4) Lines do not connect to multiple strings of characters at an end.

To recognize CSF, the following construction rules are used in KARD. The rules include defining, (1) A line, (2) Connecting line, (3) Characters representing atoms formed from short lines, (4) Strings representing radicals formed from characters, (5) Arcs (including single, double, triple) formed from connecting lines, (6) Nodes made by strings of characters and arcs connecting to the strings, (7) Imaginary nodes indicated by mutual connection of arcs. These rules are all used in bottom-up search. However, these rules may cause generating multiple interpretations for the same area or may give an incorrect interpretation to a complex area. In order to avoid these miss-interpretations, verifying rules are embedded in the Node level of conceptual hierarchy. The description shown below is a verifying rule for nodes made by characters CH2 and connecting arcs to them.

```
RULE 10 $CORRECT-NODE, $STR-CH2 $CONNECTED-ARC
    HAS_ID $STR-CH2
    SUCH_THAT (
        HAS_RELATION $CONNECTED-ARC
        COUNT_ARC
        EQUAL 2
    )
    LABEL $CORRECT-NODE
END_RULE
```

In this description, COUNT_ARC is a macro statement defined elsewhere. This rule means that, if a node, which is made by a character string

CH2, has arc segments related to it by the identifier $CONNECTED-ARC, and if the number of arcs are equal to 2, then give the identifier $CORRECT-NODE to the node. This rule automatically turned applicable to invoke after segments $STR-CH2 and relation $CONNECTED-ARC are both successfully extracted. One of the other verifying rules is shown below. This rule means that, if there is an open-ended single arc identified by $SINGLE-ARC whose end doesn't connect to a node, and if there is only one imaginary-node $IM-CH2 near the arc, then let the open-ended arc connect to the imaginary-node. TX and TY are parameters for predicate AREA, restricting the search area of selective predicate HAS_ID into TX by TY size around each obtained end-point. TD is the threshold value for predicate CONNECT_TO, indicating the distance between nodes and end points of arcs.

```
RULE 20 $IM-CH, $SINGLE-ARC $IM-CH2 $ENDPOINT $CONNECT-TO-NODE
        HAS_ID $SINGLE-ARC
        FOR_EACH (
            LET ARC
            SUBSEGMENT $ENDPOINT
            SUCH_THAT (
                HAS_RELATION $CONNECT-TO-NODE
                NOT_EXIST
            )
            FOR_EACH (
                LET ENDPOINT
                AREA TX TY
                INITIATE
                HAS_ID $IM-CH2
                CONNECT_TO ENDPOINT TD
                COUNT 1
                RELATE ARC $CONNECTED-ARC
                RELATED ENDPOINT $CONNECT-TO-NODE
                LABEL $IM-CH
                DELABEL $IM-CH2
            )
        )
        END_RULE
```

## 3.2 EXPERIMENTS AND RESULTS

Figure 4(a) shows an input image example. KARD initially extracts the primitives from it by pattern matching and puts them into the Segment Memory. After that, extraction processing, based on the construction rules, starts. Figure 4(b) shows the segments extracted by construction rules for double-arcs, each of which consists of two lines that are parallel and have almost the same length. Figure 4(c) shows the final result, which is generated by reconfiguring the extracted nodes network. In Fig.4(c), small squares represent extracted imaginary nodes. Figure 4(d) shows the segments that are detected to be incorrect interpretations from multiple interpretations by checking with verifying rules. Figure 5 shows the result for an input image in which there are drawing mistakes. KARD finds the contradictions between the patterns and definitions, indicating them with the dotted line boxes in the reconfigured drawing, shown in Fig. 5. This self-checking function is very useful to decrease time consumed during check jobs by users after automatic recognition.

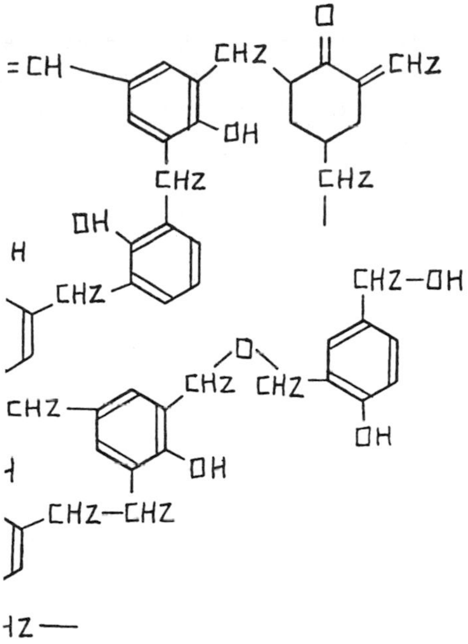

(a) Input Image Example.

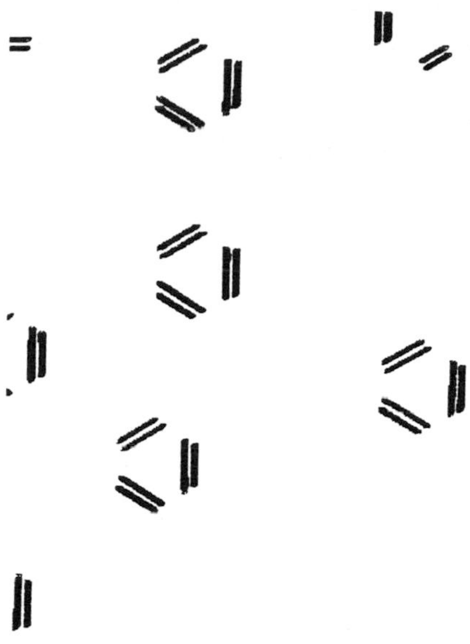

(b) Segments Extracted by
Construction Rules for Double-arc.

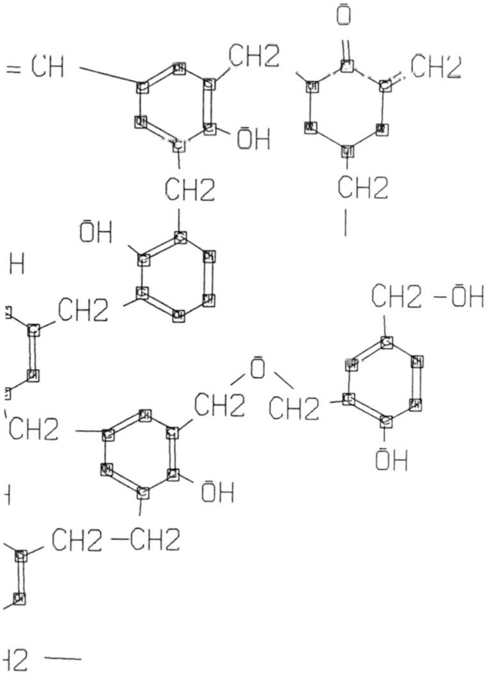

(c) Reconfigured Drawing,
Based on Extracted Nodes.

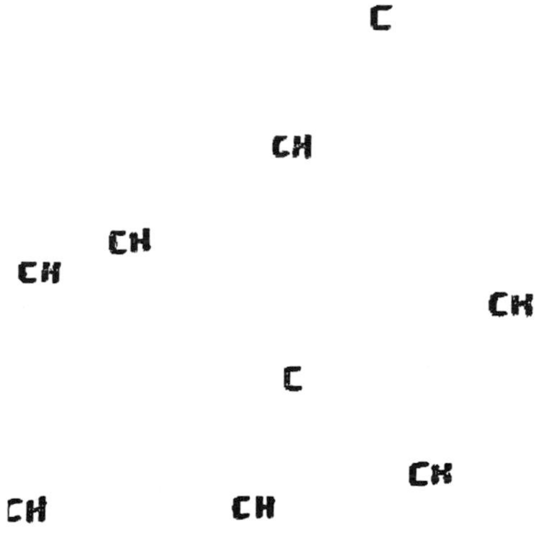

(d) Contradicting Segments
by Verifying Rules.

Fig. 4    Application to Chemical Structure Formula.

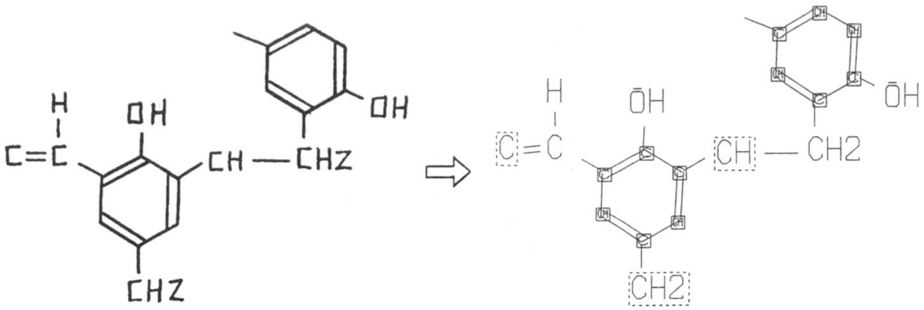

Fig. 5    Extracting Nodes Contradicting Specifications.

## 4. CONCLUDING REMARKS

This paper has described KARD configuration and its functions. Individual construction rules are hierarchically described corresponding to a class of objective patterns or relations. Its activation mechanism, that is controlled based on data-driven-like strategy, not only improves the modularity to describe, but also provides a fast search mechanism for rules which would be applicable. KARD application to CSF shows the ability to find contradictions to the construction rules by itself. KARD enables that knowledge-based approach, to cope with varieties in target drawings, can be adopted for drawing recognition, all at a reasonable speed.

Further studies are going on for control mechanism, implementing effective top-down searches for the target patterns, and for user-friendly description method and its compilation to construction rules.

## ACKNOWLEDGEMENT

The authors are grateful to Mr.Asai for providing the chance for this work, and to the members of the Pattern Recognition Research Laboratory in the C&C Information Technology Research Laboratories.

## REFERENCES

[1] H.Bunke, "Experience with several methods for the analysis of schematic diagrams", Proc. of 6th ICPR, pp710-712, 1982.
[2] H.Harada, Y.Ishii, "Recognition of freehand drawings in chemical plant engineering", IEEE workshop on CAPAIDM, pp146-153, 1985.
[3] T.Matsuyama, "Knowledge organization and control structure in image understanding", Proc. of 7th ICPR, pp1118-1127, 1984.
[4] T.Kanade, "Model representations and control structures in image understanding", Proc. of 5th IJCAI, pp1074-1082, 1977.
[5] R.A.Brooks, "The ACRONYM model based vision system", Proc. of 6th IJCAI, pp105-113. 1979.
[6] A.M.Nazif, M.D.Levine, "Low level image segmentation. An expert system", PAMI vol.6 No.5, pp555-577, 1984.
[7] D.M.McKeown,Jr., W.A.Harvey, J.McDermott, "Rule-based interpretation of aerial imagery", PAMI Vol.7 No.5, pp570-585, 1985.

# EXTENDED SYMBOLIC PROJECTIONS AS A KNOWLEDGE STRUCTURE FOR SPATIAL REASONING

Erland Jungert

FOA, National Defence Research Institute

Box 1165, S-581 11 Linköping

Sweden

Abstract

In earlier work it has been demonstrated that symbolic projections can be used as a spatial knowledge structure. Here it will be shown how the basic language used in the symbolic projections can be extended. The motivation for this extension is the need for a means by which to perform spatial reasoning in, e.g. digitized images or maps.

## 1. Introduction

The importance of spatial reasoning is growing and stems from not only the need to control autonomous vehicles and robots, but also upon the increasing need to analyze various kinds of images, e.g. satellite images or maps. This paper describes a basic knowledge structure which includes fundamental properties useful for performing spatial reasoning in digitized images and maps. The spatial structure underlying the knowledge structure is based on a work originally made by Chang et al. (1). The structure is called Symbolic Projections, and its principles are relatively simple and straightforward. The original work was applied to two dimensions, but the method can be applied to three dimensions as well. The basic idea is to project the positions of all objects in a scene or image along each coordinate axis and then generate a string corresponding to each one of the axes. Each string contains all the objects in their relative positions; that is, one object is either equal to or less than any of the others. Figure 1 shows how simple objects can be projected along the x- and y-coordinate axes. The original method included just two relational operators for indicating the relative positions of objects in an image or scene. The two operators are "equal to" and "less than". The strings are called the U- and the V-strings where the U-string corresponds to the projections of the objects along the x-axis, the V-string to the y-axis. For a more thorough description of the method see (1).

Ideas similar to the work described here have been demonstrated by Truvé (2). Another approach is Natural Constraints described by Winston (3). However, these techniques require a lot of pre-processing. A further difference between symbolic projections and the other two methods is that symbolic projections are best suited for describing relative positions of objects or sub-objects, which is of importance in spatial reasoning within maps. The other two methods merely discuss the shape of objects.

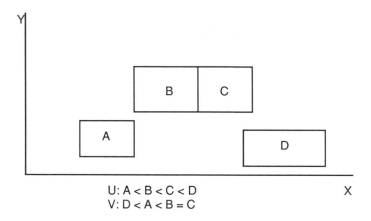

U: A < B < C < D
V: D < A < B = C

Figure 1. Example of the original principles of symbolic projections.

Both the original and the extended method of symbolic projections can be applied to various kinds of spatial reasoning. Especially, the extended method can be applied to  problems such as relative position, binary relations, planning and navigation. Using symbolic projections for reasoning about relative positions is trivial, therefore no focus is made on that aspect per se. Reasoning about shape and design has been discussed by Chang and Jungert in (4) and will not be considered further here. In this paper the extension of the knowledge structure and its application to spatial reasoning will be demonstrated in various situations for identification of binary relations. A discussion on how to apply queries to scenes with various types of objects is also given.


2. The basic data structure

We have chosen to represent the objects of interest by means of run-length-code (RLC). Hence, an object is described by a set of lines, where those lines are represented by their respective start points and lengths. The start points consist of a X- and a Y-coordinate. However, it is not sufficient to describe an object with just these attributes. Other object attributes are needed, such as name and type. In the final application many different application-dependent attributes will be needed, but this is not of any importance for this discussion. A natural way of representing the objects is  to further separate the object description from its extension. Using a relational database system the following relations are adequate:

Extension(X,Y,length,type,nc)

Object(<u>name</u>,<u>Yk</u>,<u>Xk</u>,nc)

Application-dependent attributes have been omitted in these relations. The attribute nc is a number code of the object and is used in this model as a logical link between the object and its extension. nc is used instead of the name just to save memory space. Yk and Xk are coordinate values used as a key to identify an object uniquely. There exist three different object classes, i.e closed, linear and point objects. However, for a more thorough description of the RLC-technique, the reader is referred to (5).

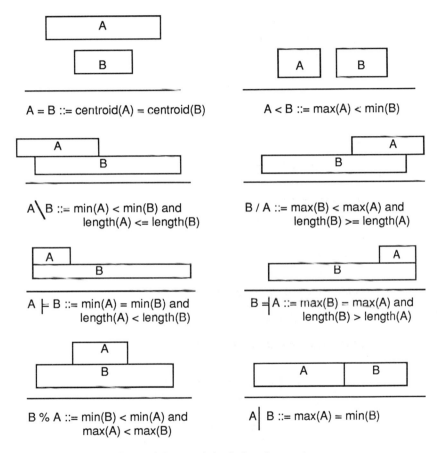

Figure 2. Illustrations of the spatial relational operators.

3. The knowledge structure

Given a set of pictorial objects and a set of spatial relational operators, a 2-D string over the complete set of objects is defined as:

U: i1 x1 i2 x2 ..... in, V:...i1 x3 ... i2 x4 ... im

where i1,i2...im...in are members of the set of pictorial objects and x1,x2... are members of the set of spatial relational operators. The pictorial objects can be identified either by their names or by any symbols. The set of operators is {\,%,I,I=,=I,/,=,<,~} where the operators are used to specify spatial relationships between pictorial objects.  U: is a label that denotes the string of symbolic projections along the x- axis while V: corresponds to the symbolic projections along the y-axis. The order of the objects along each coordinate axis corresponds to the order of the objects in the 2-D string; this correspondence must always be maintained. The order of the objects in the V-string is some permutation of the objects in the U-string. The definitions of the operators are found in table 1 and are illustrated in figure 2.

| local operator | definition |
|---|---|
| \ | $min(i) < min(j)$ and $length(i) <= length(j)$ |
| % | $min(i) < min(j)$ and $max(j) < max(i)$ |
| I | $max(i) = min(j)$ |
| I= | $min(i) = min(j)$ and $length(i) < length(j)$ |
| =I | $max(i) = max(j)$ and $length(i) > length(j)$ |
| / | $max(i) < max(j)$ and $length(i) >= length(j)$ |
| = | $centroid(i) = centroid(j)$ |
| < | $max(i) < min(j)$ |

Table 1. Spatial relational operators in symbolic projections.

Objects with more complicated structures can be decomposed  and their overall structures described by means of symbolic projections. This is illustrated in figure 3. To simplify decomposition of objects in order to preserve all relations in compound objects, a method which describes compound objects hierarchically is proposed.

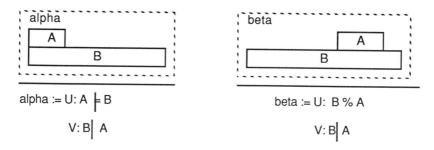

$$alpha := U: A \models B$$
$$V: B| A$$

$$beta := U: B \% A$$
$$V: B| A$$

Figure 3. Decomposition of objects by means of local relations.

On object level, symbolic projections can be used to represent the orientation of an object by identifying unique nodes of the object. Figure 4 illustrates the symbolic projections of a rectangle. The symbolic projections can be represented on two levels, i.e. on an external level where a single node is represented as <Object>.<node> or on an internal level where <Object>.<string> represents the relative relations of all nodes along one of the coordinate axis. Hence, such an object can be opened for inspection. In the first case the node can be integrated into a global string just like any other object, while in the latter case the string must be represented alone.

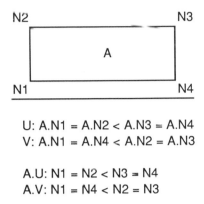

U: A.N1 = A.N2 < A.N3 = A.N4
V: A.N1 = A.N4 < A.N2 = A.N3

A.U: N1 = N2 < N3 = N4
A.V: N1 = N4 < N2 = N3

Figure 4. Symbolic projections applied to object nodes.

## 4. Heuristics used in the knowledge structure

To be able to apply the technique of symbolic projections to spatial reasoning using inference rules, some kinds of heuristics must also be used. The alternative chosen here is based upon two observations. The first observation originates from the fact that since all objects of interest are composed of RLC-lines, it is easy to split the objects along those lines. The second observation comes from the fact that even though all objects have arbitrary extensions, they can easily be regarded as rectangles; alternatively, they can be enclosed within rectangles. These two observations lead to the possibility of first splitting the objects, then enclosing the new sub-objects inside rectangles. The rectangles generated in this way can be handled by means of symbolic projections. The strategy chosen here for splitting the objects is based on the following rule:

An object is split wherever a run-length-code line is the tangent of a point on the edge of the object or when a run-length-code line is the tangent of a hole inside the object.

Hence, a line that splits an object always includes a point where the object is split into three sub-objects; that point is here called a split point. An object can, of course, include more than one split point. A sub-object corresponds to an area, which is called a tile. By enclosing the tiles in rectangles symbolic projections can be applied in a simple manner. An illustration of this can be seen in figure 5.

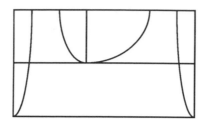

Figure 5. Three adjacent tiles enclosed within rectangles.

## 5. Rules

The use of the spatial knowledge structures in inference rules, as a means for identification of object relations, has also been discussed in (2) by Chang and Jungert. However, it is necessary to develop this technique further and use the extended operators. A rule which on a local level describes two objects situated beside each other, edge to edge, can be defined as:

       beside:: if U: O1 I O2
                V: O1 = O2
                then (beside O1 O2)

Observe that there is an implicit "and" between the U- and the V- string.
Another example is:

       at_top_left::if U:O2 I= O1
                    V:O1 I O2
                    then (at_top_left O2 O1)

These types of rules can be used in both forward and backward chaining, as well as in various kinds of queries for identification of relations that correspond to the rules. Queries are discussed in section 6.

Objects occurring in a rule do not always have to be situated directly adjacent to each other. Furthermore, the first object matched in the condition of the rule does not have to be the only object for which the relation is true. An example of this can be seen in figure 6, which illustrates objects situated diagonally to each other. The relation is not only true for the objects A and B but also for all objects in between. Therefore, a rule must consider all these cases as well. A rule of this type can look like:

       diagonal:: if U: O1 $0 I O2
                  V: O1 $0 I O2
                  then (diagonal O1 O2)

where $0::=[I \; MO]$. $0 is a substring which might occur zero or more times and MO corresponds to an arbitrary object. Hence all objects on the same diagonal will be found when the rule is fired.

Among other things, we are concerned with the shortest path problem in a digitized map. For this reason relationships among tiles are of importance, and it is especially necessary to keep track of sequences of tiles. A tile sequence might correspond to a more complex structure in the map such as, an island or a peninsula. A sequence is labelled with "R:". Hence, an example from the shortest path problem which illustrates a left turn around an arbitrary object will look like:

    if R: l,j,k
      U: j < k
      V: i l j and i l k
    then (direction-in j south-north)(context-in j left-turn)

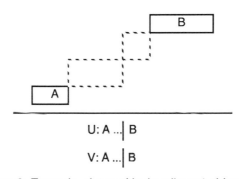

        U: A ...| B
        V: A ...| B

Figure 6. Example of transitively adjacent objects.

This rule corresponds to a path where an entity, which could either be a ship or a vehicle of some kind, is heading south, makes a left turn around an object and, after the turn, begins a northern course. The consequent of this rule corresponds to an elementary step of a plan, which includes the direction of the entity and a description of the local context in which the entity will be acting.

6. Queries

Posing queries is one way of using the rules. For example, if we apply the "beside" rule above to the objects in figure 1, then the following query can be made:

    (beside C ?X)

The answer to this query is obviously "failure" since object D, which is the last object of the U-string does not satisfy the relationship C I D.

If instead the query is changed to:

(beside B ?X)

then a search is performed along both strings, where ?X temporarily is bound to the different objects to the right of B in the U-string. It is easy to see that this type of query is related to Prolog. However, when searching among the objects, only those objects situated after B in the U-string are considered. Hence, this string is just searched once. The V-string, on the other hand, is searched once for all objects after B. Consequently, the problem of backtracking a tree structure like in Prolog is simplified.

Queries of the following types are, of course, also permitted:

(beside ?X ?Y)

(beside ?X A)

The technique can also be used in rules, e.g.:

if (beside A B) then ......

7. Conclusions and Future Research

Currently, not all problems connected to the use of symbolic projections as a knowledge structure have been explored. However, the method seems promising and the experiences so far show that it can be used in several applications. This work will, in the future, concentrate on route planning and navigation. Presently, work is going on in an effort to solve the problem of finding the shortest path between two points in a digitized map.

In the shortest path problem, the technique just described is used in a two step method. The first part uses the knowledge-based technique to give a rough plan oriented description of the path. This description of the path contains a number of steps where each step includes the main direction of the entity and the context in which it is navigating. The plan is then used to control the second, algorithmic step in generating the optimal path. The second part of this application is currently operable, so the shortest path can be found for any given plan. The rules that make up the knowledge base in the first step have also been defined and verified. A simple inference engine is also implemented and used in the first part of the system, i.e. interpreting the rules and generating the plan.

Acknowledgements

I would like to thank Peter Holmes for his help proof-reading this paper and for his valuable suggestions concerning the contents. Mats Ekman was also very helpful when preparing the final version of this paper on the Macintosh.

References

(1) S. K. Chang, Q.-Y. Shi and C.-W. Yan, "Iconic Indexing by 2D Strings", IEEE Transactions on Pattern Analysis and Machine Intelligence, May 1987, Vol PAMI-9, No 3, pp 413-428.

(2) S. Truvé and W. Richards, "From Waltz to Winston (via the Connection table)", Proceedings of the First International Conference on Computer Vision, June 8-11, London, England, pp 393-404.

(3) P. H. Winston, "Artificial Intelligence", Addison-Wesley, Reading, Mass., 1977.

(4) S. K. Chang and E. Jungert, "A Spatial Knowledge Structure for Image Information Systems Using Symbolic Projections", Proceedings of the National Computer Conference, Dallas, Texas, November 2 - 6, 1986, pp 79-86.

(5) E. Jungert, "Run-Length-Code as an Object-Oriented Spatial Data structure", Proc. of the IEEE Workshop on Language for Automation, August 27-29, 1986, Singapore, pp 66-70.

# Knowledge-based road network extraction on SPOT satellite images

J. Van Cleynenbreugel      F. Fierens      P. Suetens      A. Oosterlinck

ESAT-MI2, Katholieke Universiteit Leuven
De Croylaan 52b, B-3030 Heverlee, Belgium

### Abstract

Automated delineation of linear cultural structures can help to improve the classification of remotely-sensed images. This topic also provides an excellent testbed for knowledge-based computer vision research. In this paper, a road network extraction system, useful on SPOT satellite images, is described. By applying semantic model-fitting operators, an initial spatial segmentation is obtained. To analyse the resulting primal road network, declaratively stated knowledge about generic appearances of roads and crossroads on SPOT images is used. As a result a more detailed description of the network can be obtained. Advantages and drawbacks of the use of existing knowledge base tools for this computer vision task are reported.

## 1    Spatial analysis of remote sensing data

Machine interpretation of satellite multispectral data usually relies on spectral classification of individual pixels. However, extraction of planimetric features, either natural (rivers, lakes) or man-made (roads, built-up area), requires the additional ability to recognize geometrical properties and spatial relations. The outlining of e.g. road structures - a labour intensive task for a human operator - has many useful applications in cartography, landscape investigation and geographic information systems. A first practical application of road network extraction we have in mind, is the automatic enhancement of thematic maps. Generally, such a map contains an interpretation of a number of environmental parameters such as vegetation areas or bio-ecological patterns. It can be deduced from the raw data based on spectral signature. However, road structures, which are valuable guidelines for a human reader of such maps, cannot be obtained by this technique. Due to the availability of high resolution satellite imagery, such as the pictures generated by the SPOT HRV sensors, automatic spatial analysis techniques can be considered as appropriate for this task.

Edge and line detectors and region-based methods are well-known spatial segmentation techniques. Unfortunately, the cues detected by these local-oriented algorithms are mostly incomplete and error prone. This imperfect result cannot be improved by sophisticated low-level operators because global context and model-knowledge are missing. Possible methodologies to overcome these difficulties are being proposed in the emerging field of 'knowledge-based computer vision' (KBCV). Here the applicability of knowledge-based programming systems to the problem of correcting and refining an initial segmentation is investigated. By introducing declaratively stated 'world knowledge' in all stages of the feature elicitation process, a flexible integration of low-level numerical calculations and high-level symbolical inferences is aimed at.

For the interpretation of remotely sensed images, different 'world knowledge' sources are available, external to the raw image data [TAILOR]. These include expertise of human analysts, knowledge of structures to be expected and their interrelationships and other data such as maps and previous interpretations. Obviously, a KBCV road detection system for map enhancement, will largely profit from generic spatial knowledge of roads, crossroads and road networks. We will show that a basic vocabulary to deal with this knowledge, can be described using current expert system building tools.

## 2 Road extraction on satellite imagery

Automatic linear feature extraction has been recently recognized as a research topic for AI-based analysis of remotely-sensed images [PARIKH,YEE,WANG,ZHU]. Conceptually, the problem solving strategy is adhering to the signals-to-symbols paradigm of computational vision [FISCHLER 87]. This means that a symbolic description of the results of low-level image processing operators (i.e. edge and line detectors) are used by high-level knowledge-driven reasoning mechanisms to obtain a complete delineation of the desired features. We have adopted this methodology to the problem of extracting road networks from SPOT images.

The SPOT satellite produces 10 meter panchromatic and 20 meter multispectral images. Due to this resolution, low level operators, which intrinsically apply spatial knowledge can be considered to detect road fragments. Indeed, a road has relatively constant width (three pixels or less), it is contrasting with the adjacent terrain and along its track there is a uniform variation of the gray level intensity.

By implementing these specifications into a local operator, a semantic model fitting detector for road extraction can be designed. An operator originating from mathematical morphology is proposed in [DESTIVAL]. In our approach, we use the Duda road operator (DRO) [FISCHLER 81]. This DRO applies to every pixel a sequence of four masks, designed to detect the presence of a road - i.e. a straight line segment having uniform intensity and high contrast with the surroundings - in each of the four directions. By adopting the same basic principle to the detection of crossroads, we are able to create masks sensitive to road crossings. (See Figures 1 and 2).

Of course, the output of these low level operators is not perfect. Natural properties of the earth surface and errors in the digitization process cause gaps in the detected road segments . On the other hand, line-like structures, such as borders of woods and fields, can be falsely recognized as road fragments. Contextual knowledge should be applied to solve these ambiguities. To be able to reason with such knowledge, a tracking program is used to collect the low level output into structural entities. As a result, two types of primitives are instantiated: nodes (crossroads) and road segments. Road segments are subdivided into connections (connection lines between two crossroads), semi-connections (lines beginning but not ending in a crossroad), and free (unconnected) lines. Using these primitives an initial road network is set up. It is our intention to update and verify this road network using KBCV techniques.

# 3  Knowledge-based road network analysis

Existing knowledge-based programming tools require a symbolic description of the domain of discourse. No inference engine has yet been developed to incorporate geometrical and spatial reasoning based on an iconic rather than on a symbolic representation. Although we have to pay for this drawback in terms of limited description power and loss of isomorphic representation, the symbolic encoding of extracted features is the only possible way of analysis, given today's digital computers [FISCHLER 87]. The primitives used in our system (nodes and road segments) can be straigthforwardly symbolized. Nodes are described by their pixel positions in the image and by the connections and semi-connections starting from the node. Road segments are described by the pixel positions of their track in the image, from which secondary features such as length, global direction and possible adjacent nodes can be easily determined. We also store a symbolic 'label-image' to denote the spatial relationships of the extracted primitives. In this label-image, each pixel belonging to a primitive (node or road segment) is labeled with the unique identification mark (a symbolic pointer) of the corresponding primitive. This additional data structure makes it possible to cope with the 'pattern-matching problem' occurring when traditional knowledge base tools are used in image analysis.

The current knowledge base contains knowledge about the generic appearance of road segments and crossroads on SPOT images. It is mainly used for geometrical reasoning about perceptual grouping. Based on relations such as proximity, collinearity and visibility, actions of the following nature are performed: connecting road segments and nodes - possibly by 'filling gaps' -, deleting 'suspicious' nodes, clustering 'close' nodes, delineating entire road pieces, ... . The chosen software environment mainly supports the rule-based programming style. We will illustrate by an example how geometrical knowledge is encoded using this knowledge representation. Suppose a road piece (a concatenation of almost equally sloped connections) is being built up. The following rule describes a possible situation encountered during this process:

```
IF    there is a ROADPIECE from NODE1 to NODE2 having a DIRECTION
AND   there is a SEMI-CONNECTION starting at NODE2
                having almost the same DIRECTION
THEN  assert it is POSSIBLE-TO-EXTEND ROADPIECE via SEMI-CONNECTION
AND   call the routine LOOK-AT-THE-END-OF for this SEMI-CONNECTION
```

This rule states that it is worthwile to explore the neighborhood at the end of a semi-connection, if that semi-connection is aligned to an already established road piece. The routine LOOK-AT-THE-END-OF generates a region of interest to describe this neighborhood (see Figure 3) and scans this region for the occurence of other primitives (by accessing the label-image). If other primitives are found, new facts are added to the global database to symbolically describe these spatial relations. These new facts (e.g. TWO-CLOSE-COLLINEAR-SEMI) are used to trigger other rules in order to continue the road piece delineation, e.g.

```
IF     there is a ROADPIECE from NODE1 to NODE2
  AND  it is POSSIBLE-TO-EXTEND ROADPIECE via SEMI-CONNECTION
  AND  there is a fact TWO-CLOSE-COLLINEAR-SEMI relating
                        SEMI-CONNECTION to ANOTHER-SEMI-CONNECTION
  AND  ANOTHER-SEMI-CONNECTION starts from NODE3
  THEN extend ROADPIECE to NODE3
```

The control flow in our approach is basically data-driven. However, top-down reasoning is invoked by context-generated predictions about missing segments. These hypotheses can be verified by locally resegmenting the original image data. This ability of model-driven reexamination is a main feature of KBCV [FUA]. Hypotheses can be created at different levels of the analysis. Indeed, during the course of the process, the structural pattern of the road network is growing towards an instantiation of a more specific model (e.g. a rural, urban or residential pattern). Each specific model imposes its own specific road appearance knowledge. To give an example, let us suppose that the network under analysis exists of a number of highly connected nodes - so there is evidence for an urban pattern. In this case, small subpatterns not connected to the main network will be hypothesized as being spatial segmentation errors. However verification techniques for these high level hypotheses are not yet implemented in the current system. Research is going on to investigate effective ways to solve these problems.

# 4 Discussion

Our prototype system is implemented on a TI Explorer LX LISP-machine. The knowledge base is coded in the ART[1] environment, making extensively use of the underlying object-oriented LISP-FLAVORS world. The image processing modules are written in PASCAL.

The theoretical usefulness of knowledge-based programming for the analysis of remote sensing data has been widely recognized (e.g. [TAILOR]). Practically, however,

---

[1] ART is a trademark of Inference Corporation.

the resulting systems turn out to be extremely time consuming. This is mainly due to what we would like to call the 'pattern matching problem'. This problem occurs when general knowledge base tools are applied to computer vision problems. Indeed, usually only a small number of different symbolic primitive types are needed in those problems, while there are massive amounts of instantiations. The instantaneous input of all these data into such systems cause severe problems to their pattern matching capabilities [VAN CLEYN]. In order to overcome this fundamental problem, we are selectively inputting data into the global facts database. On the one hand this can be done by using backward chaining rules - a control mechanism available in ART -. These rules are fetching data from the underlying LISP environment when they are needed in ART. On the other hand, by context-driven exploration of the label-image (e.g. the second rule above) new primitive instantiations are added to the ART database as soon as they become present in newly found relations. This architecture has led to an efficient implementation of our system.

In other research on road network extraction [WANG,ZHU], it is proposed to postpone the treatment of road junctions until the symbolic inference level. In our opinion, however, crossroads belong to the basic vocabulary describing a road network. Thus, by initially extracting crossroad-like entities from the image data, a richer symbolical description is generated for the subsequent reasoning. Work is also started to include region-based segmentation methods in our road network delineation process. Indeed, roads and regions have a complementary nature. The inclusion of region-like primitives will enable the description of new types of road appearance knowledge.

To further extend the capabilities of the current system, additional domain-dependent knowledge needs to be included. Available knowledge to improve a segmentation of remotely-sensed images can be split into two categories: a priori knowledge and expertise on exploiting spectral, spatial and temporal distributions of the image data. Of course, the amount of knowledge to be included is related to the practical application one has in mind. Since our primal purpose is to detect as many roads as possible to enhance a thematic map, it is straightforward to expect existing maps to be useful sources of a priori knowledge. Unfortunately, reliable maps are often obsolete on or not available for the area of interest. Therefore, we have decided not to make use of existing maps, at the moment. The inclusion of maps would be an interesting new direction in this research.

Spectral information can be used in combination with temporal information (time of day, time of the year), information about weather conditions and regional knowledge of the terrain, to validate road segments established by the lower level geometrical rules. Thus a large part of the future system will have to be devoted to expert knowledge about spectral signature analysis.

# Acknowledgements

This research is based on SPOT data under a SPOT-IMAGE(R) license acquired in collaboration with EUROSENSE TECHNOLOGIES N.V., Belgium.

# References

[DESTIVAL]      Destival, I. Le Men, H. *Detection of linear networks on satelitte images* Proc. 8th. Int. Conf. Pat. Rec. 86 (1986) 856-858

[FISCHLER 81]   Fischler, M. Tenenbaum, J. Wolf, H. *Detection of roads and linear structures in low-resolution aerial imagery using a multisource knowledge integrating technique* Com. Gr. Im. Pr. 15 (1981) 201-223

[FISCHLER 87]   Fischler, M. Firschein, O. *The eye, the brain and the computer* Addison Wesley 1987

[FUA]      Fua, P. Hanson, A. J. *Resegmentation using generic shape: locating general cultural objects* PR Letters 5 (1987) 243-252

[PARIKH]      Parikh, J. A. *Automatic Techniques for Extraction of Geological Fracture Patterns* Pattern Recognition in Practice II (1986) 373-383

[TAILOR]      Tailor, A. et al. *Knowledge-based interpretation of remotely sensed images* Image and Vision Comp. 4.2 (1986) 67-83

[VAN CLEYN]   Van Cleynenbreugel, J. et al. *Knowledge-based improvement of automatic image interpretation for restricted scenes: two case studies* submitted for publication to Image and Vision Comp. (april 1987)

[WANG]      Wang, F. Newkirk, R. *A Knowledge-based System for Highway Network Extraction* Proc. IGARSS 87 (1987) 343-347

[YEE]      Yee, B. *An Expert System for Planimetric Feature Extraction* Proc. IGARSS 87 (1987) 321-325

[ZHU]      Zhu, M. Yeh, P. *Automatic Road Network Detection on Aerial Photographs* Proc. IEEE CVPR 86 (1986) 34-40

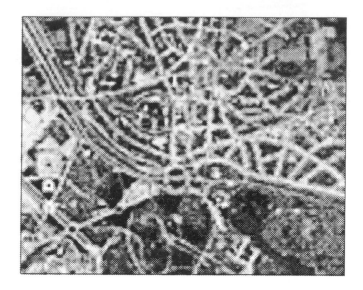

Figure 1: *Part (2.5 × 2 km²) of a SPOT image, obtained by taking the ratio of the XS1 band image to the XS3 band image*

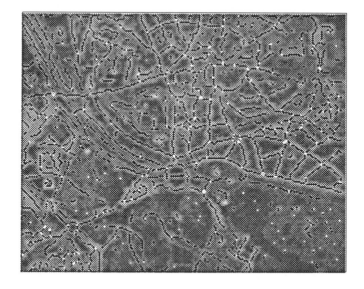

Figure 2: *Result of low level extraction on Figure 1: road segments are presented as black, crossroads as white*

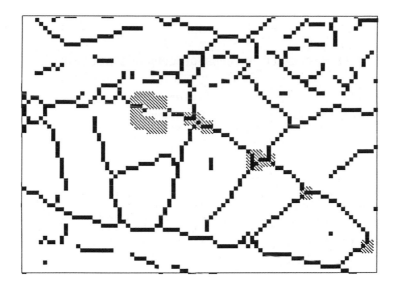

Figure 3: *A region of interest (the interior of the U-shaped boundary) is created at the end of a semi-connection, aligned to the road piece indicated by the highlighted nodes*

# MEDIAN-BASED METHODS OF CORNER DETECTION

E R Davies

Machine Vision Group, Department of Physics
Royal Holloway & Bedford New College
Egham Hill, Egham, Surrey TW20 0EX, UK

## Abstract

This paper examines the 'local ordered grey-level' corner detector and compares it with detectors based on second order variations of the intensity function.  It finds that the method is essentially identical to the Kitchen and Rosenfeld (KR) detector for slowly varying intensity functions, though it is slower and more susceptible to noise.  In many applications  these disadvantages can be eliminated by thresholding the local intensity gradient.

## 1.  Introduction

In many applications of machine vision a vital first stage in  the analysis  of images is the location of specific types of object.  This task can be highly  computation-intensive  - especially if objects can appear in a variety of orientations in three  dimensions.   For  this reason  it  is  common practice to locate objects indirectly, by first finding and identifying salient features such as straight sides, round holes, slits, surface markings and  so  on [1,2].  Corners form one of the most important classes of features  that  can  be  used  for  this purpose.   Thus it is not surprising that a number of corner detection schemes have been developed over the last few years [3-9].

Perhaps the most surprising fact about grey-scale corner detection is the wide variety of means  that have been devised for this purpose. Apart  from  the  obvious  method  of  applying  template  matching schemes [4],  second  order differential operator approaches have been widely used [3,5,6,7], and these  are  augmented by the 'local ordered grey-level' approach [8], and a scheme based on the generalised  Hough transform [9].   To  some  extent  these  different  approaches serve different  purposes:  for  example  the  last  of  these  schemes  was suggested for applications where corners  are liable to be blunted, as often happens with food products.  Finally, some schemes seem to  have rather different characteristics which might be particularly useful in specialised  types  of  applications:  an  example  is  Beaudet's 'DET' operator, which leads to maximal corner-signals (of opposite sign) on either side of the edge bordering the corner [3].

Of the other second order corner detectors, three have now been proven formally identical, following rather different initial development stages. These are the Dreschler and Nagel (DN) approach [5], the Kitchen and Rosenfeld (KR) approach [6], and the Zuniga and Haralick (ZH) approach [7]. That they are mathematically identical is not surprising as this implies only that the same underlying phenomenon is being measured in each case. In this paper we re-examine the local ordered grey-level approach of Paler et al (PFIK). This is a highly effective technique, which seems to be based on a totally different premise. It would be useful if its mechanism could be related to these other corner detectors - if it were understood in more detail it might be possible to improve it.

In section 2 we summarise the properties and relationships of the second order corner detectors. In section 3 we describe the PFIK approach, developing a new understanding of its operation. Finally, in section 4 we investigate it experimentally.

## 2. Corner detectors based on second order intensity variations

By definition, corners in grey-scale images occur in regions of rapidly changing intensity levels. By this token they are detected by the same operators that detect edges in images. However, corner pixels are much rarer than edge pixels, so it is necessary to have operators that detect corners directly without unnecessarily locating edges. To achieve this sort of discriminability it is clearly necessary to consider local variations in image intensity up to at least second order. For this purpose we proceed by expanding the local intensity variation as the second order function:

$$g(X) = g(X_o) + g_x x + g_y y + (1/2)[g_{xx}x^2 + 2g_{xy}xy + g_{yy}y^2] + \ldots \quad (1)$$

where $X = (x,y)'$, the primes indicating transpose, and the suffices indicating partial differentiation with respect to x and y, all taken at the origin $X_o(0,0)'$. The symmetric matrix of second derivatives is

$$G = \begin{bmatrix} g_{xx} & g_{xy} \\ g_{yx} & g_{yy} \end{bmatrix} \qquad \text{where } g_{xy} = g_{yx} \qquad (2)$$

and gives information on the local curvature at $X_o$. A suitable axes rotation will transform G into diagonal form:

$$\begin{bmatrix} g_{xx}^{\,''} & 0 \\ 0 & g_{yy}^{\,''} \end{bmatrix} = \begin{bmatrix} K_1 & 0 \\ 0 & K_2 \end{bmatrix} \tag{3}$$

where we have reinterpreted appropriate derivatives as principal curvatures at $X_0$.

We are particularly interested in rotationally invariant operators, and it is significant that the trace and determinant of a matrix such as G are invariant under rotations. Thus we obtain the Beaudet operators [3]

$$\text{Laplacian} = g_{xx} + g_{yy} = K_1 + K_2 \tag{4}$$

and $\text{Hessian} = \det(G) = g_{xx}g_{yy} - g_{xy}^2 = K_1 K_2 \tag{5}$

It is well known that the Laplacian operator responds to lines and edges and hence is not particularly suitable as a corner detector. Beaudet noted that the Hessian (his 'DET' operator) has significant values near corners: it should therefore form a useful corner detector. However, DET responds with one sign on one side of a corner and with the opposite sign on the other side of the corner, and rather more complicated analysis is required to deduce the presence and exact position of a single corner [5,10].

To find other rotationally invariant corner detectors other workers have started from physical considerations. Kitchen and Rosenfeld calculated the projection of the local rate of change of gradient direction vector along the horizontal edge tangent direction, and showed that it is mathematically identical to calculating the horizontal curvature K of the intensity function g. To obtain a realistic indication of the strength of a corner they multiplied the horizontal curvature by the local intensity gradient:

$$C = K[g_x^2 + g_y^2]^{\frac{1}{2}}$$

$$= (g_{xx}g_x^2 - 2g_{xy}g_x g_y + g_{yy}g_y^2)/(g_x^2 + g_y^2) \tag{6}$$

Finally, they used the heuristic of non-maximum suppression to further localise the corner positions.

Recently, Nagel has shown that the KR corner detector using non-maximum suppression is very similar to the DN corner detector [10]. In addition, Shah and Jain [11] have shown that the ZH corner detector is essentially equivalent to the KR corner detector, the difference being that in the former case the cornerness measure is simply the local horizontal curvature K, but this measure is only applied to edge points: i.e. the ZH corner detector makes edge detection explicit in the operator, hence eliminating a number of false corners that would otherwise have been induced by noise.

The near-equivalence of these three corner detectors need not be overly surprising, since as remarked earlier different methods should reflect the same underlying phenomena.


## 3.  The PFIK corner detector

The PFIK corner detector contrasts with the second order intensity variation methods outlined above in being much less complex mathematically, but at first appearing somewhat ad hoc in nature. The technique applies a median filter to the input image, and then forms an image that is the difference between the input and the filtered images. This difference image contains a set of signals which are interpreted as local measures of cornerness. However, one major worry about the method is that it will by its nature unearth all the noise in the original image and present this as a set of 'corner' signals.

To see that the method can in principle detect corners, we first note that in the absence of significant noise, strong signals would not be expected in areas of background. In addition, strong signals are not expected near edges, it being well known that median filters do not shift edges significantly. In fact the principle of the PFIK corner detector lies in "the insensitivity of the median filter to features with dimensions smaller than half the size of the filter window" [8]. This means that the corner can be brought to a position covering the central pixel of the window without causing any change in the filter output - hence giving a strong difference signal and indicating a corner. This gives the method a different characteristic from other corner detectors in that a maximal response is obtained within the corner rather than on the edge bordering the corner.

Paler et al show that the signal strength obtained from the operator is proportional to (a) the local contrast, and (b) the 'sharpness' of the corner (here to be interpreted as the angle through which the boundary turns) [8]. Since it is assumed here that the corner turns through a significant angle within the filter neighbourhood, the difference from the second order intensity variation approach is a major one. Indeed, it is an implicit assumption in the latter approach that first and second order coefficients describe the local intensity characteristics reasonably rigorously, the intensity function being inherently continuous and differentiable. Thus the second order methods may give unpredictable results with sharp corners where directions change within a few pixels' range.

In spite of these problems of principle, it is worthwhile to try to relate the PFIK method to the second order intensity variation approaches. We investigate the situation further below.

## 3.1 Re-analysis of the operation of the PFIK detector

To analyse the performance of the PFIK corner detector we assume that the grey-scale intensity varies only a small amount within the median filter neighbourhood region. In this situation there is some hope of relating the performance of this corner detector to low order derivatives of the intensity variation.

First we assume a continuous analogue image and a median filter operating in an idealised circular neighbourhood. In addition, we ignore noise in developing the basic theory. Next we note a simple property of the median filter: for an intensity function that increases monotonically with distance in a direction x", but which does not vary in the perpendicular direction y", the median within the circular window is equal to the value at the centre of the neighbourhood. This finding is in accord with the property stated earlier, that the median does not shift symmetric edges. However, it is more general, in that the edge profile need not be symmetric within the vertical plane of the x"-axis, so long as there is no y"-variation. Hence the median corner detector will give zero signal if the horizontal curvature is locally zero. We assume that no higher order derivatives are present which could complicate this view.

Let us now see the effect of introducing a small local curvature. Looking down on our circular window we see a set of intensity contours, each having roughly circular shape and approximately equal curvature (Figure 1). The centre of the contour containing the median value of intensity will not now pass through the centre of the window, but will be displaced to one side along the negative x"-axis. Further, the signal obtained from the corner detector will depend on this displacement. If the displacement is D, it is easy to see that the corner signal is $Dg_{x"}$, since $g_{x"}$ allows the intensity change over the distance D to be estimated. The remaining problem is to relate D to the horizontal curvature K.

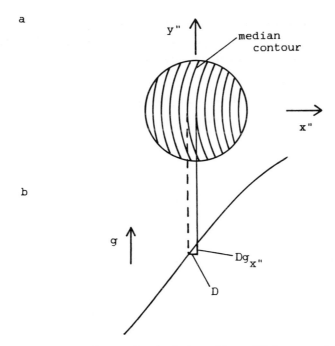

<u>Figure 1  Contours of constant intensity within a neighbourhood</u>

(a) shows the contours of constant intensity within a small
neighbourhood. Ideally these are parallel, circular and of
approximately equal curvature. The contour of median intensity does
not pass through the centre of the neighbourhood. (b) shows a
cross-section of the intensity variation, indicating how the
displacement D of the median contour leads to an estimate of corner
strength.

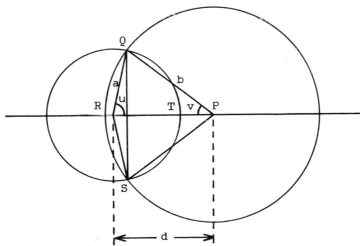

<u>Figure 2  Area of overlap between a circular neighbourhood and the
region inside a circular arc of radius b</u>

To calculate D, we reformulate the problem in geometrical terms. In fact we need to find at what distance d from the centre of curvature the area of a circular neighbourhood of radius a is bisected by the circular arc of radius b (= 1/K).

From Figure 2 the area of sector PQRS is $vb^2$, while the area of triangle PQS is $b^2\sin v \cos v$. Hence the area of segment QRS is

$$B = b^2(v - \sin v \cos v) \qquad (7)$$

Making a similar calculation of the area A of segment QTS, we deduce the area of overlap (Figure 2) between the circular neighbourhood of radius a and the area inside the circular arc of radius b. For a median filter this is equal to $\pi a^2/2$.

Hence $\quad F = a^2(u - \sin u \cos u) + b^2(v - \sin v \cos v) - \pi a^2/2 = 0 \quad (8)$

where $\quad a^2 = b^2 + d^2 - 2bd\cos v \qquad (9)$

and $\quad b^2 = a^2 + d^2 - 2ad\cos u \qquad (10)$

In the spirit of our second order approximation to the local intensity variation, we assume that a ≪ b. Under these circumstances, v is small, u ≃ π/2 and d ≃ b. Hence we find

$$v \simeq a/b \qquad (11)$$

Setting D = b - d $\qquad (12)$

after some manipulation we obtain D in the form

$$D = a^2/6b = Ka^2/6 \qquad (13)$$

since K = 1/b is the local curvature.

Hence the corner signal is

$$C = Dg_{x''} = Kg_{x''}a^2/6 \qquad (14)$$

Notice that C has the dimensions of intensity (contrast), but that as in the formulation of Paler et al the sharpness of the corner also appears - here in the form a/b = aK.

What we have shown here is that the local signal from the median-based corner detector is proportional to horizontal curvature and to intensity gradient. This makes it formally identical to the three second order intensity variation detectors discussed in section 2. However, we have only made this direct comparison under circumstances where second order variations in intensity give a complete description of the situation. Clearly the situation might be significantly different when corners are so sharp that they turn through a large proportion of the total angle within the chosen size of neighbourhood. In addition, noise might be expected to affect

performance differently in the different cases. We discuss some of
these factors in the context of our experimental results. Meanwhile,
it appears that there ought to be no difference in the positions at
which median and second order derivative methods locate corners.


## 4. Experimental results

Experimental tests with the PFIK approach to corner detection
showed that it is a highly effective procedure. Corners are detected
reliably (Figure 3), and signal strength is indeed roughly proportional both to local image contrast and to corner sharpness. Noise is
more apparent for 3x3 implementations and this makes it better to use
5x5 or larger neighbourhoods to give good corner discrimination.
However, even when using a 5x5 neighbourhood, background noise is
still highlighted as anticipated earlier. It seems that some means is
required of reducing this effect. In addition, the method is rather
slow in operation - particularly with 5x5 and larger neighbourhoods.

On the other hand no particular discontinuity in properties seemed
to occur as corners were made progressively more or less sharp (e.g.
with the aid of Gaussian smoothing operators). Indeed, the method
seemed well behaved in this respect.

a          b          c

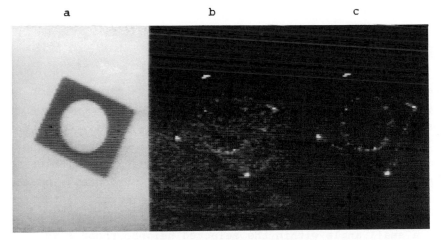

Figure 3  Performance of the original and improved corner detectors

(a) is the original image of a metal part, (b) is the result of
applying a PFIK detector, and (c) is the result of including a
suitable gradient threshold. Image (a) has 64 grey levels: the
considerable amounts of background noise are saturated out in the
photograph (a), but are evident from (b). 5x5 neighbourhoods were
employed in these tests.

Because of the proven equivalence in principle between the three major second order derivative corner detectors, only the KR detector was used for comparison with the median-based method. On comparing the results for the two cases, the following observations were made: (1) the corner signals appeared at approximately the same locations in the two cases - in accordance with the theory of section 3.1; (2) as anticipated, the background noise was greater for the median approach.

To make the median method more generally useful, noise has to be reduced and speed enhanced. For this reason we have tried a two-stage recognition process in which edge detection is followed by median corner enhancement, following the style of the ZH method. We have shown this method achieves both aims at the same time. The result is superior to that for the KR method in giving less interference from remanent edge signals and other artefacts, though the noise level remains somewhat higher. When setting up either algorithm, the edge detection threshold must not be raised too high since at corners the edge magnitude is typically only one half of its size on those parts of object boundaries where horizontal curvature is low.

Typical speed improvement factors of at least 8 were noted - as for the image shown in Figure 3. (In this case a 3x3 Sobel type of edge detector was used, this being followed by a 5x5 median corner enhancer: a conventional serial computer (PDP-11/73) implementation was used for the tests.)


## 5. Concluding remarks

This paper has examined the local ordered grey-level approach to corner detection and compared it with three well-known corner detectors based on second order derivatives of the local intensity function. Theory has shown that contrary to initial expectations this median-based approach measures the same underlying characteristics of the image in arriving at a local measure of corner strength. Indeed, as originally formulated it is mathematically almost identical to the KR method when horizontal curvature is low so that the corner turns through only a small angle within the selected neighbourhood size.

Noise levels are significantly reduced by thresholding the intensity gradient magnitude, but remain higher than for the KR method. On balance this means that the median-based approach should only be used when image noise is not excessive. Thresholding intensity gradient magnitude has the additional advantage of significantly speeding up the algorithm so that its speed is comparable to that of the KR method.

Overall, this work has highlighted the value of the initially rather odd procedure of taking the difference between the output of a median filter and the original image as a corner-enhanced image. It has shown that the method is in fact closely related to other corner detectors that were systematically designed for the purpose. It has also shown how the speed and noise rejection properties of the method may be improved.

## Acknowledgement

The author is grateful to the UK Science and Engineering Research Council for financial support during the course of this research.

## References

1. R. C. Bolles and R. A. Cain "Recognising and locating partially visible objects: the local-feature-focus method", Int. J. Robotics Res., $\underline{1}$, no. 3, pp. 57-82 (1982)

2. E. R. Davies "A comparison of methods for the rapid location of products and their features and defects", pp. 111-120 in P. A. McKeown (ed.), Proc. 7th Int. Conf. on Automated Inspection and Product Control, Birmingham (26-28 March 1985)

3. P. R. Beaudet "Rotationally invariant image operators", Proc. 4th Int. Conf. on Pattern Recogn., Kyoto, pp. 579-583 (1978)

4. J. Bretschi "Automated Inspection Systems for Industry", IFS Publications Ltd, UK, Ch. 10 (1981)

5. L. Dreschler and H.-H. Nagel "Volumetric model and 3D-trajectory of a moving car derived from monocular TV-frame sequences of a street scene", Proc. IJCAI, pp. 692-697 (1981)

6. L. Kitchen and A. Rosenfeld "Gray-level corner detection", Pattern Recogn. Lett., $\underline{1}$, no. 2, pp. 95-102 (1982)

7. O. A. Zuniga and R. Haralick "Corner detection using the facet model", Proc. IEEE CVPR Conf., pp. 30-37 (1983)

8. K. Paler, J. Föglein, J. Illingworth and J. Kittler "Local ordered grey levels as an aid to corner detection", Pattern Recogn., $\underline{17}$, no. 5, pp. 535-543 (1984)

9. E. R. Davies "Corner detection using the generalised Hough transform", Proc. 2nd Int. Conf. on Image Processing and its Applications (24-26 June 1986), IEE Conf. Publication no. 265, pp. 175-179 (1986)

10. H.-H. Nagel "Displacement vectors derived from second-order intensity variations in image sequences", Comput. Vision Graph. Image Process., $\underline{21}$, pp. 85-117 (1983)

11. M. A. Shah and R. Jain "Detecting time-varying corners", Comput. Vision Graph. Image Process., $\underline{28}$, pp. 345-355 (1984)

# APPLICATION OF THE PROJECTED HOUGH TRANSFORM IN PICTURE PROCESSING

Ulrich Eckhardt

Institut für Angewandte Mathematik, Universität Hamburg

Bundesstraße 55, D-2000 Hamburg 13


Gerd Maderlechner

ZT ZTI INF 122, SIEMENS AG

Otto-Hahn-Ring 6, D-8000 München 83

**Abstract.**

The main result of this paper is that a projection of the classical Hough transform for line detection onto a subspace of the parameter space (accumulator) will yield a useless trivial result if the composite operator consisting of projection and Hough transform is assumed to be linear and translation invariant.

## 1. Introduction

The Hough transform (or Radon transform) is an integral transform which assigns to a two-dimensional function $\beta(x,y)$ (the **picture** or **image**) the set of all integrals of this function along lines. In its classical formulation it was given by Radon (1917):

$$H(\beta)(p, \alpha) := \int_{-\infty}^{\infty} \beta\left(\begin{matrix} p \cos \alpha + t \sin \alpha \\ p \sin \alpha - t \cos \alpha \end{matrix}\right) dt.$$

Hough (1962) made the observation that in binary images the maxima of this transformation correspond to lines in the image. In the meantime this concept was generalized by different researchers and it turned out to be a very useful tool in many applications of picture processing.

There are numerous attempts reported in the literature to reduce the dimension of the image space (the so-called accumulator) of the transform. There are two reasons for doing so:

The Hough transform assigns to each two-dimensional function a two-dimensional function. Since the latter has to be calculated point by point, the computational effort for carrying out the transformation (the sampling effort) becomes large. The sampling effort can be reduced by data compression techniques.

After the Hough transform has been calculated, a search for maxima becomes necessary. Also this search is far more easier in one dimension than in two dimensions.

These arguments gain considerably weight if generalizations of the Hough transform are discussed whose image space has a dimension higher than two (Ballard 1981).

In the present paper the classical Hough transform for lines is investigated. It is shown that it is not possible to retain simultaneously three favourable properties when the Hough transform is projected onto a one-dimensional subspace of the parameter space:

- Linearity of the projection,
- Translation invariance of the projection,
- A nontrivial result of the projection.

This negative result can be generalized to a more general variant of the Hough transform, at the cost, however, of deeper functional analysis. Therefore, this generalization will be the subject of a separate investigation.

## 2. Basic Concepts

An **image** is a function $\beta(P)$ associating to each point $P=(x,y)^T$ of the plane a real number. We assume that the integral of the absolute value of $\beta$ exists and that $\beta$ vanishes outside a bounded set R. Some examples for images are: binary images ($\beta$ takes only values 0 and 1), gray tone images ($0 \leq \beta \leq 1$), gradient images ($\beta$ is assumed to be the length of the gradient vector at point P). In the context of this paper we are mainly interested in binary images.

For analyzing and understanding the content of an image, the identification of certain **features** is important. In this paper we concentrate ourselves on linear features. For investigating the question whether a linear feature is contained in the image, we first parametrize all lines in the plane by number pairs (a,b). The set of all parameter pairs belonging to lines, the so-called

**accumulator**, is denoted by A. We assume that there is a one-to-one correspondence between parameter pairs (a,b) ε A and lines in the plane.

Let $\ell(a,b)$ be the line corresponding to (a,b) ε A. The line integral (whenever it exists)

$$H(\beta)(a,\ b) = \int_{\ell(a,b)} \beta(P)\ d\sigma$$

($\sigma$ denoting the arc length on the line $\ell(a,b)$) is the Hough transform (or Radon transform) of the image $\beta$ (see Hough 1962, Duda, Hart 1972, Deans 1983, Radon 1917). Hough (1962) observed that in binary images a maximum value of $H(\beta)(a,b)$ indicates that there is a feature on the line $\ell(a,b)$.

The computational trick applied in the Hough transform is to evaluate the integrals (in a discretized form as sums) for a finite set of accumulator points idependently. Hence the method allows to process the picture in one pass and it fits very well to parallel computer architectures (Merlin, Farber 1975, Yalaman-chili, Aggarwal 1985, Gerig 1987).

There are generalizations of the Hough transform to other features than lines (see e.g. Ballard 1981). In this paper we concentrate ourselves on line features for easier presentation. A generalization of the results of this paper, which requires deeper analysis, will be published elsewhere.

One main obstacle for using the Hough transform on general purpose computers is the fact that it is very elaborate to perform it. Moreover, the identification of maxima in a two-dimensional accumulator might become cumbersome and difficult.

There are numerous approaches in the literature for reducing the computational effort of the Hough transform (Brown, Sher 1982, Neveu, Dyer, Chin 1986, O'Rourke 1981, Sloan 1981) by applying clever storage techniques for the accumulator. Reducing the number of relevant points in the image e.g. by skeletonization might also enhance the computational efficiency of the Hough transform (Kushnir, Abe, Matsumoto 1985). Here we investigate a different approach. When the contents of the accumulator are projected onto a subspace of dimension one, at least the effort for identifying

the extrema is reduced at the cost of loosing information. This
approach was also proposed by different authors, specifically for
higher dimensional accumulators (Ballard, Sabbah 1983, Biland,
Wahl 1986, Gerig, Klein 1986, Gerig 1987, Silberberg, Davis,
Harwood 1984).

## 3. Motions and Invariances

In the context of lines, motions of the plane play a distinguished
role. A motion is an affine linear transformation of the plane
leaving the Euclidean distance and the orientation of angles
invariant. Given a point $P=(x,y)^T$, a motion has the general form

$$M\ P := \begin{pmatrix} x \cos \phi + y \sin \phi + x_0 \\ -x \sin \phi + y \cos \phi + y_0 \end{pmatrix}$$

with fixed vector $P_0=(x_0,y_0)^T$. We list some properties of motions:

A motion has a nontrivial rotational part (i.e. nonzero rotation
angle) if and only if it has exactly one fixed point. In this
case it is a rotation of the plane by an angle $\phi$ around the
fixed point.

If $\cos \phi = 1$ then the motion corresponds to a pure translation
of the plane by a vector $P_0$. If $P_0$ is not the zero vector, each
line parallel to $P_0$ will be mapped into itself by the
translation.

To each pair of lines in the plane there corresponds uniquely
one motion mapping one of the lines into the other. The motion
is a translation if and only if the lines are parallel.

The motions are a group, specifically the product of two motions
is a motion and there exists for each motion an inverse motion.

Without loss of generality we assume that the Hough transform
$H(\beta)(a,b)$ is to be projected with respect to parameter b. Other
parametrizations can be easily treated by reparametrizing A.
Assume therefore that parameter a is fixed.

Let $L_a$ be the set of all lines $\ell(a,b)$ with fixed first parameter
a. $M_a$ is the set of all motions defined by line pairs in $L_a$. $M_a$ is
assumed to be a subgroup of the group of all motions of the plane.
This means that for any two motions in $M_a$ the product is also
in $M_a$.

Given a function h(a,b) of two variables. A **projector** Π is an operator associating to h a function (Πh)(a) of the first variable only. Assume that M is a motion in $M_a$. Then for each parameter b there exists a parameter $b_M(b)$ such that $M\ell(a,b)=\ell(a,b_M(b))$, hence

$$H(M\beta)(a, b) = H(\beta)(a, b_M(b))$$

for all pictures β. In other words: The function $b_M(b)$ compensates for the motion M by a transformation of the parameter b. It is natural to require that for all M in $M_a$ and for any function h(a,b) in the domain of the projector Π the function h'(a,b):= :=$h(a,b_M(b))$ is also in the domain of Π and

$$\Pi h'(a) = \Pi h(a).$$

A projector having this property is said to be **compatible with the motions in $M_a$**.

Given a fixed line $\ell_0:=\ell(a,b_0)$ in $L_a$ and a translation vector Q parallel to ℓ. We require that the composite operator ΠH is **line translation invariant with respect to $\ell_0$**, i.e.:

$$\Pi H(\beta)(a) = \Pi H(\beta_Q)(a)$$

for all images β where $\beta_Q$ is the translated image $\beta_Q(P):=\beta(P+Q)$.

Assume that ΠH is not line translation invariant with respect to $\ell_0$ and consider an image containing only a single line element on $\ell_0$. Then the value of ΠH depends on the position of this line element on $\ell_0$ which is certainly not desirable.

We are now able to formulate a Theorem:

**Theorem:** Assume that the composite operator ΠH is continuous and linear and that it is line translation invariant with respect to a line $\ell_0$ in $L_a$. Assume further that the projector Π is compatible with the motions in $M_a$.
Then the projected Hough transform has the form

$$H_b(\beta)(a) := \Pi H(\beta)(a) = C(a) \cdot \int_R \beta(P)\, dP$$

where C(a) is a constant not depending on β.

For proving the Theorem we first note that by Riesz' Representation Theorem (See e.g. Adams 1975) the composite operator has the form

$$\Pi H(\beta)(a) = C(a) \cdot \int_R g(P) \cdot \beta(P) \, dP$$

where g(P) is a function which is essentially bounded on R. By virtue of the line translation invariance we can conclude that g is constant on $\ell_0$. Since $\Pi$ is compatible with motions in $M_a$, g is also constant and has the same value on all lines in $M_a$.
A detailed proof for a more general situation is given in a manuscript of the authors (1987).

The assertion of the Theorem implies that in case all conditions of the Theorem are fulfilled, the projected Hough transform is a multiple of the mean value of the image and therefore it carries no information at all. Consequently, if a useful result of the projection is required, we have to use either a nonlinear or a non translation invariant projector.


5. Linear Projections

Assume that β represents a binary picture containing prominent directions, for example a document, a flow diagram etc. We want to adjust this picture by identifying the prominent directions. In contrast to the situation with the ordinary Hough transform for lines we are not interested in the individual lines in the picture.

Any projection of the form

$$(\Pi h)(a) = \int g(b) \, h(a,b) \, db$$

with suitable g is of course continuous and linear. It is compatible with all motions in $M_a$ if and only if g(b) is constant. Without loss of generality let $g \equiv 1$ for all b. There remains only the condition of line translation invariance which needs closer investigation.

Example 1: (a,b)=(m,p) and $\ell(m,p)$ is given by the slope-intercept representation of a line

$$y = m x + p.$$

This parametrization was originally used by Hough (1962). It was recommended quite recently by Biland and Wahl (1986).

a) For fixed m, the motions in $M_m$ are the translations parallel to the y-axis. One has

$$H_p(\beta)(m) := \int_{-\infty}^{\infty} H(\beta)(m, p) \, dp = (1 + m^2)^{1/2} \cdot \int_R \beta(P) \, dP.$$

Obviously, this operator is line translation invariant for any translation vector with slope m.

b) If p is fixed, the group of motions in $M_p$ is given by all rotations with center $(0,p)^T$. We have

$$H_m(\beta)(p) := \int_{-\infty}^{\infty} H(\beta)(m, p) \, dm =$$

$$= \int_R (x^2 + (p - y)^2)^{1/2}/x^2 \, \beta(P) \, dP.$$

This expression can become singular when there are features on the y-axis. Since this projection does not fulfill the line invariance condition, it becomes hard to interpret the results of its application.

**Example 2:** $(a,b)=(\alpha,p)$ and $\ell(\alpha,p)$ is given by Hesse's normal form

$$x \sin \alpha - y \cos \alpha = p.$$

This parametrization is usually applied in the Radon transform (Deans 1983).

a) For fixed $\alpha$, obviously all conditions of the Theorem are met, hence

$$H_p(\beta)(\alpha) := \int_{-\infty}^{\infty} H(\beta)(\alpha, p) \, dp = \int_R \beta(P) \, dP.$$

b) For fixed p one has

$$H_\alpha(\beta)(p) := \int_0^{2\pi} H(\beta)(\alpha, p) \, d\alpha =$$

$$= \int_{r>p} \beta(P)/(r^2 - p^2) \, dP$$

with $r^2 = x^2 + y^2$.

This projection is not line translation invariant. If the picture contains only a line segment with fixed center, then $\Pi H$ will be maximal if the line segment points towards the origin. $\Pi H$ will become larger as the line segment is moved from outside towards the periphery of a circle around the origin with radius p; it becomes singular, if the line segment touches the periphery. The interior of the circle is invisible for $\Pi H$.

**Example 3:** For a fixed number S with $x^2 + y^2 < S^2$ for all P $\varepsilon$ R a line is parametrized by $(\alpha, \phi)$:

$$x \sin \alpha - y \cos \alpha = S \sin(\alpha - \phi).$$

This parametrization is closely related to Wallace's "Muff"-transform (Wallace 1985). It is known in the computer tomography literature as "fan beam" geometry (see e.g. Deans 1983).
a) For fixed $\alpha$ one has

$$H_\phi(\beta)(\alpha) := \int_0^{2\pi} H(\beta)(\alpha, \phi) \, d\phi =$$

$$= \int_R \beta(P)/(S^2 - (y \cos \alpha - x \sin \alpha)^2)^{1/2} \, dP.$$

The composite operator is line translation invariant for all lines with direction $\alpha$.
b) The projection in direction $\alpha$ is not interesting here.

At a first glance, the projection of Example 3 looks very promising. Experiments with realistic pictures, however, were not very encouraging. The more details were present in the picture the more constant its projection becomes.

## 6. Conclusions

We can conclude from the results of the examples that the severely non translation invariant projection (Example 1.b) is difficult to interpret. If the projection is not translation invariant, the contribution of a specific feature in the image to the projected Hough transform depends on its location in the picture. It is therefore impossible to distinguish faint details at a good position from strong details at a position of poor visibility.

It seems to be more preferable to apply the ordinary Hough

transform to a "window" within the image which gives controlled visibility and also reduces the sampling effort considerably.

On the other hand, if the projection is only moderately non translation invariant (Example 3), it approaches the conditions of the Theorem and therefore it ought to be nearly constant.

We can therefore conclude that the condition of translation invariance should not be abandoned. There remains only the possibility to apply a nonlinear projector. In the literature a large amount of examples can be found for nonlinear projectors (Ballard, Sabbah 1983, Gerig, Klein 1986, Gerig 1987, Silberberg, Davis, Harwood 1984 and others).

## References

Adams RA (1975) Sobolev Spaces.
  New York, San Francisco, London: Academic Press

Ballard DH (1981) Generalizing the Hough transform to detect arbitrary shapes.
  Pattern Recognition 13:111-122

Ballard DH, Sabbah D (1983) Viewer independent shape recognition.
  IEEE Trans. PAMI-5:653-660

Biland HP, Wahl FM (1986) Understanding Hough space for polyhedral scene decomposition.
  IBM Zürich Research Laboratory, RZ 1458 (# 52978) 3/25/86

Brown CM, Sher DB (1982) Hough transformation into cache accumulators: Considerations and simulations.
  TR 114, Department of Computer Science, University of Rochester

Deans SR (1983) The Radon Transform and Some of Its Applications.
  New York, Chichester, Brisbane, Toronto, Singapore: John Wiley and Sons

Duda RO, Hart PE (1972) Use of the Hough transform to detect lines and curves in pictures.
  Communications of the ACM 15:11-15

Eckhardt U, Maderlechner G (1987) Projections of the Hough transform.
  Manuscript Universität Hamburg

Gerig G, Klein F (1986) Fast contour identification through efficient Hough transform and simplified interpretation strategy.
  IAPR - afcet: Eighth International Conference on Pattern Recognition. Paris, France, October 27-31,1986

Gerig G (1987) Segmentierung zur symbolischen Beschreibung von Strukturen in Grauwertbildern.
  Zürich: Dissertation ETH Nr. 8390

Hough PVC (1962) Method and means for recognizing complex patterns.
  U.S. Patent 3,069,654. Washington: United States Patent Office, December 18, 1962

Kushnir M, Abe K, Matsumoto K (1985) Recognition of handprinted Hebrew characters using features selected in the Hough transform space.
  Pattern Recognition 18:103-114

Merlin PM, Farber DJ (1975) A parallel mechanism for detecting curves in pictures.
  IEEE Trans. C-24:96-98

Neveu CF, Dyer CR, Chin RT (1986) Two-dimensional object recognition using multi-resolution models.
  Computer Vision, Graphics, and Image Processing 34:52-65

O'Rourke J (1981) Dynamically quantized spaces for focusing the Hough transform.
  In: Proceedings of the Seventh International Joint Conference on Artificial Intelligence, 24-28 August 1981, University of British Columbia, Vancouver, B.C., Canada, pp. 737-739

Radon J (1917) Über die Bestimmung von Funktionen durch ihre Integralwerte längs gewisser Mannigfaltigkeiten.
  Ber. Verh. Sächs. Akad. Wiss. Leipzig, Math.-Nat. Kl. 69:262-277

Silberberg TM, Davis L, Harwood D (1984) An iterative Hough procedure for three-dimensional object recognition.
  Pattern Recognition 17:621-629

Sloan KR (1981) Dynamically quantized pyramids.
  In: Proceedings of the Seventh International Joint Conference on Artificial Intelligence, 24-28 August 1981, University of British Columbia, Vancouver,B.C., Canada, pp. 734-736

Wallace RS (1985) A modified Hough transform for lines.
  IEEE Computer Society Conference on Computer Vision and Pattern Recognition, June 19-23, 1985, San Francisco, California, pp. 665-667. Silver Spring: IEEE Computer Society Press. Amsterdam: North-Holland Publishing Company

Yalamanchili S, Aggarwal JK (1985) A system organization for parallel image processing.
  Pattern Recognition 18:17-29

# An Efficient Radon Transform

Violet F. Leavers[†]
Mark B. Sandler[*]

## Abstract

A new algorithm is presented whereby the Radon transform may be computed in a time commensurate with real-time computer vision applications. The computation and storage requirments are optimized using the four-fold symmetry of the image plane and the properties of the transform. A hybrid technique of multi-tasking and asynchronous parallel processing is proposed and a suitable architecture is suggested.

## 1 . Introduction

The classic paper[1] in which the concept of the Radon transform was first introduced has had far-reaching effects in many branches of science. Use of the transform has been widely exploited in the field of computerized tomography but its use in the area of computer vision has been limited to the detection of straight line segments where typically the Hough transform[2], a special case of the Radon transform[3], is used for the detection of linear features in digital images[4].

The Hough transform may be used to detect shapes other than straight line segments. A comprehensive review of the Hough transform, its applications and implementations is given by Illingworth and Kittler[5]. A major drawback of the technique is that each new shape requires that the kernel of the transformation be rewritten in a form particular to that shape. Transform spaces of a minimum dimensionality of four[6] are required to accumulate the results of the transformation and each recasting of the transformation allows the detection of only one particular shape. An image composed of different shapes would require successive transformations with respect to each particular shape. Attempts to define fast, efficient algorithms and implementations for the detection of curves have been restricted by these considerations.

It has been shown[7] that the Radon transform may be retained as the generic transformation in a technique which allows any analytically defined shape to be detected. The task is thus reduced to the optimization of a well defined problem with inherent symmetry and properties which may be exploited to produce an efficient algorithm and implementation.

Ballard[6] and Kimme et al.[10] have both demonstrated a technique whereby the computation of the Hough transform may be accelerated, but without formalizing the approach. This paper both sets the approach in a formal framework and extends it to give further computational advantages. To be particular,

[†] Department of Physics, King's College, The Strand, London WC2R 2LS.
[*] Department of Electrical Engineering, King's College, The Strand, London WC2R 2LS.

it is shown in [6,10] that the gradient information obtained, for example using the Sobel edge detector, may be used to focus the computational effort in appropriate regions of the transform space. The work described here uses this and employs the table-lookup technique to speed up the computation further still.

## 2 . The Radon transform

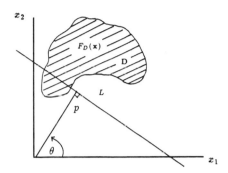

Fig.1 Graphical representation of the Radon Transform.

The Radon transform may be written in the convenient form suggested by Gel'fand et al.[8]

$$\Re\{F(\mathbf{x})\} = H(p,\xi) = \int_{-\infty}^{\infty} d\mathbf{x}\, F(\mathbf{x})\delta(p - \xi \cdot \mathbf{x}) \tag{1}$$

$F(\mathbf{x})$ is a function defined on a domain $D$. In two dimensions, $\delta(p - \xi \cdot \mathbf{x})$, represents a delta function distribution situated along a line, $L$, with equation $p - \xi \cdot \mathbf{x} = 0$ where $\xi$ is a unit vector in the direction of the normal to that line and $p$ is the algebraic length of the normal. It is of particular interest to consider the case in which the general function $F(\mathbf{x})$ is replaced by a particular function $F_D(\mathbf{x})$, where

$$F_D(\mathbf{x}) = \begin{cases} 1, & \text{in } D; \\ 0, & \text{otherwise.} \end{cases}$$

Fig 1 illustrates the Radon transform of such a function. The shaded region represents the function $F_D(\mathbf{x})$. The line $L$ acts as a probe or detector function and $F_D(\mathbf{x})$ as the object function. Whenever the line $L$ and the domain $D$ intersect the value of the integral is equal to the length of the intersection; otherwise it is zero.

This definition corresponds to the transformation of a binary image and is required by the present theory as the shapes extracted from digital images will be represented as binary edge maps.

It is known[5,7,9,10] that the maxima generated in transform space correspond to the tangents to the curve in image space at the points where curve and tangent have a common normal.

## 3 . Discretization of the Transform

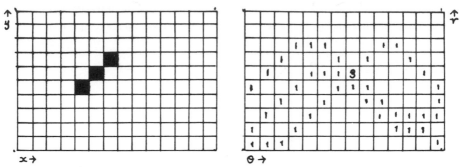

Fig. 2 Discrete representation

of the Radon transform

The transformation may be computed using the normal parametrisation:

$$p_j = x_i \cos \theta_j + y_i \sin \theta_j \tag{2}$$

which may also be expressed as:

$$p_j = (x_i^2 + y_i^2)^{\frac{1}{2}} \cos \left( \theta_j - \tan^{-1} \left( \frac{y_i}{x_i} \right) \right) \tag{3}$$

where the $i$, $j$ subscripts refer to ordered pairs in the image and the transform space respectively. Equation (3) then becomes:

$$p_j = A(x_i, y_i) \cos(\theta_j - \phi(x_i, y_i)) \tag{4}$$

This represents a cosine curve with an amplitude, $A(x_i, y_i) = (x_i^2 + y_i^2)^{\frac{1}{2}}$ and a phase $\phi(x_i, y_i) = \tan^{-1} \left( \frac{y_i}{x_i} \right)$.

For every point, $(x_i, y_i)$, of the image, $i$ is fixed and the values $p_j$ are calculated using stepwise increments of $\theta_j$. Each point, $(p_j, \theta_j)$, in the transform space is assigned a value of 1. Where curves intersect, the point of intersection will have a value equal to the number of intersecting curves. Fig 2 is an illustration of the discretization of the transformation. Three co-linear image points are shown as black pixels and the corresponding discrete representation of the transform space, the accumulator, is incremented at the appropriate values of $(p_j, \theta_j)$.

Every value $(p_j, \theta_j)$, on a cosine curve in the transform space will refer to a possible line in image space which passes through the point $(x_i, y_i)$.

## 4 . An Efficient Algorithm

It is possible to use the form of the transformation and its properties to devise an efficient algorithm.

1 . Equation (4) states that both the amplitude and the phase of the cosine curve are functions of $x$ and $y$, i.e. they are constant for a given value of $i$ and may be pre-calculated, indexed by $x$ and $y$, and stored in look-up tables.

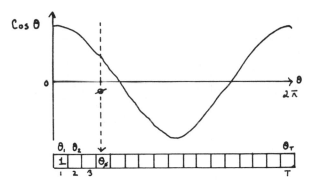

Fig. 3 Graphic representation of cosine look-up table

2 . It is known[6,7,10] that the maxima generated in the transform space correspond to the tangents to a curve in image space. This property may be exploited in order to reduce significantly the computational load.

The gradient, $\psi_i$, of the tangent to the curve at the point $P_{xy}$, which is provided at the edge detection stage of the processing, may be used to deduce an approximation to $\psi_0$, the approximate location, with respect to $\theta$, of the maxima in transform space associated with the point $P_{xy}$. Hence only those values of $p_j$ in equation (4) corresponding to values of $\theta_j = \psi_0$ and some small arbitrary number, $m$, of values adjacent to $\psi_0$ need be calculated.

In practice the value of $\phi(x, y)$ is used as a pointer to the appropriate starting value in a $1 \times T$ look-up table whose elements are the $T$ equidistant values on a cosine curve, see Fig 3

The value of $\psi_0$ provides the index of the appropriate look-up value of $\theta$ in the $1 \times T$ vector whose first element is $\theta_\phi$ and whose last element is the $(\theta_{\phi-1})$ element of the vector shown in Fig 3 , see Fig 4 , where the labels of the elements remain as shown in Fig 3

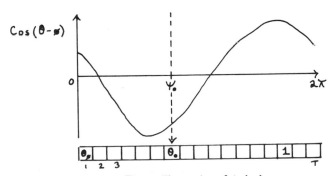

Fig. 4 Illustration of $\psi_0$ look-up

The range of $j$ in equation (3) is therefore reduced from $[1, T]$ to $[j_{\psi_0} - 2m, j_{\psi_0} + m]$; where $m$ is chosen to be appropriate to the error inherent in the edge detection process used to approximate $\psi_0$.

3. The ranges of values of the amplitude, $A(x, y)$, and the cosine term, $C(\psi_0, \phi) = \cos(\psi_0 - \phi)$, in equation (3) are finite and they may also be precalculated and stored in a look-up table indexed by $A(x, y)$ and the function $C(\psi_0, \phi)$.

Thus the computation of the transformation may be accomplished using only look-up tables and determining only those values of $p_j$ known to contribute to significant peaks in the transform space.

The algorithm can be further optimized using a multi-tasking procedure to execute look-up operations efficiently. A data flow diagram is shown in Fig 5. Once the $(x_i, y_i, \psi_i)$ data are available, only one look-up cycle is required to return the values corresponding to $\phi(x, y)$ and $A(x, y)$; $C(\psi_0, \phi)$ may then be accessed followed by $A(x, y)C(\psi_0, \phi)$. A reduction in computation time may therefore be achieved.

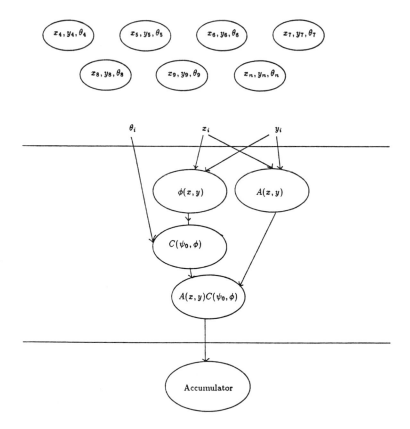

Fig. 5 Data flow diagram

| Equation 2 | Equation 4 | Efficient Transform |
|---|---|---|
| $x \cos \theta$ | $x^2$ | $A(x, y)$ and $\phi(x, y)$ |
| $y \sin \theta$ | $y^2$ | $\psi_0(\phi(x, y))$ |
| $x \cos \theta + y \sin \theta$ | $x^2 + y^2$ | $A(x, y)\psi_0(\phi(x, y))$ |
| | $(x^2 + y^2)^{\frac{1}{2}}$ | |
| | $A(x, y) \cos(\theta_j - \phi(x, y))$ | |
| Operations $3Tn$ | $n(T + 6)$ | $n(3 + 2m)$ |
| Time $1.2s$ | $114ms$ | $8.8ms$ |

Fig. 6 Comparison of Algorithms

## 5 . Comparison of Algorithms

Fig 6 is a table which compares a standard algorithm based on equation 2 with an algorithm based on equation 4 (without the use of look-up tables) and the final comparison is with the efficient algorithm. The following assumptions have been made in compiling the table:

1 A list of $n$ feature points is available, i.e. that the image has already been scanned for feature points.

2 . The processors are configured such that the operations of addition, multiplication and look-up may be performed in one machine cycle. The square-rooting operation is assumed to take two machine cycles.

3 . The clock is $10MHz$.

5 . A parameter space size of $T = 512$ is used.

6 . The number of feature points is $n = 8000$.

7 . A value of $m = 4$ is appropriate.

8 . No special architecture is assumed for the transform accumulator, i.e. two machine cycles are needed per feature point to fetch an address and to increment the contents of that address. The following calculation implies a lower time limit of $0.8ms$ irrespective of the number of processors involved in the parallel implementation of the transform.

$$Lower\ time\ limit = number\ of\ feature\ points \times 2\ clock\ cycles$$
$$= 0.8ms$$

(5)

Sequential access to the transform accumulator need not however be a holding factor as the accumulator may be structured to receive information in parallel.

Based on the preceding simplification, it can be seen that the efficient, multi-tasked algorithm is faster than the first comparison by a factor of 136 and faster than the second comparison by a factor of 47 even though the efficient implementation would require no particular hardware and may be implemented sequentially.

Implementing all three algorithms on a Microvax-II, using $T = 256$ and $m = 4$, produced corresponding ratios between timings of 71 : 31 : 1. The average timing for the efficient algorithm was $80ms$ and was achieved by starting the timing $after$ all relevant data had been paged into physical memory.

The order of the data triplets used in the transformation is not significant and hence it is possible to have a scheduler which assigns the data to slave processors. In this instance, for a number of processing elements, $P_n = 10$, the implementation would approach the assumed lower limit of the system of $0.8ms$.

## 6 . Space Saving Strategies

Where computer memory is at a premium it is possible to optimize the storage requirements of the algorithm. The correct choice of image coordinate system and attention paid to the symmetries inherent in the look-up values will significantly reduce the memory requirements of the look-up tables. It should be remembered however, that there will be a penalty in the look-up speed as sign-checks etc. must be made.

### 1 . Choice of co-ordinate sytem

For a square digital image space having $N \times N$ pixels; each pixel may be considered as a 'point', $(x_i, y_i)$, in image space, where $(x_i, y_i)$ can be considered as an address in a two dimensional array whose contents are the binary edge image. The values of $x$ and $y$ will therefore be integral.

If the origin of the image coordinate system is chosen to be a pixel located centrally in the image then the range of values of $x$ and $y$ may be limited to $[-N/2, (N/2) - 1]$. For example, a $512 \times 512$ image may be considered to be addressed from $-256$ to $255$ in each dimension. These limits are chosen to correspond with the 2's complement number system usually implemented in computer arithmetic units.

If a $T \times T$ accumulator array is used to store the results of the transformation, and it is assumed that no significant number of image points will be located further than a radial distance $N/2$ from the origin of the image coordinate system, then there need be no non-integral scaling factor involved in the quantization of the $p_j$ in discrete transform space.

$T$ is chosen to reflect the resolution required from the transformation with respect to the image space dimensions. In the present work a one to one mapping of $p$ is achieved using a value of $T = N$.

### 2 . Attention to Symmetry

When considering the look-up tables of $A(x, y)$ and $\phi(x, y)$, an eightfold saving in storage space may be achieved using the fact that

$$A(x_i, y_i) = A(x_j, y_j) \tag{6}$$

when $|x_i| = |y_j|$ and $|y_i| = |x_j|$. For example, the points:

$$(1, 127), (127, 1), (-1, -127), (-127, -1), (-1, 127), (-127, 1), (1, -127), (127, -1)$$

will each have the same value of $A(x, y)$. It is therefore only necessary to store $\left[(T/2)^2\right]/2$ values of $A(x, y)$.

A similar saving in computer memory space may be achieved when considering the $\phi(x, y)$ where:

$$\phi(x, y) = \tan^{-1}\left(\frac{y}{x}\right)$$

The range of $\theta$ in equation (3) is $[0, \pi]$ and for an $T \times T$ transform space accumulator, the step size of $\theta$, $\delta\theta$, is $\pi/T$. For $x, y$ in the range $[-N/2, N/2 - 1]$, the range of $\tan^{-1}\left(\frac{y}{x}\right)$ will be symmetric which requires that only the magnitude of the quantity be stored in a look-up table indexed by $x$ and $y$. The result may be signed according to which quadrant of the image space the $x$ and $y$ values belong. Hence only $\left[(T/2)^2\right]/2$ values of $\phi(x, y)$ need be stored.

The $A(x, y)C(\psi_0, \phi)$ look-up table may be reduced using the fact that the cosine curve is symmetric about the value of $\pi$ and a further symmetry exists about the point $\pi/2$ therefore only the values of $C(\psi_0, \phi)$ in the range $[0, \pi/2]$ need be stored.

### 7 . Suitable Architectures.

The data flow diagram shown in Fig.5 illustrates the potential to execute the Radon transform in parallel. The processing may be divided into three separate stages:

1 . The image is scanned for edge points. This may be done in parallel as each feature point is independent of any other feature point and no intercommunication is required between the processing units.

2 . A sequence of look-ups is performed using the data made available by the feature points in the image array.

3 . The result of performing the sequence of look-ups, an address in the accumulator, is used to increment the contents of that address by 1.

It is at stage 3. that the process becomes communication resource bound. It should be remembered however that not all processors will be active at a given time and if they act asynchronously will not all require access to the accumulator simultaneously. It is possible to avoid the implied bottleneck in processing if buffers of a size appropriate to the number of processors are used. If no special architecture is assumed for the accumulator the process may run at a rate determined principally by the number of feature points. Fig 7 shows a suitable parallel architecture. Four processors are shown but any number may be used with buffers of an appropriate size. In this instance an upper limit on the number of parallel processors needed to optimize the computation is set by the sequential access to the transform accumulator.

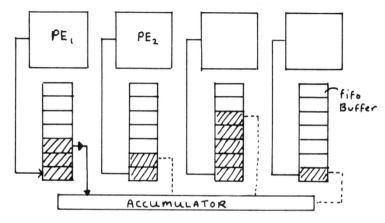

Fig. 7 Suitable architecture

## 8 . Conclusions

A new algorithm has been detailed whereby the discrete Radon transform of a digital image may be efficiently computed.

Multi-tasking and asynchronous parallel processing are suggested as being appropriate to the fast execution of the transform.

A suitable architecture for a parallel implementation is proposed. Such an architecture is attractive because no particular distribution of the image space amongst the parallel processors is required. The system may therefore be implemented on existing parallel architectures where the the image space has been distributed in such a way as to optimize processes such as convolution.

## Acknowledgements

I would like to acknowledge the National Physical Laboratory for the financial support of this project and to thank Dr. A. P. Plummer of that institution for the practical help and guidance he has given me.

I also wish to thank my supervisor, Professor R. Burge of the King's College Physics Department for his helpful suggestions. Most especially I would like to thank Nigel Arnot, our systems manager, without whose help this work would not have been completed.

## References

1 . **Radon J.** Uber die Bestimmung von Funktionen durch ihre Integralwerte langs gewisser Mannigfaltigkeiten. Berichte Sachsische Akademie der Wissenschaften Leipzig, Math-Phys Kl., 69, 262-267 , 1917.

2 . **Hough P.V.C.** Method and means for recognising complex patterns. U.S. Patent No. 3069654, 1962

3 . **Deans S.R.** Applications of the Radon transform Wiley Interscience Publications, New York, 1983]

4 . **Deans S.R.**, Hough transform from the Radon transform. IEEE Trans. Pattern Analysis and Machine Intelligence. Vol. PAMI-3, No., March 1981.

5 . **Illingworth J. and Kittler J.** A survey of efficient Hough Transform methods. Alvey Vision Club Meeting, Cambridge 1987

6 . **Ballard D.H.**, Generalizing the Hough Transform to detect arbitrary shapes. Pattern recognition, 13, 111-122, 1981.

7 . **Leavers V.F.** To be submitted as part of a PhD Thesis, London University 1987.

8 . **Gel'fand I.M., Graev M.I. and Vilenkin N. Ya.** Generalized functions, Vol 5, Academic Press, New York, 1966.

9 . **Leavers V.F. and Miller G.F.** The Radon Transformation of $\delta$-function curves. A Geometric Approach. Alvey Vision Club Meeting, Cambridge 1987.

1 0. **Kimme C., Ballard D.H. and Slansky J.**, Finding circles by an array of accumulators. Comm. of ACM. 18, 1975.

# MINERAL CLEAVAGE ANALYSIS VIA THE HOUGH TRANSFORM

R.C.Thomson and E.Sokolowska

Department of Computer Science and Applied Mathematics

Aston University, Birmingham  B4 7ET

## Abstract

The development of an image processing scheme for the analysis of cleavage cracks in minerals is described.  The scheme is designed for use on digitised rock thin section micrographs.  The cracks in a crystal image are isolated, and thresholded to create a binary image.  The Hough transform is used to detect the presence of alignments in these data.  Alignments create maxima in the transform space which are detected via the maxima in a one dimensional distribution.  This distribution is formed by first convolving the transform space with a shaping filter then taking a projection.  The cleavage orientations may be deduced from the transform, but the endpoints of the cleavage cracks cannot be similarly determined.  Instead, the extent of each cleavage present is deduced from the results of filtering the data with median operators oriented at the measured angles.  This produces useful estimates of each cleavage which will serve as the basis for further analysis.  The techniques presented may be of use in other applications areas which require the analysis of families of parallel alignments.

## Introduction

As part of a broader  study of applications of computers in geology at Aston University,  the use of image processing methods in petrography is being investigated.  Most minerals become translucent when ground down into a sufficiently thin slice.  This fact permits the microscopic study of wafers of rocks using transmitted light.  Optical microscopy using polarised light is the foundation of detailed petrographic and petrological study.  We are investigating the feasibility of automating some simple petrographic tasks through the introduction of image processing techniques in the examination of thin section micrographs.

There have been many encounters between image processing and petrography: [5], [6], [10], [16] are some key references.  However, many basic problems have yet to be solved.  The fundamental problem of delineating a mineral grain is not at all straightforward because anisotropic minerals may have different properties, such as colour, in different positions in polarised light.  Here, however, we consider another important attribute of a mineral grain - its cleavage.

The natural planes of weakness in the mineral, intersecting with the plane of the section, give rise to a texture of fine, impersistent, parallel cracks.  This is how the mineral cleavage is realised in thin sections.  There may be several sets of cleavage cracks visible in a mineral section, but usually only one or two, or none at all. The number of cleavage sets and their angular relation are very important diagnostic features. For example, figure 1 shows a section of a hornblende crystal, with its characteristic double cleavage.

When analysing a grain such as this we would like to know if the surface irregularities and cracks seen are random, or if they constitute a cleavage. The desired end product is a partition of the cracks into N+1 classes: cleavage1.... cleavageN, and non-cleavage features. For each cleavage we would like a qualitative description of its development, eg weakly or strongly developed, and its direction.

This paper is in part a case study which traces the evolution of a processing scheme designed to achieve these ends. The work is not yet complete, but existing techniques have been combined to create a novel processing scheme which takes us close to a solution, and the direction of future work is indicated.


## Data Preparation

The data shown in figure 1 was used for these investigations. This image was digitised to 256 intensity levels and stored as an array of 256 X 240 pixels. The cracks and irregularities which are our object of study were isolated by a processing sequence involving the use of a two dimensional median operator. A new image was created by replacing each pixel value by the median value found in a neighbourhood of pixels. This smoothed the image very effectively by ignoring the cracks and irregularities. The smoothed image was thresholded, connected components were found, and their outlines smoothed in a manner similar to that described by Ohlander et al. [13]. This created a mask with which the crystal of interest was isolated. A difference image was then formed by subtracting the smoothed values from the original. Thresholding the difference image eliminated the small irregularities and produced a binary image of the crack network. Finally, a standard thinning operation produced the crack image of figure 2a, from which crack orientations could be established.

At this stage an estimate of the 'edge density' should be made. Further segmentation of the image on the basis of this measurement may be indicated. This problem is under investigation and is only dealt with briefly here. Approaches to this segmentation problem are found in the work of Ohlander et al [13] and Nagao and Matsuyama [11], for example. Promising results have been obtained from a modification of Perkins's scheme for area segmentation of images using edge points [14]. An additional step has been introduced into the algorithm in order to recognise the jigsaw mosaics of small regions which the scheme generates when applied to data such as figure 2a.

One must be prepared for cracks images, such as figure 2a, to have more than one cleavage direction present. For example, there may be two sets of nearly parallel line segments or strokes, and they can be expected to intersect, as in this case. The presence of intersecting strokes biases a local edge detector such as the Sobel or Prewitt operator, and as our images contain many intersections this makes the measurement of stroke orientation by such local operators too unreliable to serve as a basis for segmentation via the selection of modes in a histogram of directions. A more global approach seemed appropriate, and the Hough transform ([2]) seemed a suitable technique to investigate.

## The Hough transform for line detection

In order to apply the Hough transform to the task of detecting line segments a suitable parametrisation must be found. Any line may be uniquely identified by two parameters. The familiar gradient and intercept parametrisation of the standard expression $y=mx+c$ is not convenient since gradient m and intercept c are both unbounded. Duda and Hart [2] championed the r,$\varphi$ parametrisation which is now standard: $r=x\cos\varphi+y\sin\varphi$, where r is the line's distance from the origin and $\varphi$ is the slope of the perpendicular from the origin to the line.

Thus a two dimensional parameter space $(\varphi,r)$ is created. This may be partitioned into a set of 'pigeonholes', so forming the accumulator array for the transform procedure. The creation of the Hough transform may then be viewed as a voting process where each point in the input picture votes for all the lines to which it could possibly belong, and the corresponding entries in the accumulator array are incremented. Because of the parametrisation chosen, the pigeonholes receiving a point's votes will lie along a sinusoidal curve in the parameter (Hough) space. Since all the points on a line yield the same parameters, say r1 and $\varphi$1, all the sinusoids generated for that line intersect in Hough space at this single point $(\varphi 1,r1)$, and each sinusoid increments it. This should produce a local maximum in Hough space, signalling the presence of the line in the input picture and describing its exact position.

The Hough transform is commonly implemented for binary images by scanning through the input data, and for each (non-zero) point in the image, stepping through $\varphi$ values in discrete steps, finding the corresponding r value from the parametrisation equation, and incrementing the appropriate array entry. The Hough transform may also be viewed as a process where, for each point in parameter space, the corresponding line in the input picture is identified, all values lying along that line are summed, and this sum is placed in the accumulator at the appropriate pigeonhole. In the continuous case these two processes would be equivalent. In the discrete case the former method is to be preferred for accuracy and efficiency, but the alternative viewpoint is nevertheless useful when interpreting the transform results.

## Interpreting the Hough transform

The local maxima in Hough transform space should correspond to alignments of points in the original image space. The r and $\varphi$ coordinates of the peak identify the line, but further processing will be required in order to locate the endpoints of the line segment(s) which created the peak. Some form of two-dimensional clustering technique is sometimes used to find the peaks in Hough space. Dudani and Luk [3] used a computationally simpler two-stage method using projections which may usefully be outlined here. First the accumulator values were projected on to the $\varphi$ axis. This distribution was smoothed with a running mean operator and the local minima selected. These points defined a partition of the Hough space into parallel sided corridors which were in turn projected on to the r axis. These distributions were then smoothed and local minima found. This resulted in a partition of the transform space into rectangles each containing a peak.

Figure 2b shows synthetic data created for test purposes which has been masked off to match the real crystal outlines. Figure 3b shows the results of applying the Hough transform to this data, with higher

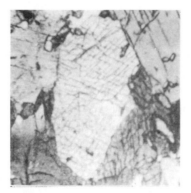

Figure 1

Figure 2a

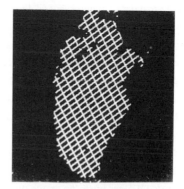

Figure 2b

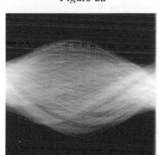

Figure 3a

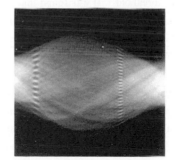

Figure 3b

Figure 4a

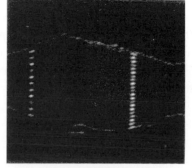

Figure 4b

values shown by the brighter grey tones. The two sets of parallel lines in the input data are revealed by the two sets of peaks lying along lines of constant φ in transform space. Figure 3a shows the Hough transform of the real data set (figure 2a). Notice that in both transforms there are regions of high values for φ values near 0 and 180 degrees - ie for near vertical lines. This effect is due to the elongated shape of the input picture. Viewing the transform as summing along lines in the picture space, it is evident that for our data nearly vertical lines are longer, contain more points, and so produce higher values in the parameter space. Maxima like these hamper the detection of 'valid' peaks in transform space.

The maxima in Hough space corresponding to straight line segments have a characteristic 'butterfly' shape, as can be observed in figure 3b. Leavers and Boyce [9] exploit this feature by convolving the Hough space with a filter designed to focus the butterfly shape into a sharper peak which is more easily identified. Applying this convolution greatly improved the definition of the maxima, both for the synthetic test data and the real data. Figures 4a and 4b show the results of the convolution for the data of figures 3a and 3b respectively.

The next step was to locate these maxima accurately. First tests were made using the convolved synthetic data Hough transform of figure 4b. The maxima were well defined, and nearly all peaks could be found correctly by simply thresholding and finding the centre of each isolated component. (It was envisaged that more sophisticated methods would be necessary to deal with less idealised data) Line segments in the image associated with each peak found in the transform space now had to be identified, at the same time rejecting the points which seemed to be more closely associated with other alignments.

Each peak location defined a line in the original picture, and a tracking process was initiated which searched along this line and endeavoured to find the pixels which had created the peak. With the aim of rejecting points from other lines, the search procedure looked for continuous sequences of 1s with lengths above a given threshold. It was found that the search corridor had to be extremely narrow, otherwise pixels from other lines fell into the tracking corridor and invalidated the search procedure. This indicated that the level of accuracy in the peak determination and location stages necessary for a successful search using this method could not be achieved with real, non-idealised data. In more than one sense, attempts to track individual lines at such close spacings were misguided.

The directions of the cleavages could, however, be estimated from the Hough transform data. The near parallel alignments constituting the mineral cleavage cracks are represented in transform space by a family of peaks with φ coordinate values clustered around the φ value corresponding to the cleavage orientation. The smoothed distribution of the accumulator values projected on to the φ axis, described above as the first stage of the Dudani and Luk method, may therefore be expected to show a strong peak marking each cleavage direction. Before taking the projection, however, it proved necessary to convolve the transform space with the butterfly filter, to reduce the distorting effects of the spurious maxima in the data, described above. Figure 5a shows the projection on to the φ axis of the unmodified Hough transform of figure 3a. Figure 5b shows the projection of the transform space after convolution with the butterfly filter (figure 4a). Two strong peaks in the distribution are now easily recognised, identifying the cleavage directions.

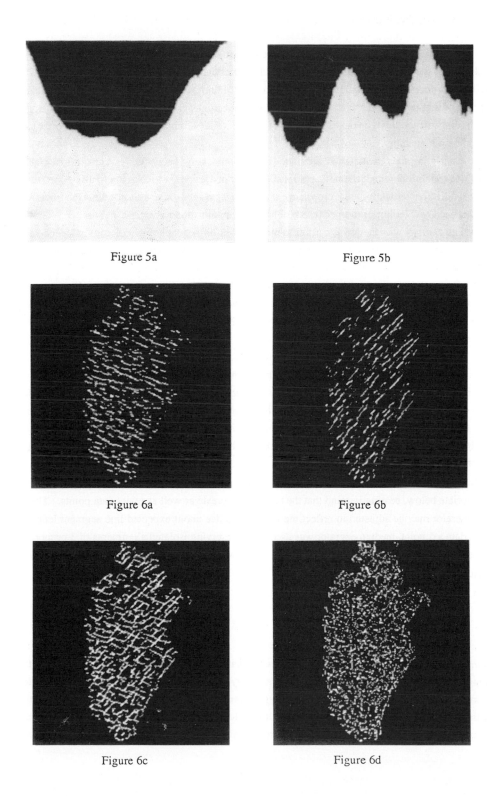

Figure 5a

Figure 5b

Figure 6a

Figure 6b

Figure 6c

Figure 6d

<u>Separating the cleavages</u>

On re-examination of the crack image the task of separating the two cleavage sets was seen to be analagous to the task of separating the wavefields in vertical seismic profiles (VSPs). The VSP is a well established geophysical technique for the generation of high resolution seismic reflection images in the vicinity of a borehole. Hardage [8] is a useful reference. A feature of the VSP is that the upgoing and downgoing wavefields appear as two sets of near-parallel alignments with different orientations, so providing our analogy.

Translating the relevant VSP techniques into a processing sequence for our original cracks image gave rise to the following scheme: apply a shearing transformation to the data to align one set of cracks horizontally (or vertically, as appropriate), apply a simple median operator - described below - across (down) each row (column) to reject rival, oblique alignments, then reverse the shear. The term 'shear' is used in an analogy with the physics usage to mean the shifting of each row (column) independently, in this case in order to bring some non vertical (non-horizontal) feature in the image into a true vertical (horizontal) alignment.

Clearly there is no need to physically shift the data up and down since the median operator can be applied along a set of zigzag paths through the data which are least error approximations to the oblique paths. Such paths may be chain encoded (Freeman [7]) , and Ehrich [4] describes a scheme for directional averaging which employs such paths.

The operation of taking the median in a window of values can be greatly simplified for binary data. It is only necessary to find the sum over the window and check that it exceeds half the window length; the sum itself can be efficiently maintained as the operator moves through the data by a simple 'add a term, drop a term' method. The median can be further generalised by varying the threshold value for the sum over the window. In this way we reach a one dimensional form of the smoothing operation described by Ohlander et al. [13]. Another variation available for binary data is a 'run length filter', mentioned above, which screens out points which are not part of a sequence of 1s reaching some specified length. Because of the variations possible we may use the looser term 'selection operator' in place of 'median', where appropriate below, bearing in mind that the median can create as well as reject data points. The length of this operator may be adjusted to reflect the user's prejudice about expected line segment lengths. With these data a 5 point median operator was used, thus preserving isolated alignments of 3 or more collinear points. Longer operators may be used in order to limit the influence of rival, oblique alignments, i.e. to reduce spatial aliasing.

<u>Results and discussion</u>

The two dominant cleavage alignment directions in the real data were found from the projection of the Hough transform convolved with the Leaver and Boyce butterfly filter (figure 5b) and a simple median operator was applied to the original cracks image at these two angles. Figures 6a and 6b show the results of the two passes; figure 6c shows the result of a logical OR operation applied to these two images. Comparing this image with the original (figure2a), this simple process can be seen to have analysed the data effectively. Figure 6d shows the result of subtracting the data of figure 6c from the original data of figure 2a. One may consider figures 6c and 6d as estimates of the signal and the noise respectively.

The noise image may be analysed to see if it reveals any further structure. This has not been undertaken, but a visual inspection identifies the single near vertical alignment close to the centre of the image which resulted from a strong (non-cleavage) crack in the mineral grain.

The oblique median processing took under 2 seconds for this image (on an HLH Orion 1/05 mini-computer). The times for thinning, Hough transform and the convolution of transform space were respectively 5, 19 and 3 seconds.

We may observe that the processing route followed suggests a conceptually simple and useful modification to the Hough transform as described above. We can reduce the biasing inherent in the transform by restricting the set of lines for which each point in the input image votes:- a point should not vote for a line if a selection operator (such as the median) for that line, applied at the point, rejects the point. The proposed modification has not yet been implemented. Early tests have shown that elongated or irregular pictures such as the synthetic test data set will still lead to spurious maxima in transform space. Such attempts to restrict the voting range of image points are not new. Brown [1] considers the problem in depth. O'Gorman and Clowes [12] and Perkins and Binford [15] used local edge direction information since this defines the $\phi$ value closely, permitting solution of the parametrisation equation, and only a handful of votes need be made by each point. (Inaccuracies in the local direction determinations, described above, made this method unworkable with our data.)

The scheme presented here does not yet provide a complete solution to the problem as outlined in the introduction. So far, we have made estimates of each cleavage present. This does not give a partition of the cracks in the strict mathematical sense of a family of disjoint sets, since the two estimates have points in common, but what we have is appropriate to the true situation. It is anticipated that a qualitative description of the cleavage development may be derived by analysing the results of applying sequences of selection operators to the data. The information derived may also serve as input to a further segmentation analysis, since it should be possible to recognise areas with different cleavage characteristics.

Elements of the novel processing route detailed above may be of interest to image processing researchers in other applications areas which require the analysis of families of parallel alignments.

Acknowledgment

Figure 1 is reproduced with permission from "An Introduction to the Practical Study of Crystals, Minerals and Rocks" by K. Cox, N. Price and B. Harte, published by McGraw-Hill Book Company (UK) limited 1967.

References

[1]   Brown, C.M.   Inherent bias and noise in the Hough transform.  IEEE Trans. Pattern Anal. Mach.
      Intell., **PAMI-5**, 493-505, Sept 1983.

[2]     Duda, R.O. and Hart, P.E.   Use of the Hough transform to detect lines and curves in pictures. Commun. ACM, **15**, 11-15, Jan 1972.

[3]     Dudani, S.A. and Luk, A.L.   Locating straight line edge segments in outdoor scenes.   Pattern Recognition, **10**, 145-157, 1978.

[4]     Ehrich, R.W.   Detection of global edges in textured images.   IEEE Trans. Comput., **C-26**, 589-603, June 1977.

[5]     Ehrlich, R., Kennedy, S.K., Crabtree, S.J. and Cannon, R.L.   Petrographic image analysis, I. Analysis of reservoir pore complexes.   J. Sediment. Petrol., **54**, 1365-1378, Dec 1984.

[6]     Fabbri, A.G.   Image Processing of Geological Data, Van Nostrand, New York, 1984.

[7]     Freeman, H.   Boundary encoding and processing, in Picture Processing and Psychopictorics, 381-393, (B.S.Lipkin and A.Rosenfeld, Eds.), Academic Press, New York, 1970.

[8]     Hardage, B.A.   Principles of Vertical Seismic Profiling, Geophysical Press, Amsterdam, 1983

[9]     Leavers, V.F. and Boyce, J.F.   The Radon transform and its application to shape parametrization in machine vision.   Image andVision Computing, **5**, 161-166, May 1987.

[10]    Montoto, M., Bel-Lan, A. and Montoto, L.   Microscopic quantification of textures and fissures in rocks by digital image processing.   Proc. 3rd Int. Cong. Int. Assoc. Eng. Geol., Sec.II, Vol 2, 51-60, (Servicio Geologica de O.P., Madrid), 1978.

[11]    Nagao, M. and Matsuyama, T.   A structural analysis of complex aerial photographs, Plenum Press, New York, 1980.

[12]    O'Gorman, F. and Clowes, M.B.   Finding picture edges through collinearity of feature points. IEEE Trans. Comput., **C-25**, 449-456, Apr 1976.

[13]    Ohlander, R., Price, K. and Reddy, D.R.   Picture segmentation using a recursive splitting method.   Comput. Graphics Image Process., **8**, 313-333, 1978.

[14]    Perkins, W.A.   Area segmentation of images using edge points,   IEEE Trans. Pattern Anal. Mach. Intell., **PAMI-2**, 8-15, Jan 1980.

[15]    Perkins, W.A. and Binford, T.O.   A corner finder for visual feedback.   Comput. Graphics Image Process., **2**, 355-376, Dec 1973.

[16]    Pong, T-C., Haralick, R.M., Craig, J.R., Yoon, R-H. and Chin, W-Z.   The application of image analysis techniques to mineral processing.   Pattern Recognition Lett., **2**, 117-123, Dec 1983.

# ABOUT MOMENT NORMALIZATION AND COMPLEX MOMENT DESCRIPTORS

A. Abo-Zaid, O.R. Hinton, E. Horne

Electronic Engineering Labs.,
University of Kent,
Canterbury, Kent.

## 1. INTRODUCTION

Moments are one of the most useful features that can be extracted from an image. They can be invariant to translation, changes in size, intensity and rotation of the object which forms the image. The low order moments of an image intensity distribution are often used to locate the image centroid and to make image size and orientation measurements. Higher order moments have been used in 2-D pattern recognition [1-4], and in 3-D object recognition schemes [5].

The versatility of moments for treating a general problem in image manipulation and analysis is becoming increasingly well known. In all cases the usefulness of the moments method stems from two factors:

i) Moments have very convenient transformation properties when the image undergoes a size change, contrast change, a translation and/or rotation in the image plane.

ii) An image has a unique approximate reconstruction in terms of a finite set of its moments.

Two ways exist to compute the moments of an image:

i) Directly via integration over the image plane in digital pattern recognition.

ii) By evaluating at the Fourier plane origin derivatives of the FT in optical pattern recognition, where the image is present on a film. For real-time image analysis this method requires the use of a spatial light modulator with a rapid cycle time.

There are many forms of moment invariants; ordinary and Hu moments [4,7], radial and angular moments [6], Zernik moments [4,8], Upsilon invariants [9], and complex moments [10, 12].

Section 2 of this paper deals with the normalization of ordinary moments, while Section 3 gives an approach to the "complex moments descriptor" which provides a complete set of invariants without any additional transformation.

## 2. ORDINARY AND Hu MOMENTS NORMALIZATION

Given an image characterized by an interior intensity function $f(x,y)$ in the 2-D plane, the moment of order $(p,q)$ is defined as:

$$M_{pq} = \int_{-\infty}^{\infty}\int_{-\infty}^{\infty} x^p y^q\ f(x,y)\ dxdy \qquad (2.1)$$

there are theorems which guarantee the existence and uniqueness of $M_{pq}$ provided that $f(x,y)$ has a finite value. The range invariant moment is given by the central moment $\mu_{pq}$:

$$\mu_{pq} = \int_{-\infty}^{\infty}\int_{-\infty}^{\infty} (x-\bar{x})(y-\bar{y})\ f(x,y)\ dxdy \tag{2.2}$$

where $\bar{x},\bar{y}$ are the center of the image:

$$\bar{x} = \frac{M_{10}}{M_{00}}\ ,\ \ \bar{y} = \frac{M_{01}}{M_{00}}\ ,\ \ \ \mu_{00} = M_{00}$$

A previous method for normalization of moments with regard to change in size involves the normalization of $\mu_{pq}$ by $\mu_{00}$ to produce the central normalized moment $\eta_{pq}$:

$$\eta_{pq} = \frac{\mu_{pq}}{\mu_{00}^{\frac{p+q+2}{2}}} \tag{2.3}$$

The normalized central moment $\eta_{pq}$ may be used to cancel the effect of rotation using the relation [4]:

$$n'_{pq} = \sum_{r}^{p}\sum_{s}^{q} (-1)^{q-s}\ \binom{p}{r}\binom{q}{s}\ (\cos\theta)^{p+s-r}(\sin\theta)^{q-s+r}\ \eta_{p+q-r-s,r+s} \tag{2.4}$$

where:

$$\tan2\theta = \frac{2\mu_{11}}{\mu_{20}-\mu_{02}}\ ,\ \text{choose } \theta \text{ such that } \mu_{20} < \mu_{02} \text{ and } \mu_{30} > 0$$

Alternatively Hu vectors can be calculated from the normalized central moments as follows:

$$\phi_1 = \eta_{20} + \eta_{02}$$
$$\phi_2 = (\eta_{20} - \eta_{02})^2 + 4\eta_{11}^2$$
$$\phi_3 = (\eta_{30} - \eta_{12})^2 + (3\eta_{21} + \eta_{03})^2$$
$$\phi_4 = (\eta_{30} + \eta_{12})^2 + (\eta_{21} + \eta_{03})^2$$
$$\phi_5 = (\eta_{30} - 3\eta_{12})(\eta_{30} + \eta_{12})\ [(\eta_{30} + \eta_{12})^2 - 3\ (\eta_{21} + \eta_{03})^2]$$
$$\quad + (3\eta_{21} - \eta_{03})(\eta_{21} + \eta_{03})\ [3(\eta_{30} + \eta_{12})^2 - (\eta_{21} + \eta_{03})^2]$$
$$\phi_6 = (\eta_{20} - \eta_{02})\ [(\eta_{30} + \eta_{12})^2 - (\eta_{21} + \eta_{03})^2]$$
$$\quad + 4\eta_{11}(\eta_{30} + \eta_{12})(\eta_{21} + \eta_{03})$$
$$\phi_7 = (3\eta_{12} - \eta_{30})(\eta_{30} + \eta_{12})\ [(\eta_{30} + \eta_{12})^2 - 3\ (\eta_{21} + \eta_{03})^2]$$
$$\quad + (3\eta_{21} - \eta_{03})(\eta_{21} + \eta_{03})\ [3(\eta_{30} + \eta_{12})^2 - (\eta_{21} + \eta_{03})^2]$$

$$\tag{2.5}$$

the above vector is invariant under image rotation. Due to the term $\mu_{00}^{\frac{p+q+2}{2}}$ the dynamic range of $\eta_{pq}$ as well as the Hu vector is large. For this reason it is generally represented on a logarithmic scale. However, use of a logarithmic scale destroys the sign of the moments.

A further factor that is ignored in the normalization is the sensitivity to change in contrast between two images i.e. the more general invariants of two images $f_1(x,y)$ and $f_2(\bar{x},\bar{y})$ should remain unchanged under the following transformation:

$$f_1(x,y) = kf_2(\hat{x},\hat{y}) \; ,$$

$$\begin{bmatrix} \hat{x} \\ \hat{y} \end{bmatrix} = c \begin{bmatrix} \cos\theta & \sin\theta \\ -\sin\theta & \cos\theta \end{bmatrix} \begin{bmatrix} x \\ y \end{bmatrix} + \begin{bmatrix} a \\ b \end{bmatrix} \tag{2.6}$$

where:

$\theta$     arbitrary rotation

$(a,b)$     object translation

$k$     change on image contrast

$c$     an arbitrary scale factor

Maitra [11] suggested the use of an alternative set (instead of Hu vector) $\beta_1,\ldots,\beta_6$ to replace the Hu vector such that:

$$\beta_1 = \frac{\sqrt{\phi_1}}{\phi_1} \qquad \beta_2 = \frac{\phi_3}{\phi_2} \cdot \frac{\mu_{00}}{\phi_1}$$

$$\beta_3 = \frac{\phi_4}{\phi_3} \qquad \beta_4 = \frac{\sqrt{\phi_5}}{\phi_4} \tag{2.7}$$

$$\beta_5 = \frac{\phi_6}{\phi_4} \qquad \beta_6 = \frac{\phi_7}{\phi_5}$$

without applying the normalization (2.3). However, change in size, $c$, has the effect:

$$\mu'_{pq} = \mu_{pq} \cdot c^{p+q+2/2}$$

which is dependent on the order of the moments, while change in contrast, $k$, has the effect:

$$\mu''_{pq} = \mu_{pq} \cdot k$$

which is independent of the order of the moment $\mu_{p,q}$. Since $(\mu_{20}+\mu_{20})$ is independent of rotation, we can use both $\mu_{00}$ and $(\mu_{20} + \mu_{02})$ to cancel both contrast and size changes, i.e. from the central moment $\mu_{pq}$ find the normalized central moment $\eta_{pq}$:

$$= \frac{\mu_{pq}}{\mu_{00}} \cdot \left(\frac{\mu_{00}}{\mu_{20}+\mu_{20}}\right)^{\frac{p+q}{2}} \tag{2.8}$$

The normalized central moments of (2.8) are not only invariant to size and contrast, but also have a decreased dynamic range due to the term:

$$\frac{1}{\mu_{00}} \left(\frac{\mu_{00}}{\mu_{02}+\mu_{20}}\right)^{\frac{p+q}{2}} \quad \text{instead of} \quad \frac{1}{\mu_{00}^{\frac{p+q+2}{2}}}$$

In consequence a logarithmic transformation is no longer required. Fig. 1 shows two simulated images 1-a, 1-b. Image 1-a is generated from 1-b by decreasing the intensity function such that:

$$\hat{f}(x,y) = \tfrac{1}{2}\, f(x,y)$$

and by quadrupling the size such that each pixel of the image 1-a is replaced by 4 pixels of intensity $\hat{f}(x,y)$. Moment normalization by the two methods is performed and the Hu vector is calculated. The results (table 1-a, 1-b) emphasize the decrease in the dynamic range and the invariance of the resulting moments using (2.8) to size and contrast variations.

The differences which are apparent arise due to quantization effects in the image 1-b.

3.   COMPLEX MOMENT DESCRIPTOR

Complex moments are a recent approach for deriving moment invariants. They form an intermediate step between ordinary moments and moment invariants.

Definition:

The complex moments of order $(p,q)$ for a two dimensional function $f(x,y)$ are given by:

$$C_{pq} = \int\!\!\int_{-\infty}^{\infty} (x+iy)^p (x-iy)^q f(x,y)\,dxdy \tag{3.1}$$

where $p,q$ are non-negative integers, $p \geq q$ and $i = \sqrt{-1}$. If $f(x,y)$ is real non-negative, the contrast of the image, $C_{pp}$ is a real non-negative number, while $C_{pq}$ is the complex conjugate of $C_{qp}$. The complex moment of order $(p,q)$ is a linear combination of the ordinary moments $M_{rs}$ with the relation:

$$r + s = p + q = m$$

In polar  coordinates the complex moment of order $(p,q)$ is:

$$C_{pq} = \int\!\!\int r^{p+q} e^{\,j(p-q)\theta} f(r,\theta)\, rdrd\theta \tag{3.2}$$

where:

$$f(r,\theta) = f(r\cos\theta, r\sin\theta) = f(x,y)$$

from (3.2) the relation between complex moments and Zernike polynomials becomes apparent [10]. It can be shown that Zernicke polynomials are obtained from the complex moment kernels: ·

$$r^{p+q} \cdot e^{i(p-q)\theta}$$

The complex moments are both very simple and quite powerful in providing analytic characterization for moments invariants. From (3.1), it is clear that when the image is rotated by angle $\theta$, the new moments may be expressed by:

$$\tilde{C}_{pq} = C_{pq} e^{i(p-q)\theta}$$

In order to normalize complex moments for the transform given in (2.6), [12], suggested the following:

1. Adjust $C_{10} = 0$, which corresponds to cancellation of translation
2. If $C_{00} = \alpha$, $C_{11} = \beta$ then k,c in (2.7) are related by:

$$c = \frac{\alpha}{\sqrt{\beta}} \left( \frac{M_{20} + M_{02}}{M_{00}} \right)^{\frac{1}{2}}$$

$$, k = (\alpha^2 / \beta) \cdot \frac{M_{20} + M_{02}}{M_{00}^2}$$

(3.3)

using these parameters to transform $f_1(x,y)$ into the normalized version $f_2(x,y)$,

$$f_2(x,y) = kf_1(x,y)$$

The value of c in (3.3) is independent of image contrast and the value of k is independent of image scale.

For rotation, cancellation can be achieved by using the relation:

$$C_{rs} \cdot C_{tu}^n + C_{sr} \cdot C_{ut}^n$$

where r,s,t,u,n, are given by the following [12]:

$$(r-s) + n (t-u) = 0$$

(3.4)

The drawbacks of this approach are:

1. Instead of normalization of a few moments, each pixel requires normalization as in (3.3).

2. The expression of (3.4), to cancel the effects of rotation is computationally expensive. Moreover, it creates dependency in complex moments.

An algorithm is proposed here which is based on the calculation of normalized central moment, given in Section 2, as the first phase and then employs the linear mapping properties for the cancellation of rotation effects in the second phase.

Given:

$$C_{pq} = \int_{-\infty}^{\infty}\int_{-\infty}^{\infty} (x+iy)^P(x-iy)^q f(x,y) \; dxdy$$

$$= \int_{-\infty}^{\infty}\int_{-\infty}^{\infty} \sum_{r=0}^{p} \binom{P}{r} x^r (iy)^{p-r} \cdot \sum_{s=0}^{q} \binom{q}{s} (-1)^{q-s} x^s (iy)^{q-s} f(x,y) dxdy \qquad (3.5)$$

(3.5) shows that the complex moment of order m is a linear combination of ordinary moments of the same order. The normalized complex moments are derived from the normalized ordinary moments:

$$C_{pq} \text{ normalized} = C_{pq}^n = \sum_{r+s=m} W_{r,s} \; \eta_{r,s}$$

where $w_{r,s}$ is a constant given by (3.5):

$$C_{pq}^n = \sum_{r+s=m} W_{r,s} \; \mu_{r,s} \cdot \frac{1}{\mu_{00}} \cdot \left(\frac{\mu_{00}}{\mu_{02}+\mu_{20}}\right)^{\frac{r+s}{2}}$$

$$= \sum_{r+s=m} W_{r,s} \; \mu_{r,s} \cdot \frac{1}{\mu_{00}} \left(\frac{\mu_{00}}{\mu_{20}+\mu_{02}}\right)^{\frac{p+q}{2}} \qquad (3.6)$$

$$= \frac{1}{\mu_{00}} \left(\frac{\mu_{00}}{\mu_{02}+\mu_{20}}\right)^{\frac{p+q}{2}} \cdot \sum_{r+s=m} W_{r,s} \; \mu_{r,s}$$

$$= NF_{p,q} \cdot C_{pq}$$

where $NF_{p,q}$ is the normalization factor given in (2.8):

$$NF_{p,q} = \frac{1}{\mu_{00}} \left(\frac{\mu_{00}}{\mu_{20}+\mu_{02}}\right)^{\frac{p+q}{2}}$$

If $C_{p,q}^c$ is the complex central moment calculated at the centroid of the image by the relation:

$$C_{10} = 0, \text{ then:}$$

$$C_{00} = \mu_{00},$$

$$NF_{p,q} = \frac{1}{C_{00}} \cdot \left(\frac{C_{00}}{C_{11}}\right)^{\frac{p+q}{2}} \qquad (3.7)$$

(3.7, 3.6) show that the normalized complex moments may be calculated as a linear combination of ordinary normalized moments. Alternatively they can be derived directly as follows:

1. Find the complex central moment $C_{pq}^c$ by moving the origin to image centroid calculated by $C_{10} = 0$

2.  Find the normalized central complex moment $C_{pq}^n$ :

$$C_{pq}^n = C_{pq}^c \cdot \left[\frac{1}{C_{00}} \cdot \left(\frac{C_{00}}{C_{11}}\right)^{\frac{p+q}{2}}\right] \tag{3.8}$$

For rotation, applying (3.4) means that we are going to higher order without any gain in information.  Moreover, (3.4) creates dependency in the complex moments.

An alternative is to take $C_{21}$ as a reference component and find the normalized central complex moment which is invariant to rotation of the object.  We have called this the "Complex Moments Descriptor".  We define the complex moments descriptor $CD_{pq}$ as:

$$\text{Let } C_{pq}^n = |C_{pq}^n| \, e^{i\phi_{pq}}$$

$$CD_{pq} = |CD_{pq}| e^{i\beta_{pq}} \qquad \text{with:} \tag{3.9}$$

$$|CD_{pq}| = |C_{pq}^n| \quad , \quad \beta_{pq} = \phi_{pq} - (p-q)\,\phi_{21}$$

Lemma:

The complex moments descriptors defined by (3.9) are invariants under size change, contrast change, translation and/or rotation.

Proof:

(1)  For translation, size, and contrast change, (3.6) provides the proof.

(2)  For rotation.

Given an image with normalized central complex moment $C_{pq}^n = |C_{pq}^n| \, e^{i\phi_{pq}}$.
The complex moment descriptor $CD_{pq}$ is:

$$CD_{pq} = |C_{pq}^n| \cdot e^{i\left[\phi_{pq} - (p-q)\phi_{21}\right]} \tag{3.10-a}$$

if the image undergoes rotation by angle $\alpha$ then the normalized central complex moment $\tilde{C}_{pq}^n$ is:

$$\tilde{C}_{pq}^n = |C_{pq}^n| \cdot e^{i\tilde{\phi}_{pq}}$$

$$= |C_{pq}^n| \cdot e^{i\left[\phi_{pq} + (p-q)\alpha\right]}$$

$$\text{and } \tilde{C}_{21}^n = |\tilde{C}_{21}^n| \, e^{i\tilde{\phi}_{21}} = |\tilde{C}_{21}^n| \cdot e^{i\left[\phi_{21} + \alpha\right]}$$

and the complex moments descriptor $\tilde{CD}_{pq}$ is:

$$\tilde{CD}_{pq} = |\tilde{C}_{pq}^n| \, e^{i\left[\tilde{\phi}_{pq} - (p-q)\tilde{\phi}_{21}\right]}$$

$$= |\grave{\tilde{c}}_{pq}^{n}| \cdot e^{i\left[\phi_{pq} + (p-q)\,\alpha - (p-q)(\phi_{21} + \alpha)\right]}$$

since $|\grave{\tilde{c}}_{pq}^{n}| = |c_{pq}^{n}|$           (3-10,b)

$$\therefore \quad \grave{CD}_{pq} = |c_{pq}^{n}| \, e^{i\left[\phi_{pq} - (p-q)\phi_{21}\right]}$$

$$= CD_{pq}$$

from (3-10,a), (3-10,b) the Lemma's proof is complete.

Another advantage of the complex moments descriptor is that normalization for rotation is independent of contrast and size change normalization. This means that normalization for rotation can be done in parallel with normalization for contrast and size changes, directly after the complex central moments calculation.

Table 2-a, 2-b shows the polar complex moments for image 1-a, and 1-b, calculated at reference axes with rotation angles 12°, 25°. Tables 3-a, 3-b show the complex moment descriptor calculated by the transform (3.9). It can be seen that it retains the same value irrespective of the angle of rotation.

## 4. CONCLUSION

A new normalization factor is given. Its application produces a normalized image with regard to intensity variations and scale changes. Further, in the same operation the dynamic range of the moment vector is reduced, such that higher order moments can be used without recourse to logarithmic representation.

The complex moments descriptors provides a complete set of invariants without any considerable calculation for rotational changes. This is achieved by using the phase of a reference component ($C_{21}$, $C_{32}$, ...) to cancel the effect of rotational angle variations by simple relation.

The simulation results presented demonstrate the efficiency of both the proposed normalization factor and the complex moment descriptor.

## REFERENCES

1. M.R. TEAGUE, "Optical Calculation of Irradiance Moments", Applied Optics, vol. 19, No. 8, 1980, pp. 1353:1356.

2. M.R. TEAGUE, "Image Analysis via the General Theory of Moments", J. opt. Soc. Am., vol. 70, no. 8, 1980, pp.920:930.

3. Y.N. HSU, "Rotation Invariant Discrimination Between Almost Similar Objects", Applied Optics, vol. 22, No. 1, 1983, pp. 130:132.

4.  P. REEVES, "Shape Analysis of Segmented Objects Using Moments", Proceeding IEEE Computer Society Conf. on Pattern Recognition and Image Processing, August 1981, pp. 171:176.

5.  S.A. DUDANI & GHEE, "Aircraft Identification by Moment Invariant", IEEE, T. Computer, C-26, 1977, pp. 39:45.

6.  S.S. REDDI, "Radial and Angular Moment Invariant for Image Identification", IEEE, PAMI-3, No. 2, 1981, pp. 240:242.

7.  C. TEH, "On Digital Approximation of Moments Invariants", Computer Graphics and Image Processing, 33, 1986, pp. 318:326.

8.  HOSSACK, "Moment Invariant for Pattern Recognition", Pattern Recognition Letters, 1, 1983, pp. 451:456.

9.  N. DROVNYCHENKO, "Upsilon Invariants: A Uniform Set of Moment Invariants", SPIE, vol. 504, 1984, pp. 40:44.

10. ABO-MOSTFA, "Recognitive Aspects of Moments Invariants", IEEE, PAMI-6, No. 6, 1984, pp. 698:706.

11. S. MAITRA, "Moment Invariants", Proceeding of IEEE, vol. 67, No. 4, 1979, pp. 697:699.

12. ABO-MOSTFA, "Image Normalization by Complex Moments", IEEE, PAMI-7, No. 1, 1985, pp. 45:55.

```
0    0    0    0    8    0    0    0    0
0    0    0    0   10   12    0    0    0
0    0    0    0   12   14   16    0    0
0    0    0    0    0    0   18   20    0
0    0    0    0    0    0   20   22   24
0    0    0    0    0    0   22   24    0
0    0    0    0   20   22   24    0    0
0    0    0    0   22   24    0    0    0
0    0    0    0   24    0    0    0    0
```

Fig 1-a  (k=2,c=1)

Table 1-a :

(1) normalized moments &normal method :

```
1.000000
0.000000        -0.000000
0.004332        -0.001557        0.011993
0.000059         0.000009       -0.000569       -0.000271
0.000037        -0.000012        0.000053       -0.000001        0.000310
0.000002        -0.000000       -0.000004       -0.000000       -0.000020       -0.000018
******
```

(2) normalized  moments & 2nd method :

```
1.000000
0.000000        -0.000000
0.265346        -0.095380        0.734654
0.028106         0.004218       -0.272612       -0.129743
0.139078        -0.043507        0.197822       -0.002703        1.164451
0.047890        -0.005564       -0.104508       -0.010664       -0.574035       -0.530695
```

(3) Hu moments & normal method :

```
0.016324         0.000068         0.000003         0.000000
-0.000000        -0.000000        -0.000000
```

(4) Hu moments &2nd method :

```
1.000000         0.256640         0.735897         0.075540
-0.005513        -0.032372        -0.000336
```

*******************************

Table 2-a (Complex Moments in Polar):

* theta=12.0

```
C[2][0]= 0.506594 ,   358.073886
C[3][0]= 0.857843 ,   243.523162
C[2][1]= 0.274849 ,   285.138425
C[4][0]= 0.200610 ,   257.500288
C[3][1]= 1.029543 ,   341.106508
C[2][2]= 1.699150 ,     0.000000
C[5][0]= 1.833912 ,   224.230639
C[4][1]= 2.039503 ,   247.953905
C[3][2]= 0.922412 ,   295.145431
```

* theta=25.0

```
C[2][0]= 0.506598 ,   332.077404
C[3][0]= 0.857845 ,   204.528931
C[2][1]= 0.274841 ,   272.139665
C[4][0]= 0.200617 ,   205.515164
C[3][1]= 1.029551 ,   315.111256
C[2][2]= 1.699127 ,     0.000000
C[5][0]= 1.833820 ,   159.240130
C[4][1]= 2.039490 ,   208.958595
C[3][2]= 0.922439 ,   282.145770
```

******

Table 3-a (Complex Moments Descriptor):

* theta=12.0

```
CD[2][0]= 0.506594 ,   147.750414
CD[3][0]= 0.857843 ,   108.014589
CD[2][1]= 0.274849 ,     0.000000
CD[4][0]= 0.200610 ,   196.806614
CD[3][1]= 1.029543 ,   130.783023
CD[2][2]= 1.699150 ,     0.000000
CD[5][0]= 1.833912 ,   238.351931
CD[4][1]= 2.039503 ,   112.445359
CD[3][2]= 0.922412 ,    10.007006
```

* theta=25.0

```
CD[2][0]= 0.506598 ,   147.751438
CD[3][0]= 0.857845 ,   108.016610
CD[2][1]= 0.274841 ,     0.000000
CD[4][0]= 0.200617 ,   196.816557
CD[3][1]= 1.029551 ,   130.785290
CD[2][2]= 1.699127 ,     0.000000
CD[5][0]= 1.833820 ,   238.355100
CD[4][1]= 2.039490 ,   112.446342
CD[3][2]= 0.922439 ,    10.006105
```

```
0  0  0   0  0   0  0   0  4   4  0   0  0   0  0   0  0   0
0  0  0   0  0   0  0   0  4   4  0   0  0   0  0   0  0   0
0  0  0   0  0   0  0   0  5   5  6   6  0   0  0   0  0   0
0  0  0   0  0   0  0   0  5   5  6   6  0   0  0   0  0   0
0  0  0   0  0   0  0   0  6   6  7   7  8   8  0   0  0   0
0  0  0   0  0   0  0   0  6   6  7   7  8   8  0   0  0   0
0  0  0   0  0   0  0   0  0   0  0   0  9   9  10  10  0   0
0  0  0   0  0   0  0   0  0   0  0   0  9   9  10  10  0   0
0  0  0   0  0   0  0   0  0   0  0   10 10  11  11  12  12
0  0  0   0  0   0  0   0  0   0  0   10 10  11  11  12  12
0  0  0   0  0   0  0   0  0   0  0   11 11  12  12  0   0
0  0  0   0  0   0  0   0  0   0  0   11 11  12  12  0   0
0  0  0   0  0   0  0   0  10  10 11  11 12  12  0   0  0   0
0  0  0   0  0   0  0   0  10  10 11  11 12  12  0   0  0   0
0  0  0   0  0   0  0   0  11  11 12  12  0   0  0   0  0   0
0  0  0   0  0   0  0   0  11  11 12  12  0   0  0   0  0   0
0  0  0   0  0   0  0   0  12  12 0   0  0   0  0   0  0   0
0  0  0   0  0   0  0   0  12  12 0   0  0   0  0   0  0   0
```

Fig 1-b (k=1 ,c=2 )

Table 1-b :

(1) normalized moments &normal method :

```
1.000000
0.000000      -0.000000
0.009012      -0.003114     0.024334
0.000166       0.000025    -0.001608    -0.000765
0.000167      -0.000050     0.000222    -0.000006     0.001292
0.000010      -0.000001    -0.000022    -0.000002    -0.000114    -0.000105
```

(2) normalized moments & 2nd method :

```
1.000000
0.000000      -0.000000
0.270260      -0.093383     0.729740
0.027225       0.004087    -0.264094    -0.125689
0.149740      -0.044637     0.199983    -0.005523     1.161489
0.048322      -0.005005    -0.107123    -0.011296    -0.561047    -0.516487
```

(3) Hu moments & normal method:

```
   0.033347        0.000274        0.000026        0.000003
  -0.000000       -0.000000       -0.000000
```

(4) Hu moments &  2nd method :

```
   1.000000        0.246004        0.690621        0.070894
  -0.004855       -0.029745       -0.000296
```

********************************

Table 2-b (Complex Moments in Polar):

* theta=12.0                                    * theta=25.0

```
C[2][0]= 0.495990 ,   358.074214        c[2][0]=0.495988 ,  332.077431
C[3][0]= 0.831041 ,   243.524173        C[3][0]=0.831029 ,  204.528507
C[2][1]= 0.266250 ,   285.137469        C[2][1]=0.266261 ,  272.139037
C[4][0]= 0.192038 ,   257.398832        C[4][0]=0.191933 ,  205.425864
C[3][1]= 1.016711 ,   341.619853        C[3][1]=1.016645 ,  315.619574
C[2][2]= 1.711169 ,     0.000000        C[2][2]=1.739108 ,    0.000000
C[5][0]= 1.739061 ,   224.233712        C[5][0]=1.739108 ,  159.261410
C[4][1]= 2.003838 ,   247.795711        C[4][1]=2.003436 ,  208.789009
C[3][2]= 0.907897 ,   294.778206        C[3][2]=0.908493 ,  281.769366
```

******

Table 3-b (Complex Moments Descriptor):

* theta=12.0                                    * theta=25.0

```
CD[2][0]= 0.495990 ,   147.752640       CD[2][0]=0.495988 ,  147.752722
CD[3][0]= 0.831041 ,   108.018440       CD[3][0]=0.831029 ,  108.018058
CD[2][1]= 0.266250 ,     0.000000       CD[2][1]=.266261 ,  0.000000
CD[4][0]= 0.192038 ,   196.708968       CD[4][0]=0.191933 ,  196.729716
CD[3][1]= 1.016711 ,   131.298280       CD[3][1]=1.016645 ,  131.294865
CD[2][2]= 1.711169 ,     0.000000       CD[2][2]=1.711258 ,  0.000000
CD[5][0]= 1.739061 ,   238.359744       CD[5][0]=1.739108 ,  238.379522
CD[4][1]= 2.003838 ,   112.289979       CD[4][1]=2.003436 ,  112.278560
CD[3][2]= 0.907897 ,     9.640737       CD[3][2]=0.908493 ,  9.630329
```

# A Method of Recognizing Infrared Target Images

## He Bin

Image Processing Group, Dept. of Information and Control

Xi'an Jiaotong University

Xi'an, Shaanxi, P. R. China

*Abstract*

A method is presented in this paper for the analysis of characteristics of infrared images from anti-tank missile systems. It is shown that some of the invariant moments of these images can be calculated from the projection function of targets. Based on theoretic analysis and computer simulation results, the possibility of using only two of the invariant moments in such systems is discussed.

*I Characteristics of infrared images of targets and system requirements on target features*

A typical infrared imaging guidance head has a functional diagram as in Fig. 1. The infrared sensor receives infrared radiation from targets and translates it into video signals. Two vital components of the tracking algorithm are the preprocessing of the video signals to provide abstract target features, and the recognition of targets based on these features. Target features and movement parameters are used to form tracking strategy. Control signals can then be formed to drive the servo system of the camera to follow the target.

An infrared image describes the distribution of heat radiation from a target and its background. The infrared images considered in this paper have the following properties:

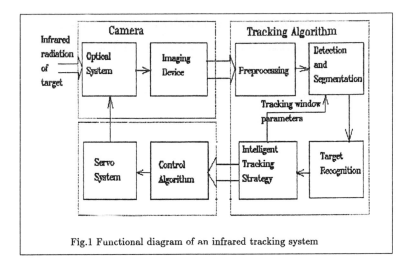

Fig.1 Functional diagram of an infrared tracking system

1] They are binary images, i.e. the target is either brighter or darker than its immediate adjacent background;

2] They do not provide information about the interior details of a target;

3] Due to the existence of a temperature field, target edges are blurred and can not be accurately defined.

Recognition and tracking is based on the representative features of a target. Therefore in the choice of target features the following should be considered:

1] Real-time response. To meet the speed requirement of a real-time system, target feature abstraction must make compromise between reliability of recognition, simplicity of hardware implementation and speed of computation;

2] Invariance. Since both the target and the tracking missile are moving the target features must be invariant with respect to translation, scaling and rotation.

3] Robustness. The target features should be sufficiently representative for the worst cases in the course of tracking, i.e. account should be taken of situations where a target may be partially covered or its thermal radiation be influenced by its surroundings;

4] Due to the low resolution of infrared imaging devices, the features chosen should be insensitive to the interior details of a target.

In [1] the author has given a detailed discussion on target feature selection. The conclusion is: In an infrared tracking system the features to be chosen should be those that are related to the shape or target point distribution. In this paper, the use of some of the invariant moments as target shape signature [2] is proposed. It is further shown that the projection function defined in the next section can be used in calculating the moments.

*II  A method for fast target feature abstraction*

It will be assumed throughout that all images are preprocessed, i.e. target edge detection and segmentation have been performed, so that they are binary with "1" representing the target area. Therefore the intensity function of an image is a binary mapping from the two dimensional space X×Y to the set {0, 1}. Such an intensity function describes only the structural information of an image. An invariant moment is a mapping from intensity functions to real numbers that remains the same while the image is translated, scaled and rotated. Ming-Huei Hu [2] has point out that theoretically there are infinitely many such invariant moments, and that only a finite number of them are needed for recognition purposes.

Let $\mu_{pq}$ denote the (p+q)th central moment and $\eta_{pq} \triangleq \mu_{pq}/\mu_{00}^r$, where $r \triangleq (p+q)/2$, p+q=2, 3, .... Then the following quantities have been shown to be invariant moments [2]:

$$\phi_1 \triangleq \eta_{20} + \eta_{02}$$

$$\phi_2 \triangleq (\eta_{20} - \eta_{02})^2 + 4\eta_{11}$$

$$\phi_3 \triangleq (\eta_{30} - 3\eta_{12})^2 + (3\eta_{21} - \eta_{03})^2$$

$$\phi_4 \triangleq (\eta_{30} + \eta_{12})^2 + (\eta_{21} + \eta_{03})^2$$

$$\vdots$$

However, the direct use of these formule would involve huge amount of computation and thus result in a complicated system. The projection method outlined below will reduce computation considerably.

As in [3], a projection function can be defined as follows.

Given an intensity function $f(x, y)$ and a direction $W$, let $Z$ be the straight line passing through $(0, 0)$ and orthogonal to $W$. At any point $z$ on $Z$, the projection of $f(x, y)$ is defined to be the line integral:

$$P_W(z) \triangleq \int_{w(z)} f(x, y) \, ds$$

where $W(z)$ is parallel to $W$ and passes through $z$. When $f(\cdot, \cdot)$ is defined on a discrete set of points (finite resolution), the integral reduces to a summation. In particular,

$$P_y(x) = \sum_y f(x, y)$$

and

$$P_x(y) = \sum_x f(x, y).$$

For a binary image $P_x(y)$ and $P_y(x)$ can be obtained by adding the 1's row- or column-wise, respectively. This procedure can be easily realized by hardware.

The central moments can be computed once the quantities $m_{ij} \triangleq \sum_x \sum_y x^i y^j f(x, y)$ are available. The calculation below shows that $m_{ij}$'s are closely related to the projection functions.

$$m_{io} = \sum_x \sum_y x^i f(x, y)$$

$$= \sum_x x^i \sum_y f(x, y)$$

$$= \sum_x x^i P_y(x),$$

and similarly

$$m_{oi} = \sum_y y^j P_x(y).$$

For $i \neq 0$ and $j \neq 0$, $m_{ij}$ cannot be calculated from the projection functions directly. However the binary nature of images can be made use of, as shown below, to compute $m_{ij}$ in the course of computing the projection functions, thus saving computing resources.

Note that for a binary image, if the target area is denoted by T, the intensity function f(x, y) is

$$f(x, y) \triangleq \begin{cases} 1 & \text{if } (x, y) \in T \\ 0 & \text{if } (x, y) \notin T \end{cases}$$

Therefore

$$m_{ij} = \sum_{(x, y) \in T} x^i \, y^j.$$

When computing the projection functions, the binary data of an image are input row-wise in series. For a particular row the value of y is fixed. Let $y'_T$ and $y''_T$ be the minimum and maximum values of y in T, and $y'_T \leq y_T \leq y''_T$ it then follows that

$$m_{ij} = \sum_{y_T = y'_T}^{y''_T} y_T^j \, [ \sum_{(x, y_T) \in T} x^i ].$$

The computation involved within the brackets can be done at the same time as $P_x(y)$ is calculated, for

$$P_x(y_T) = \sum_{(x, y_T) \in T} 1.$$

Direct reference to the projection functions instead of the intensity function itself will increase computing speed and reduce memory size (for an N×N image the memory requirement can be reduced from $N^2$ to $N \times \log_2 N$).

*III. Examples*

Some experiments have been conducted to establish the feasibility of using only $\phi_1$ and $\phi_2$ to recognize the target of an anti-tank missile. First, some basic shapes, i.e. rectangular, cross, triangular and circle are analyzed. Their locations in ($\phi_1$, $\phi_2$) space are ploted in Fig. 2. Evidently, they are distinguishable from each other in this space.

Fig. 3 shows the ranges of locations in the $(\phi_1, \phi_2)$ space of tanks and trucks. Experiments have indicated that the tank and truck areas do not overlap significantly. Thus for the purpose of recognition it is feasible to use only $\phi_1$ and $\phi_2$ as the target features.

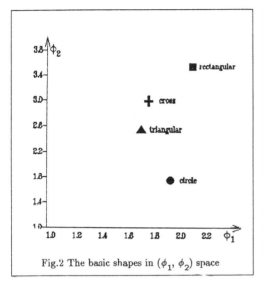

Fig.2 The basic shapes in $(\phi_1, \phi_2)$ space

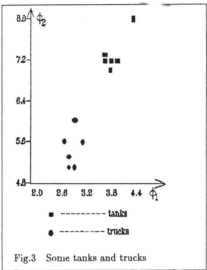

Fig.3  Some tanks and trucks

## IV. Conclusions

In [1] the author has given a detailed discussion on the computation of the invariant moments. A brief account of the conclusions from [1] in this paper has shown that the use of projection function reduces the computional burden substantially. It is also noted that in most cases $\phi_1$ and $\phi_2$ are sufficient in distinguishing a tank from its main rivals. $\phi_1$ and $\phi_2$ could also be used as inputs to the tracking strategy model [1]. Finally, it should be pointed out that deeper research is necessary for the method proposed here to have any practical application.

*V. References*

[1]     He Bin, Ms.c Thesis, NW Institute of Telecommunication, 1986.

[2]     Ming-Kuei, Hu, IRE Trans. on Information Theory, IT-8, Feb., 1962, pp179-187.

[3]     Yee-Hsun, U and Flachs G. M., Proc. of 1976 IEEE Region V Conf. Austin, TX, pp15-19.

[4]     Y. R., Wang, IEEE Trans. on Computer, Oct. 1975

# A Biologically Motivated Approach to Early Visual Computations: orientation selection, texture, and optical flow

*Steven W. Zucker*

Computer Vision and Robotics Laboratory
McGill Research Centre for Intelligent Machines
McGill University
Montréal, Québec, Canada
and
The Canadian Institute for Advanced Research

## Abstract

The problem of curve detection decomposes naturally into two stages: (i) inferring the (discrete) trace and tangent to the curve; and (ii) finding integrals through the resultant tangent field. Orientation selection is the term used by physiologists for the first of these stages; i.e., for the process of extracting the tangents to piecewise smooth curves from a two-dimensional image. We present an analysis of the orientation selection process from a computational perspective that is strongly influenced by various biological constraints. As such, it provides both a solid foundation for curve detection algorithms within computer vision systems and illustrates the insights that can be gained by analyzing biological vision systems. Formal extensions to the algorithm can also be posed that provide further insight into texture and optical flow.

## 1. Introduction

There is a fundamental chicken-and-egg problem facing the designers of computer vision systems: algorithms depend on problem formulations, and vice-versa. But for most engineering tasks, neither is specified with enough precision to completely motivate a solution to the other. Rather, there are always a significant number of open choices, and the question remains of how to decide them. Our position is that the analysis of biological vision systems can provide an insight suffcent for motivating a break in the chicken-and-egg cycle, and that at times this insight can lead to real innovation in computational algorithms. While there has always been some biological influence on computer vision [Zucker, 1987], recent evidence is that the potential for fruitful interaction is increasing. For the remainder of this paper, we shall overview one such case in point, the research in our laboratory on orientation selection, and shall illustrate how biology is not only influencing computer vision, but how computational studies are now beginning to influence the analysis of biological systems. For a more complete survey of the former, see [Zucker, 1987].

### 1.1 From Orientation Selection to Optical Flow

Orientation selection is the process by which the low-order differential characteristics of curves in images are inferred. It provides the foundation for the inference of shape and other information from static images. Optical flow, the inference of points, curves and regions of consistent motion in the retinal image, is similarly fundamental for moving images. The primacy of these two processes in physiological vision systems can be observed by noting the predominance of orientation and motion sensitive neurons in the primary visual cortex [Hubel and Wiesel 1977, Orban 1984]. As a bridge between these two well-known processes, we have introduced texture flow, the process of inferring a dense, locally parallel tangent field over a region in a static two-dimensional image. This is the kind of process that would be used in perceiving hair, wood grain or random dot Moiré patterns (see [Zucker 1985]).

## 1.2 The Geometry of Early Vision

From a geometric perspective, these three processes—orientation selection, texture flow, and optical flow—share the property of being essentially tied to the inference of consistent fields of orientation or velocity vectors in an image. Orientation selection involves the inference and localization of one-dimensional contours in a static two-dimensional image, while texture flow consists of inferring two-dimensional regions of consistent orientation structure from similarly static images. If we consider the projection of a moving point, line or surface, then an extension of the image space to include a third temporal dimension leads to the observation that motion inference involves recovering (i) the 1D curves in $(x, y, t)$ or space-time swept out by moving points in each image; (ii) the 2D surfaces in $(x, y, t)$ swept out by moving curves; and (iii) the 3D volumes swept out by moving surfaces. In this way, optical flow can be regarded as an extension of orientation selection and texture flow. Another way to view this relationship is to describe orientation selection as a special case of optical flow which factors out the time variable. This analogy has been described elsewhere [Zucker and Iverson 1987] and our present goal is to develop a general computational framework for solving all three problems. We concentrate, because of space limitations, on the orientation selection computation, since the others can then be derived from this basis.

## 1.3 Local Measurements and Contextual Interactions

In the past, computational and neurophysiological analyses of these problems have focussed primarily on measurements, which are almost always local, and have ignored the question of whether these local measurements provide globally consistent estimates. Physiologically this may reflect a bias toward single cell recordings at the expense of ignoring local circuit interactions [Gilbert and Wiesel, 1981]. These local estimates are inherently inaccurate, however, and we contend that putting them together computationally is key; in particular, since all of these processes depend on establishing a consistent global interpretation of information gathered from local measurements, the relaxation labelling approach can be applied [Hummel and Zucker 1983]. This is a formal framework for neural network style modeling which, as we show, leads to a natural functional for optimization. The key issues are thus the representation, the nature of the initial measurements, and the structure of the relaxation networks which will compute local consistency in each domain. We discuss each in turn.

## 2. Orientation Selection: Inferring the tangent field

Orientation selection is the first stage in contour recovery; we define it to be the inference of a local description of the curve everywhere along it. Formally this amounts to inferring the trace of the curve, or the set of points (in the image) through which the curve passes, its (approximate) tangent and curvature at those points, and their discontinuities [Zucker, 1986]. We refer to such information as the tangent field, and note that, since the tangent is the first derivative (with respect to arc length), the global curve can be recovered as integrals through it.

Orientation selection is modeled as a two stage process:

1. *Initial Measurement* of the local fit at each point to a model of orientation and curvature. We use a difference of Gaussians approximation to simple-cell receptive fields which is analagous to so-called line detectors in computer vision. This is taken as an initial setting for the confidence in the associated local hypothesis, and can be viewed in rough physiological terms as being proportional to the distribution of firing rates in an orientation column of simple cells convolved against a raw (positive or negative contrast) image. A model of end-stopped cortical neurons [Dobbins, Zucker, and Cynader, 1987] provides an estimate of curvature, and permits the simultaneous representation of orientation and curvature information.

2. *Interpretation* in which the initial measurements are selectively attenuated and enhanced using the relaxation labelling functional minimization to be described next.

## 2.1 Relaxation Labeling

The abstract structure of a relaxation labeling process is as follows. Let $i = (x_i, y_i) \in I$ denote discrete coordinate positions in the image $I$, and let $\lambda \in \Lambda_i$ denote the set of labels at position $i$. (In a simple model of orientation selection, think of the distinct labels as indicating distinct orientations.) The labels at each position are ordered according to the measure $p_i(\lambda)$ such that $0 \leq p_i(\lambda) \leq 1$ and $\sum_{\lambda \in \Lambda_i} p_i(\lambda) = 1 \quad \forall i$. Compatibility functions $r_{i,j}(\lambda, \lambda')$ are defined between label $\lambda$ at position $i$ and label $\lambda'$ at position $j$ such that increasingly positive values represent stronger compatibility. The network structure derives from the support that label $\lambda$ obtains from the labeling on it's neighbors $Neigh(i)$; in symbols,

$$S_i(\lambda) = \sum_{j \in Neigh(i)} \sum_{\lambda' \in \Lambda_j} r_{i,j}(\lambda, \lambda') p_j(\lambda').$$

The final labeling is selected such that it maximizes the average local support:

$$A(p) = \sum_{i \in I} S_i(\lambda) p_i(\lambda).$$

Such a labeling is said to be consistent. While the above potential function has now become rather standard in neural network modeling when the compatibility functions are symmetric, the following theorem shows that consistency can be naturally extended to asymmetric compatibilities as well.

**Theorem** With the above notation, a labeling $\{p(\lambda)\}$ is consistent iff it satisfies the variational inequality:

$$\sum_{\lambda \in \Lambda_i} p_i(\lambda) s_i(\lambda; \{p\}) \geq \sum_{\lambda \in \Lambda_i} v_i(\lambda) s_i(\lambda; \{p\})$$

for any other labeling $v_i(\lambda)$ in an appropriate convex set of labelings.

For details and proof, see [Hummel and Zucker, 1983]. An iterative, gradient ascent algorithm for achieving consistent labelings is presented in [Mohammed, Hummel, and Zucker, 1983; Parent and Zucker, 1985a]. What remains is thus a specification of the labels and compatibilities—in short, the functional $A(p)$—for orientation selection.

## 2.2 Representation

Physical, geometric, and neurophysiological constraints arise for orientation selection. First observe that artificial and biological systems for gathering images begin with positionally localized discrete sensors. Other constraints derive from the differential geometry of curves in the plane, emphasizing the importance of the trace—the set of points through which the curve passes—as well as the tangent and curvature. Each of these serves as a local model for the curve that is essential in localizing discontinuities [Parent and Zucker, 1985b].

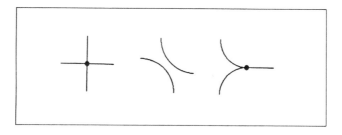

**Figure 1**  Three sets of confounding curves in the plane. In order to adequately represent [a] the representation must allow for lines of more than one orientation to co-exist at the same point (the cross). Without some element in the representation which somehow measures at least the sign of curvature it will be very difficult to separate two nearby oppositely curved lines (as in [b]). In order to represent [c], at least two differently curved but similarly oriented lines must be able to co-exist at the same point.

Another source of constraints on the representation can be derived by examining the potential interactions between curves. Examination of the three curve sets in Figure 1 shows that an adequate representation of curves in the plane requires curvature (to disambiguate between nearby inconsistently curved contours as in [b]), and must also allow for the representation of multiple curves passing through the same trace point.

Our representation is consistent with all of these points. It is based on a retinotopic grid. However, instead of containing intensity measurements, each point $i \in I$ is associated with a matrix of hypotheses about the orientations and curvatures of the curves which pass through that point. Quantizing orientation into $n$ discrete values and curvature into $m$, we have an $n \times m$ matrix of *independent* hypotheses about the existence of a curve with the given orientation and curvature passing through the point.

With the proposed discretization, there is a set of $n$ orientation labels represented by $\lambda \in \{0, \ldots, n\}$, and $\Theta_\lambda$, the orientation of the label $\lambda$, is given by $\Theta_\lambda = \epsilon\lambda$, where $\epsilon = \pi/n$. (For reasons of symmetry, it is only necessary to represent the $0 \rightarrow \pi$ half-plane.) The natural range for curvatures is limited to a given minimum radius $r_{min}$ $(\kappa_{max} = 1/r_{min})$

which is related to the discretization of the plane. Adopting the convention that negative curvatures are confined to the left half-plane (associated with a particular orientation), a similar discretization for curvature is as follows. The label is $\kappa \in \{0, \ldots, m\}$, and $K_\kappa$, the curvature of the label $\kappa$, is given by $K_\kappa = -\kappa_{max} + \kappa \Delta \kappa$, where $\Delta \kappa = 2\kappa_{max}/m$.

The notation $p_i(\lambda_i, \kappa_i)$ represents the certainty of a particular label pair at the pixel $(x_i, y_i)$, and thus the confidence in the hypothesis about the existence of a curve with orientation $\Theta_{\lambda_i}$ and curvature $K_{\kappa_i}$ at point $i$.

## 2.3 Compatibilities and Co-circularity

The compatibilities between two label pairs within a local neighbourhood are derived from an analysis of the first and second order differential geometric properties of curves in the plane. The discretization of this geometry builds upon that in [Parent and Zucker 1985b], who introduced the notion of co-circularity as a generalization of the osculating circle, or the circle that just "kisses" the curve at 3 points. Curvature can also be viewed as a relationship between neighboring tangents along the curve, and hence provides a compatibility relationship between labels in our orientation selection network. The derivation proceeds as follows (consider Figure 2.).

First, observe that, if $\lambda_i$ and $\lambda_j$ are co-circular, then the angle of the connecting line $ij$, specified as $\Theta_{ij}$, must have the same internal angle with both $\Theta_{\lambda_i}$ and $\Theta_{\lambda_j}$. Thus one has $\Theta_{\lambda_j}$ from $\Theta_{\lambda_i}$ and $\Theta_{ij}$ via the relationship $\Theta_{\lambda_j} = 2\Theta_{ij} - \Theta_{\lambda_i}$. The radius of the circle $C$ may also be derived as $r = D_{ij}/2\sin(\Theta_{ij} - \Theta_{\lambda_i})$, where $D_{ij}$ is the distance between points $i$ and $j$.

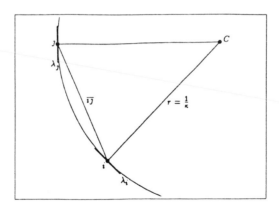

**Figure 2** The geometric relationships necessary for defining the compatibilities between two label pairs at points $i$ and $j$.

In translating these geometric constraints into a measure of compatibility between labels, the digitization of the represention becomes key. If we consider the discrete values associated with the labels in the system to be related to their continuous counterparts by some matching process, then we can define a measure of correspondence (or goodness-of-fit) between the real value and the label. Take the variable $X_i$, the value associated with a label $i$, and a quantization specified by $\Delta X$, the distance between adjacent values of $X_i$. Then a function representing the correspondence between $X_i$ and some real value $x$ should: (i) have a global maximum when $x = X_i$; (ii) decrease monotonically approaching 0 as $|x - X_i|$ increases; (iii) be tuned more closely to $X_i$ as $\Delta X$, the quantization, approaches 0. In order to ensure a locally smooth energy landscape $A(p)$ for the relaxation, it is also useful to have a this correspondence function be smooth. A gaussian centered on $X_i$ with standard deviation $\propto \Delta X$ fulfills all of these criteria as well as a symmetry condition which should be included when the sign of $x - X_i$ is unimportant. A natural choice for the proportionality constant is that value which assigns a correspondence of 0.5 when the real value is the arithmetic mean of two adjacent discrete values. This is achieved for the gaussian when $\sigma = \Delta X / 2\sqrt{2 ln 2}$.

A measure of compatibility can now be achieved by maximizing the overall correspondence of all of the digitized variables in the system. This is based on the principle that compatibility will be defined as the best correspondence that can be achieved with real valued approximations to each discrete variable while still conforming to the geometric constraints imposed by the coupling between variables. With this in mind, the distribution around $\Theta_{\lambda_i}$ and $\Theta_{\lambda_j}$ will both have $\sigma \propto \epsilon/2$ and both $K_{\kappa_i}$ and $K_{\kappa_j}$ will have $\sigma \propto \Delta \kappa/2$. The two difficult cases both have to do with the relationship between the two positions, $D_{ij}$ and $\Theta_{ij}$. For $D_{ij}$ there are two points which both have positional variations with $\sigma \propto 1/2$. Thus $D_{ij}$'s correspondence distribution should be the convolution of these two distributions, which will give a $\sigma \propto \sqrt{1/2}$. Since the positioning perpendicular to $\overline{ij}$ will also have $\sigma \propto 1/2$, the variation of the angle $\Theta_{ij}$ will have $\sigma \propto \alpha$, where $\alpha = \sin^{-1}(1/D_{ij})$. For each of our discrete variables $X$, we can now define a correspondence function $C_X$:

$$C_{\Theta_{\lambda_i}}(x) = G[\, \mu = \Theta_{\lambda_i}, \, \sigma = c\epsilon/2\,](x)$$

$$C_{K_{\kappa_i}}(x) = G[\, \mu = K_{\kappa_i}, \, \sigma = c\Delta\kappa/2\,](x)$$

$$C_{\Theta_{\lambda_j}}(x) = G[\, \mu = \Theta_{\lambda_j}, \, \sigma = c\epsilon/2\,](x)$$

$$C_{K_{\kappa_j}}(x) = G[\, \mu = K_{\kappa_j}, \, \sigma = c\Delta\kappa/2\,](x)$$

$$C_{\Theta_{ij}}(x) = G[\, \mu = \Theta_{ij}, \, \sigma = c\alpha\,](x)$$

$$C_{D_{ij}}(x) = G[\, \mu = D_{ij}, \, \sigma = c\sqrt{1/2}\,](x).$$

And the compatibility between label pairs $(\lambda, \kappa)$ at points $i$ and $j$ can be expressed as:

$$r_{i,j} = \max_{\theta_{\lambda_i},\theta_{ij},d_{ij}} \{C_{\Theta_{\lambda_i}}(\theta_{\lambda_i})\, C_{K_{\kappa_i}}(k_{\kappa_i})\, C_{\Theta_{\lambda_j}}(\theta_{\lambda_j})\, C_{K_{\kappa_j}}(k_{\kappa_j})\, C_{\Theta_{ij}}(\theta_{ij})\, C_{D_{ij}}(d_{ij})\}$$

where

$$\theta_{\lambda_j} = 2\theta_{ij} - \theta_{\lambda_i},$$

$$k_{\kappa_i} = 2\sin(\theta_{ij} - \theta_{\lambda_i})/d_{ij}, \text{ and}$$

$$|k_{\kappa_i}| = |k_{\kappa_j}| \qquad \text{(with sign determined by cocircularity)}$$

**Figure 3** An example of a set of orientation selection compatibilities for a particular discretized orientation and curvature. With $n = 8$ and $m = 7$, this class of
compatible labels is all those within a neighbourhood of 7 pixels of the central pixel
which have $c_{i,j}(1, 2; \lambda_j, \kappa_j) > 0.4$.

This approach to determining relaxation labelling compatibilities has quite general
application. It is useful whenever relaxation labelling is used to solve a problem posed in
terms of maximization of aggregate consistency where: (i) there is a set of labels, each of
which is a discrete approximation to a continuous value (as orientation and curvature were
here); (ii) information is available regarding the error distributions (or basis functions)
associated with the mapping from discrete to continuous (the smooth Gaussians); and
(iii) the notion of compatibility is defined in terms of coupling constraints between the
real-valued analogs to the discrete labels (the constraints from differential geometry).

### 2.3.1 Endstopped Neurons Code Position, Orientation, and Curvature

As is clear from the compatibility diagram in Fig. 3, there is a need to represent
information about position, orientation, and curvature within a homogeneous framework.
Fascinatingly, once these computational requirements were understood, it became possible
to relate them to a widely observed property of neurons in the visual cortex: endstopping.
In Dobbins *et al.* [1987] we develop a computational model for endstopping, and show how
it leads to quantitative predictions about the response of endstopped (simple) neurons to
curved stimuli that have now been observed. The model is of interest to researchers in
computer vision because it suggests an algorithm for estimating curvature coarsely but
reliably.

The model is based on the observation that there are simple cells, or cells with elongated receptive fields (and a clear orientation preference) whose size differs as a function
of cortical layer. In particular, there are "short" simple cells, i.e., simple cells with short
receptive fields, in layer 4, and "long" simple cells in layer 6 of area V1 in the cat visual
cortex [Wiesel and Gilbert, 1981]. Now, if we let $R_S$ denote the response of a short simple
cell, and $R_L$ denote the response of a long simple cell, both of whose receptive fields are
centered at the same retinotopic location with the same orientation preference, then their
"difference" provides an estimate of endstopping that varies with curvature (or deviation
from straightness). More precisely, letting $\phi(\cdot)$ denote a rectifying function (equal to its

argument when positive and zero otherwise), the response of an end-stopped simple cell $(R_{ES})$ is modeled by:

$$R_{ES} = \phi(c_S \cdot \phi(R_S) - c_L \cdot \phi(R_L))$$

where $c_S$ and $c_L$ are positive constants that normalize the area difference between the receptive fields.

In addition to the scalar orientation-dependent curvature measurements, the remaining part of the compatibility structure is coded as the graph of network interactions.

## 2.4 Lateral Maxima

An additional constraint is needed in the orientation selection network to ensure lateral localization of the curves. Mathematically a curve is 1-dimensional; it has extent along its length, but not along its breadth. However, the response pattern of the initial convolution (difference of gaussian) convolution kernel is not perfectly localized laterally. In fact, its response profile will be the same as a lateral cross-section of it (see Fig. 4).

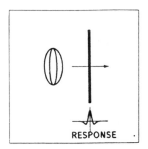

**Figure 4** As an orientation-specific DOG cell (or cosine Gabor cell) is moved laterally across a similarly oriented line, its response profile will be smeared spatially with respect to the line. We should be primarily concerned with the maximal response of this lateral envelope (the lateral maximum).

The traditional way of resolving this has been the introduction of lateral inhibition (or a negative compatibility between laterally parallel tangent labels) in the relaxation network. To accelerate convergence, however, we designed a characteristic function that actually *selects* the lateral maxima within a certain neighborhood $N_{\lambda,\kappa}$ of lateral (i.e. not along any one of the possible curves associated with a $(\lambda, \kappa)$ pair) and parallel labels (see Fig. 5). A lateral maxima condition can then be defined as:

$$m_i(\lambda_i, \kappa_i) = \begin{cases} 1, & \text{iff } \forall (j, \lambda_j, \kappa_j) \in N_{\lambda_i, \kappa_i} \ p_i(\lambda_i, \kappa_i) > p_j(\lambda_j, \kappa_j); \\ 0, & \text{otherwise.} \end{cases}$$

Support is thus restricted to being provided by those labels which have been selected as laterally maximal, effectively focusing attention onto them.

To summarize, the process of interpreting the initial measurements in terms of the compatibilities previously described can be seen as one of maximizing the average local

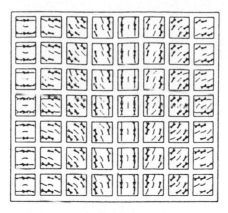

**Figure 5** The lateral maxima neighbourhoods $N_{\lambda,\kappa}$ for all $\lambda \in \{0, \ldots, n\}$ (across) and $\kappa \in \{0, \ldots, m\}$ (down). The central arc in each group is the label pair with which the neighbourhood is associated. It can be seen that the arcs in each of the neighbourhoods are lateral, parallel and have similar curvatures to the reference arc.

support

$$A(p) = \sum_{i=0}^{N} \sum_{\lambda_i=0}^{n} \sum_{\kappa_i=0}^{m} s_i(\lambda_i, \kappa_i)\, p_i(\lambda_i, \kappa_i)$$

where the support $s_i(\lambda, \kappa)$ was derived above as

$$s_i(\lambda_i, \kappa_i) = \sum_{j=0}^{N} \sum_{\lambda_j=0}^{n} \sum_{\kappa_j=0}^{m} c_{i,j}(\lambda_i, \kappa_i : \lambda_j, \kappa_j)\, p_j(\lambda_j, \kappa_j)\, m_j(\lambda_j, \kappa_j)$$

## 3. Orientation Selection: Results

An example of running the network is shown in Fig. 6. At the top we show a section of a fingerprint image, blown up so that the individual pixels are clearly visible. In the lower left of the figure are the results of the initial convolution and curvature measurements. Finally, in the lower right is set of labels onto which the network converged after only 3 iterations. The labels, which are short curved segments, indicate both the orientation (the tangent angle) and the curvature at each trace position, and hence code something like what could be represented in endstopped neurons early in the visual cortex.

## 4. From Orientation Selection to Texture and Optical Flow

The generalization from orientation selection to texture flow involves two crucial steps. Because texture flows consist of parallel tangent fields dense over a two-dimensional manifold, (i) lateral maxima selection must be changed to lateral maxima spreading; and (ii) the family of osculating circles on which co-circularity constraints are based must be generalized to an eqivalence class of concentric circles; details are in [Iverson and Zucker,

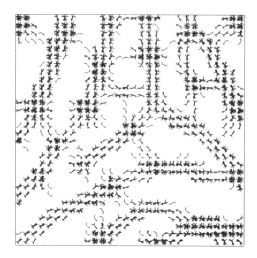
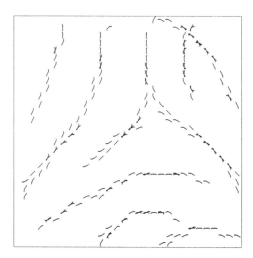

**Figure 6** Results of a simulation run on the small section of a fingerprint image. (top) The individual pixels are shown as blocks, so that the subsequent labels can be displayed at appropriate positions. (lower left) The initial hypotheses about orientation and curvature at each position. Note that there are many overlapping hypotheses along the curves as well as bogus ones between them. Such a display can be thought of in rough physiological terms as a projection onto the retinotopic plane of the significant initial responses to an image of one contrast along an orientation column. (lower right) Results of the network after 3 iterations. Note that all of the bogus responses have been eliminated within the coarse quantization (into 8 orientations and 7 curvatures) and spatial sampling employed.

1987]. Also, a sketch of extensions into the three problems of optical flow (see Sec. 1) is in Zucker and Iverson, [1987].

## 4.1 Sensitivity to Discontinuities

In addition to illustrating that the network for orientation selection works, and that it suggests a new role for endstopping, it can be shown that is have more of an input/output connection with human perception as well. In particular, Link and Zucker [1988a, 1988b] quantify human sensitivity to orientation and texture flow discontinuities; and Zucker and Iverson [1987] illustrate them for optical flow. The algorithms can be shown to have similar sensitivities [Zucker, 1986; Link and Zucker, 1988a].

## 5. Conclusions

It is often the case that problems in computer vision are only partially motivated, and in this paper we argued that insights from the study of biological vision systems can help to complete the motivation. The paper consisted largely of a survey of work in our laboratory or orientation selection, from computational, mathematical, psychophysical, and physiological directions, and hinted at how we are extending it to the analysis of texture flow and optical flow. Given the effort that has already been spent on optical flow, and the current paucity of general, robust solutions, our hope is that biology will provide the key to properly formulating the questions.

## 6. Acknowledgements

Many colleagues and students participated actively in the research program described here, and I would especially like to acknowledge the roles of Allan Dobbins, Lee Iverson, and Pierre Parent. This research was supported by the NSERC, the MRC, and by DREA.

## 7. References

1. Dobbins, A., Zucker, S.W., and Cynader, M., Endstopping in the visual cortex as a neural substrate for calculating curvature, *Nature*, 1987, **329**, 438 - 441.

2. Hubel, D., and Wiesel, T., Functional architecture of macaque monkey visual cortex, *Proceedings of the Royal Society (London) B* **198**, 1977, pp. 1–59.

3. Gilbert, C., and Wiesel, T., Laminar specialization and intra-cortical connections in cat primary visual cortex, in F. Schmidt, F. Worden, G. Adalman, and S. Dennis (eds.), *The Organization of the Cerebral Cortex*, MIT Press, Cambridge, 1981.

4. Hummel, R., and Zucker, S.W., "On the foundations of relaxation labelling processes," *IEEE Trans. PAMI* **5**, 1983, pp. 267–287.

5. Iverson, Lee, and Zucker, S.W., Orientation selection to optical flow: a computational perspective, *Proc. IEEE Workshop on Computer Vision*, Miami, 1987.

6. Link, N., and Zucker, S.W., Sensitivity to corners in Flow Patterns, *Spatial Vision*, 1988a, to be published.

7. Link, N., and Zucker, S.W., Corner detection in curvilinear dot grouping, *Biological Cybernetics*, 1988b, to be published.

9. Orban, G.A., *Neuronal Operations in the Visual Cortex*, Springer-Verlag, 1984.

10. Parent, P. and Zucker, S.W., *Radial Projection: An Efficient Update Rule for Relaxation Labelling*, CVaRL Technical Report TR-86-15R, McGill University, 1985a; *IEEE Trans. PAMI*, in press.

11. Parent, P. and Zucker, S.W., *Trace Inference, Curvature Consistency, and Curve Detection*, CVaRL Technical Report CIM-86-3, McGill University, 1985b; *IEEE Trans. PAMI*, in press.

12. Zucker, S.W., Early Orientation Selection, Tangent Fields and the Dimensionality of their Support, *Computer Vision, Graphics and Image Processing* **32**, 1985 pp. 74–103.

13. Zucker, S.W., The computational connection in vision: Early orientation selection, *Behaviour Research Methods, Instruments, and Computers*, 1986, **18**, 608 - 617.

14. Zucker, S.W., Early vision, in S. Shapiro (ed.), *The Encyclopedia of Artificial Intelligence*, John Wiley, 1987.

15. Zucker, S.W. and Iverson, L., "From Orientation Selection to Optical Flow," *Computer Vision, Graphics and Image Processing*, **37**, January 1987.

# First Steps Towards A Blackboard Controlled System for Matching Image and Model in the Presence of Noise and Distortion

Richard Baldock and Simon Towers

*Pattern Recognition & Automation Section*
*MRC Clinical & Population Cytogenetics Unit*
*Western General Hospital, Crewe Road, Edinburgh EH4 2XU, UK.*

### Abstract

In this paper we discuss some of the problems of computer interpretation of medical ultrasound images and the use of an *expert system* to control the image processing and model matching. We describe an expert system shell developed for this task and detail our preliminary application to an ultrasound scan. We model the anatomical and geometric structures involved as a network of *frames*. This and the model-matching control strategy we have employed are discussed. An example of how the strategy operates is given with reference to example images and attention is drawn to the feedback aspects of the control mechanism. Finally, possible improvements and enhancements to the work are considered.

## 1. Introduction

Very noisy or distorted images, and images containing flexible or articulated objects, are difficult to interpret, and in particular the interpretation is strongly dependent on prior knowledge and experience, and expectation of what may be present in the image.

Examples of such images are those resulting from ultrasonic scanning. This is an imaging modality that is now widely used in Medicine. The technique can provide an image of a two dimensional slice of the body but suffers from the coherence properties of the ultrasound which produces spatial noise known as "speckle". Furthermore, dense structures can produce shadowing and reverberations which show up as artifacts in the image. This results in an image that is difficult to interpret and requires a high degree of training and expertise on the part of the operator. Figure 1.1 is a typical fetal ultrasound image and illustrates the various difficulties. Despite these drawbacks, the advantages of cheapness and convenience, and because the modality is regarded as benign, have meant that the use of ultrasound scanning has spread rapidly and widely. Most image processing work associated with medical ultrasound has concentrated on reconstruction and enhancement. However, in this paper we use such images as examples of noisy and distorted material with which to consider some of the problems of image interpretation.

Because of the noise inherent in the modality, the interpretation is very difficult and strongly dependent on prior knowledge, experience and expectation. For this reason we believe that a model-based approach is essential and we expect a strong interaction between the high level knowledge and the low level processing will be necessary to interpret the image. The models required for this work will necessarily be complicated and involve flexible and deformable objects for which parameters must be bound during the matching process. This means that we must allow and expect considerable *feedback* from the partially instantiated model to the low level processing so that the matching can be performed incrementally.

The complexity of the task and the fact that we will want to encode high level symbolic knowledge, such as for example fetal anatomy, as well as expertise from radiologists and many heuristics and rules, mean that we use a knowledge-based or *expert* system approach. This has the advantage of flexibility for when we wish to consider other application domains.

In section 2 of this paper we describe the expert system tools we have developed to explore this problem. In section 3 we outline the structure of our models, how they have been implemented and in section 4 we discuss our model matching algorithm. In this section we also present the results of our initial implementation. Section 5 is a brief summary and a discussion of enhancements and developments being

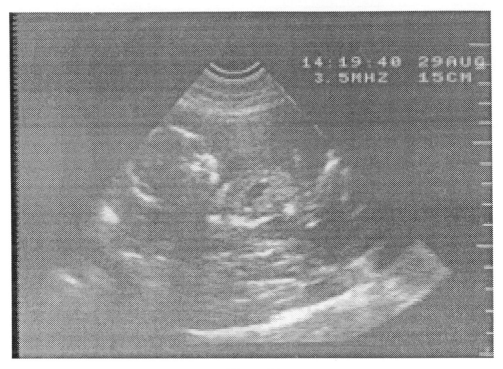

**Figure 1.1**

A fetal ultrasound scan showing the head, torso and some of the limbs. The noise level and distortion is typical of scan frames used for feature measurement.

considered.

## 2. Expert System Tools

### 2.1 Requirements of a Knowledge-Based System

Our basic aim was to see how knowledge-based systems could be used to encode high level knowledge and use it to control a complex image processing and model matching task. Of particular interest was to see how feedback could be implemented and controlled within the system. With this in mind we list our initial requirements which are then discussed in more detail:

- Data driven or *forward chaining* when required.
- Within the data driven part, the system must allow flexibility in both the knowledge-representation (eg mixtures of rules and procedures) and the control mechanism. For example, where a rule base is used it must provide:
    (i) a means of selecting appropriate rules (*meta-level control*)
    (ii) a means of forming a (dynamic) hierachical ordering of rules in order to restrict attention to the most relevant ones
    (iii) a flexible and dynamically modifiable way of selecting which rule from a set should be executed (*conflict resolution strategy*)
- Must allow use of practically any data structures: eg atoms, lists, records and frames.

- Must allow goal-driven (*backward chaining*) and planning operations.
- Debugging tools.
- Explanation and trace facilities.
- Must easily interface to lower level languages, for example C, FORTRAN or PASCAL.
- If possible it should interface to "AI languages" such as PROLOG or LISP, where a lot of work has already been done in the area of knowledge-based systems.
- Easy access to the source language to allow the full power and flexibility of that language.

Although the system will operate in a goal-driven way (for example it may have the goal "interpret image"), at the lowest levels, and to initiate any analysis, the image will have to be handed to a module which will simply process it and produce some higher level results. Within this module the control is *data-driven* and will depend upon the input image. If the control knowledge is encoded as *if-then* (production) rules then the typical control strategy is to find rules for which the *if* <condition> is satisfied and then execute the *then* <action>. This is termed *forward-chaining* and we expect this type of processing to be important at all levels, although to the user it may not be apparent. In this type of processing we will require full flexibility, so that not only the selection and execution order of the rules/procedures is under some higher level control but also perhaps the rules themselves, or at the very least, any parameters that are used within them.

Since we do not know beforehand how the data should be stored, we must allow any sort of data structure to be defined. This is related to the last point, that the source language must be available to the user because, although it would be nice to have an English-like interface to shield the user from programming details, this would be difficult to set up and would almost certainly be too constraining.

The interface to "C" and other languages is important because there already exist procedures for most of the image handling and processing tasks. Secondly languages such as POP11 or LISP, which are very good for list processing and matching and better for expressing the AI ideas, are not good at number crunching and so it should be more efficient to hand such tasks to procedures written in another language.

## 2.2 Implementation

To satisfy these requirements we have developed some expert system tools, implemented as an expert sytem shell, which we refer to as SBS.

Our first consideration was what language to use. Given the above requirements the simplest choice is POP-11 in the POPLOG environment because:

(i) it is an integrated software development environment providing incremental compilers for PROLOG, LISP and POP-11

(ii) it allows intermixing of these languages

(iii) it allows easy access to "C" and any other compilable code

(iv) POP-11 is a language similar to and with all the power of LISP but with a much richer and more readable syntax.

Our next consideration was the overall architecture or organisation of the system. We have chosen to design it as a "blackboard" system. The original blackboard model was developed at Carnegie-Mellon for the speech understanding system HEARSAY-II (Erman *et al* 1980) and has been successfully employed since (eg Nii and Fiegenbaum 1978, Hayes-Roth 1985, Russell and Lane 1986 and Rake and Smith 1987). A blackboard architecture is comprised of at least three elements: a shared data region (called the blackboard), a set of "*experts*", and a scheduler (Ensor and Gabbe 1986). The blackboard is a data base which is shared by the experts for communication. The experts contain rules, procedures etc which express the domain expertise of the system and these experts respond to each other through changes on the blackboard. The scheduler controls execution of the experts according to information in goal queues and on the blackboard. The inherent modularity of such architectures is particularly useful for systems solving problems with complex information interdependencies and diverse knowledge types. Furthermore, the modularity of the experts and formalisation of the communication means that it is easy to plug in or remove experts. This is, of course, only a way of organising the various modules and their communication and doesn't provide any solution to the actual image processing task but it should allow the final system to be more flexible and more easily modifiable.

Full details of the operation and syntax of SBS are given in the "SBS User Guide" (Baldock, Ireland and Towers 1987a). Figure 2.1 is a schematic diagram of SBS where the arrows indicate lines of communication which can be seen to be only between the blackboard and the "experts".

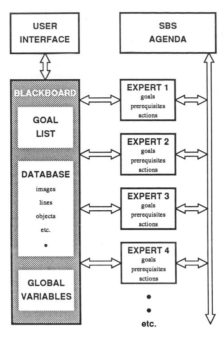

**Figure 2.1**

Schematic diagram of SBS and the relations between experts and blackboard.

Operation of the system can be summarised as follows. At any time, the head of the goal list† is the goal/sub-goal which the system is attempting to satisfy. Initially the goal list is empty and the user is asked to enter a goal. After this the goal list is altered by experts adding or deleting goals, until either the goal list becomes empty, indicating that the initial goal has been satisfied, or no expert can be found which can satisfy the present goal/sub-goal. This mechanism can be summarised as follows:

1. User enters initial goal.
2. If the goal list is empty, the system exits and indicates success.
3. Each expert compares the head of the goal list with the list of goals it can satisfy. If the expert can satisfy the goal then the expert is added to the "agenda".
4. The agenda is sorted by the priorities of the experts.
5. If there are experts on the agenda, the highest priority expert is *executed* (which can involve goals being added or deleted from the goal list — see below) and control returns to step 2.
6. The system exits and indicates failure.

Each expert divides into two parts. The first is a list of goals which the expert can satisfy and to each goal there is a corresponding prerequisite in the form of a condition-action pair. The second part contains the rules and procedures of the actions of the expert. *Execution* of an expert is a two stage process:

1. The first part of the "prerequisite" (corresponding to the goal being considered) is tested to determine whether the conditions for satisfactory application of the expert's "actions" are satisfied.
2. If the prerequisite conditions are not satisfied, the second part of the "prerequisite" is executed causing sub-goals to be added to the goal list. Execution of the present expert is terminated and the system attempts to select another expert, as described above, to satisfy the new sub-goal. If the prerequisites are satisfied the system goes on to execute the actions of the expert.

The actions of the expert basically involve running a production rule mechanism on a user-defined rule base. The rules within each expert are grouped into "contexts", and within each context the rules are ordered according to a priority parameter which may be changed dynamically. Processing control will

---

† In the current version the goal list is implemented with a "stack" architecture.

remain within a context until no rules can fire or until an explicit "exit" call has been made. It should be noted that if the actions of another expert are required from within a rule base, then this can only be achieved by putting the appropriate goal on the goal list, and quitting the current expert. Since the rule base associated with any expert need only comprise one rule whose <action> part can just execute procedures, then normal procedural control is provided for.

It will be clear from the above that the blackboard system/experts provide the backward-chaining and planning aspects of the control mechanism, while the experts' actions provide the forward chaining and procedural parts.

## 2.3 Data Structures

SBS has been designed in such a way that the user can use any data structures that are desired. For our work, however, we have found *frames* to be particularly useful for representing image features, models etc.

The word *frame* has been applied to a variety of "slot-and-filler" declarative representation structures, mostly following the work of Minsky (1975). Minsky described "a framework for representing knowledge", including how to "reason" within such a paradigm, and considered human cognitive processes. In this work we do not consider a calculus for the frames but simply use them as a convenient data structure. In particular we use the implementation of frames by Towers (1987).

A frame consists of a collection of *slots* that describe aspects of the objects. These slots can be filled with any data item (including other frame instances). Associated with each slot may be a set of conditions that must be met by any *filler* for it and if appropriate slots can be instantiated with a default value. Procedural information may also be associated with a slot and two special classes of procedure are provided. These are *if-needed* (executed if a value for the slot is ever requested – the determined value then replaces the procedure as the slot filler) and *daemon* (executed every time a value for the slot is requested) procedures.

Relations between frames are readily included by defining a relationship slot. However, two particular types of relation are provided. The first is the *is-a* relation which provides for *inheritance* and allows specialisation classes to be defined. In this implementation, multiple inheritance allows classes to inherit information from a number of super-classes, with a precedence list to resolve possible conflicts between super-classes supplying the same slots etc. The second built in relation is *component-of* so that *composite* frames can be defined. This means that a set of frames describing sub-parts of a common object can be grouped together under a single frame. A component frame may be otherwise unrelated to its composite parent and so there is no inheritance along this relationship.

## 3. Models

The choice of model representation depends on the weight attached to competing requirements (Clark 1987). From the point of view of the generation, verification and inspection of a model structure, the model elements or primitives and their relationships should be explicitly represented. An example of such a representation is the network described in Ballard and Brown (1982) where the nodes represent image elements and the arcs relationships. However for the matching algorithm to be efficient a great deal of heuristic or "procedural" knowledge specific to the model is required. If all this control knowledge is incorporated in the model then the model will be less easy to understand and modify. Our representation is an attempt to accommodate both requirements.

Our basic model structure is a tree of nodes where each node is either *composite* (a non-terminal node) or *primitive* (a terminal node). The reason for a hierarchical structure is to allow the systematic building of large and complex structures from simpler models. To supplement the model, a further node type is permitted but with restrictions as to which other nodes it can be connected to. The additional node is a *relation* which can exist between any components *of the same composite*. This restriction isn't necessary but it allows an easier partitioning of the model during the matching process. Allowing such relations implies that our model is a tree of networks. It should also be pointed out that our composite nodes are just a specialised form of relation similar to the *partitions* of Ballard and Brown (1982). With this type of structure it is easy to build explicit models of geometric or anatomical structures, an example of a geometric model is shown in figure 3.1. This is the geometrical model used for the fetal ultrasound scan considered in the next section, although it is certainly the case that more sophisticated shape descriptions will be required for this and other models.

In the system described in this paper each node is represented as a frame, and in this way procedural

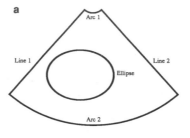

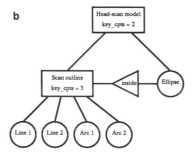

**Figure 3.1**

Diagram **a** is the prototype geometric model of a transverse ultrasound scan of a fetal head. Diagram **b** is the graphical form of the same structure. The rectangular, circular and triangular nodes denote composite, primitive and relation nodes respectively.

knowledge can be incorporated into the model (for example, heuristic matching functions can be be bound to the model). The model structure of composites, primitives and relations provides an explicit description at an anatomical or image primitive level and procedures and heuristic knowledge can appear in slots of each node either explicitly or be inherited from *super-frames*.

In this pilot version of the system, we have only implemented geometric models involving primitives such as lines and arcs. The composite frame in this case has only four slots: time-stamp, confidence, transformation and key-features. It also has a list of components and a list of relationships. The time-stamp denotes when the slot values were last changed and is used by the model-matching expert to determine which node to match next. In the current models we have not defined a confidence but a slot has been provided in the expectation that some form of *degree of belief* for each node will be essential (although how such a confidence is to be calculated has not been resolved yet). The transformation is the set of geometric transformation parameters (scale, shift and rotate) required to transform the component coordinate frame to that of the composite coordinate frame. In the matching of a rigid model there will be a single such transformation with free parameters which, when an instance of the model is found in the image, will become the mapping from model coordinates to image coordinates. Later, instead of a fixed transformation slot, there will probably be a *transformation algorithm* slot, of a which a Euclidean transformation is one example. The key features slot is a way of including the simplest form of matching control knowledge, namely *saliency*. In our models the components are ordered (left to right in fig 3.1b), and the value of the key features slot is an integer indicating the number of components necessary or important for matching the parent composite.

## 4. Model Matching

### 4.1 Matching Algorithm

As well as encoding the position, orientation and scale of structures, the models also need to describe deformations to allow for biological variation, flexion and articulation. This implies that any form of direct template matching may involve impossibly large search spaces. Our general strategy is therefore to attempt to constrain the search space by matching initially to primitives derived from the image by a bottom-up or data-driven process. We would expect that in many cases, there will be a requirement to reinforce initial primitive matching (both as regards confidence and accuracy of size, orientation and position estimation) by generation of special matched filters and their re-application to the image. It is likely that for a complex image this cycle will be repeated many times as different parts of the structure are matched, or the match reconsidered, and this feedback loop will be crucial to the success of the matching process.

The matching problem thus divides into two stages. The first is a match to primitives that have been derived from the image by some initial processing in order to find a set of sufficiently constrained hypotheses. The second is to confirm and refine, or reject these hypotheses by again matching directly to parts of the image.

A further assumption we have made for convenience is that any *composite* that is marked as a key-feature of a higher node, is a model in its own right, and so is independently matchable. This means that it is only necessary to consider primitives of a single composite at any one time which simplifies the matching process. We will relax this restriction in future implementations.

Our matching procedure can now be summarised:

1. Record the start time† of the matching process.
2. Depth-first search of the model tree, considering only out-of-date nodes, until a key primitive is encountered. When all components of a composite are matched:
   i) update appropriate transformation parameters
   ii) mark the composite node up to date
   iii) backtrack to the composite's parent node
   Repeat until all features required by the current goal are up-to-date, or until all key-features are found and then repeat for non-key features.
3. If the primitive is sufficiently constrained to allow a direct match to the image then refine
4. If the primitive is not sufficiently constrained then
   i) form a list of all key primitives of the same composite
   ii) use relations between primitives to form a list of possible matches of primitives on the blackboard to the key primitive list
   iii) order the list according to how well each match fits the model
   iv) for the best hypothesis, solve all the constraints to find the narrowest limits on parameters
   v) if constraint manipulation for this hypothesis returns false or the hypothesis can not be verified then remove it from the list and return to iv), otherwise accept the hypothesis and refine.
5. Make the matched primitives up-to-date
6. Update any other "siblings" via relationships
7. Backtrack to parent node and continue at step 2.

We have implemented this algorithm as a model matching "expert" within our expert system and provided the necessary procedures for each stage for the matching of models consisting of simple geometric objects such as arcs and lines. During the initial matching phase when nothing is known about the position, orientation and scale of the object the expert forms, in effect, a relational graph of the model primitives which is then matched with primitives on the blackboard. For the primitives which we have considered, the relation involved is the relative angle. For line primitives this will be reasonably accurate whereas the length of an image line is unlikely to be correct because with noisy images most lines will be broken.

The matching of the relational graph provides a list of possible matches, many of which can be eliminated by considering other relations between the primitives. We intend to implement this as a constraint manipulation process in a similar manner to Brooks (1981) and Fisher and Orr (1987) but in the current system the constraints are satisfied, or proved inconsistent, by numerically minimising a sum of error functions where each function corresponds to matching one of the primitives.

---

† *Time* here refers to a counter which is incremented at various points during the matching cycle.

In our implementation this procedure is subdivided into processes modelled on the geometric reasoning tasks described by Orr and Fisher (1987). For this application the two tasks involved are LOCATE and MERGE. LOCATE takes an image primitive and a model primitive as arguments and returns a transformation (referred to as a *position* by Orr and Fisher) which will map the model primitive on the image primitive. Each of the transformation parameters is represented by an upper and lower bound within which the true value must lie. In our case where we cannot assume the image line length is correct these bounds must be rather large. MERGE takes two transformations as arguments and returns a single transformation with parameter bounds consistent with both arguments or returns false if the two arguments are inconsistent. The MERGE we have implemented in fact will accept an arbitrary number of argument transformations. Fisher and Orr (1987) use LOCATE and MERGE to set up a network encoding all the parameter correlations and using the bounds from MERGE as starting values, the network is evaluated to find a maximum parameter space consistent with all the constraints. This of course may be null. In our case the network evaluation is replaced by a minimisation of an error function which could, in principle, yield the same information.

## 4.2 Matching an Ultrasound Scan

As a preliminary test, the algorithm outlined in the preceding subsection has been used to locate the outline of the ultrasound scan. This will be necessary for orientation and scaling purposes and is therefore a useful task to start with. Although in any final system the position, size and orientation of the outline will be fairly accurately known, in this test we make no such assumptions so that all aspects of the matching process are involved. To further test the robustness of the method we deliberately assume angles are known less accurately than they are, and we have not "tuned" the edge detector for this type of image so that the various lines are shorter and more fragmented.

The actions of the experts in solving this matching problem are illustrated in figures 4.1 (a-d). Figure 4.1a shows the original ultrasound image of a fetal head taken with a sector scanner, so the shape of the outline is bounded by two lines and two arcs. This is the model descibed in section 3.

The first goal, entered by the user, is `match model scan []`. This asks the matcher expert to find an instance of a model defined by the frame type `scan` anywhere in the image. The matcher finds that the search is unconstrained and so puts further goals in the goal list. In this example they are `find line` and `find arc` which are the key primitives found at the first non-composite level in the model.

The *line* and *arc* experts look for straight and circular segments of *polylines* respectively and so each in turn would enter `find polyline` on the goal-list. However, once the polylines are on the blackboard, the second expert to be invoked "realises" the data is available and so does not re-issue the goal.

Polylines are a sequence of connected vertices and can describe arbitrary shapes. In this example however, we have imposed certain constraints on the shape of polylines so that they will correspond more closely to perceived lines in the image. We have also assumed that the lines of interest can be detected by a derivative type filter. These constraints and assumptions are expressed as a series of *rules* in the polyline expert, and are easily modified (see Baldock, Ireland and Towers (1987b) for full details of the extraction of the polylines, lines and arcs from the image).

The polylines are the lowest level graphical primitive and are obtained directly from the image and therefore, provided the image is on the blackboard, the goal-directed or planning stage terminates at this point and the system can execute the goals in sequence. The initial polylines located by the polyline expert are not shown but the derived lines and arcs are shown in figure 4.1b. These lines and arcs are used to generate a list of possible matches by considering only the relative angles of the lines and arcs. Each primitive can be matched independently to define regions of transformation parameter space which must contain the true transformation if that particular match is correct. In fact each match may provide a number of regions corresponding to discrete ambiguities and all such possibilities must be considered. If there are a number of primitives to be matched then the correct transformation must lie in the intersection of the parameter spaces and many putative matches are at this "merging" stage ruled out because the intersection is null.

Unfortunately the possible matches remaining after the above process are not sufficiently constrained to permit a direct search for the best fit transformation.This is illustrated in figure 4.1c where the hatched region indicates the region within which the left-hand side of the scan is predicted to occur. This prediction is very poor because algebraic relations between the allowed values of parameters have been ignored. The correlations between parameters are expressed as an error or constraint function attached to each of the transformation frames returned by LOCATE. The last stage of the matching algorithm that we have implemented takes a list of constraint functions and a starting set of bounds as arguments and returns a new set of bounds that simultaneously satisfies all the constraints. For the example we are considering here

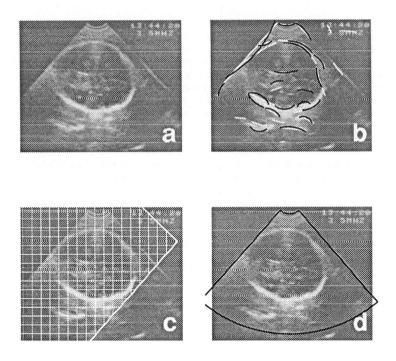

**Figure 4.1**

a: original image, b: located Lines (white) and Arcs (black), c: range of posssible positions of the left-hand edge after a naive merge of the permitted transformation parameter ranges, d: final scan outline after constraining with proper account taken of parameter correlations.

this results in a near exact match and is shown in figure 4.1d.

The last stage of verification and refinement is not yet fully implemented and so is not shown.

## 5. Summary and Discussion

In this paper we have considered some of the problems encountered when trying to interpret noisy images. For this task we have developed an expert system shell based upon a blackboard architecture. Some parts of this shell have proved useful (in particular the production rule mechanisms incorporated within the experts' actions), while other parts, such as the backward-chaining/planning aspects of the control mechanism, have been little used as yet. However, we believe that these parts will become increasing important as our models become more complex thus requiring more "intelligent" planning of the operations to be performed.

We have implemented simple geometric and relational models using frames as data structures. We hope in the next stage of our work to increase the complexity of these models. In particular we are interested in the modelling of objects with inherent variation and articulation. Furthermore we intend to build more of the control and strategy knowledge into the model. For example, the heuristic of using the relative angles between primitives to reduce the number of matches is at present in the matching expert. This should be a *relation* between primitives in the model, and then the matcher will be modified to make use of such relations. This will mean model dependent matching expertise can be built into the model structure so that the matching algorithm can be domain independent. Such control knowledge will either be put in by the user or could be learnt from a training set of images.

Although our primary control strategy for model matching is goal-directed, we begin processing in an inherently data-driven way. That is, *polylines* are defined by a set of production rules, which are then used to identify these items in the image. The polylines are then processed by other experts each of which have other primitives (lines and arcs) described in the experts' *actions*. This initial processing has been done using quite simple image processing routines (for example, first derivative of gaussian as the edge finder), since we were interested in demonstrating methods only. Nevertheless, the overall control mechanism has been able to overcome the deficiencies of the initial image processing.

The next stage of the work demonstrated that the initial primitives found in the image can be used as "cues" to guide the model-matcher to initial image-model feature matches. The geometric constraints implied by these matches can then be used to find the best match. Finally, a stage of verification can be used in which "matched filters" are applied to the image in order to accurately fix the parameters of the model instance.

So far, matches at the lowest level are all in terms of geometrical mappings in which only scale, orientation in the image plane and origin vary. This is a meagre matching strategy which will be extended to include region-based, colour-orientated, topological, syntactic and parametric matching.

At present, most of the model matching strategem is defined within a single "expert". In future we intend to separate the elements into separate experts to allow the planning mechanism to generate variations in the strategy to suit different images and goals.

Although we are at an early stage of implementing the details of the matching strategy, the basic elements of it have been demonstrated.

## 6. Acknowledgements

This work was funded by the Medical Research Council and Alvey grant MMI-134. We would like to thank Norman McDicken and Roger Wild for valuable discussions on the fetal ultrasound problem and John Ireland for his work on the development of SBS.

## 7. Bibliography

**Baldock** R.A., J. Ireland and S.J. Towers, "SBS User Guide", *MRC CAPCU internal report* (1987a)

**Baldock** R.A., J. Ireland and S.J. Towers, "A Pilot Study of Knowledge-Based Control for Image Processing", *MRC CAPCU internal report* (1987b)

**Ballard** D.H. and C.M. Brown, "Computer Vision" (Prentice-Hall, New Jersey; 1982)

**Brooks** R.A., "Symbolic Reasoning Among 3-D Models and 2-D Images", *Artificial Intelligence* **17** (1981) 285-348

**Clark** P., "Rule-Based Systems in Image Processing", *Turing Institute report* (1987) unpublished.

**Ensor** J.R. and J.D. Gabbe, "Transactional Blackboards" *Art. Intell. in Eng.* **1** (1986) 80-84

**Erman** J.R., F. Hayes-Roth, V.R. Lesser and R. Reddy, "The Hearsay-II Speech Understanding System: Integrating Knowledge to Resolve Uncertainty", *ACM Computing Surveys* **12** (1980) 213-253

**Fisher** R.B. and M.J.L. Orr, " Solving Geometric Constraints in a Parallel Network", *Proc. of 3rd Alvey Vision Conf., Cambridge* (1987) 87-95

**Hayes-Roth** B., "A Blackboard Architecture for Control", *Artificial Intelligence* **26** (1985) 251-321

**Minsky** M., "The Psychology of Computer Vision" ed P. Winston (McGraw Hill, NY; 1975)

**Nii** H.P. and E.A. Fiegenbaum, "Rule-Based Understanding of Signals in Pattern Directed Inference Systems" (Academic Press; 1978)

**Orr** M.J.L. and R.B. Fisher, "Geometric Reasoning for Computer Vision", *Image and Vision Computing* **5** (1987) 233-238

**Rake** S.T. and L.D.R. Smith, "The Interpretation of X-ray Angiograms using a Blackboard Control Architecture", *Proceedings of the Symposium on Computer Assisted Radiology* (Springer-Verlag, Berlin; 1987) to be published

**Russell** G.T. and D.M. Lane, "A Knowledge-Based System Framework for Enviromental Perception in a Subsea Robotics Context", *IEEE J. of Oceanic Eng.* **OE-11** (1986) 401-412

**Towers** S.J., "Frames as Data Structures for SBS", *MRC CAPCU internal report* (1987)

# LINEAR ALGORITHM FOR MOTION ESTIMATION:

## HOW TO HANDLE DEGENERATE CASES

T.S. Huang and Y.S. Shim

Coordinated Science Laboratory

University of Illinois

1101 W. Springfield Ave.

Urbana, IL 61801

U.S.A.

## ABSTRACT

For determining motion/structure of a 3-D rigid object from point correspondences over two perspective views, a linear algorithm was developed in Refs. 1 and 2. This algorithm fails when the 3-D points under observation satisfy certain geometrical constraints, as demonstrated in Refs. 3 and 4. In the present paper, we show that the linear algorithm can be resurrected in these degenerate cases.

## I.  INTRODUCTION.

The problem of determining 3-D motion and structure from image sequences has attracted much attention in recent years. In particular, a linear algorithm has been developed by Longuet-Higgins[1], and Tsai and Huang [2] for determining 3-D motion/structure of a rigid object from two perspective views. This algorithm requires 8 (or more) point correspondences over the two views. A necessary and sufficient condition for this algorithm to fail has also been established [3,4]. In this paper, we show that in these degenerate cases where the above condition holds, the linear algorithm can nevertheless be resurrected. The modified procedure requires, in addition to solving the 8 (or more) linear equations, the least-squares solution of three polynominal equations.

## II.  REVIEW OF THE 8-POINT ALGORITHM.

### A.  Problem Statement

We shall use the following notations. The object-space coordinates are denoted by lowercase letters, and the image-plane coordinates by uppercase letters. The coordinates of points before the motion are unprimed, those after the motion are primed. Thus

$(x,y,z)$ = coordinates of object point before motion
$(x',y',z')$ = coordinates of object point after motion
$(X,Y)$ = coordinates of image point before motion
$(X',Y')$ = coordinates of object point after motion

We assume that the image plane is at z = 1, the origin of the image plane is on the z-axis, and the X- and Y- axes are parallel to the x- and y- axes, respectively. The point (X,Y) is the central projection of the point (x,y,z) with respect to the origin (0,0,0).

From kinematics,

$$\begin{bmatrix} x' \\ y' \\ z' \end{bmatrix} = R \begin{bmatrix} x \\ y \\ z \end{bmatrix} + T \tag{1}$$

where R is a rotation (right-handed orthonormal) matrix and T a translation vector

$$T = \begin{bmatrix} t_1 \\ t_2 \\ t_3 \end{bmatrix} \tag{2}$$

our problem is:

Given- N image point correspondences

$$(X_i, Y_i) \leftrightarrow (X'_i, Y'_i)$$

$$i = 1, 2, \ldots, N.$$

Find-    The motion parameters
         T (to within a scale factor) and R.

## B. The 8–Point Linear Algorithm

It can be readily shown that if we define

$$E = \begin{bmatrix} e_1 & e_2 & e_3 \\ e_4 & e_5 & e_6 \\ e_7 & e_8 & e_9 \end{bmatrix} \triangleq GR \tag{3}$$

where

$$G = \begin{bmatrix} 0 & -t_3 & t_2 \\ t_3 & 0 & -t_1 \\ -t_2 & t_1 & 0 \end{bmatrix} \tag{4}$$

then

$$[X' \ Y' \ 1] \ E \begin{bmatrix} X \\ Y \\ 1 \end{bmatrix} = 0 \tag{5}$$

which is linear and homogeneous in the nine unknowns $e_1, e_2, \ldots, e_9$.

From the N point correspondences, we have

$$
B \begin{bmatrix} e_1 \\ e_2 \\ \cdot \\ \cdot \\ \cdot \\ e_9 \end{bmatrix} = 0 \qquad (6)
$$

where

$$
B \triangleq \begin{bmatrix} X'_1X_1, \ X'_1Y_1, \ X'_1, \ Y'_1X_1, \ Y'_1Y_1, \ Y'_1, \ X_1,Y_1, \ 1 \\ \cdot \\ \cdot \\ \cdot \\ X'_NX_N, \ X'_NY_N, \ X'_N, \ Y'_NX_N, \ Y'_NY_N, \ Y'_N, \ X_N,Y_N, \ 1 \end{bmatrix}. \qquad (7)
$$

Assuming the rank of B is 8, we can solve (6) to get kE, where k is an unknown scale factor.

Once kE is obtained, several methods are available [1,2,5] to decompose it uniquely to find T (to within a scale factor) and R.

## C.  Degenerate Cases

The linear algorithm fails if the rank of B is less than 8 (in which case we say that degeneracy occurs).  A necessary and sufficient condition for degeneracy can be stated geometrically if we assume that the object is stationary and the camera is moving [3].  Let the origin of the camera system be 0 and 0' before and after the motion, respectively.  Then, assuming $T \neq 0$, the rank of B is less than 8 if and only if the N 3-D points lie on a quadratic surface passing through 0 and 0'.

## III.  HOW TO RESURRECT THE 8-POINT LINEAR ALGORITHM IN DEGENERATE CASES.

## A.  Basic Idea

It is important to note that although the linear algorithm as described in Section II.B fails if Rank (B) < 8, it does not necessarily mean that a unique solution to the motion parameters cannot be found by other methods.  In fact, we shall show presently that the linear algorithm with appropriate modifications can be used even in the degenerate cases.

The basic idea is as follows.  Let

$$
\text{Rank (B)} = M < 8. \qquad (8)
$$

Then there are

$$
K = 9-M \qquad (9)
$$

linearly independent vectors in the null space of B.  A set of these vectors can be found by solving Eq. (6).  Putting each of these vectors in the form of a $3 \times 3$ matrix, we obtain a set of K E-matrices which we shall call $E_i$; $i = 1, 2, \ldots, K$.  Then a general solution to Eq. (6) is

$$
E = \sum_{i=1}^{K} a_i E_i \qquad (10)
$$

where the $a_i$'s are arbitrary constants.

The thing left to do is to find values of $a_i$'s such that E is in the form of (3), i.e., it is decomposable into the product of a skew matrix and a right-handed orthonormal matrix.

## B.  Decomposability Conditions

We show that the decomposability conditions for E can be expressed in the form of three simultaneous polynominal equations with the $a_i$'s as unknowns.

Let

$r_i$ = ith row of R
$\varepsilon_i$ = ith row of E
(i = 1, 2, 3)

Then Eq. (3) can be written as

$$\varepsilon_1 = -t_3 r_2 + t_2 r_3 \qquad \text{(a)}$$
$$\varepsilon_2 = t_3 r_1 - t_1 r_3 \qquad \text{(b)} \quad (11)$$
$$\varepsilon_3 = -t_2 r_1 + t_1 r_2. \qquad \text{(c)}$$

Our problem is to find conditions on $\varepsilon_1, \varepsilon_2, \varepsilon_3$ such that they can be expressed as in (11), where $t_1, t_2, t_3$ are real numbers and $\begin{bmatrix} r_1 \\ r_2 \\ r_3 \end{bmatrix}$ is a right-handed orthonormal matrix.  These conditions can then be expressed in terms of the $a_i$'s via (10).

Lemma  Any two 3-vectors $\varepsilon_1$ and $\varepsilon_2$ can be expressed as

$$\varepsilon_1 = -t_3 r_2 + t_2 r_3 \qquad (12)$$

$$\varepsilon_2 = t_3 r_1 - t_1 r_3 \qquad (13)$$

where $t_1, t_2, t_3$ are real numbers and $\begin{bmatrix} r_1 \\ r_2 \\ r_3 \end{bmatrix}$ is a right-handed orthonormal matrix.

[Proof] From (12) and (13),

$$\varepsilon_1 \times \varepsilon_2 = t_3 (t_1 r_1 + t_2 r_2 + t_3 r_3). \qquad (14)$$

Eqs. (12), (13), (14) can be written as

$$A \begin{bmatrix} r_1 \\ r_2 \\ r_3 \end{bmatrix} = \begin{bmatrix} \varepsilon_1 \\ \varepsilon_2 \\ \varepsilon_1 \times \varepsilon_2 \end{bmatrix} \qquad (15)$$

where

$$A \triangleq \begin{bmatrix} 0 & -t_3 & t_2 \\ t_3 & 0 & -t_1 \\ t_3 t_1 & t_3 t_2 & t_3^2 \end{bmatrix}. \qquad (16)$$

Case 1- If $\varepsilon_1 \times \varepsilon_2 = 0$, then we can choose $r_3$ as the normalized vector of $\varepsilon_1$ or $\varepsilon_2$. Then, $t_3 = 0$, and we do not have to worry about $r_1$ and $r_2$.

Case 2- If $\varepsilon_1 \times \varepsilon_2 \neq 0$, then

$$\det (A) = \|\varepsilon_1 \times \varepsilon_2\|^2 \neq 0.$$

We solve (15) to get

$$r_3 = [t_3^2(\varepsilon_1 \times \varepsilon_2) + t_2 t_3^2 \varepsilon_1 - t_1 t_3^2 \varepsilon_2] / \det (A) \qquad (a)$$
$$r_2 = [t_2 t_3(\varepsilon_1 \times \varepsilon_2) - t_3(t_1^2 + t_3^2)\varepsilon_1 - t_1 t_2 t_3 \varepsilon_2] / \det (A) \qquad (b) \quad (17)$$
$$r_1 = [t_1 t_3(\varepsilon_1 \times \varepsilon_2) + t_1 t_2 t_3 \varepsilon_1 + t_3(t_2^2 + t_3^2)\varepsilon_2] / \det (A). \qquad (c)$$

It can be readily verified that $r_1, r_2, r_3$ form a right-handed orthonormal basis, if $t_1, t_2, t_3$ satisfy:

$$t_2^2 + t_3^2 = \|\varepsilon_1\|^2$$
$$t_1^2 + t_3^2 = \|\varepsilon_2\|^2 \qquad (18)$$
$$t_1 t_2 = -(\varepsilon_1 \cdot \varepsilon_2).$$

[End of Proof]

Now we proceed to find conditions on $\varepsilon_1, \varepsilon_2, \varepsilon_3$ such that $\varepsilon_3$ can be expressed as in (11c). Let

$$\varepsilon_3 = \mu r_1 + v r_2 + \omega r_3. \qquad (19)$$

Then we want to find conditions such that

$$(\mu, v, \omega) = (-t_2, t_1, 0) \qquad (20)$$

From (11), the direction of $\varepsilon_3$ can be determined by:

$$\varepsilon_3 \cdot (\varepsilon_1 \times \varepsilon_2) = 0 \qquad (21)$$

and

$$\varepsilon_3 \cdot r_3 = 0 \qquad (22)$$

with the help of (17a) and (21), Eq. (22) becomes

$$t_1(\varepsilon_2 \cdot \varepsilon_3) - t_2(\varepsilon_1 \cdot \varepsilon_3) = 0. \qquad (23)$$

Multiplying (23) by $t_1$:

$$t_1^2 (\varepsilon_2 \cdot \varepsilon_3) - t_1 t_2(\varepsilon_1 \cdot \varepsilon_3) = 0$$

Then by (18) and (25),

$$(\|\varepsilon_3\|^2 + \|\varepsilon_2\|^2 - \|\varepsilon_1\|^2) (\varepsilon_2 \cdot \varepsilon_3) + (\varepsilon_1 \cdot \varepsilon_2) (\varepsilon_1 \cdot \varepsilon_3) = 0 \qquad (24)$$

From (11c), the magnitude of $\varepsilon_3$ is determined by

$$\|\varepsilon_3\|^2 = t_2^2 + t_1^2 \qquad (25)$$

which becomes, with the help of (18):

$$\|\varepsilon_3\|^4 = (\|\varepsilon_2\|^2 - \|\varepsilon_1\|^2)^2 + 4(\varepsilon_1 \cdot \varepsilon_2)^2. \qquad (26)$$

Eqs. (21), (24), and (26) are the decomposition conditions. To check, we rewrite them in terms of $\mu,\nu,\omega,t_1,t_2,t_3$ using (11a), (11b), and (19):

$$t_3(t_1\mu + t_2\nu + t_3\omega) = 0 \tag{27}$$

$$(t_1^2 + t_2^2)\omega - t_3(t_1\mu + t_2\nu) = 0 \tag{28}$$

$$\mu^2 + \nu^2 + \omega^2 = t_1^2 + t_2^2. \tag{29}$$

Solving, we get

$$(\mu,\nu,\omega) = (-t_2,t_1,0) \tag{30}$$

or

$$(\mu,\nu,\omega) = (t_2,-t_1,0). \tag{31}$$

Note that via (10), Eqs. (21), (24), (26) can be written in terms of the $a_i$'s. These are polynominal equations of degrees 3, 4, and 4, respectively. The equations are homogeneous, reflecting the fact that the $a_i$'s can only be determined to within an unknown scale factor. We can conceptually setting one of the $a_i$'s to 1, and solve for the others. Thus: If the number of $a_i$'s is K, the number of unknowns in the three equations is (K-1). The interesting cases are:

| Rank(B) = M = | 8 | 7 | 6 | 5 |
|---|---|---|---|---|
| Number of unknowns = K-1 = | 0 | 1 | 2 | 3 |
| Number of equations = | 3 | 3 | 3 | 3 |

The case of M=8 is the nondegenerate case where the original linear alrogithm works and the solution to motion/structure is unique. When M=7 or 6, we have more equations than unknowns, so the solution to the $a_i$'s is very likely unique. When M=5, the number of equations is equal to the number of unknowns. Since the equations are nonlinear (polynominal), there are likely more than one (but a finite number of) solutions to the $a_i$'s. For each solution to the $a_i$'s, we obtain an E (using Eq. (10)) to within a scale factor, from which we get a solution to the motion and structure. For $M \le 4$, the number of equations becomes smaller than the number of unknowns. Therefore, the number of solutions to the $a_i$'s (and hence to motion and structure) become infinite. In fact, the solution space is a continuum.

For the cases M=7, 6, and 5, a good way to solve the three polynominal equations for the $a_i$'s is to find a least-square solution subject to the constraint

$$\sum_{i=1}^{K} a_i^2 = 1. \tag{32}$$

Iterative methods can be used to obtain the solution. Since we do not know a priori the number of solutions, global search is needed. The computation can be tedius, especially for M=5.

## C. Summary of the Algorithm

Step 1: By solving (6), find a set of basis vectors of the null space of the matrix B. If Rank(B) = M, then the number of such vectors is K=9-M.

Step 2: Using (10), express $e_i(i=1,2,\ldots,9)$ in terms of $a_j(j=j,2,\ldots,K)$.

Step 3: Construct the three polynominal equations (21), (24), and (26); and solve them for the $a_i$'s.

Step 4: For each solution of the $a_i$'s get E from (10), and decompose it (using the techuique of Ref. 1, 2 or 5) to obtain the motion parameters.

## IV. COMPUTER SIMULATION RESULTS.

### A. Seven Points in General Positions, Rank(B) = 7

In every case we have tried, the solution is unique. We shall give one example here.

Ground truth: 3-D object coordinates of 7 points before motion-
(2, 2, 2), (3, 1, 3), (-2, 2, 2), (2, -2, 3),
(-1, -3, 3.5), (-4, -3, 2.5), (3, 0, 3).

Rotation-
Direction of rotation axis = (1, 1, 1)
Angle of rotation = 30°
Translation = (1, 0, 1)

Given point correspondences:

| i | $X_i$ | $Y_i$ | $X'_i$ | $Y'_i$ |
|---|---|---|---|---|
| 1 | 1 | 1 | 1 | 0.666666 |
| 2 | 1 | 0.3333333 | 1.3464 | 0.3535899 |
| 3 | -1 | 1 | -0.1616507 | 0.1676698 |
| 4 | 0.6666667 | -0.6666667 | 1.672028 | -0.7320508 |
| 5 | -0.2857143 | -0.8571429 | 0.5793637 | -1.142226 |
| 6 | -1.6 | -1.2 | -0.3312093 | -1.437365 |
| 7 | 1 | 0 | 1.57735 | 0.08931641 |

## Solution:

Step 1- Rank(B) = 7

$$E_1 = \begin{bmatrix} 0.22912069 & 1 & 0.1671754 \\ -1.101394 & 0.5376813 & 0.487313 \\ -0.5702385 & -0.7751201 & 0 \end{bmatrix}$$

$$E_2 = \begin{bmatrix} 0.510991 & 0 & -1.623915 \\ -0.6215896 & 0.3593681 & 0.5473321 \\ 0.7621039 & -0.8392533 & 1 \end{bmatrix}$$

Step 2-

$$E = a_1E_1 + a_2E_2$$

Thus, $e_1 = 0.2291069\, a_1 + 0.510991\, a_2$, etc.

Step 3- Since in this simulation the data are essentially noise-free, instead of finding the least-squares solution of Eqs. (21), (24), (26), we take an easier route. We first construct Eq. (21) and set $a_2 = 1$:

$$0.02635941\, a_1^3 - 0.01565024\, a_1^2 + 0.01741159\, a_1 + 0.01595911 = 0.$$

The three roots of this equation are:

$$-0.582126, \ 3.734082, \ 2.785306.$$

For each root we get E via (10) and substitute into Eqs. (24) and (26). Only the second root satisfies these two equations. Thus, we choose

$$a_1 = 3.734082$$

Step 4-

$$E = a_1 E_1 + E_2 = \begin{bmatrix} 1.366495 & 3.734082 & -0.9996085 \\ -4.734287 & 2.367114 & 2.366999 \\ -1.367176 & -3.733616 & 1 \end{bmatrix}$$

Finally, using the method of Ref. 5 we decompose E to get:

Rotation axis direction = (0.5772734, 0.5773939, 0.5773835)
Rotation angle = 29.99962°
Translation = (4.099894, -0.0006235445, 4.100011)

## B. Eight Points On Vertices Of A Cube.

This case is degenerate as stated in Ref. 1. We found that Rank(B) = 7 and that the solution to motion/structure is unique.

## C. Six Points In General Positions, Rank(B) = 6.

In every case we have tried, the solution to motion/structure is unique.

## D. Five Points In General Positions, Rank(B) = 5.

In each case we have tried, the number of solutions to motion/structure is 2.

## V. CONCLUDING REMARKS

The linear algorithm for determining motion/structure (of a 3-D rigid object from point correspondences over 2 perspective views) fails when the matrix B in Eq. (7) has a rank less than 8. In this paper, we have described an approach to handling such degenerate cases. This approach becomes particularly simple when Rank (B) = 7, in which case (in addition to linear processing) one needs only to solve a 3rd-order polynomial equation in one variable.

We note that the orders of the polynomial eqs. (21), (24), and (26) are 3, 4, and 4, respectively. When Rank (B) = 7, there is only one unknown in these equations; therefore, the number of solutions to motion/structure is at most 3. When Rank (B) = 6, there are 2 unknowns; the number of solutions is at most 3 x 4 = 12. When Rank (B) = 5, there are 3 unknowns; the number of solutions is at most 3 x 4 x 4 = 48.

## Acknowledgement

This work was supported by the National Science Foundation under Grant IRI-8605400.

# REFERENCES

1.  H.C. Longuet-Higgins, A Computer Program for Reconstructing a Scence From Two Projections, *Nature*, Vol. 293, pp. 133-135, 1981.

2.  R.Y. Tsai and T.S. Huang, Uniqueness and Estimation of 3-D Motion Parameters of Rigid Bodies with Curved Surfaces, *IEEE Trans. PAMI*, Vol. 6, No. 1, pp. 13-27, 1984.

3.  H.C. Lonquet-Higgins, The Reconstruction of a Scene From Two Projections - Configurations That Defeat the 8-Point Algorithm, *Proc. 1st Conf. AI Applications*, Dec 5-7, 1984, Denver, CO., pp. 395-397.

4.  X. Zhuang and R.M. Haralick, Two-View Motion Analysis, *Proc. Int. Conf. ASSP.*, March 1985, Tampa, FL.

5.  T.S. Huang, Determining Three-Dimensional Motion and Structure From Two Prospective Views, in "Handbook of Pattern Recognition and Image Processing," ed. by T.Y. Young and K.S. Fu, Academic Press, 1986; pp. 333-354.

# On Token-Matching in Real Time Motion Analysis.

Henrik I Christensen & Erik Granum

Laboratory of Image Analysis,
Institute of Electronic Systems,
Aalborg University, Denmark.

**Keywords:**

Dynamic scene analysis, robot vision, image sequences, probabilistic relaxation, Support functions.

## 1. Introduction.

Serious discussions about real time motion analysis in a general sense in 1987, will refer to special hardware, special methods and/or a rather constrained scenario.

One of the most promising examples from the literature uses a "back tracking" scheme. Sethi & Jain (1987) assumes smooth and well-behaved motion of feature points and they achieve tracking by optimizing "smoothness of motion". Their method can be fast since it is based on feature points such as corners; this results in a small amount of data for the optimization. They have tested the system on various scenarios, ie. a sequence from a "superman" movie and laboratory scenes, but they have not reported time-usage. Wiklund and Granlund (1987) have suggested a binary image differencing method where tracking is based on comparison of measured and predicted images. A real-time operation must here rely on special hardware for the image differencing. This method has been demonstrated using off-line computation on a sequence of driving cars. However, none of these methods have capabilities of handling occlusions.

Granum and Munk (1986) have also proposed a method where predicted frames are matched with measured frames. They are matching frames by tokens, where the tokens are objects described by feature vectors. Hence input is taken from a fast image analysis system which produces frame descriptions in terms of lists of object-feature vectors at frame rate.

The token matching problem of their approach is the topic of this paper.

## 2. The "scenario".

The potential of real-time operation is based on constraints of the complexity of the scenario, a minimum or non special hardware and a special method, which may not be particular special after all.

Constraints of scene are

All objects observed are in a slice in space which is perpendicular to the camera axis and as deep as the depth of focus of the camera.
Only planar (2D) motion is considered (but occlusions may occur).

Objects are easily distinguisable from the background and occluding/touching objects appear as one object.

The image acquisition and analysis system employed produces for each observed object in each frame, a set of object discriptive features and the object position in the frame (e.g. object centroid).

The motion analysis system operates with a world model of all individual objects seen so far, – including their descriptive features, their current position, velocity and acceleration. Motion parameters used are at least with respect to linear motion and may or may not include angular change in trajectory and object rotation (velocity and acceleration).

The total set of motion parameters is used in a prediction of the position of the objects in the next frame, such as to minimize ambiguity and prepare a quick match. This on the other hand leaves us basically with only position and descriptive features as information for the matching process.

Two sample implementations of this approach have been made. Munk (1986) used a rule supported method to explicitly foresee occlusions and compute an estimate of next frame which expressed such occluding objects as one object. Christensen (1987) have avoided many of these rules and simplified the estimation. Instead his method relies more heavily on matching by relaxation, which is then supposed automatically to cope with occlusions directly. It is the matching problem of the last implementation which is of concern here.

The "scenario" for the matching process of this real-time approach can be summarized as follows.

a) The ambition of real-time operation calls for a method which
   – requires a minimum of information from the preprocessing system.
   – uses a minimum of sophistication in the matching process itself.
b) Objects (= tokens) of the observed frame are to be matched with objects in an estimated version of the same frame.
c) An object in the observed frame may correspond to two or more objects currently occluding.
d) An object in the estimated frame is a single object, if and only if, it has previously been observed as such.
e) The maximum number of objects per frame is limited to, – say 10.
f) Standard hardware and software should suffice for implementation, and time of execution should be less than one frame interval.

## 3. Real time token matching.

Token matching is associated with an inherent ambiguity (Ullman, 1979), and a relaxation approach is chosen, as it has the potential of coping with ambiguity using conventional numerical methods.

Relaxation methods may be discrete, fuzzy and probabilistic. The discrete methods are considered to be too rigid, and the fuzzy methods seems to have little to offer compared with the probabilistic methods. The latter are resonably well described in the literature and supported by more analytical tools (see survey by Kittler and Illingworth, 1985).

Price (1985) compares four different probabilistic relaxation methods:

A gradient approach (Price and Faugeras, 1981)
An optimization approach (Hummel and Zucker, 1983)
The product rule (Peleg, 1981)
The "original" method (Rosenfeld et. al., 1976)

The first two seem to perform best (low error rates), but algorithmic complexity seems to rule them out for our real time application. The third method is based on statistics of the population of objects per frame. As we assume a very limited number of objects per frame, Peleg's method may not be very useful for us. The last method is possibly the fastest and it can operate even on our limited scenario. Goshtasby and Page (1984) has used it for a labeling problem similar to ours (Image registration).

The updating formula of the "original" method is:

$$p_i^{(k+1)}(\lambda) \;=\; \frac{p_i^{(k)}(\lambda)*[1+S_i^{(k)}(\lambda)]}{\sum\limits_{j} p_i^{(k)}(\lambda_j)*[1+S_i^{(k)}(\lambda_j)]} \tag{1}$$

where (see figure 1)

$p_i^{(k)}(\lambda)$ is the matching strength associated with the matching of the measured token $t_i$ with the predicted token $\lambda$ in the k'th iteration.

$S_i^{(k)}(\lambda)$ is the label support function which expresses compatibility of labeling $t_i$ with $\lambda$ in the k'th iteration given the labeling of neighbouring tokens.

The denominator of (1) normalizes each row in the relaxation matrix to sum to one after each iteration.

The iterative procedure of relaxation is then in pseudo code:

Initialize (k=0; $p_i^{(0)}(\lambda)$)
while ( stop criteria not OK )
{
    Compute support function $S_i^{(k)}(\lambda)$
    Compute updating $p_i^{(k+1)}(\lambda)$
    (including rowwise normalization)
    k=k+1
}

Predicted/estimated tokens

| | | $\lambda_1$ | $\lambda_2$ | $\lambda_3$ |
|---|---|---|---|---|
| M e a s u r e d | t o k e n s | | | |
| | $t_1$ | $p_1^{(k)}(\lambda_1)$ | $p_1^{(k)}(\lambda_2)$ | $p_1^{(k)}(\lambda_3)$ |
| | $t_2$ | $p_2^{(k)}(\lambda_1)$ | $p_2^{(k)}(\lambda_2)$ | $p_2^{(k)}(\lambda_3)$ |
| | $t_3$ | $p_3^{(k)}(\lambda_1)$ | $p_3^{(k)}(\lambda_1)$ | $p_3^{(k)}(\lambda_1)$ |

Fig. 1 Organisation of relaxation matrix, illustrating
the "Rosenfeld et. al" terminology used.

To make it all work we thus have to define initialization, support function and stop criteria.

## 3.1. Initialization.

The initial probabilities:

$$p_i^{(0)}(\lambda) = p(\lambda \mid t_i) \text{ for } \sum_{\lambda'} p(\lambda' \mid t_i) = 1. \tag{2}$$

I.e. all $t_i$ are considered separately and an a-priori likelihood of matching each $\lambda$ is calculated. The process is much like an ordinary classification (evaluation of similarity) and we want these estimates to be as close to the final matching as possible using all information available.

As the strengths for all potential labels of a given $t_i$ is required to sum to one, a problem may arise in situations where a new token (object) enters the field of view, ie. it has no match partner in the previous/estimated frame. In order to handle this an artificial object is introduced, the "no-label" token. This label should have preference only when none of the other tokens from the estimated frame have.

The information given here is descriptive features and position leaving us only with a choice of how to weight these features against one another. Having real time implementation in mind we choose a high preference for similarity of position.

From the knowledge of the motion parameters an individual tolerance on the estimate of each object's position could be computed from the velocities of the objects. However, this possibility is not used yet.

As our artificial token (no-label) has no descriptive features and no unique position, the normal formula for initial strength cannot be used here. Given the requirement it should have preference when the others fail, we use eqn. (3) for this label:

$$p(no-label) = 1-\max_{\lambda}(p_i^{(0)}(\lambda)) \tag{3}$$

As this label should be used for introduction of new objects, eqn. (3) is only applied if a token is close to the boundary of the field of view, i.e. if the object is in the middle it can not be a new one and hence $p_i(no-label)$ should equal 0.

## 3.2. Support function,

From eqn. (1) it can be derived that the support function should obey the following criteria, in order to ensure convergence towards the optimal labeling.

a) $S_i^{(k)}(\lambda)$ should be in the range $[-1;1]$.
b) If the labeling in question is supported by neighbouring tokens it should be positive.
c) If the labeling might be inconsistent the support should be negative.
d) If the labelings are independent or if insufficient information is available the
   support-function should equal zero, ie. no preference is recommended.

A general version of the support function may be expressed as described by Price (1985):

$$S_i^{(k)}(\lambda) = \sum_j \sum_{\lambda'} r_{ij}^{(k)}(\lambda,\lambda')p_j^{(k)}(\lambda')+\alpha F_i(\lambda) \tag{4}$$

where

$r_{ij}(\lambda,\lambda')$ is a parameter which describes the influence of the labeling $t_j-\lambda'$ on labeling $t_i-\lambda$. This parameter will typically express scene constraints, e.g. whether two labels can match with a single token and visa versa.

$F_i(\lambda)$ is a feature match function which can be used to incorporate feature information in the updating process.

$\alpha$ expresses the importance of image data versus scene constraints.

The purpose of the support function is to influence and speed up convergence by imposing controlling information in each iteration. The example of eqn. (4) gives pro-vision for quite a variety of information. We do not have any new information directly available and computing it as well as using it may easily challenge the "real time ambi-tion".

For a start we want to experiment with an extremly simple support function which is heuristicly developed:

$$S_i^{(k)}(\lambda) \;=\; 2 \;\star\; \frac{p_i^{(k)}(\lambda)}{\sum\limits_{j} p_i^{(k)}(\lambda_j)} \;-\; 1 \tag{5}$$

Essentially what this means is that for each iteration the matrix at a stage of computation is normalized column-wise before the row-wise normalization of eqn. (1).

This can also be formulated as propagation of mutual certainty inherent in the initial matrix. Each iteration is fast and convergence to a unique labeling will take place if such a labeling exists and sufficient information is available. For the simple scenes we have considered so far (see section 5 for examples), convergence takes places in 1-5 iterations.

We cannot use the support function (eqn. (5)) for the no-label token, as these tokens are independent, i.e. the no-label for different tokens should not influence each other. Here we promote the no-label if no other labels achieves a "good" support, and we use the following heuristic formula for the no-label:

$$S_i^{(k)}(no{-}label) \;=\; -\; \max_{\lambda}(S_i^{(k)}(\lambda)) \tag{6}$$

### 3.3. Stop criteria.

The labeling process should continue until a clear match trend appear, i.e. we don't need the final result. Here we consider

Consistency
Magnitude of convergence trend
Computation time (no of iterations)

Given convergence takes place, one should not stop before we have a consistent labeling, i.e. we require that a token does not participate in an occlusion and a split at the same time. To check for a trend in the matching we use a heuristic bi-level thresholding scheme. If a strength is below

$$0.9 \;\star\; \max_{\lambda}\; (p_i^{(k)}(\lambda))$$

it should also be below

$$0.5 \;\star\; \max_{\lambda}\; (p_i^{(k)}(\lambda))$$

before we stop, this should ensure sufficient convergence. This method will ensure that strengths are either approximately equal or they differ by a factor larger than 2.

In order to have a real-time matching the relaxation should converge in a few iterations, otherwise it will use to much time. If convergence has not taken place after n iterations, the process might as well be terminated and the result either be used or rejected, depending on the degree of convergence.

## 4. Implementation.

The matching method has been tested in an implementation, which is based on the methods outlined in section 2 and 3. the implementation is called DANTE. Prior to presenting some results various formulas and assumption are described.

In our implementation we use an estimation which is based on translational velocity and acceleration only. In occlusions no exact information is available for the updating of these parameters. Hence we assume that the acceleration is constant.

As we aim at real-time analysis our preprocessing system is only capable of producing a feature vector containing area, sum of itensities (IOD), bounding rectangle and position of centroid for each object. Given these features we calculate the initial strengths as follows:

$$p_i^{(0)}(\lambda) = \frac{2}{3} * \frac{a}{a+distance(t_i,\lambda)} + \frac{1}{6} * \frac{\Delta area(t_i,\lambda)}{maxarea(t_i,\lambda)} + \frac{1}{6} * \frac{\Delta IOD(t_i,\lambda)}{max\_IOD(t_i,\lambda)} \qquad (7)$$

Here a is a distance weight factor, which is equal to IMAGESIZE/20. This results in a high preference for similarity in position. Our initial experiments has shown that this parameters often is application dependent.

For the no-label we use eqn. (3) if the label is close to the boundary (IMAGESIZE/10) otherwise this strength equals zero. After all the initial strengths has been calculated, they are normalized row-wise to sum to one.

In our stop criteria we allow a maximum of 20 iteration, before we stop the matching process.

A number of synthetic sequences with varying complexity has been used in a timing of our implementation. These measurements has shown that the motion analysis is capable of analyzing about 5 frames/sec, given the scene contains less than 5 objects and using a standard UNIX microcomputer (68020, 16 MHz).

## 5. Experimental results.

In this section we will present and discuss some results, which has been obtained using the implementation outlined above and a number of synthetic image sequences.

The presentation form and initial performance is illustrated by the sequence in figure 2.

The rectangles in figure 2 is an axis parallel bounding rectangle approximation of the measured objects (limitation imposed by preprocessing system). The lines through these rectangles show the path of object centroids, as it was estimated by DANTE. In figure 2.a is shown a split, i.e. a growing object appears to be two objects and the

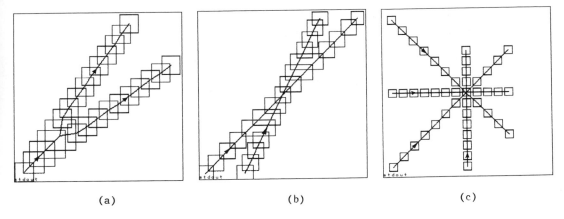

(a)                          (b)                          (c)

Fig. 2 Superimposed sequences containing simple linear motion.

system accepts that as soon as it is detected. In figure 2.b two individual objects have been detected prior to the occlusion. The estimator maintains them as such, and estimates their individual appearences (seperate trajectories). The matching copes with the ambiguity of matching one observed with two estimated tokens. Hence a capability of handling occlusions seems available. In figure 2.c four objects meet in the middle of the field of view and again the system maintains a correct tracking.

In figure 3.a is shown an example where the the motion parameters are time varying and an occlusion which last 2 frames occur.

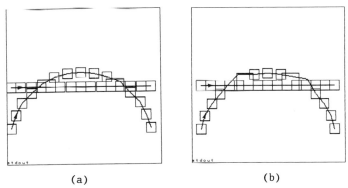

(a)                          (b)

Fig. 3 A superimposed sequence with objects which
have time varying motion parameters.

Again the system performs an almost perfect tracking. Small "bumps" appear in the circular path during the occlusion, since we assume the highest order motion parameters (acceleration) are constant during occlusions.

In figure 3.b the sequence from figure 3.a is used again, only this time the object with circular path has been given a small offset, which results in longer occlusions.

As it appears from the paths detected by DANTE, the tracking is erronous during the occlusions, i.e. a major error arises. This is mainly due to the assumption of constant motion parameters. If we for instance incorporated motion parameters suited for description of circular paths this problem would not arise or it would be less prominent. Despite the erronous tracking during occlusions it can be seen that the overall tracking is satisfactory.

The sequence in figure 4 has been designed to go beyond the limitations in the system, concerning the motion description. The sequence is outlined in figure 4.a., i.e. an object moves from the bottom left corner to the upper right corner with constant velocity while a larger object moves in a semi circle within the field of view. The trajectories have been designed so that an occlusion lasts for 1/3 the total sequence. During this occlusion one of the objects have a major change in motion parameters, hence the prediction is expected to fail.

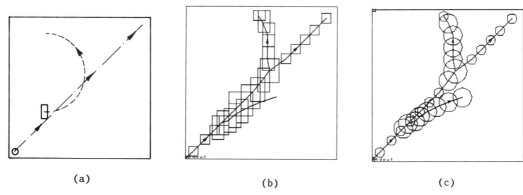

(a)         (b)         (c)

Fig. 4 A sequence which shows limitations in our current motion description.

In figure 4.b is shown the superimposed measured frames and the trajectories, while figure 4.c shows the estimates calculated by DANTE. The results clearly shows that the estimation is confused, i.e. as the estimate for the larger object moves away from the measured one, the system realises that the prediction must be incorrect, as we have a high preference for similarity in position. This estimate is then rejected and only one of the objects is maintained. When the occluding objects reappear this object is then split into the two original ones.

## 6. Conclusion.

A token matching scheme for high-level motion analysis has been developed. The goal is real-time usage for a constrained scenario. The demand for real-time has forced an unsophisticated method, which simply propagates certainties through normalizations.

Matching has been performed between a measured and an estimate of the same frame. The experiments has shown that the matching method is capable of handling occlusions even in the case of rather poor estimates. The problems observed for very poor estimation, are clearly due to lack of sophistication in the estimators usage of motion information. In other words we have a number of problems to attend to and solve before the weaknesses of the matching scheme will appear.

**References:**

Christensen, H.I., 1987
    Monitoring Moving Objects in Real Time,
    M.Sc Thesis, Institute of Electronic Systems,
    Aalborg University, Denmark.

Goshtasby, A. & Page, C.V., 1984
    Image matching by a probabislitic relaxation labeling process,
    Proceedings from Seventh International Conference on Pattern Recognition, pp. 307.

Granum, E. & Munk, K.H., 1986
    Monitoring moving objects in real time,
    Description of FTU-project,
    Institute of Electronic Systems,
    Aalborg University, Denmark.

Hummel, R.A. & Zucker, S.W., 1983
    On the foundation of relaxation labeling processes,
    IEEE PAMI-5, No. 3, May 1983, pp. 267.

Kittler, J. & Illingworth, J., 1985
    Relaxation Labeling algorithms - a review,
    Image and Vision Computing, Vol 3. 1985, pp. 206

Munk, K.H., 1986
    Bevaegelsesanalyse ved hojniveau billedrepraesentation,
    (Motion Analysis using High Level Image description),
    M.Sc Thesis (in Danish), Institute of Electronic Systems,
    Aalborg University, Denmark.

Peleg, S., 1980
    A new probabilistic relaxation scheme,
    IEEE PAMI-2, No. 4, July 1980, pp. 363.

Price, K.E., 1985
    Relaxation matching techniques - A Comparison,
    IEEE PAMI-7, No. 5, September 1985, pp. 617.

Rosenfeld et. al, 1976
    Scene labeling be relaxation operators,
    IEEE SMC-6, No. 6, June 1976, pp. 421.

Sethi, I.K. & Jain, R., 1987
    Finding Trajectories of Feature Points in A Monocular Image Sequence
    IEEE PAMI-9, No. 1, Januar 1987, pp. 56

Ullman, S., 1979
    Interpretation of visual motion,
    MIT Press, Massachusetts, USA.

Wiklund, J. & Granlund, G.H., 1987
    Image Sequence Analysis for Object Tracking,
    5th Scandinavian Conference on Image Analysis, June 1987, pp. 641

# Determining 3-D Structure of Scene from Image Sequences Obtained by Horizontal and Vertical Moving Camera

Masanobu YAMAMOTO

Computer Vision Section, Electrotechnical Laboratory

1-1-4,Umezono,Tsukuba-shi,Ibaraki-ken,305,JAPAN

### Abstract

The stereo vision is one of the simplest methods for acquiring three-dimensional (3-D) information. A problem then is that sometimes it is difficult to establish a correspondence between the left and the right images, in such cases as (1) multiple correspondence, (2) occlusion, (3) position reversals, and (4) horizontal edge. This paper proposes a method to determine the three-dimensional structure of the scene from the sequences of images obtained by the moving camera. As the first step, a two-dimensional image is constructed from the sequence of images, in which the apparent locus of motion is represented as segments. The correspondence problem in this step is simplified as the detection of segments on the synthetic image. By examining the relations among the detected segments, the occlusions can be detected, and the correspondence can be established where the positional reversals happen. By moving the camera not only in one direction, but also in orthogonal directions, the unique correspondence can be established, independently from the direction of the edge. An input system was constructed, which can accept a large number of motion stereo image sequence with a high speed, and some complex three-dimensional structures of the scenes were actually determined.

## 1   Introduction

The stereo vision is frequently considered because of its simplicity in the input of the images, among various methods of acquiring three-dimensional (3-D) information. The small parallex stereo [8] [14], where the distance between view points is small, can determine the 3-D information using the gradient method. Its computation is simple, while the accuracy of the measurement is a problem.

In order to improve the accuracy of measurement, it is necessary to increase the distance between the two view points. Then, establishment of the correspondence between the two images is problem. As a unit for establishing correspondence, features such as edge or the region between edges are often utilized. The coarse-to-fine strategy [3], relaxation method [1] and the dynamic programming [13] [12] can search efficiently for the optimum correspondence from a large number of possibilities. A precondition for the application of those search methods is , however, that the order of the corresponding elements should be preserved and the occlusion should not occur, in principle. Furthermore, a common problem in the binocular vision is that the unique correspondence is difficult to establish between on the edges parallel to the epi-polar line. From such a point of view, there have been studies on the multiple correspondence unit [4] and utilization of the image model [16].

On the other hand, a multi-view stereo images can be acquired, which are obtained by placing several cameras between the left and right view points [9] [10] [17] [5] [11]. In the multi-view images, the ambiguity in the correspondence between the left and right images can be checked using the images from other view positions. The correspondence is also possible for the cases of occlusion and positional reversals. Furthermore, by using the images from upper or lower view, the correspondence between horizontal edges can also be established. Processing multi-view stereo images is normally based on the iteration of search processes. But this paper proposes a method , in which the search for the corresponding pair is made unnecessary, by increasing the number of view points. In the method, the number of view points is increased, until the stereo pair composed of the adjacent view points form the small-parallax stereo pair. The multi-view stereo images obtained by such a construction is called *motion stereo image sequence.*

The motion stereo image sequence can also be considered as a dynamic image sequence obtained by moving the camera in the direction perpendicular to the visual axis. In this image sequence, the far object moves slowly , while the close object moves rapidly. Using the visualized locus method, the motion trajectory of the point on the object is represented as a segment on the two-dimensional synthetic image. From such a view point, the correspondence problem becomes a simple task of detecting the segment from the synthetic image. By providing interpretations for the mutual relations among the detected segments, it is possible to detect the occlusion and to establish the correspondence for the case of positional reversals. Furthermore, by moving the camera in orthogonal directions, the unique correspondence can be established between horizontal edges.

Thus, by applying the visualized locus method [6] [15] [19] for the motion stereo image sequence, the correspondence can be established in a simple and fast way, while maintaining the merits of the multi-view stereo image [18]. The method can be extended to the case, where the object is rotating in a quasi-static way [7], or the view point is moving along the visual axis [2]. In the method using motion stereo image sequence, however, the simplicity of the input, which is one of the merits in the stereo vision, is lost. From such a view point, a motion stereo image sequence input system was developed, which is combination of a precise moving mechanism for the video camera and a video disc device. The motion stereo image sequence is obtained from this dedicated system, and the 3-D of the complex scene is recovered, indicating the effectiveness of the proposed method.

# 2  Principle

## 2.1  Extraction of 3-D Information by The Visualized Locus Method

The coordinate $O - XYZ$ of the scene is set as in Fig.1. The view point is set on $X$-axis and visual axis is aligned with $Z$-axis. The scene is projected on a plane $Z = F$ parallel to $XY$-plane with the focal distance $F$. The coordinate $o - xy$ of the projection plane is set so that the intersection with the visual axis is the origin, and axis are parallel to those of the scene.

The motion stereo image sequence is taken by moving the camera along $X$-axis with step $\delta x$. By arranging the images in the taken order, 3-D image is constructed as in Fig.1. Let the $X$-coordinate of the n-th view point be $U$, i.e., $U = n \cdot \delta x$, where $n$ is an integer. Then the point $P(X, Y, Z)$ on the object is mapped to the point $p(X', Y', F)$ on the image plane with the following relation.

$$\frac{X - U}{X' - U} = \frac{Y}{Y'} = \frac{Z}{F} \tag{1}$$

Letting $k_x$ and $k_y$ be the scale factor along $x$- and $y$-direction of the projection coordinate in regard to the scene coordinate,

$$\begin{cases} x = k_x(X' - U) \\ y = k_y Y' \end{cases} \tag{2}$$

By substituting eq.(2) into eq.(1) and rearranging, considering that $U = n \cdot \delta x$ ,

$$\begin{cases} \frac{Z}{k_x F} x = X - n\delta x \\ \frac{Z}{k_y F} y = Y \end{cases} \tag{3}$$

The second equation of eq.(3) indicates that the motion trajectory of the projecting point of point $P$ with the motion of the camera, is reconstrained on the horizontal cross-section of the 3-D image. The first equation of eq.(3) indicates that the trajectory is a straight line with the gradient $-Z/(k_x F\delta x)$ proportional to the depth $Z$. This straight-line trajectory is called *path line*, and the magnitude of the gradient is called the slope of the path line.

If the image of the point $P$ is on an edge, the corresponding path line is represented on the image as a straight edge on the horizontal cross-section image. Then, the correspondence problem between images is reduced to the detection of straight edges. If the straight edge, i.e., the path line can be detected, the 3-D coordinate of the corresponding point $P$ can be reconstructed as follows.

Fig.2 shows the horizontal cross-section image at $y = k_y FY/Z$ and the path line of point $P$. The vertical axis indicates the number of the view points, being numbered in the order of taking the image. The horizontal axis indicates the horizontal coordinate of the image. The point $q_1(x_1, n_1)$ on the path line corresponds to the projection point of $P$ at the $n_1$-th view point, and $q_2(x_2, n_2)$ corresponds to the projection point of $P$ at the $n_2$-th view point. It follows from eq.(3) that

$$\frac{Z}{k_x F} x_1 = X - n_1 \delta x \tag{4}$$

$$\frac{Z}{k_x F} x_2 = X - n_2 \delta x \tag{5}$$

It follows from eq.(4) and (5) that

$$Z = \frac{n_2 - n_1}{x_1 - x_2} k_x F \delta x \tag{6}$$

The slope $l_x$ of the path line is determined by the least-square approximation. Replacing $(n_2 - n1)/(x_1 - x_2)$ by $l_x$, the depth $Z$ is given by

$$Z = l_x k_x F \delta x \tag{7}$$

$Y$-coordinate is given by eq.(3) as

$$Y = y l_x \delta x k_x / k_y \tag{8}$$

Using a point $(x, n)$ on the path line, $X$-coordinate is given from eq.(3) as

$$X = (x l_x + n) \delta x \tag{9}$$

In order to improve the accuracy, the values obtained from all points on the path line are averaged.

$$X = \frac{1}{N} \sum_{i=1}^{N} (x_i l_x + n_i) \delta x \tag{10}$$

where $(x_i, n_i)$ is the point on the path line, and $N$ is the number of such points.

When the projection of the point $P$ is on an edge which is horizontal or almost horizontal, the path line either dose not appear, or is of a low accuracy if it appears. For such a case, the camera is moved along $Y$-axis, and the motion stereo image sequence is obtained along the vertical direction. Constructing the 3-D image from this image sequence, the horizontal edge clearly appears on the vertical cross-section image. Using the vertical cross-section image , 3-D coordinate of point $P$ is given as follows.

$$\begin{cases} X = x l_y \delta y k_y / k_x \\ Y = \frac{1}{M} \sum_{i=1}^{M} (y_i l_y + m_i) \delta y \\ Z = k_y F l_y \delta y \end{cases} \tag{11}$$

where $(y_i, m_i)$ is the point on the path line, and $M$ is the number of such points. $l_y$ is the slope of the path line. $k_x F$ or $k_y F$ and the aspect ratio $k_y/k_x$ of the camera are experimentally determined.

## 2.2 Detection of Occlusion and Correspondence for Position Reversals

Consider a problem as shown in Fig.3 (a), where 3-D structure of two square columns placed in depth direction is to be restored. Among the motion stereo image sequence of the scene, the images with camera at the leftmost, center and the rightmost positions are shown in Fig.3 (b). Fig.3 (c) is the synthesized cross-section image at the position of the solid-line in the original image. The points $a, b, \ldots, h$ on the edge of the square column correspond to the path lines $A, B, \ldots, H$ on the cross-section image. By examining the relation among the path lines on the cross-section image, the following observations are made.

(a) There are produced occlusions on the side of the column, depending on the camera position. It is the case of points $a$ and $c$, for example, where the far point $c$ is hidden behind the near point $a$. On the cross-section image, a path line with a larger slope corresponding to the far point is interrupted by the path line with smaller slope corresponding to the near point. Consequently, when a path line is found in the cross-section image, which is terminated , an occlusion of the point corresponding to that path line is detected.

(b) It may happen depending on the position of the camera that the order of points is reversed, as in the case of points $a$ and $e$. In this case, the far point $e$ is once hidden behind the near point $a$ in the course of the camera movement. On the cross-section image, the path line $E$ corresponding to the far point $e$ is interruped by the path line $A$ corresponding to the near point $a$. Consequently, when path lines which are on the same straight-line are found on the cross-section image, the correspondence can be established by tracing the path line, inspite of the positional reversal.

The condition that several path lines are on the same straight-line, is determined as follows. As is shown in Fig.4, let a set of several path lines be represented by a single-valued function $f(n)$ of the camera position $n$. Let the segment connecting the end points of $f(n)$ be $g(n)$. Let the maximum distance between $f(n)$ and $g(n)$ be defined by $d_m = \max \| f(n) - g(n) \|$ . If the maximum distance is within a certain permissible range, $f(n)$ is considered as a single path line. In this paper, the permissible limit is set as 2. This condition is called the *integration criterion*.

One of the remarkable properties is that the 3-D coordinate of the corresponding point can be reconstructed as far as the path line can be observed, whether there occurs the positional reversals or occlusion.

# 3   Motion Stereo Image Sequence Input System

The motion stereo image sequence input system is composed of the camera carrier, the video disc (Victor Co., VM-1000M) to store the obtained image from the video camera (Sony Co., XC-37) and the personal computer (Sanyo Co., MBC-225) to control those units. Fig.5 shows the camera carrier. The video camera is set on the carrier constructed by two slide-packs (THK Co.) which perpendicularly intersect each other. The camera motion in horizontal and vertical direction is guided by each slide-pack, and is precisely controlled by the ball-screw mechanism, which is directly connected to the step-motor.

The maximum movement is 500 $mm$ both for horizontal and vertical directions. The motion pitch can be set arbitrarily, with the minimum being 25 $\mu m$ for both directions. The video camera is a CCD camera with standard 16 $mm$ TV camera lens. The personal computer sends the pulse signal to the step motor in the camera carrier and the instruction, such as start, image taking, next move and stop to the video disc.

The images taken for each small step are successively stored in the video disc. The disc can store up to 600 frames. The input system can receive motion stereo image sequence of 128 images in the horizontal and vertical directions respectively in approximately 2 minutes.

Fig.6 shows the whole processing system for the motion stereo image sequence. The portion surrounded by the dashed-line is the input system. The images once stored in the video disc are quantized into $512 \times 512$ pixels with 256 gray levels, by the digitizer (Toshiba Co., TOSPIX). The images are smoothed into $128 \times 128$ pixels and the data is transferred to the minicomputer (Prime 750). Since the total data for images are tremendous, the image data are transferred to a large-scale computer (Fujitsu Co., M-380) for generation of the cross-section image and extraction of the 3-D information.

# 4   Experiments

This section describes an example of generation of cross-section image from an image sequence, extraction of path line and recovery of 3-D information. The apparent motion of an object resulting from the camera motion is represented as an image as follows. The scene is the laboratory room containing tripod and monitor equipment, and the motion stereo image sequence is given by the camera moving in the horizontal direction. The motion pitch of the view point is 3 $mm$ and the number of images taken is 128. Fig.7 shows the images from the leftmost, center and rightmost view points.

## 4.1　Extraction of Path Line

It is seen from the characteristic image of Fig.8 that the path line can be visualized. The path line extracted by the following algorithm.

**Path line extraction algorithm**

**Step 1 (Extraction of path line candidates)** The intensity gradient for each pixel is calculated. The point with the magnitude of the gradient exceeding a certain threshold is retained. The point with the local maximum of the horizontal or vertical derivative is searched and retained. By connecting the remaining pixels by 8-neighborhood, a line image is obtained, composed of a number of segments. The isolated points are deleted, being regarded as noise. Fig.9 shows the result of this extraction. In the following, the suffix indicates the line number.

The obtained line image may contain a large number of segments, which are inconsistent with the property of the path line, as well as an element, which is incomplete to be regarded as a path line. In this sense, the segments extracted at this stage are called path line candidates.

**Step 2 (Partitioning into segment sets)** The path line must be a segment. Consequently, the path line candidate is partitioned into a set of segments.

**step 2.1 (Elimination of cross-point)** If three or more lines intersect at a point, the path line candidate is sectioned at that point.

**step 2.2 (Conversion into single-valued function)** The path line candidate is partitioned so that the result is a single-valued function with regard to the view point number.

**step 2.3 (Partitioning of piecewise-linear line)** The path line candidate, which does not satisfy the integration criterion, is considered as a piecewise-linear line composed of different path lines. The path line is then partitioned at the point with the maximum distance along the horizontal direction between the path line and the auxiliary line connecting both ends of the path line. In general, the point of partitioning is the point at the corner of the piecewise-linear line. Fig.10 shows the result of partitioning the path line.

**Step 3 (Extension and connection)** Each of the segments in Fig.10 is a path line. Among those, there are path lines which are fragments of an originally continuous path line. For such a case, the path line is extended and connected to another path line, in order to restore the complete path line from its fragments. The path lines are extended in the ascending order of the slope. In other words, the path line are extended from the ones corresponding to the nearest points to the camera. The path line is extended to both directions along the line connecting both ends. Before extending a path line, it is examined whether or not there exists another path line in the extending direction. If there does not exist another path line, the path line can be extended. If there exists another path line, the following connection procedure is tried.

**step 3.1 (Connection)** Consider extending two path lines as a single path line, if the integration criterion is satisfied and the closer end points of these path lines are connected by a segment. If the integration criterion is not satisfied, either one of the following extension stop or extension continue processes is executed.

**step 3.2 (Extension stop)** If the slope of the other path line is smaller than the extending path line, it follows by **2.2** (a) that the point of the scene corresponding to the extending path line is hidden behind the point of the scene corresponding to the another path line. Consequently, the extension is stopped before the other path line.

**step 3.3 (Extension continue)** If the slope of the another path line is larger than that of the extending path line, the situation is reverse to that of the extension slope. Consequently, the extension is further continued intersecting the other path line. The result of path line extension is shown in Fig.11.

**Step 4 (Integration interrupted path line)** This procedure integrates the path lines which are interrupted by the apparent positional reversals. As was discussed in **2.2** (b) , if two path lines satisfy the integration criterion, they are considered as a single path line. The result of processing is shown in Fig.12. The interrupted path lines such as 8, 63, and 9, 29, are integrated in Fig.12.

**Step 5 (Correspondence between cross-section images)** The path line extractions are performed for all cross-section images. Then, 3-D coordinates of points in the corresponding scenes are determined from the path line by the method described in **2.1**. If the result of reconstruction is preserved as the 3-D contour line of the object, it is convenient not only for the display of the result, but also for the object recognition as an advantage research.

If the path lines are close in the consecutive cross-section images, the points corresponding to the path lines in the scene are connected to form the 3-D contour line. The extent of closeness of path line is represented as follows. As is shown in Fig.13, let the two path lines be $f(n)$ and $h(n)$. Let the number of view points, for which at least one of the path lines is defined, be $N_1$. Let the number of view points for which $\| f(n) - h(n) \| \leq w_t$ be $N_2$. If the ratio $N_2/N_1$ is above a certain threshold, the two path lines are decided as close. In this experiment, the threshold is set as 0.9, and $w_t$ is set as 2. If there exist more than one path lines which are close to the path line $f(n)$, the one with the largest ratio $N_2/N_1$ is chosen.

## 4.2   Determining 3-D Structure

The result of reconstruction of the 3-D structure of the scene of Fig.7 is shown in Fig.14. The solid-line is 3-D contour line of the tripod and the dashed-line is its projection on the three projecting planes perpendicularly intersecting each other. As the next step, the effect of added vertical motion is examined.

For the scene with a monitor on the desk, the motion stereo image sequences with orthogonal motions are given as the input. The pitch of the camera motion is 1.25 mm. The number of images is 128 each for horizontal and vertical directions, resulting in 256 in total. Fig.15 is a sample of the motion stereo image sequence, which is the one with the camera at the center. Fig.16 (a) and (b) are samples of horizontal cross-section image ($y = 70$) and vertical cross-section image ($x = 45$), respectively. The white line in Fig.15 is the cross-section positions.

Fig.17 is the result of reconstruction of 3-D structure from the horizontal motion stereo image sequence. Fig.18 is the result obtained by superposing the reconstruction from the vertical motion stereo image sequence.

In this experiment, $k_x F = 240$, $k_y/k_x = 1.18$.

## 5   Conclusion

This paper proposed a method to determine the 3-D structure of the scene from the motion stereo image sequence obtained by moving the camera.

Using a dedicated high-speed input system, a large number of motion stereo image sequences was acquired. By means of the proposed method, the correspondence problem is simplified to the detection of segments on the 2-D synthesized image generated from the motion stereo image sequence. By examining the mutual relations among the detected segments, it is easy to detect occlusion and establish the correspondence for the case of positional reversals. Furthermore, by moving the view point not only in a particular direction but also in orthogonal direction, a unique correspondence can be established, independently of the direction of the edge. Lastly, 3-D structure of a fairly complex scene was restored, demonstrating the usefulness of the proposed method.

One of the problems left for further study is the improvement of the processing speed. The dedicated system can receive the image sequence with high speed, however, it requires a considerable time at present. From such a point of view, parallel processing and hardware implementation should be considered. Another problem is that the result of restoration is not satisfactory in this paper, if the method is to be extended to the problem of environmental model building or object recognition. It would be required to design a more precise moving carrier and to perform a quantitative evaluation of the measurement accuracy.

## Acknowledgments

The author would like to thank for the suggestions by Dr. Y.Shirai, Head of Control Div., as well as the discussions with Dr. M.Oshima, Head and members of the Computer Vision Sec.. He also thanks for the assistance in the construction of the camera carrier given by Mr. K.Tanazawa and members of the Research Implementation Div.

# References

[1] S.T. Barnard and W.D Thompson. Disparity analysis of images. *IEEE Trans. on Pattern Analysis and Machine Intelligence*, vol.PAMI-2,no.4:333–340, 1981.

[2] R.C. Bolles and H.H. Baker. Epipolar-plane image analysis; a technique for analyzing motion sequences. In *Proc. of 3rd ISRR*, pages 192–199, 1985.

[3] W.E.L. Grimson. Computational experiments with a feature based stereo algorithm. *IEEE Trans. on Pattern Analysis and Machine Intelligence*, vol.PAMI-7,no.1:17–34, 1985.

[4] K. Ikeuchi. Determining depth map from a pair of needle maps by apair of photometric stereo systems with region matching. *Trans. of Institute of Electronics and Communication Engineers of Japan*, vol.J68-D,no.10:1761–1768, 1985.

[5] T. Itoh and A. Ishii. Stereo vision correspondence processing by three-view-stereo. In *Proc. of 29th Conv. of Information Processing Society of Japan*, pages 2M–3, 1984.

[6] J.F Jarvis. Automatic visual inspection of glass-metal seals. In *Proc. of 4th IJCPR*, pages 961–965, 1978.

[7] T. Kaneko. *Three-dimensional measurement using quasi-static rotation of an object*. Technical Report PRL-85-22, Institute of Electronics and Communication Engineers of Japan, 1985.

[8] B.D. Lucas and T. Kanade. An iterative image registration technique with an application to stereo vision. In *Proc. of 7th IJCAI*, pages 674–679, 1981.

[9] H.P. Moravec. Visual mapping by a robot rover. In *Proc. of 6th IJCAI*, pages 598–600, 1979.

[10] T. Ohmori and I. Morishita. Object detection using multi-view stereo images. *Trans. of SICE*, vol.18,no.7:716–722, 1982.

[11] Y. Ohta and K. Ikeda. On the three-view stereo. In *Proc. of 29th National Confference of Information Processing Society of Japan*, pages 2M–4, 1984.

[12] Y. Ohta and T. Kanade. Stereo by intra- and inter-scan line search using dynamic programming. *IEEE Trans. on Pattern Analysis and Machine Intelligence*, vol.PAMI-7,no.2:139–154, 1985.

[13] Y. Ohta, Y. Masai, and K. Ikeda. Interval matching method of stereo images using dynamic programing. *Trans. of Institute of Electronics and Communication Engineers of Japan*, vol.J68-D,no.4:554–561, 1985.

[14] K.F. Prazdny. Determining the instantaneous direction of motion from optical flow generated by a curvilinearrly moving observer. *Computer Graphics and Image Processing*, vol.17:238–248, 1981.

[15] Y. Sasaki and T. Furukawa. A synthesis algorithm of arbitrary intermediate viewing angle images from several pairs of stereograms. *Trans. of Institute of Electronics and Communication Engineers of Japan*, vol.J63-D,no.9:813–814, 1980.

[16] F. Tomita. *Stereo matching based on region boundary segments*. Technical Report CV-38-1, Information Processing Society of Japan, 1985.

[17] M. Yachida. Recognition of three-dimensional object using multi-view stereo images. *Nikkei Mechanical*, vol.157:82–91, 1984.

[18] M. Yamamoto. Determining three-dimensional structure by visualized locus method. In *Proc. of National Confference of Institute of Electronics and Communication Engineers of Japan*, pages S18–12, 1981.

[19] M. Yamamoto. Motion analysis by visualized locus method. *Trans. of Information Processing Society of Japan*, vol.22,no.5:442–449, 1981.

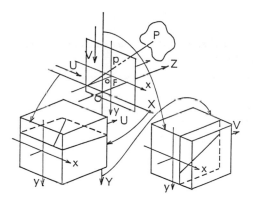

**Fig.1** Visualization of apparent motion.

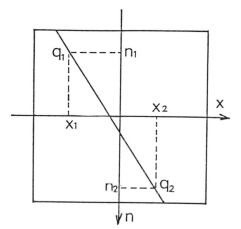

**Fig.2** A path line on the cross-section.

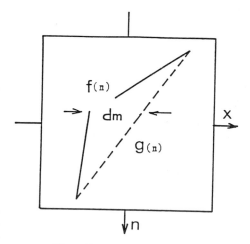

**Fig.4** Path lines on a line.

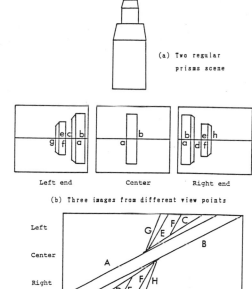

(a) Two regular prisms scene

(b) Three images from different view points

(c) Cross section

**Fig.3** Occlusion and positional reversals.

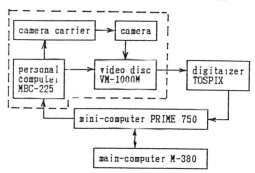

**Fig.6** A processing system for position based image sequence.

**Fig.5** Camera carrier.

466

(n=1)                    (n=64)                    (n=128)

Fig.7 Laboratory scene.

x

n

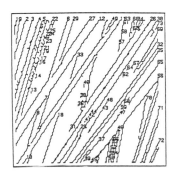

Fig.8 Cross section at $y = 64$.

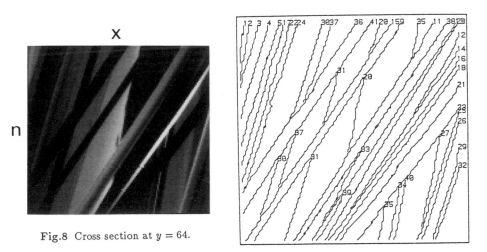

Fig.12 Detected path lines.

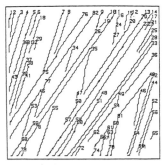

Fig.9 Result of Step 1.          Fig.10 Result of Step 2.          Fig.11 Result of Step 3.

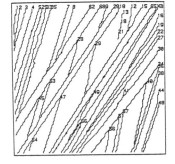

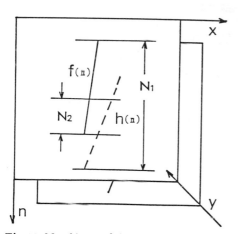

Fig.13 Matching path lines between adjacent cross section.

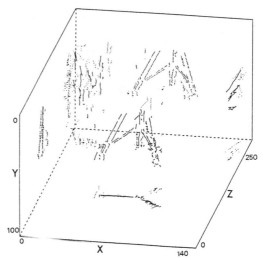

Fig.14 3-D structure of the scene to Fig.7.

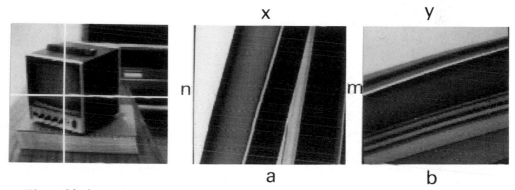

Fig.15 Monitor scene

Fig.16 (a) Horizontal cross section at $y = 70$.
(b) Vertical cross section at $x = 45$.

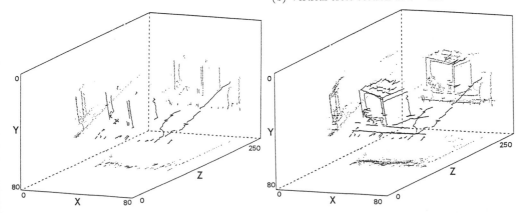

Fig.17 3-D structure from horizontal motion stereo image sequence.

Fig.18 3-D structure from horizontal and vertical motion stereo image sequences.

# Optical Flow Estimation Using Line Image Sequences

*Philippe Thévenaz & Heinz Hügli*
*Institut de microtechnique de l'Université de Neuchâtel*
*2 rue A.-L. Breguet, CH-2000 Neuchâtel (Switzerland)*

## Abstract

This paper presents and evaluates a method for measuring the speed of objects in line image sequences. In a line sequence, a line corresponds to a fixed line position in the real scene, and the objects move against it. The line image sequence is a space-time two dimensional image giving a good record of moving objects. The method uses two such line image sequences and estimate the object speed by optical flow computation. Unidirectional movement of the objects is assumed which simplifies the optical flow computation and makes it a simple method to implement. The usefullness and performance of the method is shown by an example comprising several vehicles of different speed. The performance evaluation shows good linearity and low error.

## 1.    Introduction

### 1.1.    PREVIOUS WORK ON OPTICAL FLOW

Optical flow estimation by intensity gradient based techniques has been investigated by many workers [5], [6], [7]. They mainly show how to compute a multidimensional flow field, that not only gives rise to the velocity magnitude, but also to its direction. Unfortunately, this cannot be done without assuming some a priori knowledge [10], [11], [13], [14], because of the aperture problem, that basically specifies that motion can locally only be measured along the intensity gradient.

### 1.2    LINE IMAGE SEQUENCE

The scope of this paper covers the simpliest of these assumptions, namely the assumption that the motion is along a straight line of known direction. According to that, we use a line image camera that produces a space-time two-dimensional image [1]. Such a camera shoots only one line image at a time, and always aims at the same place; a time sequence is collected and the line images are put aside. The two-dimensional image produced is spatially defined along one axis, and temporally along the other. Such an image is quiet different from an ordinary one. When nothing moves, the background only is shot, and no significant feature is present in the image. When an object crosses the line, then it leaves a trail on the record; if it crosses the line slowly, then it will have a longer trace than when it goes faster. Using such a camera, we will be able to survey every moving object crossing the line of acquisition on a path perpendicular to it. This sort of camera is also used for order decision, e. g. in horse races or bicycle races.

### 1.3.    METHODS FOR MEASURING SPEED

We have seen that a moving object has a longer trace when it goes slow than when it goes fast.

Knowing a priori its real length, and measuring the length of its trace (that is, its duration), we could determine its speed; but the real length of an object is usually not available, so we have to resort to other schemes. One of them is obvious: it is to automatically identify the object and then fetch its length from a table. The other schemes take advantage of a second line image camera, aiming at a place just in front of the first one (figure 1). By knowing the space interval $\Delta x$ between the lines, and by timing the appearance of locally identifiable features, it is possible to extract speed measurements valid for these features. This is termed a correspondence scheme [8]. The next method used for measuring velocity is the Fourier Method [2], [4], [12]. In this case, we assume that only one object is moving. That assumption lets us predict that one image is the shifted version of the other. The amount of shifting is proportional to the inverse of the speed and can be measured by calculating the phase difference between the Fourier Transforms of each image.

### 1.4.    OPTICAL FLOW

The last scheme is also termed the method of differentials [3], [9]. Its interest resides in the fact that it can compute locally the optical flow, without any a priori knowledge. We will develop this method below, adapting it to a pair of line image sequences.

## 2    Optical flow of line image sequences

### 2.1.    DEFINITION

The optical flow is a method for computing a velocity field from a set of two or more images. In our case, the field obtained is scalar. It represents the value $V_x(Y, T)$ of the speed measured on every point of the line image sequences $(i_1(Y, T), i_2(Y, T))$, where Y relates to the spatial axis and T to the time axis.

### 2.2    COMPUTATION

Let us consider a set of general time-varying images:

$$i = f(x, y, t) \tag{1}$$

Developing them in a Taylor series expansion we get:

$$f(x+\Delta x, y+\Delta y, t+\Delta t) = f(x, y, t) + \Delta x \cdot (\partial f/\partial x) + \Delta y \cdot (\partial f/\partial y) + \Delta t \cdot (\partial f/\partial t) + \varepsilon_1 \tag{2}$$

In that expression, $\varepsilon_1$ represents the higher order terms, that we will consider as negligible. If anything moves in the image, then it will be possible to track it and find many sets $(\Delta x, \Delta y, \Delta t)$ such that:

$$f(x+\Delta x, y+\Delta y, t+\Delta t) = f(x, y, t) \tag{3}$$

Whenever such a set exists, we can write:

$$\Delta x \cdot (\partial f/\partial x) + \Delta y \cdot (\partial f/\partial y) = - \Delta t \cdot (\partial f/\partial t) \tag{4}$$

In our case, we know that the motion is perpendicular to the line of acquisition:

$$\Delta y = 0 \tag{5}$$

If the set is not trivial, that is if $\Delta t \neq 0$, then we have:

$$(\Delta x/\Delta t) \cdot (\partial f/\partial x) = - (\partial f/\partial t) \tag{6}$$

From this equation, we can extract the velocity $V_x$, with no further reference to the particular set we used:

$$V_x = \Delta x/\Delta t = - (\partial f/\partial t)/(\partial f/\partial x) \tag{7}$$

To do that, the necessary conditions are i) the time and space derivatives should be defined, and ii) the space derivative in the motion direction has to be non-zero. This last condition means that the moving object shouldn't be of constant intensity.

Let us consider now a set of two discrete line image sequences taken at locations $X_1$ and $X_2$:

$$i_1 = f(X_1, Y, T) = f_1(Y, T) \tag{8}$$
$$i_2 = f(X_2, Y, T) = f_2(Y, T) \tag{9}$$

Choose some points of these images, remembering that the y-coordinate has no effect on the velocity:

$$A = f(X_1, Y, T_1) \tag{10}$$
$$B = f(X_1, Y, T_2) \tag{11}$$
$$C = f(X_2, Y, T_1) \tag{12}$$
$$D = f(X_2, Y, T_2) \tag{13}$$

It can easily be shown that the velocity (7) can be approximated by:

$$v_x(A, B, C, D) = - (\Delta X/\Delta T) \cdot ((B + D - A - C)/(C + D - A - B)) \tag{14}$$

Where $\Delta X = X_2 - X_1$ is the distance betwen the two acquisition lines, and $\Delta T = T_2 - T_1$ is the time interval between two shots. Note that the condition i) has disappeared, whilst condition ii) is still valid.

### 2.3. CONFIDENCE

Let us now have a look at the sensitivity of that method. What we want to know is the consequence of an error on the gray levels specified in (10) through (13). For that purpose, we will use again a Taylor series expansion, where the higher than first order terms $\varepsilon_2$ are dropped:

$$v_x(A+\Delta A, B+\Delta B, C+\Delta C, D+\Delta D) = v_x(A, B, C, D) + \Delta A \cdot (\partial v_x/\partial a) + \Delta B \cdot (\partial v_x/\partial b) + \Delta C \cdot (\partial v_x/\partial c) + \Delta D \cdot (\partial v_x/\partial d) + \varepsilon_2 \tag{15}$$

We term:

$$\Delta v_x = v_x( A+\Delta A, \; B+\Delta B, \; C+\Delta C, \; D+\Delta D) - v_x(A, \; B, \; C, \; D) \tag{16}$$

That gives:

$$\Delta v_x = -2 \cdot (\Delta X/\Delta T) \cdot (((B - C) \cdot (\Delta A - \Delta D) + (D \;\; A) \cdot (\Delta B - \Delta C))/(C + D - A - B)^2) \tag{17}$$

Considering that the errors are of same magnitude:

$$|\Delta A| = |\Delta B| = |\Delta C| = |\Delta D| = \Delta E \tag{18}$$

We have in the worst case approximation:

$$|\Delta v_x| = 4 \cdot |\Delta X/\Delta T| \cdot ((|B - C| + |D - A|)/|(B - C)^2 - (D - A)^2|) \cdot \Delta E \tag{19}$$

Finally, we define the sensitivity S, and the relative sensitivity $S_r$ by:

$$S = |\Delta v_x|/\Delta E \tag{20}$$
$$S_r = S/|v_x| = 4 \cdot ((|B - C| + |D - A|)/|(B - C)^2 - (D - A)^2|) \tag{21}$$

### 2.4. THRESHOLDING

It is clear that when $S_r$ is high, a low confidence has to be set on $V_x(Y, T)$, since any small error (for example: quantization) has a great effect on the measured velocity. Indeed, we could introduce a measure for that confidence, that would be like $1/S_r$; but this step is not necessary. Rather, we choose a threshold $S_{r0}$, above which we no longer accept $V_x(Y, T)$ as reliable. Finally, we have the optical flow field:

$$V_x(Y, T) = \begin{cases} v_x(A, B, C, D) & \text{if } S_r(A, B, C, D) < S_{r0} \\ \text{undefined} & \text{else} \end{cases} \tag{22}$$

## 3. Experiments and results

### 3.1. EXPERIMENT

To verifiy the usefullness and performance of the method, we constructed a bench on which some train models could be run. A single motor was used, but three different pulleys allowed three different speeds at a time. The transmission was designed to allow two pulling directions for each wire. We used a CCD video camera to look at the scene. From each frame, we retained two adjacent columns of pixels to simulate the two line image cameras. The acquisition rate was 12.5 [Hz].

### 3.2. RESULT: EXAMPLE

Figure 2 shows one of the two line image sequences obtained (the other is visually indistinguishable from the first one). Three models have a negative speed (first floor), and three others a positive one (second floor). The time axis is horizontal; the past-future direction is from left to right. Its range is about 41 [s]. Notice a property of line image sequences: although some models were moving to the left and some to the right in the real scene, the line image sequence shows only left-going models. The reason is simply that they move head first and tail last. Superimposed over the image are frames enclosing each model. These frames are the result of some segmentation process we don't describe here.

Figure 3 shows the full optical flow field associated with figure 2. One can see that much noise is present, but at least the shape and direction (light: positive, dark: negative) of each model can be recognized. Nevertheless, the high level of noise forbids us from simply thresholding $V_x(Y, T)$ in order to segment the image.

Figure 4 shows the relative sensitivity field; the less sensitive measurements are coded more darkly. In this image, it is not difficult to find a threshold $S_{r0}$ that conserves only points where confidence is sufficient. We see that most such points are located where the intensity gradients are large, that is, where simultaneously the denominator and numerator of the last term of expression (7) are large.

Figure 5 shows the result of relative sensitivity thresholding. White encodes accurate measurements. Grey encodes points above the $S_{r0}$ threshold, for which the confidence is insufficient. Black stands for undefined velocity as well as for undefined relative sensitivity. The threshold used was $S_{r0} = 100\%$; it means that the correct velocity could have had twice the measured value, or as well have been zero.

Figure 6 shows the figure 3, masked with figure 5. A lot of noise has disappeared, and velocities are now contrasted enough to recognize the velocity gradations between models.

The next step is to investigate the correctness of these measurements. For this purpose, we will compute the mean and standard deviation of measured velocities for each model. Figure 7 shows the computations performed within each model frame, before and after thresholding. Note that the frame shape is well suited to all models but the motorcyclist, for which the zero-velocity points have a priori some influence. The last column of figure 7 shows the real speed. All units are in $[\Delta X \cdot s^{-1}]$, that is the number of times the distance between the two acquisition lines is covered during one second.

Looking at these results, we can see that a sharp improvement over the measurement accuracy has been obtained. The correspondence between the real speed $v_r$ and the measured speed is good. The thresholding operation has been able to reduce the standard deviation by a factor of 3.

### 3.3.    RESULT: LINEARITY

The last step is to evaluate the accuracy under very good conditions. We resort to a special moving object, depicted in figure 8.This particular pattern is a space-varying sinusoidal pattern, that was mounted on the tender models. Such a pattern is well suited to optical flow measurements, because its intensity gradient is non-zero almost everywhere. We made a lot of measurements, varying the motor speed between each one.

The data obtained are plotted against the real velocity in figure 9. We see that the linearity of the measurements is excellent, over more than one decade range. The mean square best fit line has a slope m = 1.0453. The difference from the true unity can be explained by some errors made during the calibration process of real speed measurements. The offset of this line is 0.0603 [$\Delta X \cdot s^{-1}$], which is quiet negligible. The normalized correlation coefficient is $\rho_{xy}$ = 0.9757, which ascertains that the results show good linearity.

## 4.  Conclusion

We have developed a method based on optical flow for measuring velocity with a set of two line sequence cameras, assuming unidirectional motion. The characteristic of this method is that the speed measurement is based on the image gradient, and its advantage is that of a local measurement which does not require knowledge about the shape of the objects to measure. This method has proven to be usefull in most cases where the moving objects offer sufficiently smooth and large intensity variations. In practice and under very good conditions, the linearity is excellent over more than one decade range, while the error is quiet low. In common practical situations, the measurement is noisy but can be significantly reduced by confidence thresholding. Typically, the standard deviation is reduced by a factor of three.

## 5.  Acknowledgements

This work was supported by the swiss *Commission pour l'Encouragement de la Recherche Scientifique* under contract number 1511 and C$^{ie}$ des Montres Longines SA.

## 6.  References

[1]  Aoki M., "Detection of Moving Objects Using Line Image Sequence", *Proc. Seventh Int. Conf. Pattern Recognition, pp. 784-786, 1984.*

[2]  Arking A. A., Lo R. C., Rosenfeld A., "An Evaluation of Fourier Transform Techniques for Cloud Motion Estimation", *TR-351 (January 1975) Computer Science Departement, Univeristy of Maryland, College Park/MD.*

[3]  Cafforio C., Rocca F., "Methods for measuring small displacements of television images", *IEEE Trans. IT-22, pp. 573, 1976.*

[4]  Haskell B. G., "Frame-to-Frame Coding of Television Pictures Using Two-Dimensional Fourier Transforms", *IEEE Trans. Information Theory IT-20, pp. 119-120, 1974.*

[5]  Horn B. K. P., Schunk B. G., "Determining Optical Flow", *Artificial Intelligence, Nº 17, pp. 185-203, 1981.*

[6]  Kahn P., "Local Determination of a Moving Contrast Edge", *IEEE Trans. Pattern Analysis and Machine Intelligence, Vol. PAMI-7, Nº 4, pp. 402-409, July 1985.*

[7]  Kearney J. K., Thompson W. B., Boley L. D., "Optical Flow Estimation: An Error Analysis of Gradient-Based Methods with Local Optimisation", *IEEE Trans. Pattern Analysis and Machine Intelligence, Vol. PAMI-9, Nº 2, pp. 229-244, March 1987.*

[8]  Lawton D. T., "Processing Translational Motion Sequences", *Computer Vision, Graphics and Image Processing, Nº 22, pp. 116-144, 1983.*

[9]   Limb J., Murphy J., "Estimating the Velocity of Moving
      Images in TV Signal", *Comp. Graph. Image Proc., Nº 4, pp.
      311-327,* 1975.

[10]  Murray D. W., Buxton B. F., "Scene Segmentation from Visual
      Motion Using Global Optimisation", *IEEE Trans. Pattern
      Analysis and Machine Intelligence, Vol. PAMI-9, Nº 2, pp.
      220-228,* March 1987.

[11]  Prager J. M., Arbib M. A., "Computing the Optic Flow: The
      MATCH Algorithm and Prediction", *Computer Vision, Graphics
      and Image Processing, Nº 24, pp. 271-304,* 1983.

[12]  Roese J. A., Pratt W. V., "Combined Spatial and Temporal
      Coding of Digital Image Sequences", *Proc. SPIE 66, pp.
      172-180,* 1975.

[13]  Thompson W. B., Barnard S. T., "Lower-Level Estimation and
      Interpretation of Visual Motion", *Computer,* August 1981.

[14]  Ullman S., "Analysis of Visual Motion by Biological and
      Computer Systems", *Computer,* August 1981.

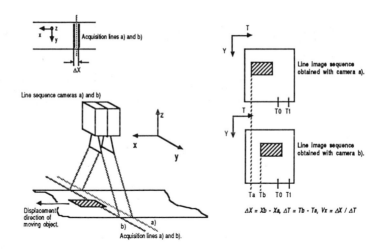

Figure 1: A set of two line cameras is used to implement speed measurements.

Figure 2:  Line image sequence $i_1(Y, T)$, showing six models with a superimposed framing.

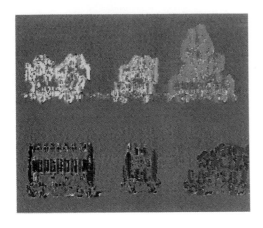

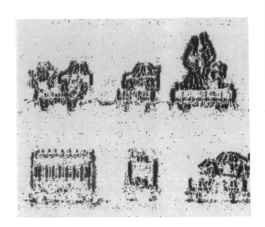

Figure 3: Optical flow field over the full image. Positive velocities are light and negative are dark. The neutral grey level codes zero-velocities as well as undefined velocities.

Figure 4: Relative sensitivity field. A high relative sensitivity (low confidence) is lighter than a low one (high confidence). Undefined relative sensitivities are mapped to white (lowest confidence).

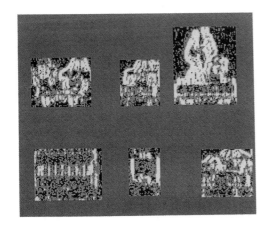

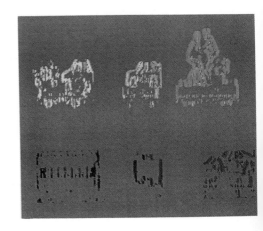

Figure 5: Result of thresholding. The white pixels encode the retained velocity measures.

Figure 6: Figure 3 masked with figure 5.

| Object | v | σ | $v_t$ | $σ_t$ | $v_r$ |
|---|---|---|---|---|---|
| Two cars | 27.29 | 29.30 | 31.90 | 11.07 | 32.72 |
| Upper car | 21.29 | 19.34 | 25.18 | 6.71 | 27.03 |
| Motorcyclist | 14.00 | 19.34 | 16.97 | 3.59 | 16.72 |
| Coach | -19.75 | 28.29 | -29.66 | 11.66 | -32.72 |
| Tank | -14.76 | 17.40 | -23.08 | 6.14 | -27.03 |
| Lower car | -13.60 | 11.71 | -16.63 | 4.20 | -16.72 |

Figure 7: Comparison of unthresholded average velocity v, thresholded velocity $v_t$ and real velocity $v_r$. The corresponding standard deviations σ and $σ_t$ are also given.

Figure 8: Special pattern used to establish figure 9. The direction of movement was perpendicular to the sinus crests.

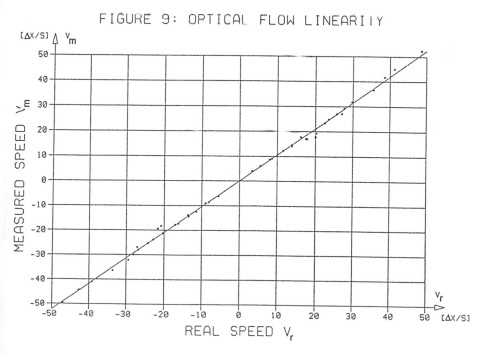

FIGURE 9: OPTICAL FLOW LINEARITY

# Three Dimensional Measurement by Stripe Line Pattern

Huang Zhi

Instrumentation Laboratory, KTH

S-100 44 Stockholm, Sweden

## *Abstract*

A method for 3-D measurement using a stripe line pattern has been developed
and tested. Both fundamentals and experiment result are presented in the paper.
Only one projected pattern is used during measurement and only one image of
TV-camera is needed for 3-D shape calculation. The measuring system developed
here can be easily used for practical applications.

## 1. Introduction

Triangulation range finding is extremly used in depth or 3-D measurement. Y. Shirai used a scanning system for 3-D measuring, in which a complete depth picture
was obtained either by moving scene object or by moving the scanning light [3] [4].
M. D. Altschuler used a laser-projected dot matrix for 3-D measurement, in which
a depth picture of $N \times N$ size was obtained by use of $\log(N + 1)$ patterns and
associated images [5] [6]. A space coded pattern based on PN-sequences was used
by P. Vuylsteke and A. Osterlink [7]. This method gives depth picture of scene
object using only one intensity picture and no movement of mechanical part is
needed in the measurement.

Recently, stripe line pattern was used by W. F. Wang et al [8] [9]. In their
method, two stripe line patterns, which are orthogonal to each other are projected
onto surface to be measured. The deformed grid pattern on the surface is used for
3-D shape calculation.

In this paper, a new method, which has been developed and tested in Instrumentation Laboratory, Royal Institute of Technology, Sweden, is presented for
measuring 3-D shape of surface. Only one projected stripe line pattern is used
during the measurement and only one TV-camera image is used for 3-D shape calculation. Both the experiment system and calculation of 3-D shape presented here
are simpler than most triangulation measuring systems. It can be conveniently
used in practical applications.

The basic idea of the method and the experiment system are given in section 2.
Analysis of normal vector and calculation of surface shape are topics of sections 3
and 4. Section 5 presents details about calculating 3-D shape from input picture.
Section 6 includes a brief discussion about the system properties.

## 2. Basic idea of stripe line system

The experiment system is shown in Fig. 1. A projected pattern, which consists of parallel and equi-spaced stright lines, is projected by an ordinary slide projector onto the surface $A$ to be measured. Due to the fact that TV-camera is viewing the surface from a direction, which is different from that of projecting light beam, a deformed pattern is recorded by TV-camera. This deformation is automatically analyzed by computer to obtain 3-D information of the surface $A$. In the experiment the projector and the TV-camera are put far away from the surface $A$ so that the projecting light between projector and the surface and the imaging light between TV-camera and surface can be considered as parallel light.

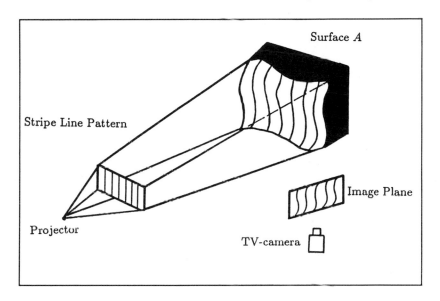

Figure 1. Experiment System

A drawing of the geometry of the system is shown in Fig. 2. For convenience of analysis and with no loss of generality, base plane of Fig. 2 is chosen as the coordinate plane $XOZ$ (paper plane), which is perpendicular to the projected pattern $P_a$ and image plane $P_i$. The stripe lines of the projected pattern are also perpendicular to the paper plane. $L_p$ is the optical axis of the projector and $L_i$ is the optical axis of the TV-camera. The intersection point of $L_p$ and $L_i$ is chosen as the origin of the coordinate system. A line, which divides the angle between $L_p$ and $L_i$ into equal parts, is chosen as the $Z$ axis. The $X$ axis is in the paper plane. The $Y$ axis becomes a point in Fig. 2.

When the surface $A$ coincides with coordinate plane $XOY$, the stripe line in the image is the same as that of projected pattern. When $A$ does not coincides with $XOY$ plane the image $P_i$ will be a deformed stripe lines, as shown in Fig. 1. In the condition of parallel illumination and parallel imaging light the shape of lines in the image is only decided by direction of the surface $A$, which can be calculated from the image and by which the 3-D shape of $A$ can be reconstructed.

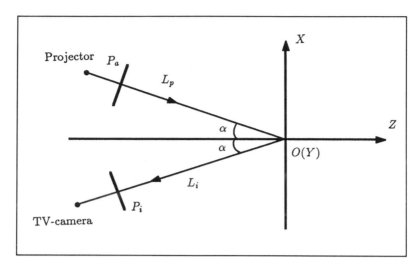

Figure 2. Plane drawing of Fig. 1

## 3. The surface normal from the deformed lines

In the following discussion, the surface normal is represented by angles $\sigma$ and $\tau$, where $\sigma$ is defined as the angle between the $L_p$ and $N_a$ (projection of the normal of surface $A$ in the $XOZ$ plane) and $\tau$ is defined as the angle between normal of surface $A$ and $XOZ$ plane. The definitions of $\sigma$ and $\tau$ are shown in Fig. 3.

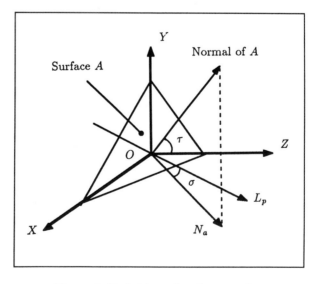

Figure 3. Definition of angles $\sigma$ and $\tau$

The shape parameters for lines in the image are represented by the distance $(dx)$ between lines along the scanning direction and the displacement $(X_d)$ of a line at a certain distance along the direction orthogonal to scanning line. In our case, $X$ direction is chosen as the scanning direction. The definitions of line shape parameters are shown in Fig. 4.

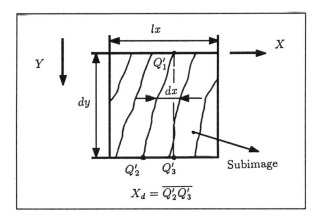

Figure 4. Definition of line shape parameter

If the system parameters of projector and TV-camera are known it is easy to find the relation among the normal angles, ($\sigma$ and $\tau$), $dx$ and $X_d$. As shown in the Fig.5, let the angle between $L_p$ and $OZ$ axis be $\alpha$ and the pitch of stripe lines

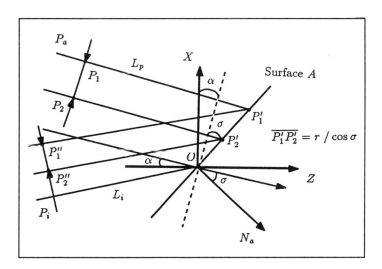

Figure 5. Relation between $\sigma$ and $dx$

of projected pattern be $r$. Two points $P_1$ and $P_2$, which are on the neighbour lines in the projected pattern, are projected onto the surface $A$, which has normal angles $\sigma$ and $\tau$. The distance between two projected points, $P_1'$ and $P_2'$, on the surface $A$ is:

$$r' = \frac{r}{\cos \sigma}$$

and the distance $(dx)$ between $P_1''$ and $P_2''$, which are image points of $P_1'$ and $P_2'$ respectively, in the image is:

$$dx = \frac{r}{\cos \sigma} \cos(\sigma + 2\alpha)$$

The angle $\sigma$ can be written as:

$$\tan \sigma = \cot(2\alpha) - \frac{dx}{r \sin(2\alpha)} \tag{1}$$

The geometrical relation for $X_d$ calculation is shown in Fig. 6, where a flat surface $A$ is measured. It is formed by projecting Fig. 1 onto the paper plane. $Q_1$ is a

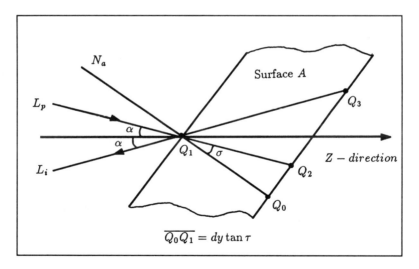

Figure 6. Relation between $X_d$ and surface normal

projected point of a point($B_1$) on a stripe line of the projected pattern($P_a$) and $Q_2$ is a projected point of another point($B_2$) on the same stripe line as that $B_1$ is on. $Q_3$ is a point on the surface $A$, whose image point $Q_3'$ formed by TV-camera is on the line which passes through the image point $Q_1'$ of $Q_1$ and perpendicular to $X$-direction, as shown in Fig. 4. Obviously, if the tilt angle $\tau$ of surface $A$ is non zero the image point $Q_2'$ of $Q_2$ will not be on the line $\overline{Q_1'Q_3'}$. In other words, the image point $Q_2'$ is displaced by the tilt angle $\tau$. Let the distance between $B_1$

and $B_2$ on the projected pattern be $dy$, $X_d$ $(\overline{Q'_2 Q'_3})$ can be represented by angles $\sigma$ and $\tau$ according to the geometrical relation given in Fig. 6:

$$X_d = dy \tan(\tau)[\tan(\sigma + 2\alpha) - \tan \sigma] \cos(\sigma + 2\alpha)$$

Angle $\tau$ can be written as:

$$\tan \tau = \frac{X_d}{dy[\tan(\sigma + 2\alpha) - \tan \sigma] \cos(\sigma + 2\alpha)} \tag{2}$$

In the above discussion the magnification ratio between projected pattern and TV-camera image is assumed to be 1. If the ratio is not equal to 1, a ratio constant should be included in Eqs. (1) and (2).

## 4. Height from normal angles

In general situations, only relative height can be obtained from the normal angles and some boundary conditions are needed to obtain absolute height. In our experiment the surface boundary is first detected and the height of the first boundary point of each row (or each column) is set to be zero. From this starting point the absolute height of each point, which belongs to the same row (or the same column) as that the first point belongs to, can be reconstructed. Let the starting boundary point be $x_0$, the current surface point be $x_c$, and the normal angles of each point $x_i$ be $\sigma(x_i)$ and $\tau(x_i)$. Height calculation proceeds according to the formula:

$$H(x_c) = \sum_{i=0}^{c} \tan[\sigma(x_i)] \cos[\tau(x_i)] \tag{3}$$

## 5. Processing steps in the experiment

The computer processing can be divided into four steps, pre-processing of input image, shape detection for deformed stripe lines, normal angles and surface height calculation.

### a. Pre-processing

For our purpose, the important information of the input image is the deformed stripe lines, these pre-processing algorithms are designed to obtain the good binary line picture from the input image.

The input picture is first processed by a local maximum enhancement program, which operates on the local area of each pixel, such as its $3 \times 3$ neighbours. If the grayvalue of the pixel is greater than the average value of its neighbours its value is not changed, otherwise the value of the pixel is set to be equal to zero [10].

The enhanced picture is then processed by a local maximum detecting program, which detects local maximum points of specified size and specified direction by gear backlash smoothing method [11]. The local maximum points are set to be white and others are set to be black.

**b.** Line shape detection

The binary picture generated in the step **(a)** is first divided into a number of small sub-pictures. Each sub-picture represents a patch on the original surface $A$.

The $dx$, the distance between lines in the $X$-direction, can be obtained either by calculating the number of black points along the $X$-direction in each sub-image or by using of a texture density function.

The texture density function $(D)$ is defined as $D = lx/dx$, where $lx$ is the length of sub-image in the $X$-direction (as shown in Fig. 4). Because $lx$ is already known and the $D$ is the number of white points in the $X$-direction, it is easy to get $dx = lx/D$ from the binary line picture.

For the $X_d$, the displacement of a line in the $X$-direction, the each line of a sub-image is tracked by a line tracking algorithm and the difference between $X$-coordinates of starting and end poins of each line ($Q'_1$ and $Q'_2$ in the Fig. 4) contributes to $X_d$.

**c.** Normal angle calculation

After the $dx$ and $X_d$ have been obtained, the normal angles can be calculated directly according to Eq. (1) and Eq . (2).

**d.** Height calculation.

From normal angles of the surface, the surface height can be calculated directly according to the Eq. (3).

Figs. 7 – 12 present the results of our initial experiment. Figs. 7 and 10 are input pictures of a ball and a pyramid, which are illuminated by stripe line light. Figs. 8 and 11 are binary line pictures of Figs. 7 and 10 respectively. Figs. 9 and 12 are 3-D pictures, which are reconstructed from Figs. 7 and 10 respectively. The $256 \times 256$ TV-camera image and $16 \times 16$ sub-image are used in the experiment. The surface of objects to be measured are diffuse reflectors and the colour of whole area on the surface is similar so that the ratios of signal to noise in the input pictures are good enough to obtain reasonable binary line pictures. In order to avoid the difficulty of normal discontinuities at edges the sharp edges of the surfaces have been smoothed before experiment.

## 6. Discussion about the stripe line system

Because only one projected line pattern is used in the system and only line information is used for 3-D shape calculation both the set-up of the system and the calculation of surface shape is simpler than most triangulation 3-D measuring systems. Most of calculations for obtaining 3-D shape can be finished by hardware.

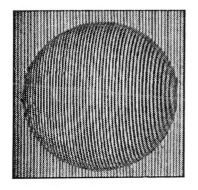

Fig 7. Ball illuminated by stripe line

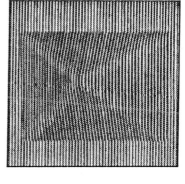

Fig 10. Pyramid illuminated by stripe line

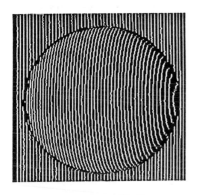

Fig. 8. Binary line picture of Fig 7.

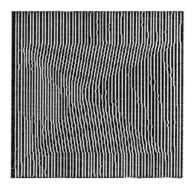

Fig. 11. Binary picture of Fig. 10.

Fig. 9. 3-D picture of Fig. 7.

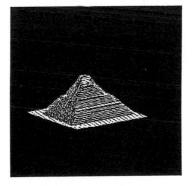

Fig. 12. 3-D picture of Fig. 10.

The stripe line system can be conveniently applied to practical problems. However, there are also some limitations for the stripe line system, which are summarized as follows:

a. The parallel illumination and parallel imaging light are assumed in the disccusion above. Although this condition for some practical purposes is not strict, the care should be taken, that is, the size of the object to be measured should be small enough comparing to the distance between the projector and the object, as well as the distance between TV-camera and object.

b. Surface to be measured should be smooth enough to obtain a good stripe binary picture and sub-image average. If there are sharp edges on the surface the stripe line method will give erroneous result in the area around the edges.

c. Resolusion of TV-camera image should be good enough for the requirements of measuring accuracy because average values of sub-images are used to replace the value of each point of that subarea of surface. In our experiment $256 \times 256$ image is used. For the practical problem the $512 \times 512$ image should be used in order to obtain better result.

The author gratefully acknowledge Prof. Rolf B Johansson of Instrumentation Laboratory, KTH for his valuable guidance and great support.

## *References*

1. R. A. JARVIS: *A perspective on range finding techniques for computer vision*, IEEE Trans on, Vol.PAMI-5, No. 2, 1983, pp. 122-139.

2. F. R. LIVINGSTONE and M. RIOUX: *Development of a large field of view 3-D vision system*, SPIE, Vol. 665, 1986, pp. 188-194.

3. Y. SHIRAI: *Recognition of polyhedrons with a range finder*, Pattern Recognition, Vol. 4, 1972, pp. 243-250.

4. Y. SHIRAI: *Object recognition using three-dimensional information*, IEEE Trans on, Vol. PAMI-5, 1983, pp. 353-361.

5. M. D. ALTSCHULER, B. R. ALTSCHULER, and J. TABOADA: *Measuring surfaces space-coded by a laser-projected dot matrix*, SPIE, Vol. 182, 1979, pp. 187-191.

6. B. R. ALTSCHULER, J. TABOADA: *Laser electro-optic system for three-dimensional (3-D) topographic mensuration*, SPIE, Vol. 192, 1979, pp. 192-196.

7. P. VUYLSTEKE and A. OOSTERLINCK: *A coded illumination pattern based on PN-sequences for 3-D robot vision*, IJCAI, June, 1986.

8. Y. F. WANG: *3D object describtion from stripe coding and multiple views*, P5SCIA, 1987, Stockholm, p. 669.

9. N. SHRIKHANDE: *Surface normals from striped light*, P5SCIA, 1987, Stockholm, p. 649.

10. T. KASVAND: *Iterative edge detection*, CGIP, Vol. 4, 1976, pp. 245-253.

11. O. R. MITCHELL et al: *A max-min measure for image texture analysis*, IEEE Trans on, Vol. C-26, 1977, pp. 408-414.

# APPLICATIONS OF MEASURES OF UNCERTAINTY IN DISCRIMINANT ANALYSIS

David Hirst & Ian Ford
Department of Statistics, University of Glasgow, Glasgow G12 8QW

Frank Critchley
Department of Statistics, University of Warwick, Coventry, CV4 7AL

## 1.  INTRODUCTION

Recently, various methods have been developed for measuring the uncertainty associated with estimates of the probabilities of group membership or related quantities in discriminant analysis.   Most of this work has centred round the problem of constructing interval estimates (Schaafsma and Van Vark, 1979; Rigby, 1982; Ambergen and Schaafsma, 1984; Van der Sluis and Schaafsma, 1984; Critchley and Ford, 1984, 1985; Critchley, Ford and Rijal, 1987, 1988; Davis, 1988).   It would appear that reliable methods of interval estimation are now available in the contexts of multivariate normal data with equal or unequal covariance matrices (Critchley, Ford and Hirst, 1988; Hirst, Ford and Critchley, 1988).

The aim of the current paper is to review existing methodology and to  change the focus of attention from development and evaluation of formal statistical procedures to that of investigating the usefulness of these techniques to the practitioner interested in the application of the methodology to practical problems in statistical pattern recognition.

In Section 2 we motivate the problem using a practical example.   In Section 3 we review the existing methodology, since this methodology may be unfamiliar to workers in the wider field of pattern recognition, and in subsequent sections explore various areas where these techniques may be employed.

## 2.  MOTIVATING EXAMPLE

Aitchison and Dunsmore (1975, Chapter 1) discuss a data set consisting of 8 features measured on 31 patients suffering from a rare syndrome of hypertension (Conn's syndrome).   In 20 of the patients the condition is known to be caused by a benign tumour (Adenoma) and in the remaining 11 the cause is known to be a more diffuse condition (Bilateral Hyperplasia).   The aim is to use the given feature data to classify future patients by disease category so that appropriate treatment can be administered.   Fig. 1 contains a scatter plot for the variables Renin and Potassium with Adenomas denoted by 1 and Bilateral Hyperplasias by 2.   Also shown on the plot are data for 4 patients (labelled A, B, C, D) of unconfirmed type.   All analysis on this problem will be reported in terms of log transformed data as recommended by Aitchison and Dunsmore (1975).   From the plot, it is clear that, with respect to the two variables plotted, there is reasonable, but not complete, separation between

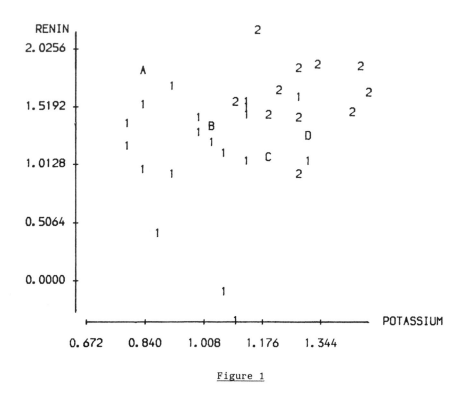

Figure 1

the two populations. It should also be fairly clear from the plot that we should not be equally certain about our diagnoses for the four new cases. Case A is atypical for both groups but looks more like an Adenoma than a Bilateral Hyperplasia. Case B looks like an Adenoma. Case C is borderline and case D looks more like a Bilateral Hyperplasia than an Adenoma. Our uncertainty about these new cases arises from two sources. The first source of uncertainty is due to the true, but unknown, odds of each case being an Adenoma rather than a Bilateral Hyperplasia and the second source is due to the error in estimating the odds based on a finite and, in this case, relatively small data set. The main motivating feature for our research is the fact that this second source of uncertainty can be fairly substantial and the magnitude of this uncertainty will depend not only on the sizes of the training sets but also on the location of the feature vector for the actual case under study. This has led various researchers to study the distributional properties of estimators of the probabilities of group membership and in particular to investigate methods of interval estimation for this or related quantities. Progress has been made in the areas of logistic discrimination (Anderson, 1972) and discrimination under the assumption of a multivariate normal distribution for the feature vectors within groups. In this paper we concentrate on the second of these areas.

## 3. REVIEW OF EXISTING METHODOLOGY

Consider the two population discrimination problem in which we are given, as training data, independent random samples $x_{ij}$; $i = 1, 2$; $j=1,\ldots,n_i$, of fixed sizes from the two populations. For $i=1, 2$ let $f_i(\cdot)$ denote the probability density function for the $i$th population and assume that the prior probability $\pi_i$ of a new case arising from that population is known. Let x be the feature vector for a case of unknown type. Then the posterior log-odds of x coming from population 1 is the known constant $\log(\pi_1\pi_2^{-1})$ plus $\theta$ where

$$\theta = \log\{f_1(x)/f_2(x)\}$$

The $x_{ij}$'s are assumed to arise from multivariate normal distributions $N_p(\mu_i,\Omega_i)$.

In the case where $\Omega_1 = \Omega_2 = \Omega$ it is easy to show that

$$\theta = \tfrac{1}{2}\{\alpha_2^2 - \alpha_1^2\},$$

where $\alpha_i^2$ is the squared Mahalanobis distance $(x-\mu_i)^T\Omega_i^{-1}(x-\mu_i)$. In the case of unequal covariance matrices,

$$\theta = \tfrac{1}{2}\Sigma(-1)^i\{\alpha_i^2 + \log \det \Omega_i\},$$

Our aim is to construct an interval estimate for $\theta$.

Let the training sample mean vectors, unpooled and pooled adjusted sum of squares and crossproducts matrix be denoted by $\bar{X}_i$, $S_i$, $i=1,2$, and $S$ respectively.

In the equal covariance case, Moran and Murphy (1979) show that the minimum variance unbiased estimator for $\theta$ is,

$$\hat{\theta} = (N-p-1)(\bar{X}_1-\bar{X}_2)^T S^{-1}\{x-\tfrac{1}{2}(\bar{X}_1+\bar{X}_2)\}+\tfrac{1}{2}p(n_1^{-1}-n_2^{-1}),$$

where $N = n_1+n_2-2$.

Schaafsma (1982) and Critchley and Ford (1984) show that the variance of $\hat{\theta}$ is given by

$$
\begin{aligned}
(N-p)(N-p-3)\mathrm{var}(\hat{\theta}) = \ & (N-p+1)\{\theta-\tfrac{1}{2}(N-1)(n_1^{-1}-n_2^{-1})\}^2 \\
& + (N-p-1)[\Phi\{(N-1)(n_1^{-1}+n_2^{-1})+\Delta^2\}-\tfrac{1}{2}\Delta^4] \\
& + \tfrac{1}{2}(N-1)(N-p-1)\{2p(n_1^{-2}+n_2^{-2}) \\
& - (N+1)(n_1^{-1}-n_2^{-1})^2\} .
\end{aligned}
$$

where $\Phi = \tfrac{1}{2}\{\alpha_1^2 + \alpha_2^2\}$ measures the average atypicality of observation x from the two population and $\Delta^2 = (\mu_1-\mu_2)^T\Omega^{-1}(\mu_1-\mu_2)$ is the squared Mahalanobis distance between them. The exact distribution of $\hat{\theta}$ appears intractable although invariance arguments, given in Critchley and Ford (1985), show that it depends only upon the three parameters $\theta$, $\Phi$ and $\Delta^2$. Critchley and Ford (1985) consider two methods of interval estimation for $\theta$ in the case of equal covariance matrices, based on the assumption of equal covariance matrices and assuming approximate Normality of the distribution of $\hat{\theta}$.

Similar results are available for the unequal covariance matrix case. Critchley, Ford and Rijal (1987) consider an approach to interval estimation based on approximate normality for this case.

Rigby (1982) has derived a Bayesian solution based on a four moment approximation to the posterior distribution for $\theta$ in the unequal covariance case. Unpublished work by Rigby contains similar results for the equal covariance matrix case.

Critchley, Ford and Rijal (1988) show how strong Lagrangian methods can be utilised to construct interval estimates based on the Profile Likelihood (Kalbfleisch and Sprott, 1970; Kalbfleisch, 1979).

More recent work by Davis (1987) contains useful results on the sampling cumulants of $\hat{\theta}$ and related statistics, which can be utilised, using a technique of Peers and Iqbal (1985), to construct confidence intervals for $\theta$. Unfortunately, it would appear that this technique can only be applied to the equal covariance matrix case.

Critchley, Ford and Hirst (1988) and Hirst, Ford and Critchley (1988) have evaluated the above methods empirically. They conclude that, in the equal covariance matrix case, the Bayesian method and the approach of Davis can be used to construct interval estimates with confidence probabilities very close to the target value. The methods of Critchley & Ford (1985) and the Profile Likelihood method appear to be less reliable in this respect. For the unequal covariance matrix case the Bayesian approach again performs best. It is interesting that the Bayesian approach has good sampling properties since it is not explicitly designed to have such properties.

Despite the fact that the different methods have different sampling theory properties, Critchley, Ford and Hirst (1988) note that, in a practical example, the various methods produce intervals for $\theta$ which have very similar qualitative properties and which would lead to similar conclusions in practice. However, an analysis of the Conn's Syndrome data reveals that this is, in fact, not always true.

Table 1 contains approximate 95% confidence intervals for $\theta$ and for the probability of membership $P_A$, of the Adenoma group (assuming that $\pi_1 = \pi_2 = \frac{1}{2}$) based on the Profile, Bayesian and approximate Normality assumption for $\hat{\theta}$. Intervals are given for the four unclassified cases labelled A, B, C and D in Fig. 1. In this case four of the variables have been used in the analysis namely age, potassium, carbon dioxide and renin, and unequal covariances have been assumed. The results for cases C and D illustrate quite clearly that intervals for $P_A$ can be extremely wide, representing substantial uncertainty about how a classification should be made. The results for Cases A and B illustrate that quite different intervals can be produced by the different methods. The Profile and Bayesian methods would allocate both cases to the Adenoma group with complete confidence while the Normality approach would reflect total uncertainty about the correct diagnosis.

|      |   | Profile | Method Bayesian | Normality |
|------|---|---------|----------|-----------|
|      | A | (9.0,61.0) | (5.7,52.4) | (-9.6,31.4) |
|      |   | (1.0,1.0) | (1.0,1.0) | (0.0,1.0) |
|      | B | (6.0,28.0) | (3.2,23.6) | (-3.3,13.5) |
|      |   | (1.0,1.0) | (0.96,1.0) | (0.04,1.0) |
| Case | C | (-0.2,7.4) | (-1.9,5.0) | (-2.8,2.3) |
|      |   | (0.45,1.0) | (0.13,0.99) | (0.06,0.91) |
|      | D | (-2.4,4.2) | (-3.8,2.3) | (-3.9,0.9) |
|      |   | (0.08,0.99) | (0.02,0.91) | (0.02,0.71) |

Table 1:  In the table the upper interval and lower
intervals are for $\theta$ and $P_A$ respectively

## 4. APPLICATIONS

We turn now to a discussion of practical applications of these procedures.

### 4.1. Assessment of individual cases

When studying individual cases it is important to remember that it is the probability of group membership, conditional on the given feature vector, which is important and not the overall misclassification properties of the method being used. In fact, in certain contexts, discrimination procedures with relatively poor misclassification properties may be useful in practice, if a reasonable number of individuals can be classified with certainty.   Screening tests are an important example.   Here it might be useful to subdivide cases into categories based on their estimated probabilities of group membership.   We feel that the uncertainty associated with estimates of these probabilities of group membership should play a role in this activity.   A simplistic scheme, in a two group classification situation, might classify cases as Group 1 (or 2) if a 95% confidence interval for the probability of membership of Group 1 is completely above (or below) 0.5.   Other cases would be sent for further investigation.

A second example of the usefulness of interval estimates is illustrated by genetic counselling.   Here, women may be quoted estimated probabilities that they will give birth to children with genetic defects, based on tests which have been carried out on them.   These estimates could be subject to substantial uncertainties which could result in a woman being given, mistakenly, very favourable or unfavourable advice.   In practice, an interval estimate might be very wide, implying that, at least for that particular woman, the tests have been totally uninformative.

2(a)   Re-substitution (and Jackknifed Method)

Classified Type

|  |  | 1 | 2 |
|---|---|---|---|
|  | 1 | 19 | 1 |
| True Type |  |  |  |
|  | 2 | 0 | 11 |

2(b)   Interval Method

Classified Type

|  |  | 1 | 2 | Unclassified |
|---|---|---|---|---|
|  | 1 | 17 | 1 | 2 |
| True Type |  |  |  |  |
|  | 2 | 0 | 4 | 7 |

Table 2:   Classification Tables

## 4.2.   Assessment of discriminant rule performance

Often, there is no option of sequential decision making (e.g. sending cases for further tests) and a decision rule for discrimination has to be formulated and assessed.    A  popular  method  for  assessing  performance  constructs  a  table  of classifications and misclassifications depicting how cases in the training set (or in a separate trial set) are allocated when the discriminant rule is applied to each case.    It is well known that this information can be biased if the classification matrix is based on the same data which was used to set up the discriminant rule. Jackknifing is a popular technique for alleviating this bias.

We  propose  an  alternative  simple  procedure  which  we  feel  reflects  more accurately the uncertainty involved in a discriminant rule due to the finiteness of training data sample sizes.   We propose that the classification matrix should be based  on  an  examination  of  interval  estimates  for  the  probability  of  group membership, resulting in a third category corresponding to cases where the 95% confidence interval includes 0.5.    Table 2 illustrates this procedure as applied to the Conn's Syndrome data. The data used in the analysis are the four variables, age, potassium, carbon dioxide and renin, and an unequal covariance matrix assumption has been made.    The Table 2(a) gives the classification matrix for rules based on the estimated probabilities of group membership using both Jackknifed and Re-subsitution methods.    In this example, these matrices turn out to be identical. The table for the three category Interval Estimate based method is given as Table 2(b).    It has 9 cases which have intervals which include 0.5.

3(a)  Method of selection : Interval estimation
      Variables selected   : Sodium, Potassium

### Method of Classification

|  |  | Re-substitution Classified Type | | | Jackknifing Classified Type | | | Interval Estimation Classified Type | | |
|---|---|---|---|---|---|---|---|---|---|---|
|  |  | 1 | 2 | | 1 | 2 | | 1 | 2 | Uncertain |
| True | 1 | 19 | 1 | 1 | 18 | 2 | 1 | 16 | 0 | 4 |
| Type | 2 | 1 | 10 | 2 | 2 | 9 | 2 | 0 | 6 | 5 |

3(b)  Method of selection : Jackknifing
      Variables selected   : Potassium

### Method of Classification

|  |  | Re-substitution Classified Type | | | Jackknifing Classified Type | | | Interval Estimation Classified Type | | |
|---|---|---|---|---|---|---|---|---|---|---|
|  |  | 1 | 2 | | 1 | 2 | | 1 | 2 | Uncertain |
| True | 1 | 18 | 2 | 1 | 18 | 1 | 1 | 14 | 1 | 4 |
| Type | 2 | 2 | 9 | 2 | 2 | 9 | 2 | 1 | 6 | 4 |

Table 3:  Classification Matrices for variables chosen
          by different variable selection routines

The actual intervals for the probabilities of group membership for the training data are displayed in Figure 2.    The intervals for Adenomas are depicted by continuous lines and those for the Bilateral Hyperplasias by dashed lines.    The point estimates for the probabilities are marked by an 'X' and the Jackknifed estimates of these probabilities are marked by a 'J'.    It is interesting to note that the Jackknifed estimates are always within the interval estimates.    Note also that the intervals can be very wide and include 0.5 even when both point estimates are close to 0 or 1.

4.3.  The Application of Interval Estimation to Variable Selection.

One possible application of interval estimation for $\theta$ is in the area of variable selection.    Given a large number of variables the problem is to choose a subset which is adequate for discrimination purposes.

One possible procedure would be a forward stepwise method as follows:-

(1)  Regard an observation as 'confidently classified' if a 95% confidence
     interval for $\theta$ does not contain zero.

(2)  Calculate the discriminant function for each variable in turn and choose

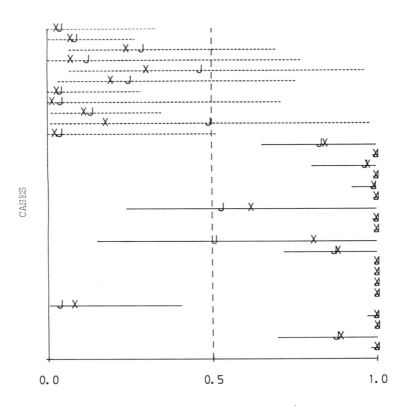

CASES

0.0                    0.5                    1.0

Prob(member of Adenoma group)

Figure 2

the one which confidently classifies the most observations correctly.

(3) Add each unselected variable in turn to the previously selected subet
    and select the combination which confidently classifies the most
    observations correctly.

(4) Repeat stage (3) until there is no further improvement.

When this procedure was used on the Conn's data, it selected the variables
sodium and potassium.   The classification matrices are shown in Table 3.   An
all-subsets search has shown that this is in fact the (unique) optimal combination
of variables for interval classification.   It has also shown that the (unique)
optimal subset for jackknifed classification is the four variables of Section 3.   We
note that, in any given example, the optimal variables for jackknifed classification
are not necessarily those for interval  classification.   For comparison, a similar
stepwise selection procedure was investigated using as  a criterion for subset
assessment the total number of observations correctly classified after Jackknifing.
The results are given in Table 3(b).

## 5. DISCUSSION

We have reviewed work on the problem of interval estimation for the probability of group membership for the two population problem assuming multivariate normality. Extensions to the multigroup problem are straightforward. Note that in different practical contexts alternative schemes might be appropriate for the definition of the unclassified category. For example 0.5 might not always be a logical boundary if prior probabilities of group membership are not equal. Alternatively, we might only want to confidently classify cases if the interval for the probability of group membership lies above $C_1$ or below $C_2$, for appropriate $C_1$ and $C_2$. The arguments for the use of these techniques, in contexts where information arrives sequentially or where further data can be sought, are strong. Our initial investigations of the application of these techniques in the assessment of discriminant rule performance and in variable selection are encouraging. Clearly more work is required in this area and we would hope to report more fully on these topics in the near future.

## REFERENCES

Aitchison, J. & Dunsmore, I.R. (1975). _Statistical Prediction Analysis_, Cambridge University Press.

Anderson, J.A. (1972). Separate sample logistic discrimination. _Biometrika_, _59_, 19-35.

Ambergen, A.W. and Schaafsma, W. (1984). Interval estimates for posterior probabilities, applications to Border Cave. In Multivariate Statistical Methods in Physical Anthropology. (G.M. Van Vark & W.W. Howells, eds.). D. Reidel Publishing Company.

Critchley, F. and Ford, I. (1984). On the covariance of two noncentral F random variables and the variance of the estimated linear discriminant function. _Biometrika_, _71_, 637-8.

Critchley, F. and Ford, I. (1985). Interval estimation in discrimination: the multivariate normal equal covariance case. _Biometrika_, _72_, 109-116.

Critchley, F., Ford, I. and Hirst, D. (1988). An evaluation of methods of interval estimation for the odds ratio in discrimination. To appear in the Proceedings of the Fifth International Symposium on Data Analysis and Informatics, Versailles, 1987. North Holland.

Critchley, F., Ford, I. and Rijal, O. (1987). Uncertainty in discrimination. Proceedings of the Conference DIANA II held in Liblice, 1986. Mathematical Institute of the Czechoslovak Academy of Sciences, Prague, 83-106.

Critchley, F., Ford, I. and Rijal, O. (1988). Interval estimation based on the profile likelihood: strong Lagrangian theory with applications to discrimination. _Biometrika_, _75_, 21-28.

Davis, A.W. (1987). Moments of linear discriminant functions, and an asymptotic confidence interval for the log odds ratio. _Biometrika_, _74_, 829-840.

Hirst, D., Ford, I. and Critchley, F. (1988). Interval estimation in discrimination a simulation study. Submitted for publication.

Kalbfleisch, J.G. and Sprott, D.A. (1970). Application of likelihood methods to models involving large numbers of parameters. _J.R. Statist. Soc._, _B_, _32_, 175-208.

Kalbfleisch, J.G. (1979). _Probability and Statistical Inference II_. New York: Springer-Verlag.

Moran, M.A. and Murphy, B.J. (1979). A closer look at two alternative methods of statistical discrimination. _Appl. Statist._, _28_, 223-232.

Peers, H.W. & Iqbal, M. (1985). Asymptotic expansions for confidence limits in the presence of nuisance parameters with applications. J.R. Statist. Soc. B, 47, 547-554.

Rigby, R.A. (1982). A credibility interval for the probability that a new observation belongs to one of two multivariate normal populations. J.R. Statist. Soc. B, 44, 212-220.

Schaafsma, W. (1982). Selecting variables in discriminant analysis for improving upon classical procedures. In Handbook of Statistics, Vol.2 P.R. Krishnaiah and L.N. Kanal, eds), Amsterdam, North Holland.

Schaafsma, W. and Van Vark, G.N. (1979). Classification and discrimination problems with applications II. Statist. Neerlandica, 33, 91-126.

Van der Sluis, D.M. and Schaafsma, W. (1984). POSCON - a decision-support system in diagnosis and prognosis based on a statistical approach. In Compstat 1984 (T. Havranek et al, eds) Vienna: Physica-Verlag.

# IMPROVING THE DISCRIMINATION OF SYNTHETIC DISCRIMINANT FILTERS

S. K. MAYO


GEC Research Limited, Hirst Research Centre
East Lane, Wembley, Middlesex, HA9 7PP, UK

## ABSTRACT

Synthetic Discriminant Filters (SDF) are theoretically capable of distortion invariant multiclass recognition. However a serious practical limitation is the trade-off between invariance and specificity. Three techniques were investigated for improving the ability of the SDF to perform 2-D rotation invariant recognition of an industrial component from amongst similarly shaped objects. The first technique involved extracting features from the correlation image. A trade-off was found between the number and/or complexity of features which must be extracted and the number of training set images in the SDF. The second technique was edge enhancing the SDF and/or test images. Edge enhancing the test images gave greater discrimination improvement than did edge enhancing the SDF. The third method was phase only filtering. Phase only SDFs gave a dramatic improvement in discrimination between training set targets and clutter although rejection of non training set targets increases. Increasing the number of training set image remedied this.

## 1. INTRODUCTION

Synthetic Discriminant Filters (SDF) are theoretically capable of distortion invariant multiclass pattern recognition (Hester and Casasent 1980, Caulfield 1982). Essentially an SDF is a weighted linear superposition, h, of N training set images $f_i$ of distorted views of the classes to be recognised. Weights $a_i$ are chosen so that the correlation between SDF and $f_i$ has a specified central value $c_i$ i.e. $h = \sum a_i f_i$ for i=1 to N and $(f_i x h)_o = c_i$ where x denotes correlation and the subscript o denotes the central correlation value. It is usually assumed that the peak correlation value occurs at the centre of the correlation image. Typically all rotations, scales and views of objects of the same class i are assigned the same peak correlation value $c_i$, whereas objects of a different class j are assigned a different peak value $c_j$. $c_i$ can be set to zero for classes which are to be rejected although it is seldom possible to specify all unwanted objects (clutter). Thus in principle, the SDF overcomes the two main disadvantages of the Matched Spatial Filter (MSF) i.e. lack of distortion invariance and inability to recognise more than one class.

However a serious practical limitation of the SDF is that it becomes less target specific the more images are included in the training set, and correlations between SDF and clutter can produce large peaks. Also, distorted views of the target which were not included in the training set can give unpredictable correlation peaks. These two effects cause misclassification and the aim of this paper is to assess three techniques for reducing such misclassifications.

The three techniques are (i) Correlation feature extraction. Additional features, other than just the peak height, such as width, perimeter and volume, are extracted from the correlation image. Ideally one would like to extract as few as possible highly discriminatory additional features in order to minimise CPU time required. (ii) Edge enhancing SDF and/or test images and (iii) Phase only SDFs. The latter two techniques modify the SDF so that it does not give such ambiguous peak heights for targets and clutter.

This work arose during development of an optical correlator for industrial inspection (Cooper et al) but the technqiues discussed are equally applicable to optical or digital correlation. All work reported here was obtained by computer simulations using digital correlation.

## 2. SDF SYNTHESIS

The object to be recognised (the "target"), which is used in all three methods discussed in this paper, is an industrial component - a crankshaft from a working model petrol engine. We have also used three similar shaped objects (clutter) against which to discriminate the target. Binary images of target and clutter were used and are shown in the top half of Figure 1. The training set images were obtained by rotating the binary image of the target about its centroid. The SDF weights are all unity for equal energy rotated images and the SDF was made by digitally summing the rotated images. A digital SDF synthetised from a training set of 8 rotations of the target (i.e. every 45 degrees) is shown in Figure 2a.

There are several practical problems in making and using an SDF. For example (i) training set images should be summed with their centroids superimposed (ii) if training set images do not have the same energy, negative weights can arise which cannot be implemented in a photographic optical correlator, though they present no problems in a holographic or digital system (iii) if the illumination of test images varies appreciably from that of the training set then the absolute size of the correlation peak will scale accordingly (iv) the central correlation value it not necessarily the peak. However such considerations are beyond the scope of this paper.

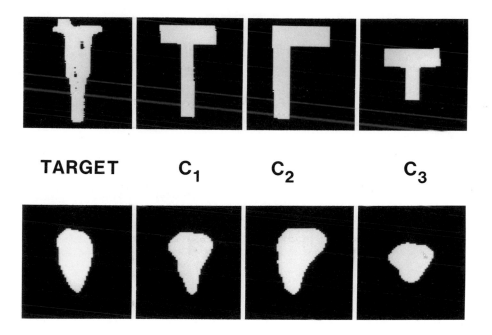

**TARGET          C₁          C₂          C₃**

FIGURE 1: (upper) Binary images of target and clutter. (lower) Thresholded
binary correlation images corresponding to images above (see text)

### 3. CORRELATION FEATURE EXTRACTION

Several training set images and the three clutter images were digitally
correlated with the SDF of Figure 2a. A non training set view of the target
with a 22.5 degree rotation was also correlated. The correlation image was
then thresholded at half the peak height, producing a binary image with a
single simply-connected central region from which we extracted all features
except peak height and grey volume. The lower half of Figure 1 shows the
binary thresholded correlation images corresponding to the test image
immediately above it.

The features extracted from the correlation images are listed in Table 1.
They fall into two categories (i) "simple" features such as peak height,
area, volume and perimeter, which can be computed very quickly using only
boolean and integer addition operations and (ii) "complex" features such as
moments and ratios which involve more complex and time consuming operations
such as multiplication and division. Speed is essential if the recognition
or rejection decision is to be made in a few milliseconds as is required
in real time applications. Simple features are discussed first.

## KEY TO TABLES

```
im   = image type (t, n or c - see below)
t    = training-set target
n    = non training-set target
c    = clutter
rot  = rotation angle of target
h    = peak height
P4   = length of 4-connected perimeter (pixels)
P8   = lenght of 8-connected perimeter (pixels)
A    = area (pixels)
V    = volume (=sum of pixel values)
E    = total energy in correlation image (=sum of pixels squared)
SNR  = Signal-to-noise ratio of correlation image defined as volume
       above half peak threshold over volume below
Imax = 2nd order moment about axis of greatest inertia
Imin = 2nd order moment about axis of least inertia
m1   = 1st invariant moment (= s = "spread")
m2   = 2nd invariant moment
e    = elongation (= [Imax - Imin]/[Imax + Imin])
c    = concavity (= [A'-A]/A, where A' is area of convex hull)
```

NOTE: all quantities except ratios are in arbitrary units

## TABLE 1

|  |  | simple features | | | | | complex features | | | | | | |
|----|-----|------|-----|-----|------|------|-----|-----|------|------|-----|-----|-----|-----|
| im | rot | h | P4 | P8 | A | V | E | SNR | Imax | Imin | m1 | m2 | e | c |
| col |  | 1 | 2 | 3 | 4 | 5 | 6 | 7 | 8 | 9 | 10 | 11 | 12 | 13 |
| | | | | | | targets | | | | | | | | |
| t | 0 | 5744 | 238 | 182 | 2346 | 4168 | 113 | 2.10 | 965 | 209 | 213 | 19 | .64 | .028 |
| t | 90 | 5760 | 244 | 185 | 2394 | 4250 | 122 | 1.78 | 1033 | 212 | 217 | 21 | .66 | .008 |
| t | 45 | 5724 | 258 | 171 | 2357 | 4185 | 115 | 2.05 | 990 | 208 | 216 | 20 | .65 | .018 |
| t | 180 | 5701 | 232 | 177 | 2322 | 4150 | 111 | 2.22 | 905 | 213 | 207 | 16 | .62 | .017 |
| n | 22.5 | 5374 | 258 | 182 | 2673 | 4894 | 130 | 2.56 | 1158 | 296 | 204 | 15 | .59 | .017 |
| mean | | 5661 | 246 | 179 | 2418 | 4329 | 118 | 2.14 | 1010 | 228 | 213 | 18 | .63 | .018 |
| std | | 145 | 11 | 5 | 129 | 284 | 7 | .25 | 85 | 34 | 5 | 2 | .03 | .006 |
| | | | | | | clutter | | | | | | | | |
| c1 | 0 | 5101 | 258 | 192 | 2389 | 4199 | 113 | 2.10 | 954 | 278 | 216 | 14 | .55 | .077 |
| c2 | 0 | 5297 | 284 | 210 | 3067 | 5652 | 149 | 2.68 | 1575 | 434 | 213 | 15 | .57 | .067 |
| c3 | 0 | 4958 | 202 | 140 | 1841 | 3341 | 89 | 2.41 | 301 | 261 | 166 | 1 | .07 | .031 |
| Useful? | | Y | N | Y | N | N | N | N | N | N | N | N | Y | Y |

## 3.1  Simple features

The simple features  extracted are given in columns  1 to 5 of Table  1 (see
key  to  tables for  details). The  final  row  of  Tables 1  to 3  labelled
"Useful?"   contains either a Y (YES) or N (NO) giving a quick indication of
whether or not that feature  discriminates between all target views  and all
clutter.   In this case peak height alone can be used to discriminate between
target and clutter but in  general this is not true.   Thus we  attempted to
determine which  additional simple  features, or  combinations  thereof, can
provide additional discriminatory information.

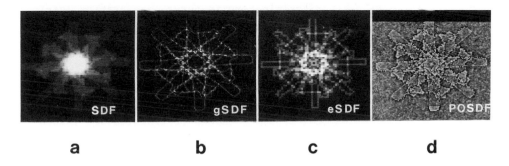

**a**          **b**          **c**          **d**

FIGURE 2:   Various types of rotation SDFs discussed in text

Simple features discriminate  quite well  between training  set  targets and
clutter objects  c2 and c3 (which have  reasonably different shapes  to the
target).   For example  absolute thresholds  can be set.   Alternatively the
mean values of features for target (both training set and non  training set)
can be  computed and  any objects  which  lie more  than a  given  number of
standard  deviations  from  the  mean  rejected.   The means  and  standard
deviations of  the various fetaures  are given  in Table 1.   However simple
features do not reject clutter object  c1 (which has the most  similar shape
to the target) and they also reject  the non training set target  (i.e. 22.5
degree rotation).   In practice one can never include all possible rotations,
scales,  views, etc,  of the  target(s) in  the  SDF training  set,  but the
combination of SDF design and correlation feature extraction  must (ideally)
be capable of recognising all views of a given target and so the  problem of
recognition of non training set targets must be overcome.

Two possible solutions to  this problem  were investigated (i)  include more
distortions  in the  training set  until  the desired  recognition of  non
training set images is achieved and (ii) extract additional,  more "complex"
features from the correlation image,  in the hope that rejection  of similar

shaped objects will improve.  The latter strategy is discussed first.


## 3.2  Complex features

The complex features  extracted  from the  correlation image  are  listed in columns 6 to  13 of  Table 1 (see  key for  details). The  first  6 complex features  did not give  any better  discrimination than the  simple ones i.e they also rejected c2 and c3 but did not discriminate between c1 and the non training set target (22.5 degree rotation).  However the final two features, elongation and concavity, did discriminate between these latter two objects. Higher order invariant  moments should  provide more discrimination  but are considered  too time consuming  for real  time digital computation.  Noting from  Table 1  that  the most  discriminatory features  are  ratios, various ratios of features in Table 1 were computed, to see if  discrimination could be improved.  Some of  these are shown in Table  2 which  shows that simple ratios of  features  are  often  better  discrimination  than  the  features themselves.


## 3.3  Effect on discrimination of increasing number of training set images

Now  the  alternative  strategy  for  improving  SDF  discrimination -i.e. increasing  the number  of views of  the target(s)  in the training  set -is considered.  The above  experiment was repeated but using  an SDF made from 16  rotations of the target i.e.  every 22.5 degrees (c.f.  only  8 rotations were used above).  A non training set target with a  rotation of 10 degrees was used.  The results for simple features are given in Table 3 below which should  be compared with Table 1.  c1 is the only clutter object for  which results are given, since it proved the most difficult to reject using  the 8 rotation SDF.  Table 3  shows  that increasing  the number  of  SDF training images to 16 and extracting only simple features, successfully discriminates between the non training set target and the clutter object c1. As for  the 8 rotation SDF, even better discrimination was obtained using ratios of simple features  (not shown). Also as  most  of the  interior of  a  binary  image contains no shape information,  edge moments (not shown) were  computed from the correlation images of the lower half of Figure 1 but these did  not give improved discrimination.


## 4. EDGE ENHANCING

It is well  known that edge  enhancing test  images or  filters  can improve discrimination, albeit often at the expense of distortion invariance.  Thus the effects of  edge  enhancing  the  test  images  and/or  the  SDF  were investigated.

TABLE 2

| im rot | | hA/V | $I_{min}/I_{max}$ | $m_2/m_1$ | S/E |
|---|---|---|---|---|---|
| | | | targets | | |
| t | 0 | 32.4 | .217 | .088 | .332 |
| t | 90 | 32.4 | .205 | .095 | .329 |
| t | 45 | 32.3 | .210 | .092 | .331 |
| t | 180 | 31.9 | .235 | .080 | .335 |
| n | 22.5 | 29.3 | .256 | .071 | .344 |
| mean | | 31.7 | .225 | .089 | .334 |
| std | | 1.2 | .019 | .006 | .005 |
| | | | clutter | | |
| c1 | 0 | 29.1 | .291 | .065 | .394 |
| c2 | 0 | 28.8 | .276 | .069 | .376 |
| c3 | 0 | 27.3 | .866 | .001 | 2.32 |
| Useful? | | N | Y | Y | Y |

TABLE 3

| im rot | | h | P8 | A | V |
|---|---|---|---|---|---|
| | | | targets | | |
| t | 0 | 10897 | 190 | 2604 | 474396 |
| t | 22.5 | 10915 | 189 | 2594 | 472969 |
| n | 10 | 10843 | 181 | 2623 | 479864 |
| mean | | 10885 | 187 | 2607 | 475743 |
| std | | 31 | 4 | 12 | 2972 |
| | | | clutter | | |
| c1 | 0 | 9978 | 194 | 2519 | 447773 |
| Useful? | | Y | Y | Y | Y |

TABLE 4

| column | | 1 | 2 | 3 | 4 | 5 | 6 |
|---|---|---|---|---|---|---|---|
| SDF test image | | SDF bin | gSDF bin | gSDF edge | SDF edge | eSDF edge | eSDF bin |
| im rot | | | | target peaks | | | |
| t | 0 | 5744 | 887 | 331 | 518 | 287 | 473 |
| t | 90 | 5760 | 879 | 321 | 521 | 290 | 475 |
| n | 22.5 | 5374 | 871 | 222 | 537 | 210 | 450 |
| mean | - | 5626 | 879 | 291 | 525 | 262 | 466 |
| std | - | 178 | 7 | 49 | 8 | 37 | 11 |
| | | | | clutter peaks | | | |
| c1 | 0 | 5105 | 831 | 187 | 354 | 151 | 401 |
| CTR | | .91 | .95 | .64 | .67 | .58 | .86 |

TABLE 5

| column | 1 | 2 | 3 | 4 | 5 |
|---|---|---|---|---|---|
| N | 8 | 16 | 36 | 8 | 8 |
| SDf test | POSDF bin | POSDF bin | POSDF bin | ePOSDF edg | ePOSDF bin |
| im/rot | | | peak height | | |
| | | | targets | | |
| 0 | 10661 | 9437 | 3379 | 4462 | 3422 |
| 90 | 9896 | - | - | 4477 | 3183 |
| 22.5 | 3457 | 9325 | - | 1769 | 2213 |
| 10 | - | 4584 | 3147 | - | - |
| 5 | - | - | 2857 | - | - |
| mean | 8005 | 7782 | 3128 | 3569 | 2939 |
| std | 3231 | 2262 | 214 | 1273 | 523 |
| | | | clutter | | |
| c1 | 3905 | 3807 | 2109 | 1221 | 2099 |
| CNR | 1.13 | .83 | .74 | .69 | .95 |

## 4.1  Edge enhancing the SDF and/or test images

The 8  rotation SDF  of Figure  2a  was edge  enhanced by  application  of a simple gradient operator and the resulting filter, a gradient SDF (gSDF), is shown  in Figure 2b.  This filter was then correlated with the binary images of the target and clutter object cl.  The peak heights obtained are shown in column 2 of Table 4 (for comparison  the corresponding peaks of Table  l are given in column 1).  Columns l and 2 cannot be compared  directly since the correlation peak decreases  anyway when edge enhanced filters  and/or images are correlated.  However the  final row of Table 4  shows the ratio of peak height produced by clutter object cl to the mean of the peak produced by the targets, and this shows whether there has been any significant improvment in discrimination. We call  this the Clutter-to-Target Ratio (CTR).  Comparing columns  l and  2 shows  that  edge enhancing  the SDF  filter  without edge enhancing  the test images  did not  improve discrimination,  since  the CTR actually  increases from  .91 to .95.  Column 3  gives the peak correlation between gSDF and "edge enhanced" test images (edge images obtained  from the binary  images). The CTR  has decreased  to .64, representing  a significant improvement in  discrimination.  Column 4  gives the  results obtained when edge  test images were correlated with  the SDF made from binary  images and clearly  that  gives  almost  as  good  an  improvement  in  discrimination (CTR = 0.67). The final two columns of Table 4 are discussed in  Section 4.2 below.

Edge enhancing the SDF need only be done once, offline.  On the other hand, edge enhancing the test scene must be done in real time and may be too time-consuming in a digital system,  although in  an optical correlator  the test scene can be edge  enhanced essentially instantaneously by inserting  a high pass spatial frequency filter in the test scene beam.


## 4.2  SDF made from edge images

An "edge  SDF" (eSDF) was made from  8 rotations (i.e. every 45  degrees) of edge  images of the target and  is shown in Figure 2c.  Column 5 of Table 4 gives the  peak height of  correlations between  eSDF and edge  test images. This has clearly improved the discrimination, giving a CTR of 0.58.  Column 6 shows the results of correlating the eSDF with the binary test images. The CTR of .86 is lower than that of column 1 (.91) and thus some improvement in discrimination was  obtained.  There  are  many other  techniques  for  edge enhancing an image or filter, such as frequency domain high  pass filtering, which were not investigated and the edge enhancing techniques used above may not be optimal.

# 5. PHASE ONLY SDF

Oppenheim and Lim (1981) demonstrated that a significant part of the information content of an image is contained in its Fourier phase component, in that when the original amplitude spectrum is discarded and reset to a constant, the reconstructed image looks like a noisy, edge enhanced version of the original. They attribute this to the fact that (i) phase contains the positional information and (ii) discarding amplitude tends to boost high spatial frequencies. Horner and Gianino (1984) subsequently discovered that using a phase only MSF or SDF gives a dramatic increase in height and sharpness of the correlation peak, albeit at the expense of signal-to-noise.

Digital phase only SDFs were made as follows: the Fourier Transform of the ordinary SFD was taken giving an amplitude and phase component. The phase only SDF (POSDF) is the inverse Fourier transform of this phase function and a constant (unity) amplitude spectrum. Figure 2d shows the POSDF obtained from the SDF of Figure 2a.

Peak heights of the correlation between various of these POSDFs and targets and clutter are given in Table 5. Columns 1 and 2 give results for POSDFs made from 8 and 16 component rotations SDFs. In both cases the peak height of the correlation with the clutter object cl falls dramatically to under half that of the training set images. However the peak of the non training set target also drops by a similar amount. Column 3 of Table 7 shows the effect of increasing the number of training set images in the POSDF to 36 i.e. every 10 degrees. The decrease in clutter correlation peak is not quite so dramatic but the correlation peak for the non training set target (5 degree rotation) is now well above that of the clutter. Thus it is possible to use POSDFs to improve the discrimination against clutter without rejecting non training set targets if the number of training set images is increased. Column 4 shows the results for an ePOSDF, the phase only version of the eSDF made from 8 rotations of edge images. Comparing Column 4 with column 1 shows the effect of using edge images rather than binary images - i.e. although the non training set target peak is much less than that of the training set targets, it does not fall below that of the clutter and it is possible to set a threshold which would reject the clutter but not the non training set target. Column 5 is similar to column 4 except that the test images were binary rather than edge images. It is also possible to set a suitable threshold in this case. The discrimination of the ePOSDF could be further improved by increasing the number of training set images.

The POSDF results are neatly summarized by the value of the ratio of clutter to non training set peak (CNR) given in the final row of Table 5.

## 6. CONCLUSIONS

In theory SDFs provide 3-D view invariant multiclass recognition although in practice it is often difficult to reject clutter whilst accepting non training set targets. Three techniques were investigated for improving SDF discrimination in the recognition of an industrial component.

The first method - correlation feature extraction - was effective when only a few simple and rapidly computed features, such as area, perimeter and volume, were extracted from the correlation image. Sufficient numbers of training set images must be used to synthesise the SDF otherwise non training set targets are rejected. Extracting too many or too complicated features from the correlation image seems pointless, since if this is necessary, direct feature extraction from the test image itself should be more efficient. Taking ratios of features often improves discrimination.

The second method was to edge enhance the SDF and/or test images. Edge enhancing the test images greatly improved discrimination whereas edge enhancing the SDF alone had little effect. The best results were obtained when edge images were correlated with an SDF made from edge only images.

Phase only SDFs gave sharper and higher correlation peaks for training set targets. Although correlation peaks of clutter fell dramatically by up to a half that of training set targets, so did peaks for non training set targets and thus recognition was not necessarily improved. However when the number of training set images was increased a significant improvement in discrimination occurred. ePOSDFs gave even better discrimination when correlated with edge images, but if binary test images are be used this is not necessarily so. Future work will involve applying these techniques to scale and 3-D view invariant and multiclass recognition.

### ACKNOWLEDGEMENT

Part of this work was funded under ESPRIT project P1035.

### REFERENCES

Hester C.F. and Casasent D.     Applied Optics, Vol 19, p 1758 (1980)
Caulfield H.J.                  Applied Optics, Vol 21, p 4391 (1982)
Oppenheim A.V. and Lim J.S.     Proc. IEEE Vol 69, No 5, pp 529-541 (1981)
Horner J.L. and Gianino P.D.    Applied Optics, Vol 23, p 812 (1984)
Horner J.L. and Gianino P.D.    SPIE 519 Conference on Analogue Optical Processing and Computing pp 70-77 (1984)
Cooper I.R., Nicholson M.G. and Petts C.R.    IEE Proceedings, Vol 133, Part J, No. 1, pp 70-76 (1986).

# OBSERVER: A PROBABILISTIC LEARNING SYSTEM FOR ORDERED EVENTS

*Keith C. C. Chan, *Andrew K. C. Wong and **David K.Y. Chiu

| | |
|---|---|
| *PAMI Laboratory | **Department of Computing and |
| Department of Systems Design Engineering | Information Science |
| University of Waterloo | University of Guelph |
| Ontario, Canada, N2L 3G1 | Ontario, Canada, N1G 2W1 |

## ABSTRACT

Given a sequence of observed events which are ordered with respect to time or positions and are described by the coexistence of several discrete-valued attributes that are assumed to be generated by a random process, the *inductive prediction problem* is to find the probabilistic patterns that characterize the random process, thereby, allowing future events to be predicted. This paper presents a probabilistic inference technique for solving such a problem. Based on it, a learning program called the OBSERVER has been implemented. The OBSERVER can learn, inductively and without supervision, even if some observed events could be erroneous, occasionally missing, or subject to certain degrees of uncertainty. It is able to reveal the patterns and regularities inherent in a sequence of observed events and can not only specify, in a clearly defined way, the happenings in the past but also gain insight for prediction. The proposed technique can be applied to solve different problems in artificial intelligence (AI) and pattern recognition (PR) where decisions concerning the future have to be made.

## 1. Introduction

Most of the pattern recognition (PR) tasks are concerned with the categorization of unordered events (e.g. symbols, objects, situations, etc.) into different classes. However, if events are ordered, patterns can be acquired by inductive learning from a *sequence of events* such that future events can be predicted [11]. The learning process can be regarded as *inductive prediction*.

We have identified three different types of IP problems: the *deterministic* (DIP), the *non-deterministic* (NIP) and the *probabilistic* (PIP) inductive prediction problem. For example, predicting the next letter in a sequence such as *lmnmnonopopq* ... is deterministic since the succeeding letter is completely determined by the preceding ones. Predicting the next object in the sequence shown in Fig. 1 [2] is non-deterministic since only some of its attributes (e.g. the number of nodes) can be determined with certainty, whereas its shape cannot be determined. Predicting the weather conditions based on past observations is probabilistic due to the inherent randomness of the process.

The NIP problem is more difficult to solve than the DIP problem since more plausible future attribute values must be considered during the learning process. By the same reasoning, the PIP problem is more difficult to solve than the NIP problem. In this paper, a statistical technique is proposed to handle the PIP problem. It is non-parametric and can be employed to deal with discrete-valued data.

## 2. Related Research

Methods that deal with different types of IP problems can be found in diverse areas such as statistics and econometrics, PR and control. For example, in time series analysis, the pattern in a set of ordered events is assumed to be made up of different components such as trend, seasonal, cyclical and erratic fluctuations. By decomposing the pattern into its component parts, forecasting methods like moving-average, exponential smoothing or Box-Jenkins methods can be employed depending on the types of components identified. This has the disadvantage of requiring subjective judgment in model identification. Also, it is necessary to assume that the future value of an attribute is independent of the

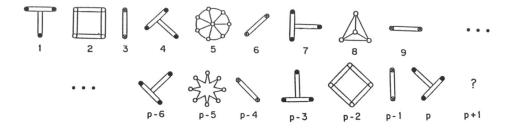

**Fig. 1.** A Sequence of Figures [2]

Figures in the sequence can be grouped together into subsequences of triplets so that the nodes of the figures in each subsequence have textures in the order: solid black, blank, cross; and the corresponding shapes are always: T-junction, any shape, bar. The orientation of the T-junction changes by -45 degrees each time with respect to its last appearance whereas that of the bar changes by +45 degrees in the similar manner. The number of nodes of the middle figure in each triplet alternates between 4 and 8.

past of the others. To analyze multivariate time series, econometric techniques (causal or regression analysis) can be used. However, assumptions about white noises may be an oversimplification of the true states of affairs. Moreover, some of these techniques, like the multivariate ARIMA, are difficult to be understood and are unpopular. Both the time series and the causal or regression techniques are very inefficient if the independent variables take on discrete values. The need for dummy variables in the analysis increases, to a great extent, the complexity of the task. Furthermore, these techniques are not appropriate if the dependent variable also assumes discrete values. In such case, the time series may be regarded as a Markov Chain. Its analysis, however, also suffers from similar limitations as univariate analysis.

In syntactic PR, grammatical inference is concerned with the determination of a formal grammar (rules) that can generate given strings of symbols under the assumption that each symbol is described by one attribute. To handle random events, stochastic grammars has to be constructed, a large sample of different sequences are necessary for analysis. This implies that more than one observation are required at a particular time.

Unlike works in statistics and econometrics, PR and control, works in psychology and AI emphasize less on parameter learning and the achievement of stable reliable performance. They are not based on sophisticated mathematical theory but are more concerned with cognitive modeling. For example, efforts have been made to explain how concepts are acquired from sequences of letters and numbers [11,7,14,4,10,6,12,3,9]. However, their extension to solve IP problems involving observations described by more than one attribute (other than a letter or a number) is not obvious. Furthermore, they cannot tolerate any 'noise' in a sequence.

Recent AI approaches are able to deal with sequences of observations described by two or more attributes. These approaches are either data-driven (e.g. THOTH [13]) or model-driven (e.g. SPARC [2, 8]). THOTH is capable of solving the DIP problem whereas SPARC is able to deal with the more general NIP problem. The solution strategies employed by them are rather slow and inefficient. For example, in THOTH, an exhaustive search for maximal common generalizations is conducted to find the underlying patterns of a sequence of observations. In case of SPARC, the program conducts a nearly exhaustive depth-first search of the possible model space which, without some good heuristics to reduce its size, may contain as many as $10^{137}$ possible rules in an application [2]. In the presence of uncertainty, more plausible generalizations or rule models have to be considered. Therefore, to be more practical in domains where certainty is unattainable, an efficient solution to the PIP problem is needed.

In all, the methods mentioned above are either incapable of handling the PIP problem or are not appropriate for analyzing a sequence of observations described by more than one attribute whose values are represented symbolically or numerically by categorical labels. This paper presents an approach to handle this type of PIP problem efficiently. With the patterns represented as rules, the method can be used for different applications in in AI and PR.

## 3. A Learning Method for Ordered Events

In this section, we present a learning method is proposed to solve the PIP problem. It is divided into four phases: 1) event transformation -- derivation of additional attributes from originally observed ones; 2) detection of temporal relations -- examination of the sequence of transformed events to see if there exists any relation among values of the same or different attributes of different events observed at different time (the relations are positional/spatial if the observations are ordered with respect to their positions); 3) generation of rules from detected relations -- generation of a set of rules, based on the detected temporal relations, to characterize the sequence of observations; 4) prediction -- deduction from the induced rules to predict future events. To improve the efficiency of the method in a 'noisy' environment where some observations could be erroneous, occasionally missing, or subject to certain degrees of uncertainty, a probabilistic inference technique [1, 16, 17] is used.

### 3.1. Definitions and Notations

A random phenomenon is usually characterized by a sequence of joint events (observations) observed at different time: $\underline{X}_1, \underline{X}_2, \ldots, \underline{X}_{t-1}, \underline{X}_t, \cdots$. A joint event (an observation) observed at time $t$ can be considered as the outcomes (values) of $n$ component events (attributes): $\underline{X}_t = (X_{t1}, X_{t2}, \cdots, X_{tn})$. Each of the random variables, $X_{tj}$, may take on a finite set of possible values (outcomes): $O(X_{tj}) = \{x_{j_k} \mid k = 1, \ldots, M_j\}$. An actual observed sequence can be denoted as: $\underline{x}_1, \underline{x}_2, \ldots, \underline{x}_{t-1}, \underline{x}_t, \cdots$, where $\underline{x}_t = (x_{t1}, x_{t2}, \ldots, x_{tn})$ is a realization of $\underline{X}_t$.

With the above notations, the random events observed prior to $\underline{X}_t$ can be represented as $\underline{X}_{(t-\tau)} = (X_{(t-\tau)1}, X_{(t-\tau)2}, \cdots, X_{(t-\tau)n})$ where $\tau$ is the time lag or the number of time units by which $\underline{X}_{(t-\tau)}$ is observed before $\underline{X}_t$.

### 3.2. Phase 1: Transformation of Events

If the initially observed events are inadequate in describing the underlying patterns in an event sequence, relevant information can be included by adding *derived* attributes for the learning process. For instance, new attributes may be derived from the other attributes using predefined transformation of the form:

$$f : (X_{ti}, X_{(t-\tau)j}) \rightarrow X_{(t+h)p}, \quad p > n \tag{1}$$

where $f$ is a function that takes the values of two attributes observed at $\tau$ units apart and maps them into a third one, $X_{(t+h)p}$ at $h$ time unit from $t$ ($i$, $j$ and $p$ are attribute indices respectively). An example of such a function is:

$$X_{(t+h)p} = X_{ti} - X_{(t-\tau)j}. \tag{2}$$

A new attribute representing the result of such a transformation is called a derived attribute of *second-order*. Derived attributes involving functions of more attributes can also be considered. Furthermore, besides arithmetic functions, functions of other kinds such as logical operators can be defined.

### 3.3. Phase 2: Detection of Temporal Relations

To determine which observed or derived attribute values may provide information for prediction, we have to identify the statistically *relevant*, or *irrelevant* ones. The irrelevant values reflect chance perturbations of the process and are screened out to improve the accuracy of the prediction.

To determine whether or not a value of the $j$ th attribute of an observation is relevant for predicting those of the $i$ th one, it is necessary to determine if a statistically significant temporal relation exists between $x_{(t-\tau)j}$ and the observed outcomes of $X_{ti}$ . This can be achieved by comparing the observed and the expected frequency of the joint outcomes $(x_{(t-\tau)j}, x_{ti})$ for all $x_{ti} \in O(X_{ti})$. The hypothesis that 'there exists a temporal relation between $x_{(t-\tau)j}$ and $X_{ti}$' can be tested using the following test statistic:

$$
D = \sum_{x_{ti} \in O(X_{ti})} \frac{(obs\ (x_{(t-\tau)j}, x_{ti}) - exp\ (x_{(t-\tau)j}, x_{ti}))^2}{exp\ (x_{(t-\tau)j}, x_{ti})} \tag{4}
$$

where $obs\ (x_{(t-\tau)j}, x_{ti})$ and $exp\ (x_{(t-\tau)j}, x_{ti})$ are frequencies of the observed and expected joint outcome $(x_{(t-\tau)j}, x_{ti})$ respectively. Since $D$ approximates the chi-square distribution $\chi^2_{(M_i -1)}$ [1, 16, 17], we can assert that a statistically significant relationship exists between $x_{(t-\tau)j}$ and outcomes of $X_{ti}$ by accepting the hypothesis if $D$ exceeds the chi-square value at a certain significance level.

In a similar manner, a subset of observed values of the $j$ th attribute that are temporally related to a subset of those of the $i$ th attribute at a time difference $\tau$ can be identified and paired together. A set of such outcome pairs, denoted by $E_{ji}^{(\tau)}$, is called a *temporally related event set* of the $j$ th attribute with respect to the $i$ th attribute at time lag $\tau$. It yields important information about the future events. For example, if $(x_{(t-\tau)j}, x_{ti})$ is in $E_{ji}^{(\tau)}$, it implies that $x_{(t-\tau)j}$ is relevant for predicting the values of $X_{ti}$ at $\tau$ time units later. Conversely, outcomes which are not in $E_{ji}^{(\tau)}$ are statistically irrelevant and are discarded during the learning process.

Once the temporally related event set is found, we can determine whether it provides significant information for the later prediction process. To do this, we use an information measure called *interdependence redundancy* [15] which is defined as:

$$
R(E_{ji}^{(\tau)}) = \frac{I(E_{ji}^{(\tau)})}{H(E_{ji}^{(\tau)})} \tag{5}
$$

where $I(E_{ji}^{(\tau)})$ is the expected mutual information between pairs of related outcomes of the $i$ th and the $j$ th attributes with a time lag $\tau$ and $H(E_{ji}^{(\tau)})$ is the respective Shannon's entropy.

The interdependence redundancy measure has the following desirable properties: a) its value is bounded between zero and one inclusively; b) a value of zero indicates that the pairs of outcomes in $E_{ji}^{(\tau)}$ are completely independent of each other whereas a value of one means that they are totally dependent on one another; c) it provides a measure of the degree of dependence or association between the pairs of outcomes; and d) it is easy to show that the following test statistics:

$$
2N \times I(E_{ji}^{(\tau)}) = 2N \times R(E_{ji}^{(\tau)})H(E_{ji}^{(\tau)}) \tag{6}
$$

where $N$ is the total number of observations in the sequence is the familiar log likelihood ratio statistic for testing whether the pairs of outcomes in $E_{ji}^{(\tau)}$ are statistically dependent on each other [15]. If the result of the test is positive, $E_{ji}^{(\tau)}$ would then provide significant information for prediction. The patterns in the sequence are revealed after all statistically significant temporal relations are detected.

### 3.4. Phase 3: Generation of Rules from Detected Temporal Relations

The detected relations can be represented by a graph which we call *temporal-relation graph*. Fig. 2 illustrates two nodes of such a graph together with three of their incidence edges.

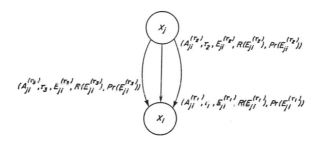

**Fig. 2.** A Component of A Temporal-Relation Graph
Subsets of outcomes of $X_i$ and $X_j$ are temporally related to each other at three different
time lags $\tau_1$, $\tau_2$ and $\tau_3$.

The nodes represent the attributes $X_i$ and $X_j$. Statistically significant temporal relations between them are represented by directed arcs $A_{ji}^{(\tau_k)}$, $k = 1,2,3$. $A_{ji}^{(\tau_k)}$ takes on the value '1' (true) if a significant temporal relation exists between a subset of outcomes of $X_j$ and that of $X_i$ at a certain time lag $\tau_k$ otherwise it takes on the value '0' (false).

If $A_{ji}^{(\tau_k)}$ has value '1', additional values associated with the arc are: 1) the time lag $\tau_k$; 2) the set of temporally related outcomes $E_{ji}^{(\tau_k)}$; 3) the interdependence redundancy measure $R(E_{ji}^{(\tau_k)})$ (which provides a quantitative estimation of the strength of the relation between the subset of temporally related outcomes) and 4) the probability distribution $Pr(E_{ji}^{(\tau_k)})$ associated with the outcomes in $E_{ji}^{(\tau_k)}$. Once the temporal-relation graph is constructed based on the detected relations, a set of rules can be derived. Let us consider the example given in Fig. 2. Suppose that $x_i \in O(X_i)$, $x_j \in O(X_j)$ and $(x_i, x_j) \in E_{ji}^{(\tau_2)}$, and let $Pr(x_i \mid x_j$ at $\tau_2) = p$. The following rule can then be generated:

If $X_j$ takes on the value $x_j$ then that $X_i$ has the value $x_i$ at a time lag $\tau_2$ is with probability $p$.

The above rule indicates that a value $x_j$ of the $j$th attribute is temporally related to $x_i$ of the $i$th attribute. In other words, $x_j$ is relevant for predicting the value of the $i$th attribute which will occur $\tau_2$ units later in time.

### 3.5. Phase 4: Prediction

To test if $\hat{x}_{(t+h)i}$ is the most plausible value for the $i$th attribute $h$ time units later from $t$, we have to combine the evidence provided by the set of rules that contain information about the relevant values for predicting the future value for the $i$th attribute. The strength of the supporting evidence for the hypothesized value depends on how strong the relevant values are related to it and how many of such there are. The hypothesized values supported by the strongest evidence can be considered as the most plausible prediction for the $i$th attribute. To measure the strength of the evidence, a quantitative measure called the Prediction Surprisal (*PS*) (called the Normalized Surprisal in [1, 16, 17]) is proposed. The greater the value of *PS*, the less its supporting evidence.

Suppose that we have found a set of induced rules that predict relevant values for the $i$th attribute. Let us denote this set of values by $C$ and let $|C| = M$. To measure how strong the available evidence is for the hypothesized value, we use the *PS* of $\hat{x}_{(t+h)i}$ given $C$ defined as:

$$PS(\hat{X}_{(t+h)i} = \hat{x}_{(t+h)i} \mid C) = \frac{I(x_{(t+h)i} \mid C)}{M \sum\limits_{x_{ij} \in C} R(E_{ji}^{(h)})} \tag{7}$$

where $I(x_{(t+h)i} | C)$ is the weighted conditional information defined on $C$ [1, 16, 17] and $R(E_{ji}^{(h)})$ is the interdependence redundancy between subsets of outcomes of $X_{tj}$ and $X_{(t+h)i}$ as given in (5).

The most plausible value for the $i$ th attribute is hence the value with the smallest $PS$. If two or more values of the same attribute have the same $PS$ value which is also the smallest, then more than one plausible value for that attribute will be predicted. If the supporting evidence for any hypothesized value is inadequate, prediction will be refrained instead of making an inaccurate one. If there is no relevant value for predicting a particular value of an attribute, then either the attribute is completely non-deterministic or we have inadequate observations.

## 4. Experimental Results

The inductive learning method has been implemented in a computer program called OBSERVER. It has been tested with various sequences of observations and some experimental results are presented here.

### 4.1. Experiment 1: A Sequence of Playing Cards

Suppose the OBSERVER is given a layout (the mainline) of a game of Eleusis (Fig. 3) [5]. It is required to discover the secret rule that generates this sequence of cards and to predict the next card. For example, a secret rule could be 'if the rank of the card is higher than or equal to that of the previous one, its suit will also be one suit higher (modulo 4); otherwise, if the rank of the card is lower than or equal to that of the previous one, then its suit will be three suit higher (modulo 4)'.

The OBSERVER is given, as input, the rank and suit of each card in the sequence. It begins the learning process by deriving additional attributes like 'color', 'facedness', 'primeness' and 'parity'. Functions, like the difference in suit (modulo 4) between two adjacent cards or how the ranks of the cards should be compared, are also defined [2].

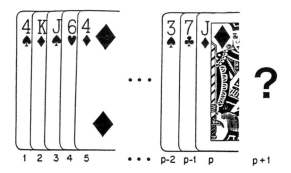

**Fig. 3.** A Sequence of Cards in a Game of Eleusis
The rank and suit of the card at position $p + 1$ are to be predicted.

To determine which of these observed and derived attributes may be relevant for predicting future cards, the relations among the attribute values of the cards in the sequence are detected and a set of rules formulated based on them.

To test if the next card is three higher than the present one in suit, a set of rules that provides us with such information is found. The set include the following rules (Note that the last card in the sequence is a Jack of Diamond):

If the rank of a card is Jack then
   that the suit of the next card is 3 higher is
   with a probability of 0.93.

If the rank of a card is greater than the next one then
   that the suit of the next card is 3 higher is
   with a probability of 1.00.

The *PS* value for 'the suit of the next card is three higher than the present one' is determined to be 0.0153 and that for 'the suit of the next card is one higher' is 0.961. Therefore, the OBSERVER will play a card that has a lower rank than Jack and the suit of the card will be 'club' since the last suit of the last card is a 'diamond'. The exact rank of the card is not predicted due to inadequate evidence.

It is interesting to discover that, besides the secret rules that the *Dealer* of the game has in mind, some other rules are also generated. For example:

If the rank of a card is Queen then
   that the suit of the next card is 3 higher is
   with a probability of 0.93.

If the rank of a card is King then
   that the suit of the next card is 3 higher is
   with a probability of 1.00.

It should be noted that these rules are unexpectedly generated because according to our secret rule, the suit of the next card is independent of the exact rank of a card in the sequence. However, from the above rules, we can see that this is not always the case. If the last card is high in rank (e.g., Jack, Queen or King), then it is more likely for the next card in the sequence to have a lower rank and thus the probability for its suit to be three higher than the previous card is much greater than for it to be one higher. In fact, if a card in the sequence is, say, a 'king of spade', then the next correct card will be either the same or smaller in rank and its suit will be the 'heart'. Similarly, we can predict, with complete certainty, that if a card in the sequence is an 'ace', then the suit of the next card will be one higher than the suit of the present one.

The results of this experiment shows that OBSERVER is able to discover rules which are not immediately obvious to a human. It also performs better than SPARC which is unable to find the secret rule for this game [2].

### 4.2. Experiment 2: A Sequence of Geometric Figures

Suppose that OBSERVER is given a sequence of figures [2] (Fig. 1), the problem is to predict the next one. The observed attributes (properties) of each figure. include the shape, the number of nodes, the node texture and the figure orientation [2]. Here, only the four observed attributes are taken into consideration in the learning process. No derived attributes are considered.

After the induction of rules based on the detected relations among the figures, predictions can be made. By combining the evidence provided through these rules, the *PS* value for the hypothesized outcome of 8 nodes for the next figure of the sequence in Fig. 1 is determined to be 0.183 by the OBSERVER. In a similar way, the *PS* value for the hypotheses that the number of nodes of the graph to be predicted are 2, 3, and 4 are determined to be 1.01, 0.954, and 0.244 respectively. Therefore, the next figure in the sequence is predicted to have 8 nodes. Similarly, the values of the other attributes can also be determine and the next figure is predicted to have 8 blank nodes and that its orientation is irrelevant (not-applicable). It's shape, however, is not predicted since none of the induced rules provide relevant information about it. These predictions are consistent with what is expected (Fig. 1).

It is interesting to note that, based on the most recently observed figure (i.e. a T-junction at +135 degrees), a human observer may be unable to tell whether the next figure has 4 or 8 nodes. One may not know the number of nodes for the figure without looking back three positions (i.e, the middle figure of the subsequence of the last period). The OBSERVER, however, is able to predict correctly that the next figure has eight nodes based on the last figure alone. In fact, it is learned that if the last figure is a T-junction at +135 degrees the next one will definitely have eight nodes. Therefore, with OBSERVER, the hidden pattern in the sequence of figures which even a human observer is not immediately aware of, can be automatically detected. The experiment also shows OBSERVER's ability to deal with sequences with nested periodic structures, a problem which SPARC is unable to solve [2].

### 4.3. Experiment 3: A Sequence of Movements

A hypothetical scenario is devised to demonstrate the capability of the OBSERVER to discover rules that govern the interdependence of movements of a set of objects. Suppose four snails are moving in a 5×5 matrix (Fig. 4) and the OBSERVER is taking a snapshot of the matrix at fixed time intervals.

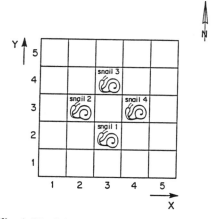

Fig. 4. The Initial Positions of The Four Snails

Suppose also that one of these snails is the leader and it makes one move every time interval and that the movements of the others should depend on it. However, the snails are not always obedient to their leader and may take a wrong move intentionally or unintentionally. If the past positions of all four snails (Fig. 5) are observed, the OBSERVER's task is to discover which of them is the leader and how the other snails are supposed to obey it thereby predicting their most probable positions.

The original set of attributes which is given to the OBSERVER contains four attributes representing the positions of the four snails. Since it may be more interesting to consider the movements of the snails than their positions, new attributes that describe their movements are defined. This attributes take on the values 'East', 'South', 'West', or 'North' (Fig. 4).

After detecting this temporal relations among the movements of different snails, rules are generated. From these rules, the next position of, say, snail 3 is predicted to be north of its previous position since there is strong evidence for this particular move. The PS value for this move is 0.126 compared with 1.99, 0.8 and 1.99 for the snail to move East, South and West respectively. In a similar manner, the moves for snails 2 and 4 can be determined. It is found that the movement of snail 1 is independent of those of any other snail (in fact, it moves randomly and its next position is unpredictable) and that the movement of all the other snails are almost always dependent on its movements most, but not all, of the time. Hence, the OBSERVER concludes that snail 1 is the leader among them.

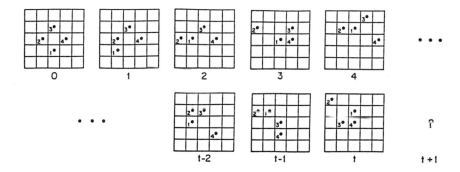

**Fig. 5** A Sequence of Snapshots Showing The Positions of The Snails

From the experimental results, we have found that the inferences drawn by OBSERVER are in compliance with the rules the designer specified for each snail before the experiment. Snail 2 obeys snail 1 all the time by moving towards the same direction whereas snail 3 obeys snail 1 about 80% of the time and moves to the opposite direction 20% of the time. Snail 4 is the least obedient for it moves to a direction that is opposite to that of snail 1 only when snail 3 obeys snail 1, otherwise it moves either to the East or to the West. This experiment illustrates the efficacy of OBSERVER in dealing with uncertain events. Also, it gives correct prediction of snails' next movements even though the relative positions occupied by them in the next time interval have never been observed before.

## 5. Concluding Remarks

In this paper, we have defined the PIP problem and have presented and a new probabilistic inference technique to handle it. It is implemented in the OBSERVER program which is able to make predictions in the presence of uncertainty and to account for the probabilistic pattern inherent in a sequence of observations. The experimental results show that it is able to solve IP problems involving complicated patterns which systems such as SPARC fails to discover [2]. It is believed that OBSERVER is more accurate and efficient than existing systems which, to our knowledge, cannot handle the PIP problem. The strength of OBSERVER also lies in its capability to construct, without supervision, prediction rules based on conceptual relations while allowing probabilistic variation. For this reason, it can be used in different application areas in PR and AI where certainty is not attainable and a probabilistic answer based on random observation is more appropriate than an exact one.

## 6. References

1.  Chiu, D.K.Y., and Wong, A.K.C., 'Synthesizing Knowledge: A Cluster Analysis Approach Using Event-Covering', *IEEE Transactions on Systems, Man and Cybernetics*, SMC-16, 2 (1986) pp.251-259.

2.  Ditterich, T.G., and Michalski, R.S., 'Discovering Patterns in Sequences of Events', *Artificial Intelligence*, 25 (1985) pp.187-232.

3.  Ernst, G.W., and Newell, A., *GPS: A Case Study in Generality and Problem Solving*, Academic Press, New York, NY (1969).

4.  Fredkin, E., 'Techniques Using LISP for Automatically Discoveving Interesting Relations in Data', in Berkeley, E.C., and Bobrow, D.G., (eds.), Information International, Cambridge, Mass. (1964).

5.  Gardner, M., On playing the new Eleusis, the game that simulate the search for truth', *Scientific American*, 237 (1977) pp.18-25.

6. Kilburn, T., Grinsdale, R.L., and Sumner, F.H., 'Experiments in Machine Learning and Thinking', in *Proceedings of the International Conference on Information Processing*, Butterworths, London (1959) pp.303-309.

7. Kotovsky, K., and Simon, H.A., 'Empirical Tests of a Theory of Human Acquisition of Concepts for Sequential Events', *Cognitive Psychology*, 4 (1973) pp.399-424.

8. Michalski, R.S., Ko, H., and Chen, K., 'Qualitative Prediction: The SPARC/G Methodology for Inductively Describing and Predicting Discrete processes', in Dufour, P., and Lamsmeerde, A. van, (eds.), *Expert Systems*, Academic Press (1986).

9. Persson, S., 'Some Sequence Extrapolating Programs: A Study of Representation and modeling in Inquiring Systems', Rept. No. STAN-CS-66-050, Department of Computer Science, Standford University, Standford, CA (1966).

10. Pivar, M., and Finkelstein, M., 'Automation using LISP, of inductive inference on sequences', in Berkeley, E.C., and Bobrow, D., (eds.), *The programming language LISP*, Information International, Cambridge, Mass. (1964).

11. Simon, H.A., and Kotovsky, K., 'Human Acquisition of Concepts for Sequential Patterns', *Psychological Review*, 70 (1963) pp.534-546.

12. Solomonoff, R.J., 'Training Sequences for Mechanized Induction', in Yovits, M., Jacobi, G.T., and Goldstein, A.D., (eds.), *Self-Organizing System*, Spartan Books, Washington, D.C. (1962) p.425-434.

13. Vere, S.A., 'Induction of Relational Productions in the Presence of Background Information', *Proceedings of the Fifth International Joint Conference on Artificial Intelligence* (1977).

14. Williams, D.S., 'Computer Program Organization Induced from Problem Examples', in H.A. Simon, and L. Siklossy (eds.), *Representation and Meaning: Experiments with Information Processing Systems*, Prentice Hall, Englewood Cliffs, New Jersy (1972) pp. 143-205.

15. Wong, A.K.C., Liu, T.S., 'Typicality, Diversity, and Feature Pattern of an Ensemble', *IEEE Transactions on Computers*, 24, 2 (1975) pp.158-181.

16. Wong, A.K.C., and Chiu, D.K.Y., 'An Event-Covering Method for Effective Probabilistic Inference', *Pattern Recognition*, 20, 2 (1987) pp.245-255.

17. Wong, A.K.C., Chiu, D.K.Y., and Lascurain, M. de, 'Synthesizing Statistical Knowledge from Incomplete Mixed-Mode Data', *IEEE Transactions on Pattern Analysis and Machine Intelligence*, PAMI-9, 6, (1987), pp.796-805.

# PATTERN CLASSIFICATION IN DYNAMICAL ENVIRONMENTS: Tagged Feature-Class Space and Univariate Sequential Classifier

Qiuming Zhu
School of Engineering and Computer Science
Oakland University
Rochester, MI 48309-4401

## ABSTRACT

This paper presents a statistic pattern recognition and machine learning based classification system paradigm. It focuses on solving problems underlying environments where the attributes of the system exhibit strong uncertainties. Configurations of classifiers therefore have to undergo continual changes during the running process. The classifier discussed here is characterized by a tagged feature-class representation, a dimension-wise univariate discrimination scheme, a default hierarchy of classification, as well as a logic-based learning strategy. Concepts of distinguishability and univariately distinguishable classes under classification are studied. Procedures developed for forming an univariately distinguishable class-feature space by learning are described.

**Key words and Phrases:** Tagged feature-class space, Distinguishability, Univariately distinguishable, Univariate sequential classifier, Logic-based learning, Goal-directed induction

## I. INTRODUCTION

Conventional pattern recognition systems are attributes invariant. They have following attributes of a classifier determined before the process: (1) a set of classes to which samples are to be assigned, (2) a set of features by which samples are evaluated and categorized. Only values of these features are changed dependent on the situations. Outcome of a classification in such environment is always a unique assignment of a sample to one of the known classes.

In many real world problems, however, the environments of the classifiers do not possess such static behavior. Answers to questions of what classes and how many classes the problem will have, what features and how many features will be presented are uncertain and not pre-definable. Examples are found such as in searching an unexplored natural scene, diagnosing diseases, verifying an engineering design, processing speeches and natural languages, etc., where situations and events are so diverse and varying from time to time. Uncertainties of classes and features are main characteristics of such environments. Both the number of features and classes are unforeseeable. Generally, these problems request the attributes of the classifiers to be variant too, and no a priori knowledge about these variations are available. After all we have to realize the fact that everything is constantly changing in this world we are living in. Pattern classification in such dynamically changing environment has not been paid much attention, and therefore been well studied.

A pattern classification system operating in the dynamic environment must (1) not depend on the predefined attributes, and (2) be able to manipulating the changes by gaining knowledge of the environment from its own running experiences. In this paper, we investigate (1) a statistic pattern recognition technique based univariate sequential classifier that bears no constrains to the variations of classes and features, and (2) a logic based learning strategy to make the classifier adaptive to the dynamic changes of the environment.

Traditional statistic pattern recognition technique is mathematically well formulated [Fukunaga, Duda]. Usually, features to distinguish various classes are represented as a feature vector, denoted as $\underline{X}$. The multidimension space spanned by all possible occurrences of the feature vectors is called the feature space, $\Omega(\underline{x})$. Clusters of feature vectors form a partition of this feature space, which are designated as classes in terms of high intraclass and low interclass similarities from the evaluation of these feature vectors. The surfaces, also called decision boundaries, of making these partitions are represented by the discriminant function, $g_i(\underline{X})$'s. Classifier that applies Bayes decision theory minimizes the probability of misclassifications. It assigns a sample to class c which shows largest value of the discriminant function based on the *a posteriori* probability. Non-parametric technique uses a sequence of training samples, $\{s_i\}$, to derive uniformed $g_i(\underline{X})$'s for discrimination. Piecewise linear discrimination applies a number of linear functions each of them distinguishes two subsets of classes. Sequential pattern recognition method was deliberately studied by Fu [Fu] and his colleagues on both statistic and structure techniques. The method evaluates features and makes classification based on the accumulation of feature values evaluated in sequence.

Recently, Holland [Holland] presented a tagged feature classifier paradigm. The notion allows the appearance of an arbitrary number of features (conditions) to a classifier. Boolean compounds of features were studied there. The first part of work in Section II of this paper is a direct extension of Holland's notion to the domain where features possess statistic distribution properties. A dimension-wise univariate sequential discrimination scheme is described in Section III. While a logic-based goal-directed learning strategy is discussed, Section IV illustrates how the feature-class space dynamically varies with respect to the changes of the environment. Section V gives a summarization.

## II. TAGGED FEATURE-CLASS REPRESENTATION

### II.1. Class-Feature Characteristics

A class is called "established" such that it has been defined by the classification process. It is also called "old class" to distinguish from the "new class" which is just brought in by a sample but has not been verified yet.

The occurrence and availability of features of a coming sample s to be classified by the system have the cases of

1. a feature $f^i$ is presented in sample s. It is tagged as "1". We use $f_s{}^i$ to denote this feature and its value. $|f_s{}^i|$ denotes the tag, therefore, $|f_s{}^i| = 1$.

2. a feature $f^i$ is not presented in sample s. We do not have value of this feature. When it is referred by a corresponding class feature, however, it is tagged as "0", i.e, $|f_s{}^i| = 0$.

The feature vector of sample s is denoted as $f_s$.

The appearance of features for a class established in the system has the cases of

1. a feature $f^i$ is presented for classification in class c. It is tagged as "1". We use $f_c{}^i$ to denote the feature, and $p(f_c{}^i)$ its probability density function. $|f_c{}^i|$ denotes the tag, therefore, $|f_c{}^i| = 1$.

2. a feature $f^i$ is not presented in class c. We have no probability density function for it. When it is referred by other classes or samples, however, it is tagged as "0", i.e., $|f_c{}^i| = 0$.

3. a feature $f^i$ is presented in class c but is uncertain of its validity in classification. It is tagged as "#". We use $f_c{}^i$ to denote this feature and $p(f_c{}^i)$ as its probability density function. $|f_c{}^i|$ denotes the tag, i.e, $|f_c{}^i| = $#. It may be a new feature that hasn't been confirmed , or an old feature its strength is too weak to be valuable for classification.

The feature vector of class c is denoted as $f_c$.

Usually an univariate Gaussian density function is assumed for $p(f_c{}^i)$. $\mu_c{}^i$ is the mean value and $\sigma_c{}^i$ the variance.

A correspondence from $f_s{}^i$, feature $f^i$ in sample s, to $f_c{}^i$, feature $f^i$ in class c, exists when $f_s{}^i$ is tagged "1" and $f_c{}^i$ is tagged "1" or "#". A correspondence is denoted by "==". Therefore

$$f_s{}^i == f_c{}^i \quad \text{if } (|f_s{}^i| = 1) \text{ and } (|f_c{}^i| = 1 \text{ or } |f_c{}^i| = \#)$$

When $f_s{}^i == f_c{}^i$, a matching degree $d_m(f_s{}^i, f_c{}^i)$ is defined as the value of $f_s{}^i$ over the probability density function of $f_c{}^i$. Normalize the matching degree to the range of 0 to 1, we get

$$\begin{cases} \int \ d_m(f_s{}^i, f_c{}^i) = 1 & \text{when } f_s{}^i = \mu_c{}^i; \\ 0 \le d_m(f_s{}^i, f_c{}^i) < 1 & \text{otherwise} \end{cases}$$

In case of $p(f_c{}^i)$ being a Gaussian density, the matching degree is

$$d_m(f_s{}^i, f_c{}^i) = \sqrt{2\pi}\, \sigma_c{}^i\, p(f_c{}^i) = \exp[-1/2\,((\,f_s{}^i - \mu_c{}^i\,)/\sigma_c{}^i\,)^2]$$

Define an inclusion from $f_s{}^i$, feature $f^i$ in sample s, to $f_c{}^i$, feature $f^i$ in class c, such that $f_s{}^i$ and $f_c{}^i$ are correspondent and the matching degree of $f_s{}^i$ over $p(f_c{}^i)$ is greater than a pre-defined threshold. An inclusion is denoted by "<=". Therefore

$$f_s{}^i <= f_c{}^i \quad\quad \text{if } f_s{}^i == f_c{}^i \text{ and } d_m(f_s{}^i, f_c{}^i) \ge \xi_c{}^i$$

where $\xi_c{}^i$ is called inclusion threshold.

The matching degree of $f_s{}^i$ over $p(f_c{}^i)$ can be attached to the notation of inclusion when necessary. Such as

$$f_s{}^i \overset{0.6}{<=} f_c{}^i$$

denotes the inclusion of $f_s{}^i$ to $f_c{}^i$ with matching degree 0.6.

The value range of $f_c{}^i$ on which probability density $p(f_c{}^i)$ is above the threshold $\xi_c{}^i$ is called discriminant scope of feature $f_c{}^i$, denoted as $dis(f_c{}^i)$.

## II.2. Sample-class Consistencies

Above definitions are given with respect to individual feature. The relations from the feature vector of a sample to the feature vector of a class are defined as following:

A consistency from sample s to class c is defined as:

for all i with $|f_c{}^i| = 1$, $f_s{}^i <= f_c{}^i$.

A consistency requires that feature vector $f_s$ carries all features that are presented as certain classification feature in $f_c$ and the inclusion conditions are satisfied. One example is

```
c:  1  1  1  1  1  1  1  0  0  #  #  0  0  0
s:  1  1  1  1  1  1  1  1  1  1  0  0  0  0
    i  i  i  i  i  i           n
```

where row c represents the features in class c, row s represents the features in sample s. "1", "0", and "#" denote the tag of the corresponding feature. Notation "i" bellow each column indicates an inclusion of features in that column. "n" means insignificant of the inclusiveness, Blank implies inclusion is not applied to that column.

A complete-consistency is defined as:

for all i with $|f_c{}^i| = 1$ or $|f_s{}^i| = 1$, $f_s{}^i <= f_c{}^i$

A complete-consistency exhibits strong evidence that sample s should be classified as class c. One example is

```
c:  1  1  1  1  1  1  1  1  1  #  #  0  0  0  0
s:  1  1  1  1  1  1  1  1  1  1  0  0  0  0  0
    i  i  i  i  i  i  i  i  i
```

A semi-consistency is defined as

for all i with $|f_s{}^i| = 1$, if $|f_c{}^i| = 1$ then $f_s{}^i <= f_c{}^i$

A semi-consistency implies that feature vector $f_s$ does not carry all features tagged 1 in $f_c$, neither does the $f_c$ present all features tagged 1 in $f_s$. But inclusion holds if both tagged 1. A semi-consistency provides some possibility for sample s to be classified as class c. one example is

```
c:   1 1 1 1 1 1 1 # # 0 0 0 0
s:   1 1 0 1 1 0 1 0 1 1 0 0 0
     i i   i i   i   n
```

Other occasions besides the above three will involve some kinds of exclusions between features. They are called missing-consistency.

The norm of a feature vector $f_c$ is the number of features tagged "1". It is denoted as $\|f_c\|$.

The consistency rate is defined as $r_c = M / \| f_c \|$, where M is total number of feature pairs $(f_s^i, f_c^i)$ with $f_s^i <= f_c^i$. For example

```
c:   1 1 1 1 1 1 1 1 # # 0 0
s:   1 1 1 1 1 1 0 1 1 0 1 0
     i i i i i i   i
```

has consistency rate $r_c = 7/8$.

The missing-consistency rate is defined as $r_{mc} = M_c / \|f_c\|$, where $M_c$ is the total number of feature pairs $( f_s^i, f_c^i )$ such that $f_s^i$ ~<= $f_c^i$ (~<= denotes an exclusion). for example

```
c:   1 1 1 1 1 1 1 1 # # 0 0
s:   1 1 1 1 1 1 0 1 1 0 1 0
     i i i e c i   e
```

has missing-consistency rate $r_{mc} = 3/8$, where notation e stands for an exclusion of features in the column.

## II.3 Sample-class Mal-matchings (MMs)

When a sample comes to the classification system in dynamical environment, the classifier makes assignment towards the established classes in terms of the consistency measure. New class is claimed when the coming sample is not able to be assigned to any old class. The correctness of an assignment for a sample by the classifier is declared as:

1. NM --- normal-matching; which means a statistically correct decision is made. The sample is either assigned to an old class or declared as a new one.
2. MM --- mal-matching; which means a mistake happens.

The mal-matchings are further categorized into following three types:
1. MMI --- Maladapted-matching; sample s is mistakenly claimed to be a new class s but actually it belongs to an old class c;
2. MMII --- Malapropos-matching; sample s is mistakenly assigned to an old class k but it actually belongs to (1) another old class c, or (2) a new class n which has not been established yet;

3. MMIII --- Maladroit-matching; sample s is assigned to a subset $\{c_j\}$ of classes with more than one members. The actual class of sample s may belong to (1) an old class c in $\{c_j\}$, (2) an old class c outside $\{c_j\}$, (3) a new class n not established in the system yet.

The key issue for the classification system, to be described in next sections, to adapt to the uncertainties of the environment is on the detection and elimination of these mal-matchings by a goal-directed inductive learning process .

## III. UNIVARIATE DISTINGUISHABILITY AND THE CLASSIFIER

Following definitions specify the relations among the samples, classes, and features in the classification system.

Classes $\{\ c_i\ \}$ in a classification system are <u>distinguishable</u> if there are features presented in due time at which a set of decision boundaries can be determined such that a sample s is uniquely assigned to one of the classes in the class-feature space $\Omega(\underline{X})$ in terms of certain criteria. The criteria can be either the minimization of probability of error, the maximization of Fisher's linear discriminant, or the minimization of mean-square-error of misclassification.

Classes are <u>linearly distinguishable</u> if the decision boundaries formed for the distinguishable classes are all able to be expressed in linear equations, i.e, hyperplanes.

Two classes $c_i$, and $c_j$ are <u>univariately distinguishable</u> if there exists one feature $f^i$ among the features presented in both classes, $|f_{ci}{}^i| = 1$ and $|f_{cj}{}^i| = 1$, that makes these two classes distinguishable.

**Theorem 1.** One feature is necessary and sufficient to classify a sample from two classes that are univariately distinguishable.

The truth of this theorem is evident. We call the feature that makes two classes univariately distinguishable the <u>discriminant feature</u> of these two classes.

Classes $\{c_i\}$ are <u>univariately distinguishable</u> if for any pair of classes in the system there exists one feature $f^i$ presented in both classes that makes them univariately distinguishable. Geometric interpretation of univariately distinguishability is that decision boundary between any two classes is perpendicular to an axis. Therefore

**Theorem 2.** Distinguishable classes are not sufficiently to be univariately distinguishable.

Prove: There are cases where class regions are formed without any surface perpendicular to an axis, as shown in Fig. 1. Therefore univariately distinguishable is a stronger condition than classes distinguishable.

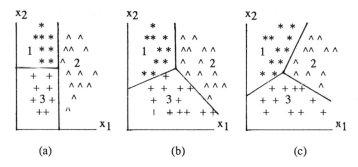

Fig.1. In a two dimensional feature space (a) class 1, 2, and 3 are univariately distinguishable; (b)class 1 and 2 are univariately distinguishable; (c) classes are not univariately distinguishable.

Classes are said that are <u>partially univariately distinguishable</u> if there exists a set of discriminant features that make a subset of the classes univariately distinguishable.

For the task of distinguishing a sample from classes, it is not necessary to explicitly find out these discriminant features for every pair of the classes. The key to solve the problem is illustrated by the univariate classification procedure stated below:

Procedure Univariate_classification;
1. Form a candidate set $C_{set} = \{c_1, c_2, ..., c_n\}$ which includes all classes established in the system.
2. For every feature $f_s^i$ of sample s and corresponding feature $f_c^i$ of class c in $C_{set}$, if $f_s^i \sim<= f_c^i$ then remove class c from $C_{set}$.
3. Assign sample to remaining classes in $C_{set}$.

Above procedure will terminate with the outcomes of
1   no classes remain in the candidate list;   In this case the sample may be  a new class.
2   only one class remain in the candidate list;   This class is univariately distinguishable from all others.
3   more than one classes remain in the candidate set;   In this case we say these classes are not univariately distinguishable.

The univariate classification procedure uniquely assigns sample s to its belonging class $c_k$ if class $c_k$ is univariately distinguishable against all other classes in $C_{set}$, and all discriminant features are presented in sample s.  Therefore we conclude

**Theorem 3.** If all discriminant features of univariately distinguishable class c are presented by sample s and for all i; $f_s^i <= f_c^i$, then sample s will be uniquely assigned to class c by the univariate classifier.

A **discriminant** procedure will further classify sample c against the classes remaining in $C_{set}$

from the univariate classifier in terms of the consistency rate $r_c$, missing-consistency rate $r_{mc}$, and the matching degree $d_m(f_s^i, f_c^i)$'s.


# IV. BY LEARNING TO FORM UNIVARIATE DISTINGUISHABLE SPACE

The learning system carries out the tasks of: (1) inspect and verify the decisions made by the classifier; (2) detect MM misclassifications, induce and generate heuristics for successive modifications of attributes of the classifier.

## IV.1 Sequential Exploration of Feature Density Functions

(a)*Sequential Accumulation Method* Traditionally accumulation method for feature distribution estimation uses only in-class samples. The parameters $\mu_i$ and $\sigma_i$ of a feature density function $p(f^i)$ for a class c is learned by Bayes estimation:

$$\mu_i(n) = 1/n \sum_{k=1, .., n} f_s(k) = (n-1)/n \, \mu_i(n-1) + 1/n \, f_s(n)$$

$$\sigma_i(n) = 1/n \sum_{k=1,..,n} (f_s(k) - \mu_i(n-1))^2 = (n-1)/n \, \sigma_i(n-1) + 1/n \, (f_s(n) - \mu_i(n-1))^2$$

where $\mu_i(n)$, $\sigma_i(n)$ denote the $n^{th}$ exploration of $\mu_i$ and $\sigma_i$ of $p(f^i)$. $f_s(k)$; $k = 1, ., n$ are the feature values from the sample that is classified as class c.

(b) *Regression method* Regression method uses both in-class samples and out-class samples to make explorations of the feature density functions. Let $\mu_{0i}(n-1)$ and $\sigma_{0i}(n-1)$ be the $(n-1)^{th}$ mean and variance of $p(f^i)$ for feature $f^i$ in class $C_0$. $\mu_{0i}(n)$, $\sigma_{0i}(n)$ the mean value and variance by taking count of $n^{th}$ sample s which has feature $f^i$ valued as $f_{si}(n)$. $C_1$ is the class that sample s is actually assigned. The following formula give the adjusted $\mu_{0i}(n)$, and $\sigma_{0i}(n)$ in cases of $n^{th}$ sample s is classified as $C_0$, i.e, $C_1 = C_0$, or in reverse, $C_1 \neq C_0$.

$$\mu_{0i}(n) = \mu_{0i}(n-1) + d_m(f_{si}(n), f_{0i}(n)) (f_{si}(n) - \mu_{0i}(n-1)) \qquad \text{if } C_1 = C_0;$$
$$\mu_{0i}(n) = \mu_{0i}(n-1) - d_m(f_{si}(n), f_{0i}(n)) (f_{si}(n) - \mu_{0i}(n-1)) \qquad \text{if } C_1 \neq C_0;$$

and

$$\sigma_{0i}(n) = \sigma_{0i}(n-1) + c_{0i} (0.5 - d_m(f_{si}(n), f_{0i}(n))) |f_{si}(n) - \mu_{0i}(n-1)| \quad \text{if } C_1 = C_0;$$
$$\sigma_{0i}(n) = \mu_{0i}(n-1) - c_{0i} d_m(f_{si}(n), f_{0i}(n)) |f_{si}(n) - \mu_{0i}(n-1)| \qquad \text{if } C_1 \neq C_0;$$

where $c_{0i}$ is a coefficient.

IV.2. Logic-based Learning to Explore Univariately Distinguishable Class-feature Space

(a) *Goal-directed Induction* An univariately distinguishable feature-class space is explored by a goal-directed induction process. A cooperative game of learning automata strategy [Thathachar] is applied. The process makes adjustments of the class-feature space in corresponding to the occurrences of MM mis-classifications. When an MM is identified, process is directed to corresponding procedures for each MM pattern. An **Inclusion** procedure makes a sample feature $f_s^i$ include in the discriminant scope of feature $f_c^i$ if the sample belongs to c. An **exclusion** procedure makes a sample feature $f_s^i$ exclude from the discriminant scope of feature $f_c^i$ if the sample not belongs to class c. The inclusion and exclusion operation performed on same feature of two classes make this feature a discriminant feature of that two classes.

As a simple example of such learning process, assuming an MMIII occurred and sample s is identified as old class c, the procedures are:

1. For all features with $|f_s^i| = 1$, call **Inclusion**$(f_s^i, f_c^i)$
2. For every class k in $\{c_i\}$
   2.1 Find feature $f^i$ such that

$$d_m(f_s^i, f_k^i) = \underset{j}{\text{MIN}}\, d_m(f_s^j, f_k^j) \quad \text{For all j; } |f_s^j| = 1$$

   2.2 Call **Exclusion**$(f_s^i, f_k^i)$

(b) *Changes of Class Attributes* Adding classes is simply handled by adding rows in the class feature space when new class is recognized. New class which has not been verified by learning process is initially marked "#". Classes established must be broad enough to "cover" the likely possibility of the occurrences, and at the same time specific enough to distinguish among feature vectors. Class splitting happens when two classes are so frequently mis-classified in MMII and MMIII. Splitting process creates a new class which has feature vector taking the intermediate values of the joint part of the features from the original two classes. It enhances the construction of univariately distinguished class-feature space. Deleting and merging classes is a risker task than adding and splitting classes. Once a class is established in the system, deleting is suggested only when it was without any occurrences for a certain long period of time. Merging process is carried out on classes that have complete consistencies on most of their common features.

(c) *Changes of Feature Attributes* Any new sample may bring in feature increase if it contains a feature which is not presented before. This feature is put into the class feature space with initial mark "#". For example, when the fifth feature is added to the feature vector of class c, the following case happens:

old feature vector of class c:   1 1 1 0 0 0
new feature vector of class c:   1 1 1 0 # 0

When the re-occurrences of the fifth feature in class c exceeds certain level or verified by other criteria, the mark "#" is changed to "1".

Reducing the number of features is an important way to speed up the classification process. It is also necessary for system be able to handle large size of the number of feature attributes and their variations in dynamic environment. The frequency of feature appearance is evaluated by recording its presences in samples. The strength of a feature is measured in terms of how many classes it distinguishes in a classification process. Features that constantly make poor discrimination when invoked have there strength steadily decreased. Feature is vanished from a class if in a long time of sequence the samples assigned to that class do not bear that feature. This feature is marked "#" before it is really sure to be removed. When a feature vanishes from all classes, it is deleted from the class feature space. When two features exhibit constantly similar behavior in making discrimination, one of them is removed. Correlated features are detected and combined. New feature may also be formed by linear transformations of some old features. The above process requires much domain-specific knowledge built in the system.

## VI. SUMMARIZATION

Pattern Classification is a general purpose task underlying many application systems. The dynamic changing characteristic of the environment makes the classification task difficult from applying traditional pattern recognition techniques. It has been seen that in order to create a meaningful classification in dynamic environment, a system must be equipped with sound background knowledge for handling the uncertainties. The univariate sequential classifier described here also allows to create, add, and compile knowledge and experiences in the system's running practice. The structure permits both value tuning and rule construction tasks in the learning process. Similarity and transferability of the technique from attribute space to structural space are very obvious. Applications of above classifier are therefore not limited to situations where conditions possess probability characteristics.

## REFERENCES

[1] Frey, P.W, "A Bit-Mapped Classifier", BYTE, November 1986, pp.161-172

[2] Duda, R. O, and Hart, P. E, "Pattern Classification and Scene Analysis", John Wiley & Sons, 1973

[3] Fukunaga, K., "Introduction to Statistical Pattern Recognition", Academic Press, 1972

[4] Fu, K. S., "Sequential Methods in Pattern Recognition and Machine Learning", Academic Press, New York, 1968

[5] Holland, J.H., "Escaping Brittleness: The Possibilities of General-purpose Learning Algorithms Applied to Parallel Rule-Based Systems","Machine Learning II" Morgan Kaufmann Publishers, Los Altos, Ca, 1986, pp.593-623

[6] Thathachar, M.A.L, and P.S.Sastry, "Learning Optimal Discriminant Functions Through a Cooperative Game of Automata", IEEE Transactions on Systems, Man, and Cybernetics, Vol. SMC-17, No.1, January/February 1987, pp.73-85

# APPLICATION OF A METHOD OF MANAGING EVIDENTIAL REASONING
## TO DECISION TREE CLASSIFIER

Ling Liu      Bao-kai He
Dept of Applied Mathematics
Chengdu College of  Geology
Chengdu,  Sichuan
The People's Republic of China

Abstract---The possibility and advantage of applying a method of manag-
ing evidential reasoning to decision tree classifyer is discussed. Relative algorithms are proposed and some experiments have been conducted.
Results are very good.

## I. Introduction

The decision tree classifier has been widely used in various pattern
recognition problems[2], especially those problems with a large number
of classes and/or features. In comparison with usual classifier it can
speed up,because it makes a difficult decision problem become a series
of simple ones. Besides, in the case that there is a hierarchical dependence relationship between features[3], decision tree classifier is the
most appropriate one for classification. When designing a tree classifier
many problems must be considered[2]. One of these important problems is
the control of error accumulation. A.V.Kulkarni et al[5]and Q.R.Wang et
al[4]proposed different methods to tackle the problem. The former used
the hieristic search technique in state space. The latter used a second
time search conducted by some fuzzy membership function. In this paper,
we would point out that by using J.Pearl's method[1]of manging evidential
reasoning and under certain conditions, the error accumulation can be
solved. We can also obtain many other advantages as well.
    For the convenience of discussion, in section II, J.Pearl's method
is introduced. In section III, the transformation from a tree classifier
to the domain of J.Pearl's method is given. characteristics of this kind
of tree classifier are discussed and two algorithms are proposed in
section IV and V respectively. Finally, results of some experiments are
discussed.

## II. Introduction of J.Pearl's Method

### A. The Domain

H={h1,...,hn} is a finite set of hypotheses known to be exhaustive. Certain subsets of H have semantic interest, and they form a tree. Every node contains its son. The conjunction of brothers is empty. The root is H and leave is hi, i=1,...,n. Initially each singleton hypothesis has a measure of belief Bel(hi)=P(hi). The Bel of a internal node is the sum of its sons. For H, there is Bel(H)=1. Every node has some corresponding evidences--es directly bearing upon it but saying nothing about its descendants.

### B. Bel Updating

When e which directly bears upon S(a node) is obtained, Bel(S) will be changed as follows:

$$Bel'(S)=a_s \lambda_s Bel(S)$$
$$\lambda_s =P(e/S)/P(e/-S)$$
$$a_s =(\lambda_s Bel(S)+1-Bel(S) )^{-1}$$

Bels of other nodes in the tree will be updated according to some rule[1].

Under the condition required by[1], Bel(S) is the a posterior probability for every node S in the tree.

## III. Transformation from a Tree Classifier to the Domain of J.Pearl's Method(shortly P-Method)

### A. Tree Classifier and the Procedure of Classifying

Figure 1. is a tree classifier. Every leave has a class label wi. Its ancestors are concerned with some sets of classes. For example, S01={w1, w2,w3 }.Every node contains its son(if there is any). The conjunction of any two sons are empty set(overlap is not considered). Each internal node Si has a corresponding feature Xi. In general, Xi can distinguish Si's sons, but can not distinguish any son's descendants further.

The meaning of "Xi can distinguish Si's sons" can be understood like this: if Si has L sons, Si1,...,Sil, then Xi's domain Ri contains at least L disjoint parts Ri1,...,RiL. When Xi is in Rij, j=1,...,L, unkown sample Y is decided to belong to Si's jth son Sij.

For every unknown Y, the classifyer always extracts its feature. X0 first which corresponds to the root S0. According to the value of X0, a decision about which son S of S0 Y is belong to is made. Then the corresponding feature of S is extracted and the further decision is made, ..., until Y reaches one leave node wi, and Y∈wi is the final solution. The path of dashline in figure 1. is a procedure of classifying.

B. Transformation to the Domain of P-Method

For any tree classifier T described in A., we can construct a tree T' such that T' satisfies the condition of the domain of P-Method. We describe the construction unformally.

First, let T' maintains the topology of T; Second, replace leave label wi with hi≙Y∈wi; Third, replace internal node Si with Si'≙Y∈Si; Fourth, for every Si, if it has L sons Si1,...,SiL, from A., we know that there are corresponding Ri1,...,RiL. Replace Xi of Si with eij≙Xi∈Rij of Sij', j=1,...,L. The construction is finished. Figure 2. is the corresponding T' of T in Figure 1..

Then we show that T' satisfies the condition of the domain of P-Method.

From Si⊃Sij in T, we can see that Si'⊃Sij' in T'. From Sijs are disjoint subsets of Si, we can obtain that Sij' are disjoint subsets of Si'. Because Xi can distinguish sons of Si but can not distinguish any son's descendants, eij can distinguish Sij' from other son of Si' but can not distinguish any descendants of Sij'. That means eij directly bears upon Sij'.

This shows that T' satisfies the condition mentioned in the domain of P-Method.

C. The Classifying Procedure in a P-Method Tree Classifier

Initially, every node S in the tree is assigned a measure of belief Bel(S)=P(S). The Bel of a internal node is the sum of Bels of its sons. The Bel of root is 1.

After each feature extraction, the Bel of every node has to be updated according to the value of features. When all useful features have been extracted, the node hi with the biggest Bel in leaves is the solution.

IV. Characteristics of P-Method Tree Classifier

A. The Classification According to the Biggest Bel Is Bayes Classification

According to the transformation from a tree classifier to the domain of P-Method, evidence e is the result of feature extraction, then parallel to (2) in 1 we have

$$\begin{cases} P(Xi/hj)=P(Xi/Si) & hj \ Si \\ P(Xi/hj)=P(Xi/-Si) & hj \ -Si \end{cases} \qquad (1)$$

Under the condition that

$$P(X1,...,Xm/hj)=P(X1/hj)...P(Xm/hj) \qquad j=1,...,n \qquad (2)$$

and according to Bayes Rule, from (1) we can prove that for any node S in the tree, Bel(S) is the a posterior probability. The classification according to the biggest a posterior probability is Bayes classification.

Then the error accumulation in a conventional tree classifier is naturally solved.

B. Parallel Processing Can Be Done

This is because P-Method itself has a very high parallel ability 1 .

C. After each feature extraction a Solution Can Be Obtained

In a conventional tree classifier, we get the solution only until the feature corresponding to the lowest internal node has been extracted. In P-Method classifier, we can get a solution after each feature extraction according to the biggest Bel rule. This means classification still can be conducted even in the case that not all features can be obtained. In general,however, more feature are extracted more satisfactory the solution is.

D. Feature Extraction Can Be in a Random Order

In a conventional tree classifier, feature extraction must be in a strictly top-down order. In a P-Method tree classifier,feature extraction can be in any order. For instance, it can be in top-down order, or in bottom-up order, and it can begin at any level,...,etc.

This makes it possible that we can arrange the order so that the extraction cost is increasing.When some Bel(hj) is big enough or satisfies some criterion, feature extraction can be stoped and computing time can be saved.

E. The information in Bels of Internal Nodes Can Be Used

When the solution about leave node is not satisfactory, solutions about higher level nodes are meaningful in many practical situations.


## V. Algorithms


It is difficult and not necessary to construct a algorithm considering all the characteristics mentioned in section IV. One of these two algorithms proposed here uses some.

A. Algorithm 1

Algorithm 1 uses hi which has the biggest Bel in leaves to guid feature extraction and Bel updating( so that not all nodes will be updated every time). The a priori probability of hi is used as heuristic information for extraction. Only those leaves whose Bels may exceed that of hi will be updated.

We suppose that there is always a leave node hi whose Bel is the biggest. This is true in many practical situations.

Every time the feature Xi to be extracted is corresponding to a node Si which is in the path from hi to the root. Bigger the Bel(hi), lower the level Si is in. This is because we suppose that lower the level,bigger

the ability of the feature to distinguish hi frome other leaves. If
Bel(hi) is small, hi has no guiding ability. The feature in the as high
as possible level will be extracted, like in a conventional tree classifier will be done.

Algorithm 1

    Input:  a tree

    Begin

        step 1:  find the hi which has the biggest Bel in leaves

        step 2:  find nodes and features in the path from hi to the root

        step 3:  calculate

                   Bel(hi)-1/n      (n is the number of leaves)

                decide which level's feature will be extracted according

                to the difference

                if  there is no feature can be extracted

                    then  give hi as the solution and stop

                    else  extracted the feature and set "having been

                          extracted" sign

        step 4:  update Si and its ancestors(Si is directly beared upon

                by e)

              update hi

              if $\lambda_{S_i}$ 1  then  update those leaves which are not Si's

                      descendants

        step 5:  find the leaves hj which has the biggest Bel in leaves

              if  Bel(hj) satisfies some criterion

                  then  give hj as solution and stop

                  else  if  j=i  then  goto step 2

                          else  j==> i and goto step 3

    End (algorithm 1)

## B. Algorithm 2

In algorithm 2, features are extracted in a top-down order strictly.
Every time those features are extracted whose corresponding node S has
the biggest Bel in its level, and only those nodes' Bels are updated
which are in the same level with the son of Sor which are leaves above
the level,as shown in figure 3..

The consideration is that the possibility of nonnecessary features
having been extracted is smaller if we extracte features according to
the Bels of higher level first. This is because higher the level is,
bigger the Bels are. Another advantage of extracting feature top-down
is that updating is easy.

When S which has the biggest Bel in its level is a leaf, but Bel(S)

is not satisfactory, those features whose corresponding node S' having the biggest Bel in non-leave nodes in the same level will be extracted.
A list OPEN is used to record nodes considered currently.

    Algorithm 2

      Input:  a tree

      Begin

        step 1:  put the root SO in OPEN

        step 2:  find the node S which has the biggest Bel in OPEN

                if  S is leave  then if  Bel(S) satisfies some criterion

                            then  give S as the solution
                                    and stop

                          else  find S' and
                                  extracte features corres-
                                  ponding to S'
                                  (if there is no such S'
                                    then  give S as
                                        solution and
                                        stop)

                    else  extracte features corresponding
                      to S

           (Si,  , are obtained, Si is the son of S or S',and is
             directly beared upon by e)

        step 3:  update Si
                find all other sons of nodes in OPEN, and update them
                store updating terms in them(those terms will be used
                when lower level nodes are updated)
                put them in NEW(another list)
        step 4:  remove non-leave nodes from OPEN
                update the remains
                (NEW U OPEN)==>OPEN
                goto step 2

    End (algorithm 2)

C. About These Two Algorithms

  When there is big difference between Bels of leaves,algorithm 1 makes full  use  of the information.

  Algorithm 2 is simple and easy to realize.

  These two algorithms can be seen as algorithms which search for  the optimum node. One measurement for search algorithm is abmissibility. Because Bels of nodes in tree classifier are changing continually,  we define one kind of admissibility.

Definition 1:   A S'-admissible algorithm is one which, when it stops, give the leave as the solution which has the biggest Bel.

Both algorithm 1 and algorithm 2 are S'-admissible. Here we give the proof for algorithm 2.For the sake of clarity,two other definitions and a lemma are given below.

Definition 2:   X is a node, if and only if X is in OPEN, IO(X) is true.

Definition 3:   X is node, if and only if IO(X) or IO(one of X's ancestors) is true, PIO(X) is true.

Lemma:   $\forall hj, j=1,\ldots,n$, at every time's excution of step 2, PIO(hj) is true.

prove:                    (using inductive method)

  initial       at the first time's excution of step 2,from step 1,we know IO(SO) is true,then $\forall hj$,PIO(hj) is true(frome definition 3).

  hypothesis    at the nth excution of step 2, $\forall hj$,PIO(hj) is true

  prove         if after the nth excution of step 3 and step 4, $\forall hj$, PIO(hj) is still true, then at the n+1th excution of step 2, it is true.

          at the nth excution of step 3 and step 4,

          if IO(hj) is true, because hj is leave, from step 4 we know that IO(hj) is still true, then PIO(hj) is true(definition 3).

          if IO(hj) is not true, according to hypothesis, PIO(hj) is true, that is to say one of hj's ancestor Y is in OPEN, step3 put Y's all sons in OPEN, one of which must be hj's ancestor or hj itself, so PIO(hj) is still true (definition 3).

        then at the n+1th excution of step 2, $\forall hj$, PIO(hj) is true.

        according to inductive rule, the lemma is proved. //.

Theorem:  Algorithm 2 is S'-admissible.

prove:

        the node S which is given as the solution when algorithm 2 stops at step 2 satisfies that $\forall X$, if IO(X) then Bel(X) Bel(S) (see algorithm 2).

        note that:   $\forall hj, hj \neq S$, if IO(hj), from above we know that

                Bel(hj)<Bel(S)

            if not IO(hj)

              ∵ PIO(hj) is true    (lemma)

              ∴ there is a Y=ancestor of hj and IO(Y) is true

              ∴ Bel(Y)<Bel(S)

$\because$ Bel(hj)<Bel(Y)    (Bel(Y)=the sum of
Bels of its sons)

$\therefore$ Bel(hj)<Bel(S)

then $\forall$hj,hj$\neq$S, Bel(hj)<Bel(S) is true,

that is to say algorithm 2 is S'-admissible. $\cdot$//$\cdot$

## VI. Experiments

Two experiments with algorithm 2 have been conducted.

In the first experiment, samples are produced by computer simulation. Every feature Xi is from N($\mu$,1),that is p(Xi/hj)~N($\mu$,1),j=1,...,n.Means of different classes are different.The reason why such kind of data is used is that e0,H and H0 can be calculated and e0$\cdot$H/H0--the upper limit of the error rate of conventional tree classifier[2] can be got. We can make the comparison of e0$\cdot$H/H0 and the error rate e of algorithm 2. From[2],we know that e0 is the biggest error rate of node in the tree. If all nodes' error rates eis are the same and equal to e0',then e0 is e0' and the upper limit e0$\cdot$H/H0 is closer to the real error rate of conventional tree classifier. In the experiment, we let eis equal to each other. The tree we constructed has ten classes. 1000 samples, 100 for each class, are produced to test algorithm 2. Its error rate e and other data are calculated and listed below:

    e0=0.1357
    H=3.32
    H0=0.664
    e0$\cdot$H/H0=0.6785
    e=0.263

We can see that e is much smaller than e0 H/H0, so we can say that algorithm 2 and then P-Method tree classifier really can control error accumulation.

In the second experiment, samples to be classified are rocks in air photograph. The value of feature is discrete. The value can be 1,0,-1, corresponding $\lambda_s$ being P(e/S)/P(e/-S), 1, P(-e/S)/P(-e/-S) respectively. P(e/S),P(e/-S) are estimated by expert. Featuer extraction is done by people. Those which are typical and used in teaching are all correctly classified by algorithm 2.

## VII. Conclusion

The evidential reasoning method proposed by J.Pearl can be used in tree classifier. This kind of tree classifier has many good characteristics.

It can overcome error accumulation which is a serious problem in large tree classifier. There are still many interesting problems need further investigation.

## References

[1] J.Pearl, "Resaerch note on Evidential Reasoning in a Hierarchy of Hypotheses", Artifial Intelligenc AI-28, pp9-15, 1986

[2] Q.R.Wang and C.Y.Suen, "Analysis and Design of a Decition Tree Based on Entropy Reduction and Its Application to Large Character Set Recognition", IEEE Tr.Vol PAMI-6, pp406-417, 1984

[3] M.Ben-Bassat and L.Zaidenberg, "Contextual Template Matching: A Distance Measure for Patterns with Hierarchically Dependent Features", IEEE Tr.Vol PAMI-6, pp201-211, 1984

[4] Q.R.Wang and C.Y.Suen, "Large Tree Classifier with Heuristic Search and Global Training", IEEE Tr.Vol PAMI-9, pp91-103, 1987

[5] A.V.Kulkarni and L.N.Kanal, "Admissible Search Strategies for Parametric and Nonparametric Hierarchical Classification", in proc. of 4th IJCPR, Japan, Nov. 1978

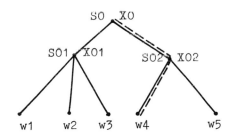

Figure 1. A Tree Classifier T

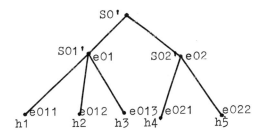

Figure 2.   T' of T

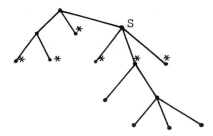

Figure 3. Nodes with a * Will Be Updated

# APPROXIMATE STRING MATCHING:
## INVESTIGATIONS WITH A HARDWARE STRING COMPARATOR.

O. Owolabi, J. D. Ferguson
Department of Computer Science
University of Strathclyde
Glasgow G1 1HX, UK.

## 1. INTRODUCTION

There has been a growing and widespread interest in the problem of approximate string matching. The inexact nature of data from human input and the existence of errors within information systems pose difficult problems for computer processing. A number of approximate string matching methods have been developed to overcome these problems. These software methods have been utilized in a variety of applications ranging from the correction of spelling errors in systems programs *(Morgan 1970)* to passenger name retrieval in airline reservation systems *(Davidson 1962)*.

These methods are also applicable in pattern recognition systems *(Hall and Dowling 1980)*. Patterns ranging from characters *(Lu 1978)* to ship targets *(Parvin 1984)* have been represented as character strings. Recognition then consists of matching character strings often in an approximate manner. Speech recognition often deals with strings of phonemes or symbols representing sounds *(White 1976)*. An attempt is then made to match a spoken utterance against a dictionary of known utterances.

However, a major problem remains with applications that require the search of a large dictionary or database. Efficient techniques exist for finding exact matches in databases organised in a manner that avoids exhaustive search. Nevertheless, combining these techniques with error correction remains a formidable problem. Hence, exhaustive searches are often necessary to locate the best match. For this reason the software methods for approximate string matching are most efficient in situations where the search space is limited.

This paper examines an alternative approach to approximate string matching applications with a large search space, utilising a special purpose microprocessor marketed by Proximity Technology - the PF474 *(PF474 Product data book 1984)*. The device is designed to search large dictionaries, comparing each entry with a given input string and then returning pointers to the best 16 matches together with their similarity or "proximity" values.

The first section of this paper contains a description of the algorithm used by the Proximity device and compares it with the dynamic programming method *(Wagner & Fischer 1974)*. This is followed by details of the Proximity microprocessor and its implementation in a 68000 Multibus workstation. Finally, the results of performance tests run on the device and its suitability for practical applications are outlined.

## 2. ALGORITHMS

An extensive survey of methods of approximate string matching is given in the paper by *Hall and Dowling (1980)*. The techniques described fall into two basic categories:

(a) Those methods that measure the distance between two strings by enumerating the number of transformation operations needed to change one string to another. Possibly the most popular of these methods is the dynamic programming technique. The algorithm used by the Proximity computer also falls in this category.

(b) Techniques that reduce strings into some code or abbreviation. If two strings reduce to the same code they are regarded as being closely similar. Examples of this technique are found in the Soundex method and the work of *Blair (1960)*.

In addition to requiring exhaustive searches, these methods sometimes suffer from inaccuracies, with widely different strings returning the same code or very similar strings yielding different codes.

## 2.1. The Dynamic Programming Method

With this technique three elementary operations are defined, namely substitution, insertion and deletion. Combinations of these primitives allow any string to be transformed to any other. The operations act on individual characters with a cost associated with each as follows:

| substitution | $a \rightarrow b$ | $cost = \gamma(a,b)$ |
| insertion | $\lambda \rightarrow a$ | $cost = \gamma(\lambda,a)$ |
| deletion | $a \rightarrow \lambda$ | $cost = \gamma(a,\lambda)$ |

where $\lambda$ is the null character.

Thus the string x = "ab" can be transformed into the string y = "bac" by the sequence of elementary operations:

$$\lambda \rightarrow c, \quad b \rightarrow \lambda, \quad c \rightarrow b, \quad \lambda \rightarrow c$$

which give in succession:

ab, cab, ca, ba, bac

at a cost of:

$$\gamma(\lambda,c) + \gamma(b,\lambda) + \gamma(c,b) + \gamma(\lambda,c).$$

The *edit distance* $\gamma(x,y)$ between two strings x and y is defined as the cost of the transformation of minimum cost from x to y.

Given two strings $x = a_1..a_n, \ y = b_1..b_m$.

Let

$$x(i) = a_1..a_i, \text{ and } D(i,j) = \delta(x(i),y(j));$$

where $\delta(x(i),y(j))$ is the edit distance between x(i) and y(j).

The edit distance is computed using the function:

$$D(i,j) = \min \begin{cases} D(i-1,j-1) + \gamma(a_i,b_j) \\ D(i-1,j) + \gamma(a_i,\lambda) \\ D(i,j-1) + \gamma(\lambda,b_j) \end{cases}$$

where

$\gamma(\alpha,\beta) = 1$ for *all* $\alpha$, $\beta$ *in* $A \cup \lambda$ and $\gamma(\alpha,\alpha) = 0$ for *all* $\alpha$ *in the alphabet A*.

Thus the distance between x and y will be D(n,m). In a dictionary search the string with the smallest distance to the search string is regarded as the most similar.

## 2.2. The Proximity Function

While the dynamic programming method computes the minimum number of direct edit operations that will transform a string x into a string y, the Proximity device evaluates a term called the THETA function *(PF474 Product data book 1984)*. The value returned by this function ranges from 0, for totally different strings, to 1 for an exact match.

The computation of the THETA function involves the use of three parameters for each letter in the alphabet, namely the *weight (W)* with range {0..7}, the *bias (B)* with range {-2,-1,0,1,2} and the *compensation (C)* with range {0..7}.

While the dynamic programming method performs a straightforward comparison between two strings x and y, the similarity value returned by the Proximity algorithm is the result of computing the function:

$$\frac{2 * (x\ compared\ with\ y)}{(x\ compared\ with\ x) + (y\ compared\ with\ y)}$$

In these comparisons the weight is used to specify the importance of each character, the bias to indicate the importance of the beginning or the end of the string and the compensation to adjust the comparison for missing characters. Each comparison is performed both forwards and backwards using the forward weight $W_f = W$ for the forward comparison and the reverse weight $W_r = W_f + B$ for the backward comparison.

Compared to a distance measure, like the dynamic programming method, the Proximity algorithm exhibits a number of interesting characteristics that could enhance the quality of the match, namely:
* The ability to weight individual characters making it possible to place emphasis on those thought more important (e.g. vowels might be deemed to carry more information than consonants in some applications).
* The possibility of biasing the match towards the start or ending of a string. Thus certain portions of the string may be made to influence the match more than others.
* The fact that the coefficient computed in the THETA function is more suited for displaying the relative differences between strings.

## 3. THE PROXIMITY PF474: PROCESSOR DESCRIPTION AND INTERFACE DESIGN

The Proximity algorithm examined above is implemented the PF474 microprocessor. This section describes the functionality of this device and its application in the WICAT 150S - a Multibus 68000 workstation operating under Unix.

### 3.1. The Proximity Processor

The PF474 is a VLSI device containing all the circuitry required to perform string comparison operations. To other circuit components the device appears as a set of 1024, 8-bit registers. Internally the PF474 is made up of two main subunits - the Computation unit that evaluates a similarity value for two strings, and the Ranker that sorts, in order, the n strings most similar to the search string. The Ranker works in parallel with the Computation unit, ordering the result of a previous operation while the next computation is in progress.
The Proximity registers are organised as follows:

* The CONTROL section that oversees the operation of the chip.
* The PARAMETER section that allows the user to assign weights to the symbols used in the strings under comparison.
* The STRING section, where strings are loaded before comparison.
* The RANKED list. This area stores the result of the matching operations. Pointers to the n strings most similar to the search string, along with their similarity values, are stored in order of the similarity value.

The PF474 can operate in two modes. In MEMORY MAPPED mode, the host processor must be used to transfer strings into the string registers. A command is then written to the control section to initiate a matching operation. At the end of each comparison the Proximity device waits until the next dictionary string and command are written. In the DMA mode, the query is again written by the host processor, however this is followed by a DMA command to the control section. The PF474 then retrieves the next dictionary string from memory, a byte at a time, until it fetches a NULL character. The starting address of the next string is then written to the Proximity device to initiate another DMA cycle. This procedure is repeated until two consecutive NULL characters are fetched signifying the end of the dictionary.

3.2. Multibus Implementation

At the start of the project, two design criteria were recognised:

(1) The interface should allow the PF474 to operate at full speed, in DMA mode, thus obtaining maximum throughput.
(2) The host processor and the system bus (Multibus 1) performance should not be reduced during the operation of the Proximity device.
To realise these aims a dual-ported memory design was adopted with the on-board memory dedicated to holding the data dictionary.

A schematic of the interface is given in Fig. 1. This design supports the two operating modes of the PF474. In the first, the memory mapped mode, the PF474 is entirely under host processor control. In the second, the DMA mode, control is passed to the Proximity processor once a search of the dictionary is initiated. The host cpu regains control when the search is complete or when a hardware reset is initiated.

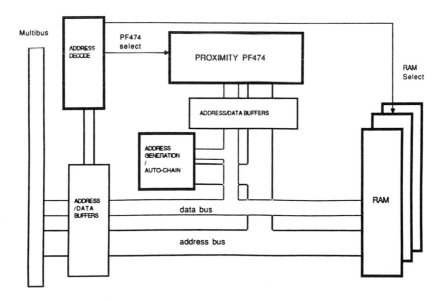

Fig. 1: Multibus Interface to Proximity PF474.

There are five major functional units forming the interface:

(1) *Address Decode Circuitry:* A flexible design utilising small DIL switches allows the interface to be placed with a one Mbyte resolution anywhere within the host processor's address space.

(2) *Multibus Data and Address Buffers:* These buffers serve two functions on the interface. Firstly they provide a safe interface to the bus standard. Secondly they provide a means of isolating the PF474 and the on-board memory from the host processor during DMA accesses of the dictionary.

(3) *Proximity PF474 Processor:* The PF474 occupies 2Kbytes of the host system's memory. To avoid the addition of byte swapping circuitry all the PF474's registers lie on an even address boundary.

(4) *On-Board RAM:* The interface contains 512 Kbytes of dual-ported RAM that can be accessed either directly by the host processor through the Multibus interface or by the Proximity device. In DMA mode the PF474 has complete control over the on-board memory allowing it to fetch strings, a byte at a time. The DMA operation is terminated either by a reset signal from the host processor or when two consecutive NULL characters are detected in the search dictionary. In normal operation the host cpu addresses the RAM as 16 bit words allowing the search dictionary to be quickly loaded prior to use.

(5) *Address Generation - Auto-Chain Circuitry:* During DMA operation the PF474 provides 16 address lines allowing it to access a 64Kbyte address space. It was envisaged that dictionaries of the order of several hundred Kbytes would be required in some applications. With this in mind a separate counter was used to provide 19 address lines, allowing the Proximity device to address up 0.5 Mbytes of continuous memory.

In the DMA mode the PF474 will stop after fetching one complete string from memory, i.e., after detecting the terminating NULL. The host cpu will then have to write the address of the next dictionary string to the PF474's DMA registers to initiate the fetch of the next string. To overcome this problem additional hardware was added to replace this host cpu function. Fig. 2 illustrates the logic of the NULL detection and auto-chain circuitry.

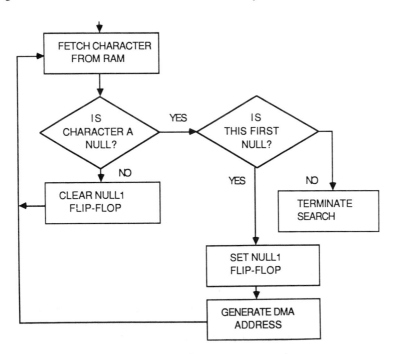

Fig. 2: Null Detection/Auto-chain Logic.

In operation the circuit continuously monitors every byte fetched by the Proximity device. A simple latch is used to record the occurrence of a NULL character in the data stream. If a NULL is detected, the latch is set and signals generated to initiate another DMA cycle. On the next cycle, detection of any character other than an NULL resets the latch and DMA continues. If however a second NULL is detected then the DMA operation is terminated, with the PF474 and the on-board memory returning to host cpu control.

## 3.3. The Software Interface

The hardware is hidden from the user by device drivers that are invoked in the user programs through Unix system calls. Two different approaches are adopted depending whether the PF474 is used in memory mapped mode or DMA mode. The following summarises the activities in each case.

To program the system using memory-mapped mode:
> (a) Open device drivers.
> (b) Set Proximity parameters.
> (c) Pass search string to device drivers.
> (d) Repeatedly pass in the next dictionary string
>    to device driver until end of dictionary.
> (e) Retrieve similarity values for, and pointers
>    to, the n strings most similar to search string.

To program the system using Direct-Memory-Access mode:
> (a) Load dictionary into on-board RAM.
> (b) Set up the symbol parameters.
> (c) Pass search string to device driver.
> (d) Select DMA option and write to DMA registers.
> (e) Poll for end of DMA operation.
> (f) Retrieve similarity values for and pointers
>    to the n strings most similar to search string.

The latter mode offers better performance, allowing the device to run without software intervention until the dictionary search is completed.

## 4. PERFORMANCE

### 4.1. Speed

Tests carried out using the Multibus implementation of the PF474 with a 24,000-word dictionary of average length 10 characters took an average time of about 1 second to compare an input string with every dictionary string. This result agrees well with the throughput analysis presented in the PF474 technical manual. To provide a comparison with a software method, the dynamic programming algorithm was coded in C. When used with the same dictionary, the program took about 29 seconds to compare the search string with every dictionary string.

While the time for the dynamic programming method could be improved by the use of a more powerful machine, the Proximity device provides a low cost method of procuring good performance.

## 4.2. Matching accuracy

The description of the Proximity algorithm outlined in section 2.2 highlighted certain characteristics that could enhance the quality of a match.

Consider a dictionary that includes the two words "cart" and "parts". On searching for the string most similar to "part", the Proximity device and the dynamic programming method will return the values shown Table 1.

|  | DP | Proximity |
|---|---|---|
| part/parts | 1 | 0.80 |
| part/cart | 1 | 0.75 |

Table 1.

While the dynamic programming method returns 1 in both cases, the Proximity returns a value which results in better recall.

## 5. APPLICATIONS

Approximate string matching has received attention in connection with spelling checking and correction programs *(Peterson 1980, Pollock & Zamora 1984, Durham, et. al. 1983)*. It is obvious that this device has the potential for use in an interactive spelling corrector. Fig. 3 outlines a possible structure for such an application. The checking part of the program has already been implemented; the correction part will require the use of a window based editing system.

Another area of interest relates to the application of the PF474 in the retrieval of information from a database with potential errors either in the stored strings or in the query strings. *Mor and Fraenkel (1982)* have reported a study in which they attempt to use three operators - deletion, exchange and rotation - to "mend" single character errors in conjunction with hashing for full text retrieval. Good performance was credited to the method in applications where the size of the dictionary of significant words was a small part of the memory requirement. However, for applications running into several thousand entries the memory requirement and the multiple hash function computations make the Mor and Fraenkel method unattractive.

One application requiring approximate string matching with a large dictionary is the FACT database system developed at the University of Strathclyde *(McGregor & Malone 1981)*. The Fact database is an entity-relational system incorporating generic information processing capability suited to deductive reasoning. In the scheme envisaged, the Proximity device would only be used if a search of the database failed to find an exact match for the desired string. Fig. 4 shows an outline of the Proximity assisted search system for the FACT database.

The result of a search could be communicated to the user in one of the following ways:
- The string most similar to the input string may be returned.
- The n most similar strings may be returned for the user's consideration.
- An error threshold could be used in order that only strings with a
  similarity value above this are returned.

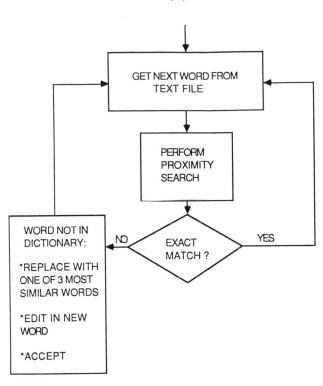

Fig. 3: Spelling Corrector Application.

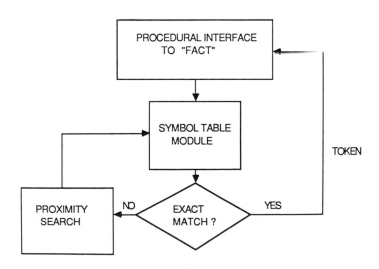

Fig. 4: A Proximity-assisted Search on FACT System Symbol Table.

# 6. CONCLUSION

A number of software algorithms exist that support an efficient search for an exact match of an input string in a large dictionary or database. Techniques also exist for approximate string matching. However, their effectiveness is limited to relatively small databases. In contrast, the special purpose architecture of the Proximity microprocessor yields an efficient method of performing approximate matching with large dictionaries. In addition, the Proximity device can be adjusted for sensitivity, as well as providing the best 16 matches ranked in order. Further, the design outlined allows the device to be used in parallel with the host processor, resulting in enhanced overall system performance.

The implementation described uses a dual ported memory arrangement making the interface suitable for a wide range of systems employing Multibus. The design could be easily adapted to work with any asynchronous bus system.

## References

Blair, C. R. 1960. A program for correcting spelling errors. *Informat. Contr. 3* ,60-67.

Davidson, L. 1962. Retrieval of misspelled names in an airline reservation system. *Comm. ACM 5* (3), 169-171.

Durham, I., Lamb, D. A. & Saxe, J. B. 1983. Spelling correction in user interfaces. *Comm. ACM 26* (10), 764-773.

Hall, P. A. V. & Dowling, G. R. 1980. Approximate string matching. *Comput. Surv. 12* (4), 381-402.

Lu, S. Y. & Fu, K. S. 1978. A sentence-to-sentence clustering procedure for pattern analysis. *IEEE Trans. Sys., Man, and Cybern. 8* (5), 381-389.

McGregor, D. R. & Malone, J. R. 1981. The FACT database: a system based on inferential methods. *in Information Retrieval Research.* Oddy, R. N., C. J. van Rijsbergen, Williams & P. W. (Eds.). London: Butterworths.

Mor, M. & Fraenkel, A. S. 1982. Retrieval in an environment of faulty texts of faulty queries. *in Improving Database Usability and Responses.* Peter Scheuemann(Ed.). New York: Academy Press, 405-425.

Morgan, H. L. 1970. Spelling correction in systems programs. *Comm. ACM 13* (2), 90-94.

Parvin, B. A. 1984. A structural classifier for ship targets. *in Proc. 7th Int. Conf. Pattern Recognition,* 550-552.

Peterson, J. L. 1980. Computer programs for detecting and correcting spelling errors. *Comm. ACM 23* (12),676-687.

PF474 product data book 1984. Proximity Devices: Florida.

Pollock, J. J. & Zamora, A. 1984. Automatic spelling correction in scientific and scholarly text. *Comm. ACM 27* (4), 358-368.

Wagner, R. A. & Fischer, M. J. 1974. The string-to-string correction problem. *J. ACM 21* (1), 168-178.

White, G. M. & Neely, R. B. 1976. Speech recognition experiments with linear prediction bandpass filtering, and dynamic programming. *IEEE Trans. Acoust., Speech, Signal Proc. 24* (2), 183-188.

# SYNTHESIS OF ATTRIBUTED HYPERGRAPHS

# FOR KNOWLEDGE REPRESENTATION

# OF 3-D OBJECTS

S.W.Lu

Department of Computer Science Concordia University
Montreal Quebec Canada H3G 1M9


A.K.C.Wong

Department of Systems Design University of Waterloo
Waterloo Ontario Canada N2l 3G1

## ABSTRACT

This paper continues our work on knowledge representation of 3-D objects. For recognition and location of 3-D objects, Attributed Hypergraph Representation has been introduced. The new research concentrates on development of synthesis of attributed hypergraph, which is capable of synthesizing several AHR's derived from the various views of an object into a complete AHR of the entire object. The resulted AHR is automatically stored in the database as a model AHR for further object recognition. This algorithm is implemented on a Grinnell Imaging System driven by a VAX 11/750 running VMS.

## I Introduction

In robot vision and task planning, an adequate representation of a real world object should enable a system to model the object or scene automatically by synthesizing data from the image of the real world. The challenge to artificial intelligence and knowledge engineering in development of intelligent manufacturing system is to provide more general and flexible knowledge representation for effective communication and control of robots.

To represent 3-D objects in data form suitable for manipulation and recognition, various approaches have been made. The most common ones are boundary representation [6], constructive solid geometry representation[8], sweep representation[2] and decomposition representation[4]. More recent development can be found in [1]. Most of these methods are feasible to acquire the geometric information from object image, but they lack the flexibility for effective recognition if the orientation of the object varies, or certain parts are occluded. Furthermore, with most of these systems, the knowledge of the prototype objects has to be input by the users.

We have developed a general flexible knowledge representation system using Attributed Hypergraph Representation as basic data structure [9, 10]. In this paper we propose a attributed hypergraph synthesis method. The complete AHR of an object can be obtained directly through synthesizing the AHR's derived from the scanned images of the various views of the object. The advantages of this system are that it furnishes a more direct and simple approach to the representation, recognition and location of objects. The advantages of the synthesis method are that it provides a flexible way to modeling objects and assigns the system a certain learning capability.

To gather more information, several images obtained from different views of a 3-D object should be used. We have developed a method by which AHR's obtained from different views can be combined (synthesized) to form a single AHR that yields a AHR of the entire object.

We introduce the hypergraph synthesis for two purposes:

1) To combine two image view hypergraphs (IVH's) of a candidate object image in the object recognition process.

From the image of each view of an object, we obtain an AHR which represents the geometric structure of only those edges and faces of that object visible from the vantage point of the laser scanner. Sometimes, from a single image of the object, the object can not be distinguished. In this case, another IVH should be obtained for further recognition in order to resolve the ambiguity. We then synthesize the two IVH's into one which contains all the information obtained about the object from both views. The comparison of the AHR synthesized from the IVH's with model AHR's in the database may yield a unique matching. The object then can be recognized by the vision system.

2) To build a model AHR for a new object in the learning phase.

The model AHR's in the knowledge base could be constructed from direct physical measurements or through learning using information derived from images of different views. Thus, several IVH's of the new model can be derived and synthesized into a model AHR, which can represent the entire model and allow the use of geometric or other surface information at various levels.

## II. Attributed Hypergraph Representation

an attributed hypergraph representation (AHR) has been developed for representing 3-D objects and constructing knowledge base for objects[3]. Here, we shall define the AHR of 3-D objects.

**Definition 1** An *attribute pair* is an ordered pair $(A_n, A_v)$ where $A_n$ is the attribute or property name of the object and $A_v$ is the attribute value.

For example, an attribute pair can be used to describe the area of a face of a 3-D model. The name $A_n$ may stand for the attribute "area" and $A_v$ the measure of the area.

**Definition 2** An *attribute set* is an m-tuple $< p_1, p_2, \ldots, p_i, \ldots, p_m >$ where each element in the tuple is an attribute pair.

For our 3-D model representation, the attribute set is used to record the properties of a surface or relation between surfaces. For example an attribute set for describing a triangular surface is

S : < (area, 30), (type, planar), (number of edges, 3) >

**Definition 3** An *attributed vertex* is a vertex with an associated attribute set called a vertex attribute set. An *attributed edge* is an edge with an associated attribute set called an edge attribute set.

**Definition 4** An *attributed graph* of an object is a graph $G_e = (V_e, A_e)$ where $V_e = \{v_1, \ldots, v_p, \ldots, v_q, \ldots, v_m\}$ is a set of attributed vertices and $A_e = \{\cdots, a_{pq}, \ldots, \}$ is a set of attributed edges. The edge $a_{pq}$ connects vertices $v_p$ and $v_q$ with an attributed relation.

**Definition 5** An *elementary area attributed graph* $G_e = (V_e, A_e)$ is an attributed graph for representing a face bounded by distinct and well-defined edges, where 1) $V_e$ is a set of attributed vertices representing the boundary segments of the face and 2) $A_e$ is the set of attributed edges representing the relations between the segments.

For example, a triangle area can be represented by:

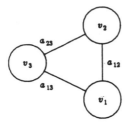 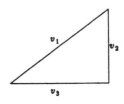

a) Graph          b) Area

Fig. 1 Elementary Area Attributed Graph

$$G^e = (V^e, A^e) \qquad where$$
$$V^e = \{ v_1, v_2, v_3 \} \qquad A^e = \{ a_{12}, a_{23}, a_{13} \}$$
$$v_1 = < (type, line), (length, 5) >$$
$$a_{12} = < (type, boundary), (angle, 53.1\ ') >$$

A *primitive block* of an object is a block bounded by surfaces such that there is no way to decompose further without creating edges on the surfaces. Hence a pyramid, a column, a cylinder and a sphere can be a primitive block of an object.

**Definition 6** A *primitive block attributed graph* is an attributed graph $G_p = (V_p, A_p)$ which represents a primitive block of an object. The attributed vertex set $V_p$ represents the faces and the attributed edge set $A_p$ represents the geometrical relations between faces.

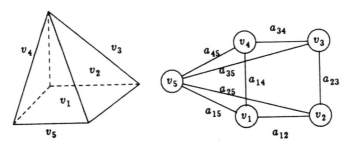

a) Block          b) Graph

Fig. 2 Primitive Block Attributed Graph

As an example, the primitive block graph of a block in Fig. 2 can be represented by:

$$G^p = (V^p, A^p) \qquad where$$
$$V^p = \{ v_1, v_2, v_3, v_4, v_5 \}$$
$$A^p = \{ a_{12}, a_{23}, a_{34}, a_{14}, a_{15}, a_{25}, a_{35}, a_{45} \}$$
$$v_1 = < (type, plane), (area, 5), (\# \ of \ edges, 3) >$$
$$a_{12} = < (type, line), (angle, 87\ ') >$$

To provide a high level object representation while retaining structural relations among the object components, the hypergraph is introduced.

**Definition 7** A *hypergraph* [12] is defined to be an ordered pair $H = (X, E)$ where $X = \{ x_1, x_2, \ldots, x_n \}$ is a set of vertices and $E = \{ e_1, e_2, \ldots, e_m \}$ a set of the hyperedges such that

(1) $e_i \neq \emptyset$ $(i = 1, \ldots, n)$,

(2) $\bigcup_i e_i = X$; $|X| = n$ and $|X|$ is called the order of the hypergraph.

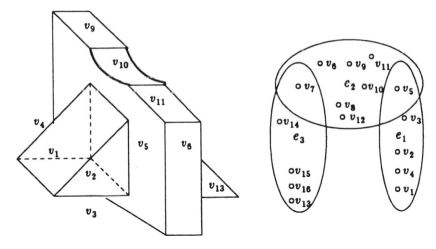

(a) Model            (b) Hypergraph of the model

Fig. 3 A Model and Its Attributed Hypergraph

**Definition 8** An *object attributed hypergraph* $H_{\bullet} = (X_{\bullet}, E_{\bullet})$ consists of a set of attributed vertices $X_{\bullet}$ and a set of hyperedges $E_0$. Each vertex is associated with an elementary area attributed graph representing a face, and each hyperedge is associated with a primitive block attributed graph representing a primitive block.

Attributed hypergraph representation can be constructed for models and organized into a database. An object can be recognized by finding the monomorphism of its AHR onto a model AHR in the database[9].

## III. Basic Operations on Graphs

To facilitate the graph or hypergraph synthesis process, two basic operations on graphs are introduced. They can be applied to the primitive area attributed graphs as well as elementary block attributed graphs associated with different image view graphs of the same object.

(1) *Intersection* of two attributed graphs

An intersection graph $G_{is}(V_{is}, A_{is})$ of two attributed graphs $G_1(V_1, A_1)$ and $G_2(V_2, A_2)$ is a largest common attributed subgraph of the two attributed graphs. In this paper we present a geometric transformation approach based on the knowledge of the attributes and the geometric relations between different view images. Consider two image view graphs representing two images of an object corresponding to two different views of the object. Thus, there exist a certain geometrical relation between the two images. Suppose that the second image is obtained from a different view angle relative to that of the first image. A spatial transformation T can be used to transform a region in the first image to a corresponding region in the second image. This method is illustrated by following example.

Figs. 4 (a) and (b) are two images of different views of an object. Their corresponding elementary block attributed graphs (Figs. 4 (c) and (d) ) can be expressed respectively as:

$$G_1 = (V_1, A_1), \quad where \quad V_1 = (v_1', v_2', v_3', v_4')$$
$$A_1 = (a_{1,2}', a_{2,3}', a_{1,4}', a_{2,3}', a_{3,4}') \quad and$$
$$G_2 = (V_2, A_2), \quad where \quad V_2 = (v_2'', v_3'', v_4'', v_5'')$$
$$A_2 = (a_{2,3}'', a_{3,4}'', a_{4,5}'', a_{3,5}'', a_{2,5}'')$$

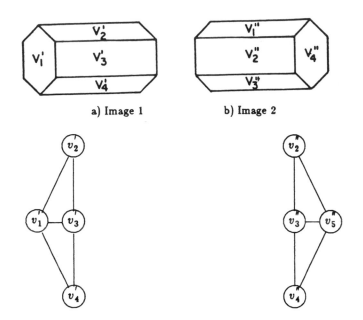

c) Graph $G_1$ for Image 1  d) Graph $G_2$ for Image 2
Fig. 4 Two Images of Different Views
of a Block and Their Associated Image View Graphs.

For each surface in each image, an orientation reference $n_i$ (see section 2) is attached to it. The normal of planar surface and the axis of conic or cylindrical surface become the orientation references. Let a geometric relation between two images be represented by a geometric transformation $T$. By checking the surface orientation reference attributes of the vertices and their transformation we establish the correspondences:

1)  $v_i' \Leftrightarrow v_j''$  if $T(n_i') \doteq n_j''$ and $\bar{v}_i' \leftrightarrow \bar{v}_j''$  *orientation transformation condition*

2)  $a_{pq}' \Leftrightarrow a_{kl}''$  if $T(n_p') \doteq n_k''$ and $T(n_q') \doteq n_l''$  *( adjacency preserving condition*

If both of the above conditions are satisfied, we then include these matched vertices $(v_i', v_j'')$ as a new vertex $v_r$ in the intersection. We call $v_r$ an intersection vertex. We relate the edge subscript of the two original graphs with that of intersection vertex by two relations $\eta_1(r)$ and $\eta_2(r)$ respectively such that $l = \eta_1(r)$ and $j = \eta_2(r)$. We can then obtain the intersection vertices and their adjacency relations in the form of adjacency matrix as follows:

Let $G_1$ and $G_2$ be:

$$I' = \left[ a_{pq}' \right] \quad where$$

$$a_{pq}' = \begin{cases} \bar{v}_p' & \text{if } v_p \in V_1, \ v_q \in V_1 \text{ and } p = q \\ \bar{a}_{pq}' & \text{if } v_p \in V_1, \ v_q \in V_1 \text{ and } a_{pq}' \in A_1 \\ 0 & \text{otherwise} \end{cases}$$

and  $$I'' = \left[ a_{lk}'' \right] \quad where$$

$$a_{lk}'' = \begin{cases} \bar{v}_{lk}'' & \text{if } v_l \in V_1, \ v_k \in V_1 \text{ and } l = k \\ \bar{a}_{lk}'' & \text{if } v_l \in V_1, \ v_k \in V_1 \text{ and } a_{lk}'' \in A_2 \\ 0 & \text{otherwise.} \end{cases}$$

The intersection adjacency matrix then becomes:

$$I_{in} = \left[ a_{rs} \right] \quad \text{where } v_r \in V_{in}, \ v_s \in V_{in} \text{ and}$$

$$a_{rs} = \begin{cases} 0 & \text{if } \bar{a}'_{q_1(r)q_1(s)} \neq \bar{a}''_{q_2(r)q_2(s)} \\ \bar{a}'_{q_1(r)q_1(s)} & \text{if } \bar{a}'_{q_1(r)q_1(s)} = \bar{a}''_{q_2(r)q_2(s)} \end{cases}$$

The adjacency relations in $G_1$ and $G_2$ are preserved in $G_1 \cap G_2$. The intersection graph $G_{in}(V_{in}, A_{in})$ is shown in Fig. 5 (a).

(2) *Union* of two attributed graphs

First we denote a union of two attributed sets $a_1$ and $a_2$ by $a_1 \oplus a_2$. Let $a_1$ be $< \ldots, (p_{si}, p_{si}), \ldots >$ and $a_2$ be $< \ldots, (p_{si}, p_{si}'), \ldots >$ where $p_{si}$ is the name of i-th attribute, and $p_{si}$ and $p_{si}'$ are its values in the respective set. If $p_{si}$ is nil and $p_{si}'$ is not, then the resulted attribute pair in the union is $(p_{si}, p_{si}')$. In this manner, the union of all attributed values for $p_{si}$'s can be obtained.

Then we form a union vertex set by including the pair of the matched vertices as a single vertex and all the unmatched vertices in both sets. Let $G_{un}(V_{un}, A_{un})$ be the union attributed graph. Its adjacency matrix can be obtained and expressed as:

$$I_{un} = \left[ a_{rs} \right] \quad \text{where } v_r, \ v_s \in V_{un} \text{ and}$$

$$a_{rs} = \begin{cases} \bar{a}'_{q_1(r)q_1(s)} \oplus \bar{a}''_{q_2(r)q_2(s)} & \text{if } v_r, v_s \in V_{in} \\ \bar{a}''_{q_2(r)q_2(s)} & \text{if } v_r \notin V_{in} \text{ and } v_{q_2(s)} \in V_2 \\ \bar{a}'_{q_1(r)q_1(s)} & \text{if } v_r \notin V_{in} \text{ and } v_{q_1(s)} \in V_1 \\ 0 & \text{otherwise} \end{cases}$$

All adjacency relations in both $G_1$ and $G_2$ are preserved.

In our example, the matched vertex pairs in both attributed graphs are $(v_2', v_2'')$, $(v_3', v_3'')$, and $(v_4', v_4'')$, and their matched edge pairs are $(a_{2,3}', a_{2,3}'')$ and $(a_{3,4}', a_{3,4}'')$. Then $v_2, v_3, v_4$ are included in the intersection graph and $a_{2,3}, a_{3,4}$ are determined according to the recorded subscript relation.

The union operation then leads to:

$$G_{un}(V_{un}, A_{un}) = G_1(V_1, A_1) \cup G_2(V_2, A_2) \quad \text{where}$$

$$V_{un} = V_1 \cup V_2 = (v_1, \ldots, v_4, v_5) \text{ and}$$

$$A_{un} = A_1 \cup A_2 = (a_{1,2}, a_{1,3}, a_{1,4}, a_{2,3}, a_{3,4}, a_{2,5}, a_{3,5}, a_{4,5}).$$

The adjacency relation of the union graph is identical to those in both $G_1$ and $G_2$. The union graph is shown in Fig. 5 (b).

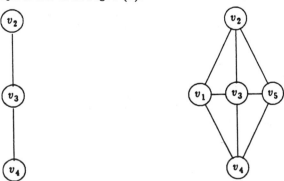

(a) Intersection of $G_1$ and $G_2$.　　　(b) Union of $G_1$ and $G_2$.
Fig. 5 Operation of $G_1$ and $G_2$.

# IV Attributed Graph Synthesis

To synthesize two attributed graphs, two levels of graph synthesis is desirable.

## 1. Elementary Area Graph Synthesis

For a face of an object with certain edges invisible in one image but visible in another, a graph synthesis procedure can be applied to obtain the elementary area attributed graph with complete geometric information of that face.

## 2. Primitive Block Graph Synthesis

Before discussing the primitive block graph synthesis procedure, we introduce two categories of edges identifiable in a range image:

1   Marginal edges : also as known as jump edges or edges between an image region of a face and the background.

2   Inner edges : edges formed by regions of adjacent faces of an object.

The procedure of synthesis is then outlined as follows:

1   Obtain a primitive block graph from the image.

2   Mark each marginal edge of the block in the image view graph. Record the elementary area vertices with marginal edges in a list M.

3   Find the normal of each face containing a marginal edge. For each of those faces, determine the relation between the surface orientation reference and the axis of the range finder. Rotate the object (or move the range finder) with orientation reference less than 60˚ such that the new view contains more of the previously invisible faces and reveals more of their relations with the known faces in the block.

4   Obtain the primitive block graph for the new image and mark the marginal edges.

5   Form the union of the two attributed graphs.

6   Check the marginal edges in the union graph. If an edge is a marginal edge in one view but is an inner edge in another view, then the edge is no longer considered as a marginal edge after the synthesis. Check the vertex set and remove the those without marginal edges from M.

7   If no vertex of the union graph is in M, the union graph formed represents the entire object, otherwise go to step 3 for further synthesis.

## 3. Primitive block attributed graph synthesis algorithm

In this section, the algorithm is presented in pseudo-codes.

Input: 1) A group of the attributed graphs to be synthesized.
$$G = \{G_1, G_2, \cdots, G_i \cdots\} \quad where \quad G_i = (V_i, A_i) \text{ with adjacency matrix } I_i.$$
2) A family of marked marginal sets: $M = \{M_1, M_2, \ldots, M_i \cdots\}$,
where $M_i = \{v_{i1}, v_{i2}, \cdots, v_{im}\}$ and $v_{im}$ is a vertex with marginal edges.
Note: Elements in both G and M could be derived from images of different views during the synthesis process.
Output: 1) A synthesized graph $G_r$ with an adjacency matrix $I_r$.
2) A set of newly marked marginal edges: $M' = \{v_1^r, v_2^r, \ldots, v_b^r\}$
where r indicates the result after r-th union operation in the synthesis process.
Procedure { Graph Synthesis }
begin
   $k = 1$;  $G_r := G_1$;  $V_r := V_1$;  $A_r := A_1$;  $M' := M_1$; { Initiation }
while $M'$ is not empty
    begin { while loop }
      $k := k +1$ ; read $G_k$;
     $G_r := G_r \cup G_k$ ; { perform the union operation to $G_r$ and $G_k$ }
    { $I_r$ extension }
        Let the vertex $v_i$ be the new vertex in the $G_r$.
        Extend the adjacency matrix $I_r^{k-1}$ to $I_r^k$ by adding a new column and
        a new row associated with $v_i$.

```
{ update M' }
      read M_k;
      Check the vertices with marginal edges in the list M';
      if v is in two different elementary graphs
      and its marginal edges become inner edges then
          M' := M' - { v }; M' := M' ∪ M_k
end { while loop }
```

# V Hypergraph Synthesis

For two hypergraphs $H_1(X_1, E_1)$ and $H_2(X_2, E_2)$, the synthesis process is organized in two stages to obtain the synthesized hypergraph $H_r(X_r, E_r)$.

First, two sets of hyperedges are considered. Let $e_p \in E_1$ and $e_q \in E_2$. If $e_p$ and $e_q$ correspond to an identical primitive block of the object, then the primitive block graph synthesis can be applied to them. For each hyperedge in $H_1$ the comparison is performed to search for its counterpart in $H_2$. If found the synthesis procedure is applied to that hyperedge and its counterpart and transfer the synthesized hyperedge into the set of hyperedges $E_r$ in the resulted hypergraph $H_r$. For hyperedges with no counterpart, they can be directly transferred into $E_r$ in the synthesized hypergraph by an union operation.

Next the sets of vertices are to be considered (note that each vertex in the hypergraph is an elementary area attributed graph). By comparing the attributes and the orientation reference of the vertices, we can determine if a vertex in $X_1$ and a vertex in $X_2$ are corresponding to the same face of the object. Then the elementary area graph synthesis procedure is performed to those vertices, and as a result the synthesized vertex can be transferred into the resulted hypergraph $H_r$. Finally the new adjacency matrix for the resulted hypergraph is constructed. The algorithm is presented in pseudo-codes as below.

Input: 1) A group of attributed hypergraphs to be synthesized.
$S = \{ H_1, H_2, \cdots, H_i \cdots \}$ *where* $H_i = (V_i, E_i)$ with adjacency matrix $I_i$.
2) A family of marked marginal sets: $M = \{ M_1, M_2, \ldots, M_i \cdots \}$,
*where* $M_i = \{ v_{i1}, v_{i2}, \cdots, v_{im} \}$ and $v_{im}$ is a vertex with marginal edges.
Output: 1) A synthesized graph $H_r$ with an adjacency matrix $I_r$.
where r indicates the result after r-th union operation in the synthesis proces
2) A set of newly marked marginal edges: $M' = \{ v_1', v_2', \ldots, v_t' \}$
where r indicates the result after r-th union operation in the synthesis process
Procedure { Hypergraph Synthesis }
begin
    k := 1;   $H_r := H_1$;   $V_r := V_1$;   $E_r := E_1$;   $M' := M_1$ { initiation }
while M' not empty
    begin { do loop }
    k := k + 1; read $H_k$
    for each $v_i$ in $V_k$ do
        if $v_i \notin V_r$ then
            extend the adjacency matrix $I_r^{k-1}$ to $I_r^k$ by adding
            a new column associated with $v_i$.
    for each $e_q \in E_k$ do
        if ( $e_p \in E_r$ and $e_q \in E_k$
            and they are corresponding to the same primitive block ) then
            $G_{e_p} := G_{e_p} \cup G_{e_q}$ { perform the union operation }
        else { $I_r$ extension }
            extend the adjacency matrix $I_r^{k-1}$ to $I_r^k$ by adding
            a new row associated with $e_q$.
    { The new elements $a_{ij}$ in $I_r^k$ are the new relations between $v_i$ and $e_j$. }

```
{ update M' }
        read M_k ;
        Check the vertices with marginal edges in the list M' ;
        if v is in two different elementary graphs
        and its marginal edges become inner edges then
              M' := M' - { v }; M' := M' ∪ M_k
end { do while loop }
```

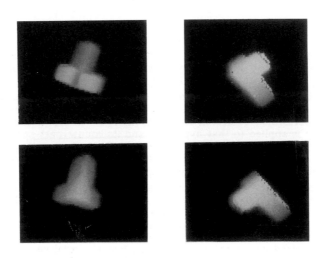

(a). The laser images for the object from several views

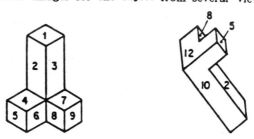

(b) Two different images with face labels

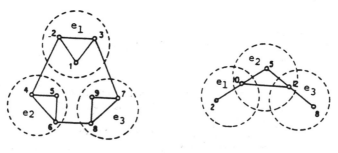

(c) Image view graphs for images in b)

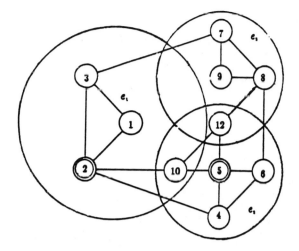

(d) Synthesized AHR for images in b)

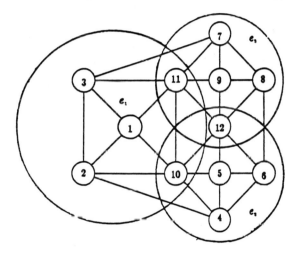

(e) Synthesized AHR for the object

Fig. 6 Hypergraph Synthesis Experiment

In the Fig. 6, the hypergraph synthesis is demonstrated. The object is shown at Fig. 6(a). The laser images for the object are obtained from several views and displayed at (b). The corresponding image view hypergraphs are shown at (c).

For the first image view hypergraph (IVH), the set of vertices with marginal edges, say $M_1$ is $\{1, 2, 3, 4, 5, 6, 7, 8, 9\}$ because each of the surfaces has marginal edges and that for the second IVH, say $M_2$ is $\{2, 5, 8, 10, 12\}$. These two IVH's are synthesised into a hypergraph. By checking the vertices in second IVH delete the vertex from $M = M_1 \cup M_2$ if marginal edges of a vertex (for example the surface 2) are inner edges in the second IVH. The union M for the synthesised hypergraph is then $\{1, 3, 4, 6, 7, 9, 10, 12\}$. In Fig. 6(d) those vertices removed from M are circled. If M still contains elements, another IVH synthesis should be conducted. In this example it takes four IVH synthesis processes before M becomes empty and the complete AHR of the object is obtained. The synthesis result is shown at (e). For most of objects, the complete hypergraph can be obtained by synthesising six or less different IVH's obtained from directions: up, down, front, rear, left, and right. In some cases, (for example a front view of a cubic contains only one surface) an extra view from left-front is required if there is no common vertex for two IVHs (one from front view and the other from left view), of the object.

## VI. Conclusion

In this paper, we have presented an attributed graph synthesis method to obtain a complete representation for 3-D objects. The method is used in our vision system to construct knowledge representation for objects, synthesis of different views of the objects is implemented on a Grinnell Imaging System driven by VAX 11/750 running VMS.

The followings summarize some of the contribution of our proposed method.

(1) The use of relative structural information of the object in AHR yields a unique representation of an object which is invariant to change of object orientation, i.e. even when the position of an object is changed as captured by the range image, the synthesis result is not affected.

(2) The graph synthesis algorithm we introduced is capable of synthesizing the AHR's derived from images taken at different views of the object. to form an AHR that represents the entire object. The complete AHR's for a collection of objects to be classified are then stored in a database. More objects to be recognized can be conveniently added to the database.

Thus it is obvious that with this new synthesis method, a great variety of tasks and task environment can now be automatically modelled.

## REFERENCES

[1] Besl P.J. and R.C. Jain "Three-dimensional object recognition", *Computing Survey,*

[2] Binford, T.O., "visual Perception by Computer", IEEE Conf. on Systems and Control, Miami, Dec. 1971.

[3] Wong A.K.C. and S.W. Lu "Representation of 3-D objects by attributed hypergraphs for computer vision"., *Proc. 1983 Intern. Conf. on Systems, Man and Cybernetics*, pp. 49-53.

[4] Jackin, Tanimoto, "Oct-trees and their Use in Representation Three Dimensional Objects", CGIP, 14 pp 249-270, 1980.

[5] Berge C. *Graph and Hypergraph*, London North-Holland Mathematical Library, pp. 389-391, 1973.

[6] Requicha, A.A.G., "Representation of Rigid Solid Objects", Computer Survey, 12.4, pp437-464, 1980.

[7] Ballard D.H. and C.M.Brown *Computer Vision*, N.Y.: Prentice Hill, 1982.

[8] Voelcker, H.B., and Requicha, A.A.G., "Geometric Modelling of Mechanical Parts and Process", Computer, 10, pp48-57.

[9] Lu, S.W., A.K.C. Wong and M. Rioux "Recognition of 3-D objects in range images by attributed hypergraph monomorphism and synthesis". *Proceeding of the First IFAC Symposium on Robot Control*, Barcelona, Spain, November, pp. 389-394, 1985.

[10] Lu, S.W. and A.K.C. Wong "Recognition of 3-D scene with partially occluded objects" *Proc. of SPIE's Conference on Intelligent Robots and Computer Vision*. pp 346-354. Oct. 1986.

# RECONSTRUCTIBLE PAIRS OF INCOMPLETE
## POLYHEDRAL LINE DRAWINGS

Seiji Ishikawa and Kiyoshi Kato

Department of Computer Science
Faculty of Engineering
Kyushu Institute of Technology
Kitakyushu  804 JAPAN

*Abstract*  The present paper describes the reconstructibility
of a polyhedron from a pair of its incomplete line drawings.
A polyhedral scene is photographed by a binocular vision
system, and a pair of polyhedral line drawings are obtained
from the pictures.  These line drawings usually have some
missing edges, which gives rise to complication in their
analysis.  There are, however, cases where a polyhedron can
be reconstructed even from the incomplete line drawings.  In
the present paper, the relation between the incompleteness
of the line drawings and the reconstructibility is studied
under a certain restricted reconstruction procedure, and the
necessary and sufficient condition is given for a polyhedron
to be reconstructed from its incomplete line drawings pair.

## 1. INTRODUCTION

Polyhedral scene analysis plays an important role in computer
vision.  Among several techniques for analysing a polyhedral scene,
line drawing analysis is one of the established methods.  A line drawing of a polyhedron is obtained by processing an image of a polyhedral
scene acquired by a TV camera.  Although most of the research [1-5]
assumes completeness of the line drawing for the benefit of the analysis, an incomplete line drawing with missing edges is usually obtained
[6-8] which gives rise to complication.  In some line drawings, their
missing edges can possibly be recovered by reexamining an original
picture [9] or by taking another picture of the same scene under
different conditions [10].  In many cases, however, a missing edge can
hardly be recovered because of the small (or no) difference of

contrast between two adjacent faces. If the defect is comparatively small, some simple ways are available such as extending an incomplete edge to reconstruct its missing part [6]. The technique [11] for guessing complete shape of an incomplete line drawing by an heuristic tree search can deal with much more defective line drawings than before [6,8]. But it does not assure that the guessed line drawing truly represents the original polyhedron.

On the other hand, for the purpose of recognising three-dimensional objects, studies have been performed on reconstructing three-dimensional shape of an object from its two-dimensional images. One of the two established techniques for this is the employment of a range finder [12,13], while the other uses binocular vision where, given a pair of images of an object photographed from different view points, the object (or part of it) is reconstructed from the corre-spondence between the images. Assuming completeness of the polyhedral line drawings obtained from the left and the right image, the polyhedron can be reconstructed [14] by employing the change of the gradients of its projected edges between the line drawings. There are, however, cases where a polyhedron is reconstructed from the line drawings with some missing edges. Whether a polyhedron is recon-structed from its incomplete line drawings depends on the location of the missing edges on the line drawings. If this relation is clarified, it may contribute to the reduction of laborious efforts toward the acquisition of complete line drawings (such as realising high contrast among all the visible faces on a polyhedron), since incomplete line drawings would be sufficient for the reconstruction. However, to date no research has been done to explore this possibility.

The present paper describes the reconstructibility of a polyhedron from a pair of its incomplete line drawings obtained by binocular vision. The reconstructibility problem is first explained by some examples; the problem is then stated using a state vector, and a tree search is introduced to exhaust the incomplete line drawings pair from which a polyhedron can be reconstructed; and finally, the necessary and sufficient condition for the reconstructibility is shown.


## 2. PREPARATION

Some fundamental definitions and assumptions are given in the following.

A polyhedron is composed of a set of *faces*. A face is surrounded by a set of *edges*. A *vertex* is an intersection of edges on a polyhedron. The *boundary* of a polyhedral line drawing is a link of all the edges that discriminate the line drawing from the background. An *inner vertex* is a vertex which is not on the boundary. An edge (A face) is *visible*, if it is observable from a view point. A polyhedral line drawing is *complete*, if all the visible edges of the polyhedron exist on the line drawing. A polyhedral line drawing is *incomplete*, if any of its visible edges are missing. A polyhedron is *reconstructible*, if all the visible faces are reconstructible. A face is *reconstructible*, if the three-dimensional coordinates of all the vertices on the face are obtained. A *reconstructible* incomplete line drawings pair is a pair of incomplete line drawings from which a polyhedron can be reconstructed.

The present research assumes binocular vision under orthographic projection by which a pair of polyhedral images is obtained. The images are processed to derive a pair of polyhedral line drawings, which are probably incomplete. A reconstructible face is classified into two categories : a face reconstructed from the correspondence between the line drawings is referred to as a face based on *primary reconstruction* or simply a *primary face*, while a face reconstructed by employing already reconstructed faces as a face based on *secondary reconstruction* or a *secondary face*.

Before going into the main subject, let us have a look at how the reconstruction proceeds. Figure 1(a) shows a pair of incomplete line drawings of a polyhedron. There the following edges have correspondence between the left and the right line drawing : edges 38 and 3'8', edges 18 and 1'8', and edges 17 and 1'7'. The polyhedron is reconstructed in the following way;

1) The direction of face 1238 is derived [14], since edges 38 and 18 have correspondence. (Note that the projection is assumed to be orthographic.) Its location is determined by specifying the origin at vertex 1, for example. This results in the recovery of the three-dimensional coordinates of the vertices 2, 3 and 8. (The three-dimensional coordinates of vertex 2, for example, is recovered, since vertex 2 is on the known face 1238, and the length and the gradient of projected edge 12 are obtainable on the image.) Thus the face 1238 is reconstructed.

2) Face 18967 is reconstructed, since edges 17 and 18 have correspondence, the face passes the origin 1, and the three-dimensional coordinates of vertices 6, 7, 8 and 9 are recovered.

3) Face 3498 is reconstructed, since it passes the recovered

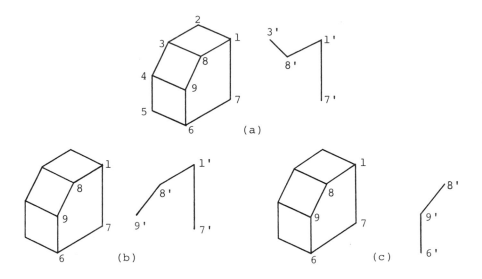

Fig.1 Incomplete line drawings pairs of a polyhedron.

vertices 3, 8 and 9, and the three-dimensional coordinates of vertex 4 is recovered.

4)   Finally, face 4569 is reconstructed, since it passes the recovered vertices 4, 6 and 9, and the three-dimensional coordinates of vertex 5 is recovered.

Among these reconstructed faces, faces 1238 and 18967 are primary faces, while faces 3498 and 4569 secondary faces.

On the other hand, a polyhedron is not reconstructed from the line drawings shown in Fig.1(b) and (c). Both the correspondence of edges 17, 18 and 89 in (b) and the correspondence of edges 69 and 89 in (c) only result in the reconstruction of face 18967.

The above argument indicates a vital aspect of the reconstructibility problem, $i.e.$, the location of corresponding edges.

The present paper analyses a complete line drawing of a polyhedron to find the condition for its reconstructibility. Therefore, in the following argument, a line drawing is supposed to mean a complete line drawing unless otherwise stated.


3. RECONSTRUCTIBLE INCOMPLETE LINE DRAWINGS PAIRS

Let us denote a line drawing of a polyhedron P by L. Let us also denote a face on L by $f_i$ ($i=1,2,\ldots,n$), an inner vertex on L by $v_j$

$(j=1,2,\ldots,m)$, and the faces meeting at vertex $v_j$ by $f_{j_k}$ $(k=1,2,\ldots,n_j)$. The sets $F$, $F_j$ and $F_i$ are defined as $F = \{f_1,f_2,\ldots,f_n\}$, $F_j = \{f_{j_1},f_{j_2},\ldots,f_{j_{n_j}}\}$, and $F_i = \{F_j|f_i \in F_j\}$, respectively. (See Fig.2 for an example.) A *state variable* $s_i$ is assigned to a face $f_i$ on L by the following rule;

$$s_i = \begin{cases} 1 \ldots & \text{face } f_i \text{ is reconstructed,} \\ 0 \ldots & \text{face } f_i \text{ is not reconstructed.} \end{cases}$$

Then, if we define a *state vector* by $s = (s_1,s_2,\ldots,s_n)$, the situation that polyhedron P is reconstructed is expressed as $s = (1,1,\ldots,1) \equiv s_0$ by the state vector.

Let us consider an inner vertex $v_i$ where $n_i$ faces meet. If arbitrary $n_i-1$ faces out of $n_i$ are reconstructed at the vertex, then the remaining face is reconstructed as well based on secondary reconstruction. By employing a state variable, this can be written in the following way;

*Proposition 1.* For $f_p \in F_j$ $(p=1,2,\ldots,n_j)$, if there exists an integer $k$ $(1 \le k \le n_j)$ such that $s_p = 1 - \delta_{pk}$, then $s_k = 1$.

Here $\delta_{ij}$ denotes Kronecker's delta.

Although a more general procedure for the secondary reconstruction could be considered, the procedure given by Proposition 1 is assumed here for the sake of simplicity.

Suppose that, given a pair of incomplete line drawings, a complete line drawing L is obtained by merging the left and the right line drawing. (We discuss this later.) The state vector $s$ of L has initially the value zero, and after primary reconstruction employing the incomplete line drawings pair, some of the faces on L are reconstructed (if any). On this stage, the state vector has a form of

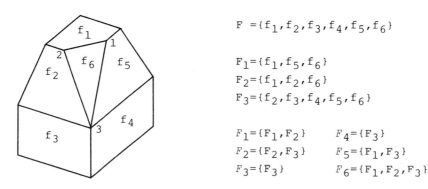

$F = \{f_1,f_2,f_3,f_4,f_5,f_6\}$

$F_1 = \{f_1,f_5,f_6\}$
$F_2 = \{f_1,f_2,f_6\}$
$F_3 = \{f_2,f_3,f_4,f_5,f_6\}$

$F_1 = \{F_1,F_2\}$ $\quad F_4 = \{F_3\}$
$F_2 = \{F_2,F_3\}$ $\quad F_5 = \{F_1,F_3\}$
$F_3 = \{F_3\}$ $\quad F_6 = \{F_1,F_2,F_3\}$

Fig.2 Representation of a polyhedral line drawing.

$ = (1,0,0,1,...,0,1,1)$ where the number of nonzero components is equal to that of the primary faces on L. Whether a polyhedron is reconstructed from the incomplete line drawings pair depends on if $ reaches the final state $_0$ after the iterative application of Proposition 1 to $. In order to derive the state vectors that can reach $_0$, we apply the following procedure which is the reverse process of Proposition 1 to the final state $_0$ and its descendants. This is performed systematically by employing a tree search.

_Procedure 1._ For an arbitrary $f_i(\in F)$ such that $s_i = 1$, if there exists $F_j(\in F_i)$ such that, for all $f_p(\in F_j)$, $s_p = 1$, let $s_i = 0$.

The above procedure can be formulated as

$$s_i : = s_i \left(1 - \max_{F_j \in F_i} \left\{ \left[ \frac{1}{n_j} \cdot \sum_{f_p \in F_j} s_p \right] \right\} \right) \equiv h(s_i) \; ,$$

where $n_j$ denotes the number of the elements of $F_j$, and $[x]$ denotes the largest integer not more than $x$.

In the tree search, the start node is $_0$ whose size is defined by a given line drawing L, and each node on the tree corresponds to a state vector $. Node $ is expanded by the following procedure;

_Procedure 2._
```
    begin
      for i: = 1 to n do
        begin
          u: = h(s_i);
          if u < > s_i then
            let (s_1,...,s_{i-1},u,s_{i+1},...,s_n) be a successor
        end
    end.
```

Before going into the tree search algorithm, a relation between two vectors is defined.

_Definition._ For arbitrary real-valued vectors $x = (x_1, x_2, ..., x_n)$ and $y = (y_1, y_2, ..., y_n)$, $x \geq y$ if $x_i \geq y_i$ $(i=1,2,...,n)$.

_Algorithm of the tree search._
1) Let the lists OPEN, CLOSED and RESULT be emptied.
2) Put the start node $_0$ on OPEN.
3) If OPEN is empty, then go to 7).
4) Select the first node $ on OPEN and expand it by Procedure 2. If $ is expanded, put all the successors last on OPEN, and put $ on CLOSED.

5)   Unless $ is expanded: if there exists $' on RESULT such that
     $ ≥ $', put $ on CLOSED; if there exists $' on RESULT such that
     $ < $', replace $' by $ on RESULT and put $' on CLOSED; otherwise
     put $ on RESULT.

6)   Go to 3).

7)   Let the nodes on RESULT be the solutions.

This tree search algorithm is a breadth-first search.   The tree
search terminates after a finite number of iteration, since a state
vector has a finite number of components.   A tree T is yielded by
applying the algorithm to the state vector of a line drawing L.   Every
node on T corresponds to a reconstructible pair of incomplete line
drawings, since it is able to backtrack to $_0 on T.   Conversely, every
reconstructible incomplete line drawings pair has its state vector
after primary reconstruction on T, since T is exhaustive.   Thus we
have the following proposition;

*Proposition 2.*   A polyhedron is reconstructible from an incomplete line
drawings pair, if, and only if, its state vector exists on T.

Our attention is, however, focused on the end nodes on the list
RESULT.   These end nodes are referred to as *irreducible state vectors*,
while the other nodes not on RESULT as *reducible state vectors*.   An
example of a searched tree and the list RESULT is given in Fig.3(a).
Figure 3(b) shows a reconstructible pair of incomplete line drawings
corresponding to one of the irreducible state vectors in (a).

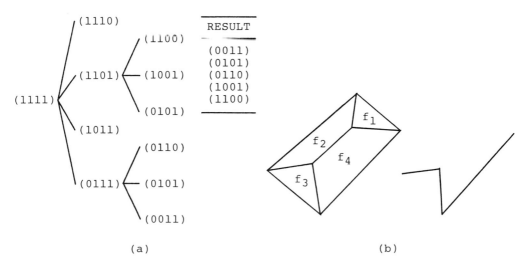

(a)                                        (b)

Fig.3 An example of the searched tree and a reconstructible pair of
      incomplete line drawings corresponding to the irreducible state
      vector (0011).

## 4. THE CONDITION FOR THE RECONSTRUCTIBILITY

A complete line drawing L of a polyhedron P produces a tree T by the search algorithm. Each node on T corresponds to a state vector of a reconstructible pair of incomplete line drawings. We have the following proposition with respect to the state vectors on T;

*Proposition 3.* If a state vector $s_i$ is an ancestor of a state vector $s_j$ on T, $s_i \geq s_j$ holds.

*Proof.* If we denote the state vector obtained from applying Procedure 1 to an arbitrary state vector $s$ by $t$, $s \geq t$ holds. As $s_i$ is an ancestor of $s_j$, the iterative application of Procedure 1 to $s_i$ leads to $s_j$. Therefore $s_i \geq s_j$ is concluded. (Q.E.D.)

Note that the equality is included in Proposition 3.

*Proposition 4.* Let us denote the state vectors of two incomplete line drawings pairs which give the same line drawing L by $s_i$ and $s_j$, respectively. If a polyhedron is reconstructible from the line drawings pair with $s_j$, and $s_i \geq s_j$ holds, then a polyhedron is reconstructible as well from the line drawings pair with $s_i$.

*Proof.* Since a polyhedron can be reconstructed from the incomplete line drawings pair with $s_j$, by Proposition 2, state vector $s_j$ exists on the tree T which is derived from L. This means that there is a path from $s_j$ to the start node $s_0$ on T, and the path indicates the order Proposition 1 is applied to the components of $s_j$. The application of Proposition 1 in this order to the components of $s_i$ results in $s_0$, since each zero component of $s_i$ changes to unity when the corresponding component of $s_j$ (which is zero because $s_i \geq s_j$) receives the alteration. Therefore a polyhedron is reconstructible from the incomplete line drawings pair with $s_i$. (Q.E.D.)

Let us denote the state vector of an incomplete line drawings pair which gives a complete line drawing L of a polyhedron P by $s$, and the tree obtained from L by T. By employing Proposition 2, 3 and 4, we have finally the following theorem which gives the condition for the reconstructibility.

*Theorem.* A polyhedron P is reconstructible, if, and only if, there exists an irreducible state vector $s^{irr}$ on T such that $s \geq s^{irr}$.

*Proof.* If P is reconstructible, the state vector $s$ exists on T by Proposition 2. Suppose downward tracking from $s$ leads to an end node $s'$ on T. Then $s \geq s'$ holds by Proposition 3. If $s'$ is an irreducible state vector $s^{irr}$, we have $s \geq s^{irr}$: Unless $s'$ is an irreducible state vector, there exists $s^{irr}$ on RESULT such that $s' \geq s^{irr}$ by step 5) of the tree search algorithm. Hence $s \geq s' \geq s^{irr}$.

Conversely, if there exists an irreducible state vector $s^{irr}$ on T such that $s \geq s^{irr}$, since P is reconstructible from an incomplete line drawings pair with $s^{irr}$, P is reconstructible from an incomplete line drawings pair with $s$ as well by Proposition 4.          (Q.E.D.)

As seen in Theorem, an irreducible state vector plays an important role in the reconstructibility of a polyhedron.

## 5. DISCUSSION

For automating the judgment of the reconstructibility, sets of the irreducible state vectors need to be kept in a dictionary for comparison. Given a pair of incomplete line drawings of a polyhedron, its state vector $s$ is compared with those irreducible state vectors to find $s^{irr}$ which satisfies the relation $s \geq s^{irr}$. This is, however, unlikely to be practical, since the number of irreducible state vectors in the dictionary might explode. Indeed, a set of irreducible state vectors is defined by each line drawing of a polyhedron whose shape could be arbitrary. For the practical use of the theorem, the variety of polyhedra should be limited [6] or the type of a polyhedron should be restricted [7]. If it is confined to a trihedral polyhedron, a simple theorem [15] is available instead of employing a set of irreducible state vectors.

It is assumed that union of the left and the right incomplete line drawing gives a complete line drawing of a polyhedron. This assumption is necessary for excluding shape guessing. Strictly speaking, in case that a polyhedron is not limited in kind, it can not be judged if the line drawing obtained by the union is complete, since it is unknown yet which polyhedron it represents. One way of settling this difficulty is to regard a line drawing as complete, if it does not contain any geometrical inconsistencies on it.

It should be noted that an edge on an incomplete line drawings pair can be partially missing, if only the union of the line drawings is complete.

In the present paper, restriction is given to the reconstruction procedure for simplicity. This procedure needs to be generalised. The present technique for analysing the reconstructibility problem could also be applicable to the general reconstruction case.

## 6. CONCLUSION

The reconstructibility of a polyhedron from a pair of incomplete line drawings was studied. Union of the incomplete line drawings was assumed to give a complete line drawing of the polyhedron, and a set of irreducible state vectors was obtained from the complete line drawing by a tree search. By employing these irreducible state vectors, a theorem was shown giving the neccessary and sufficient condition for the reconstructibility. Generalisation of the reconstruction procedure remains to be investigated.

## REFERENCES

[1] Guzman, A.:"Decomposition of a visual scene into three-dimensional bodies", 1968 Fall Joint Comput. Conf., 291-304 (1968).

[2] Huffman, D.A.:"Logical analysis of pictures of polyhedra", AI Group Technical Note No.6, SRI Project 7494 (1969).

[3] Winston, P.H.:"Learning structural descriptions from examples", The Psychology of Computer Vision (P.H. Winston Ed.), 157-209, McGraw-Hill (1975).

[4] Clowes, M.B.:"On seeing things", Artificial Intelligence, 2, 79-116 (1970).

[5] Waltz, D.L.:"Generating semantic descriptions from drawings of scenes with shadows", AI TR-271, MIT AI Lab. (1972).

[6] Falk, G.:"Interpretation of imperfect line data as a three-dimensional scene", Artificial Intelligence, 3, 101-144 (1972).

[7] Grape, G.R.:"Model based (intermediate-level) computer vision", AI Memo No.201, Stanford Univ. (1973).

[8] Shapira, R. and Freeman, H.:"Computer description of bodies bounded by quadric surfaces from a set of imperfect projections", IEEE Trans. Comput., C-27, 841-854 (1978).

[9] Tenenbaum, J.M.:"Accomodation in computer vision", Comput. Sci. Dept. Report No.CS182, Stanford Univ. (1970).

[10] Sobel, I.:"Camera models and machine perception", AI Memo No.121, Stanford Univ. (1970).

[11] Ishikawa, S.:"Guessing shape of a complete line drawing of a polyhedron using an heuristic tree search", Trans. Inst. Electron. Commun. Engineers Japan, J68-D, 2, 185-192 (1985).

[12] Shirai, Y.:"Recognition of polyhedrons with a range finder", Pattern Recognition, 4, 243-250 (1972).

[13] Agin, G.J. and Binford, T.O.:"Computer description of curved objects", IEEE Trans. Comput., C-25, 439-449 (1976).

[14] Ishikawa, S.:"Reconstructing faces on a polyhedron from apparent gradients of edges", Comput. Vision, Graphics, Image Process., 28, 3, 289-302 (1984).

[15] Ishikawa, S. and Kato, K.:"Reconstructibility of a trihedral polyhedron from a pair of incomplete line drawings", Trans. Inst. Electron. Inform. Commun. Engineers Japan. (to appear)

# FRACTAL CURVE AND ATTRIBUTE GRAMMAR

Fu-liang Weng, Qi Lu and Li-de Wu
Department of Computer Science
Fudan University
Qiang Gu
Shanghai Software Laboratory
Shanghai, P.R.China

## 1. INTRODUCTION

Like the winding coastlines, jumbled mountains and changeful clouds, many objects in the natural world have complicated and rough shape. However classical geometry was based on the property of smoothness and all the objects to be treated are assumed to have smooth shape. Similarly, image models also require the precondition of smoothness, usually more restrictive ones, such as linear or quardric function. In fact such descriptions are not precise. Although there is no conflict between the requirement of smoothness and description in the process of measuring or Gaussian filtering in the human visual system, we don't know exactly the degree of smoothness applied. So the assumption of smoothness seems questionable.

In recent years, a new branch of geometry, fractal geometry has been developed to deal with such problems. It treats more naturally shaped objects. As Mandelbrot, the founder of the new discipline said, fractal geometry is a powerful tool for describing many physical phenomena, and it may hopefully lead to new development in the field of image processing and pattern recognition.

Pentland [1984] proposed a method for generating image models on the basis of fractals, by which image can be described. In this paper, attribute grammar is exploited to describe a subclass of fractal curves, the non-self-cross fractal curves. The fractal curve generation and recognition algorithms are developed, which are invariant to the transform operations scale, rotation and translation. Information such as the length of the curve and the area enclosed by the curve can easily be calculated due to the advantage of attribute grammar.


## 2. FRACTAL CURVE AND ATTRIBUTE GRAMMAR

Fractal curves may be considerded not well defined according to the view of classical geometry. But there is regurality in these curves despite their uneven shapes because their generation is in the constructing-pattern, which provides the foundation for description by attribute grammar.

Definition of fractal curves:

A fractal curve model is a tuple $O = (N, r, \{\alpha_i\}_0^{N-1})$, where N is a natural number, r is a positive real number, $0 \leqslant \alpha_i < 2\pi$, $0 \leqslant i < N-1$ are the angles (see Fig. 1). If there is a sequence of points $\{n_i\}_0^N$ or a sequence of line segments $\{\overline{n_{i-1} n_i}\}_1^N$ such that
    for i = 0, 1, ... , N-1,
$$\|n_i - n_{i+1}\| / \|n_0 - n_N\| = r,$$
    and $(n_i - n_{i-1}, n_{i+1} - n_i) = \cos\alpha_i$, with $n_{-1} = n_N$ ,    (1)
then O is called consistent and $\{n_i\}_0^N$ is called to belong to or satisfy model O. In this paper only consistent fractal curve models are considered and for simplicity the consistent fractal model will be called fractal model later on.

It is easy to see that all the possible sequences $\{n_i'\}_0^N$ satisfying the model are the same in the sense of the transform operations -- scale, rotaion and translation. That is to say, any two sequences $\{a_i\}_0^N$ and $\{b_i\}_0^N$ satisfying the same model can be related in the form:
$$a_i = T * R * S(b_i),    i = 0, ... , N,    (2)$$
where S, R and T are the scale, rotation and translation operators, respectively. Reversely, if $\{b_i\}_0^N$ belongs to the model O, $\{a_i\}_0^N$ satisfies (2) then $\{a_i\}_0^N$ also belongs to model O.

Given fractal curve model $O = (N, r, \{\alpha_i\}_0^{N-1})$ and any two different points $(n_0, n_N)$, a sequence of points $\{n_i\}_0^N$ can be generated such that they satisfy (1). The piecewise linear curve $\overline{n_0 n_1} \cup \overline{n_1 n_2} \cup ... \cup \overline{n_{N-1} n_N}$ will be denoted as $X_1(n_0, n_N)$.

Notice that if the fractal model is consistent, then there is only a unique sequence which satisfies (1) and its start and end points are $n_0$, $n_N$, respectively.

Given ($n_0$, $n_N$), fractal curve is defined as follows:

$$X_1(n_0, n_N)$$

$$X_2(n_0, n_N) = \overset{N-1}{\underset{i=0}{U}} X_1(n_i, n_{i+1})$$

. . . . . . . . . . . . . . . . . . . . . .

$$X_m(n_0, n_N) = \underset{i-1}{U} X_{m-1}(n_i, n_{i+1})$$

. . . . . . . . . . . . . . . . . . . . . .

$$X = \lim_{m \to \infty} X_m(n_0, n_N) \qquad (3)$$

The curve X above is called fractal curve belonging to fractal model $O = (N, r, \{\alpha_i\}_0^{N-1})$ with endpoints $n_0$ and $n_N$ (see Fig 1.).

The generation of n can be recursively expressed as:

$$n1 = rR(\alpha_0) * (n_0 - n_N) + n_0$$
$$n_{i+1} = R(\alpha_i) * (n_i - n_{i-1}) + n_i, \quad i=0, 1, \ldots, N-1. \quad (4)$$

where $R(\beta)$ is a matrix .

$$R(\beta) = \begin{pmatrix} \cos\beta & , & \sin\beta \\ -\sin\beta & , & \cos\beta \end{pmatrix} \qquad \text{and} \quad n_{-1} = n_N .$$

The recursive property of fractal curve makes it possible that it can be expressed by using syntactic method.

Given the above defintion, (3) and (4), we can offer the attribute grammar description.

The attribute grammar G is a five-tuple ($V_N$, $V_T$, $V_{attr}$, P, S), where $V_N$ is the set of non-terminal symbols, $V_N = \{A_1, \ldots, A_N, S\}$, $V_T$ is the set of terminal symbols, $V_T = \{a_1, a_2, \ldots, a_N\}$, S is the set of the starting symbols, which have no ancestor, $S = \{s\}$, and the set of productions P is given as follows:

$$
\begin{aligned}
&(0) \quad S ==> A_1 A_2 \ldots A_N \; . \\
&(1.1) \quad A_1 ==> A_1 A_2 \ldots A_N \; . \\
&(1.2) \quad A_1 ==> a_1 \; . \\
&\qquad \ldots \ldots \ldots \ldots \\
&(N.1) \quad A_N ==> A_1 A_2 \ldots A_N \; . \\
&(N.2) \quad A_N ==> a_N \; .
\end{aligned}
\qquad (5)
$$

As for the attribute declaration set $V_{attr}$, each $A_i$ and $a_i$ has an inherited attribute $A_i$.vector and $a_i$.vector, respectively, and $X.vector = \begin{pmatrix} X.vector/s \\ X.vector/e \end{pmatrix}$, where X.vector/s and X.vector/e are the start point and the end point, respectively. S has an exogenous attribute S.vector. The semantic function of each production can be described as:

$$
(0) \quad A'_j . vector/s = \begin{cases} S.vector/s & j = 1 \\ A'_{j-1}.vector/e & 1 < j <= N \end{cases}
$$

$$
A'_j . vector/e = \begin{cases} rR(\alpha_0)*(A'_i.vector/s - A'_0.vector/s) + A'_i.vecotr/s & j = 1 \\ R(\alpha_{j-1})*(A'_j.vector/s - A'_{j-1}.vector/s) + A'_j.vector/s & 1 < j < N \\ S.vector/e & j = N \end{cases}
$$

$$
(i.1) \quad A'_j . vector/s = \begin{cases} A_i.vector/s & j = 1 \\ A'_{j-1}.vector/e & 1 < j <= N \end{cases}
$$

$$
A'_j . vector/e = \begin{cases} R(\alpha_{j-1})*(A'_j.vector/s - A'_{j-1}.vector/s) + A'_j.vector/s & 1 <= j <= N-1 \\ A_j.vector/e & j = N \end{cases}
$$

$(i.2) \quad a_i.vector = A_i.vector$

where $A'_j$ means the nonterminal $A_j$ on the right side of production.

Informly speaking, each nonterminal symbol corresponds a piecewise linear curve and each terminal symbol a line segment. Their attributes are the coordinates of the start and end points.

Note that the above formule comes from (4). In the following discussion, the derivation of syntax tree is done level by level to ensure that the resulted tree is a N-ary full tree. The termination of the derivation is controled by the attribute value of the nonterminals, which is dependent on specific problems.

It is easy to see that for any syntax tree T, if any node R is assigned an attribute value VAL, then attribute value of every other node can be determined by propagating VAL at node R throughtout the tree. We use EVALU(T,R,VAL) to denote such an evaluation procedure.

It should be declared that in production rules, the function of the $a_i$ is not limited to be primitive, but extended to the control of termination.

### 3. GENERATION AND RECOGNITION OF FRACTAL CURVE

Three problems are to be discussed in this section. The first one is how to generate fractal curve. The second and third ones are recognition of a complete and partial fractal curve respectively. It's necessary to make the following assumptions. Only $X_k(n_0, n_N)$, $k \leqslant K$, where K is a fixed number, is under consideration, for we cannot obtain infinitely accurate data due to the limitation of precision of the measuring instrument. All the fractal curves considered are non-self-crossing. Since a good variety of natural curves such as coastline have the property of being non-self-crossing, what has been discussed in the paper is still widely applicable. The control strategy is given in this section, by which the above three problems can be completely solved.

### 3.1 THE GENERATION OF FRACTAL CURVE

Fractal curve have been sucessfully generated to produce natural pictures in Norton [1982], therefore it has a wide application in computer graphics.

Here the production $A_i ==> a_i$ in (5) is used solely to control the levels of fractal curve, i.e., the levels of derivation of the corresponding syntax tree. In other words, production $A_i ==> a_i$ is deliberately introduced to control the termination of the fractal curve generation. Given fractal model $(N, r, \{\alpha_i\}_0^{N-1})$ the process of generation is simply to derive a full tree T according to the syntax of attribute grammar, at the same time the attributes are evaluated through EVALU(T,ROOT(T),$(n_0,n_N)$)), where $(n_0, n_N)$ is the attribute at the node ROOT(T).It means that we only need to input some parameters to obtain the corresponding curve, so the technique is easy to apply (see Fig. 2, Fig. 3 and Fig. 4).

## 3.2 THE RECOGNITION OF FULL FRACTAL CURVE

The problem can be expressed as:

Given a fractal model $(N, r, \{\alpha_i\}_0^{N-1})$, and a sequence of points P(0), ..., P(M), where M=N (L<=K), it should be decided whether the piecewise linear curve with {P(i)} as its vertices is a fractal curve of the given model.

The control procedure is rather simple:

(1) Establish a L-level full synatx tree T according to the grammar of the model.

(2) Let the left most leaf node be denoted as LMLN, evaluate the attributes of T through EVALU(T, LMLN, (P(0), P(1))) according to the model.

(3) Denote the list of all the leaf node of T from left to right as $L_1$, $L_2$,..., $L_M$. If match({$L_i$.vector} , {(P(i-1), P(i))} ) is true, then return "success" else "fail", where the function match is to see whether the two arguments are almost the same by using the similarity measure in which the distance may be $\| \cdot \|_1$, $\| \cdot \|_2$, and $\| \cdot \|_\infty$, etc.

## 3.3 THE RECOGNOTION OF PARTIAL FRACTAL CURVE

This task is different from Sect.3.2. Here $M \neq N^L$ for the sequence of points P(0), ..., P(M). According to the assumptions mentioned above, the derivation level of fractal curve is supposed not to exceed a fixed number K. The non-self-cross property assures that fractal curve can be expressed in terms of ordered points or ordered line segments, which makes it possible to check if these ordered line segments can match a part of a fractal curve.

In the match algorithm, two nodes of the current syntax tree T are of importance. One is the start node S and the other is the current node C expressed by the paths from ROOT(T) to themselves. The two paths are in the form of sequence of numbers $S-(s_1, s_2, \ldots, s_k)$ and $C=(c_1, c_2, \ldots, c_k)$, where $s_i$ and $c_i$ refer to the node on ith level of T which is the s th and c th son of their father respectively. The initial value of S and C are (1), and they will be expanded during the matching process. We use N(S) and N(C) to indicate the specific node in T expressed by S and C respectively. It's easy to see that T can be uniquely determined by S and C.

For brevity and clearity, a flowchart is adopted to describe the general idea of the recognition algorithm(see Fig. 5 and Fig. 6).

In Fig. 5, $\{N_T(j)\}$ is a sequence of points corresponding to the attributes of the leaf node sequence from N(S) to N(C). And the procedure nearest_non_failure_right_brother(S) = $\min$(node | node = right_brother$^n$(S), n >= 1 & $(tail^j(node) \notin failureset, 1<=i<=D))$, and $tail^i(node)=(n_{k-i+1}, \ldots, n_k)$ and D=k, if node=$(n_1, \ldots, n_k)$. The procedure right_brother is in fig.6, where S/T means the part of S in T , incr is the marker of whether S has been just expanded: incr = 1, yes; incr = 0, no.

## ACKNOWLEDGEMENT

The authors wish to thank Prof. Pavlidis for his lecture on fractals.

## REFERENCES

1.L.V.Gool et al, "Survey: Texture Analysis Anno 1983", CVGIP 29, No.3 NY, 1985.

2.B.B.Mandelbrot, "Fractals: Form, Chance and Dimension", Freeman, San Fransisco, CA, 1977.

3.A.Norton, "Generation and Display of Geometric Fractals in 3-D", Computer Graphics, Vol.16, No.3, NY, 1982.

4.A.Pentland, "Fractal-based Description of Natural Scenes", IEEE Trans. on PAMI, Vol.6, No.6, Washington DC, 1984.

574

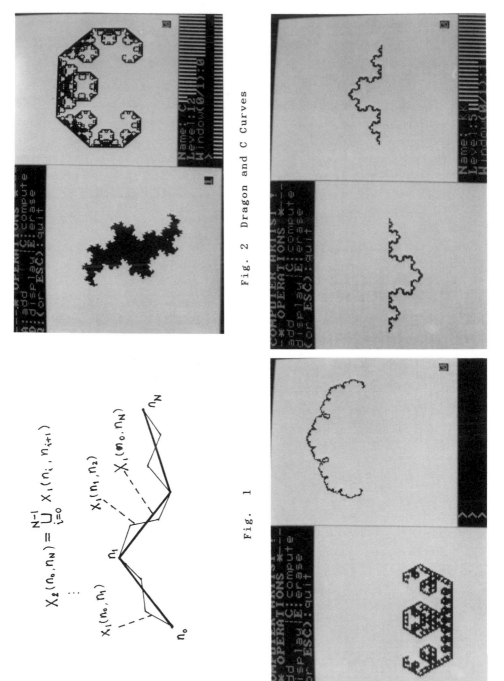

$$X_2(n_0, n_N) = \bigcup_{i=0}^{N-1} X_1(n_i, n_{i+1})$$

Fig. 1

Fig. 2   Dragon and C Curves

Fig. 3   W and G Curves

Fig. 4   Koch Curves

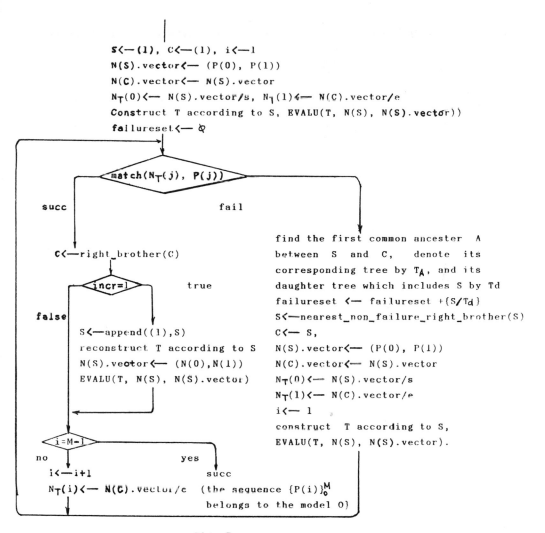

Fig. 5

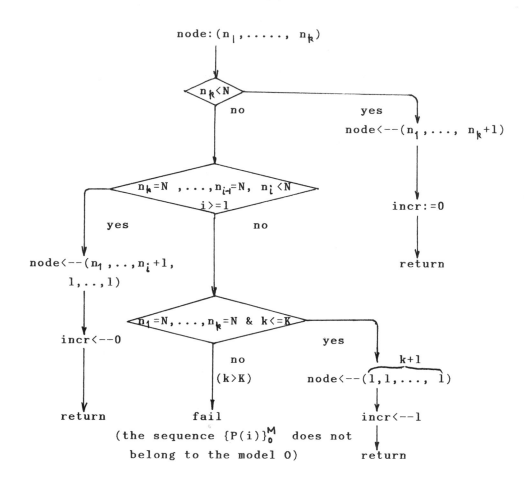

Fig. 6

# FAST AND RELIABLE IMAGE ENHANCEMENT USING FUZZY RELAXATION TECHNIQUE

Hua Li and Hyun S. Yang

Dept. of Electrical and Computer Engineering
University of Iowa
Iowa City, IA 52242, U.S.A.

## Abstract

In this paper, we propose a fuzzy relaxation technique that exploits fuzzy membership functions for gray level transformation. This technique enhances image contrast very effectively and expeditiously; different order of fuzzy membership functions and different rank statistics are tried to improve the enhancement speed and quality, respectively. We provide the proof of the convergence of our relaxation algorithm, and illustrate some experimental results.

## 1. Introduction

Since its emergence in 1965, fuzzy set theory has received a lot of attention from researchers in many different scientific fields; over 4,000 papers have been published in relation to both theoretical or applied aspects of fuzzy set theory [5]. Some of them deal with applications of fuzzy set theory for high and/or low level image analysis [2,3,6,7,8,9,10].

Fuzzy set theory could be distinguished from conventional mathematics in the sense that it has no well defined boundaries; the transition between full membership and no membership is gradual [5]. However, since it is a generalization of set theory, definitions, theorems, and proofs for fuzzy set theory always hold for non-fuzzy set theory [4].

It is generally believed that image processing bears some fuzziness in nature due to the following factors.

[1] Information being lost while three dimensional shape or scene is projected into two dimensional image.

[2] The lack of the quantitative measurement of image quality. (One of the annoying problems in image processing is how to define the quality of a given image. The judgement is subjective since it is based on visual perception.)

[3] Ambiguity and vagueness in some definitions. (For instance, there is no crisp boundary between edges and nonedges or between homogeneous regions and nonhomogeneous regions.)

[4] Ambiguity and vagueness in interpreting the result generated by low level image processing.

Using the fuzzy set theory, we might handle these uncertainties. In what follows, in Section 2, we will briefly review the definition of an image in terms of fuzzy set theory. In Section 3, we will propose a fuzzy relaxation technique that exploits S fuzzy membership functions; we provide the proof of the convergence of the proposed relaxation algorithm. In Section 4, we will then show some experimental results on image enhancement based on this technique.

## 2. Definition of Image by Fuzzy Set Theory

As described in [8], an image can be defined in terms of fuzzy set theory as follows: for an M by N image X with L number of gray levels ranging 0 to L-1, each pixel can be considered as a fuzzy singleton whose membership function ranges from 0 to 1. Thus

$$X = \bigcup_{i=1}^{M} \bigcup_{j=1}^{N} P_{ij}/x_{ij}$$

where $P_{ij}$ / $x_{ij}$ is defined as a fuzzy membership function associated with the variable $x_{ij}$. Therefore an image X can be analyzed by fuzzy mathematics. For more detail as to this definition, [3] and [8] are referred.

## 3. Fuzzy Relaxation Algorithm

Relaxation is a general computational technique where computations are iterated until certain parameter measurements converge to a set of values. In this section, we propose a relaxation algorithm that is based on a fuzzy membership function and exploits image histogram as a parameter; at each iteration, image histogram is modified by a fuzzy membership function. Image enhancement can be achieved with a few iterations, and the image could be finally binarized if the iteration continues until convergence. This technique provides a way to handle the uncertainty of image histogram, and enhances image faster and more reliably. In addition, since we adopt sub-region process, it is possible to be executed in parallel.

First, a given image X is divided into sub-regions $X_i$, where i = 1,2,...,N. Each subregion of the image can then be characterized by the different rank statistics such as minimum, maximum, standard deviation, mean, mode, and median. We design this algorithm in such a way that it changes the pixel values into smaller ones if they are near the local minimum or changes them into larger ones if they are near the local maximum. To deal with noisy images, one might choose the local minimum and maximum differently. For example, the gray levels of 10% and 90% of the local maximum can replace the local minimum and the local maximum, respectively; or gray levels of two times standard deviation smaller and greater than the mean might be used also. To accomplish this, the S membership function, which is one of the two standard fuzzy membership functions [8], has been used as a transformation function (Fig. 1). Note that, after transformation, the gray levels closer to the parameter $a$ becomes smaller, while the gray levels closer to the parameter $c$ becomes larger due to the non-linearity of the fuzzy membership function. Higher order functions can expedite this process since their slopes become stepper.

The entire procedure of the algorithm can be described as follows:

[1]  Partition the image into subregion.

[2]  Choose proper rank statistics according to the given image properties.

[3]  On each sub-region compute the rank statistics; in other words, determine a, b, and c.

[4]  Transform the gray levels using fuzzy membership function characterized by parameters determined in step [2].

[5]  Scale fuzzy membership into the gray levels.

[6]  Go back to step [3] and repeat until the image is sufficiently well enhanced.

We define the fuzzy membership function $S(x;a,b,c)$ in such a way that the parameter b can be any value between a and c:

$$S(x;a,b,c) = \begin{cases} 0 & \text{if } x \leq a \\ S_1 & \text{if } a < x \leq b \\ S_2 & \text{if } b < x \leq c \\ 1 & x > c \end{cases}$$

where

$$S_1(x;a,b,c) = \frac{(x-a)^2}{K_1}$$

$$S_2(x;a,b,c) = 1 - \frac{(x-c)^2}{K_2}$$

$$K_1 = (b-a)(c-a)$$

$$K_2 = (c-b)(c-a)$$

The parameters $K_1$ and $K_2$ are determined by solving the following equations:

$$\begin{cases} S_1(x;a,b,c) = 0 & \text{if } x = a \\ \frac{d}{dx} S_1(x;a,b,c) = 0 & \text{if } x = a \\ S_1(x;a,b,c) = S_2(x;a,b,c) & \text{if } x = b \\ \frac{d}{dx} S_1(x;a,b,c) = \frac{d}{dx} S_2(x;a,b,c) & \text{if } x = b \\ S_2(x;a,b,c) = 1 & \text{if } x = c \\ \frac{d}{dx} S_2(x;a,b,c) = 0 & \text{if } x = c \end{cases}$$

These equations satisfy the following conditions: (1) the low part of S function $(S_1)$ should pass through point a and also its first derivative at a should be zero; (2) The upper part of S function $(S_2)$ should pass through the point c and also its first derivative at c should be zero; (3) $S_1$ and $S_2$ should meet at point b and their first derivatives at b should be equal.

This membership function has been chosen since it has a desirable nonlinear property for our purpose. Similarly, we can define the third order S fuzzy membership functions.

$$S_1(x;a,b,c)=\frac{(x-a)^3}{K_1}$$

$$S_2(x;a,b,c)=1+\frac{(x-c)^3}{K_2}$$

with

$$K_1=(b-a)^2(c-a)$$
$$K_2=(c-b)^2(c-a)$$

the parameter K's can be determined following the similar conditions used for the 2nd order function; note that at a and c, the second derivatives must be zero, and at b, the 2nd order derivatives of $S_1$ and $S_2$ must be identical.

$$\begin{cases} \dfrac{d^2}{dx^2}S_1(x;a,b,c)=0 & \text{if } x=a \\[2mm] \dfrac{d^2}{dx^2}S_1(x;a,b,c)=\dfrac{d^2}{dx^2}S_2(x;a,b,c) & \text{if } x=b \\[2mm] \dfrac{d^2}{dx^2}S_2(x;a,b,c)=0 & \text{if } x=c \end{cases}$$

At each iteration, the fuzzy membership is modified as

$$P'_{ij} = \begin{cases} S_1(P_{ij}) & \text{if } a \leq cP_{ij} < b \\ S_2(P_{ij}) & \text{if } b \leq cP_{ij} < c \end{cases}$$

New pixel values are computed using this function S(x;a,b,c).

Convergence of histogram into bimodal using the 2nd order S fuzzy membership function can be proved as follows.

Case 1: When the transformation is defined by the function $S_1$.
Given

$$\mu_i(x_i)=\frac{(x_i-a)^2}{K_{1i}}$$

$$x_{i+1}=\mu_i(x_i)c$$

where

$$a \leq x_i \leq b,$$

and

$$0 \leq \mu_i(x_i) \leq 1$$

then after scaling, we have $c\mu_i(x_i)$, to show convergence, one needs to show:

$$x_{i+1} < x_i$$

or

$$\frac{c(x_i-a)^2}{(c-a)(b-a)} < x_i$$

or

$$F(x_i) = c(x_i-a)^2 - x_i(c-a)(b-a) < 0$$

It is not difficult to show this parabolic function has the following properties:

$$F(a) < 0$$
$$F(b) < 0$$

and the extremum

$$F_{min}(\frac{(c-a)(b-a)}{2c} + a) < 0$$

therefore

$$x_{i+1} < x_i$$

**Case 2:** When the transformation is defined by the function $S_2$. Following the similar way as we did in Case 1, it can be shown that

$$x_{i+1} > x_i$$

The proof of convergence for the higher order functions can be done similarly.

In Fig. 2a and b are shown examples of the convergence of pixel values in 3 X 3 region using the second order and the third order membership functions. Note that pixel values converge faster by the third order function.

## 4. Experimental Results

Two 128 X 128 gray tone images with 256 gray levels were chosen to test the algorithm. Each image was divided into 16 sub-regions of size 32 X 32 and each sub-region overlaps 2 pixels with its neighboring sub-regions. In each subregion, a fuzzy relaxation was performed to enhance the contrast. In Figs. 3a and b are shown enhanced images using the second order S fuzzy membership function; in Figs. 4a and b are illustrated enhanced images using the third order S fuzzy membership function. Note that dark part of the image becomes darker while bright part becomes brighter, implying that the contrast is well enhanced.

## 5. Concluding Remarks

In this paper, a fuzzy relaxation algorithm based on the second and higher order S fuzzy membership functions was proposed for the purpose of image enhancement; we also provided the proof of the convergence of this relaxation algorithm. In the future, we would like to compare the performance of the fuzzy relaxation technique with that of the probabilistic relaxation technique.

## 6. References

[1] A. Barr and E. Feigenbaum, Handbook of Artificial Intelligence, Vol. 3, William Kaufmann, Inc., 1982.

[2] V. Goetcherian, "From Binary to Gray Tone Image Processing Using Fuzzy Logic Concepts," **Pattern Recognition,** Vol. 12, pp. 7-15, 1980.

[3] T. L. Huntsberger et. al., "Interactive Fuzzy Image Segmentation," **Pattern Recognition,** Vol. 18, No. 2, pp. 131-138, 1985.

[4] A. Kandel, Fuzzy Mathematical Techniques with Applications, Addision-Wesley, 1986.

[5] A. Kaufmann and M. Gupta, Introduction to fuzzy Arithmetic, Van Nonstrand Reinhold Co. Inc., 1985.

[6] Y. Nakagawa and A. Rosenfeld, "A Note on the Use of Local Min and Max Operations in Digital Picture Processing," **IEEE SMC-8,** Vol. 11, pp. 632-635, 1978.

[7] Y. Nakagawa and A. Rosenfeld, "Some Experiments On Variable Thresholding," **Pattern Recognition,** Vol. 11, pp. 191-204, 1979.

[8] K. Pal and Robert A. King, "On Edge Detection of X-ray Images Using Fuzzy Set," **IEEE PAMI-5,** No. 1, pp. 69-77, 1983.

[9] A. Rosenfeld, "The Fuzzy Geometry of Image Subsets," **Pattern Recognition,** Vol. 2, pp. 311-317, 1984.

[10] L. Vanderheydt, F. Dom, et. al., "Two Dimensional Shape Decomposition Using Fuzzy Set Theory Applied to Automated Chromosome Analysis," **Pattern Recognition,** Vol. 13, PP. 147-157, 1981. [11] W. K. Pratt: Digital Image Processing, Part 4, John Wiley & Sons, 1978.

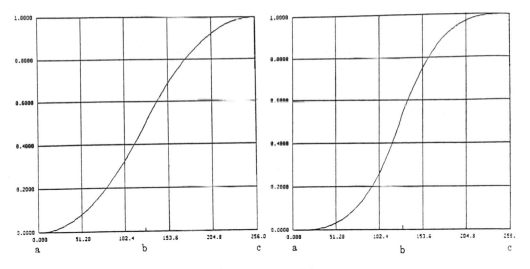

(a) the second order membership function　　　　(b) the third order membership function

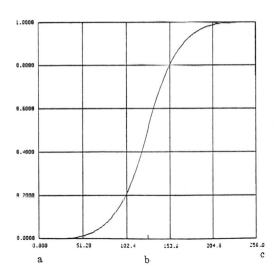

(c) the fourth order membership function

Fig. 1: S Membership Functions.

```
iteration #  0          iteration #  4          iteration #  8

12   11   32             0    0    0            0    0    0
45   36   47            66    6   67           67    0   67
52   39   67            67   39   67           67   64   67

iteration #  1          iteration #  5          iteration #  9

 0    0   20             0    0    0            0    0    0
47   28   51            67    1   67           67    0   67
58   35   67            67   43   67           67   67   67

iteration #  2          iteration #  6

 0    0   12             0    0    0
55   23   59            67    0   67
65   36   67            67   49   67

iteration #  3          iteration #  7

 0    0    4             0    0    0
62   15   65            67    0   67
67   37   67            67   57   67
```

(a)

```
iteration #  0          iteration #  3          iteration #  6

12   11   32             0    0    0            0    0    0
45   36   47            67    2   67           67    0   67
52   39   67            67   43   67           67   67   67

iteration #  1          iteration #  4

 0    0   15             0    0    0
52   26   56            67    0   67
62   36   67            67   54   67

iteration #  2          iteration #  5

 0    0    3             0    0    0
64   14   66            67    0   67
67   38   67            67   65   67
```

(b)

Fig. 2: Illustrated here are examples showing the convergence of the relaxation algorithm based on the second order function (a) and the third order function (b).

(a)

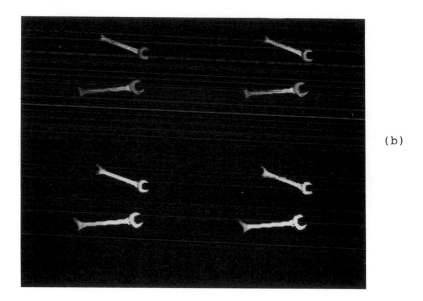

(b)

Fig. 3: Illustrated here are stripe images (a) and tool images (b) enhanced by fuzzy relaxation algorithm based on the second order S fuzzy membership function; the upper left image is original, the upper right, lower left and lower right are the enhanced images after the first, second, and third iterations respectively.

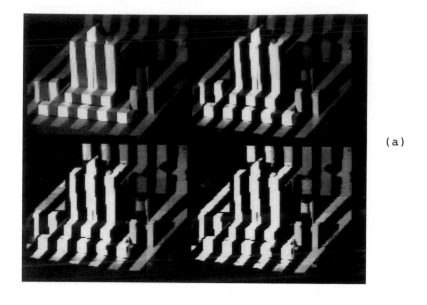

(a)

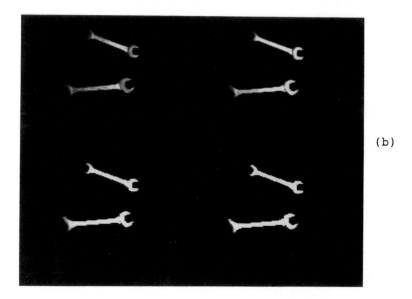

(b)

Fig. 4: Depicted here are stripe images (a) and tool images (b) enhanced by fuzzy relaxation algorithm based on the third order S fuzzy membership function; the upper left image is original, the upper right, lower left and lower right are the enhanced images after the first, second, and third iterations respectively.

ON THE CHOICE OF REGULARISATION PARAMETER
IN IMAGE RESTORATION

J.W. Kay
University of Glasgow, Scotland, UK.

This paper considers the application of the method of regularisation within the context of the restoration of degraded two-dimensional images. In particular, several recipes for choosing an appropriate degree of regularisation are described and their performance compared with reference to test-images. Some of these methods require the availability of a data-based noise-estimator; a neighbourhood noise estimator is proposed and its performance is discussed.

## 1.   INTRODUCTION

The method of regularisation has been employed in many diverse areas in order to derive solutions to ill-posed inverse problems. In such problems a solution fails to exist or is non-unique or, more commonly, the solution does not depend continuously on the initial data in the sense that small perturbations in the given data produce unstable variation in the solution. The review article [1] provides an interesting summary of applications related to early vision processes.

The basic rationale of the method of regularisation is as follows. Given an observed image g - "the data" - obtained from a true image f, we choose as our reconstruction of the underlying scene, that f which minimises

$$\Delta(f,g) + \lambda\Phi(f) \qquad\qquad (1.1)$$

In (1.1), $\Delta(f,g)$ represents a measure of the discrepancy between g and f, while the functional $\Phi(f)$ is a measure of the roughness of the reconstruction of the true scene. The parameter, $\lambda$, is the regularisation or smoothing parameter; it represents a trade-off between fidelity to the data and the degree of roughness in the reconstruction of the underlying scene.

The choice of an appropriate regularisation parameter remains an important aspect of the application of the method of regularisation within the context of image restoration. An important goal is to develop an objective choice of $\lambda$ that is purely data-based. We assume in the sequel that no a priori information is available regarding the true scene; where such information is available, it may be used to guide the reconstruction process [2].

Several recipes have been described in the literature for choosing an appropriate $\lambda$; see [3], [4], [5]. Recently [6] conducted a comparison of several of these methods with reference to the restoration of a simple one-dimensional image. The purpose of this work is to report some initial experiences of the comparison of different recipes within the context of the restoration of two-dimensional images.

We begin by formulating the regularisation approach to two-dimensional image restoration. The recipes for the choice of regularisation parameter - described in [6] - are then outlined. A canonical form for this problem is presented and this provides simple algebraic forms for the quantities required to compute the regularisation parameter. We then introduce a data- based noise estimator and finally present an application of our methodology to test images.

## 2. FORMULATION

We consider a linear, additive, Gaussian model for the two-dimensional $n \times n$, pixellated, image $g$:

$$g = Hf + \epsilon$$

where $g$ and $f$ are $n^2 \times 1$ vectors (stacked as in a raster scan), $H$ is a known $n^2 \times n^2$ point-spread matrix representing a blurring process and $\epsilon$ is a random noise vector and is distributed as $N(0, \sigma^2 I)$, where $I$ denotes the $n^2 \times n^2$ identity matrix

We employ the quadratic discrepancy measure

$$\Delta(f,g) = \|g - Hf\|^2$$

and we take the regularisation functional as

$$\Phi(f) = f^T C f$$

where $C$ is a non-negative smoothing matrix. Hence the regularised reconstruction of the true scene is the solution of the quadratic optimisation problem:

$$\underset{f}{\text{Min}} \{\|g - Hf\|^2 + \lambda f^T C f\}$$

which is given by

$$\hat{f}(\lambda) = (H^T H + \lambda C)^{-1} H^T g$$

### Point-Spread Matrix Structure

In general $H$ will be a row-stochastic matrix of block-Toeplitz form in which each block is of Toeplitz form. The block-bandwidth of $H$ indicates the extent of the blurring process; that is, if the light intensity at each pixel spreads into a $b \times b$ contiguous region of pixels, then the block-bandwidth of $H$ is $b$. Often $b$ will be small and the bandwidth within each block, also $b$, will be small and so $H$ will have a highly sparse, banded structure. We assume that $H$ is non-singular, although, alternatively, a generalised inverse could be utilised.

### Smoothing Matrix Structure

The choice of smoothing matrix, $C$, is achieved using finite differences of the entries of $f$. The order of differences used is termed the order of regularisation. When this order is $p$, the structure of $C$ is $C = Q_p^T Q_p$, where $Q_p$ is a $(n-p)^2 \times n^2$ matrix of the form $Q_p = D_p \otimes D_p$ ($\otimes$ denotes the Kronecker product), $D_p$ is a $(n-p) \times n$ matrix having $(i,k)$th entry $(-1)^k \, {}^p C_k$ $(j=i,\ldots,i+p; i=1,\ldots,n-p; k=j-i)$ and ${}^p C_k$ is a binomial coefficient. C is also a block-Toeplitz matrix in which each block is of Toeplitz form. Both the block-bandwidth and the bandwidth within each block are of size 1+2p. We assume that $Q_p$ has full rank $(n-p)^2$ and thus C also is of rank $(n-p)^2$.

### 3. CHOICES OF REGULARISATION PARAMETER

We consider four recipes for choosing the regularisation parameter $\lambda$.

Chi-squared choice

The rationale of this method – also called the Discrepancy Principle; see [7] – is that the differences between the observed data g and the prediction of g, $\hat{g}(\lambda) = H\hat{f}(\lambda)$, given by the model should match the errors in the input data. The Chi-squared choice is denoted by $\lambda_{CHI}$ and defined as the solution of the equation

$$RSS(\lambda) = n\sigma^2 \qquad (3.1)$$

where $RSS(\lambda) = \|g-\hat{g}(\lambda)\|^2$ .

This recipe implicitly assumes that there are n degrees of freedom available for the estimation of error. However, this makes no allowance for the loss in degrees of freedom involved in constructing $\hat{f}(\lambda)$. A recipe which attempts to remedy this deficiency was proposed in [8] and [9] and named the

Equivalent Degrees of Freedom Choice

This choice is denoted by $\lambda_{EDF}$ and defined by the solution of the equation

$$RSS(\lambda) = \sigma^2 EDF(\lambda) \qquad (3.2)$$

where $EDF(\lambda) = n - tr\{K(\lambda)\}$ and $K(\lambda) = H(H^TH + \lambda C)^{-1}H^T$ $\qquad (3.3)$

EDF($\lambda$) is interpreted as the equivalent degrees of freedom for the estimation of error.

In [8], [9] and [6] it is demonstrated that $\lambda_{CHI}$ tends to over-smooth relative to $\lambda_{EDF}$ in some inverse problems. Note that, in general, $\lambda_{EDF} < \lambda_{CHI}$. A potential drawback of both of these methods is that an a priori value for $\sigma^2$ is required. In practice we require a wholly data-based choice of $\lambda$ and so we consider the

Generalised Cross-Validation Choice

We define $\lambda_{GCV}$ as the minimiser of

$$GCV(\lambda) = RSS(\lambda)/\{EDF(\lambda)\}^2 \qquad (3.4)$$

This method – proposed in [12] – is motivated with prediction in mind as a fully data-based version of the value of $\lambda$ that minimises the total predicted mean squared error, defined as

$$TP(\lambda) = E\{\|\hat{g}(\lambda) - Hf\|^2\} \qquad (3.5)$$

where the expectation is taken with respect to the probability distribution of $\epsilon$. We denote the $\lambda$ which minimises TP($\lambda$) by $\lambda_{TP}$; it is that value of $\lambda$ which ensures that, on average, the observed data g will have been most closely predicted by $\hat{g}(\lambda)$. In practice, $\lambda_{TP}$ is not available and we include it here for the purpose of comparison only.

It would seem reasonable to suppose that $\lambda_{GCV}$ should be used in practice because it is completely data-based; however [6] has reported some practical problems with this method. So it is worthwhile to entertain $\lambda_{CHI}$ and $\lambda_{EDF}$; to do so, we require to provide a consistent estimator of $\sigma^2$.

## Neighbourhood Noise Estimation

For a given order of finite differences p, we propose as an estimator of $\sigma^2$

$$S_p = g^T Q_p^T Q_p g / tr\{Q_p^T Q_p\}$$

where $Q_p$ is defined in Section 2 and

$$tr\{Q_p^T Q_p\} = (n-p)^2 z_p : z_p = \sum_{r=0}^{p} \sum_{s=0}^{p} (P_{C_r} P_{C_s})^2$$

The estimator $S_p$ is the mean of the $(n-p)^2$ _empirical estimators_ of $\sigma^2$ obtained by moving a $(p+1) \times (p+1)$ window around the image and calculating in each neighbourhood

$$e_{a,b} = z_p^{-1}\{\sum_{r=0}^{p} \sum_{s=0}^{p} (-1)^{r+s} P_{C_r} P_{C_s} g_{a+r,b+s}\}^2 \quad (a,b = 1,2,\ldots,n-p)$$

where $(a,b)$ denotes the pixel in the upper left-hand corner of the moving window and $g_{a+r,b+s}$ denotes the observation at pixel $(a+r,b+s)$. It can be shown that $S_p$ is a consistent estimator for $\sigma^2$, since

$$E(S_p) = \sigma^2 + \|Q_p Hf\|^2 \Big/ \{(n-p)^2 z_p\}$$

$$var(S_p) = 2\sigma^4 \Big/ (n-p)^2 + 4\|Q_p Hf\|^2 \sigma^2 \Big/ \{z_p (n-p)^4\} \, ,$$

provided that $\|Q_p Hf\|^2$ is bounded for large n. However, it is desirable to reduce the bias of Sp. When, in a given neighbourhood, f is a discretised polynomial of degree less than, or equal to, p-1, the bias of the empirical estimate of $\sigma^2$ is zero. Hence it follows that the major component of the bias will occur where the given neighbourhood contains an edge of the underlying scene. Therefore the performance of the estimator Sp can be improved in particular by (a) trimming out the bias or (b) employing an intelligent edge detector which can identify neighbourhoods containing an edge and then delete the contribution of the corresponding empirical estimates from Sp. These ideas are currently under investigation.

## 4. A CANONICAL CHARACTERISATION

In order to facilitate the analysis, both theoretically and computationally, it is convenient to express the formulae of Section 3 in terms of the spectral decomposition of the matrix

$$Q = (H^{-1})^T C H^{-1}$$

Suppose that Q has eigenvalues $q_1$, $q_2$, ..., $q_n2$ and corresponding orthonormal eigenvectors $u_1$, $u_2$, ..., $u_n2$. It can be shown that the formulae of (3.1, (3.2), (3.4) and (3.5) become

$$\lambda_{CHI} : \sum_{i=1}^{n^2} \left[\frac{\lambda q_i}{1+\lambda q_i}\right]^2 |v_i|^2 = n\sigma^2 \tag{4.1}$$

$$\lambda_{EDF} : \sum_{i=1}^{n^2} \left[\frac{\lambda q_i}{1+\lambda q_i}\right]^2 |v_i|^2 = \sigma^2 \sum_{i=1}^{n^2} \frac{\lambda q_i}{(1+\lambda q_i)} \tag{4.2}$$

$$\lambda_{GCV} : GCV(\lambda) = \sum_{i=1}^{n^2} \left[\frac{\lambda q_i}{1+\lambda q_i}\right]^2 |v_i|^2 \Bigg/ \left\{\sum_{i=1}^{n^2} \frac{\lambda q_i}{(1+\lambda q_i)}\right\}^2 \tag{4.3}$$

$$\lambda_{TP} : TP(\lambda) = \sum_{i=1}^{n^2} \left[\frac{\lambda q_i}{1+\lambda q_i}\right]^2 |u_i^* Hf|^2 + \sigma^2 \sum_{i=1}^{n^2} (1+\lambda q_i)^{-2} \tag{4.4}$$

where $v_i = u_i^* g$. (* denotes complex conjugate transpose).

Computationally, it is required to perform an eigenanalysis of the matrix Q, although when H and C are sparse it is more efficient to solve the generalised eigenproblem

$$(C - \theta H^T H)x = 0$$

in order to determine $\{q_i\}$ and $\{u_i\}$.

However, we now consider an approximation which provides a fast computational solution.

## 5. CIRCULANT APPROXIMATIONS

Given that the matrices H and C are large, banded and of Toeplitz type, we approximate them by block circulant matrices; see [13], [14]. Given the theoretical work developed in [15], little will be lost by such approximations. As a result of this, the eigenanalysis outlined in Section 4, can be performed using three two-dimensional inverse Fast-Fourier Transforms (FFT). The reconstruction of f can then be obtained from a two-dimensional FFT, and may be expressed in the following way.

$$\hat{f}(\lambda) = \sum_{i=1}^{n^2} \frac{h_i(w_i^* g)}{(|h_i|^2 + \lambda c_i)} w_i .$$

The canonical expressions of Section 4 now may be written as:

$$\lambda_{CHI} : \sum_{i=1}^{n^2} \left[ \frac{\lambda c_i}{|h_i|^2 + \lambda c_i} \right]^2 |x_i|^2 = n\sigma^2 \tag{5.1}$$

$$\lambda_{EDF} : \sum_{i=1}^{n^2} \left[ \frac{\lambda c_i}{|h_i|^2 + \lambda c_i} \right]^2 |x_i|^2 = \sigma^2 \sum_{i=1}^{n^2} \frac{\lambda c_i}{(|h_i|^2 + \lambda c_i)} \tag{5.2}$$

$$\lambda_{GCV} : GCV(\lambda) = \sum_{i=1}^{n^2} \left[ \frac{\lambda c_i}{|h_i|^2 + \lambda c_i} \right]^2 \Bigg/ \left\{ \sum_{i=1}^{n^2} \frac{\lambda c_i}{(|h_i|^2 + \lambda c_i)} \right\}^2 \tag{5.3}$$

$$\lambda_{TP} : TP(\lambda) = \sum_{i=1}^{n^2} \left[ \frac{\lambda c_i}{|h_i|^2 + \lambda c_i} \right]^2 |w_i^* Hf|^2 + \sigma^2 \sum_{i=1}^{n^2} \frac{|h_i|^4}{(|h_i|^2 + \lambda c_i)^2} \tag{5.4}$$

Here $x_i = w_i^* g$ and the $\{h_i\}$, $\{c_i\}$ and $\{w_i\}$ are the eigenvalues of H and C respectively, and the common unit eigenvectors of all the block-circulants of order $n^2$. The eigenvalues $\{c_i\}$ and $\{h_i\}$ may be calculated from the equations:

$$h_i = \sum_{r=0}^{n-1} \sum_{s=0}^{n-1} \alpha_{rs} \omega^{(re+sf)} \tag{5.5}$$

$$c_i = \sum_{r=0}^{n-1} \sum_{s=0}^{n-1} \kappa_{rs} \omega^{(re+sf)} \tag{5.6}$$

where $\{\alpha_{rs}\}$, $\{\kappa_{rs}\}$ denote the first rows of H and C, respectively, and

$$e = [i/n] , \quad f = i \bmod n, \quad \omega = \exp(2\pi\sqrt{(-1)}/n)$$

The $\{w_i\}$ are the columns of the matrix $U_n \otimes U_n$, where $U_n$ is the $n\times n$ unitary Fourier matrix with $(k,\ell)$th entry $n^{-\frac{1}{2}}\omega^{k\ell}$ ($k=0,1,\ldots,n-1$; $\ell=0,1,\ldots,n-1$). We now discuss the application of these developments to a test image.

## 6.  AN APPLICATION

We now apply our methodology to the test image display in Fig. 1. This is a piecewise constant image, of size 64×64, having grey levels 100, 120, 150, 180. This image was blurred using a 3×3 blurring operator with mask

$$M = \begin{bmatrix} 0.05 & 0.06 & 0.05 \\ 0.06 & 0.56 & 0.06 \\ 0.05 & 0.06 & 0.05 \end{bmatrix}$$

This choice of M results in the following specification of the point-spread matrix H.

$$H = bl\text{-}toep(H_1, H_0, H_1)$$

that is a block-Toeplitz matrix having the matrix $H_1$ on the super and sub block diagonals and $H_0$ on the block diagonal and

Fig. 1  true scene (f)

Fig. 2  blurred scene (Hf)

Fig. 3  degraded image (g)

$$H_0 = \text{toep}(0.06, 0.56, 0.06)$$
$$H_1 = \text{toep}(0.05, 0.06, 0.05)$$

The blurred image is displayed in Fig. 2.

Second order regularisation was employed in the reconstruction process and so the smoothing matrix C is given by

$$C = Q_2^T Q_2 \; : \; Q_2 = D_2 \otimes D_2 \; : \; D_2 = \begin{bmatrix} 1 & -2 & 1 & & & \\ & 1 & -2 & 1 & & \\ & & & & & \\ & & & 1 & -2 & 1 \end{bmatrix}$$

The following circulant approximations were used to specify the matrices H and C.

$H = \text{bl-circ}(H_1, H_0, H_1)$

$H_0 = \text{circ}(0.56\ 0.06\ \ldots\ldots\ 0.05)$

$H_1 = \text{circ}(0.06\ 0.05\ \ldots\ldots\ 0.05)$

$C = \text{bl-circ}(6C_1,\ -4C_1,\ C_1,\ \ldots,\ C_1,\ -4C_1)$

$C_1 = \text{circ}(6\ -4\ 1\ \ldots\ldots\ 1\ -4)$

The neighbourhood noise estimator $S_2$, defined in Section 3, was used to estimate the noise variance $\sigma^2$. Note that no attempt was made to correct the bias involved in this estimation process. The true noise standard deviation was chosen to be 2, and in this particular example, $S_2$ was 2.71, while the estimated standard deviation of the actual noise, used in the experiment was 1.97. The reconstructions obtained using the CHI, EDF, GCV and TP methods are displayed in Figs. 4, 5, 6, 7, respectively.

We observe that for this particular example, each of the recipes CHI, EDF and GCV over-smoothes, in that order, relative to TP and that the reconstructions are rather blurred around the edges of the test image. While the quality of these reconstructions is disappointing, the main point of the example is to compare the degrees of smoothing imposed by the different methods.

This work provides some examples of initial experiments conducted with the aim of providing an objective and automatic choice of regularisation parameter. It is too early to attempt to generalise from the results of these simple experiments. Apart from the development of a 'bias-trimmed' neighbourhood noise estimator, our experimental work is currently examining the effects of varying the components, f, H, C and $\sigma$, in order to determine the effect of these parameters on the regularised reconstruction.

## ACKNOWLEDGEMENT

I wish to thank Professor D.M. Titterington and Dr. A.M. Thompson for several stimulating conversations.

Fig. 4    restoration using the
          CHI method

Fig. 5    restoration using the
          EDF method

Fig. 6    restoration using the
          GCV method

Fig. 7    restoration using the
          TP method

REFERENCES

[1]  T. Poggio, V. Torre and C. Koch (1985).  Computational Vision and Regularisation Theory. Nature, Vol. 317, 314-319.

[2]  D.S. Sharman, K.A. Stewart and T.S. Durrani (1986).  The use of Context in Image Restoration.  Presented at the BPRA (Scotland) conference on Adaptive Image Analysis at Heriot-Watt University, May, 1986.

[3]  A.R. Davies and R.S. Anderssen (1986).  Optimisation in the Regularisation of Ill-posed Problems. Journal of the Australian Mathematical Society (Series B), 28, 114-133.

[4]  D.M. Titterington (1985).  Common Structure of Smoothing Techniques in Statistics. International Statistical Review, 53, 141-70.

[5]  P. Craven and G. Wahba (1979).  Smoothing Noisy Data with spline functions: estimating the correct degree of smoothing by the method of generalised cross-validation. Numer. Math., 31, 377-403.

[6]  A.M. Thompson, J.C. Brown, J.W. Kay and D.M. Titterington (1987).  A comparison of methods of choosing the smoothing parameter in image restoration by regularisation.  In preparation.

[7]  C.W. Groetsch.  The Theory of Tikhonov regularisation for Fredholm equations of the first kind. Research Notes in Mathematics No.105, Pitman.

[8]  P. Hall and D.M. Titterington (1987).  Common structure of techniques for choosing smoothing parameters in regression problems.  J.R. Statist. Soc. B, 49, No.2, 184-198.

[9]  P. Hall and D.M. Titterington (1986).  On some Smoothing Techniques used in Image Restoration.  J.R. Statist. Soc., 48, No. 3, 330-343.

[10] V.F. Turchin (1967).  Solution of the Fredholm equation of the first kind in a statistical ensemble of smooth functions.  USSR Comp. Math. and Math. Phys., 7, 79-96.

[11] V.F. Turchin (1968).  Selection of an ensemble of smooth functions for the solution of the inverse problem.  USSR Comput. Math. and Math. Phys., 8, 328-339.

[12] G.H. Golub, M. Heath and G. Wahba (1979).  Generalised cross-validation as a method for choosing a good ridge parameter.  Technometrics, 21, 215-223. validation as a method for choosing a good ridge parameter. Technometrics, 21, 215-223.

[13] A.K. Jain (1978).  Fast Inversion of Banded Toeplitz Matrices by Circular Decompositions.  IEEE Trans. A.S.S.P., Vol. ASSP-26, No. 2, 1978.

[14] R.C. Gonzales & P. Wintz (1987).  Digital Image Processing.  Second Edition. Addison-Wesley.

[15] R.M. Gray.  On the Asymptotic Eigenvalue Distribution of Toeplitz Matrices.  IEEE Trans. Inf. Th., Vol. IT-18, No. 6, Nov. 1972.

# SOME NOTES ON REPEATED AVERAGING SMOOTHING

Li-Dong Cai

**Department of Artificial Intelligence, University of Edinburgh**
**5 Forrest Hill, Edinburgh EH1 2QL, UK**

## Abstract

Gaussian smoothing can be accomplished with the Repeated Averaging Smoothing (RAS) method, a technique based on statistical theory. It can also be done with Diffusion Smoothing (DS) method, a technique based on the diffusion equation. The difference between the origins of RAS and DS is great. In this paper, we make explicit the relationship between RAS and DS. These notes show that RAS mask is a special case of diffusion explicit smoothing (DES) scheme, RAS's scale proportion coefficient depends on the diffusion coefficient, etc.. Thus, diffusion implicit smoothing scheme with a changeable time step (DISCT), which is better than DES, will also be better than RAS in terms of both the computational stability and complexity, especially in the scaled space.

**Keywords** : repeated averaging, Gaussian, explict, implicit, diffusion smoothing, cross mask, numerical stability and complexity.

# 1. Introduction.

In computer vision, most input data is polluted by noise. It is a fundamental problem to have a proper filter in the early visual processing. Much research investigates this issue and many techniques are proposed. Among them, Gaussian smoothing (GS) is appreciated for its elegant properties [YUI83], [WIT83]; and a widely used technique is repeated averaging smoothing (RAS), which appeals "to the central-limit theorem and implement Gaussian filtering using repeated averaging with the 3×3 mask ...". "Iterating n times approximately corresponds to filtering with a Gaussian whose standard deviation is proportional to $\sqrt{n}$" [BRA85]. Its mask is shown as below:

$$\frac{1}{24} \times \begin{array}{|c|c|c|} \hline 1 & 2 & 1 \\ \hline 2 & 12 & 2 \\ \hline 1 & 2 & 1 \\ \hline \end{array}$$

Recently, diffusion smoothing (DS) technique has been investigated in [KOE84] and [CAI87], they showed the equivalence between GS and DS. To implement the smoothing, an effective numerical scheme called DISCT for directly solving the diffusion equation is proposed in [CAI87]. DISCT has a lower computational complexity than that of Gaussian convolution.

Note that the DS technique works on the basis of the diffusion equation, thus it works on a non-statistical basis. As the difference between the origins of RAS and DS is so great, it is interesting to find a possible relationship between both effective techniques, as well as that known between GS and DS. This is the motivation of the research in this paper.

Such a link has been found and is presented in the notes in the next section.

## 2. Six Notes On Repeated Averaging Smoothing (RAS).

**Note 1.** *Repeated averaging smoothing (RAS) is a special case of diffusion smoothing (DS) with the equation:*

$$\frac{\partial u}{\partial t} = \frac{1}{6} \Delta u \tag{2}$$

**Proof** : In recursion, RAS technique's mask (1) can be denoted as:

$$u_{i,j}^{k+1} = \frac{12}{24} u_{i,j}^k + \frac{2}{24} (u_{i-1,j}^k + u_{i+1,j}^k + u_{i,j-1}^k + u_{i,j+1}^k) + \frac{1}{24} (u_{i-1,j-1}^k + u_{i+1,j+1}^k + u_{i-1,j+1}^k + u_{i+1,j-1}^k)$$

which corresponds to the numerical difference scheme:

$$u_{i,j}^{k+1} = ( 1 - \frac{\tau}{2h^2} ) u_{i,j}^k + \frac{\tau}{h^2}( \frac{2}{24} \; o\!\!+\!\!o \; + \; \frac{1}{24} \; \times \; ) \tag{3}$$

with a time step $\tau = 1$ unit and a spatial step $h = 1$ unit, where the symbols

$$o\!\!+\!\!o \equiv u_{i-1,j}^k + u_{i+1,j}^k + u_{i,j-1}^k + u_{i,j+1}^k \tag{4}$$

and

$$\times \equiv u_{i-1,j-1}^k + u_{i+1,j+1}^k + u_{i-1,j+1}^k + u_{i+1,j-1}^k \tag{5}$$

Substitute the following Taylor expansions in (3) for those nodes around the node (i,j) and for the time k:

$$u_{i,j}^{k+1} = [I + \tau\frac{\partial}{\partial t}]u_{i,j}^k + O(\tau^2) \tag{6}$$

$$u_{i-1,j}^k = [I - h\frac{\partial}{\partial x} + \frac{h^2}{2!}\frac{\partial^2}{\partial x^2} - \frac{h^3}{3!}\frac{\partial^3}{\partial x^3}]u_{i,j}^k + O(h^4) \tag{7}$$

$$u_{i+1,j}^k = [I + h\frac{\partial}{\partial x} + \frac{h^2}{2!}\frac{\partial^2}{\partial x^2} + \frac{h^3}{3!}\frac{\partial^3}{\partial x^3}]u_{i,j}^k + O(h^4) \tag{8}$$

$$u_{i,j-1}^k = [I - h\frac{\partial}{\partial y} + \frac{h^2}{2!}\frac{\partial^2}{\partial y^2} - \frac{h^3}{3!}\frac{\partial^3}{\partial y^3}]u_{i,j}^k + O(h^4) \tag{9}$$

$$u_{i,j+1}^k = [I + h\frac{\partial}{\partial y} + \frac{h^2}{2!}\frac{\partial^2}{\partial y^2} + \frac{h^3}{3!}\frac{\partial^3}{\partial y^3}]u_{i,j}^k + O(h^4) \tag{10}$$

$$u_{i-1,j-1}^k = [I - h(\frac{\partial}{\partial x}+\frac{\partial}{\partial y}) + \frac{h^2}{2!}(\frac{\partial}{\partial x}+\frac{\partial}{\partial y})^2 - \frac{h^3}{3!}(\frac{\partial}{\partial x}+\frac{\partial}{\partial y})^3]u_{i,j}^k + O(h^4) \tag{11}$$

$$u_{i+1,j+1}^k = [I + h(\frac{\partial}{\partial x}+\frac{\partial}{\partial y}) + \frac{h^2}{2!}(\frac{\partial}{\partial x}+\frac{\partial}{\partial y})^2 + \frac{h^3}{3!}(\frac{\partial}{\partial x}+\frac{\partial}{\partial y})^3]u_{i,j}^k + O(h^4) \tag{12}$$

$$u_{i-1,j+1}^k = [I - h(\frac{\partial}{\partial x}-\frac{\partial}{\partial y}) + \frac{h^2}{2!}(\frac{\partial}{\partial x}-\frac{\partial}{\partial y})^2 - \frac{h^3}{3!}(\frac{\partial}{\partial x}-\frac{\partial}{\partial y})^3]u_{i,j}^k + O(h^4) \tag{13}$$

$$u_{i+1,j-1}^k = [I + h(\frac{\partial}{\partial x}-\frac{\partial}{\partial y}) + \frac{h^2}{2!}(\frac{\partial}{\partial x}-\frac{\partial}{\partial y})^2 + \frac{h^3}{3!}(\frac{\partial}{\partial x}-\frac{\partial}{\partial y})^3]u_{i,j}^k + O(h^4) \tag{14}$$

we can get

$$\frac{\partial}{\partial t}u_{i,j}^k = \frac{1}{6}\Delta u_{i,j}^k + O(\tau+h^2) \tag{15}$$

This is one discrete form of the diffusion equation (2) at the node (i,j) and time k, hence difference equation (15) or (3) will converge to (2) when $\tau$ and h tend to zero.

**Q.E.D.**

**Note 2.** *RAS's scale proportion coefficient should be* $\sqrt{\frac{1}{3}}$.

**Proof :** Diffusion equation (2) can be described in a general form:

$$\frac{\partial u}{\partial t} = b\,\Delta u \tag{16}$$

where the parameter $b \geq 0$ is called the diffusion coefficient.

The solution of equation (16) is well known as:

$$u(x,y,t) = \frac{1}{4\pi bt}\int_{-\infty}^{\infty}\int_{-\infty}^{\infty} exp(-\frac{(x-\xi)^2+(y-\eta)^2}{4bt})\,u(\xi,\eta,0)\,d\xi d\eta \tag{17}$$

Let $\sigma^2 = 2bt$ or $\sigma = \sqrt{2bt}$, and

$$g(x,y,\sigma) = \frac{1}{2\pi\sigma^2}exp(-\frac{x^2+y^2}{2\sigma^2}) \tag{18}$$

we have

$$u(x,y,t) = g(x,y,\sigma) * u(x,y,0) \tag{19}$$

where the symbol * denotes the convolution operator.

Hence $\sigma$ here is just the scale parameter of Gaussian convolution.

From (2), it should have $b = \dfrac{1}{6}$ in equation (16), so

$$\sigma = \sqrt{\frac{t}{3}} \tag{20}$$

While $t = 1, 2, ..., n$, we have $\sigma = \sqrt{\dfrac{1}{3}}, \sqrt{\dfrac{2}{3}}, \cdots, \sqrt{\dfrac{n}{3}}$. Thus, after n times repeating, RAS will approach Gaussian smoothing at the scale level $\sigma = c\sqrt{n}$. Obviously this proportion coefficient c should be:

$$c = \sqrt{\frac{1}{3}} \tag{21}$$

As shown above, this conclusion is obtained without any prior assumption in statistics or probability theory.

**Q.E.D.**

The coefficient b may have many values. If choose $b = \dfrac{1}{2}$ as in [CAI87], then we have $\sigma = \sqrt{t}$. It shows that the parameter b determines the diffusion rate, (thus the recursion times,) leading to a surface smoothed at a specific scale level. The diffusion coefficient b is also an important factor in the numerical stability condition as will be shown in Note 5.

RAS recursion works with only the current values, so it is an explicit recursion. In fact, it is a specific form of diffusion explicit smoothing (DES) scheme [CAI87] which calculates the next time's values directly from the current time's values.

**Note 3.** *RAS mask is a specific form of DES scheme.*

**Proof:** Discretise the diffusion equation (16)

$$\frac{\partial u}{\partial t} = b\, \Delta u$$

at the node (i,j) and time k as below:

$$\frac{\partial u}{\partial t} = \frac{1}{\tau}(u_{i,j}^{k+1} - u_{i,j}^{k}) + O(\tau) \tag{22}$$

$$\frac{b}{2}\Delta u = \frac{b}{2h^2}(\;\diamond + \diamond - 4u_{i,j}^{k}\;) + O(h^2) \tag{23}$$

$$\frac{b}{2}\Delta u = \frac{b}{4h^2}(\;\times - 4u_{i,j}^{k}\;) + O(h^2) \tag{24}$$

So its explicit difference scheme and cut-off error $E(\tau,h)$ are:

$$u_{i,j}^{k+1} = (1-6b\beta)u_{i,j}^{k} + \frac{b\beta}{2}(\;2\,\diamond + \times\;) \tag{25}$$

$$E(\tau,h) = O(\tau+h^2) \tag{26}$$

$$\text{where } \beta = \frac{\tau}{2h^2}$$

Let $b = \frac{1}{6}$, $\tau = 1$ and $h = 1$, then $\beta = \frac{1}{2}$ and equation (25) comes out as:

$$u_{ij}^{k+1} = \frac{12}{24} u_{ij}^k + \frac{1}{24} ( 2\;\text{——} + \text{✕} )$$

its square mask is just RAS mask (1):

$$\frac{1}{24} \times \begin{array}{|c|c|c|} \hline 1 & 2 & 1 \\ \hline 2 & 12 & 2 \\ \hline 1 & 2 & 1 \\ \hline \end{array}$$

**Q.E.D.**

From the general form of DES scheme (25), it is easy to get more square masks. E.g., if we change the time step to $\tau = 2$, then $\beta = 1$, the mask turns to:

$$\frac{1}{24} \times \begin{array}{|c|c|c|} \hline 1 & 2 & 1 \\ \hline 2 & 0 & 2 \\ \hline 1 & 2 & 1 \\ \hline \end{array} \tag{27}$$

And when $\tau = 3$, then $\beta = \frac{3}{2}$ and we get an interesting mask:

$$\frac{1}{24} \times \begin{array}{|c|c|c|} \hline 1 & 2 & 1 \\ \hline 2 & -4 & 2 \\ \hline 1 & 2 & 1 \\ \hline \end{array} \tag{28}$$

The weighting at the central node is now a negative number! But it works well.

In addition, deducing square masks from the general DES can have the advantage shown in the next note.

**Note 4.** *Some 3×3 square mask deduced from the general DES can work faster.*

**Proof:** Given time (or scale) range, it is trivial that masks, such as (27), whose time step $\tau > 1$ will leap to the expected time (or scale) level faster than the RAS mask whose $\tau = 1$.

**Q.E.D.**

So far, for DES, we have had the normal cross and the oblique cross masks in [CAI87] and the square mask here. The square mask might be decomposed as the linear combination of the normal and the oblique cross masks. For instance, we have

$$
\begin{array}{|c|c|c|}
\hline 1 & 2 & 1 \\
\hline 2 & 12 & 2 \\
\hline 1 & 2 & 1 \\
\hline
\end{array}
\;=\; 2\times\;
\begin{array}{ccc}
 & 1 & \\
1 & 4 & 1 \\
 & 1 & \\
\end{array}
\;+\;
\begin{array}{ccc}
1 & & 1 \\
 & 4 & \\
1 & & 1 \\
\end{array}
\tag{29}
$$

Nonetheless, they are independent in the senses of their different time step, different numerical stability and even different diffusion coefficient b. As an example, the next note will be a comparison of the numerical stability between the normal cross mask and the square mask deduced from the same diffusion equation.

**Note 5.** *The square mask is less constrained with respect to numerical stability.*

**Proof:** Suppose we apply DES with equation (16):

$$
\frac{\partial u}{\partial t} = b\,\Delta u
$$

The normal cross mask's numerical stability condition (see [CAI87]) is

$$
\frac{\tau}{2h^2} = \beta \le \frac{1}{8b}
\tag{30}
$$

so

$$
\tau \le \frac{h^2}{4b}
\tag{31}
$$

With a similar analysis (see Appendix), the square mask's stability condition is:

$$
\frac{\tau}{2h^2} = \beta \le \frac{1}{4b}
\tag{32}
$$

so

$$
\tau \le \frac{h^2}{2b}
\tag{33}
$$

Hence, for the same diffusion equation, the square mask has a larger stable range for choosing a time step $\tau$, however, it is, at most, twice larger than the normal cross mask's.

**Q.E.D.**

By using the absolutely stable DISCT numerical scheme:

$$
\frac{1}{\tau}(u_{i,j}^{k+\frac{1}{2}} - u_{i,j}^{k}) - \frac{1}{2h^2}(u_{i+1,j}^{k+\frac{1}{2}} - 2u_{i,j}^{k+\frac{1}{2}} + u_{i-1,j}^{k+\frac{1}{2}}) = 0
\tag{34.x}
$$

$$
\frac{1}{\tau}(u_{i,j}^{k+1} - u_{i,j}^{k+\frac{1}{2}}) - \frac{1}{2h^2}(u_{i,j+1}^{k+1} - 2u_{i,j}^{k+1} + u_{i,j-1}^{k+1}) = 0
\tag{34.y}
$$

we can release the constraint on the time step. And a larger time step means a lower cost in the computing, so we have the next and the last note as below.

**Note 6.** *DISCT technique is better than RAS in the Multi-Scale Space.*

**Proof:** In Note 3, we have proven RAS mask is a specific form of DES scheme, or a conditionally stable scheme with a unity time step in computing. And [CAI87] has shown that in the multi-scale space the complexity of DISCT scheme is $(KM^2)$ which is lower than DES scheme's $O(K^2M^2)$, where k is the maximal scale value and $M\times M$ is the image size. Thus, the same conclusion can be applied to RAS.

**Q.E.D.**

Further research on the diffusion coefficient b might be useful to understand the smoothing itself, but would be beyond the scope of this paper.

## 3. Conclusion.

It has been shown that Repeated Averaging Smoothing mask is a special case of the explicit scheme for Diffusion Smoothing, hence in the multi-scale space the time step changeable implicit scheme proposed in the previous paper [CAI87] will be better in terms of both the computational stability and the complexity.

**Acknowledgement**

This research is supported by an Edinburgh University Postgraduate Studentship. Thanks are given to Dr. R.B. Fisher for supervision.

**References:**

[BRA85]   Brady, M., Ponce J., Yuille A. and Asada H., "Describing Surfaces", MIT A.I. Memo 822, 1985.

[CAI87]   Cai, L.-D., "Diffusion Smoothing on Dense Range Data", DAI WP-200, Department of A.I., University of Edinburgh, 1987.

[KOE84]   Koenderink, J.J., "The Structure of Images", Biological Cybernetics 50, 1984, pp.363-370.

[WIT83]    Witkin, A., "Scale-Space Filtering", Proc. 7th IJCAI, Karlsruehe, 1983, pp.1019-1021.

[YUI83]    Yuille, A.L. and Poggio, T., "Scaling Theorems for Zero Crossings", MIT A.I. AIM-722, 1983.

## Appendix: Stability Analysis of the Square Mask Diffusion Smoothing.

The general diffusion equation (16)

$$\frac{\partial u}{\partial t} = b\,\Delta u \tag{A.1}$$

may use the DES scheme with the square mask:

$$u_{i,j}^{k+1} = (1-6b\beta)u_{i,j}^k + \frac{b\beta}{2}(\,2\ \text{o}\!-\!\!+\!\!-\!\text{o}\ +\ \times\,) \tag{A.2}$$

It can be seen as a "generalised (weighting changeable)" RAS mask also.

Similar to the Fourier separation analysis in [CAI87], $\lambda$, the factor of error increase per time step $\tau$ will be:

$$\lambda = (1 - 6b\beta) + \frac{b\beta}{2}[\,(\,e^{-i\theta_1} + e^{i\theta_1} + e^{-i\theta_2} + e^{i\theta_2}\,) + (\,e^{-i(\theta_1+\theta_2)} + e^{i(\theta_1+\theta_2)} + e^{-i(\theta_1-\theta_2)} + e^{i(\theta_1-\theta_2)}\,)\,]$$

or

$$\lambda = (1 - 6b\beta) + 2b\beta\,(cos\theta_1 + cos\theta_2 + cos\theta_1\,cos\theta_2)$$

Because

$$-1 \le (cos\theta_1 + cos\theta_2 + cos\theta_1\,cos\theta_2) \le 3$$

we have

$$1 - 8b\beta \le \lambda \le 1$$

Hence, from the requirement:

$$|\lambda| \le 1$$

we obtain the stability condition:

$$0 < \frac{\tau}{2h^2} = \beta \le \frac{1}{4b} \tag{A.4}$$

or

$$0 < \tau \le \frac{h^2}{2b} \tag{A.5}$$

Let $b = \frac{1}{6}$, $h = 1$ and $\tau = 1$, this is just the case of RAS: (A.2) turns out as

$$u_{i,j}^{k+1} = \frac{12}{24}u_{i,j}^k + \frac{1}{24}(\,2\ \text{o}\!-\!\!+\!\!-\!\text{o}\ +\ \times\,) \tag{A.2.RAS}$$

with the square mask

$$\frac{1}{24} \times \begin{array}{|c|c|c|} \hline 1 & 2 & 1 \\ \hline 2 & 12 & 2 \\ \hline 1 & 2 & 1 \\ \hline \end{array}$$

Note that when $b = \dfrac{1}{6}$ and $h = 1$, the stability condition (A.5) promises

$$\max \tau = 3$$

that means some potential capability awaits developing. We can choose a time step larger than RAS's $\tau = 1$ to form new masks, (like (27) or (28) etc. in Section 2.,) so as to obtain the same result faster, and this is one of the advantages of using DS technique instead of RAS technique.

# COLOR ENHANCEMENT ALGORITHM FOR
# REMOTELY SENSED FALSE COLOR IMAGE,
# USING UNIFORM COLOR SCALE

Johji TAJIMA, Minoru MURATA, Hisao AIBA, Hidetoshi TAKAOKA*, Jiro KOMAI**

NEC Corporation, 4-1-1 Miyazaki, Miyamae-ku, Kawasaki 213, Japan
*)Sumitomo Metal Mining Co.,LTD., 5-11-3 Shimbashi, Minato-ku, Tokyo 105
**)Earth Resources Satellite Data Analysis Center, 2-4-5 Azabudai, Minato-ku,
Tokyo 106

## 1. Introduction

In remote sensing, non-visible light spectral channel images are used for earth observation. Landsat MSS (Multi-Spectral Scanner) uses five channels, including near- and far-infrared ones, for example. To make the image visible, the channels are usually shifted and CRT red, green and blue guns are controlled by the infrared, red and green channel signals, respectively. Such a display method is called a false color display. This colorization is compatible with conventional color infrared pictures. Earth resource exploration experts can analyze such images with conventional know-how capabilities. However, from an earth resource exploration viewpoint, the method is not ideal. Rather, a representation, in which color variation in an image is emphasized as much as possible, is favorable. One of the authors developed a false color enhancement algorithm[1] by which Euclidean distance in an original feature space is approximately mapped to color difference that human eyes detect and a displayable region in a color space is maximally used. As color difference was evaluated by the $L^*u^*v^*$ coordinate (one of uniform color space), this algorithm will be refered to as "LUV algorithm" in this paper.

Though this algorithm always offers very great color enhancement, evaluation comments by earth resource exploration experts were as follows.

"Though color difference is enhanced very much and rock category differences are very clear, displayed color is not natural and imcompatible with conventional false color image and rock identification is difficult."

On the other hand, Kaneko[2] had developed an algorithm by which most information involved in many channels was able to be condensed into three principal channel images and displayed color was compatible with conventional color infrared pictures. Principal components were calculated from many Landsat pictures. First three components, $y_1$, $y_2$ and $y_3$, are represented by Eq.(1) using original four channel components $x_1$, $x_2$, $x_3$ and $x_4$.

$$y_1 = 0.334x_1 + 0.603x_2 + 0.676x_3 + 0.263x_4$$
$$y_2 = -0.283x_1 - 0.661x_2 + 0.577x_3 - 0.389x_4 \qquad (1)$$
$$y_3 = -0.900x_1 + 0.428x_2 - 0.076x_3 - 0.041x_4$$

The first, second and third components are called "brightness", "greenness" and "yellowness", respectively. The most important point is that the first component is always oriented to the brightness and the brightness is used as brightness in displayed images, too. In Kaneko's paper, "brightness" means that all original components $x_1$, $x_2$, $x_3$ and $x_4$ are combined positively with the first principal component $y_1$. By the algorithm, color enhancement is also accomplished to some extent. However, the main aim of Kaneko's algorithm is to make an image which contains more information than is displayed in three-channels and is compatible with conventional false color pictures.

This paper proposes a new color enhancement algorithm that is based on the LUV algorithm, but which preserves brightness and hue. In the algorithm, the "brightness" is dealt with as in Kaneko's algorithm.

## 2. The LUV Algorithm

At first, the LUV algorithm[1] is summarized here. Three channels for false color display are denoted as $(f_1, f_2, f_3)$. $f_1$, $f_2$ and $f_3$ are coordinates usually assigned to R(ed), G(reen) and B(lue), respectively. Computer image analysis deals with color distance between $(f_1, f_2, f_3)$ and $(f_1', f_2', f_3')$ with Euclidean distance $D_f$.

$$D_f = \sqrt{(f_1'-f_1)^2 + (f_2'-f_2)^2 + (f_3'-f_3)^2} \qquad (2)$$

To visualize the distance analysed by a computer, $D_f$ should be proportional to or, at least, linearly converted to color difference perceived by human eyes.

The LUV algorithm uses $L^*u^*v^*$ space -- one of the uniform color spaces recommended by CIE -- for color difference evaluation. The $L^*$, $u^*$ and $v^*$ values are calculated from CIE-1931 XYZ coordinate values using Eq.(3) (see, for example [3]).

$$\begin{cases} L^* = 116(Y/Y_0)^{1/3} - 16 & (Y/Y_0 > 0.008856) \\ \quad\; 903.29(Y/Y_0) & (Y/Y_0 \leq 0.008856) \\ u^* = 13L^*(u'-u'_0) \\ v^* = 13L^*(v'-v'_0) \end{cases} \qquad (3)$$

$$\text{where,} \quad u' = 4X/(X+15Y+3Z)$$
$$v' = 9Y/(X+15Y+3Z),$$

$Y_0$, $u'_0$ and $v'_0$ are Y, u' and v' values for illumination source. X, Y and Z values can be obtained from (R,G,B) values for the color monitor used by employing a linear matrix.

It is assumed that an image is enhanced most effectively, if image color distribution is mapped into the entire displayable region in the $L^*u^*v^*$ space. For that purpose, mean values $(f_{10}, f_{20}, f_{30})$ and covariance matrix $\Sigma$ about the image color distribution are calculated and the shape is fitted into the displayable region shape with the least distortion. Using mean values $(L^*_0, u^*_0, v^*_0)$ and covariance matrix $\Sigma_0$ about the displayable region shape in the $L^*u^*v^*$ space, the conversion from $(f_1, f_2, f_3)$ to $(L^*, u^*, v^*)$ is represented by Eq.(4)

$$\begin{pmatrix} L^* \\ u^* \\ v^* \end{pmatrix} = O_0 \cdot \begin{pmatrix} \sigma_{01} & 0 & 0 \\ 0 & \sigma_{02} & 0 \\ 0 & 0 & \sigma_{03} \end{pmatrix} \cdot \begin{pmatrix} 1/\sigma_1 & 0 & 0 \\ 0 & 1/\sigma_2 & 0 \\ 0 & 0 & 1/\sigma_3 \end{pmatrix} \cdot O^{-1} \cdot \begin{pmatrix} f_1 - f_{10} \\ f_2 - f_{20} \\ f_3 - f_{30} \end{pmatrix} + \begin{pmatrix} L^*_0 \\ u^*_0 \\ v^*_0 \end{pmatrix} \quad (4)$$

where $O$ is an orthogonal matrix which diagonalizes $\Sigma$ and where $O_0$ is another orthogonal matrix which diagonalizes $\Sigma_0$. The relations are shown in Eq.(5).

$$\Sigma = O \begin{pmatrix} \sigma_1^2 & 0 & 0 \\ 0 & \sigma_2^2 & 0 \\ 0 & 0 & \sigma_3^2 \end{pmatrix} O^{-1}$$

$$(5)$$

$$\Sigma_0 = O_0 \begin{pmatrix} \sigma_{01}^2 & 0 & 0 \\ 0 & \sigma_{02}^2 & 0 \\ 0 & 0 & \sigma_{03}^2 \end{pmatrix} O_0^{-1}$$

$$\sigma_1^2 \geqq \sigma_2^2 \geqq \sigma_3^2, \qquad \sigma_{01}^2 \geqq \sigma_{02}^2 \geqq \sigma_{03}^2$$

By Eq.(5), the image color distribution center is positioned to the displayable region center and the three image color distribution principal axes are assigned to the displayable region principal axes in a regular order (from the greatest variance to the smallest variance). Individual pixels $(L^*, u^*, v^*)$ are determined by Eq. (4) and $(R, G, B)$ for display is obtained by Eq.(3) and the $(X, Y, Z)$ to $(R, G, B)$ linear conversion.

The image color distribution depends on used images. The displayable region shape in the $(L^*, u^*, v^*)$ space is determined by three color monitor primary color chromaticities and a chromaticity for white standard. Figure 1 shows displayable region cross sections with various $L^*$ values. Table 1 shows statistics on the region shape; $(L^*_0, u^*_0, v^*_0)$, $\Sigma$ and principal axes.

The LUV algorithm applications to two remotely sensed images ("Ruddygore" and "Mungana") are shown in Photos 1 and 2. Photos 1(a) and (b) show the conventional false color images and Photos 2(a) and (b) show the images enhanced by the LUV algorithm. Table 2 shows the statistics on image color distributions for the scenes shown in the Photos. Color variation is very strongly enhanced in every picture. CRP (Color Representing Power), defined as color distribution volume in the $L^*u^*v^*$ space[1], is also indicated with color distribution statistics in the $L^*u^*v^*$ space in Tables 3 and 4. Table 3 shows the statistics for conventional false color display (Photos 1) and Table 4 shows the statistics for LUV algorithm result (Photos 2). Comparing CRPs, it is seen that the LUV algorithm enhances image color distribution more than 100 times.

## 3. Problems in the LUV Algorithm

The enhanced images were evaluated by earth resource exploration experts, who

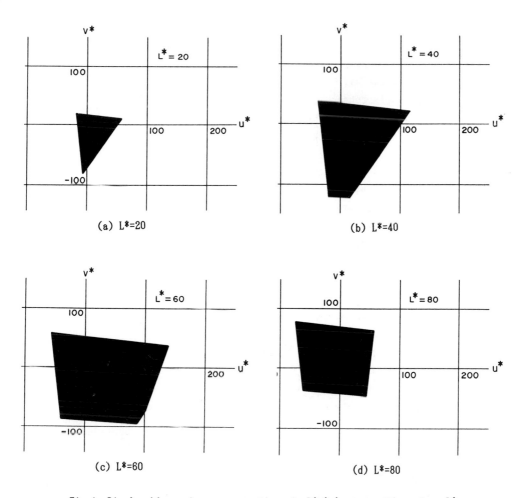

Fig.1 Displayable region cross sections in L*u*v* space with various L* values.

Table 1 Statistics on displayable region shapes.

Table 2 Statistics on color distribution in original $(f_1, f_2, f_3)$ space.

| $L^*_0$ | 57.66 | | |
|---|---|---|---|
| $u^*_0$ | 17.13 | | |
| $v^*_0$ | -10.70 | | |
| $\Sigma_0$ | 351.7 | -187.9 | 304.7 |
| | -187.9 | 1826.6 | -201.3 |
| | 304.7 | -201.3 | 1741.9 |
| $\sigma_0^2$ | 2058.0 | 1587.7 | 274.4 |
| $O_0$ | 0.197 | -0.077 | 0.977 |
| | -0.730 | -0.677 | 0.094 |
| | 0.655 | -0.732 | -0.190 |
| CRP | 29943 | | |

| | Ruddygore | | | Mungana | | |
|---|---|---|---|---|---|---|
| $f_{10}$ | 177.94 | | | 165.77 | | |
| $f_{20}$ | 142.79 | | | 157.26 | | |
| $f_{30}$ | 140.33 | | | 90.66 | | |
| $\Sigma$ | 522.8 | 169.6 | -42.6 | 746.5 | 350.6 | 143.3 |
| | 169.6 | 830.2 | 486.2 | 350.6 | 507.8 | 91.7 |
| | -42.6 | 486.2 | 468.5 | 143.3 | 91.7 | 99.4 |
| $\sigma^2$ | 1188.4 | 543.7 | 89.4 | 1028.5 | 257.2 | 67.9 |
| $O$ | 0.174 | -0.938 | 0.298 | 0.801 | 0.573 | 0.173 |
| | 0.821 | -0.029 | -0.570 | 0.571 | -0.818 | 0.067 |
| | 0.544 | 0.344 | 0.765 | 0.180 | 0.045 | -0.983 |

were used to identify rock categories by such images. Pertinent comments were as follow.

(a) In Photo 2, geological difference is very clearly represented as color difference and a rock boundary is easily discriminable.

(b) However, as displayed hues are different from conventional false color display (Photo 1), conventional analysis know-how cannot be applicable. Therefore, after investigating rock boundaries by the enhanced image, analysis by conventional display is also necessary.

(c) The shading in enhanced images is unnatural.

It was requested that drawbacks (b) and (c) should be eliminated.

It is clearly understood that color compatibility between two algorithms does not hold. The orthogonal matrix $O^{-1}$ transforms every pixel vector, rotating axes from original $f_1$, $f_2$ and $f_3$ to principal axis directions.

Table 3  Statistics on color distribution in $L^*u^*v^*$ space for conventional false color display.

|  | Ruddygore | | | Mungana | | |
|---|---|---|---|---|---|---|
| $L^*_0$ | 81.12 | | | 82.15 | | |
| $u^*_0$ | 12.85 | | | 5.13 | | |
| $v^*_0$ | 2.96 | | | 26.72 | | |
| $\Sigma$ | 25.85 | -33.97 | 17.86 | 21.04 | -0.82 | 24.11 |
|  | -33.97 | 137.03 | 10.47 | -0.82 | 65.44 | -15.43 |
|  | 17.86 | 10.47 | 47.15 | 24.11 | -15.43 | 46.18 |
| $\sigma^2$ | 146.87 | 56.76 | 6.40 | 77.38 | 49.81 | 5.48 |
| O | 0.262 | -0.441 | -0.858 | 0.260 | 0.491 | 0.831 |
|  | -0.963 | -0.070 | -0.259 | -0.770 | 0.625 | -0.128 |
|  | -0.054 | -0.895 | 0.443 | 0.582 | 0.607 | -0.541 |
| CRP | 231 | | | 145 | | |

Table 4  Statistics on color distribution in $L^*u^*v^*$ space for enhanced display by the LUV algorithm.

|  | Ruddygore | | | Mungana | | |
|---|---|---|---|---|---|---|
| $L^*_0$ | 57.68 | | | 58.10 | | |
| $u^*_0$ | 15.71 | | | 15.17 | | |
| $v^*_0$ | -8.66 | | | -6.12 | | |
| $\Sigma$ | 299.1 | -110.2 | 173.3 | 294.3 | -50.0 | 42.8 |
|  | -110.2 | 1640.1 | -191.5 | -50.0 | 1431.3 | -142.0 |
|  | 173.3 | -191.5 | 1411.3 | 42.8 | -142.0 | 1072.1 |
| $\sigma^2$ | 1771.4 | 1311.2 | 267.9 | 1483.8 | 1023.5 | 290.3 |
| O | 0.124 | -0.088 | 0.988 | 0.052 | -0.033 | 0.998 |
|  | -0.850 | -0.523 | 0.060 | -0.942 | -0.332 | 0.038 |
|  | 0.512 | -0.848 | -0.140 | 0.330 | -0.943 | -0.048 |
| CRP | 24945 | | | 20997 | | |

However, image color distributions are different from image to image and rocks or a geological entity cannot be identified by their color alone. Comparing column vectors in two O's in Table 2, though the second principal axis direction of Ruddygore color distribution is near $f_1$ axis, that for Mungana color distribution is near the $f_2$ axis. Their third principal axes are also differently oriented.

As every eigenvector in O is rotated to become a corresponding eigenvector in $O_0$, the first principal axis is rotated to about the $(-u^*, v^*)$ direction, that is, magenta→green, the second principal axis is rotated to about $(-u^*, -v^*)$ direction, that is, yellow→cyan, and the third principal axis is rotated to about $L^*$ direction, that is, brightness.

The shading unnaturality described in (c) is explained as follows. In ordinary cases, the first principal axis is oriented in the brightness direction[2]. However, the first principal axis of the displayable color region is oriented in the magenta

→green direction. Therefore, the brightness direction in the original data is usually mapped to yield green→magenta color variation. Human eyes discriminate rock categories by chromaticity or hue difference. Shading variation does not influence the judgement. Because the LUV algorithm rotates the brightness variation into chromaticity variation, unnaturality takes place.

## 4. New LUV Algorithm

In this section a new algorithm, which is an improvement for the LUV algorithm, is proposed. The policy for the improvement is as follows.

(a) A highly effective enhancement, obtained by the LUV algorithm, should be maintained.

(b) The brightness direction in original data should be preserved. Here, the brightness concept by Kaneko is used.

(c) Hue (especially redness) should be made compatible with conventional false color display.

For this purpose, a new coordinate system $(\rho, \gamma, \lambda)$ is introduced, where $\lambda$ means brightness, $\rho$ means redness, and $\gamma$ is the direction perpendicular to the $\lambda - \rho$ plane. The origin is positioned at the center of the color distribution. The relation between this coordinate system and (R,G,B) for conventional false color display is shown in Fig.2. In this section, (R,G,B) is used instead of $(f_1, f_2, f_3)$, not only for usual false color images, in which $f_1$, $f_2$ and $f_3$ are assigned to R,G and B, respectively, but also other images, used for display (for example, an image synthesized by Kaneko's algorithm), can be enhanced by the new algorithm.

The direction vector $(r_0, g_0, b_0)$ for brightness axis $\lambda$ is taken to be parallel to the vector from origin to distribution mean $(R_0, G_0, B_0)$. Next, a plane which involves $\lambda$ and R axes is assumed and the $\rho$ axis is determined to be perpendicular to

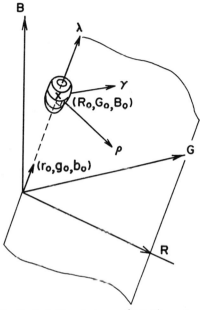

Fig.2 Relation between (R,G,B) system and $(\rho, \lambda, \gamma)$ system.

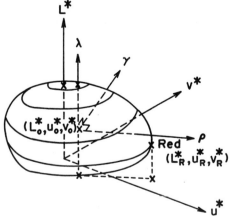

Fig.3 Relation between $(\rho, \lambda, \gamma)$ system and (L*,u*,v*) system.

the $\lambda$ axis and involved in this plane. Last, the $\gamma$ axis is obtained merely by calculating a vector product for $\lambda$ and $\rho$. The rotation is indicated by matrix $O\lambda$.

Figure 3 shows a relation between $(\rho,\gamma,\lambda)$ and $(L^*,u^*,v^*)$. The origin of the $(\rho,\gamma,\lambda)$ coordinate system is positioned at the center of gravity about the dis- playable color region in the $(L^*,u^*,v^*)$ space. The $\lambda$ axis (brightness) is made parallel to the $L^*$ axis. The $\rho$ axis is so determined that the $\lambda-\rho$ plane involves the red point $(L^*_R,u^*_R,v^*_R)$ that is the color coordinate conversion result from $(R,G,B)=(1,0,0)$.

The above discussion is only about axis rotation. Color distribution in the original space is normalized and finally fitted to the entire displayable color re- gion shape, in the same fashion as the old LUV algorithm. A resulting transforma- tion is presented in Eq.(6).

$$\begin{pmatrix}u^*\\v^*\\L^*\end{pmatrix}=O_0'\begin{pmatrix}\sigma'_{01}&0&0\\0&\sigma'_{02}&0\\0&0&\sigma'_{03}\end{pmatrix}O_0'^{-1}\cdot O\rho\cdot O\lambda\cdot O\begin{pmatrix}1/\sigma_1&0&0\\0&1/\sigma_2&0\\0&0&1/\sigma_3\end{pmatrix}O^{-1}\begin{pmatrix}R-R_0\\G-G_0\\B-B_0\end{pmatrix}+\begin{pmatrix}u^*_0\\v^*_0\\L^*_0\end{pmatrix}\qquad(6)$$

(b)                            (a)

Part (a) is for color distribution normalization and part (b) is for fitting to the displayable color region shape. Though matrices $O$ and $O_0'$ are same as those for Eq.(4) and Eq.(5), the vector order for $O_0'$, $(u^*,v^*,L^*)$, is changed from $O_0$, $(L^*,u^*,v^*)$.

## 5. Procedure to calculate $O\lambda$ and $O\rho$

It is assumed that R,G and B axes should be rotated so that they become paral- lel to $\rho$, $\gamma$ and $\lambda$ axes after rotation, respectively. For calculation, the rota- tion process for $O\lambda$ is divided into two phases.
(i) The coordinate system is rotated arround the R axis by an angle $\alpha$, so that the rotated G axis coincides with the $\gamma$ axis.
(ii) Next, the coordinate system is rotated around the $\gamma$ axis by an angle $\beta$, so that the B axis coincides with the $\lambda$ axis.
Then, $O\lambda$ is expressed by Eq.(7).

$$O\lambda=\begin{pmatrix}\cos\beta&\sin\alpha\sin\beta&-\cos\alpha\sin\beta\\0&\cos\alpha&\sin\alpha\\\sin\beta&-\sin\alpha\cos\beta&\cos\alpha\cos\beta\end{pmatrix}\qquad(7)$$

As the direction vector along the $\lambda$ axis was defined as $(r_0,g_0,b_0)^t$, and indi- vidual row vectors for $O\lambda$ are orthogonal with each other, then Eq.(8) holds.

$$g_0\cdot\cos\alpha+b_0\cdot\sin\alpha=0\qquad(8)$$
$$\sin\beta=r_0$$

Angles $\alpha$ and $\beta$ are solved as Eq.(9).

$$\alpha=\tan^{-1}(-g_0/b_0)\qquad\text{and}\qquad|\alpha|\leq\pi/2$$
$$\beta=\sin^{-1}r_0\qquad\text{and}\qquad|\beta|\leq\pi/2\qquad(9)$$

$O\lambda$ can now simply be obtained with $\alpha$ and $\beta$.

The process to calculate $O\rho$ is not difficult. As this rotation is around the $\lambda$ axis, $O\rho$ is represented by Eq.(10).

$$O\rho = \begin{pmatrix} \cos\phi & \sin\phi & 0 \\ -\sin\phi & \cos\phi & 0 \\ 0 & 0 & 1 \end{pmatrix} \tag{10}$$

Putting $(u^*,v^*)$ values for red as $(u^*_R,v^*_R)$, this point was defined to be on the $\lambda$-$\rho$ plane and $\gamma=0$. Then, Eq.(11) holds.

$$(u^*_R-u^*_0)\sin\phi + (v^*_R-v^*_0)\cos\phi = 0 \tag{11}$$

Finally, the angle $\phi$ is obtained as Eq.(12).

$$\phi = \tan^{-1}\{-(v^*_R-v^*_0)/(u^*_R-u^*_0)\} \quad\text{and}\quad |\phi| \leqq \pi/2 \tag{12}$$

Using the above mentioned procedure, all terms in Eq.(6) can be computed. The eight matrices can be, of course, summarized into one 3x3 matrix. Therefore, the computational cost for the new LUV algorithm application to image data is the same as that for the old LUV algorithm.

## 6. Experimental Results and Evaluation

The new LUV algorithm was also applied to the previous image data (Photos 1(a) and (b)). Photos 3(a) and (b) indicate the results. Color difference was very much enhanced, but brightness and hue directions were preserved. The enhanced image color distribution statistics are shown in Table 5. Color distribution shape resembles the displayable color region shape. CRPs are as large as those for the old LUV algorithm results.

These pictures were evaluated by the earth resource exploration experts, again. Their comments were as follow.

"There is no unnaturality in image color or tone. Planted field distribution and rivers can be more explicitly analyzed than by conventional false color display. Moreover, limestones look dark and it is easier to extract outline of the rock."

As it is indicated from Eq. (6), that $\rho$, $\gamma$ and $\lambda$ axis directions depend on the color distribution and the mean color of total image is fitted to $(L^*_0, u^*_0, v^*_0)$, the color correspondence between original false color image and the image result determined by the new LUV algorithm are not exactly the same. However, this chromaticity shift is not evaluated as being an

Table 5 Statistics on color distribution in $L^*u^*v^*$ space for enhanced display by the new LUV algorithm.

|  | Ruddygore | | | Mungana | | |
|---|---|---|---|---|---|---|
| $L^*_0$ $u^*_0$ $v^*_0$ | 57.31 16.39 -10.95 | | | 57.86 15.10 -5.49 | | |
| $\Sigma$ | 322.7 -185.3 272.0 | -185.3 1648.2 -197.5 | 272.0 -197.5 1481.8 | 301.4 -60.7 61.3 | -60.7 1462.3 -112.0 | 61.3 -112.0 1103.6 |
| $\sigma^2$ | 1841.7 | 1362.9 | 248.0 | 1499.1 | 1073.8 | 294.4 |
| O | 0.200 -0.787 0.583 | 0.098 0.608 0.788 | 0.975 0.101 -0.199 | 0.063 -0.958 0.281 | -0.054 -0.284 -0.957 | 0.997 0.045 -0.069 |
| CRP | 24950 | | | 21769 | | |

disadvantage of this new algorithm. Human eye's color adaptation capability seems to contribute to this good evaluation.

## 7. Conclusion

The improved LUV algorithm could highly enhance the false color image with preserved brightness and hue sensation. The resulting pictures met with approval. The algorithm was implemented as a library software and is planned to be used at Earth Resources Satellite Data Analysis Center.

There was a problem in this algorithm being used at a public center. Because this algorithm fully makes use of human color perception characteristics, displayed color should be same as that denoted by the computed (R, G, B) value. It is very important to calibrate color monitors used at the computer center so that an individual primary color brightness is proportional to each value. This problem had been also solved by the authors[4]. Using devices calibrated in such a manner, effective display was obtained.

## ACKNOWLEDGEMENT

The authors thank Mr.Asai, Manager of Pattern Recognition Laboratory, NEC Corporation and Mr.Nakada, Manager of Aerospace Engineering Department, NEC Corporation, for helpful encouragement.

## REFERENCES

[1] J.Tajima:"Uniform Color Scale Applications to Computer Graphics",CVGIP,Vol.21, No.3,pp,305-325,March,1983.
[2] T.Kaneko:"Color Composite Pictures from Principal Axis Components of Multispectral Scanner Data",IBM J.RES.DEVELOP.,Vol.22,No.4,pp.386-392,July,1978
[3] D.B.Judd and G.Wyszecki:"Color in Business, Science, and Industry",Third Ed., Wiley,1975
[4] J.Tajima and Y.Yui:"Color Reproduction Simulation for Color Printing",IECE Japan, IE84-78,Dec.,1984 (in Japanese)

 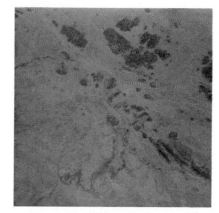

(a) Ruddygore                    (b) Mungana

Photo 1  Conventional false color images.

 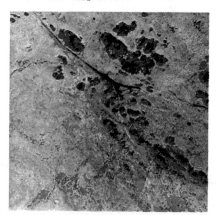

(a) Ruddygore                    (b) Mungana

Photo 2  Images enhanced by the LUV algorithm.

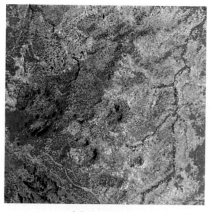 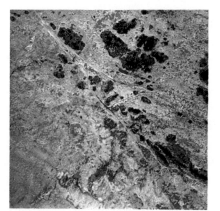

(a) Ruddygore                    (b) Mungana

Photo 3  Images enhanced by the new LUV algorithm.

# OCR OF ARABIC TEXTS

Adnan Amin

Kuwait University, Mathematics Department
P.O. Box 5969, 13060 Safat Kuwait

ABSTRACT

This paper presents a method for the recognition of multi-fonts Arabic texts
entered from a scanner (300 dpi). The technique for the recognition presents the
following steps:
digitization, line sparation, word separation, segmentation of a word into
characters, indentification of each character and finally recognition of the word.

KEY WORDS

Character recognition, Document input, Arabic character, Segmentation.

## 1. Introduction

Character recognition is an area of pattern recognition that has been subjected
to many research works during the last twenty years. This is due to the fact that
recognition and processing of (hand-) printed texts is a basic function that should
be automated in order to improve man-machine communication. Speech recognition
provides another man - machine interface that has grown up into a distinctive discipline of pattern recognition.

New generations of computer gave new impulse to the research on this topic.
Japan, USA and Europe become more and more intersested in the development of reading
machines (OCR) (Andersson 71) for many different purposes.

At the beginning, research was mainly focussed on the recognition of printed
and hand-peinted characters (SUEN 80), including chinese, Kanji, etc., and of postal
addresses (Focht 76) for automatic sorting of letters. In these fields of application, a great effort has been spent to develop fast and cheap equipments in order to
be able to transform paper documents into machine readable files inside a more general
strategy for office automation (Cassey 85).

The first subject of our research was the recognition of isolated Arabic characters and we realized two different systems, know as IRAC for Interactive Recognition

of Arabic Characters, for which a graphic tablet has been used.  The former is a
structural method adapted to recognition of Arabic characters (Amin 80) and the
latter can be applied to different type of graphisms and makes use of a graph
representation (Amin 83).  We have progressed our research to realize three methods
for the recognition of Arabic word (Amin 82), (Amin 84), (Amin 85).  The recognition of printed Arabic texts is an important step in the development  and extension
of man-machine communication in the Arabic world.

The nature of Arabic text or script differs from latin in many structural ways.
Arabic text is normally cursive.  There are 29 different characters.  The shape of
a character depends on its position in the word (at the begining, in the middle,
at the end or isolated).  Arabic characters are mainly composed of curves.  Sixteen
letters of the character set have points either above, below or on the writing line.
Some characters also contain an horizontal or a vertical bar, or a zig-zag.

The first difficulty  encountered  is the classical problem of segmentation
which has taken on an added dimension in our cases owing to the specificty of Arabic
script.  The second problem we had to solve was to recognize a character in any position within a word.  Our solution has been based on horizontal and vertical projection of the image of the character and on the use of histograms to avoid skeletonization.

The basic problem of printed (hand) word recognition are similar to, the spoken
words  recognition problems and some techniques of pattern recognition developed in
this area can be used.  In spoken words recognition, we have to solve the problems
of insertion, deletion and substitution of basic units like phonemes (Mari 79) and
many algorithms have been implemented.  One of the most popoular is the VITERBI
algorithm that specifies a probabilistic approach (Forney 73).  The mean advantage
of this approach is to allow an automatic learning procedure.

In this paper, we will describe the technique we have adopted for automatic
recognition of multi-font print Arabic texts.  It consists in the following
steps :

1.  Digitization and preprocessing:

    a.  digitization of the printed Arabic text,

    b.  separation and juxtaposition of lines to form a single line of digitized
        text,

    c.  identification and separation of subwords in the text.

2.  Segmentation of the subwords into characters (using a histogram) and ident-
    ification of the character.

3.  Recognition of the word

    Using the tree representation lexicon

Each of the part 1, 2  and  3  will be described in one of the following section of the paper.


## 2.  Digitization  and Preprocessing

The image obtained from the text is converted to a binary matrix of "zeros"
(white) and "ones" (black).  The zero elements of the matrix represent the background, while the one elements represent the character.  The next step transforms the
sample into  single line of text by making an horizontal projection.  We use a fixed
threshold to separate the pairs of consecutive lines.

Then, the line is segmented into word and sub-groups of words (a portion of a
word including several connected characters) from a vertical projection.  We use an
averge threshold computed from all the spaces found in the line to decide wether two
consecutive groups must be separated.


## 3.  Segmentation

The segmentation into characters is based on an original algorithm using the
properties of the Arabic characters:  all Arabic characters have a length much greater
than their width.  The segmentation consists in calculating the averge value (Mc)
of all the connect columns of the histogram of the word.

$$Mc = (1 \ / \ Nc) \ \Sigma \ Cic$$

Where * Nc is the number of columns,
      * Cic  is the number of black points for each column.

Figure 1 illustrates the segmentation of an Arabic word into characters.

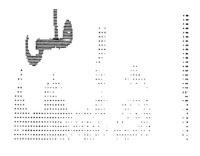

a printed Arabic word and its segmentation
into characters by using an histogram

# 4.  Recognition

## 4.1  Smoothing

This process is carried out to eliminate the noise.  We were inspired by
mathematical morpholigy (Serra 82).

Let  X  be a point in the image and a,b,c,...h its neighbors (Figure 2).

| a | b | c |
|---|---|---|
| d | x | e |
| f | g | h |

Figure 2:   a point and its eight neighbors

We have first applied an opening followed by a closing but this method is not
satisfying.  We implented another method that consists to replace the value of each
point by the value of the following logical expressions:

$$X \leftarrow X + bg(d + e) + de(b + g)$$
$$X \leftarrow X \ (g + bd + be + ah + cf)$$

The former intends to restore the missing points (holes) while the latter intends to delete noise and loosely connected edge points (Figure 3).

Figure 3: results obtained after smoothing

## 4.2  Extraction of the primitives

During the scanning of each line (row) of the image of the character, all connected points are assigned with K order. The points that are separated by a sufficient space are assigned with a K+1 order (Amin 86).

Figure 4:  illustrates the vertical and horizontal scanning
of the character  WAW.

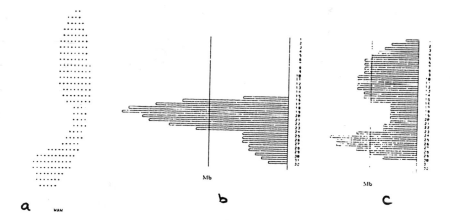

Figure 4:

        a:   Character  WAW

        b:   vertical scanning

        c:   horizontal scanning

Here are different steps of our algorithm:

1.  String generation:

    a:  Build the histogram of each order.

    b:  Compute the average value of each histogram.  The eventual group of dots
        and secondary segments are taken into account.

$$Mb = (1 / Nbp) \ \Sigma \ (1 / Hi) \ \Sigma \ Pj$$

      Nbp = number of primitives,

      Hi  = height of the primitive i,

      Pj  = number of black points of each line  j  of the projection.

    c:  Character string; each row (line) is coded by  Z  (there is no black
        point), X (horizontal bar) and Y (vertical bar).

        Z  if  $Pj = 0$

        Y  if  $0 < Pj \leq Mb$

        X  if  $Pj > Mb$.

2.  Simplification  of the code of the string: the goal of this operation is
    to eliminated the noise and the redundances.  We use 52 different rules,
    and here are some examples of these:

```
 1:  ZZZZ ⇒ Z
 2:  XXXX ⇒ X
 3:  YYYY ⇒ Y
 4:  ZYYY ⇒ Y
 5:  ZXXX ⇒ X
 6:  XXZZ ⇒ X
 7:  YYXX ⇒ if (Y<3) or ((Mb-Y)<3) then X else YX
 8:  YZZZ ⇒ if (Y<3) or ((Mb-Y)<3) then Z else YZ
 9:  XXXY ⇒ if (Y<3) or ((Mb-Y)<3) then X else XY
10:  YYYX ⇒ if ((X-Mb)<4) then Y else YX
```

For example, in the Figure 5, the initial string corresponding to the horizontal projection of the character  LAM  is:

YYYY YYYY YYYY YYYY YYYY YYXX XXXX XXZZ

This string is transformated into:

Y    Y    Y    Y    Y    X    X    X

After the redundances have been eliminated, it becomes finally  YX.

In the same way, the vertical projection for the same character is:

ZZZZ ZZZZ ZZZZ ZZZX XXXX YYYY YYYY YYYY

It becomes first ZZZXXYYY that is simplified into XY.

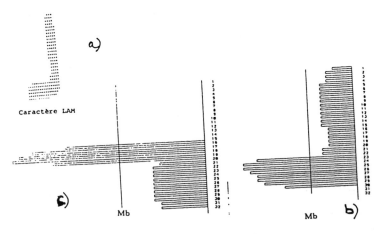

Figure 5: vertical and horizontal scanning of the
character LAM.

a:   character LAM

b:   horizontal scanning

c:   vertical scanning

### 4.3  The dictionary

The dictionary is constituted of four decision trees according to position of the character within the word, each branch of the trees representing a primitive. This structure allows to find  rapidly the character and to distinguish character that have the same shape but appear in different position within a word.

The recognition consists  in finding a path through a tree, using the primitive classes of the  descreption of the character (X, Y) to be recognized as instructions to choose which arcs to take.  The terminal node of the path gives the ASCII code of the recognized character .

### 4.4  Word recognition

The dictionary is composed of trees that are identical to the character ones, but the nodes  are  labeled  with character names.  Characters extracted from the list of the primitives allows to follow a path in the dictionary.  On the same way that a primitive allows  to follow a path in the character trees.  Each node of the dictionary is associated with a boolean variable indicating if the path joining the root to the  terminal node corresponds effectivelly to an existing word.

The main  advantage of this method is to avoid both the use of digrams and trigrams (Riseman 71), and to restrict the memory occupation.

The set of hypothesis constitute a lattice supplied by the segmentation stage. The identification of the word so represented consists in searching in the lattice a path  corresponding to a word in the dictionary.

## 5.  Experimental result  and conclusion

We present in this paper a structural approach for the recognition of Arabic multi-font texts.

All the  algorithms described in this paper were written in PASCAL and run on an IBM PC  a compatible system.  The input device was a high resolution, 300-dot per inch scanner

We obtained a 90% recognition rate for Arabic characters (Figure 6).

الأنظمة المتكاملة لمعالجة المعلومات العربية المتعددة اللغات

ان حلول التعريب المقترحة هنا ، تتلخص في توفير أنظمة متكاملة سواء في مجال الأجهزة او في التطبيقات، مما يمكن من معالجة المعطيات المتعددة اللغات عربي/لاتيني. وعليه تشمل الأنظمة المحتويات التالية :

3- حل كل المشاكل الخاصة وكتابة على مستوى النهايات الطرفية أو على مستوى أجهزة إدخال وإخراج المعلومات نفسها مما يوفر تلاؤما تاما وكاملا بين معالجة المعطيات العربية واللاتينية. وقد تم تعميم فكرة التلاؤم هذه على جميع المستويات بغرض الاستعمال على كافة التطبيقات اللاتينية الموجودة أصلا مع سهولة فائقة في تعريبها وجعلها ملائمة لاستخدامات وظروف المستعمل العربي.

4- إحتواء أجهزة إدخال وإخراج المعلومات على نظام تحليلي ذو كفاءة عالية يقوم أوتوماتيكيا باختيار الشكل الصحيح لكل حرف عربي وفقا لوضع الحرف داخل الكلمة ، مع العلم أن كل حرف له كود واحد مهما تعددت الأشكال المعبرة عنه . علاوة على ذلك يشمل النظام التحليلي معالجة الحالات الخاصة ببعض الحروف في اللغة العربية، مثل حالة اللام ألف، وحالة الأشكال المختلفة لحركات التشكيل عند إستعمالها مع الشدة () ، وذلك بطريقة تسمح بأن يكون إستعمال المعطيات متلائما تماما مع توصيات المنظمة العربية للمواصفات والمقاييس ( أسمو ) وفي نفس الوقت يتم إظهار وترئية المعطيات العربية بطريقة متآلفة ومتلائمة مع المستعمل العربي.

الأنظمة المتكاملة لمعالجة المعلومات العربية المتعددة اللغات
ان حلول التعريب المقترحة هنا ، تتلخص في توفير أنظمة متكاملة سواء في مجال الأجهزة** او في التطبيقات، مما يمكن من معالجة المعطيات المتعددة اللغات عربي/لاتيني. وعليه تشمل الأنظمة المحتويات التالية :
3- حل كل المشاكل الخاصة وكتابة على مستوى النهايات الطرفية أو على مستوى أجهزة إدخال وإخراج المعلومات نفسها مما يوفر تلاؤما تاما وكاملا بين معالجة المعطيات العربية وال*تينية. وقد تم تعميم فكرة التلاؤم هذه على جميع المستويات بغرض الاستح*ل على كافة التطبيقات اللاتينية الموجود* أصلا مع سهولة فائقة في تعريبها وجعلها ملائمة لاستخدامات وظروف المستعمل العربي.
4- إحتواء أجهزة إدخال وإخراج المعلومات على نظام تحليلي ذو كفاءة عالية يقوم أوتوماتيكيا با***ر الشكل ال*ح* لكل حرف عربي وفقا لوضع الحرف داخل الكلمة ، مع العلم أن كل حرف له كود واحد مهما تعددت لأشكال المعبرة عنه . علاوة على ذلك يشمل النظام التحليلي معال*ة الحالات الخاصة ببعض الحروف في ا*لفة العربية، مثل حالة السلام ألف، وحالة الأ*كال المختلفة لحركات التشكيل عند إستعمالها مع الشدة () ، وذلك بطريقة تسمح بأن يكون إستع*ل الم*طيات متلائ*ا تماما مع ترصيات المنظمة العربية للمواصفات والمقاييس ( أسمو ) وفي نفس الوقت يتم إظهار وترئية المعطيات العربية بطريقة متآلفة ومتلائمة مع المستعمل العربي.

Figure 6: Sample Arabic text for which we obtained a 90% recognition rate. The recognition speed was about 3 characters per second.

## REFERENCES

(Amin 80) A. Amin, A. Kaced, J.P. Haton and R. Mohr
"Handwritten Arabic Characters Recognition by the IRAC system". Proc. 5th International Conference on Pattern Recognition, Miami beach, Florida, USA, pp 729-731 (1980)

(Amin 82) A. Amin
"Machine recognition of handwritten arabic words by the IRAC II system", Proc. 6th
Inter national  Conference on Pattern Recognition, Munchen, Germany pp 34-36 (1982).

(Amin 83) A. Amin and A. Shoukry
"Topological and statistical analysis of line drawings"  Pattern Recognition Letters,
pp. 365-374 (1983).

(Amin 84) A. Amin, G. Masini and J.P. Haton
"Recognition  of handwritten arabic word and sentences"  Proc. 7th International
Conference on Pattern Recognition, Montreal, Canada (1984).

(Amin  85) A. Amin
"IRAC:  Un systeme pour la reconnaissance et la comprehension de l'arabe ecrit et
imprime"   These d'ETAT, CRIN, Universite de NANCY I (1985).

(Amin 86) A . Amin and G. Masini
"Machine  Recognition of multi-font printed Arabic texts"  Proc. 8th International
Conference on Pattern Recognition, Paris, France, pp  392-395  (1986)

(Andersson 71) P.L. Andersson
"OCR  enters the practical stage"  Datamation, Vol. 17, pp  22-27, Dec. (1971).

(Gassy  85)  R. G. Cassey and K.Y. Wong
"Text recognition in a document analysis system"  Proc.  IEEE Global Telecomm.
Conference, New  Orleans (1985).

(Focht 76)  L. R. Focht and A. Burger
"A  numeric  script recognition  processor for postal zip code application ", Proc.
of Int.  Conference of Cybernetic Society, pp  489-492 (1976).

(Riseman 71) E. M. Rise man and R. W. Ehrich
"Contextual Word recognition using binary digrams"  Proc. IEEE Trans.  On Computers,
Vol. C-20, No 4, pp 397-403 (1971).

(Serr a 82) J. Serra
"Image analysis and mathematical morphology"  Academic Press, London (1982).

(Suen 80) C. H. Suen, M . Berthod and S. Mori
"Automatic  recognition  of handprinted characters:  the state of the art" Proc.
IEEE, Vol. 68, No . 4, pp  469-487  (1980)

# GRAMMATICAL ANALYSIS OF ENGLISH BY STATISTICAL PATTERN RECOGNITION

Eric Steven Atwell

Centre for Computer Analysis of Language And Speech (CCALAS)
Artificial Intelligence Division, School of Computer Studies
Leeds University, Leeds, U.K.
(EARN/BITNET: eric%leeds.ai@ac.uk)

ABSTRACT:

Artificial Intelligence and Computational Linguistics researchers are currently debating the value of 'Deep' knowledge-representations in language processing and related computations.. Incorporating deep knowledge as well as surface statistical pattern recognition requires much greater processing, but it has been assumed that, for many applications of Artificial Intelligence, purely surface statisitical analyses cannot yield useful results. One NLP application provides a counter-argument to this widespread tenet: a system for grammatical error detection, using only probabilistic, Markovian, pattern-matching was devised, and in tests compared favourably with a much larger system which computed deep grammatical analyses of each sentence. Those who argue that statistical pattern recognition has no place in Computational Linguistics or Artificial Intelligence have still to prove their case.

## 1 STATISTICAL PATTERN RECOGNITION IN NLP AND AI

This paper deals with one specific Natural Language Processing expert system, to detect errors in Word Processed text. However, perhaps more importantly, this provides us with an analogy or lesson for a more general point of interest in Computational Linguistics and Artificial Intelligence. A topic of current debate in NLP and AI research is the level of 'Deep Knowledge Modelling' required in useful 'intelligent' systems (Refs 1-5). Unfortunately, there is no clear domain-independent definition of what constitutes 'deep' as opposed to 'surface' knowledge. Deep knowledge is supposed to encompass the underlying physical laws and principles governing a domain, as contrasted with the 'surfacy' description of a problem which can be more readily elicited from a human domain expert, or from statistical 'training' of a model from sample data using statistical pattern recognition techniques. Rather than attempt a clear definition, many proponents of deep knowledge modelling rely on description by example. For instance, an Expert System to solve routing problems in circuit design could be based on 'surfacy' rules about which components are usually used and combined by human experts; but, it is argued, if 'deep' knowledge about the underlying laws of physics and electronics (e.g. Ohm's Law) could be integrated into the knowledge base, the Expert System could produce better solutions and/or cope with a wider variety of circuit design problems. Alternatively, a system equipped with some sort of deep knowledge might be better equipped to 'learn' qualitative (as opposed to quantitative, statistical) knowledge about a domain 'from first principles': the deep knowledge here essentially consists in general concept discovery techniques (Refs 6-10).

## 2 DRAWBACKS OF DEEP KNOWLEDGE

However, R&D groups wishing to develop practical, commercially marketable Intelligent Systems should be wary of embracing deep knowledge modelling until a number of questions have been resolved. Firstly, there is no general agreement on how to represent domain-specific deep knowledge such as Ohm's Law in an Expert System, or how to integrate such deep knowledge into an Expert System, even for apparently well-suited examples such as the circuit design modeller. Secondly, even if deep knowledge could be exploited in specific special cases, this does not necessarily tell us how to integrate and use deep knowledge in other Systems, including general-purpose shells. Finally, perhaps most importantly from the practical point of view of building Systems for today's market rather than for academic experimentation, there is insufficient empirical evidence that deep knowledge modelling will actually improve performance except in special cases. If currently-available systems work well in a wide variety of domains without deep knowledge modelling, why complicate matters just because some academic researchers believe intuitively that deep knowledge is Good?

# 3 DEEP AND SURFACE RULES IN COMPUTATIONAL LINGUISTICS

Natural Language processing is probably the longest-established branch of Artificial Intelligence; in fact, Computational Linguistics may well predate Artificial Intelligence, since one of the earliest applications proposed for the code-breaking machines of the Second World War was Machine Translation. The terms "deep" and "surface" are used in Natural Language Processing to describe syntactic descriptions or analyses of sentences; a surface analysis is limited to readily-discernible phrase structure, whereas a deep analysis represents something closer to the underlying meaning-structure, possibly with hidden or transformed elements, markers and features, etc. Noam Chomsky is credited with first drawing the deep/surface distinction; in (Ref 11), he showed that several syntactic constructs in English could not be described straightforwardly using surface rules, and he went on to propose a deep level formalism which could deal with these problems more elegantly and parsimoniously. The arguments in favour of deep analysis of English grammatical structures are dealt with in more detail in most introductory texts on Natural Language Processing, for example, (Refs 12,13). Here I will simply illustrate the case with a couple of examples.

One problem with a purely surface analysis of grammar is that pairs of sentences with different surface structures can involve the same or very similar meanings. For example, "Eric kissed Charlie" and "Charlie was kissed by Eric" mean the same thing; but in the first sentence, "Eric" is the Subject and "Charlie" is the Object, while in the second sentence the surface roles are interchanged. The solution proposed by Chomsky, and widely adopted by other Computational Linguists, is that while the surface analyses are different, they both have the same deep structure. The deep rules (commonly called the Base Component of the grammar) can generate a single same analysis for both sentences. Deep analyses are mapped onto surface structures via a series of Transformations in Chomsky's model; the difference between the two sentences results from the application of an optional Passivization Transformation in one sentence but not the other.

A converse problem can also occur in English: two sentences apparently with the same or very similar surface structure may have quite different deep analyses. The most oft-quoted example of this is the contrast between "John is easy to please" and "John is eager to please". According to surface syntax rules, both sentences have essentially the same structure. However, in the underlying deep analysis, in the first sentence someone should be pleasing John, while in the second sentence it is John who should be pleasing someone. It is commonly argued that without deep knowledge of underlying grammatical structure, a Natural Language Processing system cannot cope adequately with such distinctions.

# 4  DEEP KNOWLEDGE IN CURRENT NLP THEORIES AND APPLICATIONS

Issues such as the nature of the deep/surface distinction, the formalisms to be used in deep and surface rules, and the central importance of deep structures in language processing, have been explored and discussed at length by the computational linguistics community over the past three decades.  Many variants of Chomsky's original model have been suggested (for example, Augmented Transition Networks (Ref 14); Lexical Functional Grammar (Ref 15); Generalized Phrase Structure Grammar (Ref 16)).  Some prefer to avoid the terms "deep" and "surface", as these have become closely associated with Chomskyan Transformational-Generative theories of grammar; however, in practice all involve some near-equivalent to Chomsky's distinction between surface analysis and deeper representations.

It is computationally much more expensive to compute the deep parses of input sentences, but it is argued that this deep analysis is necessary for useful applications.  The application area I have most knowledge of is error-detection and proofreading of Word Processed English text; most systems being developed to detect syntactic errors in English text assume that a fairly deep analysis is essential, to cope with the full range of syntax found in unrestricted Word Processed documents and still manage to reject ill-formed sentences.  This assumption has led to huge, unwieldy and expensive systems such as IBM's EPISTLE (Refs 17,18): the designers reported that the EPISTLE system required a 4Mb virtual machine (although a more efficient implementation is under development).  Other systems for dealing with grammatically ill-formed input (e.g. Refs 19-25) are generally designed for Natural Language Query systems (for software systems such as DataBase packages or Expert Systems); because of the restricted application, such systems may assume it is reasonable to restrict the English the user is allowed to use, which allows deep analyses to be attempted without unreasonable processing overheads.  For example, the experimental system described in (Ref 20) involved a deep, semantic analysis, but the dictionary only dealt with about fifty words!  Such systems, limited to a subset of English, cannot be used in the Word Processing domain: it is *not* reasonable to restrict the input allowed in general Word Processed documents.

# 5 A TEST SYSTEM BASED ON STATISTICAL PATTERN MATCHING

I have tested the assumption that deep knowledge modelling is essential for this domain, by designing and testing a system to detect errors using only highly restricted surface knowledge of English syntax. This system is based on Constituent-Likelihood grammar (Refs 26,27), and its syntactic knowledge is limited to first-order Markovian probabilistic rules of surface word-class cooccurrences. The system first uses a dictionary, suffixlist and other default routines to assign a set of putative tags to each word; then, for each sequence of ambiguously-tagged words, the likelihood of every possible combination or 'chain' of tags is evaluated, and the best chain is chosen. The likelihood of each chain of tags is evaluated as a product of all the 'links' (tag-pair-likelihoods) in the sequence; tag-pair likelihood is a function of the frequency of that sequence of two tags in a sample of tagged text, compared to the frequency of each of the two tags individually. An important advantage of this simple Markovian model is that word-tagging is done without 'deep' parsing: there is no need to work out deep-level constituent-structure trees before assigning unambiguous word-tags to words. The Constituent-Likelihood model was originally used to assign grammatical word-class markers to every word in a million-word collection of English text samples, the LOB Corpus (Refs 28-31); no attempt was made at 'deeper' analysis because this would have been computationally much more difficult. For error-detection, an additional stage in the analysis is required: once each word has been assigned a "best-in-context" tag, tag-cooccurrences are again checked. The likelihood of even the "best" tag may be very low, which is commonly indicative of a grammatical infelicity; when it is below a threshold, the message "ERROR" is output along with the accompanying word.

The error detection technique is described in more detail elsewhere (see Refs 32 and 33). Signal error detection by statistical techniques is used in other applications of pattern recognition (such as speech recognition or computer vision), but computational linguists have in the past assumed that Markovian models are too simple to describe the complex structure of English grammar. Attempts to use Hidden Markov models and other pattern recognition techniques to *discover* a statistical grammar of English from raw text have had only limited success (see, for example, Refs 34-39), so many computational linguists have dismissed pattern recognition techniques completely. For the purpose of the argument presented in this paper, the most important point is how error detection rates for this purely surface-knowledge-based system compare with those of much more complex and computationally expensive systems attempting deeper, fuller grammatical analysis.

# 6  COMPARISON OF DETECTION RATES

Error-detection by this system is much simpler than using a 'full-blown' parser, and yet, surprisingly, the success rate promises to be comparable. Unfortunately, there is no 'full-blown' parser for grammatical error-detection commercially available for direct comparisons; IBM's EPISTLE, for example, is an internal research vehicle only. To make some sort of comparative assessment, I took samples of text containing errors, and manually classified these errors according to the type and complexity of systems required to detect them. The errors were grouped into four classes:

A: non-word error-forms, where the error can be found by simple dictionary-lookup; These are spelling errors detectable by standard WP spelling-checkers, which are purely surface-knowledge-driven; for example: *As the news pours in from around the world, beleagured (SIC) Berlin this weekend is a city on a razor's edge.* (Ref 40)

B: error-forms involving valid English words in an invalid grammatical context, the kind of error the purely surface-based approach could be expected to detect (these may be due to spelling or typing or grammatical mistakes by the typist, but this is irrelevant here: the classification is according to the level of knowledge required by the detection program); for example: *Unlike an oil refinery one cannot grumble much about the fumes, smell and industrial dirt, generally, for little comes out of the chimney except possibly invisible gasses. (SIC)* (Ref 41)

C: error-forms which are valid English words, but in an abnormal grammatical/semantic context, which a system restricted to surface knowledge would not detect, but which *could* conceivably be caught by a very sophisticated parser incorporating deep knowledge of English grammar; for example: *The raie which would have to be paid in these circumstances would be those (SIC) of first-year operatives and not those (SIC) of "other worker."* (Ref 42)

D: lexically and syntactically valid error-forms which would require "intelligent" semantic analysis for detection (that is, which even a parser with deep knowledge could not cope with); for example: *She did not imagine that he would pay her a visit except in Frank's interest, and when she hurried into the room where her mother was trying in vain to learn the reason of his visit, her first words were of her fiancee (SIC).* (Ref 43)

Since the classification was of necessity intuitive rather than empirical, the statistics elicited cannot be claimed to be definitive. In particular, I was probably over-generous in the number of cases I assumed a deep-knowledge-based parser could correctly detect. One important overall impression is that different sources show widely different distributions of error-classes. For example, a sample of 150 errors from three different sources shows the following distribution:

i) Published (and hence manually proofread) text:
   surface knowledge sufficient (A 52% + B 28%): 80%
   deep knowledge required (C): 8%
   undetectable even with deep knowledge (D): 12%


ii) essays by 11- and 12-year-old children:
   surface knowledge sufficient (A 36% + B 38%): 74%
   deep knowledge required (C): 16%
   undetectable even with deep knowledge (D): 10%


iii) non-native English speakers:
   surface knowledge sufficient (A 4% + B 48%): 52%
   deep knowledge required (C): 12%
   undetectable even with deep knowledge (D): 36%


AVERAGE:
   surface knowledge sufficient (A 31% + B 38%): 69%
   deep knowledge required (C): 12%
   undetectable even with deep knowledge (D): 19%


Clearly, a system lacking the ability to attempt deep analyses of input sentences is liable to miss more errors. However, the degradation in performance predicted by the above figures may well be acceptable in practice, particularly given the large savings in processing time (and the fact that even the best 'deep parser' would still leave some errors undetected).

# 7 CONCLUSION

My conclusion is that, although 'deep' knowledge may be needed for ideal, highly-sophisticated Natural Language grammatical analysis systems, useful pragmatic solutions can be designed without it. This has been demonstrated for the non-trivial problem of error-detection in Natural Language text. I am not arguing that deep knowledge modelling has no place in Computational Linguistics or Artificial Intelligence research; indeed, this avenue of investigation promises to give us new insights into human reasoning techniques and other thorny theoretical problems. However, even if it turns out that human experts in a particular domain actually reason using something analogous to some combination of deep knowledge and probabilistic pattern recognition in problem solving, we need not assume that current 'shallow' computer pattern recognition algorithms in the domain must necessarily be augmented with deep knowledge. It must first be demonstrated empirically that the extra overheads are justified by significantly improved performance. R&D teams should wait for proponents of Deep Knowledge Modelling to prove their case before committing themselves.

## REFERENCES

1) Cohn, A G 1985 "Deep Knowledge Representation Techniques" in M Merry (ed), *Expert Systems 85: proceedings of the fifth technical conference of the British Computer Society Specialist Group on Expert Systems* Cambridge University Press.

2) Hayes, P J 1979 "The Naive Physics Manifesto" in D Michie (ed), *Expert Systems in the Micro Electronic Age* Edinburgh University Press

3) Forbus, K 1984 "Qualitative Process Theory" in D Bobrow (ed), *Qualitative Reasoning about Physical Systems* North Holland

4) Alvey Directorate 1985 *IKBS Report on the first Workshop on Deep Knowledge* Institution of Electrical Engineers

5) Alvey Directorate 1986 *IKBS Report on the second Workshop on Deep Knowledge* Institution of Electrical Engineers

6) Atwell, E S 1987 "A parsing expert system which learns from corpus analysis" to appear in W Meijs (ed), *Corpus Linguistics and Beyond: Proceedings of the ICAME 7th International Conference on English Language Research on Computerised Corpora* Rodopi, Amsterdam.

7) Davis R and D Lenat 1982, *Knowledge Based Systems in Artificial Intelligence* McGraw Hill

8) Cunningham, J 1985 "Comprehension by model-building as a basis for an expert system" in M Merry (ed), *Expert Systems 85: proceedings of the fifth technical conference of the British Computer Society Specialist Group on Expert Systems* Cambridge University Press.

9) Atwell, E S 1987 "Transforming a Parsed Corpus into a Corpus Parser", to appear in *Proceedings of the ICAME 8th International Conference on English Language Research on Computerised Corpora* (forthcoming)

10) Atwell, E S 1987 "An Expert System for the Automatic Discovery of Particles" to appear in *Proceedings of the International Conference on the Study of Particles* (forthcoming).

11) Chomsky, N 1957 *Syntactic Structures* Mouton, The Hague

12) Winograd, T 1983 *Language as a cognitive process; volume 1: syntax* Addison-Wesley

13) Johnson, T 1985 *Natural Language Computing: the commercial applications* Ovum, London

14) Woods, W 1970 "Transition Network Grammars for Natural Language Analysis" in *Communications of the Association for Computing Machinery* 13(10): 591-606

15) Bresnan, J and R Kaplan 1982 "Lexical-Functional Grammar: a formal system for grammatical representation" in Joan Bresnan (ed), *The Mental Representation of Grammatical Relations* 173-281, MIT Press

16) Gazdar, G, E Klein, G Pullum, and I Sag 1985 *Generalized Phrase Structure Grammar* Blackwell, Oxford

17) Heidorn, G E, Jensen, K, Miller, L A, Byrd, R J, and Chodorow, M S, 1982 "The EPISTLE text-critiquing system" in *IBM Systems Journal* 21(3): 305-326

18) Jensen, K, Heidorn, G E, Miller, L A, and Ravin, Y 1983 "Parse fitting and prose fixing: getting a hold on ill-formedness" in *American Journal of Computational Linguistics* 9(3-4): 147-160

19) Carbonell, J and P Hayes 1983 "Recovery strategies for parsing extragrammatical language" in *American Journal of Computational Linguistics* 9(3-4): 123-146

20) Fass, D, and Y Wilks 1983 "Preference semantics, ill-formedness, and metaphor" in *American Journal of Computational Linguistics* 9(3-4): 178-187

21) Granger, R 1983 "The NOMAD system: expectation-based detection and correction of errors during understanding of syntactically and semantically ill-formed text" in *American Journal of Computational Linguistics* 9(3-4): 188-196

22) Hayes, P J, and G V Mouradian 1981 "Flexible Parsing" in *American Journal of Computational Linguistics* 7(4): 232-242

23) Kwasny, S, and N Sondheimer 1981 "Relaxation techniques for parsing grammatically ill-formed input in natural language understanding systems" in *American Journal of Computational Linguistics* 7(2): 99-108

24) Weischedel, R, and J Black 1980 "Responding intelligently to unparsable inputs" in *American Journal of Computational Linguistics* 6(2) 97-109

25) Weischedel, R, and N Sondheimer 1983 "Meta-rules as a basis for processing ill-formed input" in *American Journal of Computational Linguistics* 9(3-4):161-177

26) Atwell, E S 1983 "Constituent-Likelihood Grammar" in *Newsletter of the International Computer Archive of Modern English (ICAME NEWS)* 7: 34-67, Norwegian Computing Centre for the Humanities, Bergen University.

27) Atwell, E S (forthcoming), "Constituent-likelihood grammar" to appear in Roger Garside, Geoffrey Sampson and Geoffrey Leech (eds) *The computational analysis of English* Longman

28) Atwell, E S, G Leech and R Garside 1984, "Analysis of the LOB Corpus: progress and prospects", in J Aarts and W Meijs (ed), *Corpus Linguistics* Rodopi.

29) Leech, G, R Garside, and E S Atwell 1983a, "Recent developments in the use of computer corpora in English language research" in *Transactions of the Philological Society* 1983: 23-40.

30) Leech, G, R Garside, and E S Atwell 1983b "The Automatic Grammatical Tagging of the LOB Corpus" in *Newsletter of the International Computer Archive of Modern English (ICAME NEWS)* 7: 13-33, Norwegian Computing Centre for the Humanities, Bergen University

31) Johansson, S, E Atwell, R Garside and G Leech 1986, *The Tagged LOB Corpus* Norwegian Computing Centre for the Humanities, Bergen.

32) Atwell, E S 1986, "How to detect grammatical errors in a text without parsing it", Department of Computer Studies Research Report 212; to appear in *Proceedings of the Association for Computational Linguistics Third European Chapter Conference, Copenhagen, Denmark* (forthcoming).

33) Atwell, Eric Steven (forthcoming) "Measuring grammaticality of machine-readable text" to appear in *Proceedings of the 1987 XIV International Congress of Linguists, Berlin, East Germany*

34) Wolff, J G 1976 "Frequency, Conceptual Structure and Pattern Recognition" in *British Journal of Psychology* 67:377-390

35) Wolff, J G 1978 "The Discovery of Syntagmatic and Paradigmatic Classes" in *ALLC Bulletin* 6(1):141

36) Atwell, Eric Steven 1986 *Extracting a Natural Language grammar from raw text* Department of Computer Studies Research Report no.208, University of Leeds

37) Atwell, Eric Steven 1986 "A parsing expert system which learns from corpus analysis" in Willem Meijs (ed) *Corpus Linguistics and Beyond: Proceedings of the 1986 Seventh International Conference on English Language Research on Computerised Corpora, Amsterdam, Netherlands* Rodopi, Amsterdam

38) Atwell, Eric Steven, and Nikos Drakos (forthcoming), "Pattern Recognition Applied to the Acquisition of a Grammatical Classification System from Unrestricted English Text" to appear in *Proceedings of the 1987 Association for Computational Linguistics Third European Chapter Conference, Copenhagen, Denmark*

39) Atwell, Eric Steven (forthcoming) "An Expert System for the Automatic Discovery of Particles" to appear in *Proceedings of the 1987 International Conference on the Study of Language Particles, West Berlin, West Germany*

40) Thomas, A N 1961, "Now Kruschev Hots Up" in *News of the World* July 9 (LOB Corpus text sample A21)

41) 'The Walrus' 1961, "Of Shoes and Ships and Sealing Wax" in *Yachting World* December (LOB Corpus text sample E18)

42) (Anonymous) 1961, "Editorial Points" in *Hair and Beauty* 41: 6 (June) (LOB Corpus text sample E34)

43) Hamblin, H 1961, "Give Back My Dreams" in *Smart Novels* February 6 (LOB Corpus text sample P17)

# A METHODOLOGY FOR EFFICIENCY ESTIMATION OF THE SPEECH SIGNAL FEATURE EXTRACTION METHODS

Zdravko Kačič and Bogomir Horvat
University of Maribor
Faculty of Technical Sciences
Smetanova 17, 62000 Maribor, Yugoslavia

ABSTRACT. This paper deals with a basis of methodology for speech signal feature description. Speech signal is described by three sets of features (the set of all descriptive features, the set of all selected features, and the set of all characteristic features ). Feature description methods are described by three sets of maps ( descriptive feature map, selected feature map, and characteristic feature map ). As an example two feature description methods are considered - zero - crossing method and method of formant frequency energy classes (variant a and b ). Efficiency of a single method being used in the recognition process has been estimated on the basis of experimental results. It is shown that the Fourier transformation as a map of descriptive features is more convenient as a measurement of time interval lenght. The mapping rule in variant b of the method of formant frequency energy classes gives a more convenient map of selected features than the mapping rule in variant a. With these maps the smallest features overlapping and consequently a better average recognition accuracy ( greater than 92.5 % ) can be achieved.

## 1. Introduction

Successful realization of speaker - independent continuous speech recognition system initially requires a proper solution of speech signal "features overlapping" problem.
Problem of features overlapping isnt't successfuly solved yet. Commercial speaker - independent continuous speech recognition systems with large vocabulary are not yet available on the market [1]. They exist as prototypes only and their vocabulary is limited to 10 words [1].
In systems recognizing isolated words, there is a great difference in vocabulary extent between speaker-depenedent and speaker-independent systems ( 20000 words at speaker - dependent and 40 words at speaker - indepenedent systems ) [1,3].
The reason for an enormous difference in vocabulary extent can here be found in inadequate solution of the features overlapping problem, too.

The speech signal can be recognized on the basis of phonetic units
( words, syllables, phonemes ... ).
Phonetic units can be described by miscellaneous feature description
methods [2,3,4]. Those describe speech features in different ways.
A final result of phonetic unit feature description process is mostly
an n - dimensional feature vector.
The set of feature vectors of the same phonetic unit ( when a phonetic
unit was uttered by a set of different speaker ) presents a cluster in
n - dimensional space.
Overlap of different clusters in n-dimensional space is different and
depends on feature description method used in feature description
process.
Each cluster represents features of a phonetic unit ( this is also
true for a particular feature vector ), therefore the overlap of two
or more clusters may be called a feature overlapping of different
phonetic units.
Feature overlapping mostly means recognition error in the recognition
process .
If we want to achieve high recognition accuracy the smallest feature
overlapping of different basic phonetic unit and the smallest
dispersion of feature vectors of same basic phonetic unit must be
assured.
Our paper deals with some basic terms in the methodology for
efficiency estimation of the speech signal feature extraction methods.
Further development of methodology should make it possible to select
or define "optimum" feature description methods for particular
phonetic unit.


2. Description of speech signal features


Speech signal features description process usually consists of two
stages. In first stage speech features are "mathematically described"
(e.g. calculation of frequency specter, measurement of interval lenght
between two successive zero crossing of a signal, calculation of LPC
coefficients, ...).
The final result of second description is mostly composed in an n-
dimensional feature vector, which is then used in the recognition
process. With this great reduction of data is usually achieved. As
a second description various variants of zero-crosing method, various
variants of method of formant frequency energy classes etc. may be
used.
Of course more "intermediate description" is possible to achieve
better description of speech signal features, but the final result is
again, in most cases, an n-dimensional feature vector.
Furthermore we will presume feature description process composed of
two descriptions.
Feature extraction process shall be described by means of three sets
of speech signal features and three sets of map.

The three sets of features are: the set of all descriptive features, the set of all selected features and the set of all characteristic features. Each of the sets should be mapped with the following sets of maps : descriptive feature map, selected feature map, and characteristic feature map. Such a distribution of speech signal features has been assumed to estimate the convenience of a single feature extraction method which shall be used in the feature extraction process.

Let us describe briefly each single set of features and the sets of maps.

## 2.1. Sets of features

### 2.1.1. Set of the phonetic unit utterances - $\mathcal{A}$

$$\mathcal{A} = \{A_1, A_2, \ldots A_n, \ldots A_N\},$$

N – the number of different phonetic units

$$A_n = \{A_{n1}, A_{n2}, \ldots A_{nm}, \ldots \},$$

$A_{nm}$ –the m – th articulation of the n – th phonetic unit

$$A_{nm} = \{a_{nm1}, a_{nm2}, \ldots a_{nm1}, \ldots a_{nmL}\},$$

L – the number of basic phonetic units ( frames ) of the m – th utterance

$a_{nm1}$ – the l – th basic phonetic unit of the m – th utterance of the n-th phonetic unit

$$a_{nm1} = \{a^1_{nm1}, a^2_{nm1}, \ldots a^u_{nm1}, \ldots a^U_{nm1}\},$$

U – the number of elements ( samples ) in the l-th frame.

### 2.1.2. Set of all descriptive features - D

$$I = \{descriptions\}$$

$$D = \{D_i, i \in I\}$$

$D^i$ – the set of descriptive features described by the i-th description

$$D_i = \{D_{i1}, D_{i2}, \ldots, D_{in}, \ldots D_{iN}\},$$

$D_{in}$ – the set of descriptive features of the n-th phonetic unit described by the i-th description

$D_{in} = \{D_{in1}, D_{in2}, \ldots, D_{inm}, \ldots \}$,

$D_{inm}$ - the set of descriptive features of the m-th utterance of the n-th phonetic unit

$D_{inm} = \{D_{inm1}, D_{inm2}, \ldots D_{inm1}, \ldots D_{inmL}\}$,

L - the number of basic phonetic units of the m-th utterance of the n-th phonetic unit

$D_{inml}$ - the set of descriptive features of the l-th frame of the m-th utterance of the n-th recognition base element

$D_{inml} = \{d^1_{inml}, d^2_{inml}, \ldots, d^k_{inml}, \ldots d^K_{inml}\}$,

K - the number of descriptive features.

## 2.1.3. Set of all selected features - S

$I = \{descriptions\}$

$S = \{S_j, j \in I\}$

$S_j$ - the set of selected features defined by the j-th description

$S_j = \{S_{j1}, S_{j2}, \ldots, S_{jn}, \ldots S_{jN}\}$,

N - the number of different phonetic units

$S_{jn}$ - the set of selected features of the n-th phonetic unit defined by the j-th description

$S_{jn} = \{S_{jn1}, S_{jn2}, \ldots, S_{jnp}, \ldots \}$,

$S_{jnp}$ - the p-th selected feature of the n-th phonetic unit defined by the j-th description

$S_{jnp} = \{s^1_{jnp}, s^2_{jnp}, \ldots, s^R_{jnp}\}$,

R - the number of elements of the p-th selected feature.

## 2.1.4. Set of all characteristic features - C

$I = \{descriptions\}$

$C = \{C_e, e \in I\}$,

$C_e$ - the set of characteristic features defined by the e-th description

$C_e = \{C_{e1}, C_{e2}, \ldots, C_{en}, \ldots, C_{eN}\}$,

N - the number of different phonetic units

$C_{en}$ - the characteristic feature of the n-th phonetic unit defined by the e-th description

$C_{en} = \{C_{en1}, C_{en2}, \ldots, C_{enw}, \ldots \}$,

$C_{enw}$ - the w - th characteristic feature of the n-th phonetic unit defined by the e-th description

$C_{enw} = \{c^1{}_{enw}, c^2{}_{enw}, \ldots, c^V{}_{enw}, \ldots c^V{}_{enw}\}$,

V - the number of elements of the w-th characteristic feature.

## 2.2. Sets of maps

## 2.2.1. Set of descriptive feature maps - $F_D$

- elements of the set are mapping the set of phonetic unit uterances into the set of descriptive features

$F_D = \{f_{Di}, D_i \equiv D \}$,

$i \in I$

$$f^i{}_{nml} : \quad \bigcup_{l=1}^{L} \bigcup_{m=1}^{\infty} \bigcup_{n=1}^{N} a^u{}_{nml} \longrightarrow \bigcup_{l=1}^{L} \bigcup_{m=1}^{\infty} \bigcup_{n=1}^{N} d^{h(u)}{}_{inml}$$

$$h : \{1,2, \ldots U\} \longrightarrow \{1,2, \ldots K\}$$

The map h depends on the used description.

## 2.2.2. Set of selected feature maps - $G_S$

- elements of the set are mapping the set of descriptive features into the set of selected features

$G_S = \{g_{Sj}, S_j \equiv S \}$,

$j \in I$

$$g^j{}_{up} : \quad \bigcup_{l=1}^{L} \bigcup_{m=1}^{\infty} \bigcup_{n=1}^{N} d^k{}_{inml} \longrightarrow \bigcup_{p=1}^{\infty} \bigcup_{n=1}^{N} s^{r(k)}{}_{jnp}$$

$$r : \{1,2, \ldots K\} \longrightarrow \{1,2, \ldots R\}$$

The map r depends on the used description .

## 2.2.3. Set of characteristic feature maps - $G_c$
- elements of the set are mapping the set of descriptive features
into the set of characteristic features

$$G_c = \{g_{c_e}, C_e \subseteq C\},$$

$$e \in I$$

$$g^e_{um1} \quad : \quad \bigcup_{l=1}^{L} \bigcup_{m=1}^{\infty} \bigcup_{n=1}^{N} d^k_{inm1} \quad \longrightarrow \quad \bigcup_{w=1}^{\infty} \bigcup_{n=1}^{N} c^{v(k)}_{enw}$$

$$v : \{1,2, \ldots K\} \longrightarrow \{1,2, \ldots V\}$$

The map V depends on the used description .

The elements of the characteristic features set $C_{enw}$ should be
a disjunctive sets. This is not valid for the elements of the
selected features set $S_{jnp}$.
We shall define such maps, which are mapping the set of phonetic
unit utterances into the set of characteristic features.

## 3. An example of feature extraction method

Considering the maps and sets mentioned above, as an example the two
feature extraction methods shall be considered. The first one is the
so called zero-crossing method ( method from the time domain ) and
the second one is the method of formant frequency energy classes
( frequency domain ).

## 3.1. Zero-crossing method (ZC)

There are various variants of the zero - crossing method [7]. They
have in common the mapping rule of descriptive features, i.e. measuring
the time between the two successive zero - crossings of a signal.
We shall briefly describe one of them.
Elements of the descriptive features set are defined as:

$$d_{inm1}(k) = M_k . T_\blacksquare \quad , \quad k=1,2, \ldots , K_1 \; ; \; \sum_{p=1}^{n} M_k(p) \quad , \quad n \leq U \; ; \; f_\blacksquare = 1/T_\blacksquare \qquad (3.1)$$

$M_k$ = number of successive elements $a^u_{nm1}$ with equal sign

where:
$f_\blacksquare$ is the sampling frequency
$K_1$ is the number of elements $d^k_{inm1}$ in the l-th frame
$d^k_{inm1}$ is the lenght of k-th interval

$$D_{inm1} = \{d^1_{inm1}, d^2_{inm1}, \ldots , d^k_{inm1}, \ldots d^K_{inm1}\}$$

Elements of the selected features set $S_{jn\rho}$ are defined as:

$$s_{n1\rho}(t) = (n^*_t \cdot (\tau_t + \tau_{t+1})/2)/(W \cdot (\tau_{t+1} - \tau_t)) \tag{3.2}$$

where

W          is the frame width

$\tau_t, \tau_{t+1}$  are a pair of tresholds of the t-th time class

$$S_{1n\rho} = \{s^1{}_{1n\rho}, s^2{}_{1n\rho}, \ \ldots \ s^T{}_{1n\rho}\},$$

## 3.2. Method of formant frequency energy classes (FFEC)

Like the zero-crossing method this method knows various variants as well. All variants use the discrete Fourier transformation as a map of descriptive features [3,4].
The elements of the descriptive features set $D^{jm}{}_{nL}$ are frequency samples.

$$D_{jnm1} = \{d^1{}_{jnm1}, d^2{}_{jnm1}, \ \ldots \ , d^K{}_{jnm1}\}$$

### 3.2.1. Variant a (FFECa)

To define elements of the selected features set $S_{tn\rho}$ the following prescription has been used:

$$s_{tn\rho}(m) = \left( \sum_{j=f^*{}_m}^{f^*{}_{m+1}} \log d_{1nm1}(j)^2 \right) / \left( \sum_{u=1}^{K} \log d_{1nm1}(u)^2 \right) \ ; \ m=1,2, \ \ldots \ ,R \tag{3.3}$$

$$f^*{}_m = f_m/R_f \ ; \ f^*{}_{m+1} = f_{m+1}/R_f \ ; \ R_f = f_{\blacksquare}/U \tag{3.4}$$

where

$f_{\blacksquare}$       is the sampling frequency

K          is the number of all elements in the descriptive features set $D_{1nm1}$

R          is the number of elements in the selected features set $S_{tn\rho}$

$f_m, f_{m+1}$ are the pair of thresholds of the m-th formant frequency class

$$S^t{}_{n\rho} = \{s^t{}_{n\rho 1}, s^t{}_{n\rho 2}, \ \ldots \ s^t{}_{n\rho R}\}.$$

### 3.2.2. Variant b (FFECb)

This variant defines elements of the selected features set $S^v{}_{n\rho}$ as follows:

$$s_{vn\rho}(j) = \log \ \left( \max_{r \in [f^*{}_j, f^*{}_{j+1}]} (d_{1nm1}(r)) \right)^2 / \left( \sum_{k=1}^{M} \log \ \left( \max_{t \in [f^*{}_k, f^*{}_{k+1}]} (d_{1nm1}(t)) \right)^2 \right) \tag{3.5}$$

$$f^*_j = f_j/R_f \; ; \; f^*_{j+1} = f_{j+1}/R_f \; ; \; R_f = f_=/U \; ; \; j=1,2, \ldots ,M \hspace{2cm} (3.6)$$
where

M        is the number of maximum components of all classes and the
         number of elements in the selected features set $S^v{}_{np}$
$f_m, f_{m+1}$ are the pair of thresholds of the m-th formant frequency class

$$S_{vnp} = \{s^1{}_{vnp}, s^2{}_{vnp}, \ldots s^M{}_{vnp}\}$$

Out of it arises a question how efficiency of a single map should be
estimated in order to be used in the phonetic units recognition
process .
For this purpose, the recognition results obtained by the considered
feature extraction methods mentioned above, have been used.

## 4. Experimental results

The recognition of five isolated Slovene vowels ( /a/,/e/,/i/,/o/
and /u/ ) was carried out by the recognition experiment.

| Zero - Crossing Method | | | | | Method of Formant Frequency Energy Classes | | | | | | | | | |
| --- | --- | --- | --- | --- | --- | --- | --- | --- | --- | --- | --- | --- | --- | --- |
| | | | | | variant  a | | | | | variant  b | | | | |
| recognized as  [%] | | | | | | | | | | | | | | |
| A | E | I | O | U | A | E | I | O | U | A | E | I | O | U |
| A 97.3 | 0.9 | 0.0 | 1.8 | 0.0 | 83.6 | 1.8 | 0.0 | 8.2 | 6.4 | 97.3 | 0.0 | 0.0 | 2.7 | 0.0 |
| E 0.9 | 78.2 | 10.0 | 7.3 | 3.6 | 6.3 | 70.0 | 16.4 | 2.7 | 4.6 | 0.0 | 92.8 | 5.4 | 0.9 | 0.9 |
| I 0.0 | 3.7 | 94.5 | 0.0 | 1.8 | 3.6 | 16.6 | 69.0 | 3.6 | 7.2 | 0.0 | 4.5 | 92.8 | 0.0 | 2.7 |
| O 7.3 | 22.7 | 0.0 | 63.6 | 6.4 | 13.0 | 4.5 | 1.8 | 58.1 | 21.8 | 1.8 | 0.0 | 0.0 | 92.8 | 5.4 |
| U 2.7 | 11.8 | 17.3 | 10.9 | 57.3 | 5.5 | 7.2 | 1.8 | 10.1 | 75.4 | 0.0 | 0.9 | 0.0 | 10.0 | 89.1 |

a                                                b

Table 1 a-b:   Recognition   results  of  five   isolated   vowels

One hundred and ten utterances of each vowel, pronounced by
110 different speakers, have been performed. Female-male rate was 3/7.
Classification was made on the basis of multivariate normal
distributions with equal covariances [5].
Table 1a-b shows the recognition results for a single method.
We shall now estimate efficiency of single maps, or better, their
'convenience' for the use in the phonetic units recognition process on
the basis of recognition results.
By using map rules in the zero - crossing method a somehow better
recognition accuracy was achieved only for the vowel /a/ ( 96.4% )
- less for the vowel /i/. For the vowels /e/, /o/, and /u/ a

rather worse recognition accuracy was achieved.

The reason for a worse recognition accuracy when zero-crossing method was applied, lies in the usage of the map of descriptive features.

In this method the measurement of interval lenght as a map of descriptive features was used. But measurement of interval lenght is phase dependent [6].

This is of great importance for phase changes at low frequencies ( first two formants ), which ussualy have the greatest magnitude and as such a greater influence on the zero-crossing rate.

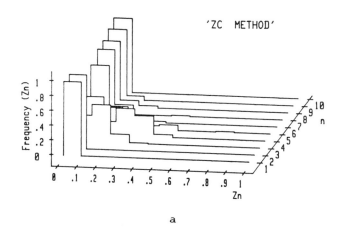

a

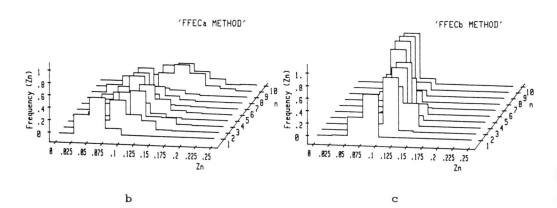

b                                    c

Fig. 1a-c : Histograms of the feature vector elements, for vowel /a/, formed by ZC a), FFECa b) and FFECb c) methods.

From the Fig. 1a it can be seen, that feature descriptions of phonetic units with measurement of interval lenght as mapping rule of descriptive features is less successful as with Fourier transformation. This is evident from the dispersion rate of each feature vector element, which is greater than the one for the other two methods.

Comparison of recognition results for variants FFECa and FFECb ( see Table 1b ) and considerations of dispersion rates of vector elements for both variants ( Fig. 1 b - c) give indication of the fact that common normalized energy of single formant frequency classes calculated by this variant was a "worser criteria" than the ratio of normalized energy of maximum components was.

A better recognition accuracy and the smallest features vector dispersion was achieved when the map of method FFECb was used. This variant gave the best average recognition accuracy - greater than 92.5 %.

## 4. Conclusions

By the speaker-independent speech recognition such feature maps should be defined that ' differences' in speech features, appearing in the case of independent speaker shall be expressed as small as possible, which means that such maps should be defined where features overlapping is as small as possible. This should be valid for maps of descriptive features ( e.g. measurement of intervals lenght - discrete Fourier transformation ) as well as for maps of selected features ( e.g. variant a - variant b of FFEC method ). The mapping rules discussed in our paper showed that the discrete Fourier transformation as the mapping rule for the descriptive feature maps and the variant b of the FFEC method as the mapping rule for the selected feature maps gave the best recognition results. With above mentioned methods the smallest feature overlapping and consequently the best average recognition accuracy has been achieved -i.e. more than 92.5 % .

References :

[1] P.Willich, "Putting speech recognizers to work", IEEE Spectrum, april 1987, pp. 55 - 57.
[2] F. Fallside and W. A. Woods , Computer speech processing , Prentice-Hall, Englewood Cliffs, NJ, 1985.
[3] R. De Mori and C. Y. Suen, New Systems and Arhitectures for Automatic Speech Recognition and Synthesis , Springer - Verlang , Berlin , 1985.
[4] R. W. Ramirez, The FFT , Prentice-Hall, Englewod Cliffs, NJ, 1985.
[5] J. C. Simon , Spoken Language Generation and Understanding , D. Reidel Publishing Company , 1980 , pp. 129 - 145
[6] James C. Anderson , "Improved zero - crossing method enhances digital speech",EDN Magazine,vol.27,No.20, oct.13 1982,pp.171-174.
[7] R.J. Niederjohn and P.F. Castelaz,"Zero-crossing analysis methods and their use for automatic speech recognition ", Proc. IEEE Comp. Soc. Workshop on Pat. Recog. and Artif. Intelligence, 1978.

# A SYSTEM FOR THE RECOGNITION OF GEOLOGICAL LINEAMENTS
## IN REMOTELY SENSED IMAGERY

Graham Oakes
Science and Engineering Research Council
Daresbury Laboratory
Daresbury, Warrington, WA4 4AD

## ABSTRACT

Lineament maps are an important intermediate step in the production of geological interpretations from remotely sensed images. A system that reduces the bias and performs the most
menial stages of lineament analysis allows interpreters to spend more time on tasks requiring
thought and judgement. The system uses standard edge- and line-detection techniques within
a structure based on a model of the human visual system. Features are recognized using
a paradigm of progressive refinement of an image description within information channels
an azimuth and spatial frequency. The system produces accurate and visually appealing
lineament maps for practical images.

## 1. MOTIVATION

A geological lineament is defined as "a mappable, simple or composite feature of a surface,
whose parts are aligned in a rectilinear or slightly curvilinear relationship and which differs
significantly from the patterns of adjacent features and presumably reflects a subsurface
phenomenon" (O'Leary et al, 1976). Lineaments recognized in remotely sensed images may
correlate with faults, joints and other tectonic features; hence the mapping of lineaments
plays an important role in general geological mapping. This is normally done using manual
photointerpretation techniques.

Burns et al (1976) note that manual interpretation introduces bias to the lineament maps:
if a scene is interpreted by two different people, or by the same person on different days,
not all lineaments are reproduced in both interpretations. Another problem is posed by
the large amount of remotely sensed imagery available and the relatively small number of
experienced photogeologists available to interpret it: there is frequently insufficient time

to take full advantage of all the information available in the images. This paper describes a system to explore the feasibility of performing the low-level, routine recognition of lineaments automatically, thus reducing bias and freeing interpreters to perform tasks requiring more thought and judgement.

## 2. SYSTEM OVERVIEW

Using a paradigm based on the human visual system, the lineament-recognition system emphasizes the use of information channels in azimuth and spatial frequency to progressively refine an image description. Images are processed in an 11-stage sequence, as shown in figure 1. These stages may be divided into five main functional groups:

(a) preprocessing,

(b) generation of information channels,

(c) primitive feature detection and refinement,

(d) recombination of information channels and final display, and

(e) semantic interpretation and control.

The semantic interpreter/controller has not yet been implemented. The algorithms used in each of the other four groups are described more fully in sections 3.1 to 3.4. The design philosophy for the system, and details of the testing performed during its construction, are given more fully in Oakes (1987).

Ideally, the system would be organized as a heirachy of parallel processors. Hardware availability precludes this, and the system is currently implemented on a VAX-11/780 computer with attached FPS-5100 series array processor. The system is currently designed to operate on a 2040x2040 pixel subscene of a single band Landsat image. Only minor modifications would be required to operate on images of different specifications or from other sensors: the current specifications were chosen simply to demonstrate the feasibility of automatic lineament recognition for images of a practical size for many geological problems.

## 3. DETAILS OF THE SYSTEM'S IMPLEMENTATION

### 3.1 Preprocessing

Preprocessing includes noise cleaning and the generation of Fourier power spectra.

Noise cleaning is achieved using a 3x3 despiking filter that outputs the wieghted average of the central grey-level and the neighbourhood mean:

output = (F x (1 - N)) + (MEAN x N)

where

F = central grey-level

MEAN = neighbourhood mean grey-level (excluding the central pixel)

N = "noisiness" = (ABS(F-MEAN) - T) / 2T

(if N < 0 then N is set to 0,    if N > 1 then N is set to 1)

T = user-defined threshold.

It can be seen that the weighting function depends on the estimated "noisiness" of the neighbourhood, using a simple piecewise-linear estimation function.

Power spectra for 512x512 subscenes of the image are calculated using standard Fourier techniques. It can be shown that these power spectra give much the same information as conventional rose diagrams (plots of lineament number or length versus azimuth), as well as being useful aids to the design of directional filters (see below). Azimuthal averages of the power spectra (calculated by averaging the power spectrum over fan-shaped windows) are particularly useful in this regard.

3.2 Generation of Information Channels

The concept of information channels is central to the lineament-recognition system. The human visual system breaks image data into several spatial frequency channels using neural networks in the retina, and into 10 or 20 azimuthal channels using orientation-specific operators in the cortex (Kronauer and Yehoshua, 1985). These channels are simulated within the lineament-recognition system by a 3-level data pyramid (giving three spatial frequency channels) and use of four azimuthal channels derived by directional filtering.

To create the data pyramid, low-resolution channels are produced by sampling every second pixel of every second line of smoothed higher-resolution channels. Smoothing is performed using a 7x7 Gaussian convolution operator. Repeating this operation twice gives a pyramid containing a 2048x2048 high-resolution channel (containing the original image), a 1024x1024 intermediate-resolution channels (containing low and intermediate frequencies only) and a 512x512 low-resolution channel (carrying the low frequency information only). The utility of this structure for implementing difference-of-Gaussian edge detectors (based on the work of Marr and Hildreth, 1980) is obvious. The structure also allows easy extraction of different types of information. For example, the low-resolution channel gives information of regional trends, and allows a large area to be examined, while the low-resolution channel allows analysis of local trends over a more restricted area. Combining results from the different channels allows accurate location of regional trends (since, where features located

at several resolutions coincide, the high-resolution channel allows precise location, while
the low-resolution channel indicates the regional significance) and the characterisation
of lineaments.

The image is separated into four azimuthal channels using standard frequency-domain filtering techniques. The transfer function (T) of the directional filter for a particular azimuth
is defined by:

$$T(r,\beta) = B(r) + (R(\beta) \times H(r))$$

where

$r,\beta$ = radial and azimuthal frequency

B  = radial blur function = $\exp(-s.r^2)$

s  = parameter controlling the standard deviation of the radial blur function

R  = azimuthal window function = $\exp(-g.[(\beta-\beta c)/\beta r]^2)$

g  = parameter controlling the standard deviation of the azimuthal window function

$\beta c, \beta r$ = cantre azimuth and half-width of the azimuthal window

H  = high-emphasis function = $(r/Rmax)^2 \times \exp(-Rtap.r^2)$

   (the Gaussian-tapered Laplacian response, as recommended by Marr and Hildreth,
   1980, for edge detection based on physiological models.)

Rmax,Rtap = parameters controlling the Laplacian response and Gaussian taper.

The filter acts as an isotropic low-pass filter (B(r)) with superimposed high-emphasis function
(H(r)) acting only in the desired azimuth window. The low-pass function preserves broad
trends, giving a framework within which the more localized trends can be interpreted (this
has been found to be highly desirable in producing enhanced images for manual interpretation:
B(r) is set equal to zero when producing images for automatic lineament detection). The
high-emphasis function enhances localized trends within the azimuth window. The window
is currently defined by a Gaussian function with standard deviation proportional to the
half-width of the window. Future versions of the filter will use a Gaussian-tapered rectangular window, as the simple Gaussian has been found to bias the results too much towards
lineaments oriented near the centre of the window.

As well as simulating processes within the human visual system, use of directional operators
may improve the signal-to-noise ratio of edge-detector output, compared to that obtained
using isotropic operators (Torre and Poggio, 1986). It may also give more accurate localization
of edges. On the other hand, the detected edges are no longer guaranteed to be closed,
as are those located by a Laplacian (under ideal conditions). As lineaments are, by definition,
not closed features, this is no handicap to the use of directional filtering. (The system
also allows images to be processed without division into azimuth channels. This is valuable
where the results may be used to aid segmentation, where closed features are desirable.)

The decision to use four azimuth channels is somewhat arbitrary, but based on the observation that images rarely contain more than four significant preferred orientations. Practical
simulation of the 10 or 20 channels of the cortex is not possible. (In any event, the human

visual system has evolved to cope with a wide range of scenes: careful selection of the azimuthal channels for a particular scene, after considering the power spectra and any other available information, should allow acceptable performance with a limited number of channels.)

## 3.3 Primitiva Feature Detection and Refinement

This stage include primitive feature detection, relaxation labelling and thresholding.

As lineaments are composed of lines and edges, standard line- and edge-detectors can be used for the primitive feature detection stage. After testing more than 60 such detectors (see Oakes, 1987, for a detailed description of this testing) the template-matching operator of Nevatia and Babu (1980) was selected for edge detection, while the semi-linear sum operator (Vanderbrug, 1975) is used for line detection. These operators were selected on the basis of their simplicity and good performance with respect to freedom from bias, linearity of response and noise immunity.

The figures-of-merit output by these detectors, for edges and lines respectively, are combined to give an overall "lineament possibility" figure to each pixel. This is done by independently scaling the edge- and line-detector outputs for the scene to the range [0,1], then merging the two results pixel-by-pixel, retaining the larger of the two figures.

The lineament possibilities are refined using the relaxation labelling algorithm of Schachter et al (1977). Again, this algorithm has been chosen for its simplicity.

The refined lineament possibilities are converted to a binary lineament decision using a combination of semithresholding, space-variant adaptive thresholding (where a different threshold is defined for each pixel, based on the histogram of lineament possibilities for the 32x32 block of pixels surrounding it) and non-maximum suppression.

## 3.4 Recombination of Information Channels and Display of Results

To produce a final lineament map, the lineament decisions in each channel must be brought together into a single map. For each pixel of the original image, the lineament decisions at each azimuth are characterised by:

FH = lineament flag for the high-resolution channel,

FI  = lineament flag for the intermediate-resolution channel, and

FL  = lineament flag for the low-resolution channel.

(The intermediate- and low-resolution channels are interpolated to match the high-resolution image using nearest-neighbour interpolation.) We wish to assign one of four labels to each pixel: LOC (local lineament), INT (intermediate lineament), REG (regional lineament) or NON (no-lineament). Initial assignment of possibilities follows the rules:

NON= ((1-FH) + (1-FI) + (1-FL)) / 3

LOC = ( FH  + (1-FI) + (1-DL)) / 3

INT = ( FH  +  FI  + (1-FL)) / 3

REG = ( FH  +  FI  +  FL ) / 3

Since each resolution channel has been processed independently, it cannot be expected that the responses will be entirely consistent. Relaxation labelling, using the algorithm of Zucker et al (1977), is therefore applied at this stage to upgrade the labelling consistency. After relaxation, the label with the highest possibility is assigned to each pixel.

The azimuthal channels are now combined to produce the final lineament map, by assigning each channel to a different colour on an IIS image display. This produces a display which differentiates between lineaments of different orientations using colour (with intersections of lineaments of different azimuths shown as a mixture of the relevant colours) and between those of different scale using intensity (local lineaments are shown at low intensity, regional ones at high intensity). This display is both simple and highly effective.

Provision is made for various cosmetic operations (eg. to span gaps in lineaments) at this stage. In practice, the system produces high-quality results without this step.

## 4. RESULTS AND CONCLUSIONS

Figure 2 shows the results produced by the system for a 512x512 subscene of a Landsat MSS band 7 image over the Dartmoor Granite. The image was acquired in January, 1979, and the combination of snow cover and low solar-illumination angle makes it an excellent target for lineament analysis, but with some problems of bias due to preferential enhancement of directional features perpendicular to the illumination direction. The total processing time for a 2048x2048 subscene of this image was approximately three days. Given parallel hardware, this processing time could be reduced by two or three orders of magnitude. The following points can be made about the results:

(a) The power spectra are dominated by power perpendicular to the illumination direction. Trends due to geological features are apparent as smaller peaks superimposed on this illumination peak: thus the power spectra are useful aids to characterising the main trends of the image, and hence defining appropriate azimuthal windows.

(b) All lineaments located by the system correlate with features in the original image. The lineament maps are both visually appealing and comprehensive.

(c) When no directional filtering is applied, the lineament maps are strongly biased towards features oriented perpendicular to the solar illumination. Directional filtering overcomes this bias.

(d) After directional filtering, the lineament maps are strongly biased towards features located at the centre of each azimuthal window. Use of a Gaussian-tapered rectangular function to define the azimuthal windows, or use of a larger number of windows (as done in the human visual system) will overcome this bias.

(e) The system fails to recognize very broad trends. This problem could be overcome by incorporating more low-frequency information in the decision-making process, ie. by using more levels in the data pyramid.

Overall, the results produced by the system are of high quality, and clearly demonstrate the feasibility of automatic recognition of geological lineaments using an approach based on progressive refinement of an image description in a number of information channels.

## Acknowledgements

The lineament analysis system was built during my postgraduate studies at Imperial College, London, using facilities provided by the geophysics section and the Centre for Remote Sensing. These studies were supported by a University of Queensland Travelling Scholarship.

## References

BURNS, K.L., SHEPHERD, J., and BERMAN, M., 1976, "Reproducibility of geological lineaments and other discrete features interpreted from imagery: measurement by a coefficient of association": Remote Sensing of Environment, 5, 267-301.

KRONAUER, L., and YEHOSHUA, Y.Z., 1985, "Reorganization and diversification of signals in vision": I.E.E.E. Transactions on Systems, Man and Cybernetics, SMC-15, 91-101.

MARR. D., and HILDRETH, E.C., 1980, "Theory of edge detection": Proceedings of the Royal Society of London, Series B, 207, 187-217.

OAKES, G., 1987, "Automatic lineament analysis techniques for remotely sensed imagery": Ph.D. Thesis, Imperial College, University of London.

O'LEARY, D.W., FRIEDMAN, J.D., and POHN, H.A., 1976, "Lineament, linear, lineation: some proposed new standards for old terms": Geological Society of America Bulletin, 87, 1463-1469.

NEVATIA, R., and BABU, K., 1980, "Linear feature extraction and description": Computer

Graphics and Image Processing, 13, 257-269.

SCHACHTER, B.J., AMOS, L., ZUCKER, S.W., and ROSENFELD, A., 1977, "An application of relaxation methods to edge reinforcement":I.E.E.E. Transactions on Systems, Man and Cybernetics, SMC-7, 813-816.

TORRE, V., and POGGIO, T., 1986, "On edge detection". I.E.E.E. Transactions on Pattern Analysis and Machine Intelligence, PAMI-8, 147-169.

VANDERBRUG, G.J., 1975, "Semi-linear line detection": Computer Graphics and Image Processing, 4, 287-293.

ZUCKER, S.W., HUMMEL, R.A., and ROSENFELD, A., 1977, "An application of relaxation labelling to line and curve enhancement": I.E.E.E. Transactions on Computers, C-26, 394-403.

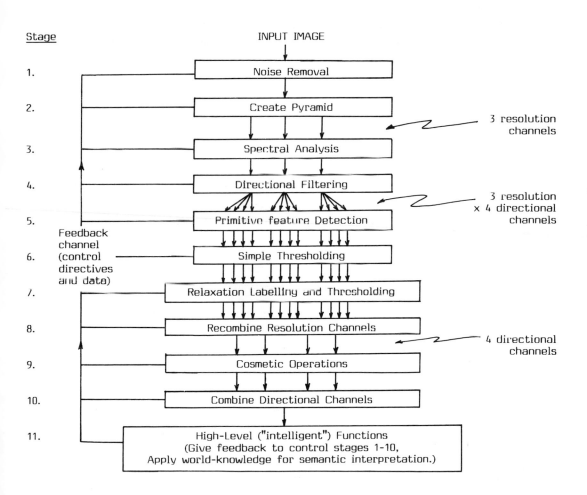

Figure 1    A Model for a Lineament Recognition System

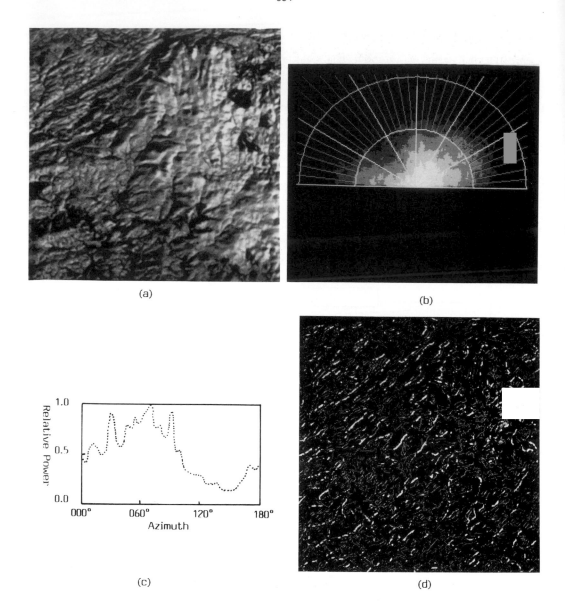

(a)

(b)

(c)

(d)

Figure 2

(a) MSS band 7 scene over Dartmoor, acquired January, 1979.
(b) Power spectrum for the Dartmoor scene (rotated through 90°, smoothed using a 5x5 median filter and quantized to 8 grey levels).
(c) Azimuthal averages of the power spectrum. (Calculated using 1° intervals, then smoothed using a 7-point triangular filter.)
(d) Lineament map produced by the lineament recognition system, without application of directional filters. Local features are shown at low intensity, regional ones at high intensity.
(e),(f) Lineaments at azimuths centred about 040° and 130°, as determined by the lineament recognition system. (The normal colour display, of three such azimuthal plots, cannot be reproduced here.)
(g) Manual lineament interpretation.

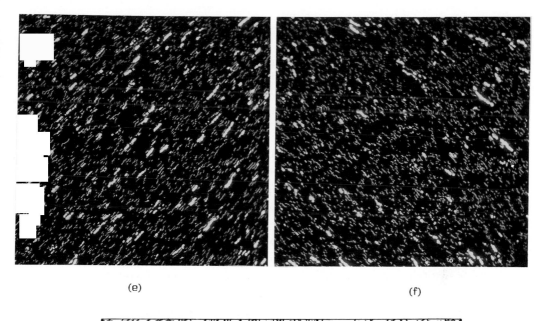

(e)                                                                                  (f)

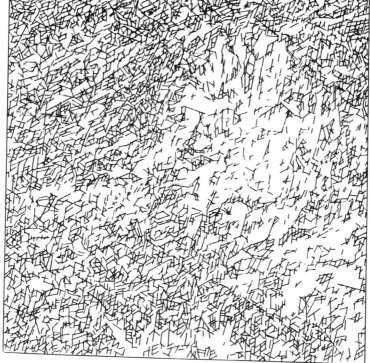

(g)

# Use of an Assumption-based Truth Maintenance System to Record and Resolve Ambiguity in Cardiac Angiograms.

S.T. Rake[1]
and L.D.R. Smith.
IBM(UK) Scientific Centre, Winchester and Brompton Hospital, London.

## Introduction

Over a number of years the IBM UK Scientific Centre and the Brompton Hospital have been interested in the analysis of medical images and, in particular, the analysis of cardiac angiograms with the aim of producing quantitative, moving, three dimensional models of the left ventricle from biplane coronary arteriograms(1,2,4).

The process of extracting data from the images (identifying and naming the arteries, tracking the centre lines, measuring the diameters at frequent intervals along the artery and identifying corresponding bifurcations in each view of each frame) can be performed manually(3) but is very time consuming for a trained cardiologist/radiologist. However, we have automated the process so that the only operator input now required is the identification of bifurcations in the first frame of each view. Thereafter bifurcations are found in all subsequent frames, and vessel sections between bifurcations are tracked and diameters measured automatically.

The techniques used in this sort of automatic vessel tracking involve algorithms that perform local analysis of the image and rely on identification of some characteristic pattern of pixels which match some form of template of an arterial centre line, edge or branch. This approach has at least three major problems.

1. There is no means of verifying that a pattern identified as a possible feature of interest really is a feature of interest. As a result, in the noisy, complex and ambiguous images obtained by arteriography this *pattern recognition* approach often results in failure of the system accurately to track the artery.
2. Because the analysis is essentially local, it is left to the operator to indicate the features of interest (in this case bifurcations of arteries) and their connectivity.
3. The operator must also identify the true structure of ambiguous features that can have a number of different interpretations.

In this paper we are particularly interested in the resolution of ambiguous features - that is, developing a unique explanation of data that can have a number of different interpretations. We describe some of the structures produced by the low level processes

---

[1] S.T. Rake is registered for a PhD at the University of Reading and the study of Truth Maintenance Systems has been conducted in conjunction with the Intelligent Systems Group of the Department of Computer Science.

that are required to allow knowledge encapsulated in a computer program (known as a *knowledge source*) to resolve the ambiguous features.

## Ambiguous Features

In any 'real world' scene (i.e. a scene that has not been specially constructed) features will appear that cannot be completely resolved by local analysis.

For instance, in cardiac angiography local analysis will not distinguish between arteries which are near the camera and arteries which are farther away. Figure 1 shows a typical image with an ambiguous feature indicated by the arrow.

Low-level processes will describe the features extracted from this region of the image, but it is the domain knowledge that will make assumptions about the actual construction of the arteries in three dimensional space. The domain knowledge knows that cardiac arteries do not actually cross on one surface of the heart, but, without data from other parts of the image or images, will not be able to decide which of the possible hypotheses is correct. Some of the possible hypotheses are shown in Figure 1

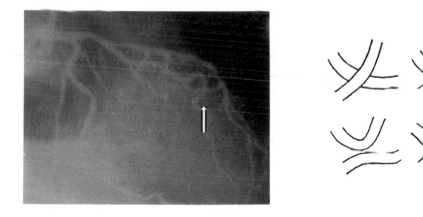

Figure 1. **Ambiguous Features:** The arrow shows an ambiguous feature in the image. The line drawings are some of the possible hypotheses about the structure of the feature

As the analysis proceeds the emerging network of arteries will constrain the possible hypotheses, and eventually allow the ambiguity to be resolved. A Truth Maintenance System (TMS) can be used to record data about ambiguous features so as to allow the ambiguity to be resolved at a later time.

## Truth Maintenance Systems

Truth Maintenance Systems have been well described in the literature (5,6,7,8) and de Kleer(6) points out that a system that incorporates a TMS has two parts, as shown in Figure 2. The problem solver is the collection of processes and knowledge sources that are applied to the image and the extracted features, while the TMS is used to record and maintain consistency within the developing solution.

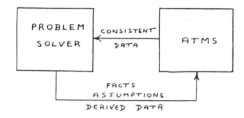

Figure 2. **TMS and Problem Solver:** The TMS is used as a recording mechanism for the data generated by the Problem Solver.

Using a TMS to record the developing solution ensures that the recorded data has a particular structure - essentially *nodes* of data support other nodes of data, with the implication that if all the supporting nodes are believed, then the supported nodes are also believed. If for some reason a supporting node is disbelieved, then the supported node is also disbelieved. That is, a TMS not only records the beliefs that the problem solver is developing, but also ensures that those beliefs are *consistent*.

In the TMS described by Doyle(5), as data is recorded by the problem solver, the status of an assumption is modified by the TMS in order to maintain the one consistent environment that the TMS allows. Since we wish to use the problem solver to make assumptions about the content of the image, and then use other evidence to verify which assumptions are valid, the Doyle approach is too uncontrolled. More appropriate is the Assumption-based TMS (ATMS), described by de Kleer(6,7,8), which allows the problem solver to manipulate the data so that many consistent sets of data can exist simultaneously, and, most crucially, gives control of the manipulation of the assumptions to the problem solver.

When an ambiguity is found, possibly after a very compute intensive process, all the possible hypotheses about the ambiguity are recorded.

Each hypothesis is recorded as an *assumption*. Each hypothesis can be based upon other data, including other assumptions. The complete set of assumptions which are necessary for an hypothesis is an *environment*. The ATMS is designed to handle multiple environments which we use to record a number of hypotheses at one time. The ATMS will also ensure that each environment is *consistent*. All the data that exists in a consistent environment is known as the *context* of that environment. If the problem solver discovers that the set of assumptions that make up an environment are found to be inconsistent, the problem solver tells the ATMS to mark the environment as *NOGOOD*. The ATMS will propagate this NOGOOD automatically through any superset environments.

## Facts, Assumptions and Derived Data

Each node of data recorded by the ATMS must be a fact, an assumption or be derived data and the data types are distinguished by their method of generation. By making the distinctions between the types of data and using the ATMS to manipulate the relationships between the data we can address the recording and resolution of ambiguity. In the angiography task in particular, and any image understanding task in general, the definitions of facts, assumptions and derived data need to be modified from those described by de Kleer(6).

### Facts

Facts are the items of data which are the 'givens' of the system: the data that are always true, in any environment. In a vision task the original image is a fact and it is probable that the data extracted by low level processes (such as the identified edges) will be recorded as facts for pragmatic reasons. The constraints that are encapsulated in the various processes and knowledge sources are not recorded as facts.

### Assumptions

In the TMS of Doyle(5) and the ATMS of de Kleer(6), assumptions are part of the initial set of data. For instance, if the ATMS is being used to solve the NQUEENS problem [2] the starting set of assumptions would be that there is a queen on every square of the board. The problem solver then applies the constraints encapsulated in the processes and knowledge sources to the set of assumptions and facts in order to eliminate any combination which is inconsistent. De Kleer(6) points out that if there are n assumptions, there will be potentially 2**n environments, with consequent implications for implementation and performance.

In image understanding it is impractical to take the de Kleer approach (i.e. assume everything at the start) since the number of assumptions would be huge, even if they could be defined. Thus there are few, if any, starting assumptions. The low level

---

[2] The NQUEENS problem requires that N queens are placed on an N by N chess board so that they cannot take each other.

processes will extract edge data and record the edge points as facts. We will defined assumptions as data items that are generated as the result of 'inspired guesswork', perhaps supported by already existing data, which the task may attempt to deny at a later stage of the task.

Data which act as parameters to the processes and knowledge sources are not defined as assumptions if they will not be changed during execution of the task.

Derived Data

These data are items that are generated by some process or knowledge source for which there is a sound computational basis, and which the task will not attempt to deny as the solution develops. Derived data may be derived from facts, assumptions and other derived data.

## Assumed Data

In the vision task it is inevitable that, at some point in the task, it will be appropriate for a knowledge source to make assumptions about the existence of data.

For instance, if the edge detector fails to identify continuous edges for part of an artery, it is possible that a 'gap jumping' knowledge source will produce the structure shown in Figure 3.

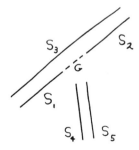

Figure 3.    **Assumed Data:**    The problem solver has assumed that the gap can be filled by the segment G in order to link segments S1 and S2. However, segment S4 and S5 may later produce evidence that the assumption is incorrect.

The assumption G is based upon the existence of segments S1, S2, S3 and the execution of a 'gap jumping' knowledge source. Since the simultaneous analysis and integration of all the data in the image is not possible, the assumption may be denied at a later time. The existence of segments S4 and S5 could mean that the assumption about segment G was incorrect. If G had not been recorded in a form that indicated that it was recorded as an 'inspired guess' then its deletion would be difficult.

## Recording a Structure as Ambiguous

The example in **Figure** 1 showed a number of hypotheses about the ambiguous feature.
Two of these hypotheses are shown in **Figure** 4.

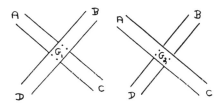

Figure 4.  **Two Interpretations:**   It is possible to interpret the ambiguous feature in at least two ways.

In order to make complete arteries it is first necessary for knowledge sources to be
invoked which will assume the presence of 'gap jumping' artery structures called G1
and G2.  The invocation of a second knowledge source will construct 'super arteries'
A-G1-C and B-G2-D.  Since the 'super artery' constructs are the ones in which the
ambiguity is revealed, the problem solver must record that A-G1-C may lay either in
front of or behind B-G2-D.  The necessary structures are shown in **Figure** 5.

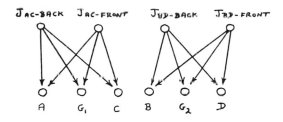

Figure 5.   **Recording the Ambiguity:**   The J nodes record the ambiguity as a number of hypotheses.

The problem solver is also aware that there is a constraint on the possible layout of the
four 'super arteries' - they will not both be on the same surface of the heart.  Thus two
of the possible environments are disallowed and recorded as

NOGOOD (J-AC-BACK  J-BD-BACK )
NOGOOD (J-AC-FRONT J-BD-FRONT)

## Developing the Solution in Multiple Environments

Since we are recording data in a form which ensures that all the data in one environment (the context of the environment) is consistent, it is possible to develop multiple hypotheses about the ambiguous structure described above. For example, suppose that it is possible to infer that there is an extension, E, of the artery D which can be tracked to its termination at X. This is shown in Figure 6.

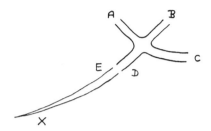

Figure 6.   **Extending Artery D:**   Artery D can be extended to meet artery E which terminates at X.

When the necessary knowledge sources have been invoked in the correct sequence, a 'super artery' node will have been built which will describe the artery D and E to its end at X. The recorded data is shown in Figure 7.

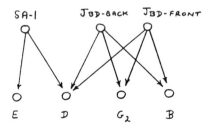

Figure 7.   **Recording the 'super artery':**   SA-1 records the artery D to E to X.

Now, if the knowledge source that builds 'super arteries' is invoked rigorously, then it will be invoked twice more to build SS-2 and SS-3, shown in Figure 8.

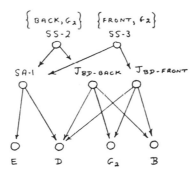

Figure 8. **Two Hypotheses:** SS-2 and SS-3 are the possible hypotheses of the extension of the ambiguous feature. The environments of the hypotheses are shown in curly braces.

We now have data which will allow the ambiguity to be resolved. If information can be obtained from other features in the image that will cause the environment of SS-2 or SS-3 to become NOGOOD, then the data will have only one structure with a consistent environment, the context of which will be the resolved ambiguity.

This example reveals one other important feature of this method of recording. The structure of the artery E is computed only once, so that either the hypothesis SS-2 or the hypothesis SS-3 can be chosen without the structure of E being rebuilt from scratch.

## Resolution of Ambiguity

Resolution of the ambiguity recorded in the various hypotheses is achieved by identifying which of the sets of assumptions (environments) are inconsistent. The example in Figure 8 does not contain enough information for this process to be completed. The necessary information can only come from analysis of other parts of the image, and from applying knowledge about the possible constraints which exist. It is possible, even likely, that there will not be sufficient information in the one image for all the ambiguities to be resolved. However, in this particular task, there is a second (biplane) view for each frame of the heart beat cycle and the identification of corresponding structures in the two views of one frame will allow many of the ambiguities to be resolved.

Other image understanding tasks would resolve ambiguities in different ways. For instance, if the task is model-based recognition of manufactured objects, then the library of models would a rich source of information to guide strategies that identify which of the recorded hypotheses is correct.

Alternatively, hypotheses could be labelled in a systematic way and a form of relaxation could be applied to separate the consistent and inconsistent environments.

## Conclusion

There are a number of important points that have been revealed in the discussion above.

It is crucial that data that is *assumed* is clearly separated from data that is *derived*. If this separation is not made, then the environments that characterise the possible unambiguous solutions will not be complete.

The recording of all possible hypotheses at the point where they are identified will mean

1. The analysis is likely to be more rigorous than if only one hypothesis is allowed to exist at a time. Multiple hypotheses allow the problem solver to develop a possible solution along a promising line but also provide a record of the existence of other solutions which will have to be addressed at some time.
2. It will not be necessary to recompute an alternative hypothesis if the environment of the one being pursued is found to be NOGOOD.

All computation and recording that leads to an hypothesis being made will be valid, even if the environment of a hypothesis is later found to be NOGOOD.

The processes and knowledge sources of the problem solver that run at the various levels (low level, world and domain) must be designed to make the distinction between assumptions and facts. The recording and consistency mechanisms offered by the ATMS cannot be considered as an 'add-on' to be included into the system at some time in the future.

The contents of the nodes recorded by the ATMS will depend upon the type of image understanding task the problem solver is addressing, and this has not been discussed. This paper has been more interested in the relationships between nodes that record, and allow later resolution of, ambiguities.

In any system that performs incremental construction and assembly of features found in an image, and those features have a number of different interpretations, some form of recording and consistency maintenance mechanism is required. This is particularly true when attempting to track and identify cardiac arteries. The modified ATMS described here offers one way of performing those functions.

## References

1. Smith L.D.R. and P.Quarendon. Four-Dimensional Cardiac Imaging. SPIE Proceedings 593, Conference on Medical Image Processing, pp 74-77, 1985.
2. Smith L.D.R. et al. A semi automatic system for the production of quantitative four dimensional cardiac images. Proceedings IEE Number 265, pp 72-76, 1986
3. Reiber J.H.C. and P.W. Serruys, Eds., State of the Art in Quantitative Coronary Arteriography. Martinus Nijhoff. 1986
4. Smith L.D.R. et al. Quantitative Moving Three Dimensional (3D) Images of the Heart and Coronary Arteries. An Automated Method of Production (Abs). Circulation, Vol. 74, Supp II, Oct 1986.
5. Doyle J. A Truth Maintenance System. Artificial Intelligence, Vol. 12, 1979
6. de Kleer J. An Assumption-based TMS. Artificial Intelligence, Vol. 28, 1986
7. de Kleer J. Extending the ATMS. Artificial Intelligence, Vol. 28, 1986
8. de Kleer J. Problem Solving with the ATMS Artificial Intelligence, Vol. 28, 1986

# INDEX OF AUTHORS